BY JANE RIDLEY

*The Letters of Edwin Lutyens
to His Wife Lady Emily*
(ed. with Clayre Percy)

Fox Hunting: A History

*The Letters of Arthur Balfour
and Lady Elcho, 1885–1917*
(ed. with Clayre Percy)

Young Disraeli

*The Architect and His Wife:
A Life of Edwin Lutyens*

*The Heir Apparent:
A Life of Edward VII,
the Playboy Prince*

THE HEIR APPARENT

THE HEIR APPARENT

A LIFE OF EDWARD VII,

THE PLAYBOY PRINCE

Jane Ridley

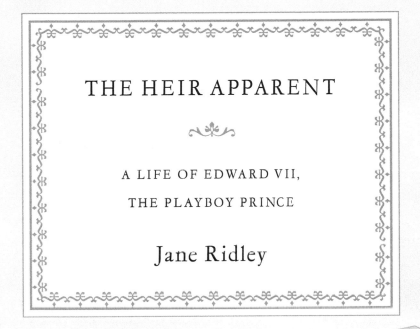

RANDOM HOUSE

NEW YORK

Published in the United States by Random House, an imprint of
The Random House Publishing Group, a division of Random House LLC,
a Penguin Random House Company, New York.

RANDOM HOUSE and the HOUSE colophon are registered
trademarks of Penguin Random House LLC.

Originally published in Great Britain by Chatto & Windus, a member of The Random
House Group, London, in 2012, as *Bertie: A Life of Edward VII.*

Portraits of the Royal Family (plate 1), Susan Vane-Tempest (plate 5),
John Brown (plate 6), Jennie Churchill (plate 8), Queen Victoria (plate 10) and
Queen Victoria's family (plate 11): all © National Portrait Gallery, London.

LIBRARY OF CONGRESS CATALOGING-IN-PUBLICATION DATA
Ridley, Jane.
The heir apparent : a life of Edward VII, the playboy prince / Jane Ridley.
pages cm
Includes bibliographical references and index.
ISBN 978-1-4000-6255-3
eBook ISBN 978-0-8129-9475-9
1. Edward VII, King of Great Britain, 1841–1910. 2. Great Britain—Kings and rulers—
Biography. 3. Edward VII, King of Great Britain, 1841–1910—Relations with
women. 4. Great Britain—History—Edward VII, 1901–1910. I. Title.
DA567.R53 2013   941.082'3092—dc23   2013002597
[B]

www.atrandom.com

2 4 6 8 9 7 5 3 1

FIRST U.S. EDITION

Book design by Dana Leigh Blanchette
Title-page and part-title photograph: © iStockphoto.com

FOR TOBY AND HUMPHREY

CONTENTS

PART ONE
Youth

PART TWO

Expanding Middle

PART THREE

King

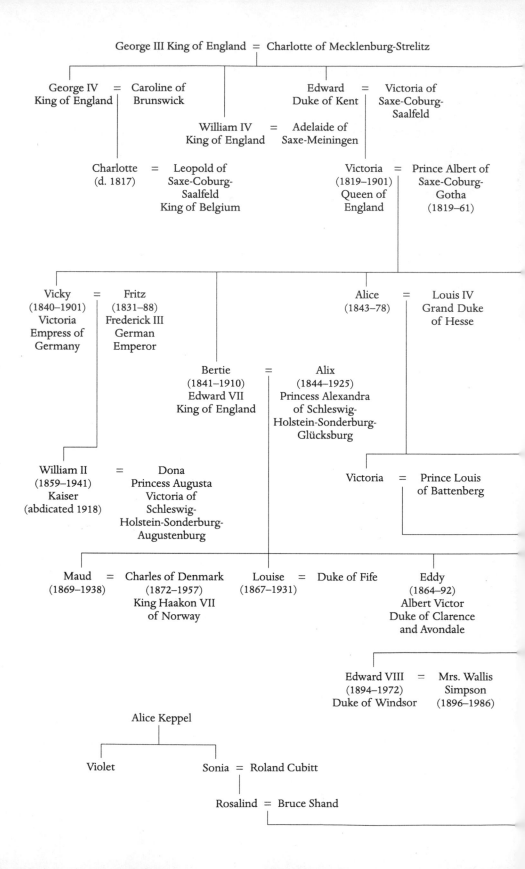

FAMILY TREE OF EDWARD VII

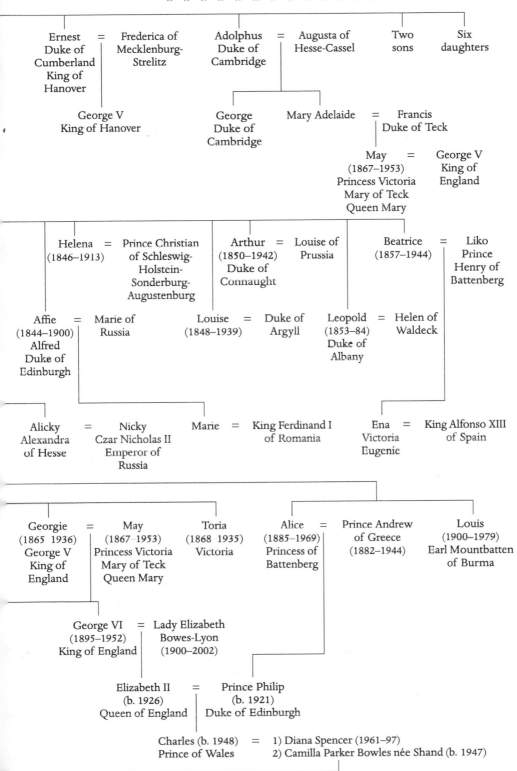

Ernest
Duke of
Cumberland
King of
Hanover
= Frederica of
Mecklenburg-
Strelitz

Adolphus
Duke of
Cambridge
= Augusta of
Hesse-Cassel

Two
sons

Six
daughters

George V
King of Hanover

George
Duke of
Cambridge

Mary Adelaide = Francis
Duke of Teck

May
(1867–1953)
Princess Victoria
Mary of Teck
Queen Mary
= George V
King of
England

Helena
(1846–1913)
= Prince Christian
of Schleswig-
Holstein-
Sonderburg-
Augustenburg

Arthur
(1850–1942)
Duke of
Connaught
= Louise of
Prussia

Beatrice
(1857–1944)
= Liko
Prince
Henry of
Battenberg

Affie
(1844–1900)
Alfred
Duke of
Edinburgh
= Marie of
Russia

Louise
(1848–1939)
= Duke of
Argyll

Leopold
(1853–84)
Duke of
Albany
= Helen of
Waldeck

Alicky
Alexandra
of Hesse
= Nicky
Czar Nicholas II
Emperor of
Russia

Marie = King Ferdinand I
of Romania

Ena
Victoria
Eugenie
= King Alfonso XIII
of Spain

Georgie
(1865–1936)
George V
King of
England
= May
(1867–1953)
Princess Victoria
Mary of Teck
Queen Mary

Toria
(1868–1935)
Victoria

Alice
(1885–1969)
Princess of
Battenberg
= Prince Andrew
of Greece
(1882–1944)

Louis
(1900–1979)
Earl Mountbatten
of Burma

George VI
(1895–1952)
King of England
= Lady Elizabeth
Bowes-Lyon
(1900–2002)

Elizabeth II
(b. 1926)
Queen of England
= Prince Philip
(b. 1921)
Duke of Edinburgh

Charles (b. 1948)
Prince of Wales
= 1) Diana Spencer (1961–97)
2) Camilla Parker Bowles née Shand (b. 1947)

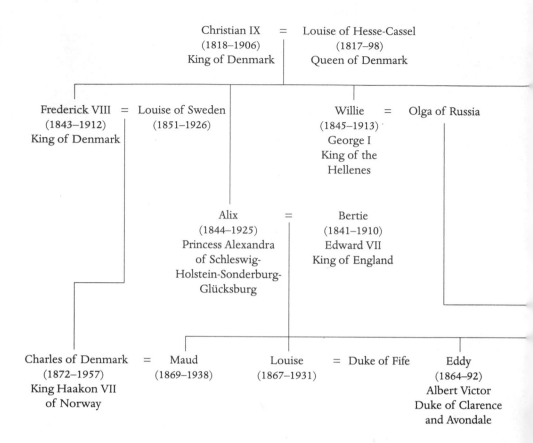

Christian IX = Louise of Hesse-Cassel
(1818–1906)   (1817–98)
King of Denmark   Queen of Denmark

Frederick VIII = Louise of Sweden
(1843–1912)   (1851–1926)
King of Denmark

Willie = Olga of Russia
(1845–1913)
George I
King of the
Hellenes

Alix = Bertie
(1844–1925)   (1841–1910)
Princess Alexandra   Edward VII
of Schleswig-   King of England
Holstein-Sonderburg-
Glücksburg

Charles of Denmark = Maud
(1872–1957)   (1869–1938)
King Haakon VII
of Norway

Louise = Duke of Fife
(1867–1931)

Eddy
(1864–92)
Albert Victor
Duke of Clarence
and Avondale

Edward VIII = Mrs. Wallis Simpson
(1894–1972)   (1896–1986)
Duke of Windsor

FAMILY TREE OF ALEXANDRA

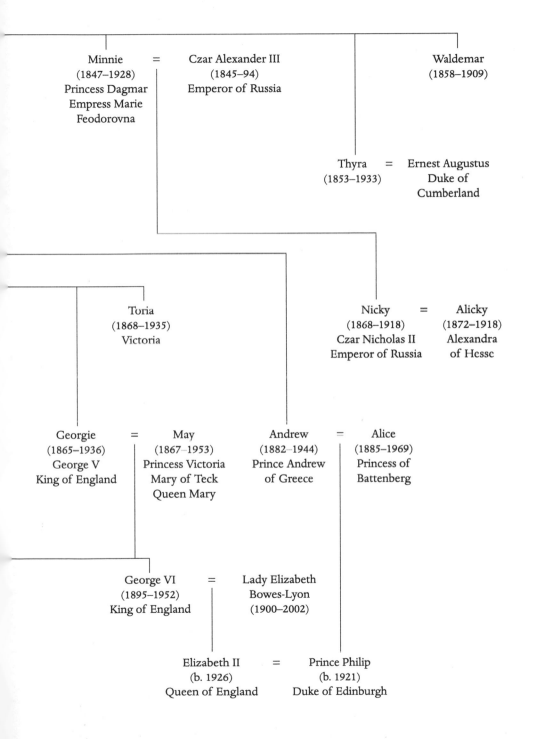

Minnie (1847–1928) Princess Dagmar Empress Marie Feodorovna = Czar Alexander III (1845–94) Emperor of Russia

Waldemar (1858–1909)

Thyra (1853–1933) = Ernest Augustus Duke of Cumberland

Toria (1868–1935) Victoria

Nicky (1868–1918) Czar Nicholas II Emperor of Russia = Alicky (1872–1918) Alexandra of Hesse

Georgie (1865–1936) George V King of England = May (1867–1953) Princess Victoria Mary of Teck Queen Mary

Andrew (1882–1944) Prince Andrew of Greece = Alice (1885–1969) Princess of Battenberg

George VI (1895–1952) King of England = Lady Elizabeth Bowes-Lyon (1900–2002)

Elizabeth II (b. 1926) Queen of England = Prince Philip (b. 1921) Duke of Edinburgh

INTRODUCTION

The Eighty-Nine Steps

I began work on this book in 2003. My original idea was to write a short life of King Edward VII, looking at his relations with women: with his mother, Queen Victoria; with his sisters; with his wife, Queen Alexandra; and, of course, with his mistresses. But then, by gracious permission of Her Majesty the Queen, I was granted unrestricted access to the papers of King Edward VII in the Royal Archives.

This was an extraordinary privilege. I find it hard to convey a sense of the vast riches I encountered in the archives at Windsor Castle. The first documents I saw concerned the Prince of Wales's childhood and education. Trolley loads of papers, meticulously cataloged and bound, gave a harrowing insight into an ambitious educational project that ended in fiasco. Where else was the upbringing of a recalcitrant boy documented as if it were an affair of state? I was the first biographer to see the papers of Edward VII for almost fifty years—since Philip Magnus, who published in 1964. Many more papers have been added since. I realized very soon that I would need to write a full biography.

The research at Windsor took me more than five years. I don't mean that I went there every day—far from it; but whenever I could, I seized a research day. I caught the train from Paddington, changed at Slough, walked from Windsor station up to the castle, passed through security checks at the Henry VIII Gate, and climbed the eighty-nine steps to the top of the Round Tower, where the archives are housed. Windsor is quite unlike any other archive; researchers work in rooms of understated grandeur, the manuscripts are preordered, awaiting your arrival, and when the bell rings for coffee at eleven o'clock the guard changes to the stirring music of a military band in the Lower Ward outside. Arriving pale and haggard (I know this from the police security photographs), I would sink into a chair beside a cart which had been loaded with my ration of papers for the day. Like a caterpillar chewing a giant lettuce leaf, I set to work, reading through the mountain of documents and transcribing them onto my laptop. When I came across gold—as I often did—I would type like a frenzied exam candidate, racing against the time when the bell rang for closing.

I made the decision that I must call my subject Bertie. None of his contemporaries addressed him by the double name of Albert Edward, which he himself disliked. Previous biographers had referred to him respectfully as the Prince of Wales or King Edward, but I wanted to avoid the formality and distancing effect of royal titles. Calling him Bertie—as his family did—brought him closer in some ways, but at the same time gave him reality as a figure from history.

The many thousands of letters that I read from Queen Victoria to Bertie were a revelation. I found it astonishing—admirable, in a way— that Victoria never learned the courtly art of dissembling. Not for her the long pause, the polite request for more information. Whatever was on her mind she poured out in her emphatic, illegible scrawl. Her correspondence with her daughter Vicky reveals her as one of the best letter writers of the nineteenth century—vivid, candid, and intensely human. Her letters to Bertie, by contrast, were often judgmental and framed in the imperative mood. Her anger leaped from the page, startling in its urgency even today.

Bertie's replies puzzled me. I have read thousands of his letters, and they are—mostly—prime examples of the masculine epistolary style sometimes known as British phlegm. He filled the page with small talk, padded out with comments on the weather or the health of acquaintances, and peppered his sentences with clichés enclosed in quotes. Little wonder that Victoria berated him for failing to enter into a vigorous and heartfelt exchange of opinions with her. There were times when I wondered whether the effort of deciphering the impenetrable loops of his grotesque calligraphy was worth the bathetic result. But then I realized that I was missing the point. For him, letter writing was a duty, not a means of self-expression; the aim was not to reveal, but to conceal, his true feelings.

So closely did Bertie guard his private life that, in his will, he ordered all his letters to be destroyed. No correspondence survives between him and his wife, Alexandra of Denmark. I wanted to place the marriage at the center of my story, but the hole in the archive seemed to make this impossible. My breakthrough came when I discovered that the National Archives of Denmark possessed three boxes of photocopies of letters written in Danish by Alix to her sister Dagmar. I booked a flight to Copenhagen and hired a translator. It was February, and I sat shivering beside my translator in the permafrost of the archive, typing as she read the fading photocopies and translated roughly out loud. Later, she worked systematically through the boxes, translating the letters that at last allowed me to see things from Alexandra's point of view.

The first phase of Bertie's life—up to the age of about thirty—has a strong story line provided by his stormy relationship with Queen Victoria and by his marriage. The second part—the thirty years until his accession aged fifty-nine, which I have called the Expanding Middle—was the hardest bit to write. A great deal is known about what he did—what time he took a train, whom he saw, how many pheasants he shot—but it is hard to find the heart of the genuine man who was

Bertie. Then I hit upon the idea of going back to my original plan of trying to work out his inner life by looking at his relationships with women.

No letters from women are preserved among Bertie's papers, but many of his letters to women survive outside the Royal Archives.* These are typically polite and discreet; but the bland contents belie their subversive purposes. Consider the situation. Royal invitations were normally formal and formulaic, issued by equerries or private secretaries and composed in the third person. Here, however, the Prince of Wales wrote to a woman in his own hand, informally and in the first person. His purpose was often to make an appointment to see the woman alone, sometimes for tea—the *cinq à sept*—or for luncheon. Though they give so little away, Bertie's missives can be read as coded messages in a royal dance of courtly love. Some, but not all, of the women became his mistresses. But that did not necessarily mean that he slept with them. The word "mistress" should perhaps be understood in the sense, today archaic, of a woman who is admired, cosseted, and courted by a man, as well as in the modern meaning, which almost invariably implies a sexual relationship.

Queen Victoria deplored Bertie's habit of letter writing, and she had good cause to do so. Time after time it got him into trouble. Writing letters implied a degree of intimacy with a woman—usually a married woman—that most Victorians judged to be improper. Today these relationships would be censured for a different reason: because they were unequal and often involved what we would see as an abuse of Bertie's power as Prince of Wales. Within Bertie's social set, it was almost impossible for a woman to resist his advances. Some of his early mistresses were destroyed by the experience.

Historians have written of the "feminization" of the monarchy under Queen Victoria, as domestic virtues and philanthropy replaced martial valor, and rulers were no longer expected to lead armies into battle. Bertie's womanizing signaled a vigorous protest against the

---

* Letters between Bertie and women that have found their way into the Royal Archives are later accessions, and do not form part of Bertie's papers.

bourgeois respectability of his parents. It made a statement about a certain type of masculinity that was entirely at odds with the gender politics of the Victorian court.

Bertie's affairs and flirtations depended upon compliant husbands. When the husbands rebelled—as Sir Charles Mordaunt did in 1870, or Lord Randolph Churchill over the Aylesford affair or, later, Lord Charles Beresford—a scandal ensued. It was the men of Bertie's circle—the so-called Marlborough House Set—who caused the crises which punctuated his life as Prince of Wales: the Mordaunt divorce, the Aylesford scandal, the Tranby Croft case, and the Beresford scandal. But what drove these men to come out in opposition to the prince was his predatory behavior toward their wives or mistresses. The functioning of Bertie's court as Prince of Wales can be understood only by exploring his links with women. To a remarkable extent, women—mistresses—are central to the dynamics of Marlborough House.

As a young man, Bertie was not always likable. I found it hard to warm to a prince who blatantly cheated on his wife and ruthlessly discarded his mistresses—even though the explanation for his behavior can be found in the unhappiness and loneliness of his loveless childhood. As Bertie reached middle age, however, he did something that is quite difficult for a royal to do, a thing that Alexandra never fully achieved: He grew up. My affection grew for this man condemned to a lifetime of indulgence and political impotence while he waited for his mother to die.

He continued to be unfaithful, but the pattern of the relationships changed. These late love affairs mattered to him; he cared more. But the evidence is elusive. I knew that Daisy Warwick was central to his life in the 1890s, but all the letters seemed to have been destroyed, leaving a silence that I was unable to penetrate. Fortunately, Daisy possessed a strong sense of her historical importance and having quarreled with the court—a motive for telling her story. It turned out that she had defied royal commands and kept copies of some of Bertie's letters. My eureka moment came when I discovered in Bertie's diary the code he used to record their frequent assignations, enabling me to reconstruct the intensity of the relationship. Alice Keppel, his last mistress, was both more public and more discreet. She enjoyed a quasi-official status as the King's *favorita*, but the correspondence that passed between them was almost all destroyed. Unlike Daisy the Babbling Brooke, Alice Keppel stayed silent, and to this day the details of her physical relationship with Bertie—if, indeed, it was physical— remain an enigma.

By September 2008, I had almost completed my research on Bertie's years as Prince of Wales, and I had written a draft of his life up to 1901. I planned only a brief concluding chapter on his life as king. I was late for my publisher's deadline, which had originally been set as 2006. When I think about the story of this book I am humbled by the patience of my long-suffering publishers, Chatto, and especially by the support I have received from my editor, Penelope Hoare. The faith of my American publisher, Susannah Porter of Random House, has also amazed me. I was contracted to write seventy thousand words, but by late 2008 the manuscript had already grown to twice that length: Inside the thin book there was a fat book struggling to get out, and my rich grazing at Windsor had piled on the words. But at least the end seemed in sight.

Then I received a telephone call from the Royal Archives. Waiting for me, it seemed, were some papers from the reign that I had not yet seen. I arrived at Windsor to find more than 150 bound volumes of documents, as well as several other important files. Any slight hope I might have entertained of publication in 2009 was dashed. I braced myself to ask for yet another extension and cleared my diary to spend a month at Windsor.

Reading through the bound files of political papers made me realize that I needed to write the history of King Edward's reign as a story. Previous biographers had treated the reign thematically, organizing their books around the filing system of the King's papers. There is always a pressure on royal biographers to write the life and times, but I wanted to convey a sense of the King's preoccupations and achievements, and I reckoned a narrative was the best way to do this. I was struck by the abrupt shift from the party-going Prince of Wales to the conscientious, even workaholic, King. The womanizing comes to a stop—well, almost. The third and final part of Bertie's life—King—was very different from the long years of waiting, yet he seemed instinctively to adapt to the role.

Having written a DPhil thesis on the Edwardian Tory party, I had absorbed the conventional view that Edward VII played a marginal part in the turbulent politics of his reign. These files told a very different story. He was effective and politically astute, he excelled as a diplomat, and (unlike Queen Victoria) he understood and adapted to the changing role of monarchy. Rather to my surprise, I found myself writing a revisionist account of the reign. I came to respect and admire Bertie: The philandering Prince of Wales turned out to be a wise, reforming king, but his intelligence and achievements had been consistently underestimated.

Why historians had got Edward VII so wrong baffled me. But then I came across a collection of nearly 1,200 letters among the papers of George V that documented the writing of the official biography of Edward VII by Sidney Lee. The dossier told a gripping tale of history in the making. These letters revealed the extraordinary efforts made by politicians such as Balfour, Asquith, and Lansdowne to write Edward VII out of history and to suppress his achievements by giving deliberately misleading accounts of his reign.

In this book I have tried to show a Bertie who was both more able and more complex than the figure we know as Edward VII. The real Bertie was obscured by authorized biographers who, in their concern to protect the reputation of the monarchy, concentrated on the politics and said little about the scandals. Equally misleading and one-sided was the alternative narrative that flourished of Bertie as prince of pleasure—a frivolous, self-indulgent lothario. His bed-hopping exploits were wildly exaggerated. His name was linked with more than fifty women, and at least ten illegitimate children were chalked up to him. The true figures are, alas, considerably more modest. I have tried to combine both sides of his life, the public and the private. To do this I have had to chip away at the patina of old anecdotes and peel back layers of hearsay that has been repeated so often that it has almost hardened into fact. It has been a lengthy business. But, like so many women in the past, I have greatly enjoyed the years I have spent in the company of HRH.

PART ONE

✥

Youth

CHAPTER 1

Victoria and Albert

1841

"Not feeling very well again and had rather a restless night," wrote Queen Victoria in her journal on 17 October 1841.[1] She was heavily pregnant with her second child.

Next day, the royal obstetrician, Dr. Locock, examined the Queen and pronounced the birth to be imminent. Much against her will, she traveled from Windsor, where she was comfortable, to Buckingham Palace, which she disliked. Fat as a barrel and wearing no stays, the twenty-two-year-old Queen expected her confinement daily. She felt "wretched" and too tired to walk.[2] Prince Albert watched his wife anxiously. He wrote in bold black ink in his large childish hand to the prime minister, warning him to be ready to appear at the palace at the shortest notice, "as we have reason to believe a certain event is approaching."[3] It was a false alarm, the first of many.[4]

Victoria had not wanted this baby, and she was furious to discover herself pregnant again only months after the birth of her first child.

She had a "vein of iron," but though she was Queen of England, she could not rule her own biology.[5] Feeling nauseous, flushed, and stupid, she was powerless to stop the control of affairs slipping from her fingers. Still more did she resent her enforced abstinence from nights of married bliss with her "Angel," Albert.

On the morning of 9 November 1841, the Queen's pains began. Only Albert, four doctors, and a midwife, Mrs. Lilly, attended the labor. At the prince's request, the prime minister, his colleagues, and the Archbishop of Canterbury did not witness the birth but, contrary to custom, waited in another room. Albert, always conscious of appearances, had insisted that the Queen "was most anxious from a feeling of delicacy that it should appear in the Gazette that at her confinement only the Prince, Dr Locock and the nurse were present in the room."[6] His own attendance at the birth, which was widely reported, gave an example to English manhood of how a modern father should behave.[7]

Delivering the royal baby was nervous work for Dr. Locock. Although this was the Queen's second confinement, her first child had been a girl, and the possibility of a male heir to the throne meant that this birth was an important political event. The job of royal obstetrician was so risky that Locock was paid danger money—an exorbitant fee of £1,000.*[8]

At twelve minutes to eleven, a boy was born. The baby was exceptionally large, the mother was only four feet eleven inches tall, and it had been a difficult birth. "My sufferings were really very severe," wrote Victoria, "and I do not know what I should have done but for the great comfort and support my beloved Albert was to me during the whole time."[9] Albert, who (according to his private secretary) was

---

* The medical bill for the birth totaled £2,500 and the doctors were solemnly informed that these lavish fees were paid solely "in consideration of HM's having given birth to a Prince and future heir to the Crown of England and that they must not be considered as forming any precedent for future payments." (RA VIC/M11/25, Sir Henry Wheatley to Albert, 11 November 1841.)

"very happy but too anxious and nervous to bear his happiness with much calmness," showed the baby to the ministers waiting next door.[10] The healthy boy was the first Prince of Wales to be born since 1762, but for his mother this was not a cause for rejoicing.

The fate of Princess Charlotte, Victoria's first cousin, could never have been far from the mind of Dr. Locock. Charlotte died in November 1817 after an agonizing fifty-hour labor, having given birth to a still-born son. Her accoucheur—the fancy French title for what was little more than an unqualified male midwife—shot himself three months later.

If Charlotte had not succumbed to postpartum hemorrhage, Queen Victoria would not have been born. Charlotte's death detonated a crisis of succession for the Hanoverian dynasty. Not only was she the sole legitimate child of the Prince Regent, later George IV, but, incredibly, she was the only legitimate grandchild of George III—in spite of the fact that he had fathered a brood of six princesses and seven princes. Not that the Hanoverians were an infertile lot. Three of the daughters of George III remained spinsters and the three princesses who married were childless; but the seven sons managed to sire an estimated twenty children between them.[11] All except Charlotte were illegitimate. The sons of George III had failed in their fundamental dynastic purpose: to ensure the succession.

When Charlotte died, Lord Byron threw open the windows of his Venice apartment and emitted a piercing scream over the Grand Canal. She was the only member of the royal family whom the people loved, and with her death the credibility of the monarchy slumped. The Prince Regent, who reigned in place of his old, mad father, George III, was lecherous, gluttonous, and grossly self-indulgent. How he had managed to father Princess Charlotte was a mystery. On his wedding night he was so drunk that he slept in the fireplace. He banished his wife and treated her with ostentatious cruelty, which made him deeply disliked. He and his brothers were the so-called wicked uncles of

Queen Victoria, and even by the rakehell standards of the day, they were dissolute.

Charlotte's death forced these middle-aged roués, with their dyed whiskers, their wigs, and their paunches, to enter into an undignified race to beget an heir. One by one they dumped their mistresses and hastened to the altar. Their choice of brides was limited by the Royal Marriages Act, introduced by George III in 1772, which made it illegal for the King's children to marry without his consent. The royal family disapproved of princes marrying into the English aristocracy, as this involved the monarchy in party politics. Under the Act of Settlement of 1701, Roman Catholics were excluded from the succession. So the royal marriage market was effectively confined to the small Protestant German courts, which acted as stud farms for the Hanoverian monarchy.

Prince Edward, Duke of Kent, was the fourth son of George III. Neither dissolute nor vicious, he was large and talkative with a certain sly cunning. He smelled of garlic and tobacco, and he was always in debt. In the army he was a stickler for uniforms and a harsh disciplinarian, heartily disliked by the rank and file. He had lived contentedly for twenty-eight years with his bourgeois French mistress, the childless Julie de St. Laurent. When the death of Princess Charlotte gave him the opportunity to supplicate Parliament to pay off his debts in exchange for trading in his bachelor status, the duke did not hesitate to discard Julie and marry a German princess. His choice was Victoire, the thirty-year-old widow of the minor German prince of Leiningen and the mother of two young children. She was also the sister of Prince Leopold of Saxe-Coburg-Saalfeld, the widower of Princess Charlotte.

The Kents shared a double marriage ceremony in 1818 with William, Duke of Clarence, the third son of George III, who married another German princess, Adelaide of Saxe-Meiningen. Two weeks earlier, the seventh brother, Adolphus, the virtuous Duke of Cambridge, his mother's favorite, had married yet another German princess, Augusta of Hesse-Cassel. Ernest, the Duke of Cumberland, who

had married a German princess four years before, and had as yet produced no children, was now hard at it. The race was on.*

Kent won. On 24 May 1819, the duchess gave birth to a daughter,
Victoria. This baby was fifth in line to the throne, coming after the
Regent and his three younger brothers.†

No one questioned Victoria's legitimacy at the time, but the rogue
gene for hemophilia that she carried throws doubt on her paternity.
Two of her daughters were carriers of the gene for the condition,
which impairs blood clotting, and one of her sons, Leopold, was a
bleeder.‡ Victoria's gene was either inherited or the result of a spontaneous mutation. Hemophilia cannot be traced in either the Hanoverian or the Saxe-Coburg family; and as the odds of spontaneous
mutation are 25,000:1, Victoria's gene has prompted speculation that
the Duke of Kent was not her biological father. According to one scenario, the Duchess of Kent, despairing of her husband's fertility, and
desperate to win the race for the succession, decided to take corrective
action and sleep with another man. Unfortunately, this lover happened
to be hemophiliac.[12]

This melodramatic hypothesis is entirely speculative, and there is
not a scrap of historical evidence to support it. The Duke of Kent was
not infertile; on the contrary, he is credited with at least two well-
attested illegitimate children.[13] Victoria, along with her eldest son, inherited unmistakably Hanoverian features, such as a receding chin and
protruding nose (her profile in old age is remarkably similar to that of
her grandfather, George III), as well as a tendency toward obesity and

* Three other brothers were unable to take part in the race for the succession. The Prince
Regent was still legally married to his estranged wife, Caroline of Brunswick, who was too
old to have another child. The second brother, Frederick, Duke of York, was married to a
Prussian princess, but the marriage was childless. Augustus, Duke of Sussex, brother num-
ber six, had ruled himself out by marrying Lady Augusta Murray in defiance of the Royal
Marriages Act.
† Next in succession after the Regent came the Duke of York (childless), then Clarence
(childless), and fourth, Victoria's father, the Duke of Kent.
‡ The hemophilia gene is carried on the X chromosome, which means that women can be
carriers, though, like Victoria, they show no symptoms.

explosive rages. Courts are hotbeds of gossip, but there was no whisper at the time that Victoria was illegitimate. Scientists believe that the faulty gene was a new mutation. At least one in four incidences of hemophilia are the result of new mutations, and this is especially likely in the case of older fathers; the Duke of Kent was fifty-one when Victoria was conceived. So the odds are that the gene, which was later to wreak havoc with both the Spanish and the Russian royal families via marriages to Victoria's granddaughters, originated in the testicles of the Duke of Kent in 1818. The genetic time bomb of hemophilia was the tragic price paid by his descendants when Kent won the race that the wits dubbed Hymen's War Terrific.[14]

Victoria's doctors and family worried not that she was illegitimate, but, on the contrary, that she had inherited the Hanoverian insanity. Mention of the madness of George III was suppressed in the nineteenth century, largely because Victoria herself was sensitive on the subject, but the royal doctors were well aware of it. It blighted the lives of the daughters of George III, who, prevented from marrying, were confined to the so-called nunnery at Windsor. In the 1960s, the mother-and-son medical historians Ida Macalpine and Richard Hunter made the diagnosis of the genetic disease porphyria. Symptoms include severe rheumatic pain, skin rashes, light sensitivity, and attacks of acute illness, but the diagnostic clincher for this rare metabolic disorder is red-stained urine. The disease had apparently bedeviled the royal family since Mary, Queen of Scots, and James I, but only caused madness in extreme cases.[15] A recent analysis of the hair of George III shows abnormal levels of arsenic. This was prescribed by his doctors, but the medication may have been counterproductive and made his illness worse.[16]

Building on the work of Macalpine and Hunter, researchers have conjectured that most of the children of George III were afflicted by some of the symptoms of porphyria. The Prince Regent was laid low by bouts of acute illness and episodes of mental confusion, and he complained of a range of porphyria symptoms, which he self-medicated with alarmingly large doses of laudanum. He and his brothers were all convinced that they suffered from a peculiar family disease.[17] The medical history of Victoria's father includes attacks of abdominal pain, "rheumatism," and acute sensitivity to sunlight, all symptoms of porphyria. Earlier biographers insisted that Victoria was completely unaffected, but the picture is not quite so straightforward.[18] One of her granddaughters, Princess Charlotte of Prussia, whose distressing medical history is fully documented, seems to have suffered from the disease. She may have inherited it through Victoria, though Victoria herself was asymptomatic, or at worst a mild sufferer.*

Much of this is speculative. The porphyria theory is known to be shaky and incapable of real proof, and it has come under attack from other medical historians. No one knows for certain what was wrong with the unfortunate George III. It is conceivable that contemporaries were right after all, and he really was mad. The latest theory is that he was afflicted by bipolar disorder.[19]

Victoria's father, the Duke of Kent, died unexpectedly of pneumonia when she was eight months old. Six days later, her grandfather, George III, also died, and she advanced from fifth to third in the line of succession.

Victoria was brought up in seclusion and (by royal standards) reduced circumstances by her mother, the Duchess of Kent, in an apartment in Kensington Palace. Her mother quarreled with George IV, "whose great wish," as her uncle Leopold told Victoria, "was to get you and your Mama out of the country."[20] Had Victoria lived in Germany, as the King desired, she would have been perceived as just another German princess. The duchess, however, was an ambitious woman, and she took great care to ensure that her daughter was brought up as heir to the English throne.

---

* Porphyria is a dominant gene, which means that each child of a carrier has a 50 percent chance of inheriting the disease. However, one of the peculiarities of the illness is that in 90 percent of those with the faulty gene, it remains latent and they show no symptoms of the illness. The gene can thus appear to skip generations and then resurface. Queen Victoria's medical history includes some of the physical symptoms of porphyria, but they are neither specific nor acute enough to make a convincing case for a diagnosis. (Rohl, Warren, and Hunt, *Purple Secret*, pp. 6–7, 117, 222–23.)

The rift between the Duchess of Kent and George IV meant that her mother kept the young Victoria under constant surveillance. She was never alone without a servant. She was not allowed to walk downstairs without someone holding her hand. At night she slept in a bed in her mother's room. She was allowed no friends. Even her half sister, Feodora, twelve years her senior, was banished, married off to the minor German prince of Hohenlohe-Langenburg, where she lived in a freezing palace in a dull court. Louise Lehzen, Victoria's governess, was appointed because she was German and knew no one of influence in England. Victoria was effectively a prisoner, with her mother acting as jailer.

In 1830, George IV died and was succeeded by his brother, the Duke of Clarence, now William IV. The Duchess of Kent became paranoid about the new King, whom she suspected of plotting to cut her out and promote Victoria as his heir. Determined to ensure that she should be regent, the duchess kept her daughter away from court. She refused to allow Victoria to attend the Coronation, and she enraged the new King by taking her around the country on quasi-official royal progresses. She was aided and abetted by Sir John Conroy, her comptroller, a scheming Irish officer who was widely believed to be her lover. No Gothic novelist could have invented a villain blacker than Conroy. He terrified Victoria with tales of plans to poison her and promote the claims to the throne of her younger uncles. When, aged sixteen, she fell seriously ill with typhoid fever, he presented her with a letter appointing him as her private secretary, and stood over her sickbed demanding that she sign it. With precocious strength of will, Victoria refused.

Victoria's isolated upbringing meant that her mother was entirely responsible for her education. Victoria spoke and wrote fluent French and German, and she excelled at arithmetic and drawing. She had lessons in history, geography, religion, music, and Latin (reluctantly).[21] She learned more than most aristocratic girls, but she did not receive the instruction in subjects such as constitutional history considered necessary for princes. As Lord Melbourne remarked: "The rest of her education she owes to her own shrewdness and quickness, and this perhaps has not been the proper education for one who was to wear the Crown of England."[22]

Victoria grew up hating and distrusting her mother. She yearned for a father figure to fill the place of the father she had barely known. But she was not lacking in self-worth. On the contrary, knowing that she was so close to the succession gave her a rare sense of entitlement. She never learned to accept authority figures; she *was* authority. Self-reliant, with a steely confidence in her own judgment, she was impulsive and volatile. No one taught her to control her temper.

At six a.m. on 20 June 1837, the Archbishop of Canterbury and the Lord Chamberlain arrived at Kensington Palace with the news that King William IV had died at midnight. Victoria insisted on seeing them by herself. Later that day, the tiny eighteen-year-old monarch addressed the Privy Council alone.

That night, Victoria moved out of her mother's bedroom.

She had escaped the duchess's plan for a regency, but only by a whisker (her eighteenth birthday had been a few weeks earlier), thanks to her own strength of character and coolness under pressure—qualities that were precisely the opposite of the demure submissiveness expected of women in what was now the Victorian era.

The dramatic events of her accession left the young Queen very isolated. She moved into Buckingham Palace, the still unfinished London residence, reviled for its vulgar raspberry-colored pillars and Queen Adelaide's sickly wallpapers; but her apartments were far apart from those of her mother, with whom she was barely on speaking terms. She found a father figure in the prime minister, Lord Melbourne. His bluff Whig worldliness gave her a much-needed political education, but her court was babyish and philistine.

Into this girlie court of late-night dancing, schoolgirl gossip, and immature politics walked Albert.

Prince Albert of Saxe-Coburg-Gotha was Victoria's first cousin. The two babies had been delivered within months of each other by the same midwife, but the cousins had met only once before. Albert's first visit to the English court had not been a success. He had fallen asleep after dinner and had suffered from bilious attacks.

When a second visit was arranged in 1839, Victoria warned her relations to expect no engagement, "for, independent of my youth, and my <u>great</u> repugnance to change my present position, there is <u>no anxiety</u> evinced in <u>this country</u> for such an event."[23] But when Albert arrived at Windsor, late and travel-stained from a bad crossing, and Victoria stood at the head of the staircase to receive him, it was a *coup de foudre*. She wrote in her journal: "It was with some emotion that I beheld Albert—who is <u>beautiful</u>."[24]

Throughout her life, Victoria was strongly attracted by male beauty, though she had few claims to beauty herself. She was short and fat, with protruding teeth. But she was the most eligible woman in the world—willful, spoiled, and twenty years old.

Five days later, she summoned Albert and proposed to him on the sofa. "We embraced each other over and over again, and he was so kind, so affectionate. Oh! to feel I was and am, loved by such an Angel as Albert was too great delight to describe! He is perfection: perfection in every way—in beauty—in everything!"[25]

Not everyone agreed. Lytton Strachey wrote of Albert's distressingly un-English looks: "His features were regular, no doubt, but there was something smooth and smug about them; he was tall but he was clumsily put together, and he walked with a slight slouch. . . . More like some kind of foreign tenor."[26]

Albert was very much a poor relation. He was born in Coburg, the second son of Duke Ernest, the ruler of the two minor German states of Coburg and Gotha, whose combined population totaled no more than 150,000. Duke Ernest ranked only twelfth in the thirty-nine states of the German Confederation. Albert's mother, Princess Louise of Saxe-Gotha-Altenburg, married the womanizing duke at the age of seventeen. Her first child, Ernest, was recognizably his father's son—dark and swarthy, he grew up a philanderer and syphilitic. But Albert, her favorite, born a year later, was different: gentle, even feminine, and intellectually precocious. He was so unlike his brother that it was rumored that he was, in fact, the son of the court chamberlain, the Jewish Baron Ferdinand von Meyern.

Years later, Albert liked to say that it was, in fact, "a blessing when there was a little imperfection in the pure royal descent and . . . some fresh blood was infused."

"We must have some strong dark blood," he would say, to correct the constant fair hair, blue eyes, and "lymphatic" blood of the Protestant German royal families who intermarried again and again.[27]

Whether there was, in fact, a little imperfection in the case of Albert himself is debatable.[28] But his personality was so different from those of his relations—he was an art lover, a scholar, and a workaholic in a family of lusty philistines—that it is tempting to speculate about his Jewish paternity. Supposing Meyern really was Albert's father and Conroy was Victoria's, this would mean, as A. N. Wilson has mischievously pointed out, that the royal families of Europe are descended from a German Jew and an Irish soldier. "Given this," comments Wilson, "it is surprising that these families manifested so few of the talents stereotypically attributed to the Irish and the Jews: such as wit or good looks."[29]

Albert's mother revenged herself on her unfaithful husband by taking lovers. When Albert was five, Duke Ernest banished his wife from court because of her affair with an officer, Alexander von Hanstein. Albert never saw his mother again. She married Hanstein, and died at age thirty, supposedly of cancer of the uterus.

The sudden disappearance of his mother traumatized Albert's childhood. Physically frail and easily tired, he was often in tears. Duke Ernest was a distant, neglectful father, and Albert's parent figure was his tutor, Christopher Florschutz, who created a secure schoolroom world for the two brothers at Rosenau, the Hansel and Gretel castle in the Thuringian Forest where Albert was born.

Albert grew up surrounded by men. Theodore Martin, his official biographer, noted approvingly that he had "even as a child shown a great dislike to be in the charge of women."[30] Uneasy and awkward with girls, he was stiff and overbearing. "Ought to pay more attention to the ladies," was Melbourne's gruff comment.[31] Albert had a horror of the sexual promiscuity that had poisoned his childhood, broken up his family, and contaminated the Coburg court.

The motherless boy learned to forget about his misery by succeeding in his lessons. His hobby was collecting and labeling objects—obsessive behavior that perhaps satisfied a need to control that can still be seen in his wife's papers, methodically filed, cataloged, and indexed in his own hand in the Royal Archives.[32] Order made him feel safe; creating and organizing his own world was perhaps his security against the chaos and loss left by his mother's disappearance.

Albert's career was shaped by his uncle Leopold, the widower of Princess Charlotte, whose death in childbirth in 1817 had cheated Leopold of his chance to rule as king or consort of England. Since 1831, Leopold had been King of Belgium, but he still clung to his ambition to control the throne of England. By arranging a marriage between his niece Victoria and his nephew Albert he would guarantee his own influence, as well as bring off a major dynastic coup for the minor house of Saxe-Coburg-Gotha.

When Albert was sixteen, Leopold dispatched his physician Baron Stockmar, who acted as his agent, to report on the boy's progress. Stockmar's verdict was mixed. Albert, he reported, was well educated, but knew nothing of European politics and was excessively prudent and unambitious. Stockmar began to groom the shy prince for the English throne. He removed him from Coburg's provincial, seedy court and sent him to the University of Bonn, where he received the best modern education of the day. Law, finance, public administration, art history, and history—all were eagerly devoured by the studious Albert. Next, he toured Italy with Stockmar; he rose each morning at six to study by the light of his green student's lamp, shunned social invitations, drank only water, and retired to bed at nine.

When Albert was twenty, Leopold and Stockmar judged him ready for his destiny. He had received an education that trained him supremely well as a public servant, but gave him no experience in dealing with human relationships. He preferred work to social life. He had lit-

tle emotional intelligence. Of women he had no experience whatsoever.

Victoria and Albert were married on 10 February 1840 in Inigo Jones's
boxlike Chapel Royal in St. James's Palace. The next day the euphoric
bride wrote to her uncle Leopold from Windsor: "Really I do not think
it possible for anyone in the world to be happier or AS happy as I am.
He is an Angel."[33]

Victoria always slept with a maid on the sofa in the next room, but
this never inhibited her enjoyment of sex. Nor did she object to the
white cotton long johns that Albert insisted on wearing to warm his
perpetually cold feet. She was annoyed to find herself pregnant almost
immediately. Later, she complained that the first two years of her married life had been ruined by the aches and sufferings of pregnancy:
"Without that—certainly it is unbounded happiness—if one has a husband one worships! It is a foretaste of heaven."[34]

Blaming her pregnancies allowed Victoria conveniently to forget
the tensions and rows that had scarred the first two years of her marriage. For all their sexual harmony, the two first cousins were locked in
a struggle for dominance. Albert had married a wife who was also a
queen, and Victoria did not let him forget it. When Albert suggested a
honeymoon, Victoria put him sharply in his place: "You forget, my
dearest Love, that I am the Sovereign, and that business can stop and
wait for nothing."[35]

Victoria clung to her power as queen, but she was uneasily conscious of her inadequacy for the role. As for Albert, he knew exactly
what he wanted: control not only of the royal family, but also of the
royal household and the monarchy itself. He had no faith in Victoria's
ability to rule. The male-dominated political world of the day legitimized his quest for power. Women had no place in England's public
sphere. A female sovereign was an anachronism, a constitutional odd-
ity. Taking control out of Victoria's hands was a matter of public interest.

Shortly after the wedding, Albert began to flex his muscles. He complained that the court was dull. Chess after dinner each night bored him; he wanted literary and scientific conversation, but the Queen feared that her education had not equipped her for intellectual topics. He sulked when Victoria refused to discuss business with him.

At first Victoria resisted, but pregnancy soon forced her to share her public duties with her husband. In June 1840, the Regency Bill passed unopposed through Parliament, making the twenty-one-year-old German prince sole regent in the event of Victoria's death. It was a triumph for Albert, who had been infuriated when Parliament had slashed his allowance a few months before—a snub intended to humiliate him.

When Victoria was seven months pregnant, Albert reported: "I have come to be extremely pleased with Victoria during the past few months. She has only twice had the sulks. . . . She puts more confidence in me daily." He noted that he was "constantly provided with interesting papers."[36] Soon twin writing desks were installed for Albert and Victoria, side by side, at both Windsor Castle and Buckingham Palace.

Victoria's first child, Vicky, the Princess Royal, was born on 22 November 1840. The baptism was held on 10 February, the anniversary of Victoria's marriage, and her uncle Leopold wrote triumphantly to her: "The act of the christening is, in my eyes, a sort of closing of the first cyclus of your dear life."[37]

Only a month after the christening, Victoria was pregnant again. "Victoria is not very happy about it," Albert told his brother.[38] She resented this second pregnancy even more than the first.

Victoria considered that serially pregnant women were "quite disgusting"—"more like a rabbit or a guinea-pig than anything else and . . . not very nice."[39] She didn't admit it, but she disliked motherhood partly because it forced her effectively to abdicate in favor of her power-hungry consort. She made a sort of sense of this by convincing herself that Albert was a higher being to whom she must surrender herself completely. In a letter to her daughter Vicky in 1858, she described her feelings for Albert: "I owe everything to dear Papa. He was my father, my protector, my guide and advisor in all and everything, my mother (I might almost say) as well as my husband. I suppose no one was ever so completely altered and changed in every way as I was by dear Papa's blessed influence. . . . When he is away I feel quite paralysed."[40]

A woman who is trying to find both a mother and a father in her husband is unlikely to be an engaged mother herself. Victoria was so needy for Albert's love and support that she had little affection to spare for her children. Her pregnancies were unwelcome by-products of her infatuation with Albert. She showed no inclination to dote on her new baby son.

CHAPTER 2

"Our Poor Strange Boy"[1]

1841–56

The new baby was named Albert Edward: Albert after his father, and Edward in memory of Victoria's father, the Duke of Kent. The name Albert pleased no one. Lord Melbourne politely harrumphed that although it was an Anglo-Saxon name, it had not been much in use since the Norman Conquest; while Albert's dreadful father, Ernest of Saxe-Coburg-Gotha, objected that the prince was not named after him.[2] Victoria referred to the child as "the Boy." When he was eighteen months old she wrote, "I do not think him worthy of being called <u>Albert</u> yet."[3] He never was. Instead, everyone called him Bertie.[4]

When Bertie was four weeks old, he was created Prince of Wales and Earl of Chester. At Albert's behest, Bertie had been given the title of Duke of Saxony as well, which annoyed Englishmen but gave him the right to inherit German lands.*[5] Victoria worried that, as heir to

---

* At birth the prince was also given the titles of Duke of Cornwall and Rothesay, Earl of Carrick, Baron of Renfrew, and Great Steward of Scotland.

the throne, the baby would take precedence over his father, and she insisted that his name should come after Albert's in the nation's prayers.

She was troubled by depression. Bertie's birth had been difficult. The doctors told her that "it was a mercy it had not been the first child as it would have been a very serious affair."[6] She was often tearful, and in letters to her uncle Leopold, she complained that she had been "suffering so much from lowness that it made me quite miserable."[7] Six weeks after the birth, she was still "much troubled" by lowness.[8] Her misery dragged on for a whole year.[9]

Postnatal depression made it hard for Victoria to bond with her new son. She claimed to dislike all babies for the first six months; they were "mere little plants," with that "terrible frog-like action."[10] She had a horror of breast-feeding, and Bertie was fed by a wet nurse, a woman named Mrs. Brough.*[11] He was a fat, healthy baby, but Victoria thought him ugly—"too frightful," she later wrote. He was also "sadly backward."[12] Never one to conceal her feelings, Victoria made no attempt to hide her boredom with the child.

Victoria blamed her depression on what she called the "shadow side" of marriage—pregnancy and the hormonal chaos that it caused.[13] But the weeks after Bertie's birth also saw a crisis in her relations with Albert. He forced a palace revolution, eliminating Victoria's closest ally: Baroness Lehzen, her devoted governess.

A Lutheran pastor's daughter with an unappealing habit of chewing caraway seeds (used as a carminative for expelling wind), Lehzen had remained close to Victoria after her marriage. A private passage linked her room to the Queen's. As well as supervising the court and issuing much-prized invitations, she was in charge of the royal nursery. By the time Bertie was born, Albert had developed an obsessive hatred of her. The "old hag" was, he said, "a crazy, stupid intriguer, obsessed with the thirst of power, who regards herself as a demi-god."[14]

---

* The Queen was delighted by Mrs. Brough, whom she thought a simple countrywoman; she was horrified to learn thirteen years later that Mrs. Brough was in fact "depraved" and in a fit of madness had murdered her own six children. (RA VIC/Y99/23, QV to King Leopold, 13 June 1854.) Mary Ann Brough was tried for murder, acquitted on plea of insanity, and died in Bethlem in 1861.

The trouble with Victoria, thought Albert, was that Lehzen had warped her character by giving her the wrong sort of upbringing.[15] Now, encouraged by his own political adviser, the wizened Baron Stockmar, he sought to promote the development of "proper moral and religious feelings" in his wife.[16] She must be taught that, like the queen bee, her chief purpose in life was reproduction, while Albert did the work of a thousand worker bees. Victoria must be isolated from anyone who might seek to influence her ideas. Stockmar had already tried to put a stop to the correspondence between the Queen and Lord Melbourne, her ex–prime minister and father figure. Now he plotted to remove Lehzen, whom he accused of scheming against Albert.

In January 1842, Victoria and Albert were staying at Claremont, fifteen miles from Windsor, where the Queen had been sent to recover her health after Bertie's birth. An urgent message arrived: Their daughter Vicky was dangerously ill. They rushed back and raced upstairs to the nursery, where they found the ailing Vicky. Albert flew into a rage, blamed Victoria for allowing Lehzen to neglect the nursery, and refused to speak to his wife for days. Victoria capitulated. She apologized, took the blame, and agreed to Lehzen's removal. Albert and Stockmar had won.

The angry notes that Victoria and Albert wrote each other during this quarrel give a glimpse of a turbulent marriage. Albert is sometimes seen as a Hamlet figure, always waiting for a better moment, with "a hidden streak of wax," but this hardly fits with his behavior over Lehzen.[17] Bullying his wife at a time when depression made her vulnerable, and removing her closest friend, reveals a cold ruthlessness that some might say amounts to cruelty.

His motives were partly political. Lehzen was the obstacle blocking his plans to reform the court, which was anachronistic, uncomfortable, and wasteful. The responsibilities of the offices of lord chamberlain and lord steward overlapped, so that, for example, the latter found the wood for a fire, while the former lit it. Albert slashed perks at Windsor such as the "Red Room Wine," a weekly allowance paid to a butler to buy alcohol, and the daily practice of installing fresh candles, which were sold off by servants if they were not used.[18] Modernizing the court brought it into line with the age of reform; it was, Albert believed, a necessary process that Victoria could never have achieved while Lehzen remained in control.

When Bertie was ten weeks old, he was christened at Windsor. For the baptism, Victoria dressed in her Garter robes adorned with a large diamond diadem. St. George's Chapel, with its banners and music, filled her with peaceful feelings; she found it "calming" to reflect that so many of her relations, in fact the entire family of George III—including her father, whom she had never known—were buried in the vault beneath the flagstones upon which she stood. "The Child" behaved well, and his mother offered earnest prayers that he might become a true and virtuous Christian and grow up "like his beloved Father!"[19]

After Lehzen was sacked, Lady Lyttelton was appointed royal governess. A well-meaning, intelligent woman in her fifties, she was, as Victoria wrote, "a Lady of Rank." Her role was to supervise the nursery and give occasional lessons.[20] Sarah Lyttelton, or "Lally" as the children called her, worshipped Prince Albert, sentimentalized the royal marriage, and wrote syrupy letters about the "babes."

In the nursery, Bertie's companion was his sister Victoria, the Princess Royal, known as Vicky. Barely a year older than Bertie, she was a paragon. At three she spoke French and could already read. At four a governess was engaged, and soon Vicky learned Latin, later reading Gibbon's Decline and Fall and Shakespeare for relaxation.[21]

Albert doted on Vicky. The relationship between father and daughter was so close that Victoria already felt excluded. The arrival of a younger sibling did not lead, as it often does, to the dethronement of the eldest child. On the contrary, Albert made no attempt to conceal his preference for Vicky. Bertie by comparison seemed backward; few children would not.

It was soon recognized that he was less gifted than his sister. Lady Lyttelton wrote reports on the children for the royal parents. She judged two-year-old Bertie "just as forward as the generality of the children and no more—but with every promise I think as to disposition and intellect."[22] At three, "he is not articulate like his sister, but rather babyish in accent." He "understands a little French," but "is altogether backward in language, very intelligent and generous, and good-tempered, with a few passions and *stampings* occasionally."[23]

The stamping and tantrums grew worse. Bertie developed a stammer. At three and a half, he refused to do his lessons, upset his books, and sat under the table.[24] His anxious parents concluded that there could be only one explanation: Bertie was retarded. What they could or would not see was that his naughtiness was attention-seeking behavior typical of a less loved second child. Albert has often been praised for stimulating Vicky's mind; it has been rightly pointed out that he must equally bear responsibility for the slow development of his son.[25] Victoria was also to blame for ignoring Bertie.

Lady Lyttelton perceived something of this. "Princey," as she called Bertie, was her favorite. She wrote encouraging reports about his "kindness and nobleness of mind."[26] But to Bertie she seems to have been little more than an affectionate presence.

Bertie unquestioningly deferred to Vicky's superiority. When he was four, he was overheard having a heated argument with her as to which of them owned the Scilly Islands. "Princess Royal said they were hers, and the Prince of Wales was equally sure they belonged to him; and another day the Princess was heard telling her brother all the things she would do when she was Queen, and he quite acquiesced in it, and it never seemed to strike either of them that it would be otherwise."[27] The nursery dynamic shifted with the arrival of a third child: Alice, born on 25 April 1843, eighteen months younger than Bertie. Vicky, as the eldest sibling, protected and mothered Alice, who was the prettiest daughter, neither as clever nor as rebellious as Vicky but more manipulative. But the tightest bond was between Bertie and Alice. "Bertie and Alice are the greatest friends and always playing together," wrote Victoria when Bertie was three.[28] The pattern of Bertie and Vicky competing for the affections of Alice endured into adulthood. In the nursery, she was Bertie's devoted slave and loyal friend. Fourteen months after Alice, on 6 August 1844, a second boy, Alfred (Affie) was born. Because of his physical resemblance to Albert and his cleverness at lessons, he became (briefly) Victoria's favorite, which did not endear him to Bertie.*

Vicky made Bertie feel inadequate. How could he compete with a precocious six-year-old who could declare, when her governess momentarily forgot the name of some minor poet: "Oh yes, I dare say you did know all about him, only you have forgotten it. *Réfléchissez*. [Think.] Go back to your *youngness*, and you will soon remember."[29] Little wonder that, at age eight, Bertie was firmly convinced that the monarchy was a matriarchy. "You see," he explained, "Vicky will be Mama's successor. Mama is now the Queen, and Vicky will have her crown, and you see Vicky will be Victoria the second."[30]

Even Queen Victoria perceived that Bertie had been "injured" by being with the clever Vicky, who "put him down by a look—or a word—and their natural affection had been . . . impaired by this state of things."[31] Because Bertie could not possibly do better than Vicky, his reaction was to rebel and refuse to do anything at all.

The education of their children was a matter of great concern to Victoria and Albert. Because Bertie was the eldest prince, his education was especially important. Ever since the Renaissance, Protestant tradition had taught that little princes must be protected from flattery by early training in moral toughness, hard work, and strict duty. (Catholic rulers, by contrast, were said to spoil their heirs from early childhood, hoping by overindulgence to make them immune to temptation.)[32] Months after Bertie's birth, Stockmar addressed a memorandum to Victoria and Albert. "The first truth by which the Queen and the Prince ought to be thoroughly penetrated is, that their position is a much more difficult one, than that of any other parents in the kingdom."

---

* The remaining five children were too young to feature in Bertie's nursery life. They were Helena, born 25 May 1846; Louise, born 18 March 1848; Arthur, born 1 May 1850; Leopold, born 7 April 1853; and Beatrice, born 14 April 1857.

The bad education provided by George III, warned Stockmar, had caused the errors of the Queen's wicked uncles, whose conduct had "contributed more than any other circumstance to weaken the respect and influence of Royalty in this country."[33] The very survival of the monarchy depended upon the education of the Prince of Wales.

The system devised by Stockmar followed the typical German model of princely education in the generation after 1815.[34] This was the method that had succeeded so brilliantly with Albert. As was the custom with princes, Bertie was to be educated in seclusion. His days were to be organized like formal schooling and strictly time-tabled.

In Bertie's case, education was also meant to be a form of treatment. He had special needs. When he was two and a half, an expert was summoned. Dr. Andrew Combe was a leading practitioner of the fashionable quack science of phrenology, the Victorian answer to a child psychiatrist. He calibrated the bumps on Bertie's head and reported that "the development of the brain was in some respects defective." When Bertie was four, Dr. Combe reported improvement, but Stockmar still judged him "essentially a nervous and excitable child with little power of endurance or sustained action in any direction."[35] The therapy prescribed by Stockmar in consequence was regular, systematic exercise of the brain. A detailed timetable was drawn up for Bertie's lessons under the direction of the governess, Miss Hildyard. From eight a.m. until six p.m., every half hour of the six-year-old prince's day was time-tabled, parceled into lessons in French, German, geography, reading, and writing on the slate and also dancing, history, and poetry.[36]

It soon became apparent that Stockmar's system was a failure. Bertie's French teacher expressed "the greatest concern" at his want of progress. When he was six, he was reading the same French book as Alice, who was neither studious nor as clever as Vicky. Lady Lyttelton, who had up till now staunchly defended Bertie's "quickness and power of learning," was compelled to report that he was "a very difficult pupil in some respects, besides his being not at all in advance of his age."[37] By the time Bertie was seven, Lady Lyttelton could no longer control the Prince of Wales.

Bertie's first language was English, and his early words, as recorded by his governess Lady Lyttelton ("Dear Mama gone! Flag should be taken away!"), were all in English.[38] He learned German in the nursery, where at an early age the children "spoke German like their native tongue, even to one another."[39] At three, he had lessons with a German governess, and by the age of five he could read German books.[40] His fluency in German interfered with his speaking of English. An actor, George Bartley, was employed to teach him elocution.[41] At sixteen, his "foreign mode of pronunciation" was very noticeable.[42] Some thought that he never lost the traces of a German accent, rolling his *r*'s in a manner that was unmistakably Teutonic. Others claimed that he spoke English in a beautifully modulated voice—no doubt the legacy of those early elocution lessons.*

Bertie was promoted from the nursery to a tutor when he was seven and a half. This was the age when Victorian boys were considered ready to be removed from the care of women and given over to men for their education. Victoria was more than happy to opt out. When he was two and a half she had declared: "I wish that he should grow up entirely under his Father's eye, and every step be guided by him, so that when he has attained the age of 16 or 17 he may be a real companion to his Father."[43] From now on, Bertie's education was directed by Albert.

On the recommendation of Sir James Clark, the royal physician, Albert engaged a tutor named Henry Birch.[44] A good-looking thirty-year-old bachelor, he was an Eton master with a string of Cambridge prizes and no experience of teaching small boys. He was installed next door to Bertie's room at Buckingham Palace, and Albert drew up a syllabus and timetable. The first few weeks were disastrous. Bertie was rude, disobedient, and rebellious. He refused to take his hat off when people bowed. He stayed in bed until late in the morning; he lost his temper whenever he attempted anything difficult. He was excitable

---

* No known sound recording of his voice survives.

and tyrannical when other little boys came to play, and unkind to his brothers and sisters. "There was at first <u>the very greatest difficulty</u> in fixing his attention," wrote Birch. "He had more than usual difficulty in writing, spelling, calculating and composing sentences, or doing grammatical exercises."[45]

Birch thought that Bertie was too young to leave the nursery. Some biographers have suggested that he was dyslexic, but there is little evidence for this. Certainly he found writing difficult, and it is possible that he was mildly dyspraxic. Albert thought Bertie's handwriting at age seven was "very feeble and unsteady."[46] In Bertie's teens, his tutors noticed that "his slowness of manipulation makes writing laborious to him."[47] The careful copperplate he inscribed in youth ballooned in careless middle age into a paleographic nightmare, suggesting that the fault lay with his motor skills rather than his unwillingness to learn.*

Victoria kept a disgusted distance from her son. The waspish diarist Charles Greville picked up rumors that "the hereditary and unfailing antipathy of our sovereigns to their Heir Apparent seems . . . early to be taking root, and the Queen does not much like the child."[48] No one wondered whether the mother's dislike was cause, as well as consequence, of Bertie's bad behavior. But then Victoria was herself a patient, undergoing a course of moral improvement under Albert's supervision. It was as if poor, bad Bertie was a lightning conductor, articulating buried family tensions.

Birch, by now desperate, consulted the royal parents. What a comfort it was, he reflected, to be able to "open one's mind fully both to the Queen and Prince, on <u>any</u> subject connected with the management of their child."[49] He decided to take a stand; the prince's naughtiness must be met with "severity."[50] Precisely what he meant by the word was not spelled out, but the answer is to be found in the diary of the royal physician, Sir James Clark. He records that in May 1849 the

---

* The doctor Frederick Treves observed Bertie at age sixty cutting his cigars with the blade of a heavy pearl-handled pocketknife. "Now I have never known anyone more clumsy with his fingers than the King and to see him use this great weapon for this small purpose was really alarming," wrote Treves. (RA VIC/Add U/28, Sir Frederick Treves, "An Account of the Illness of King Edward VII in June 1902" [typescript], p. 9.)

prince's "perverseness was such that the father decided on whipping him. The effect was excellent."[51]

Albert's whipping did not cure Bertie's naughtiness for long. That summer he was spotted by a dancing teacher standing on a chair in the corner of the billiard room as a punishment for writing badly. "I'm in disgrace," he wailed.[52]

Bertie took his lessons all alone. He saw no one except his tutors, apart from fifteen minutes with his parents at nine a.m. and again before bed. Birch found the isolation oppressive, and in his "Private Thoughts," written for Stockmar's eyes only (and which Stockmar, of course, promptly passed on to Albert), he complained that being confined day and night at Buckingham Palace was injurious to his own health and spirits.[53] It was worse for his pupil, in whom "symptoms of evil" had once again "assumed an alarming appearance." Birch decided that obedience must be enforced, however "painful" the task—Bertie must again be whipped.[54]

Birch was a grumbler. He babbled on about taking religious orders, encouraged by an offer of a fat living. This annoyed Albert, as one of the conditions of Birch's appointment was that he should be a layman. To make matters worse, Birch was a High Church Puseyite and ostentatiously refused to obey Albert's orders to attend the Presbyterian kirk while staying at Balmoral. Albert's sympathy with the Church of Scotland made him unpopular, as it raised suspicion of his German Lutheran links; Birch's scruples must have looked very much like disloyalty. Albert became convinced that the choice of Birch had been a mistake—he lacked judgment and thought too much of himself and too little of his pupil.

After about a year, though, Bertie began to improve. He kept a diary, which he dictated to Mr. Birch. On the birth of Prince Arthur in May 1850, he reflected: "I have long wished to have another brother, and at last I have got my wish. I mean to try to set a good example to him." After a summer spent on the Isle of Wight, recommended by the doctors on account of the sea air, he claimed: "At Osborne this time I think that I have learned more than when I was in Scotland, and I hope that I have done better also." As a reward, his brother Alfred

(Affie), eighteen months younger, was allowed to share a bedroom with him. "I think that Affie likes being with me and I like having him too, because it is a much better match for me than older persons." At Christmas, Mr. Birch wrote a good report for Papa, which "pleased him very much," and gave Bertie a history of Greece for good behavior. "He promised me a prize a long time ago if I was good up to Christmas." Bertie was allowed to start Latin. Mr. Birch taught him some useful phrases: *"sum bonus puer, non ero malus puer, amo magistrum"* (I am a good boy, I will not be a bad boy, I love my tutor).[55]

These virtuous sentiments were no doubt dictated by Birch, not Bertie, but Birch believed that he had found the key to Bertie's heart, and in November 1850 he implored Stockmar to let him stay.[56] It was too late. By now, Prince Albert had lost faith in Birch. He called in the phrenologist George Combe.* The brain of the Prince of Wales, reported Combe, was feeble and abnormal. The anterior lobe, devoted to intellect, was deficient in size, while the organs of "combativeness, destructiveness and self-esteem" were overdeveloped. This made him highly excitable and "liable to vehement fits of passion, opposition, self-will and obstinacy," which were not acts of "voluntary disobedience" but the result of the physiology of the brain. The treatment was not punishment but a "soothing system" of kindness, avoiding all irritation as every fit of anger made the brain more feeble.[57]

"I wonder whence that Anglo-Saxon brain of his has come," mused Albert. "It must have descended from the Stuarts, for the family have been purely German since their day." Combe, however, was of the opinion that Bertie had inherited the brain of George III—and by implication his madness. "It will be vain to treat the Prince as a normal child," he wrote.[58] This sent a shiver down Albert's spine. The Prince of Wales, he minuted, was not an ordinary boy but "a patient, who ought to be treated physiologically on principles arising out of a thorough knowledge of the faculties of the human mind."[59] By punishing him and speaking harshly to him, Mr. Birch was exacerbating his condition.

---

* George Combe, the older brother of Andrew Combe, was the leader of the phrenological movement in Britain and founder of the Edinburgh Phrenological Society.

Combe then inspected Birch's head and found the cerebral development to be inadequate. There was no doubt about it; Birch must go.

Unfortunately, Albert failed to realize that by now Birch was giving his son precisely what he craved—affection—and Bertie was thriving on it.

The Times worried that Albert was tinkering with the religious education of the Prince of Wales. Little did they know. By today's standards at least, Albert's interference was truly damaging. The public could on no account suspect that the heir to the throne was abnormal, so Albert, persuaded by Combe, arranged for surveillance of Bertie's schoolroom by phrenological spies. He appointed a librarian named Dr. Becker, who also acted as Bertie's German tutor. Becker was sent under an assumed name to Edinburgh, where he trained undercover in phrenology with Combe.[60]

That summer, the nine-year-old Bertie at last discovered that he was heir to the throne, after examining a genealogical table in his room. Becker reported that the prince's self-esteem had swollen, his intellectual organs had shrunk, and his combativeness had become uncontrollable.[61] With Birch, however, Bertie continued to be good. It was 1851, the summer of the Great Exhibition, and Bertie visited almost daily with Birch, writing notes on the exhibits. When Affie fell on his head running downstairs, Bertie noted primly in his diary: "He is so disobedient and heedless that I should not be surprised if he kills himself one of these days." On Christmas Eve at Windsor, Albert led Bertie into a room where, on a table, stood a tree surrounded by presents. Bertie oozed virtue from every pore. "Mr. Birch tells me that I am quite an altered boy in all of my dealing with him and this makes me happy."[62]

Albert must have read this, but to no avail; he was determined to sack the tutor. On 7 January 1852, Bertie wrote sadly in his private diary in his spiky handwriting: "A very unhappy day because Papa had told me that Mr. Birch must soon go away." Next day, "I was still very unhappy. Mr. Birch was so very kind as to console me and give me good advice which made me a little happier." On 20 January: "The last evening and day that I passed with dear Mr. Birch."[63]

Albert's brutal dismissal of Birch echoes his sacking of Victoria's governess Lehzen ten years before. In both cases he convinced himself that a devoted servant and confidant was a malign influence who must be removed in the interest of the "patient," his wife or son. He shut his eyes to the unhappiness this caused. He believed that both Victoria and Bertie had to be treated on moral and scientific principles for their own good. It was as if the intimacy of his wife or his son with anyone but himself represented a threat to his control over them.

Birch left a verdict on his pupil. Progress in writing and spelling was slow, he conceded, but few English boys knew so much French and German. As for Bertie's character, Birch reported: "He has a very keen perception of right and wrong, a very good memory, very singular powers of observation, and for the last year and a half I saw numerous traits of a very amiable and affectionate disposition." Bertie's problems, thought Birch, were due to lack of contact with boys of his own age, and "from himself being the centre round which everything seems to move. . . . He has no standard by which to measure his own powers." The tutor's prognosis was optimistic: "There is every reason to hope that the Prince of Wales will eventually turn out a good, and in my humble opinion a great man."*[64]

Bertie's new tutor was named Frederick Gibbs. He came on the recommendation of Sir James Stephen, the professor of modern history at Cambridge, where Albert was chancellor. Gibbs was a barrister and a fellow of Trinity College, and Stephen tried to impress Albert by describing him as a typical member of the middle class; this was hardly true, as Gibbs had been brought up by Stephen.† Dry, humorless, and

---

* Bertie never forgot Birch. Nearly thirty years later, he was still pressing Prime Minister Benjamin Disraeli to find his old tutor a job. "With regard to Mr. Birch," wrote Disraeli, "he is not unknown to me as, ten years ago, at Your Royal Highness's request, I submitted his name to the Queen for the canonry he now holds." (RA VIC/T8/1, Lord Beaconsfield to B, 5 February 1880.)

† Virginia Woolf remembered Gibbs as an old man: "He wore a tie ring; had a bald, benevolent head; was dry; neat; precise; and had folds of skin under his chin." (Virginia Woolf, *Moments of Being* [Sussex University Press, 1976], p. 74.)

lacking in both imagination and experience, he was a strange choice of tutor for the difficult Bertie.

Gibbs started badly. On his first day, he went for a walk with the two morose little boys, Bertie and Affie. "You can't wonder if we are rather dull today," Bertie told Gibbs. "We are very sorry Mr. Birch is gone. It is very natural is it not?"[65] Acting on instructions from Prince Albert, Gibbs increased Bertie's schooling to six hourly lesson periods a day, time-tabled from eight a.m. to seven p.m., six days a week. In the intervals between lessons, he was ordered to make the princes do riding, drill, and gymnastics, ensuring that they were tired out by the end of each day. Exactly why Albert decided to reject the "soothing system" of light work recommended by George Combe in favor of a program of intensive study is not clear, but it rapidly undid all the good that Birch had achieved.

Some of the more distressing papers relating to Bertie's education were destroyed on his instructions when he became king, but Gibbs kept a diary that survived.[66] He recorded little about the content of Bertie's lessons but, worried perhaps that he might be held to account, wrote detailed notes of Bertie's bad behavior. Day after day, Bertie was rude, had fits of ungovernable temper, and refused to fix his attention on lessons. He fought with Affie and pulled his hair. One day in February 1852, Gibbs wrote:

> I had to do some arithmetic with the Prince of Wales. Immediately he became passionate, the pencil was flung to the end of the room, the stool was kicked away, and he was hardly able to apply at all. That night he woke twice. Next day he became very passionate because I told him he must not take out a walking stick, and in consequence of something crossing him when dressing. Later in the day he became violently angry because I wanted some Latin done. He flung things about—made grimaces— called me names, and would not do anything for a long time.[67]

When Bertie swung a stick and hit Mr. Gibbs in a passion, Albert advised him to box the prince's ears or rap his knuckles sharply. Gibbs

37

n his room. "His Father also spoke to him, and it had a
"

methods won the confidence of the Queen, who thought
real treasure." "Our poor strange boy has improved greatly
since he came," she told Uncle Leopold.[68] Victoria was deluding herself. The more Gibbs tightened the screw, the worse Bertie became.
Photographs from this time show a boy small for his age, hanging his
head, looking down sulkily at his feet. When his German teacher,
Becker, told him off for being rude, Bertie replied: "<u>Other children
are not always good, why should I always be good? Nobody is always
good</u>."[69] Florence Nightingale met the Prince of Wales and thought
him simple, unaffected, and shy, but "a little cowed, as if he had been
overtaught."[70]

Becker addressed a memorandum to Prince Albert, pointing out
that Bertie's rages ("He stands in the corner stamping with his legs and
screaming in the most dreadful manner") were caused by exhaustion
owing to overwork.[71] This was only common sense, but Becker's pleas
were ignored by Albert, who by now had lost patience with the phre-
nologists and their prescription of a "soothing system." He seems to
have lost faith in Bertie, too. Stockmar certainly had. He told Gibbs
that the prince was "an exaggerated copy of his mother." He despaired
of Bertie and his Hanoverian inheritance, preferring Affie. "If you cannot make anything of the eldest, you must try with the younger one,"
he told Gibbs.[72] When Bertie was taken to meet the Eton boys, he was
rude and aggressive, and the headmaster complained. Stockmar gave
his medical opinion that the madness of George III was reappearing;
according to him, one of the symptoms displayed by Bertie's grandfather, the Duke of Kent, and his wicked great-uncles had been the pleasure they took in giving pain.

Bertie's solitary lessons and the long days spent alone with Gibbs were
a form of psychological cruelty; but they took place against a background of luxury and opulence, as his schoolroom moved with the
peripatetic royal family on its stately progress between Windsor, Buck-

ingham Palace, Balmoral, and Osborne.* Home for Bertie was Windsor. With its towers and battlements crowning a hilltop above the Thames, it was less a castle than a miniature city state—an enclosed world. The men of the household dressed in the Windsor uniform of red and blue designed by George III. In the lower ward, toy-town guardsmen in scarlet uniforms marched to the tunes of drums and fifes.

Osborne on the Isle of Wight, where Bertie spent most summers, was the Italianate seaside fantasy that Albert had designed with the help of Thomas Cubitt—a retreat from the grand spaces of Windsor and Buckingham Palace. At Osborne, the Queen and Albert could play at *gemütlich* domesticity. The sparkling blue of the Solent reminded Albert of the Bay of Naples, and the sculpture gallery, which he wrapped round Cubitt's square stuccoed blocks, shimmered with light, which bathed the classical sculptures he and Victoria gave each other as presents. Often mildly erotic, they hinted at the sexual dynamic of the royal marriage. Franz Xaver Winterhalter painted a giant formal canvas of the royal family, which had as its focal point the hands of Victoria and Albert forever engaged in sensuous flirtation.

Albert's dressing room was fitted with bath and cutting-edge shower, filled by running water. The German fresco on the wall showed Hercules laying aside his power and becoming a slave to the Queen of Lydia. Next door to his writing room was the Queen's bow-windowed sitting room, furnished with twin writing desks—Victoria's on the left nearest the window and Albert's on the right—and dotted with white marble casts of their children's hands. On the wall hung Winterhalter's startling painting of the nude Florinda and her ladies undressing as they prepared to bathe.

Directly above the royal suite was the children's floor. The babies and toddlers all slept together with a nurse in the night nursery, lying

* After Christmas at Windsor, the family visited Osborne before settling at Buckingham Palace. They returned to Osborne in the spring for the Queen's birthday (24 May); the early summer was divided between Buckingham Palace and Windsor, before escaping to Osborne. Balmoral was booked for August and September, leaving some children behind at Osborne; October was spent at Windsor, and Osborne was visited again early in December.

in padded wicker cots specially designed by Albert. Bertie slept close by. Light poured into the nursery from the top-lit central staircase; but the parental supervision emanating from below was oppressively claustrophobic.

In May 1853, when Bertie was twelve, the seven royal children solemnly laid the first stone of the Swiss Cottage. This Alpine chalet was Albert's attempt to relive his German childhood and instill habits of work and craftsmanship into his children. "Affie and I worked very diligently at the Swiss Cottage and Papa paid us wages," Bertie dictated to Gibbs in his journal. A week or so later he wrote: "We are getting on beautifully with our brick laying."[73]

The prefabricated Swiss Cottage, shipped over in pieces and completed by workmen on the Osborne estate, was the children's space, one of the few places where Bertie could escape the snooping Gibbs. Albert provided each child with a garden plot and tools, stamped with their initials—Pss L (Louise), P L (Leopold), and so forth—and the girls were taught to cook in the miniature kitchen; but for Bertie the Swiss Cottage was not a Petit Trianon for playing in the manner of Marie Antoinette, but a den of sin. Here he practiced secret smoking with Affie and Alice. Alice wrote from Osborne to Bertie, her "poor forsaken darling" who had been left behind at Windsor: "We went after dinner immediately to the Swiss Cottage (as you can guess) for it is generally the first place we go on arriving here." How she missed her "dearest dear": "I can't smoke paper cigars here for I have no one to smoke with you know what I mean."[74]

Eleanor Stanley, one of the ladies at court, commented on the remarkable physical likeness between Bertie and Alice. She thought them "not alike in character at all; he is retiring, shy, a little inclined to be overbearing, and rather obstinate; but with a sweet, kind expression about his eyes; she, not apparently knowing what shyness means, very sweet-tempered and not at all obstinate."[75] All the adults were taken in by Alice. She seemed so docile and lovable; but in reality she was (as Vicky wrote) a "smart little lady," skilled at dissembling and "almost never getting into trouble," even though she was Bertie's partner in crime.[76]

Osborne was followed in the autumn by Balmoral, the castle in the mountain solitude of the Scottish Highlands, which reminded Albert of his native Thuringian Forest. By 1855, the modest house that Albert had first leased in 1848 had been replaced by a new schloss in the Scots baronial style. Albert designed a Balmoral tartan in gray and purple and a white "Victorian" tartan, and there were tartan-covered chairs and tartan curtains and even tartan linoleum. Bertie spent more time with Albert at Balmoral than anywhere else, accompanying him on stalking expeditions. Stalking was Albert's passion, but he was an unorthodox sportsman. The eight-year-old Bertie described a day on the hill with his father:

> We walked on through some bogs, and we were obliged to stoop quite low, or else the deer would have seen us. Then we sat down on a rock, and Grant [stalker] looked again through his glass and said that the deer had seen us. . . . We soon saw a stag. . . . Papa shot 4 times and then he gave the two rifles to Macdonald [stalker] and then took a small one himself and ordered the dogs to be let loose. . . . For a long time we looked about for Papa, and could not find him, but at last we heard him calling Macdonald. . . . and we saw a fine stag half dead.[77]

As Bertie's account makes clear, Albert was an erratic shot.*[78]

At Balmoral when Bertie was twelve, Albert forbade him from taking a holiday, but ordered him to continue lessons as normal. Even Gibbs thought this too harsh, and he told the Queen so. Gibbs was also critical of Albert's system of seclusion, and suggested that Bertie should be allowed to meet other boys. Very occasionally a few noblemen's sons from Eton came to tea. Charles Carrington, who was to

---

* Some of the deer Albert recorded killing in his game book were young stags weighing only 70 to 80 pounds, well below the size of a full-grown beast, which weighs 180 to 200 pounds. There could be two possible explanations for this. Either Albert "made such a bad shot that he hit a beast at which he was not aiming, or he ignored the advice of his stalker (who would have been pointing out the best stag to shoot) and blazed away at anything he could. Neither explanation does the Prince much credit." (Hart-Davis, *Monarchs of the Glen*, p. 119.)

become Bertie's lifelong friend and devoted follower, a clever courtier who kept a diary, first met the prince at Buckingham Palace in 1854. He recalled that Prince Alfred was the favorite, "but I always liked the Prince of Wales far the best. He had such a kind and generous disposition and the kindest heart imaginable." But Bertie was often getting into scrapes, and he was afraid of his father, "who seemed a proud, shy, stand-offish sort of man, not calculated to make friends with children."[79]

Albert was always there, watching from the undergrowth; once he suddenly appeared from behind a bush, and Carrington fell off the seesaw from sheer fright.

Albert reinvented the "royal family" as a beacon of bourgeois domesticity. Using the new medium of photography, he projected an image of queen and consort as an adoring couple, surrounded by obedient, subdued children. The contrast with Victoria's wicked uncles could hardly be starker. But within this narrative, Albert's role as father was by no means clear. He had no model to follow. His own father, the lecherous Duke Ernest, gave an example of what not to do, but Albert had no experience of the English aristocratic paterfamilias—the dominant male who offered a benevolent example of self-assured manhood.[80] When Bertie, his difficult son, failed in his lessons and threatened to rebel, Albert was at a loss. He spied on Bertie, he whipped him, he treated him as a patient. He never tried to engage his sympathy or initiate him into the world of English manhood—but that was a world that was closed to Albert, too. Little wonder that Bertie later recalled, "I had no boyhood."[81]

The Crimean War intervened. Bertie watched his mother pin medals on to the returning soldiers and allow wounded men into the garden at Buckingham Palace, where they walked about or sat on benches listening to the band of the marines. Albert, meanwhile, was wearing himself out. Victoria and Albert's diplomatic correspondence on the war fills thirty-five folio volumes, and as Albert exhausted himself on the treadmill of duty, his popularity evaporated. He was hated for being German, and for meddling in the army, and his response was to meddle even more.* Key to Albert's diplomacy was a rapprochement with the French emperor, Napoléon III. With the Empress Eugénie, Louis-Napoléon paid a state visit in April 1855. "The Emperor is a short person," wrote Bertie. "He has very long moustachios but short hair, fair. The Empress is very pretty."[82] In August, Victoria and Albert returned the visit, taking with them Vicky and Bertie. They sailed from Osborne, serenaded by the two-year-old Leopold, who wailed (Affie told Bertie): "Ma gone in the boot to Fa, meaning mama is gone in the boat to France, also one buder [brother] why not two buder."[83]

It was the first visit of a British monarch to Paris since Henry VI in 1431, and for Bertie, the ten-day trip was a revelation. Victoria for once was in a state of euphoria. Not only was she welcomed by rapturous Paris crowds, but Albert was given equal rank, which soothed his edgy ego, while his frigid shyness was melted by the willowy Empress Eugénie. "Altogether I am delighted to see how much he likes her and admires her," wrote Victoria artlessly, "as it is so seldom that I see him do so with any woman."[84] As for Victoria, she was charmed and flattered by the emperor, who kissed and squeezed her hand, and whispered affectionate words into her ear. Lord Clarendon, the urbane courtier whose letters give a Rosencrantz and Guildenstern commentary on the court, observed that this was male attention of a sort the Queen had never known before: "She never had been made love to in her life, and never had conversed with a man of the world on a footing of equality; and as his love-making was of a character to flatter her vanity without alarming her virtue and modesty, she enjoyed the novelty of it without scruple or fear."[85] Even the dumpy Queen's homely gowns pleased the emperor, who especially admired the full white dress bursting with red geraniums that she wore with the Koh-i-Noor diamond.

The emperor made a point of paying attention to Bertie, driving

---

* One of Albert's pet projects at this time was a plan to move Westminster School to the country, pulling down the old buildings and throwing open the ground adjoining Westminster Abbey as a park for the public. Fortunately perhaps, this particular act of architectural vandalism was frustrated.

him around Paris in his curricle. "You have a nice country, I would like to be your son," said Bertie.[86] Wearing Highland dress, the British boy won the heart of the crowd. When he visited the tomb of Napoléon I in a thunderstorm and the band played "God Save the Queen," Victoria, moved at the thought of leaning on the arm of Napoléon III before the coffin of his uncle and namesake, Britain's bitterest foe, gestured Bertie to kneel, and the crowd went wild. Vicky cried when they left, and Bertie asked Eugénie if they could stay longer. "Your parents can't do without you," she replied. "Not do without us!" exclaimed Bertie. "Don't fancy that, for there are six more of us at home, and they don't want us."[87]

In Paris, Bertie was put in the charge of Lord Clarendon. "[Clarendon] thinks the Queen's severe way of treating her children very injudicious," reported Greville, "and that the Prince will be difficult to manage, as he has evidently a will of his own and is rather positive and opinionated, and inclined to lay down the law; but he is clever and his manners are good."[88]

Back home, the system of seclusion was tightened, and the children grew ever more rebellious and conspiratorial. The royal schoolroom was a hotbed of subversion. "Write your letters as well as you can," Affie told Bertie, "because Papa wishes to see them."[89] Alice managed to slip through the parental censorship and write Bertie letters that breathe naughtiness:

> Only think what I did yesterday evening with Mr. Affie we smoked paper cigars as we were alone and the room smelled <u>so strong</u> of it that <u>Tilla</u>* found it out and scolded me dreadfully for it not Affie mind you. I was <u>so</u> wretched the first day without <u>you my own</u> darling Brother I did nothing but cry when I got to bed: I put your hair in the pretty little glass locket I generally wear for I have taken the others off and even when I go in a low

---

* Tilla was the children's name for Miss Hildyard, the governess.

dress in the evening I do not take it off I treasure it so, being the only thing I have of you whom I so so dearly love and cherish.[90]

Already the fourteen-year-old prince was learning to live a secret life. With Alice he was wicked and adored. With Gibbs he was no longer openly rebellious, but tame and dull. "We are glad to have continued good accounts of you," wrote Victoria, who hoped to find her son "decidedly improved, and very quiet, and amiable and not contradictory."[91] To Uncle Leopold she wrote, "seclusion has it seems done him good."[92]

Victoria spoke too soon. A few months later, Bertie and Affie were caught smoking. The smoking itself was harmless, Gibbs thought, but the boys had used deceit to conceal it. Prince Albert intervened and punished his sons with three days' solitary confinement. He then announced that he had decided to separate them. The real reason for this was not the smoking, but because in lessons Alfred was ahead of Bertie, who was "almost stationary and his knowledge only half mastered." Being behind his younger brother irritated Bertie, whose "love of rule bore down" on Alfred, and "the result was that the Prince of Wales domineered and Prince Alfred lost his sense of independence."[93]

At eleven, Affie was sent away and given a separate establishment at Royal Lodge in Windsor Park, with an officer of the Royal Engineers as his tutor and sole companion. Bertie, meanwhile, was kept at home under the watchful eye of his father. He penned a contrite letter of apology, to which Albert sternly replied: "Our confidence can of course at present not be restored to you, but you can earn it," which seems somewhat hypocritical, considering that the smoking was not the real reason for separating the brothers.[94]

Bertie sobbed bitterly when Affie moved to Royal Lodge. "His devotion to Affie is very great and pleasing to see," wrote his mother; but she allowed Albert to deny her the pleasure of seeing it.[95] Albert had been brought up with his brother Ernest as his chief companion; but this seemed to make him all the more determined to separate his own sons, convincing himself that it was for their own good. Bertie, by contrast, was later to insist on his two sons being educated together, even though the elder, Prince Albert Victor, was woefully backward by comparison with his younger brother, Prince George.

Albert's relations with his wife were reaching a crisis point. Early in 1856, Victoria's doctor, Sir James Clark, expressed concern about her mental state. He warned that another pregnancy would endanger her mind. Albert must avoid confrontation when she was angry, as this would cause long-term damage to the Queen's brain.[96] (Much the same advice had been given by doctors about Bertie's tantrums.) By July, however, whether by accident or design, the Queen was once again pregnant, this time with Beatrice, and Albert was circling around her, petrified lest she scream—her rages upset him so.

When the family migrated to Balmoral in September 1856, Bertie was left behind at Osborne with his tutors. As an experiment, he was sent on a walking tour in the West Country under the name of Baron Renfrew; it was abruptly called off when he was recognized at Dorchester and cheered. "I do miss you so," wrote Alice from Buckingham Palace, "each time the door opens and I see Affiechaps come in I always think it is you." She had treasured up all his presents to her: "Your little drum [a charm] I mean always to wear and I have not taken it off since you gave it to me for it is fastened to my bracelet: your paintbrush is in my bag, and [I] even took it out in the railroad carriage to see that it was safe: your book on tournaments is also in my bag. . . . So think sometimes of your poor little Alice who is <u>so so</u> fond of you."[97]

At Balmoral the rain never ceased, and Albert struggled up the sodden hills for six hours each day in pursuit of stags that eluded him—for one whole week he shot nothing. Victoria, resenting her pregnancy and torn by conflicting emotions as she watched her daughter Vicky monopolize Albert's attention, was more impossible than ever. She confided in her friend Augusta, the liberal queen of Prussia, that she found no especial pleasure in the company of her elder children, and she was only really happy when Albert was with her. But when he *was* with her they quarreled, and Albert, desperate to avoid a scene, was reduced to communicating by sending letters to her room. "It is indeed a pity," he wrote, "that you find no consolation in the company of your children. . . . The root of the trouble lies in the mistaken notion that the function of a mother is to be always correcting, scolding, ordering them about and organising their activities."[98]

This was, of course, exactly what Albert was subjecting Victoria to. Few people are happy when they are scolded, and Queen Victoria was no exception.

The previous summer, Vicky had become engaged to the Prussian Crown Prince, Frederick William. Victoria tried desperately to convince herself that her fifteen-year-old daughter was, in fact, a grown woman. Albert was miserable at the thought of losing the person he cared about most in the world, but as usual succeeded in convincing himself that doing the thing that gave real unhappiness was for the greater good: Vicky's marriage was part of his long-term dynastic plan. She was to be launched on a one-woman mission to bring liberalism to Germany. He gave Vicky daily tutorials on being a well-informed monarch, and she now ate dinner with her parents when they were alone. If he could not reform Victoria, at least Albert could create his ideal woman in his daughter.

CHAPTER 3

"Neither Fish nor Flesh"[1]

1856–60

In November 1856, Bertie was fifteen. That Christmas he attended the lectures on attraction delivered by Professor Faraday at the Royal Institution. His notes, carefully penned in a neat copperplate hand ("The meaning of attraction is that one body draws another body to itself and keeps it there") are preserved in a leather-bound volume in the Royal Archives—testimony, one might think, to the industry of the royal pupil.[2] The reality was different. Bertie was laboriously prepared before the lectures by his tutor Mr. Gibbs and afterward supplied with notes; but the result, as Prince Albert noted with despair, was "an inaccurate stringing together of the notes!"[3]

A note of panic crept into Albert and Victoria's dealings with Bertie. Victoria insisted on giving Albert the title of Prince Consort, which would give him precedence over the Prince of Wales, meaning that Albert himself, and not his teenage son, became second to the Queen. Victoria often bemoaned the inconsistency that as a married woman she had sworn to obey her lord and master, while as a queen her husband was her subject—a German prince with neither rank nor defined position. Albert worried about the political risks involved in allowing his wife to promote him, which she did by an Order in Council (25 June 1857); but, as he explained to his brother, the question had become urgent because of the fear that "wicked people might succeed in bringing up the Prince of Wales against his father, and tell him that he should not allow a foreign prince to take a place before him."[4] Already, Albert saw his eldest son as a potential enemy.

In January 1857, Albert consulted his friend Lord Granville about Bertie's education. Granville strongly recommended that Bertie should be allowed to mix with other boys. After a meeting with Gibbs, who discussed the pros and cons of being Prince of Wales in a very frank and "uncourtierlike" manner, a new policy was decided.[5] Bertie was no longer to be educated in seclusion; instead, he was to be sent abroad to Germany, accompanied by a group of companions, carefully picked from the best aristocratic families.

Queen Victoria held the somewhat strange view that a king of England should not be *too* English. She considered that George III and William IV failed as monarchs because they were narrowly patriotic. England's greatest king, Victoria believed, was William III, who was a foreigner, as indeed was Albert; being foreign "gave them a freedom from all national prejudices which is very important in Princes."[6] "Dear Germany" had a special place in Victoria's affections. She told Bertie that he must learn to love it, as "it is in fact also your country—being your dear father's and yourself being a German as well as an English Prince."[7]

Foreign travel had another advantage: It removed the adolescent prince, whom Albert described as "neither fish nor flesh," from London and the pollution of aristocratic society. Both Victoria and Albert feared and loathed "the independent, haughty faultfinding fashionable set" of society.[8] Neither of them had grown up in splendor—indeed, the Queen considered that she was "brought up almost as a private individual, in very restricted circumstances, for which I have ever felt thankful."[9]

———

In July 1857, Bertie, his tutors, and a select party of four young companions, including Willie Gladstone, son of the politician William Gladstone, set off for Königswinter, near Bonn.* Before he left, Bertie wrote an essay for his tutors on how to spot the difference between friends, who "tell you of your faults," and flatterers, who please you with false compliments, and "make you despised and hated in society, and lead you into any imaginable vice."[10] Gibbs sent daily bulletins back to Albert, noting Bertie's improvement under the influence of his new friends. The level of conversation can be seen from the book of schoolboy puns titled "Wit and Whoppers" that the friends compiled: "The Prince of Wales on hearing that an insulting caricature had appeared in a popular periodical said that the Editor should be 'punched' for it."[11] According to Gibbs, Bertie's companions taught him not to be idle, and they shamed him out of his dictatorial manner of saying, "But I wish so and so." This, said Gibbs, "is just what is wanted, and what none of us can do."[12]

Gibbs complained that Bertie ordered about the equerry Henry Ponsonby as though he were a servant.[13] When Bertie managed to kiss a girl, the episode was not reported to Albert, but it reached the ears of Mr. Gladstone, who pursed his lips at the prince's "squalid little debauch."[14] The truth was, Bertie was exceptionally immature. Victoria told him that she expected to find him "grown quite a <u>Child</u> and quite a companion to us," having heard from everyone how improved he was.[15] But she didn't hear the whole story. In Switzerland, where the party traveled after Königswinter, Bertie stayed at a house in Interlaken, and the people there thought him "young and childish for his age." They noticed that his suite talked among themselves, seldom addressing Bertie when serious issues were discussed, but "treating him as a boy." He behaved like a child, too: One day he was nowhere to be found at dinnertime, and when everyone had tired of looking, he sud-

---

* Gladstone's son seems a strange companion to choose, given Victoria's later dislike of the father, but Lady Lyttelton, Bertie's former governess, was a relative of the Gladstones.

denly appeared from beneath the table.[16] This was regressive behavior for a fifteen-year-old, but Bertie had never been allowed to be a child at home.

Bertie returned in October. The whole family assembled on the staircase at Windsor to welcome him. Victoria noted in her journal that he looked "extremely well, bronzed, and bright, and is a good deal grown."[17] She wrote a letter for his sixteenth birthday in November, giving permission for him to choose his own clothes; however, "we do expect that you will never wear anything extravagant or slang."[18]

Ever since the Crimean War, Bertie had hankered after a military career, and he now prepared for the army examination, but his mother forbade him from joining the army as a profession. Politically, this was no doubt wise; the army was considered an inappropriate career for the heir to a constitutional monarchy. On the other hand, Affie was allowed to join the navy. "This is a passion which we as parents have not the right to subdue," Albert explained; but the same logic did not apparently apply to Bertie.[19] The unfairness of this must surely have made the examinations a somewhat pointless exercise. Bertie's history paper shows no evidence of reading, but a certain common sense. To the question whether kings should be elected, he answered: "It is better than hereditary right because you have more chance of having a good sovereign, if it goes by hereditary right if you have a bad or weak sovereign, you cannot prevent him reigning." Asked to trace his mama's descent from King James I, however, he managed to muddle even his own pedigree.[20]

Vicky, the Princess Royal, married Prince Frederick William (Fritz), heir to the throne of Prussia, on 25 January 1858. It was a dynastic match of great importance, the keystone of Albert's project to create a liberal Germany united under Prussia, but the celebrations were muted. At the pre-wedding ball, Buckingham Palace's grand new ballroom was only half full, and Benjamin Disraeli noted that the princes and princesses danced only with one another and looked tired. Vicky cried all the time at the thought of leaving home; but then (Disraeli again), "they say she is very childish and always cries."[21] On the morning of the wedding, the Queen was so nervous that she shook as she posed for the pre-wedding daguerreotype, which shows her as a dumpy blur beside her daughter.

At the wedding in the Chapel Royal at St. James's, Bertie wore Highland dress and acted as Vicky's supporter. The next day, Vicky wrote: "You were so good to me yesterday, dear Bertie, I shall not forget the kind affectionate way in which you said goodbye to me."[22]

Vicky was a child bride, just seventeen; Albert certainly did not see his daughter as a woman, describing her as having "a man's head and a child's heart."[23] Countess Walburga ("Wally") Hohenthal, her new German lady-in-waiting, who was only a year older, noted that "her childish roundness still clung to her and made her look shorter than she really was."[24] Vicky had a bewitching smile, which showed her small and beautiful teeth, and she was soft-voiced and gentle; but she had a will of steel. She was intellectual, stunningly tactless ("I can never say what I do not think"), and a poor judge of character, prone to taking violent likes and dislikes.[25]

Fritz was eleven years her senior. Over six feet tall, he was a Saxon chieftain with glittering blue eyes, a mane of blond hair, and thick leonine whiskers. He seemed the ideal husband, but he was indecisive and lacking in confidence. Since his first visit to England at age nineteen, he had been schooled in liberal politics by Albert, who sent him reading lists and signed his autograph book: "May Prussia be merged in Germany, and not Germany in Prussia." Fritz brought to the altar what Victoria called "the white flower of a blameless life," just as Albert had done.[26] And Vicky fell in love with him, just as Victoria had with Albert.

At Windsor, where Vicky and Fritz spent their so-called honeymoon, the ladies shivered in their evening dresses with their backs to an open window, while the Queen and her daughters toasted themselves before the fire. Fritz was invested with the Order of the Garter, looking absurd in stockings and knee breeches beneath his Prussian military tunic. When the Garter Knights retired backward out of St.

George's Hall, they stumbled over their long cloaks, which twisted round their legs, and Bertie giggled.[27]

Vicky and Fritz left England for good. Albert accompanied the couple to Gravesend. When they parted, Vicky buried her head in her father's breast in floods of tears. "I thought my heart was going to break when you shut the cabin door and you were gone," she wrote. "I miss you so dreadfully, dear Papa, more than I can say; your dear picture stood near me all night."[28] For Vicky, who idolized her father and thought him a perfect being, his decision to exile her from paradise must have seemed strangely confusing. She never resolved her ambivalence about her identity; she was an Englishwoman in Germany, and in England she seemed distinctly foreign.

Albert wrote Vicky what was probably the saddest letter of his life. "I am not of a demonstrative nature, and therefore you can hardly know how dear you have been to me, and what a void you have left behind in my heart."[29] He had lost his favorite child, the brainiest member of the English royal family since George II's wife Queen Caroline and the only one of his children with an academic mind like his.

Victoria wept more than anyone when Vicky left, but her tears were mixed with remorse. For months she had scolded Vicky, telling her that she was thankful to be rid of her. Once Vicky was married, however, and Victoria had Albert to herself, the Queen bombarded her daughter with letters. Vicky in Germany became Victoria's confidante; the frank and candid letters she poured out to her Dearest Child reveal the intimate feelings of an impulsive, emotional woman who never worried what posterity might think of her.

Vicky's marriage shifted the family dynamic. Hitherto, Victoria had had little to do with Bertie, concentrating her scolding on Vicky. Now, all the anger she had once vented on her daughter rained down on Bertie. "Oh! Bertie alas! That is too sad a subject to enter on," wrote the Queen; but enter upon it she did, and in letter after letter to Vicky she bemoaned Bertie's shortcomings. He was lazy, he was weak, he was dull. "Handsome I cannot think him, with that painfully small and narrow head, those immense features and total want of chin." "You cannot imagine the sorrow and bitter disappointment and the awful anxiety for the future which [Bertie] causes us!"[30] Vicky annoyed Victoria by remaining silent on the subject of Bertie in her replies. To Bertie, however, she wrote preachy letters, telling him that "we all ought to help one another [prove] ourselves worthy to be the children of our parents."[31]

One person who dared to speak to the Queen about her relations with Bertie was her half sister, Feodora, safely ensconced in a distant palace in provincial Germany. "Do show him love, dearest Victoria," she begged, "I know that he thinks you are not fond of him."[32] But showing love to her eldest son was something that Victoria was quite unable to do. So emotionally dependent was she on Albert that she wanted only to be the "child" of her husband. Bertie was despised for his failure to resemble his father in looks, character, or ability. Only Affie and Arthur, who both had a physical likeness to Albert, were adored; but Affie fell from grace on account of his distressing habit of telling lies.

Bertie's confirmation in April 1858 was an important rite of passage, marking his transition to adult life and independence. He prepared by reading sermons aloud to the Queen, and he was examined on the catechism for more than an hour by the Dean of Windsor in front of the Archbishop of Canterbury. The next day, wearing his Windsor uniform of blue and red, he was confirmed by the archbishop in St. George's Chapel. The Queen wore a "blue moiré antique" and prayed fervently for her son. Afterward he dined alone with his parents, and Albert gave him a fatherly talk about the dangers to which he was now exposed, warning him not to be led astray. Bertie took this in good heart, probably because he had no idea what Albert was referring to; as Victoria wrote, "thank God he is still too innocent and pure to understand, for he is as innocent as a little child."[33] The sixteen-year-old prince knew nothing of the facts of life.

Queen Victoria kept a notebook of her private thoughts entitled "Remarks Conversations Reflections," in which she poured out her anxiety about her children, Bertie especially:

He has a good heart and is very affte [*sic*], and at bottom very truthful, but his intellect alas! is weak which is <u>not</u> his fault but, what <u>is</u> his fault <u>is</u> his shocking laziness, which I fear has been far too much indulged, and which goes so far that he listens to nothing you tell him or teach him or what is said before him, but seems in a sort of dreaminess, which alarms <u>us</u> for his <u>brain</u>. He profits by nothing he learns, gives way to temper, very bad <u>manners</u> and great insubordination, all <u>most dangerous</u> qualities for his position. <u>And</u> poor Mr. Gibbs . . . has been far too indulgent and I fear has no authority over him, which is very sad . . . From his idleness, which extends to his <u>thinking</u> as well as <u>acting</u>, he leans entirely upon others and therefore will always be led more or less, the danger of which is enormous.[34]

Victoria thought the answer was to tighten the discipline, but Albert disagreed. By now he had begun to doubt the wisdom of what he called the "aggressive system" that the Queen followed toward her children. But he was powerless to stop her. Stockmar found him "completely cowed" by Victoria, who was "so excitable that the Prince lived in perpetual terror of bringing on the hereditary malady." When Lord Clarendon ventured to advise Albert to treat his children more kindly, Albert replied that he dare not confront Victoria for fear of exciting her mind, adding that "the disagreeable office of punishment had always fallen upon him." Clarendon thought that in spite of his natural good sense, Albert had been "very injudicious" in the way he treated his children, "and that the Prince of Wales resented very much the severity which he had experienced."[35]

Shortly after his confirmation, Bertie was given an establishment of his own at White Lodge, a Palladian villa built by George II in Richmond Park. Sending his teenage sons away to grace-and-favor houses to be force-fed knowledge by their tutors in seclusion formed the next stage of Albert's curriculum. At White Lodge, Bertie was accompanied by Gibbs; the Rev. Charles Tarver, his Latin tutor and chaplain; and three equerries, carefully picked young men in their twenties of the "very highest character," who were charged with giving him a good example. They received strict instructions from the Queen not to "indulge in careless self-indulgent lounging ways" such as slouching with their hands in their pockets. "Anything approaching a practical joke . . . should never be permitted."[36]

White Lodge was a dismal failure. Bertie continued to be addicted to practical jokes. On a trip to Ireland, he fired a rifle loaded with blanks at a group of boatmen and accidentally cut a man in the cheek. Victoria noted that "he was dreadfully frightened and distressed at the time—but when his father spoke to him he did not take it in that contrite spirit which one would have wished."[37] Sir James Clark, the Queen's doctor, was consulted, and prescribed a lowering diet. Luncheon: meat and vegetables, pudding best avoided, seltzer water to drink. Dinner: as light as possible, but a little heavier than luncheon, claret and seltzer in hot weather, sherry and water in cold.[38]

Lonely and bored by the reading he was made to do, Bertie made no progress. One of Bertie's gentlemen thought the problem was Gibbs, who had no influence over him. "Mr. Gibbs has devoted himself to the boy, but no affection is given him in return, nor do I wonder at it, for they are by nature thoroughly unsuited. . . . I confess I quite understand the Prince's feelings towards Mr. Gibbs."[39]

Bertie got on far better with Mr. Tarver. Shortly before he turned seventeen, he asked Tarver to explain some words "which it was impossible to make clear to him without entering somewhat fully on the subject of the purpose and the abuse of the union of the sexes."[40] Tarver did his best, and then made a hurried and embarrassed confession to Albert, whose fatherly duty he worried that he had usurped.

On Bertie's seventeenth birthday, Albert penned him a memorandum. Gibbs was to leave. ("He has failed completely over the last year and a half," said the Queen, "and Bertie did what he liked!")[41] Instead, Bertie was to have a governor. He must now embark on a study more important than any he had undertaken so far: "How to become a good man and a thorough gentleman."[42] He was to receive the Order of the

Garter and the rank of colonel. So overcome was Bertie at the prospect of liberation from Gibbs that he brought the letter to the Dean of Windsor, Gerald Wellesley, in floods of tears.

The governor was Colonel (later General) Robert Bruce, the son of Lord Elgin of the Elgin Marbles; his sister, Lady Augusta Bruce, was a close friend of the Queen, and he was in almost daily contact with Prince Albert. Bruce was a strict disciplinarian, who ruled the prince as if he were an unruly colony. Bertie was held under virtual house arrest, and it was Bruce who settled the plans for each day.

Bertie was thrilled with his new uniform, but he later recalled that he detested being made a lieutenant colonel straight away, rather than beginning at the bottom of the ladder as he had hoped. It meant that his army career was aborted.[43] He was to be a mere play soldier; a tailor's dummy in uniforms with no real military experience. Instead, he was to study at Oxford. Meanwhile, rather than stay in London ("It would not be good for him," said Albert), he was to spend his gap year in foreign travel.[44]

Bertie arrived in Rome in January 1859. Colonel Bruce's reports to Prince Albert make depressing reading. Bertie frittered away his time, showed no interest in art or classical history and, in spite of the little dinners that Bruce arranged for him to meet distinguished men, he seemed only interested in gossip, dress, and society.[45] This was not how the outside world saw him, however. One of Bertie's guests was the poet Robert Browning. To his surprise, Browning was impressed. "The prince did not talk much, but listened intelligently and asked several questions on Italian politics."[46]

From England, Albert exercised strict supervision, returning Bertie's letters with corrections to the English and grammar.[47] Bertie was made to keep a journal, which was sent back to Albert and later bound. It is a bald account of his doings—"I went with Colonel Bruce here and there"—and Albert rightly complained that it was disappointing.

Bertie was granted an audience with Pope Pius IX—the first member of the English royal family to meet the pontiff since Henry VIII broke with Rome. When Albert met Pope Gregory XVI twenty years before as a young German prince, he had conversed in Italian on the

influence of the Egyptians on Greek and Roman art.[48] Bertie, by contrast, described his encounter thus:

> The staircase was lined by the Swiss Guards, who looked very
> picturesque in their peculiar and handsome dress; we had to pass
> through many rooms, before we reached that in which the Pope
> was; he came to his door and received me very kindly, I remained
> about ten minutes conversing with him, and then took my de-
> parture.[49]

In light of his later openness toward Roman Catholicism, it is possible that Bertie was more affected by the meeting than he admitted to
his Lutheran father. "I was sorry that you were not pleased with my
journal," he told Albert, "as I took pains about it, but I see the justice
of your remarks and will try to profit by them."[50] His tutors dictated a
new version: "Whilst standing before the Pope many thoughts crowded
into my mind. . . ." Tarver was stung to defend himself. The prince
could hardly be expected to do better, he wrote, considering how small
were his "reflective and inductive powers"; he never asked questions or
read books.[51]

The tutors' failure to spark any interest whatsoever in classical history or art reflects as badly on them as it does on Bertie. His intellect,
as Albert remarked, was lively and sharp, but "of no more use than a
pistol packed in a trunk."[52] Perhaps the most valuable lesson that Bertie learned was how to deceive his keepers. He was caught writing
letters from Rome to lady-in-waiting Jane Churchill, a court beauty
who was married and nearly thirty but looked ten years younger. Years
later, Bertie told Vicky that he had been "much in love with her."[53]

When the War of Italian Unification broke out and Rome was
threatened with hostilities, Bertie was forced to cut short his stay, but
Albert refused to allow him to return home. As he explained to Bruce,
"it would be very objectionable for him to be at Buckingham Palace
during a succession of gaieties," which would prevent him from applying himself to the study that was "absolutely necessary." But Albert
was anxious to avoid "the appearance of unkindness if not of injus-

tice" by banishing Bertie fr⟍   ⟍ne. "Nothing could be so dangerous to . . . the welfare of the young Prince, and to the future influence of his royal parents over him, as any opinion upon the part . . . of the public that he was treated with unkindness. . . . There could but be two reasons for such a want of natural feeling—either unjust caprice on the part of the parents or unworthiness on the part of the son. It would be difficult to say which judgement on the part of the public would be more disastrous."[54] Albert's frankness is as chilling as his calculation is devastating—a reminder that this was the man who had "sold" the monarchy through spin, reinventing it as "the royal family" (this was Albert's phrase) and repackaging it as a middle-class domestic idyll.

Bertie was packed off to Edinburgh. Here he would be safely out of harm's way and, Albert calculated, his stay could be advertised as a bid to please the Scots. The Palace of Holyroodhouse was dull, but Bertie applied himself dutifully to lectures on science and Roman history. Albert descended and held an "educational conference" with Bertie's tutors. Bertie was allowed to join his family afterward at Balmoral, but his father insisted on two hours' study daily; when his tutors suggested that he might read a novel by Walter Scott, Albert snapped: "I should be very sorry that he should look upon the reading of a novel (even by Sir Walter Scott) as a day's work."[55]

Victoria conceded that, somewhat to her surprise, Bertie had worked better at Edinburgh than ever before, but she disliked his looks. "The nose," wrote the doting mother, "is becoming the true Coburg nose, and begins to hang a little, but there remains unfortunately the want of chin which with that very large nose and very large lips is not so well in profile."[56] Bertie was rebuked for wearing long coats and large shoes out shooting, and his hairstyle enraged the Queen: "Do not divide your hair so nearly in front and paste it down at the sides. It looks so effeminate and girlish and makes the head look so small."[57]

In October 1859, Bertie arrived at Oxford. Albert browbeat the reluctant Dean Liddell of Christ Church to agree that the prince should not have rooms in college like other students, but live in isolation with his

governor, now promoted to Major-General Bruce. Private lodgings
were rented at Frewin Hall in the Cornmarket, where he was strictly
supervised. "The only use of Oxford," wrote Albert, "is that it is a
place for study, a refuge from the world."[58] Bertie must become acquainted with Oxford's distinguished men, but avoid the contamination of his fellow undergraduates. Under the supervision of tutor
Herbert Fisher a special course of lectures was delivered to Bertie and
six carefully picked Christ Church undergraduates at Frewin Hall.
Whenever Bertie walked into a lecture or attended a cathedral service,
everyone rose and remained standing until he was seated.

Bertie resented his isolation, later claiming that it damaged his education, as no doubt it did, given his gregarious nature. His "rigidly virtuous" system and the omnipresence of General Bruce was "a good
deal laughed at."[59]

In December, Dean Liddell gave Bertie an oral examination on
English history from the Anglo-Saxons to Henry III. How this specially
designed course would prepare him for his future role is hard to see,
but his answers were "ready, clear and for the most part right." His
written examinations were less good. "His pen is not so ready as his
tongue," commented the dean.[60]

Victoria made a practice of sending Bertie a report on his behavior
at the end of each holiday, and the letter she addressed to him after
that Christmas at Windsor was particularly stinging. He had dawdled
and wasted his time—the Queen had noticed "a growing listlessness
and inattention and . . . self-indulgence" that was most dangerous. "Let
me never hear of your lying on a sofa or an armchair except you are ill
or returned from a long fatiguing day's hunting or shooting."[61]

Back at Oxford, General Bruce complained to Albert about Bertie's
lack of respect for his tutor Herbert Fisher. "After severely censoring
the intemperate tone and manner in which he not infrequently addresses those about him, I stated that such displays to a gentleman in
Mr Fisher's position were intolerable."[62] In spite of this, Dean Liddell
reported an improvement on the previous term. Bertie had worked
harder on more difficult subjects, and his oral answers were good. The

written answers still showed constraint. "They might be fuller and might be expressed in freer and more idiomatic language." Privately, the dean considered Bertie to be "the nicest fellow possible, so simple, naïve, ingenuous and modest, and moreover with extremely good wits; possessing also the Royal faculty of never forgetting a face."[63]

In spite of General Bruce's surveillance, Bertie managed to make one extremely unsuitable friend at Christ Church: Sir Frederick Johnstone. Johnstone was exactly the type of "fast" young man Albert was anxious that Bertie should avoid—a heavy-drinking member of the Bullingdon Club, devoted to gambling, horse racing, and womanizing. It was he who first led Bertie astray, opened his eyes to the possibilities of his position, and perhaps helped to rub off his harsh German accent.[64] Soon the Prince of Wales's name was to be found inscribed in the ledger of the fashionable Savile Row tailor Henry Poole, along with his measurements—chest: 33¾ inches; waist: 29¼ inches.[65] So much for the view that he was already overweight. At Frewin Hall, Bertie engaged a first-rate chef. He took up fox hunting. He was becoming a swell.

Victoria watched with dismay. She urged Bertie to refrain, as she and Albert did, from eating rich and unwholesome dishes. She implored him to be careful out hunting, a sport that she abhorred—"that horrid hunting from which it is a mercy anyone returns alive. . . . You all of you belong to the country and must not be foolhardy or imprudent. Of course this applies a thousand times more to dear Papa, who is all and all to me, without whom I shd be utterly powerless, consequently whose life is of national and European importance."[66]

Bertie's replies to his mother's letters were pathetically meek and submissive. "I am afraid that I have very little news to tell you, as every day is much the same."[67] One senses the irritation behind the Queen's complaint: "It is very discouraging when I write to you dear Child, full of anxiety for your welfare and receive nothing but an indifferent answer. . . . Try in future dear and enter a little into what Mama in the fullness of her heart writes to you."[68] Bertie's response was hardly encouraging. "I am afraid that my letters are very dull and stupid as there

your letters as much as I can." Little wonder the royal parents worried sometimes that their son was a half-wit.

Queen Victoria considered that one of the problems about being
royal was that "we <u>cannot form</u> intimate friendships <u>except</u> among our
<u>nearest relations</u>."[70] The eighteen-year-old Bertie's most intimate
friends were his sisters, and his response to his mother's bullying was
to appeal for their support. He wrote to Vicky in Berlin, complaining
about his parents' constantly finding fault. Her response was affectionate but patronizing. "Don't be cast down my darling old Bertie," she
urged, "only try and do what dear Papa wishes and you will see all will
go right and dear Mama will be pleased and satisfied."[71] Homesick and
lonely in her barracks-like palace in Berlin, reading and nursing her
new baby, Vicky had forgotten how wounding Victoria's criticisms
could be.

Alice was different. Her sharp, waiflike profile contrasted starkly
with the rich, rustling satins of her wide hooped dresses. At sixteen she
was intensely religious, with a directness and spontaneity that was perhaps the result of childhood illness; it made her strangely attractive.
Lord Clarendon described her as a bird in a cage, beating her wings
against her prison bars.[72]

This was an age of intense, romanticized brother-sister relationships, but few sisters wrote such emotional letters as Alice did to Bertie. "I am so happy when I have you dear darling, though it is but for a
short time." Again: "My good love I miss you so though we are so
constantly separated, I cannot get accustomed to it, and it makes me
quite sad to think that I must once more make my pen the interpreter
of all my feelings and thoughts." It was as if Bertie was her fantasy
lover, but she worshipped Albert, too, declaring, as Vicky had done
before her, that "there never was such a <u>perfect man</u> as Papa before,
everything that is good is united in him, everything that is great, that is
noble, that is clever, that is true, he really is almost an angel upon
earth!"[73]

Instead of lecturing Bertie, as Vicky did, Alice joined him in con-
spiring against the Queen. "Thank you very much for both your let-

ters," Alice wrote in December 1859; "the first I burned after reading it, as I do not wish to risk any false excuse for not showing it; for though you were quite excusable in your annoyance, yet the way you expressed yourself against Her was not quite respectful. Please burn the letter I sent you."[74] Bertie forwarded Victoria's letters to Alice, who replied carefully. "I think it would be better dear Bertie if, when she makes such remarks, gives you such advice, that you should not only thank her for it, but tell her you will follow it." She counseled caution: "You must remember, she is your Mother and is privileged to say such things; and though, as Vicky and I have often and long known, they are not said in the pleasantest way and often exaggerated, yet out of filial duty they must be borne and taken in the right way."[75]

Alice, now seventeen, was impatient to be married off to the inevitable German prince, and suitable candidates were invited for inspection. Prince Louis of Hesse arrived at Windsor to stay for Royal Ascot week in June, and Bertie joined the party from Oxford. The romantic Alice fell desperately in love with the red-faced, doltish Louis. The couple exchanged tear-sodden handkerchiefs when they parted, and very soon they became engaged. Clarendon, who thought Alice the brightest and most attractive of her family, regretted her engagement to a "dull boy" with a "dull family in a dull country."[76] The news was a wrench for Bertie, who wrote unhappily to Alice: "It will be a bitter pang for me to separate from you, as it will not be the same place without you, nobody will be able to supply your place, as Lenchen [Bertie and Alice's younger sister Helena] is so much younger and still so childish."[77]

Back in Oxford after Ascot, Bertie wrote Victoria a letter that could hardly fail to annoy her: "I hope that you will excuse that I have not written before, but as I had no news of any sort to give you, my letter would have been very dull, and I am afraid that it will be so now, as I have nothing of any interest to communicate to you."[78] The Oxford term ended with a Christ Church ball. Albert warned Bertie strictly that Oxford balls "are not visited by you for your amusement, but to give pleasure to others by your presence."[79] The next morning, when the doors of the Sheldonian Theatre were flung open for Commemoration, Bertie headed the procession of dons, taking precedence over

the vice chancellor on account of his rank. An audience of rowdy undergraduates gave three hearty cheers for the prince, who "graciously
acknowledged them."[80] Fame, it seemed, was not something that Bertie needed to earn by reading and applying himself to his lectures as his
father had done. He was famous just because of who he was, and the
discovery was intoxicating.

In the summer of 1860, the eighteen-year-old Bertie made his first
royal tour, to Canada and the United States.

Bertie's grandfather, the Duke of Kent, had served with his regiment in Canada in the 1790s, and Prince Edward Island was named
after him; but the idea of sending the heir to the throne on a ceremonial tour of the new world was an innovation. Like most ideas at court,
it originated with Albert, who choreographed the entire visit, even
composing memoranda supplying responses for Bertie to read to all
the addresses he received on his tour.[81]

Bertie's minder was the Duke of Newcastle, known to his friends as
Barbarossa on account of his red beard. A crony of Gladstone, the hapless but humorless duke had lived down the disgrace of his wife's adultery and divorce; he was now fleeing the scandal caused by the
elopement of his daughter Lady Susan Clinton with Lord Adolphus
Vane-Tempest, the son of the Marquess of Londonderry, who was alcoholic, violent, and insane.

Bertie and his retinue landed at the remote fishing village of St.
John's, Newfoundland, on 23 July 1860. He dutifully read aloud the
wooden speeches written for him by Newcastle, who had drafted them
from Albert's memoranda; but the journalists found the copy they
needed at the dance that evening, when the prince whirled and twirled
until two a.m. and was spotted calling the dances, correcting the back-
woods folk of this unfashionable spot. A news report appeared in the
New York press, which earned Bertie a reproof from Albert: "You always liked to order people about at dances but I trust you will keep
that longing in check." Never forget, he warned his son, "how much
and how constantly you are watched, observed and described."[82] "I am

quite aware that I am closely watched and must be careful in what I do," responded Bertie, denying that he had ordered the dancers about; but "besides if I did it would have been not to be wondered at, as I never saw so many people who knew so little about dancing."[83] A few days later, however, *The New York Herald* reported that the prince "whispered sweet nothings" to the ladies as he directed them in the dance. "His Royal Highness looks as if he might have a very susceptible nature and has already yielded to several twinges in the region of his midriff."[84] This was not what Albert wanted to hear.

When he crossed the border from Canada into the United States, Bertie traveled as Baron Renfrew. Some commented on his unimpressive looks and unfashionable clothes, but he was recognized and welcomed everywhere. At Washington he was received at the White House by President James Buchanan, and Harriet Lane, the bachelor president's thirty-year-old niece, played hostess. "I thought Miss Lane a particularly nice person and very pretty," Bertie told Victoria.[85] The royal tour climaxed with Bertie's arrival at New York on 11 October. A crowd of three hundred thousand (allegedly) showered him with flowers—which shows, Bertie modestly reported, "that the feeling between the two countries could not be better." At the Grand Ball next day, three thousand were invited but five thousand squeezed into the Opera House, causing the floor to give way. It took two hours of banging for the carpenters to put it right, and dancing did not begin until midnight.*[86]

No one had expected such overwhelming enthusiasm. Even Victoria went out of her way to give credit to her son. She insisted, however, that Bertie's reception by the Americans was due principally to "the (to me incredible) liking they have for my unworthy self."[87] Bertie returned home to Windsor in November looking extremely well. Victoria commented in her journal that he had become "very talkative," and the courtiers were amused to see him conversing in an independent sort of way with his father.[88]

---

* The ball made a lasting impression. When Bertie's grandson Edward VIII as Prince of Wales visited New York in 1919, a reception was given for all the survivors of Bertie's ball nearly sixty years before.

CHAPTER 4

Bertie's Fall

1861

After America, Bertie was sent straight back to Oxford. Even the martinet General Bruce questioned the wisdom of resuming the schoolboy discipline, but Albert insisted on the same strict rules as before. Bertie left Oxford in December with good reports. According to the dean of Christ Church, "[He] has expressed himself with increasing freedom and written at greater length than he has ever done before."[1]

Next on Albert's program for his son came a year at Cambridge. In January 1861, Bertie enrolled at Trinity College. As before, he was installed under General Bruce's supervision in a residence of his own: Madingley Hall, a large, comfortable house about four miles outside Cambridge. Bertie found it old-fashioned and very cold. For his lectures he drove in to Cambridge, where Dr. Whewell, the master of Trinity, lent him rooms in the Lodge. Here Charles Kingsley, the regius professor, came to lecture him on history. Kingsley was nervous as to whether the interpretation that he gave of the Glorious Revolution of 1689 accorded with the royal parents' historical views. "The responsibility terrifies me," he wrote. He needn't have worried. Bertie thought Kingsley one of the best lecturers he had ever heard—"though of course my experience is not very great"—and had nothing to say about the content.[2] Albert forbade him from taking notes, insisting that he write the lectures out from memory when he returned home to Madingley.[3]

On his nineteenth birthday, Bertie was given leave by Albert to smoke. Victoria told him that she hoped he would give it up, as smoking set a bad example in society and encouraged idleness, a particular danger in his case: "Your natural difficulty in applying and exerting your mind would be greatly increased & you would often think you were occupied . . . when you are puffing away in a state of dreamy idleness." Bertie's reply was diplomatic: "I should not like to make you [a] promise that I will entirely give it up, because I don't think I could keep it; at the same time I will do it as little [as] I can & I dare say that before long I shall give it up altogether."[4] These were the words of a lifelong smoker. Victoria, who detested the habit, banned him from smoking in her houses or in public, and when Bertie was at Buckingham Palace, she ordered the conservatory to be locked to prevent him sneaking out for a cigar.[5]

At Cambridge, Bertie sucked strong cigars and hunted with the drag hounds.* Bruce forbade him from asking anyone back to Madingley, but he was uneasily aware that Bertie's "love of excitement and constitutional disinclination to all serious pursuits" tended to carry him "almost unconsciously into the company of the idle and the frivolous."[6] For the first time in his life, Bertie made real friends—Charles Carrington, the boy he had played with at Buckingham Palace, and Nathaniel (Natty) Rothschild and his brother Alfred. For the Rothschilds, this was a social breakthrough, bringing access to court; for Bertie it was the beginning of a lifelong friendship that was to define his style of royalty.[7]

The drag hunt was paid for largely by the Rothschilds, and Natty noted that Bertie was not allowed expensive horses, owing to his par-

---

* A drag is a scent that is laid by a man before the hunt, rather than a live fox or hare.

ents' disapproval of hunting. "No wonder that he gets so many falls," commented Natty. "I fancy the little spirit he has is quite broken, as his remarks are commonplace and very slow. He will I suppose eventually settle down into a well-disciplined German prince with all the narrow views of his father's family."[8]

In March, Bertie was summoned home unexpectedly to Windsor to the deathbed of his grandmother, the Duchess of Kent. Victoria abandoned herself to an orgy of grief and self-pity. She had never liked her mother, but now she felt (as Albert wrote) "her whole childhood rush back once more upon her memory."[9]

No doubt Victoria was overcome by guilt and remorse at reading her mother's papers, which made her realize how much her despised parent had loved her. But even in a culture that institutionalized mourning, as the court did, the Queen's reaction seems excessive. Her mother was seventy-five, which was old by the standards of the day, and though the two women had quarreled when Victoria became queen, they had been reconciled for many years. Albert worried that the duchess's death had unhinged Victoria, and that her obsessive grief signaled a descent into madness.

"She remains almost entirely alone," he noted. "It is no easy task for me to comfort and support her and to keep others at a distance, and yet at the same time not to throw away the opportunity, which a time like the present affords, of binding the family together in a closer bond of unity."[10] The grief-stricken Queen refused to see anyone except Albert, and Albert encouraged her to give herself up to mourning, even though he knew that her seclusion was causing gossip about her mental state. He now did all her work to save her trouble, laboring at the papers on his desk like a donkey on a treadmill.[11]

Victoria refused to see her children. Bertie annoyed her the most. She made terrible scenes when he shed no tears at his grandmother's funeral at Frogmore, accusing him of lacking feelings.* As Clarendon

---

* By her own request, the Duchess of Kent was buried in a specially constructed mausoleum at Frogmore. She had a horror of being interred beside the Hanoverians in the vault in St. George's Chapel.

remarked, Bertie could do no right; if he had cried, he would no doubt have been rebuked for increasing her grief.[12] Vicky wrote to her mother begging her to avoid an estrangement. Victoria's reply was stubbornly unforgiving. "I quite agree with you, dear child—that he must be a little more tender and affectionate in his manner—if he is to expect it from me." Bertie irritated her with silly remarks. "His voice makes me so nervous I could hardly bear it."[13] To Bertie himself, however, Victoria was less angry than hurt. "Open your heart freely to your Mother," she implored him, "for she too, yearns to <u>show</u> you the love she <u>feels</u> but she must <u>meet</u> with warmth <u>&</u> tenderness! I alas! in gone by <u>&</u> days, was not as tender and affectionate to dearest Grandmama as I ought to have been (much as I loved her) <u>&</u> <u>bitterly</u> do I lament it <u>now</u>."[14]

"I can assure you," replied Bertie, "that I did not try to check my feelings"; he was "stunned" by the suddenness of his grandmother's death, and unable to realize it until some time later. "I did not like to intrude myself upon you, when dear Vicky & Alice were sympathizing with you so warmly & affectionately not because I had not the same feelings as they had, but because I thought I should be in your way."[15] As a token of his grief, he ordered writing paper with even thicker black edges.

Around this time, Prince Albert began a new file of papers, which he labeled "Bertie's Marriage Prospects." He collected letters from Vicky and from old Baron Stockmar, which he annotated in red ink. Victoria entered a note later: "Up to this place all the papers in this book were arranged by the beloved Prince Himself."[16]

Bertie was not yet twenty, but already Albert was plotting a dynastic alliance. He must marry before he was old enough to choose for himself, or, which was more likely, before he disgraced himself. That the next English queen should be a German princess was unquestioned, essential both to Albert's plans for shaping Germany's future and to his own control over the English throne. The royal family of England must continue to be German.

Albert's agent in picking a bride was Vicky. Albert had complete confidence in the judgment of his twenty-year-old daughter. For months now, Vicky had been scouring the pages of the *Almanac de Gotha,* the stud book of European royalty, and sending back reports on the available princesses. It was she who had found Louis of Hesse for Alice, and that had succeeded delightfully; but suitable princesses were in short supply.[17] Two possible candidates were Elizabeth of Wied and Anna of Hesse, the sister of Alice's fiancé Louis. Elizabeth, according to Vicky, was good-tempered and clever but boisterous and talked too much.* Anna spoke in a deep, gruff voice, her eyes twitched incessantly, and her teeth were bad.[18] The only princess who seemed at all possible was the least eligible on political grounds: Princess Alexandra of Denmark. Denmark was on unfriendly terms with Prussia, locked into a quarrel over the disputed territories of Schleswig and Holstein. Alexandra's mother's family was reputed to be bad, her father's foolish. But Vicky received glowing reports from Wally Hohenthal, now married to Augustus Paget, the English minister in Copenhagen.

At length, in June 1861, Vicky arranged to meet Alexandra. To the relief of Wally Paget, who was by now feeling somewhat responsible, she was captivated. Never had she set eyes on a sweeter creature. Alexandra was everything that Vicky was not—beautiful, tall (taller at least than the five-foot-two Vicky), slender, and gentle. She spoke English and German, but whether she was clever or not, Vicky could not tell—"though I could not perceive the slightest thing to make me think the contrary." "She has been very strictly kept for she has not read a novel of any kind."[19]

When Albert saw a photograph of Alexandra, he declared, "From that photograph I would marry her at once."[20] She was evidently "a pearl not to be lost," and the royal parents now became desperate to bag this treasure for their son. "May he only be worthy of such a jewel!" exclaimed the Queen. A Russian prince was also in the market, and Victoria worried that her "sallow, dull, blasé" son would lose the Danish pearl.[21]

---

* Elizabeth of Wied later married the King of Romania and wrote novels under the pseudonym Carmen Silva.

Bertie himself was the last to hear of these negotiations. Not until the end of May did Albert forward Alexandra's photograph: "It would be a thousand pities if you were to lose her!" he wrote.[22] Victoria thought Bertie was "evidently much pleased and interested," but Bertie wrote guardedly to Albert: "The accounts of the P[rince]ss are so very good, that it leaves me really nothing to say; but of course how to find a way of securing her, is a very difficult matter." He refused to be rushed: "You must excuse my giving you now my opinions on the subject, as I should like some time to think it over."[23]

Bertie's role in Albert's matchmaking was simple: He must fall in love with the Danish pearl. But the fact was that it was Vicky, not Bertie, who had fallen in love with Alexandra. Bertie's romantic feelings were altogether more problematic.

As a special concession, Albert agreed to General Bruce's request that Bertie should be allowed to attend a military camp at the Curragh in the summer of 1861. Bruce permitted him to mix with other officers, but only in public. "Private intercourse" with his companions was strictly policed. Two stern Grenadier officers acted as his mentors: General Ridley, "an excellent soldier and high-minded gentleman," and Colonel Henry Percy, a Crimean War hero awarded the Victoria Cross and a favorite of the Queen, who made no concessions to the prince's rank.[24]

At the Curragh, Bertie lived in general's quarters. His so-called hut consisted of a sitting room, drawing room, and dining room. The soldier's life agreed with him, and he wrote to his mother: "I will . . . do my best now to make the best use of the short time I now have before me for acquiring knowledge & instruction."[25] What sort of instruction he had in mind was left unclear. The day before, Victoria had written to her uncle Leopold in one of her flashes of self-knowledge: "Alas! Sons are like their mothers—at least the eldest are supposed to be—& so I think Bertie has avoided all likeness to his beloved father."[26]

Victoria and Albert visited the Curragh at the end of August. Bertie's hopes of commanding a company in front of his parents were dashed by Colonel Percy, who told him: "You are too imperfect in your drill, and your word of command is not sufficiently loud and distinct."[27]

Bertie had other distractions. His engagement diary contains the following entries:

6 Sept	Curragh	N. C. 1st time
9 Sept	Curragh	N. C. 2nd time
10 Sept	Curragh	N. C. 3rd time[28]

The discovery of these cryptic notes allows us to pinpoint exactly the date of Bertie's "fall." "N.C." was Nellie Clifden, a lady of easy virtue who had followed the brigade from London. Urged on by his fellow officers, Bertie escaped at night through the windows of his quarters, and made love to her in another officer's hut. As his diary reveals, this took place not once but on three occasions.[29]

Four days after the "third time," Bertie crossed to Coblenz, where he attended the maneuvers of the Prussian army.

From Coblenz, Bertie traveled through the Rhineland with Vicky and Fritz. He journeyed incognito, again using the title of Baron Renfrew. Incognito was not meant to conceal his true identity; it was a convention that excused him from ceremonial duties and meant that he was not expected to be formally received by the rulers through whose lands he traveled.[30] Bertie and his party visited Speyer Cathedral, a jewel of Romanesque architecture that had been recently restored. In the Chapel of St. Bernard, above the crypt crammed with the coffins of medieval emperors, he and Vicky happened to encounter Prince Christian of Denmark and his wife, Princess Louise, traveling with their daughter Alexandra.

This meeting, seemingly a chance encounter, had, in fact, been carefully choreographed by Vicky at Bertie's request. Alexandra, however, knew nothing. When she left the family house party at Rumpenheim Castle on the banks of the Main that morning, she was surprised at her mother telling her to wear her best dress; being a thrifty princess, she usually wore old clothes for grimy train journeys. Bertie attempted to make conversation with Princess Louise, Alexandra's mother, but this was difficult as his hushed voice was barely audible to the princess, who was almost completely deaf.

Vicky and Fritz moved away from the Danish group and pretended to admire the new frescoes in the German Nazarene style that artfully obliterated the crude medieval stonework. Vicky tried desperately to overhear the conversation; this meeting was crucial to her marriage diplomacy, the Queen had written obsessively detailed instructions from England, and Vicky was naturally nervous. At first, the encounter between Bertie and Alexandra was stilted. In the flesh, Bertie thought Alexandra a disappointment after the studio photographs, which showed an oval-faced beauty posed against a profile-flattering mirror, her tiny waist exaggerated by the big checks of her full gathered skirt. In reality, her nose was too long and her forehead too low. But after fifteen minutes or so, observers thought that "the reverse of indifference on both sides soon became unmistakeable." Perhaps because she was unaware how much was at stake, the sixteen-year-old Alexandra was not shy. Vicky noted approvingly her simple and unaffected manner, and thought her forward for her age—"her manners are more like 24."[31]

The scene at Speyer Cathedral is intensely visual, almost filmic in its immediacy. Communication was a matter of bows and curtseys, the touch of a gloved hand, an incline of the head; Alexandra could speak English—she had had English nurses since childhood—but she and Bertie barely exchanged words. Alexandra remained silent after the meeting, or at least there is no record of what she thought. Not for six months did her mother tell her of the Prince of Wales's intentions.

Bertie returned home to Balmoral mildly pleased, but in no hurry to wed. To his mother's dismay, it was evident that he was not smitten. "As for being in love," she wrote, "I don't think he can be, or that he is capable of enthusiasm about anything in this world."[32] Vicky, too, was annoyed that, after all her negotiations, Bertie was unmoved—incapable, apparently, of feeling passion for "that sweet lovely flower young and beautiful—that even makes my heart beat when I look at her—which would make most men fire and flames—not even producing an impression enough to last from Baden to England."[33] All sorts of objections now occurred to Bertie: Alexandra's family must first visit England, he didn't want children ("which for so young a man is so strange a fear," thought Victoria); he was too young—he was after all not yet twenty.[34]

At this point, Albert's patience snapped. He gave Bertie an angry lecture and the next day handed him a note of what he had said. If Alexandra and her parents came to Windsor, warned Albert, Bertie would be duty-bound to propose. If he delayed, he risked losing "a positive and present advantage for the hope of future chances which . . . probably may never occur."[35]

Albert could feel the game slipping away. From Coburg, his brother Ernest objected to a Danish match. Albert loftily brushed him aside. "I am not, as you suppose, asking 'What has it to do with you?' " he began, and then wrote a letter saying precisely that.[36] More wounding was a letter from old Stockmar, now retired to Coburg, who wrote urging the unsuitability of the match. The purpose of the marriage, he pointed out, was to correct Bertie's weakness, but so tarnished was Alexandra's family that matrimony was bound to have the opposite effect. Alexandra's mother was rumored to be a loose woman who had affairs, while her father was an imbecile. Stockmar's defection gave Albert a "dreadful shock," but he was no less determined to press the marriage.[37]

Bertie, however, had compelling reasons for delaying. Nellie Clifden was back in London. Gossips whispered that she now styled herself the Princess of Wales. It was rumored that when Bertie went to Windsor for his twentieth birthday on 9 November 1861, Nellie followed him and he smuggled her into the castle.

Nellie briefly became Bertie's mistress. Through her, and her friends among the Guards officers, Bertie made his first forays into a secret London nightlife of theaters, casinos, and women in deep décolletage. The 1860s was a decade of sexual liberation, a brief interlude of eroticism that has been obscured to posterity by Victorian prudishness and respectability. The world in which Nellie was the girlfriend of a number of young officers was not squalid or furtive; it was fashionable and fast.

This was the era in which Bertie reached manhood, and it shaped his sexuality for life. There are hints about his initiation with Nellie—though only hints, as he was already clever at hiding his tracks—in letters to his friend Charles Carrington. Referring to "our friend N," whom Carrington identified as "Nelly Clifton [*sic*] a well known 'London Lady' much run after by the household brigade," Bertie wrote:

> I hope that you will continue to like Cambridge . . . and I trust that you will occasionally look at a book, which at present (entre nous) you have not much done. You won't I'm sure forget those few hints I gave you regarding certain matters, and I have not forgotten those you gave me at the same time. I am glad to hear that our friend is in good health as I had not heard anything about her for some time. . . . PS: You won't I hope forget your promise not to show anybody any of my letters. AE[38]

By "certain matters," it seems Bertie meant carnal knowledge, horseplay, and a jokey, manly boisterousness.[39] Little wonder that he was reluctant to exchange Nellie's hoydenish charms for prudish monogamy with a flat-chested teenage Danish princess.

On 12 November, Lord Torrington, a courtier and gossip, came into waiting at Windsor and repeated to Albert the rumors about Nellie's seduction of Bertie at the Curragh. Victoria never forgot Albert's misery. "Oh! ! that face, that heavenly face of woe and sorrow which was so dreadful to witness!"[40]

Albert penned a long, self-pitying letter to Bertie, writing "with a heavy heart, on a subject which has caused me the deepest pain I have yet felt in this life." How could Bertie allow himself to have "sexual intercourse" with this woman—he couldn't bring himself to write "prostitute." "To thrust yourself into the hands of one of the most abject of the human species, to be by her initiated in the sacred mysteries of creation, which ought to remain shrouded in holy awe until touched by pure & undefiled hands." The language throbs with repressed sexual tensions. "At your age," counseled Albert, "the sexual passions begin to move in young men & lead them to seek explanation to relieve a state of vague suspense & desire. Why did you not open yourself to your father? . . . I would have reminded you [of] . . . the special mode in which these desires are to be gratified . . . by . . . the holy ties of Matrimony."[41] Albert's pen ran away with him as he painted a lurid picture of Nellie blackmailing Bertie, of illegitimate children and law cases.

Bertie was contrite. Though penitent, however, he refused to give the names of the officers who had led him into sin, and he denied that Nellie had come to Windsor. In fact, it seems there *was* a prostitute at Windsor on his birthday, but it wasn't Nellie.[42] Possibly it was a woman named Green. In November 1864, Bertie was hounded by a "blackguard" called Green, who was trying to blackmail him for events that took place "above three years ago." From the letters of the royal advisers, it seems that Green's wife had ensnared Bertie into "wickedness": There could be no doubt, they wrote, "who was the tempter and who the tempted." Green and his wife were paid an annuity of £60 in exchange for keeping silent and leaving the country to live in New Zealand.[43]

Though Bertie told his father only half the truth, Albert was mollified. But he gave his son a stark warning: "You <u>must</u> not, you <u>dare</u> not be lost; the consequences for this country & for the world at large would be too dreadful! There is no middle course possible . . . you must either belong to the good, or to the bad in this life." In the future, he told Bertie, when speeches were made about the virtue of the royal family, people would always stare at him. "The loose women of London (who form a confraternity) will consider you good sport, & look at you with an effrontery—offering their ware."[44]

Albert accurately predicted Bertie's sexual politics, but his inflamed language and fevered emotions demand explanation. Sleeping with prostitutes was not exceptional behavior for young, healthy upper-class males. As Victoria's half sister, Feodora, wrote: "It is one of the greatest trials parents can have to go through, yet, Alas! how frequent! not the less distressing though."[45] Bertie's alleged profligacy, wrote Lord Granville, "as yet consisted in losing that which few men, well fed and with animal spirits long retain."[46] No doubt Bertie's fall threatened to jeopardize the Danish wedding, which, if it was to be passed off as a love match, depended upon keeping him in a state of pent-up sexual frustration so that he fell madly in love at first sight. But Albert's over-reaction is symptomatic of his own unbalanced state. Nellie Clifden stirred painful memories of his childhood, which had been scarred by the debaucheries of his father and the adultery of his mother. And the Prince Consort was a dying man.

Ever since he had visited Coburg the previous autumn, Albert had thought he was close to death. Out driving one day, his carriage horses bolted. As the runaway horses galloped headlong toward a railway crossing, Albert flung himself out. He was cut and bruised and badly shaken. He became depressed and emotional. Out walking with his brother, Ernest, he broke down; tears streamed down his cheeks as he declared that he would never see Coburg again. When he paid a fare-well visit to Stockmar, his old mentor thought that he lacked the will to live.[47]

Albert returned to England suffering from diarrhea and stomach cramps. Ever since boyhood, he had complained of a "weak stomach," and his gastric attacks had become progressively worse and more fre-quent. Stress and overwork made him vulnerable, and to this was added the depression of a lonely man with few friends in England. Retrospective diagnosis is a tricky business, but it seems likely that Al-bert suffered from some form of chronic, recurring gastric illness.[48]

Now forty-two and a grandfather, he looked heavy, paunchy, and balding. He was always cold; when he rose early to work on dark win-ter mornings, he wore a wig to warm his bald pate.

On 25 November 1861, Bertie received a surprise visit at Cambridge from Albert, who had resolved to have it out with him. Carrington ac companied his friend to the station. Bertie seemed nervous, and Carrington stood on the platform and watched as the Prince Consort kissed his son and they drove off in a coach to Madingley.[49] It was a wet and stormy day, but Albert insisted on going for a private walk with Bertie. Bertie mistook the way, and by the time they returned, Albert was soaked to the skin, with racking pains in his back and legs. He had been tormented by sleeplessness and "rheumatism" for the past fortnight, but he stayed up talking to Bertie until one a.m.

What passed between them is not known, but the result was that Albert forgave his son.[50]

Albert returned to Windsor a sick man. "I never saw him so low," said Victoria.[51] She blamed Albert's depression and sleeplessness on Bertie's fall, which "broke him quite down." Albert himself confided in Vicky that his "shattered state" was due to worry, "about which I beg you not to ask questions."[52] Neither Albert nor Victoria could see that his anxiety over Bertie was an emotional overreaction, as much a symptom as the cause of his wretchedness.

Watching the Eton volunteers two days later, Albert shuddered inside his fur-lined coat. The day was warm, but he felt as if water were being poured down his back. Not until 7 December, after he had been miserably ill for more than two weeks, did the doctors make a diagnosis of "fever," meaning typhoid. Listless and irritable, unable to eat or sleep, Albert wandered restlessly day and night, pacing Windsor's state bedrooms in his quilted dressing gown.

In Cambridge, Bertie spent his time larking with Natty Rothschild and his hounds. "It is perhaps better to say as little as possible about the festivities here," a conscience-stricken Natty later wrote.[53] When Albert was diagnosed with typhoid, Bertie was warned that he must not return to Windsor, for fear the fever was epidemic.[54] But he received little detailed news about his father's illness, and Victoria wrote no letters to him. Vicky, on the other hand, who was pregnant in Berlin and not permitted to travel, was kept fully informed by Victoria, who wrote almost daily to her daughter.

Victoria found the diagnosis of fever oddly reassuring. Sir William Jenner promised her the prince would recover when the fever had taken its natural course, and she allowed herself to hope. She seemed not to realize that Albert had become dangerously ill. Only the eighteen-year-old Alice, who sat for long hours by her father's bedside, knew the truth.

On Wednesday, 11 December 1861, Alice wrote to Bertie telling him that Albert was "very ill, but continues to improve."[55] In fact, the doctors that evening noticed an ominous change in Prince Albert's breathing, and they feared the onset of the dreaded "congestion of the lungs," or pneumonia.[56] Later, as Alice read aloud from the Bible, Albert stopped her and asked: "Is your Mother in the room?"

"No," said Alice.

"Before you go to bed tonight I want you to write to your sister at Berlin & tell her that she must be prepared for the worst. I feel sure I shall never get over this." The next day Albert's fever was worse, he became delirious, and he vomited foul-smelling, bloodied mucus into a bowl held by Alice. Again he asked her: "Is your Mother here?" and finding her alone, he asked if she had done as he wished.

"Yes," said Alice, "but I also added that we hoped you saw danger where there was none."

"Oh," said he, "you could not say that now. I see the doctors think me in great danger."[57]

Albert never asked for Bertie nor mentioned his name. Victoria had no intention of summoning him. So it was Alice who sent a telegram to her brother in Cambridge, asking him to return to Windsor.[58] It was "cautiously worded" and gave no indication that Albert was critically ill.[59] Bertie spent Friday hunting, "rejoicing over the good news from Windsor," which he had received in Alice's earlier letter.[60] Not until he returned in the afternoon did he see the telegram, and he thought so little of it that he decided to stay for a dinner engagement with some dons, and left by the eleven o'clock train. He arrived at Windsor at three a.m., talking cheerfully. He was "appalled" to learn how ill his father really was.[61]

When Bertie saw his father at ten a.m. the next day (Saturday, 14 December 1861), Albert briefly recognized him, but his breathing was alarmingly rapid, his tongue was blackened and swollen, he could barely speak, and his face was changed. He rambled incoherently, repeating Bertie's name. The doctors still gave slight grounds for hope, and Bertie wrote to Louis, Alice's fiancé: Their father was "fighting for his life. In 24 hours we will know for sure—almighty God hear our prayers."[62]

By late afternoon, it was plain that Albert was sinking. The doctors prepared for the end. At five thirty p.m., the bed was wheeled to the center of the room, and Victoria sat on one side. *"Gutes Frauchen"* (good little wife) were Albert's last coherent words to her. He agreed to see the Prince of Wales, but when Bertie took his hand, followed by Helena, Louise, and Arthur, Albert was dozing and showed no signs of recognition. He asked for Sir Charles Phipps, and his three private secretaries trooped in one after another and kissed his hand, weeping as they did so.

As the evening wore on, Albert's breathing grew more painful and he was bathed in sweat. Victoria knelt beside him, holding his left hand, which was already cold. Alice knelt opposite her. At the foot of the bed knelt Bertie with Helena. This ghastly tableau continued for some time until the Queen could bear it no longer and rushed from the room. At ten forty-five p.m., Alice heard the struggle for breath that she knew was the death rattle, and called her back. After a few gentle breaths it was all over.

Victoria flung herself passionately upon the bed and embraced her dead husband, uttering every endearment she knew. She was removed from the room in hysterics.

Bertie followed her, threw his arms round her neck, and cried: "Indeed Mama I will be all I can to you." He promised to do his utmost to take his father's place. He told her he would "hold his life to hers." Victoria kissed him, and said, "I'm sure my dear boy you will."[63]

In the first few days after Albert died, Bertie stayed very close to Victoria. He barely left her room; he wrote letters for her and took meals to her, waiting on her like a devoted servant. The Queen was sedated with opiates, but she couldn't bear Bertie or Alice to be away from her. To observers it seemed as if the Queen and her heir were reconciled.[64] But the stark fact was that if Alice had not summoned him, Bertie would not have been present at Albert's deathbed. As it was, the death came as a profound shock, for which he was utterly unprepared.

Albert's funeral took place in wintry gloom at St. George's Chapel on 23 December 1861. Sobbing uncontrollably at being forced to tear herself away from Albert's deathbed, the Queen had already left Windsor for Osborne with Alice, Louise, and Helena; it was customary for widows not to attend their husbands' funerals, and Victoria was in no state to appear in public. Bertie was chief mourner and walked at the head of the procession behind the coffin, wearing a kilt and accompanied by the weeping eleven-year-old Arthur. (Affie was away at sea, and the hemophiliac Leopold was recuperating in the South of France.) On entering the chapel, Bertie was "very much distressed."[65] Albert's body, dressed in the uniform of a field marshal—even in death he was on duty—was lowered into a temporary resting place in the crypt below the altar, a space more like a coal hole that contained the remains of the kings of England.[66]

Naturally the doctors were blamed for the prince's death. "They are not fit to attend a sick cat," said Lord Clarendon. The diagnosis of fever was made very late, but this may have been deliberate. Sir James Clark knew his patients' psychology well enough to predict that the very word "fever," which to the Victorians spelled the killer typhoid, would cause the Queen to have hysterics and Albert to resign himself to death. But the consequence of Clark's efforts to protect Albert's peace of mind was that the Prince Consort received no professional nursing. He was attended only by Alice and his valet; he was not confined to bed but allowed to wander about from room to room.[67]

Victoria refused to permit an autopsy. Albert's doctor, Sir William Jenner, was Europe's leading authority on typhoid, and at the time there was no reason to doubt his diagnosis. But no other cases of this infectious waterborne illness were reported either at Windsor or Sandhurst, where the prince was sometimes alleged to have contracted it. The immediate cause of death was pneumonia, but Albert was weakened by an underlying illness. Some have suggested that his symptoms fit a diagnosis of stomach cancer.[68] The latest theory is that he suffered from Crohn's disease. Though unknown to medicine until the early twentieth century, this progressive inflammation of the gut could explain Albert's chronic abdominal pain, vomiting, and diarrhea.[69] He often talked about death, telling Vicky that "he would not care if God took him that moment, he always felt ready." He once told Victoria: "I do not cling to life. . . . I am sure, if I had a severe illness I should give up at once, I should not struggle for life."[70]

Looking back on the case, Sir James Clark wrote in his diary: "There was excessive mental excitement on one very recent occasion, mental depression, and exposure on two occasions to fatigue and cold."[71] This was what Victoria wanted to hear. She needed someone to blame for Albert's death. Medical opinion agreed with her that the mental excitement and depression caused by Bertie's fall, culminating in the sad, wet mission to Madingley, had killed her beloved Albert. In attempting to save their own reputations, the doctors validated the Queen's emotional rejection of her son, doing lasting damage. For years afterward, Victoria blamed Bertie for Albert's death.

CHAPTER 5

Marriage

1861–63

The sharp-eyed courtiers who scanned the Prince of Wales for signs of grief reported that the bereavement made no deep impression.[1] Bertie wrote tight letters that gave little away. To his friend Carrington he said: "I have received a sad blow in the loss of my Father, who was kindness itself to me, though I fear that I have often given him pain by my conduct."[2] He told another Cambridge friend, "I am still quite stunned by the dreadful blow . . . and can hardly yet realize it."[3]

A reporter who caught a glimpse of him off his guard noted that he "appeared very careworn, and suffering severely."[4] But the mask rarely slipped. Bertie was an emotional character and easily moved to tears, but he did not allow himself to grieve for his father's death.

Albert's death marked the beginning of a new reign. Effectively, he had been king. He had reformed the monarchy, distancing it from Victoria's "wicked uncles" and identifying the "royal family" with middle-class domestic virtue. He had reorganized its finances, cut waste, and eliminated corruption. Thanks to the savings he made on the Civil List, the Crown could live within its means without appealing to Parliament for more, significantly strengthening its political position. Osborne and Balmoral were both paid for out of savings.[5] On the other hand, he had interfered in politics, attempted to shape foreign policy, and acted almost as an unofficial member of the Cabinet. As Disraeli put it, he planned "to establish court-influence on the ruins of political party . . . with perseverance equal to that of George the Third and talent infinitely greater."[6] He had taken political business out of the hands of the Queen, who had become de-skilled; she could barely write a letter unless Albert drafted it. At dinner, politicians noticed how Albert would prompt Victoria in German, and then, like a ventriloquist's doll, she would ask the question he suggested.[7] It's worth asking the counterfactual question: What would have happened if Albert had lived? His spectacular career demonstrates just how much could be achieved by a genuinely able ruler. But his quest for power was arguably destined to set the monarchy on a collision course with Parliament. His inability to delegate and his insistence on keeping control of the court in his own hands are worrying signs. In some ways, his death was opportune. It removed the Crown from the front line of politics at a time when the rise of a robust system of two-party politics meant that retreat was essential to the monarchy's survival. At the moment of his death, however, Albert seemed indispensable. Now the entire burden of monarchy fell to Victoria, and this hysterical widow, crippled by grief, seemed of all people the least capable of bearing it.

The deeper the Queen retreated into mourning, the greater was Bertie's opportunity to seize a political role, as his father had done before him. As heir to the throne and a male, Bertie was a figure of national importance. Leaders appeared in *The Times* urging the Prince of Wales to reject a life of frivolity and follow a career of usefulness, filling the place left by his father. Inspired by court insiders, the editor of *The Times* implored the Queen not to follow the example of the Hanoverians and quarrel with her heir. Instead, she should take him into her confidence and prepare him for the duties of government.[8] Bertie read the *Times* articles with great attention, and was reportedly "very struck" by them.[9] But he seemed fatally lacking in ambition. Instead of grasping power, he allowed himself to be outmaneuvered by his mother into a position of impotence. Breaking with Hanoverian tradition, the Prince of Wales did not become the focus of opposition to the reigning monarch.

Victoria's grief was all-consuming. "Why may not the earth swallow us up?" she wailed.[10] She had leaned on Albert for everything, never donning a gown or a bonnet without his approval. In her private journal of "Remarks Conversations Reflections," the Queen poured out thousands of words of unedited grief. "Oh no more peaceful blessed nights! . . . Those w[hich] seemed a foretaste of Heaven—for their peace."[11]

It is sometimes suggested that Queen Victoria was going through menopause, but this seems unlikely.[12] She was only forty-two and was not physically ill. But she had never experienced any real misfortune in her life before, and she was suffering from an emotional breakdown. In denial about Albert's death, she slept in the marital bed with his nightshirt in her arms, his photograph and watch lying on the pillow beside her, and a marble cast of his hand within reach. Next door, in his dressing room, his papers and clothes lay as they had when he was alive, and hot water was brought each morning to his room. At Windsor, the Blue Room where Albert died was photographed and kept as a shrine, exactly as it was at the hour of his death, "even to an open pocket handkerchief on the sofa," but the bed was strewn like a coffin with white flowers.[13]

In spite of all her weeping and sad mornings, waking day after day at four a.m., Victoria insisted on performing the business of monarchy herself. "I must work and work, and can't rest," she told Vicky, "and the amount of work which comes upon me is more than I can bear! I who always hated business have nothing but that!"[14] Sitting at her twin writing table next to the beloved's empty desk, scrawling over page after page of thickly black-edged paper, she felt that she was carrying on Albert's mission.

Albert had encouraged Victoria in her obsessive mourning when her mother died, and now she clung to her grief. All the anger she felt for Albert's death was directed at Bertie. "Oh! that boy . . . I never can or shall look at him without a shudder," she wrote.[15]

Early in 1862, Victoria had a conversation at Osborne with her groom-in-waiting Colonel Francis Seymour. She received him standing in Albert's dressing room, wearing her widow's cap. A locket containing Albert's hair and his photograph hung from her neck. "I don't mind telling you as an old friend . . . that what killed [Albert], was that dreadful business at the Curragh." Seymour pleaded that Bertie's fall was the sort of error that few young men escaped, but the Queen was adamant: She could never forget that he had caused his father's illness. "She said he had nothing to remind her of him, the others Princess Royal and Alfred in particular had just something of his look, but the Prince of Wales nothing and she could not help being relieved when he was gone from her, tho' he had behaved as well as he could."[16]

On 5 January 1862, Victoria penned a memorandum. She was under pressure to keep Bertie beside her, but this, she explained, was out of the question. We always come back, she wrote, to "the one dreadful misfortune," that is, Bertie's fall; the vital thing was to prevent it happening again. Meanwhile, Bertie's character was such that "a lengthened stay . . . at Home will only lead to continued & protracted idleness." The solution was for him to travel. "If the Prince of Wales is well surrounded and is never allowed to go out alone & is moreover constantly kept reminded of all that is right & good, the Queen does not see how it is possible for him to get into mischief."[17]

Albert had planned that Bertie should complete his education with a trip to the Near East, and Victoria insisted that this should still take place. Bertie had no wish to travel, but his views were not consulted. King Leopold, who interviewed Bertie and tried to intervene with Victoria on his behalf, told Lord Clarendon that relations between mother and son were worse than ever. "It is entirely her fault as the poor boy asks nothing better than to devote himself to comforting his Mother and with that object would be delighted to give up his foreign expedition but she wouldn't hear of it and seems only anxious to get rid of him."[18] The prime minister, Lord Palmerston, tried to dissuade the Queen from sending Bertie abroad, telling her that "the country was fearful we were not on good terms, as he was so much away from home."[19] But Victoria refused to budge. "Many wish to shake my resolution and to keep him here," she told Vicky, but that would "force a contact which is more than ever unbearable to me."[20]

Not only had Bertie lost his father, but he was made to feel responsible for his death. At first he tried to please by complying with his mother's wishes. He made no attempt to resist his banishment. But Victoria's rejection left deep wounds. Bertie's pity for his grieving mother soon turned to anger. Rather than confront her, he was outwardly dutiful and obedient, but secretly he deceived her. He was resentful, too, that, in spite of all the pressure from politicians and *The Times,* Victoria excluded him from her confidence. Instead, she shared her innermost thoughts with Vicky, to whom she complained constantly about Bertie.

Before departing on his tour of the Near East, Bertie saw his mother (6 February 1862). She thought he seemed nervous at the thought of leaving. "He was low and upset, poor Boy. So was I."[21]

The Queen had ordered that the Prince of Wales should travel with his suite in deep mourning, alone and in strict incognito, and accept no invitations. Away from his mother, Bertie's spirits rose. In Venice ("charming"), the royal yacht *Osborne* anchored opposite the ducal palace, and he cruised around in gondolas all day ("a charming sensation") and paid two visits to Elizabeth, Empress of Austria, whom he found "very handsome" as well as (naturally) "charming."[22] Venetian art, however, received no mention.

In Alexandria, Arthur (later Dean) Stanley, a protégé of Albert's, joined the party. As professor of ecclesiastical history at Oxford University, his role was to provide tuition in ancient history. Bertie scrambled very fast up one pyramid and then, to Stanley's dismay, showed no interest in seeing any more dull ruins. Instead, he sat smoking and reading *East Lynne,* the bestselling novel about adultery by Mrs. Henry Wood. He insisted on the rest of the party reading *East Lynne,* too, and as they steamed in luxury down the Nile, the prince quizzed his companions. "With whom did Lady Isobel dine on the fatal night?"[23] His chief amusement was shooting crocodiles from the boat. "We are leading quite an Eastern lazy life, and smoke and drink coffee nearly all day," he told Carrington. "I trust that you have cut the acquaintance of our friend N [Nellie Clifden]."[24]

Stanley at first despaired of Bertie, who was woefully lacking in intellectual curiosity, but he was disarmed by the prince's engaging manner, his modesty, and his real efforts to conceal his boredom. He was especially impressed by the way Bertie conducted himself in interviews with high personages, where "he appears to the best advantage."[25]

In Jerusalem, Bertie was tattooed with the five crosses forming a Crusader's Jerusalem cross on his forearm.*[26] He grew his first beard. Strictly supervised by Bruce, he avoided the erotic temptations of the East, which for many English travelers formed the secret agenda of the Grand Tour. Nellie Clifden was still on his mind, however. From Constantinople he wrote to Carrington: "I am sorry to see by your letter that you still keep up an acquaintance with NC, as I had hoped by this time that that was over."[27]

With Bertie safely out of the country for four months, Queen Victoria busied herself arranging his marriage—a "sacred duty" that Albert, "our darling Angel," had left her to perform.[28] How fortunate it was that sacred duty coincided so exactly with the Queen's convenience, removing her irksome son from her home while protecting him from the dangers of bachelor life. Bertie was not consulted in the matter. The marriage was arranged entirely by the Queen and Vicky.

From Germany, Vicky reported dark rumors that Princess Alexandra had disgraced herself by having a teenage affair with an army officer.[29] This and other tales about Alexandra's family were fabrications,

---

* In 1882, the future George V was tattooed "by the same old man that tattooed Papa, and the same thing too, the 5 crosses, you ask Papa to show his arm." (RA GV/PRIV/AA36, Prince George to Princess of Wales, April 1882.)

invented by Denmark's enemies in Germany, as Vicky's investigations soon revealed. Alexandra's mother, Princess Louise, was "lively," which was code for flirtatious, but not unfaithful to her husband. The harlot of the family was Louise's sister, the Princess of Dessau, who had an illegitimate child as a result of an affair with a groom; this passion had been encouraged by her mother, Alexandra's grandmother, the old Landgravine of Hesse, who, Vicky reported, was "wicked and very intriguing—besides not being at all respectable."[30]

Ever since she was fourteen, Alexandra had been monitored by the British minister in Copenhagen, Augustus Paget, who assured Baron Stockmar that the young princess had attended only two parties in her life, both heavily chaperoned. Up until sixteen she had lived in seclusion in the nursery. "In short," wrote Paget, "it appears that the whole object of the parents has been to prevent her name being mixed up with anyone else's."[31]

Princess Louise was an ambitious matchmaker, anxious to marry her two pretty daughters, Alexandra and Dagmar, into the top league of European royalty. Her husband, Prince Christian, was an obscure and impoverished princeling, connected only remotely to the childless King of Denmark, whose heir he had been designated under the London Protocol of 1852.* He owned no estates, and his income had only recently increased from a paltry £800 to £2,000, still a modest sum. The Danish princesses' sole assets were their beauty and connections, and Princess Louise knew very well that her daughters' virtue must be strictly and conspicuously guarded if they were to hold their value in the royal marriage market.

Queen Victoria grumbled that the Danish family were "as bad as possible," but she was being disingenuous, conveniently forgetting her own Albert's lecherous father and her philandering brother-in-law, Ernest.[32] She insisted that Bertie's fall should be kept secret. Her cover was blown by the Duke of Cambridge, who wrote to Princess Louise

* This was the protocol that assigned the succession of the two duchies of Schleswig and Holstein to Denmark. Princess Louise herself was, in fact, more closely related to the King of Denmark than her husband, but as a woman she was excluded from the succession by Salic law.

(she was his cousin) revealing all, adding that Victoria and her son were on the worst of terms. Wally Paget found Princess Louise in tears with this letter in her hands, saying that Alexandra's position would be impossible if she married Bertie.[33] Victoria leaped to her son's defense, insisting that "wicked wretches had led our poor innocent boy into a scrape," that Albert and she had forgiven him "this (one) sad mistake," that she had never quarreled with him and that "she looked to his wife as being his salvation."[34] But the Duke of Cambridge's leak had shifted the advantage in this game of moral bargaining away from Victoria, giving the Danes the upper hand—all the more so as the czar of Russia now returned to the attack and announced his intention of swooping off either Alexandra or Dagmar as a bride for his son.[35]

When Bertie returned home in June 1862, Victoria found him "much improved and . . . ready to do everything I wish"—that is, he agreed to marry as soon as she desired. She told Vicky "we get on very well. He is much less coarse looking and the expression of the eyes is so much better."[36] Within a few weeks, however, Bertie was irritating his mother as much as ever. She complained that he was idle and listless, he fidgeted terribly, his voice was too loud, and his argumentative manner with the younger children exasperated her.[37]

The Queen found all talk or excitement intolerable. She always dined alone. She suffered from neuralgia, lost weight, and sometimes could barely walk. Her journal is a dreary litany of sleepless nights, headaches, and lethargy. No doubt today she would be diagnosed as clinically depressed.[38] As the months went by, her mourning continued unabated. Like Miss Havisham, her grief had become almost pathological. Prolonged grief can follow an ambiguous relationship where conflict and tensions are unresolved, leaving lingering guilt, and perhaps this was the case with Victoria. Her marriage to Albert had been intensely competitive, a battleground for power, and the Queen's worship of her Angel was a stratagem for coping with his superiority, which at another level she resented.

But she found that mourning suited her. It allowed her to withdraw from all public appearances and court functions that she found boring or disagreeable. Under cover of mourning she could do exactly as she wished. She retreated into a small inner circle, seeing only her younger children, servants, and favored ladies-in-waiting. Her favorite, Lady Augusta Bruce, the sister of Bertie's governor, always answered "Yes, ma'am" to everything she said and was promoted to a privileged permanent position at her side.[39]

Albert was beatified and transmogrified into a cult. At Frogmore, close to the sepulcher that housed the remains of her mother, Victoria supervised the construction of a mausoleum, her own version of the Taj Mahal, a rich and dramatic celebration of the angel of death. It was built on a marsh, and a fire burned constantly to keep off decay. Bertie was heard to remark that he "would take good care not to be buried in such a place."[40]

The anniversary of Albert's death, 14 December, became a holy day for the Queen and her family, commemorated each year with prayers and weeping at the mausoleum. For the rest of her life Victoria dressed in widow's cap and weeds. Alice's wedding, which took place in the dining room at Osborne in July, was more like a funeral. Victoria sat hunched in an armchair. Affie "sobbed all through and afterwards—dreadfully."[41]

General Bruce, Bertie's governor, who had contracted fever in the Near East, died shortly before Alice's wedding. On the last day of his life, he spoke of Bertie's fall.[42] For Bertie, Bruce's exit was sad but timely; Bruce had controlled him with excessive strictness. In place of a governor, Victoria appointed a comptroller and treasurer for her son: General William Knollys, a sixty-five-year-old retired soldier.* The Queen ordered Knollys to act as Bertie's mentor and to report directly to her.[43] Much to Bertie's annoyance, she insisted that Knollys should

---

* His father, another General Knollys, had been a friend of Queen Victoria's father, the Duke of Kent, and the man to whose care the duke had commended his cast-off mistress, Julie de St. Laurent.

be informed of his fall. Reluctantly, Bertie agreed, "hoping that this may be the last conversation that I shall have with you on this painful subject."[44]

Victoria, however, was obsessive on the matter; she couldn't let it go. "Poor Boy," she wrote, "who alas! cannot, as beloved Papa & good Fritz, bring 'the white flower of a blameless life' to the altar, but alas! must feel when that pure innocent girl looks at you with her fine eyes, ashamed at your unworthiness—oh! those wicked ones who 'robbed you of your virtue' as beloved Papa said. Oh! That sad stain which grieved your beloved Papa so sorely, so bitterly . . . let it not be blotted out from your own conscience but let it be your constant admonition to make up, by a future spotless life, for that which alas! can never be undone."[45]

Bertie's response to this eleven-page outburst was diplomatic. "If you only knew how much I feel for you," he wrote, "& how I see what a miserable existence you are now forced to lead, & how I often wish I could allay your suffering & sorrow, you would not I think consider me so very selfish." As for his fall, he was contrite: "I will not touch again on that unhappy subject, which I know grieved you & Papa so much, I only hope that my past conduct has made some amends."[46]

For Bertie, writing to his mother had become like negotiating with a hostile power. His letters are devoid of real feeling. Victoria's language of sin and redemption made little impression. How insincere his repentance was can be seen from a gossipy letter he wrote that same month to his friend Carrington. "I am sorry to hear that you went to such a disreputable place as the one you mention in your letter, as I hoped that you were conducting yourself better, but I fear that such is not the case . . . I hope that you have not lost Lydia Thompson's shoe?"*[47]

Freud hypothesized that men seek out prostitutes to revenge themselves on their mothers, by treating women merely as objects of sexual gratification. Bertie's hunger for the demimonde may have represented

* Lydia Thompson was an actress who sold her old dancing shoes to her admirers at the Crystal Palace.

a rebellion against his overcontrolling mother. But he always risked being found out, and whenever the Queen learned of his transgressions, she used them as an argument for refusing to allow him responsibility.

Victoria left nothing about Bertie's engagement to chance. She insisted on seeing Alexandra for herself, in order to judge "whether she will suit me."[48] She drew up an elaborate schedule for this meeting, choreographing each interview in advance. Bertie was also provided with detailed instructions as to how and where and when to propose to the princess. "It is dreadful to do all this without [Papa]," wailed the Queen, imploring Bertie by his marriage to "cast a few gleams of light on the declining years of my now utterly desolate . . . life."[49]

Traveling as Countess of Balmoral, Victoria crossed to Laeken, Uncle Leopold's Brussels palace, on 3 September 1862, and the carefully scripted audiences with Princess Alexandra and her family took place. Victoria was overcome by tears, not at the prospect of losing her son, but because she found it "horrible" to meet Alexandra's parents without Albert by her side. Alexandra, who had been warned that the Queen wished for virtue in her daughter-in-law, wore a tactful black dress and simple, girlish hair.[50] Victoria fell for her at once. Princess Alexandra, she wrote, was "a pearl," gentle and dignified and altogether more distinguished than her rather common family. "Tho' quite exhausted & worn out—& in a state of nervousness & exhaustion & sorrow hardly to be described," Victoria wrote at once giving Bertie full sanction to propose.[51]

Bertie was like an actor in a play. All he had to do was learn the lines the Queen had written for him and perform them on cue. "I think," he wrote, "that I have quite made up my mind about the young Princess, & that I should be happy with her."[52] Two days later, on 9 September, he gave a triumphant report to Victoria: "The all important event has taken place today." As scripted by his mother, Bertie had proposed to the princess at Laeken, while out walking in the garden. "She immediately said yes; but I told her not to answer too quickly but to consider over it. She said she had long ago, I then asked her if she liked me. She said <u>yes</u>. I then kissed her hand & she kissed me." Next, he asked Alexandra's parents for their consent, and "We then went to luncheon."[53]

Bertie was under every sort of pressure to fall in love with his princess. A love match, as his uncle Leopold wrote, "<u>destroys all the arguments of his affair being arranged for him without it being his choice</u>."[54] Victoria shamelessly briefed both *The Times* and Lord Russell, her minister in Germany, to deny reports of an arranged marriage, insisting that the match was in no sense political.[55] Bertie tried hard to oblige, seeming to become more enamored by the hour. Two days later he wrote to his mother: "I frankly avow to you that I did not think it possible to love a person so as I do her."[56]

No sooner was the engagement accomplished than Victoria invited Alexandra to visit her. It was less an invitation than a command. The princess was summoned to Osborne alone, without Bertie. Such was "the fear—I might almost say the horror—the Queen has of the Princess's mother's family," wrote Victoria's private secretary, General Grey, that the parents were expressly forbidden from staying.[57] Prince Christian was allowed to accompany his daughter on the crossing, but Victoria ostentatiously refused to receive him, forcing him to put up at a London hotel. When Princess Louise objected, pointing out that her daughter had never before been away from home, Victoria sent unpleasant messages via her lady-in-waiting. The Queen "has been a little disapp[ointe]d," wrote Lady Augusta Bruce, "[she] cannot help feeling an alteration in tone."[58] That the Danes must learn their place as poor relations was made painfully clear.

Alexandra arrived at Osborne by moonlight on 5 November 1862. She later confessed to being terrified, but from the moment she landed and embraced the nine-year-old Prince Leopold, who greeted her on the pier clutching a bunch of flowers, she could do no wrong. She was gentle and unaffected, she went to bed at ten o'clock, and she spent hours sitting alone with Victoria listening to her talk about Albert. So moved was Alexandra, wrote Victoria, that she "laid her dear head on my shoulder & cried"—an act of emotional intelligence that won the Queen's heart.[59] Soon the princess was being affectionately referred to as Alix.

The affection was mutual. "You cannot imagine how <u>lovable</u> the dear good Queen is," wrote Alix (in Danish) to her sister in a letter that breathes homesickness. On long drives through the rain with the Queen in an open carriage she consoled herself by reflecting how similar the Isle of Wight was to the coast of Denmark.[60]

Victoria warned Alix not to make Bertie a partisan of Denmark, and forbade her to bring a Danish maid. "It would not do for the dear young couple's happiness if Alix had a maid to whom she could chatter away in a language her Husband could not understand."[61] She complained that Bertie wrote to Alix in English rather than German, which "grieves and pains me as the German element is the one I wish to be cherished and kept up in our beloved home."[62] But Bertie's laziness about German was compounded by Alix's Danish sympathies. She had learned from her parents a horror of German, which was the language of Denmark's enemies, and she preferred to speak English when she couldn't use Danish. Victoria's command was not obeyed.

Bertie, meanwhile, was packed off on yet another foreign cruise, this time to the Mediterranean with Vicky and Fritz. As Lord Clarendon explained, Victoria wanted to keep him out of the way "till the time for Hymen is completed. Perhaps too the Queen may think that Continental temptations will be less strong than the British."[63] Like a stallion at stud, the Prince of Wales was kept in a sort of sexual quarantine.

From Rome, Vicky gave glowing reports on Bertie. "His is a nature which develops itself slowly," she told her mother, "and I think you will find that he will go on improving and that his marriage will do a good deal for him in that way."[64] This was the optimistic view. The beast, however, *would* keep rearing its ugly head. Back home, Bertie foolishly boasted about his adventures in Paris with actresses "with very little dress on" to the gossip Lord Torrington, who reported to Delane, the editor of *The Times*: "Evidently the young man is very hot and asked me a good many leading questions. I believe the marriage is hurried on with all speed for fear of <u>any</u> <u>accident</u> overtaking him."[65]

———

The wedding was set for a date in Lent, the season of sackcloth and ashes; the dress code for the court was half-mourning colors of gray, silver, and lilac, and the Queen commanded that it should take place at St. George's Chapel, Windsor, rather than London. She insisted that this had been Albert's wish, but insiders thought the Queen's real reason for cheating London's show-loving crowds of a royal wedding was the fact that in St. George's Chapel she could watch the ceremony unseen from Catherine of Aragon's closet.[66]

Alexandra arrived at Gravesend three days before the wedding. The Danish ambassador Augustus Paget, who accompanied her from Copenhagen, thought her "rather down in the mouth" during the voyage, and she had a heavy cold.[67] Bertie, who was "a good deal agitated," went to meet her.[68] He was more than ten minutes late, "which was rather unfortunate," and rushed aboard the *Victoria and Albert,* which had been sent to bring her from Antwerp, delighting the crowd by kissing her in full view.[69] The road through London teemed with cheering crowds, and in the City even the imperturbable Alix was frightened when the Life Guards charged the crush brandishing their sabers. The crowds inspired the Poet Laureate Tennyson's wedding ode:

> Sea-kings' daughter from over the sea,
> Alexandra!
> Saxon and Norman and Dane are we,
> But all of us Danes in our welcome of thee,
> Alexandra!
> Welcome her, thunders of fort and of fleet!
> Welcome her, thundering cheer of the street!

Victoria, however, read the celebrations as a tribute to her own popularity and, naturally, as recognition for Albert. The sight of any happy couple, she told Palmerston, "plunges daggers into the Queen's widowed heart, for she is always alone."[70]

At Windsor, Victoria received Alix at the foot of the great staircase with an embrace, and then retired to her room, "desolate and sad." Later, Alix knocked at her door and knelt before her "with that sweet loving expression which spoke volumes. I was very much moved and kissed her again and again."[71]

On the morning of the wedding (10 March 1863), Victoria dressed in her widow's weeds and widow's cap ("more hideous than any I have yet seen," thought Clarendon), which she enlivened with the blue ribbon and star of the Order of the Garter, worn for the first time since Albert's death.[72] She walked from the deanery over the roof leads to the royal closet, a Gothic box high up on the wall of St. George's Chapel.

Inside, the chapel was packed. The Queen's insistence on inviting her entire household left few seats for the great and the good, and invitations were highly prized. Bertie himself was allowed only four friends (Carrington was one). The adventurer Disraeli was present (on the insistence of Prime Minister Palmerston, and not, as he liked to think, because of the Queen's special regard for him), while the Duchess of Manchester, who had once served as Mistress of the Robes, was omitted, a snub that caused a lasting rift.

When the Queen entered the box, the entire congregation bowed. As Vicky processed up the aisle, magnificent in white satin trimmed with ermine, she caught sight of her mother and (wrote the Queen) "made a very low curtsey, with an inexpressible look of love and respect, which had a most touching effect."[73]

Next Bertie entered, wearing Garter robes and flanked by his supporters, his brother-in-law Fritz and his uncle Ernest of Saxe-Coburg.* He seemed pale and nervous but, some said, "more considerable" than usual.[74] He bowed to his mother and kept looking up at her, Victoria thought, "with an anxious clinging look."[75] Bertie stood waiting for what seemed an eternity, ten or twenty minutes, until at last Alix appeared. Instead of the magnificent wedding dress of Brussels lace

---

* Ernest no longer opposed the marriage. A few months before, Bertie had renounced the succession to his uncle, who was childless, in favor of his brother Alfred. At least Alix would never sit upon the throne of Coburg.

given to her by King Leopold, she wore Honiton lace patterned with roses, shamrocks, and thistles and garlanded with orange blossoms—a last-minute change of plan that signaled her role as ambassador for English fashion, though critics considered her "too sunk in greenery."[76] She was pale and trembling and red-eyed, having cried all morning at leaving her mother. Not that she was doubtful about marrying Bertie; she said to one of his sisters: "You perhaps think that I like marrying your Brother for his position but if he was a cowboy I should love him just the same and would marry no one else."[77]

Victoria was overcome during the singing of a chorale composed by Albert, but after this she recovered and looked inquisitively at the audience. Disraeli, who was nearsighted, raised his eyeglass to the royal box, and caught her icy glance. He did not venture to use his glass again. When the marriage was over, the Queen recorded, "I gave them an affectionate nod and kissed my hand to sweet Alix."[78]

Afterward, Bertie and Alix lunched with thirty-eight royal relations, while five hundred wedding guests caroused elsewhere. Not so the Queen. "I lunched alone with Baby [Princess Beatrice]."[79] The wedding guests departed in an undignified crush from Windsor station. Disraeli sat on his wife's lap on the train, while so many gems were plundered from the jewel-encrusted Maharaja Duleep Singh that he had to be locked up and sent to London by a later train. Meanwhile, Bertie and Alix departed for the honeymoon to Osborne, which, as Fritz remarked, was now a gloomy vault crammed with relics of Prince Albert.[80]

Neither Bertie nor Alix wrote accounts of the wedding. From the version Victoria gave in her journal, one might think it was she, not her son, who was the star of the occasion. Victoria was superbly skilled at dramatizing her role as queen in mourning. W. P. Frith's painting of the ceremony in St. George's Chapel, which Victoria commissioned, encapsulates the drama. The eye is instantly drawn to the lonely figure of the black-clothed Queen standing in her box, her face and widow's cap bathed in light. The bridesmaids and members of the royal family stare up at her, and seem almost oblivious of the bridal couple; but her gaze is firmly fixed on her son and his bride—neither of whom returns it, nor indeed do they look at each other, but seem absorbed in inner reflection.[81]

A few days after the honeymoon, Bertie and Alix were photographed at Windsor with Victoria beside Albert's marble bust, the "dear, dear protecting head" as Victoria called it.[82] The day before the wedding, the Queen had taken Bertie and Alix to the mausoleum at Frogmore and opened the shrine. "He gives you his blessing," she said, and joined their hands, took them both in her arms, and kissed them. "It was a very touching moment and we all felt it," she wrote.[83] The wedding photograph was an attempt to convey this. Victoria gazes theatrically up at Albert's bust, but her face in profile set off against the deep black of her mourning drapery is sharply focused, while Albert's chiseled marble features dissolve into a blur. The photographer was forced to bathe the Queen's black dress in an excess of light, which whited out Albert's head. Victoria had positioned herself deferentially below Albert on his pillar, but he had become a faceless spirit.[84] Bertie and Alix were almost irrelevant to the drama of Victoria's grief. Bertie stands behind his mother, clean-shaven for once, puffy-eyed, plump and slightly seedy, bulging out of his too-tight black coat—he had put on weight during his tours abroad.[85] Alix, in white contrasting sharply with the Queen's black, looks neither at her husband nor his parents but skittishly over her shoulder as the photographers had taught her to do. The dance between Bertie, his wife, and his mother was about to unfold.

CHAPTER 6

"Totally Totally Unfit . . . for Ever Becoming King"[1]

1863–65

After the honeymoon, Bertie and Alix traveled to Sandringham, the new house Bertie had bought in Norfolk. The countryside was bleak and wild, and people in country carts lined the road from the station to greet them.[2] The east wind blowing from the Wash made spring unendurable. "As there was all England wherein to choose, I do wish they had had a finer house in a more picturesque and cheerful situation," lamented a lady-in-waiting.[3]

At Sandringham, however, Bertie and Alix could be alone together—or at least, as alone as much as people can be when attended always by ladies-in-waiting and equerries as well as troops of servants. The flat countryside reminded Alix of Denmark, and she felt at home, she told her sister, because the house was "comfortable and cosy and not too large."[4] The couple spent all day together, walking in the garden and discussing improvements, and went to bed before eleven. "He seems very kind to her," reported lady-in-waiting Mrs. Bruce, "and so proud of her appearance, which is certainly most fascinating."[5]

The eighteen-year-old princess was young for her age and refreshingly simple. "I am very fond of soldiers," she once said; "I always think I was intended for a nursery maid."[6] The Danish court where she grew up was neither as rich nor as formal as the English monarchy. The Yellow Palace, where Alix's family lived, was a modest town house; the front door opened straight on to the street. Blue-uniformed soldiers changed the guard outside each morning, and Alix played four-handed piano in the cream and gold drawing room with its French rococo furniture. Until she married, she shared a bedroom with her sister Dagmar, known as Minnie, three years her junior, to whom she wrote rambling, homesick letters from England. She clung to cozy, cluttered domesticity, summed up in the Danish word *hygge*. Most of all, she clung to Bertie.

No letters survive between Bertie and Alix. But their marriage was closely observed, especially by Victoria. She set up a network of spies and intelligence gatherers, of private secretaries and ladies-in-waiting and doctors, who reported to her almost daily on her son and daughter-in-law. From her inner sanctums at Windsor and Osborne, she spun webs of spiderlike intricacy; the more reclusive she became, the more she needed to know and control.

The widow Queen held tight to her family. Her letters to her married daughters, Vicky and Alice, are intimate and frank, but also judgmental and contradictory, sometimes startlingly so. To them she poured out her anxieties about Bertie and his marriage. Her letters to Alice are especially outspoken; Victoria had become very close to Alice as a result of Albert's death, and she told her: "I can say every thing to you, as I can to no one else."[7]

At first, Victoria found Bertie improved by marriage. He was, she told Alice, "so amiable and ready to do anything."[8] The reports from Sandringham were "very satisfactory," and the Queen confessed herself "astonished" by the change in Bertie.[9] But the Queen's hopes that marriage had redeemed her son were soon dashed. Within weeks she was complaining that Bertie had "let himself down" to his old bad

manners.[10] Victoria considered that Alix's education had been neglected and she did nothing but write letters all day.[11] As for Bertie, he
did not do one useful thing. He never read a book. He was hopelessly
frivolous and unreflecting. She shuddered to think of "the poor country with such a terribly unfit, totally unreflecting successor! Oh! that is
awful! He does nothing!"[12] Bertie (she told Alice) "shows more and
more how totally totally unfit he is for ever becoming King."[13]

In London, the Prince and Princess of Wales were installed at
Marlborough House, which the government modernized at a cost of
£60,000. The original house, designed by Christopher Wren for Sarah,
Duchess of Marlborough, was enlarged by the government architect
Sir James Pennethorne. Louis Laguerre's spectacular saloon, decorated with scenes from Marlborough's victories, was preserved, and
so were his painted staircases. To allow the prince to accommodate
the whole of London society at a single ball, the house was remod-
eled with a lavish enfilade of Frenchified gilded state drawing rooms
and dining rooms. The interior was furnished and fitted up by the
fashionable London firm of Holland.[14] Bertie took an interest, and he
was allowed to decide such details as the lighting (candles in the princess's reception room, gas in the passage between the reception room
and visitors' rooms). But the readying and running of the house was
the responsibility of Sir William Knollys and his son Francis, and they
resented attempts by the prince to interfere with such details as writing paper or servants' livery, the more so as he constantly found
fault.[15]

No sooner had Bertie and Alix unpacked than the London Season
began. Night after night the prince and princess hosted great dinner
parties, attended banquets, appeared at the opera, and received deputations congratulating them on their marriage. Alix represented the
Queen at a drawing room at St. James's Palace. Victoria usually held
three afternoon drawing rooms each season, at which women were
presented (men were presented at levees). Mourning for Albert had
canceled court functions in 1862, and so in 1863, two thousand guests
attended, all agog to see the new princess, the girls wearing bare-

shouldered dresses with long trains and ostrich feathers.[16] From two till six p.m., Alix curtseyed continuously as six hundred unknown ladies were presented to her. She seemed pathetic and exhausted—"a white gown and a white face, two curls and a tiara," sniffed the diarist Louisa Bowater.[17] Even worse was her ordeal three days later, at a state reception at St. James's Palace, when she was obliged to walk in front of the royal party, "totally alone" behind the Lord Chamberlain, through three crowded halls. "In every room I had to make a deep curtsey and then walk on greeting to right and left! It was terrible!"[18]

At twenty-one, Bertie had been plunged into exacting responsibilities. He had no experience of London society, and his only qualification for this role was his rank. From Osborne and Balmoral, Victoria watched Bertie and Alix's every move, controlling their lives in an "extraordinary" way.[19] Where they dined out, whom they invited to Marlborough House—every name was approved by her. When Alix rode in the park, she received a sharp telling-off. Each day a detailed report was sent from Marlborough House to the Queen.[20] Victoria complained that Bertie took no care of Alix, but for Alix's exhaustion Victoria had only herself to blame. By making Bertie act as "social sovereign" in order to shield her own seclusion, she imposed a punishing schedule on her daughter-in-law.

Victoria anxiously scrutinized Alix for signs of pregnancy. Here, too, she despaired. With a twenty-two-inch waist and a thirty-two-inch chest, Alix hardly seemed built for childbearing.[21] "Are you aware," Victoria asked Vicky, "that Alix has the smallest head ever seen? I dread that—with [Bertie's] small empty brain—very much for future children."[22] Bertie insisted on going out most nights and staying up until four a.m. Alix, said the Queen, "will become a skeleton, and hopes [of pregnancy] there cannot be!!"[23]

The physician-in-ordinary to the Prince of Wales was named Dr. Sieveking. He kept a private diary of his attendance on the prince and princess: two locked black leather volumes that, by a minor miracle, have survived in a little-known archive.*

Sieveking, who was born in England to German parents and had trained in Bonn, was briefed by Victoria. Speaking German, she informed him of "the want of resistance to morbid influences" in Albert's family, and instructed him to look carefully after "those children," the prince and princess. "I thought her behaviour most gracious, her voice as clear as a bell and her smile more winning than that of any woman," wrote the doctor after his first audience with the Queen.[24] Unwittingly, he had been enlisted as one of her informers, charged to spy on Marlborough House.

Sieveking visited Marlborough House every Friday, alternating with Dr. Jenner, who visited on Tuesdays. He rarely saw Alix, but usually spoke to Bertie, who was always sensible and affable. Bertie enjoyed robust health, though he occasionally complained of a hangover. General Knollys told the doctor that the prince had "strong animal passions and is fond of good living . . . keeps late hours to his great disadvantage . . . is very good at heart, well meaning and well pleased with truthfulness among those about him—rather hot-tempered but forgiving." Sieveking also noticed that Bertie was very curious about medical subjects, cross-questioning him on topics such as hermaphroditism. Alix, thought Sieveking, had no influence over her husband, though she was "very fond" of him.[25] She was always more communicative when he was away.

Bertie knew every detail of his wife's menstrual cycle, and he freely discussed her intimate gynecological details with the doctor. When, three months after the marriage, her period ("catamenia" was the doctor's word) was two days late, Sieveking promptly forbade her from riding a horse and banned late nights and walking.[26] In spite of these precautions, her period appeared a few days later. Alix confided her

---

* Expert advice in the 1930s strongly urged that the journals be destroyed on account of their intimate subject matter. Fortunately this was ignored, and the journals were deposited in the library of the Royal College of Physicians, where they have languished ever since. I stumbled upon them in a chance trawl through a card index.

woes to the Queen, who reported to Alice that "all came on on Sunday, to [Alix's] great disappointment."[27]

Victoria (being Victoria) began to worry that Alix would never have children.[28] Alix complained of sickness, but this was dismissed as insignificant. Sieveking prescribed quinine to strengthen her. Not until a month later, in August, did he see Alix alone for the first time. He spoke German to her, in an attempt to put her at her ease, but he didn't examine her. She gave him a list of the dates of her periods, from which it appeared that she had last menstruated on 30 April, and then only for one day on 7 June. Sieveking recorded: "I expressed the opinion that the 7th June did not count and that she must reckon pregnancy, if enceinte, from the middle of May, accordingly she may be nearly three months gone."[29]

Sieveking still had doubts about the pregnancy, as the princess's figure remained unchanged. Not until a month later did Bertie report to Sieveking that her dresses were becoming too tight, "whereat I expressed my joy, as it was the first confirmatory symptom of pregnancy which had occurred." A few days later he saw the Queen, who still refused to believe that the princess was pregnant.[30]

Even after the pregnancy had become visible, Alix put on hardly any weight and felt and looked unusually well. Victoria feared the worst. "They say it is not a sign of strength," she wrote ominously.[31]

The real danger to Alix's well-being came from Denmark. In November 1863, the old King of Denmark died and Alix's father succeeded as King Christian IX. He was at once confronted with a crisis over the vexed issue of the duchies of Schleswig and Holstein. The Danish parliament had already voted to incorporate Schleswig, which was half Danish and half German (Holstein was German), into Denmark, but King Christian knew that if he signed this new constitution, he risked conflict with Germany. "Germany" meant the German Confederation, a loose grouping of thirty-nine states, but the rise of Prussia gave it a new military significance.

Vicky and her husband, Fritz, were staying at Windsor when the news came through that King Christian had signed. After a disagreeable breakfast with Fritz, who, as Crown Prince of Prussia, was "very violent" in his support for the claims of Germany, Victoria was in despair— "miserable, wretched, almost frantic without my Angel to stand by me, and put the others down, and in their right place! No respect is paid to my opinion now, and this helplessness almost drives me wild."[32] So divided were her family over this question that Victoria's uncle Leopold urged her to forbid them from discussing it in her presence.[33]

Between the conflicting claims of Denmark and Germany, Victoria's mind was soon made up. King Christian, she insisted, had brought his troubles on himself by his foolish attempt to incorporate Schleswig into Denmark, and he must face the consequences.[34] She supported the claims of the prince of Augustenburg, who was her nephew, known in the family as Fritz Holstein and married to the daughter of her half sister, Feodora.*

Victoria claimed that in opposing Denmark, she was merely doing what Albert would have done. Why oh why, she wailed, could her beloved not be here "to write those admirable memoranda which are gospel now."[35] Albert had indeed criticized the Treaty of London, which imposed a Danish ruler on the predominantly German population of Holstein. His logic went as follows: "Schleswig is entitled to insist on union with Holstein; Holstein belongs to Germany, and the Augustenburgs are the heirs."[36] But Victoria also found it convenient to claim Albert's support to vindicate her own prejudices. Naturally, she sided with "dear Germany," aligning herself with Vicky and Fritz. She despised Alix's family and thought King Christian a fool. And, by now, she had come to believe that Bertie's marriage was a mistake. Alix was "dear and amiable," but (she told Alice), "I do regret deeply the connection and feel those . . . who so strongly opposed it were right."[37]

The Schleswig-Holstein crisis roused Victoria to make her first political intervention since Albert's death. It was badly misjudged. Her

---

* Under the 1852 London treaty, the prince of Augustenburg had waived his claim to the duchies, which had been assigned to the personal rule of Christian of Denmark when he became king, but only on condition that he did not rule the duchies as part of Denmark.

support for Germany placed her in opposition to Palmerston, her prime minister, and foreign secretary Earl Russell, who urged mediation in the interests of Denmark. Palmerston argued that King Christian had not yet violated international law, but this cut no ice with the Queen, who saw the Schleswig-Holstein issue as a family quarrel where justice was on the side of the Augustenburgs. That the monarch was not supposed to pursue a foreign policy of her own but support her government's policy worried her not at all. When Russell attempted to deter the Germans by warning that Britain might be obliged to intervene on the side of Denmark, the Queen overruled him and protested to the Cabinet.[38]

The Schleswig-Holstein question was notoriously complicated—Palmerston famously quipped that only three people understood it: Prince Albert, who was dead, a German professor, who had gone mad, and he himself, who had forgotten all about it. Victoria certainly did not understand it, and she acted not as a constitutional monarch ought but (in the words of one diplomatic historian) as "a violent partisan inspired by emotion rather than reason."[39] She failed to realize that "Dear Germany" was changing. Albert's dream of a liberal, "good" Germany united by Prussia and ruled by Vicky and Fritz was melting away. In Prussia, Otto von Bismarck secretly prepared for war against Denmark, the first step in his program of uniting Germany by iron and blood, creating an autocratic royal state. By refusing support for King Christian, and blocking her ministers' efforts to mediate, Victoria was unwittingly playing into Bismarck's hands, as Denmark's diplomatic isolation allowed him to go to war and score an overwhelming military victory.

Bertie and Alix stayed at Osborne with the Queen for Christmas 1863. When the news came through that German troops were occupying Holstein, Alix dissolved into tears. Surprising everyone with her assertiveness, she insisted that the duchies belonged to her papa. Victoria was pitiless. From her desk she penned long, stern letters to her ministers: "Should war ensue between the German Powers and Denmark, in consequence of the violation by the latter of her promises respecting Schleswig . . . the Queen [could not] consider that any obligation rested upon England to come to the assistance of Denmark."[40]

Bertie and Alix retreated to Frogmore near Windsor for New Year's, thankful to escape Victoria's anti-Dane politics as well as her ban on smoking. "You need not be afraid that the new Royal Edict ag[ain]st the sinful practice of smoking will be carried out in my house," Bertie told his cousin, King Leopold's son Philip, "the more you smoke when you come, the better I shall be pleased."[41]

On 8 January, Alix complained of slight pains, but in the afternoon she insisted on being pushed in a sleigh on the ice at Virginia Water to watch Bertie playing a game of ice hockey. The cold was so intense that the photographer summoned from Windsor was forced to abandon his attempt to record the game, as the solution on the photographic plates froze solid.[42] Alix left early, and around six p.m. her pains came on more rapidly. Bertie telegrammed Dr. Sieveking in London: "Please come by earliest train and stay here tonight." At 8:50 Alix gave birth to a son who was probably two months premature, though no one was quite sure of the dates. Bertie was present in the room throughout the labor. Alix and Bertie were both distressed, fearing that the baby would die. Only the local Windsor doctor, Brown, attended the delivery. When Sieveking eventually arrived, he was met on the stairs by Bertie, who declared, "I am a father!"[43] The baby was healthy and ruddy, but tiny, weighing only 3¾ pounds.[44]

Nothing was ready. No nurse, no baby clothes, no wet nurse. At least Alix escaped the daunting presence of ministers and grand accoucheurs who might otherwise have been assembled to attend the birth of an heir to the throne. Lord Granville, a Cabinet minister, happened to be staying and acted as witness. "It was very touching to see the Prince of Wales's emotion," he wrote.[45] Lady Macclesfield, a "precise little stick" who was herself a mother of thirteen, was in attendance at Frogmore.*[46] She made the bed with clean linen, cleared away

---

* "The Queen wishes the new court to be as dull and stupid as her own" was the comment of Lord Stanley of Alderley (aka Ben Backbite) on hearing of Lady Macclesfield's appointment as Alix's lady-in-waiting. (Fulford, *Dearest Mama,* p. 289.)

the bloodied sheets, and wrapped the baby in cotton wool.[47] Because the child was premature, Alix was unable to breast-feed even if she had wished to do so, and a wet nurse was hurriedly procured from Windsor.*

After it was all over, looking into the bedroom, Lady Macclesfield saw Alix and Bertie weeping together on the bed.[48] Bertie's devotion and tenderness toward his wife was touching to behold.

The Queen at Osborne was "dumbfounded" to receive a telegram at eleven p.m. from Bertie announcing the birth.[49] She spent a sleepless night worrying what had caused this premature confinement and hastened to Windsor next day. She found Bertie "pale and worn, and so quiet and kind and happy."[50] Alix pleased her, too, the more so as she confessed that she "dislikes the whole business extremely and is utterly disgusted with it all."[51] To Victoria it all seemed like a dream, and "one wh[ich] I like to dwell on," though, of course, "it . . . c[oul]d not bring back my Angel, and I am ever, ever lonely."[52]

Victoria insisted that the baby should be called by the double name Albert Victor. Wags dubbed him "All-but on the ice," and he was always known as Eddy. At the christening, Victoria held him in her arms, and he roared throughout the ceremony.[53]

In April 1864, Fritz led the Prussian army in a crushing victory over the Danes. Victoria deplored the war, the more so as it soon became evident that Bismarck planned to ditch the Duke of Augustenburg and take over the duchies for Prussia. In spite of her dismay at Prussia's war policy, however, Victoria remained close to Vicky. "Politics must never divide relations—at least not the female part," she told her.[54] It was different with Bertie. His marriage created a division in the family. "Oh, if

---

* The temporary wet nurse, whom the Queen thought too old, was replaced by a woman named Mrs. Roe, who nursed the baby for nine months. Her husband was employed as a keeper at Sandringham, but was caught poaching and then left of his own accord. He became a constable in the Metropolitan Police, but was dismissed for drunkenness. Eventually he immigrated to America. (RA VIC/Add C07/1/0650, Francis Knollys's Memo on Wetnurses Engaged by Prince of Wales 1864–68, 20 October 1868.)

Bertie's wife was only a good German and not a Dane!" lamented Victoria.[55] "A Danish <u>partisan</u> you must <u>never</u> be," she told Bertie, "or you put <u>yourself</u> against your whole family and against your Mother and Sovereign—who (God knows!) has been as <u>impartial</u> as <u>anyone</u> ever was!" Bertie must never forget that "your connexion with Denmark is <u>only</u> of a year's standing, and . . . your whole family <u>are</u> German and you are yourself half German."[56] To Alice, her confidante among her children, the only one to whom she could pour out her "overburdened heart," Victoria wrote long, heavily underlined letters, over and again regretting Bertie's marriage, which "ought <u>not</u> to <u>have been</u>."[57] "Do try and make Bertie feel <u>how</u> shamefully <u>ungrateful</u> it is of him to be <u>unkind</u> to poor <u>Vicky</u>," Victoria implored Alice.[58] Victoria blamed the rift on Alix's scheming mother, Queen Louise.*[59] Bertie, she declared was "<u>so weak</u>" that he was "swayed by the <u>opinion</u> of the <u>last</u> person he speaks to, and he has no <u>reasoning</u> or <u>reflective powers</u>."[60] The fact was, however, that Bertie's views on the Schleswig-Holstein war were far closer to the British government's than were the Queen's.

Bertie asked to be sent Foreign Office dispatches. The Queen was predictably dismissive. The last thing she wanted was for him to communicate directly with ministers, undermining her anti-Dane policy. Bertie, she responded, could be sent a précis of the dispatches received by her. This, her secretary assured the foreign secretary, Lord Russell, would allow the Queen to control Bertie's reading of official papers, as "HRH is not, at all times, as discreet as he should be."[61] That Bertie was loose-tongued and probably too lazy to read the dispatches anyway was an unfair charge, which was often to be repeated.

The Schleswig-Holstein war ended in May 1864 with the ignominious defeat of the Danes, who were forced to surrender the duchies. Prussia's conquest of Schleswig left festering wounds, and poisoned relations between Germany and Denmark. To Alix, Prussia was henceforth known as the "robber's den."[62] Bertie's defection to what Victoria

---

* Queen Louise had more time for Bertie than Victoria did. She told Clarendon that she had studied his character, and "there was more latent ability than he was given credit for or than anyone had tried to develop, but that what she dreaded for him was want of occupation." It was a shrewd assessment. (Kennedy, *My Dear Duchess*, p. 216.)

called the "enemy's camp" was the first step in the construction of an anti-Prussian dynastic bloc by the Danish royal family.[63] Few would have guessed that Alix, the pretty, docile Danish princess, would be the linchpin in a reconfiguration of dynastic alliances.

The arranged marriage between Bertie and Alix had developed into a genuinely affectionate relationship. Alix's feelings had never been in doubt, but Bertie's devotion was now manifest. He supported Alix's family over the Danish war, though this cut him off from his mother and sisters. He was tender and protective of Alix.

Victoria's interference only brought them closer together. The Queen worried about Alix's health. Alix, commented Victoria, three months after the birth of the baby, looked terribly thin, as flat as a board with a face like a knife.[64] Victoria enlisted the aging Uncle Leopold, who was instructed to warn Bertie that it would be "a [great] national misfortune if Alix got <u>weaker</u> and <u>weaker</u>. . . . You <u>must not mince</u> the matter," the Queen told him, "but <u>speak strongly</u> and <u>frighten</u> Bertie."[65]

The Queen appointed a committee of three doctors, Sieveking, Jenner, and Sir James Clark, to report on the sanitary arrangements of the princess. Alix was to go to bed at eleven o'clock, have eight hours' sleep and take a daily walk; "at the monthly periods the exercise should be limited to a gentle walk." In the event of another pregnancy, great care must be taken to prevent a premature birth. Otherwise, the doctors warned, "a habit may be engendered likely to result in a general and permanent delicacy of health."[66] On the Queen's orders, court balls and drawing rooms were planned so that the dates did not coincide with Alix's periods.[67]

Bertie thought the doctors' report "absurd" and, according to Sieveking, showed "a good deal of temper over it."[68] No doubt Alix was distressingly thin, but most of her ailments could be put down to childbirth. She suffered from "extreme costiveness," natural enough after giving birth, but refused to accept an enema. She complained of backache, fatigue, and "general lassitude," a "want of power and disinclination to do anything," ailments that surely would be diagnosed today as postpartum depression.[69] Some of her symptoms were odd and worrying, however. Shortly after the birth of her son, she seems to have suffered a prolapsed uterus, which she described as a falling of the womb. Her nurse, Mrs. Clarke, told Sieveking that "it had come outside and was without sensation and had best be cut off."[70]

Queen Victoria corresponded regularly with Bertie—she wrote to him on average once every ten days—but she often used Sir Charles Phipps, the Keeper of the Privy Purse, to communicate her displeasure. Together with General Grey, Victoria's private secretary, Phipps had assumed a dominant position at court.[71] He had been one of Albert's close associates, and when Albert died Lord Torrington worried that the court was in for a "King Phipps reign . . . it makes me quite savage the thought, that we shall be ruled by Phipps."[72] At first, Phipps's ambitions were frustrated by Albert's German servants, especially his valet, Carl Ruland. Victoria always inclined to give favorite servants access, bypassing the household, and Ruland's ascendancy made Phipps "angry and jealous."[73] By the summer of 1863, however, Phipps and Grey together had succeeded in purging the Germans, establishing themselves as the Queen's advisers.[74]

Phipps seemed fated to write "injudicious" letters to Bertie.[75] Whenever reports reached the Queen of Alix going riding or even boating, or of Bertie accepting invitations without consulting her, he fired off a missive. This enraged Bertie, who complained about "espionage," and tale-telling.[76] "It would be really better for poor Sir Charles never to write on any subject connected with the Queen's wishes," wrote Sir William Knollys.[77]

Victoria, for her part, complained to Alice of Bertie's want of confidence in her, which meant that "none can be given in return, and much as I love Alix I am not on an intimate footing with her, I am no nearer than I was when she married, and I feel that B's marriage with her has alienated him from our relations and has made him quite a stranger and quite John Bullish!!"[78] "It hurts me and it shocks me," she wrote, "to see how stupid and obtuse he is."[79] Using King Leopold as intermediary, she demanded that Bertie should "consult me on everything concerning his own movements and concerning the management of the child, which last is my right and duty; also to point out the extreme necessity of his not making his house a foyez for Danes."[80] As she told Alice: "By law I am bound to supervise the management and education of his child or children and could if I chose take them from him—if I thought the education not good!"[81]

In September 1864, when the Schleswig-Holstein war was safely over, Bertie and Alix crossed to Copenhagen to stay with Alix's parents, bringing with them baby Eddy under the supervision of Dr. Sieveking. Victoria insisted that the baby be sent back to her at Balmoral as soon as Alix and Bertie left Copenhagen on a visit to Sweden.[82] This upset Alix and put terrible pressure on Sieveking, who expressed doubts to the Queen about sending the baby back, but "because I did not flatly contradict HM I find she has since written to the Prince to the effect that I quite agreed with her, which I certainly did not mean to convey." Bertie was "a good deal annoyed at being thwarted," and Sieveking begged him "not to put me in direct opposition to the Queen as I could not contradict her point blank."[83]

On his visit to Sweden, Bertie disobeyed Victoria's command that he and Alix should travel incognito. They stayed in Stockholm with the King, who, Bertie told Victoria, was "immensely gratified by our visit, and what would have been the use of annoying him by not going to the Palace. . . . You may be certain that I shall always try to meet your wishes as much as possible," he told her, but "if I am not allowed to use my own discretion, we had better give up travelling altogether."[84]

This display of independence was not what Victoria wanted to hear. "It is absolutely necessary," she told Bertie, "when I allow you to go abroad that the plan arranged should be strictly adhered to."[85] As a punishment, Victoria vetoed Bertie's plan to return via Paris. She called upon her ministers Palmerston and Russell to cancel it. When they refused, she was furious. "This is most annoying," she minuted, "and shows how little support the poor Queen is ever likely to get from her ministers."[86] The visit was stopped all the same. It was "a little hard," as General Grey explained, that "the disagreeable task" of controlling the movements of the Prince of Wales should be thrown entirely on the Queen. She was therefore "most anxious" that the cancellation of the trip "should be announced to HRH as coming from the Government" and not from the Queen.[87]

When Bertie and Alix stayed at Windsor on their return, however, Victoria was all smiles. Bertie, she wrote, was "most amiable" and not at all pro-Dane.[88] Alix, whom the Queen found "as dear and good as ever," complained to her sister that the court was like a nunnery where she was constantly corrected by the abbess and the nuns.[89] Victoria scolded that Bertie was childish, and she certainly treated him like a child. On his twenty-third birthday, he and Alix dined quietly with the Queen, and when she withdrew to her private drawing room, they joined the household for a party. At eleven o'clock, when they were in the middle of a round game, Victoria sent one of her pages to order them off to bed. "Down went the cards, and they retired."[90]

Meanwhile, Bertie was dogged by a character from his past: the "infernal Green," who had returned from New Zealand intent on blackmail, threatening to reveal the prince's sexual adventures with his wife three years earlier. The police inspector at Marlborough House was instructed to refuse admittance, and Green's demands for money were firmly refused. Bertie was confident that "we have nothing to fear [from] him," but he must have been on tenterhooks all the same.[91] "The great danger," as Phipps wrote, was "the Queen knowing all the worst, but I do not see how this could happen."[92]

Phipps's allusion to "knowing all" hints that Bertie's sexual adventures before his marriage had been more lurid than the record suggests. Phipps's knowing about the Green affair gave him a power that Bertie deeply resented. Far more than the scandal becoming public, he dreaded that his mother might hear of it. Whether Alix might have views in the matter was not discussed.

During the year 1865, Bertie kept a diary. The entries are brief and factual. It begins: 1 January, "Sandringham . . . In the morning we went to Church."[93] It nevertheless shows him fashioning himself as Prince of Wales. Escaping his mother's control and fleeing her dull and disapproving court, he embraced the sporting aristocracy—the shooting, hunting, gambling swells whom Prince Albert had so deplored. By nagging and spying on her son, Victoria drove him into the arms of the people whose bad influence she most feared.

In January 1865, Bertie stayed at Holkham, the home of the Earl of Leicester, who was a pioneer of the new and fashionable sport of driven pheasant shooting. Bertie wrote in his diary: "I breakfasted with the gentlemen at 9:30 wh[ich] is by Holkham time 40 minutes faster than London time, and at 10:30 went out shooting. . . . We killed 2092 head . . . 1028 pheasants and 948 hares. We killed 1000 pheasants out of the celebrated Scarborough Clump. I killed 166 pheasants to my own gun."[94]

Characteristically, Bertie recorded the times and tallies, but the diary also shows that, on a day like this, the Prince of Wales played a leading role among the gentlemen. He was the chief gun, standing in a line of shooters, which was especially nerve-racking because the guests at Holkham were among the best shots in the country. No doubt he was always placed in the best stand and his guns were the finest that London gunsmiths could craft. But the eyes of all were upon him, watching every bird that he missed. Sycophants exaggerated his skill, but Bertie was never more than an average shot, though he had "an extraordinary knack of killing birds behind him at an angle which most people find very difficult."[95] Why he was so devoted to a sport at which he did not excel is not hard to see. Expensive, exclusive, and ritualized, shooting resembled a military operation with none of its discomforts. For Bertie, the would-be army officer, shooting gave access to a man's world outside his mother's reach. In this gendered space, his role as dominant male was unchallenged.

Lord Leicester and Holkham, more than Windsor or Balmoral, inspired the regime at nearby Sandringham. Bertie had bought the house and estate in 1862.* No one could understand why he had picked it.

---

* Bertie paid £225,000 to Charles Spencer Cowper for the Sandringham estate, which wags described as six thousand acres of sand. The place had been found by Albert, and Bertie was

The house, said Sir Charles Phipps, was externally "very ugly—a white washed house with redbrick chimnies [sic] and a fanciful brown porch."[96]

The first of the Sandringham parties was held at Christmas 1864. Bertie's Cambridge friend Carrington was a guest, and he found the house "very small and inconvenient," but Bertie had already embarked on the large-scale pheasant rearing and competitive shooting that was to become such a feature of his court. They shot 809 head—a modest total by comparison with Holkham.[97] At Sandringham, too, the clocks ran fast to allow more winter daylight for shooting: Sandringham time was thirty minutes ahead of London time.

The dress code at Sandringham reflected the smartness and informality of the prince's court. The ledger of Henry Poole, the tailor of Savile Row, contains an entry in HRH's page for 1865: "blue silk smoking jacket, lined silk, silk collar and cuffs, Sandringham £13:8s."[98] This evening coat without tails was the forerunner of the dinner jacket, the first of Bertie's sartorial inventions. (He is also credited with making fashionable the turned-up trouser, after rolling up his trouser bottoms to walk through fields and, as his girth grew, undoing the bottom button of his waistcoat.)

Sandringham house parties often involved a compulsory photograph. "After luncheon," writes Bertie, "we and the whole party were photographed (in a group) . . . the result was satisfactory."[99] The group photograph, lined up on the steps of a country house with the prince seated or standing in the center, was to become his signature, an image replicated at countless house parties; Bertie, staring straight at the camera, is flanked by his hostess and the prettiest women. By contrast with Victoria and Albert, who were invariably photographed as a family, either as a couple or surrounded by their children, Bertie constructed an iconography of himself as leader of his peers.

At Sandringham, he projected lavish improvements, laying out

---

supposedly persuaded to buy it by a Cambridge friend, Henry Villebois, whose father owned the local hounds. (Charles Sebag-Montefiore Archive, Philip Magnus Papers, Lord Bradford to Magnus, 1 December 1958.)

princely kitchen gardens and pheasantries.[100] The original house was undeniably too small, but Bertie's plans panicked his advisers, who did all they could to prevent him from building an entirely new palace.[101] Bertie noted in his diary a meeting to discuss "either a site for a new house or additions to the present one. The latter course was decided on."[102] A. J. Humbert, the architect of the royal mausoleum, was engaged, and the house was enlarged piecemeal, until in 1870 a new one was at last built.

Attempting to restrain Bertie's building plans, rather than engaging a better country-house architect than Humbert, who specialized in churches, was perhaps shortsighted. But Phipps and Knollys were acutely conscious of the danger of Bertie overspending. The prince's income totaled more than £115,000. This amounted to about one-third of the Queen's income of £300,000, but she was among the very top wealth holders in the country, exceeded only by the Duke of Westminster. Bertie was in the top thirty of the rich list, in the same bracket as poorer dukes and below his friends the Duke of Sutherland (rental of £141,000) and the Duke of Devonshire (£181,000 rent). His chief source of income was the Duchy of Cornwall, with rents yielding more than £50,000, and Parliament topped this up on his marriage with an annuity of £50,000.* But this was not enough for Bertie to outshine every subject, as he was expected to do, let alone to build a house, and his expenditure regularly exceeded his income by about £20,000 a year. Rather than risk conflict with Parliament by asking for more, his advisers met the debt by drawing on his capital.[103]

Bertie's spending was fiercely curbed. When he asked for a checkbook, Sir William Knollys refused. If Bertie wrote checks, claimed Knollys, "I sh[oul]d never know how I stood with regard to the credits & debits in the Bankers Book."[104]

In London, Bertie's diary charts a routine of mornings spent riding in the public gaze in Rotten Row. He attended the House of Lords, following the advice given him by Lord Granville, who had told him to

---

* £10,000 of the parliamentary grant was apportioned as a dress allowance for Alexandra. Bertie also derived an average rental of £6,000 from Sandringham.

drop in as often as possible, not because of the debates (which were often dull), but because it was a very pleasant club.[105] He had few public duties. Victoria ordered that he must on no account be put at the head of societies such as the Royal Literary Fund or asked to make speeches. This was the sort of work that Albert had done, and which he had planned for Bertie after his marriage, but Victoria insisted that he was too young and too inexperienced.*[106]

His diary records playing whist for high stakes. "Played 8 rubbers at whist. I lost £138!!!" "I lost 7 rubbers and £101!!!"[107] But not all his companions were raffish aristocrats such as Lord Hartington or the Duke of Sutherland. George Otto Trevelyan, the Liberal MP and author, was "really intimate" with him around this time. "He used to send for me about 11 at night . . . to talk and smoke cigarettes with him in his smoking room; a beautiful little marble chamber for an hour or so. . . . He was wonderfully bright and gracious."[108] But the haughtier members of the aristocracy disapproved. After observing Bertie on a visit to the Tory grandee Lord Derby at Knowsley, where the prince sat up smoking until three a.m., Derby's son Lord Stanley wrote that "he talked a great deal, neither very sensibly nor the reverse. He is easy and pleasant in his manners: in face and figure he is growing fat, which gives an air of heaviness."[109]

On 2 June 1865, after going to Epsom races to watch the Oaks, Bertie gave a dinner party at Marlborough House, and Alix, who was eight months pregnant with her second child, "not feeling well did not come down." The obstetrician Dr. Farre was summoned, and at midnight Alix's labor pains came on. "At 1:18 she was safely confined of a boy—8 months child, but very quick labour—only Farre, Mrs. Clarke and I were present," noted Bertie.[110] This baby weighed at least two pounds more at birth than the two-months-premature Eddy. Alix had planned to breast-feed, and confided in Dr. Sieveking, telling him to keep it se-

---

* In spite of Victoria's doubts, he became president of the Society of Arts in 1863, a post formerly filled by Albert.

cret "because the Queen would not hear of it." Sieveking forbade it on medical grounds: The princess could only undertake to nurse her baby for six weeks and the child would be hand-fed thereafter.[111] So the new baby was committed to a wet nurse for nine months.

This was the future King George V, but when Victoria learned that Bertie intended to call the new prince George Frederick Ernest, she wrote: "I fear I cannot admire the names you propose for the baby." She had hoped, she said, for some fine old name, but "George only came over with the Hanoverian family."[112]

When Bertie had objected to his own double name, and asked to be known as Edward when he became king, his mother indignantly refused. As Albert Edward, Victoria explained, he was to begin a new line of kings named in memory of Albert. "I quite understand your wishes about my bearing my two names," wrote Bertie diplomatically, "although no English Sovereign has ever done so yet."[113] But he flatly refused to obey Victoria's wishes over the new baby, writing his mother a letter that Phipps thought "objectionable": "We are sorry to hear that you don't like the names that we propose to give our little boy but they are names that we like."[114]

Bertie and Alix stayed at Osborne in July, bringing with them twenty-nine servants, which Victoria thought excessive, as there was nowhere for them all to sleep.[115] "Personally we are on the most agreeable footing," Victoria told Alice, "but things are on the brink of a precipice." Bertie, she thought, was becoming less and less domestic, diverging from Alix and spending less and less time with her; yet Alix was so "indolent" that she seemed not to care. "As they go on their lives must be short," warned the Queen.[116]

CHAPTER 7

Alix's Knee

1865–67

The rift caused by the Schleswig-Holstein war was deepened by a quarrel over the marriage of the Queen's third daughter, Princess Helena (known as Lenchen). Victoria depended heavily on the support of her unmarried daughters. The first daughter who acted as her unofficial · private secretary was Alice. She was succeeded by Helena, and the Queen so despaired at the prospect of losing this daughter to marriage that she determined to find her a husband who would be prepared to live at the English court. This was a tough job description, coupled with the fact that Helena was the plainest of the princesses.[1]

Eventually, Victoria lighted on Prince Christian of Schleswig-Holstein. Penniless (by princely standards), thirty-four, prematurely bald, and a chain-smoker, he was "really a very good fellow though not handsome."[2] But Victoria could hardly have chosen a bridegroom who was more objectionable to Bertie. Christian was the younger brother of Victoria's nephew by marriage the Duke of Augustenburg, the liberal claimant to Schleswig and Holstein who had challenged King Christian of Denmark over the duchies and then been ousted when Bismarck invaded and grabbed them for Prussia and Austria. To Alix the engagement seemed a deliberate snub, especially as Victoria refused to discuss it with her. Alix could hardly bear to meet Christian.[3] Bertie, meanwhile, out of loyalty to Alix threatened to boycott Lenchen's wedding. His ally was Alice. According to Sir Charles Phipps, Alice was "the great agent in exciting dissension in the family."[4] Jealous of Lenchen's access to her mother, she worried that if Christian succeeded in gaining Victoria's confidence, she herself would be excluded forever. Outwardly she supported the match, imploring Bertie, as "the Brother who has ever been the friend of my heart and deep love of my soul," to sacrifice his feelings and act kindly toward Victoria and Lenchen.[5] But behind Victoria's back, she stirred up trouble, warning Christian not to let himself be put upon and made to live in England.[6]

Alice's meddling seems relatively harmless, but when Victoria learned about it she was furious. Like the Queen of Hearts in Lewis Carroll's *Alice in Wonderland* (which was published the same year), she was prone to bewildering changes of mood.* "Off with her head!" she roared; and Alice, who had been her favorite the year before, was disgraced. "When your parent and Sovereign settles a thing for her good which interferes with none of your rights and comforts, opposition for mere selfish and personal objects—indeed out of jealousy—is monstrous," stormed the Queen. "I cannot tell you what I have suffered."[7] Bertie swallowed his objections to the marriage, and in the topsy-turvy world of Victoria's family he now became the favorite. Blowing hot

---

* The Reverend Robinson Duckworth, who was appointed tutor to Prince Leopold in 1866, was a friend of Charles Dodgson—better known by his pseudonym of Lewis Carroll—and he was on the boating trip on the Thames with Alice Liddell and her two sisters on 4 July 1862, when Dodgson told the story that became *Alice in Wonderland*. Duckworth features in the book as the Duck in the Pool of Tears, but he had no links with the court at the time the story was written, and there is no evidence that the Queen of Hearts was a portrait of Victoria.

and cold as only she could do, Victoria declared that "Bertie has a loving affectionate heart and could never bear to be in long disagreement with his family. Towards me he is very dear and nice."[8]

The following summer, Bismarck engineered war against Austria and, with Vicky's husband, Fritz, at their head, the Prussian troops smashed Austria and Austria's German allies at the battle of Königgrätz (3 July 1866). Bismarck was merciless. Alix's grandfather, the Landgrave of Hesse-Cassel, who fought with Austria, was deprived of his sovereignty, and his country was incorporated into Prussia. Victoria's first cousin George V, the blind King of Hanover, also an ally of Austria, was dethroned, his territory absorbed into Prussia, and his family fortune—the so-called *Welfenfond*—confiscated by Bismarck. Bismarck annexed Schleswig and Holstein, in defiance of Denmark's claim to the duchies.*

Alice suffered, too. Her husband, Louis of Hesse-Darmstadt, supported Austria and was punished with the loss of part of his lands. During the war, Darmstadt was overrun by Prussian troops. Alice, who was seven months pregnant, was marooned there and became quite ill, thin and sleepless. Queen Victoria, still angry, commented tartly that "Poor Alice" was "so sharp and bitter" that "no one wishes to have her in their home."[9] In an embarrassing mix-up, the Queen placed a letter to Vicky in which she complained about Alice in an envelope addressed to Alice; though "vexed" and "distressed" by the mistake, she claimed it was good for Alice to learn what her mother thought about her.[10]

During the Austro-Prussian war, Bertie asked once more for access to government dispatches. His request was refused, as it had been at the time of the Schleswig-Holstein war.[11] But this time Bertie and Victoria were in agreement over foreign policy. Had he read the dispatches,

---

* As a concession to Denmark, the Treaty of Prague after the war provided that Schleswig should be ceded to Prussia only on condition that the Danish-speaking districts were allowed a free vote to join Denmark. In spite of strenuous efforts by Bertie, Bismarck never allowed this plebiscite to take place.

Bertie would have seen how indefatigable his mother had been in striving to prevent what she called a German civil war. She even addressed a personal appeal to her "Beloved Brother" the King of Prussia, imploring him to throw over Bismarck and sue for peace, with predictably discouraging results, as the King was no longer in control of Prussian foreign policy.

Prussia's victories strained Bertie's relations with Vicky to a breaking point. Vicky was proud of her husband, Fritz, who had commanded the Prussian troops and led his country to victory. "I cannot and will not forget that I am a Prussian," she wrote. The German states that opposed Prussia had "broken their own necks"; they had overestimated Austria's strength, knowing full well what the consequences of Austria's defeat would be, and they deserved their fate.[12]

But Vicky was conflicted. She had no sympathy with Prussian authoritarianism. She loathed Bismarck and despised her blinkered, reactionary Hohenzollern in-laws. During the war, her two-year-old son, Sigismund, died of meningitis, plunging her into deepest grief, and she was far from triumphalist about Prussia's victories. To her credit, she did all she could to stop the German wars from tearing her family apart. Struggling to keep politics out of family life, she insisted that "one must separate one's feelings for one's relations quite from one's judgement of political necessities."[13] When Bertie visited her at Potsdam that autumn, she wrote: "About Politics we will not discuss will we? They are not my doing—if they were, much w[oul]d be different. . . . I dislike Bismarck and disapprove his principles, but I cannot stand having my country abused." Vicky sympathized with Bertie's predicament: "I understand quite well what Alix's feeling must be about the fate of her relations. I feel for her and them."[14] Bertie's visit was a success. Vicky told the Queen that he was "kind and dear"—his face wore "an expression of quiet and content which is so pleasing to look at."[15]

Bertie's rapprochement with Vicky earned him more approval from Victoria. So pleased was she with her eldest son that she confided in him her anxiety about Affie, her current bête noire, whom she proposed to banish from the wicked flatterers of London society by sending him in command of a ship to Australia. "I know how much I can rely on you," the Queen told Bertie, "and how steady and well-principled you are—I feel there is no one to whom I cd appeal more properly than to you."[16]

Bertie and Alix rarely posed together, but there is one photograph that shows them standing side by side dressed for riding. Alix, slender and sleek in her tailored habit, looks doe-eyed at her prince. Bertie, slouching in his breeches and boots, avoids her gaze, staring moodily out of the photograph as if he wishes she weren't there. Victoria worried that they were drifting apart, and blamed Alix for neglecting Bertie's comfort: "She is never ready for breakfast, not being out of her room till 11 often, and poor Bertie breakfasts alone and then she alone."[17] Bertie's easy good humor meant that relations between the couple were always cordial, but he was perhaps already tiring of his sweet-natured wife; he resented her absorption in nursery life and felt suffocated by her clinging affection.

In the autumn of 1866, Alix's sister Dagmar (Minnie) became engaged to the Russian czarevitch, the future Alexander III. She had previously been engaged to his older brother, a sickly young man with a "worn aged face and pale and lustreless blue eyes," but when he died of meningitis she dutifully transferred her affections to the new heir, his vast, bearlike brother.[18] Minnie's marriage was a dynastic coup for Denmark. The daughters of the Danish Schleswig-Holstein-Sonderburg-Glücksburg family were like princesses in a fairy tale. Brought up privately and with great simplicity, Alix and Minnie had married two of the most eligible princes in Europe.[19]

Alix was pregnant once more, which meant that she was unable to travel to the wedding in St. Petersburg, and Bertie asked permission to go alone. To his surprise, Victoria gave her consent, though grudgingly ("I did not say 'I approved,' but only that 'I would not object' "); though she was unable to resist a dig, pointing out how unfortunate it was that he remained so little at home and was always "running about."[20]

In Bertie's absence, Victoria ordered her daughter-in-law to stay with her at Windsor. She took Alix driving alone with her in the afternoons, and the two women became intimate, something that Alix declared she had always wanted, though (Vicky told Victoria) "she says she is not amusing she knows, and she fears she bores you."[21] Victoria agreed that she had long wished to be friends with Alix, reporting to Bertie that "she looks thin and at times pale," but "I have talked much with her and have the highest opinion of her."[22]

Alix missed Bertie dreadfully. When he delayed his return, leaving her to celebrate her birthday alone, she consoled herself with the thought that "my angel Bertie" was well and loved by everybody in St. Petersburg.[23]

Bertie was splendidly entertained in St. Petersburg. The government was so pleased with his reception that Disraeli voted £1,000 of public money to pay for the trip. Bertie caused a sensation by dancing in his kilt at a ball, and he joined a hunt where seven wolves were killed. The Russian court was notoriously lax. The czar, Alexander II, lived openly with his mistress, while his wife lay upstairs in the Winter Palace, slowly dying from tuberculosis. Scandalous rumors of Bertie's flirtations with the pretty women of St. Petersburg reached the ears of his sister Alice.[24] This was his first significant separation from Alix, and he enjoyed himself all too obviously in the company of other women.

In England, politics that winter was deadlocked over parliamentary reform. In February 1867, the Queen reluctantly opened Parliament—a gesture of support for her Conservative ministers that she regretted, as she was hissed and booed by the pro-reform crowds. For Bertie, this was a challenge too good to resist. On 11 February, when a reform demonstration marched through London, he insisted on watching, defying the advice of General Knollys, who feared a scene. Bertie drove in his brougham through the crowds, and was recognized when he reached the United Service Club in Waterloo Place, where he "was most enthusiastically cheered," being (said Knollys) "at present very popular." Here he watched the demonstration from an upstairs window, and Knollys was struck by the irony of "this immense popular assemblage . . . supposed to entertain democratic principles—certainly anything but monarchical—defiling before the Heir Apparent of the Crown."[25]

The next day (Tuesday 12 February), Alix visited the theater and, driving home with the windows open, felt a slight pain in her shoulder. By Thursday the pains had spread, moving around her limbs, especially acute in her elbows and knee, and when Dr. Sieveking was called at nine thirty p.m. on Friday (the fifteenth), he found the princess, who was eight months pregnant, greatly distressed with severe pain in her right knee.[26] Bertie departed for a steeplechase and dinner at Windsor, judging that her malady was not "of sufficient consequence to put off going." In the evening she became worse, and Knollys sent two telegrams to Bertie, "without requiring him to come up."[27] The next morning he sent a third wire, begging him to return immediately.[28]

The Times announced that the princess had "acute rheumatism." Medical bulletins, signed by the royal doctors, Sieveking, Jenner, and Farre, were posted daily outside Marlborough House, detailing the "pain and febrile action" from which she was suffering.[29]

Alix's illness precipitated yet another premature confinement. Bertie, who told his mother he was "nervous & worried by dear Alix's illness," was called to her room at six a.m. on 20 February, having been up all night in anticipation of a crisis.[30] The doctors feared that the rheumatism would produce an "obstruction," but Alix gave birth to a baby girl after only thirty minutes of labor. Dr. Farre, the obstetrician, who arrived just in time for the delivery at six thirty, refused to allow chloroform, though the suffering princess "wished it very much."[31] The four-weeks-premature baby was very small.

In his diary, Knollys commented that the princess

> got through this part of her sorrows well and Dr. Farre does not apprehend any additional mischief from the complications attending another complaint. The other physicians however particularly Dr. Sieveking looked more serious and Lady Macclesfield who is now in waiting . . . evidently considers it a matter pregnant with <u>evil</u> consequences.[32]

What Knollys meant by "another complaint" is not clear. His wording seems curiously ambivalent, and language such as "pregnant with <u>evil</u>" is almost apocalyptic. Dr. Jenner told the Queen: "The heart still not right, the pain in the knee very obstinate and acute. At any moment the condition might become dangerous!"[33]

When Victoria visited for the first time, on 27 February 1867, she found Alix "lying very low, with her poor knee covered over and supported quite high up, so that her leg was greatly above her head!" Alix was worn, thin, and emotional—tears came to her eyes when she saw the Queen. Afterward, Jenner spoke to Victoria "very seriously" about her daughter-in-law's state.[34]

Alix was in such acute pain that she was often unable to sleep, and her restlessness could only be subdued by laudanum. After sitting up all night with her, Lady Macclesfield wrote: "The light way in which the Prince regards the Princess's illness is perfectly painful (perhaps <u>disgusting</u>) to me and to the Queen also."[35] Bertie stayed out later than ever. "The Princess had another bad night," raged Lady Macclesfield, "<u>chiefly</u> owing to the Prince promising to come in at 1 a.m. and keeping her in a perpetual fret, refusing to take her opiate for fear she should be asleep when he came. And he never came till 3 a.m.!"[36]

Jenner feared a crisis, and told the Queen that his patient stood on "the brink of a precipice."[37] Only then, when his wife was acutely agitated and fevered with a racing pulse, and the doctors injected morphia into her knee and gave her morphine to induce sleep, did Bertie seem to realize that "she <u>is</u> ill" and started to spend more time with her.[38] He moved his desk into her sickroom so that he could write letters beside her. The Queen found Alix "greatly altered" and "wretchedly ill."[39] Jenner told her on 10 March that there were symptoms he disliked. Bertie wrote to Queen Louise of Denmark asking her to come to England, and this gave rise to wild speculation that Alix was on the verge of death. *The Times* published an official denial, dismissing the rumors as "unfounded as they are extraordinary."[40]

Knollys visited, and thought her "looking very pretty" in bed, lying on her back and unable to turn or bend her knee, with a large apparatus over her legs to protect them from the bedclothes. "Her hair was loose about her shoulders, & the upper part of her figure could have formed a study for a painter."[41]

Victoria found her "very low and suffering."

"Will it never get better," sighed Alix, and laid her head on the Queen's shoulder.[42] The inflammation was made far worse by forcibly bending the knee under anesthetic and binding it in splints to straighten it. The doctors gave her chloroform for an hour and twenty-five minutes while they readjusted the leg.[43] "She was sick several times afterwards and suffered a great deal of pain," Bertie told Victoria, "partly from the alteration of the position of the knee and fr[om] exhaustion."[44] James Paget, the surgeon who was treating Alix, told the Queen that this was "very serious," though he hoped in time it "would get right." When the Queen saw Alix's leg, it "looked pitiable in all its bandages and so wasted."[45]

What was wrong with Alix?

Jenner told Queen Victoria that the doctors "had no experience of any case of the kind."[46] The ladies of Alix's household, sitting up night after night beside her bed, whispered darkly that her illness was all Bertie's fault.[47] Evil rumors began to build. Perhaps he had infected his sweet, pure wife with "Disease." Phipps was dismissive. "I fear he leads a not very healthy life," he wrote, "but I do not believe half the ill-natured stories I hear."[48] The previous year, Phipps had reported that Bertie frequented a place named the Midnight Club and complained that he "lowers himself" too much in pursuit of pleasure.[49]

"Syphilis" was the word that no one dared to mention. Rumors still persist today that Alix was the innocent victim of Bertie's lifestyle. Syphilis was epidemic in the brothels of mid-nineteenth-century Europe, and Bertie's encounters with prostitutes ever since his "fall" meant that he must have been exposed to it. If he was infected with the syphilis organism, *Treponema pallidum,* at the time of his marriage, he could hardly fail to have passed it on to Alix, as sufferers are infectious for two years. The early stages of the illness are unpleasant enough: a genital sore, then ulcers, rashes, and swollen lymph nodes. An unlucky 40 percent of sufferers experience further stages. The illness may attack the heart and sometimes the spinal cord, producing symptoms that mimic a brain tumor and end in madness. Sometimes it presents as a gumma or ulcerating tumor on the lower leg, causing a deep, gnawing pain that is worse at night and throbs remorselessly. Syphilis can damage hearing, and after her illness, Alix became increasingly deaf.[50]

Retrospective diagnosis of syphilis has become a game among biographers of nineteenth-century subjects, working without proper medical records to identify a disease that manifests in a bewildering variety of forms. Alix's case history, however, is relatively well documented, because she was attended by so many doctors. In his private diary, Sieveking described her symptoms at the start of the illness: "The right knee much swollen and very painful, the face much flushed, the tongue furred, white and creamy, the pulse above 100 . . . great restlessness and expressed fear of 'rheumatic fever.'"[51] Sieveking confirmed the diagnosis of rheumatic fever, the frightening autoimmune disease triggered by a streptococcal infection in the throat, which, in the pre-penicillin era, brought risk of death and permanent heart damage. But the diagnosis seemed not to fit. In rheumatic fever the pain moves from joint to joint, causing a "flitting polyarthritis." Alix's pains initially followed this pattern, but after a few days the pain settled in her knee. It was this symptom that baffled the doctors.

Alix's knee is proof positive that she was not suffering from syphilis, as "for all its protean manifestations in brain, skin, heart etc [syphilis] does not cause acute pain/swelling in a single joint . . . especially in the absence of symptoms in other systems."[52] Rather, she seems to have been suffering from a "septic" arthritis caused by some bacterium. Today it would respond to antibiotics. Then, there was no alternative but to stick it out.

Alix's deafness had been noticeable ever since she arrived in England, though some thought it due to "absence," inattention, or poor English.[53] Lord Stanley noted that she was "so deaf as to be unable to follow a conversation and often to answer at cross-purposes."[54] Victoria was in no doubt about the matter, writing to Vicky: "Alas! she is deaf and everyone observes it, which is a sad misfortune."[55]

According to her biographer, Georgina Battiscombe, who was herself deaf, Alix suffered from a type of deafness called otosclerosis.[56] This involves a hardening of the small bone in the middle ear; it is a genetic form of deafness that strikes only women (men are carriers), and is often thought to be brought on by pregnancy. Though Queen Louise of Denmark was deaf, there is no mention of deafness among her siblings, and only one of Alix's five children—Maud—seems to have been afflicted.

One new piece of evidence suggests a different diagnosis. Dr. Sieveking noted in his diary that, shortly after the birth of Eddy, at the urgent request of both Bertie and himself, Alix agreed to see Joseph Toynbee, who was the leading ear specialist of the day.[57] Toynbee pronounced that her deafness was "essentially nervous," and the treatment was rest; no operation was needed.*[58]

In his scientific work, Toynbee was one of the first to describe otosclerosis, yet he did not diagnose this condition in Alix. By "nervous" deafness, he meant what is today known as sensorineural hearing loss, due to changes in the acoustic nerves, which act as microphones in the inner ear. "If he diagnosed that Alix had a 'nervous' deafness," one specialist has written, "then it would be difficult to refute his finding, and this, in turn, would seem to rule out otosclerosis as the cause of Alix's progressive hearing loss."[59] Whatever its cause, deafness was a crippling handicap for a woman like Alix, whose work depended on social contact.

Alix was photographed that spring, her dark-rimmed eyes and loose hair a vision of Pre-Raphaelite beauty. For Bertie, however, the horrid cage around her leg symbolized her unavailability. Mermaid-like, she could not be a real wife.

---

* Toynbee died two years later experimenting on himself, trying to prove that tinnitus could be relieved by inhaling a lethal cocktail of hydrogen cyanide and chloroform, and then holding his nose.

Bertie's order page in the ledger of Poole the tailor includes the following:

A grey diagonal Angola Pea Coat, Silk breast facings, Silk sleevings and velvet collar £7.3s

which was delivered personally by the great Mr. Poole himself. Bertie also ordered:

a pair of black French classic trousers, braid sides. £2:14s
a pair striped doe trousers, braid sides . . . . £2:14s.

The ledger shows the tailor cleaning and pressing thirty-four white vests (waistcoats) and altering a dress coat and fancy trousers to fit the prince's expanding waistline: by June the tailor's bill came to £283:8s.6d.[60]

Bertie's destination was Paris, where he visited the International Exhibition staged by Napoléon III, reassuring the Queen that Alix, who had at last managed to sleep through a whole night, "says she don't mind it at all."[61] Before he left, he attended the baby's christening. She was named Louise; this annoyed the Queen, who made it plain that she expected a girl to be called after her. Bertie was even angrier than he had been over Victoria's interference with George's name: He declared it was a wish she "had no right to indulge or expect to be gratified," as Alix was anxious to name the baby after her own mother.[62] The child was given the second name of Victoria, but the Queen was not present at the christening—very few people were, as it took place in the sitting room at Marlborough House. Alix was wheeled in on her bed, looking "quite lovely" with a "white lace jacket trimmed with pink and a pink bow in her hair, the bed being covered with a blue silk coverlet."[63]

The Paris Exhibition was the sort of junket that Bertie most enjoyed: rubbing shoulders with crowned heads, attending a ball for two thousand guests at the British Embassy and calling on the emperor

Napoléon, whom he found "ill and worn but as kind and cordial in manner as he always has been to me."[64] In Paris, Bertie was able to pursue his own version of foreign affairs. The court of Napoléon III was notoriously depraved, and he eagerly devoured publications such as *Les Amours de Napoléon III* or *La Femme de César,* which detailed the many mistresses of the emperor.[65] The sensation of the season was Jacques Offenbach's light opera *The Grand Duchess of Gerolstein,* at the Théâtre des Variétés, which poked fun at the toy armies of the minor German states, and starred the voluptuous prima donna Hortense Schneider.

Bertie's visit to the Variétés was dramatized by Émile Zola in *Nana,* the novel about the demimonde that he wrote twelve years later, in which Bertie is thinly disguised as the Prince of Scots. Zola's research included a visit to the dressing room backstage at the Variétés, where Hortense Schneider had received the prince dressed in her costume as the Duchess of Gerolstein. Zola described the bearded, pink-complexioned prince as having "the sort of distinction peculiar to a man of pleasure, his square shoulders clearly indicated beneath the impeccably cut frock coat," and imagined him in the dressing room of the seminaked singer: "The Prince, his eyes half-closed, followed the swelling lines of her bosom with the eyes of a connoisseur." But for Zola, the prince is neither seedy nor undignified. Far from being tarnished, he transposes the demimonde into a make-believe world of kings and queens. When he drinks a toast in the actors' cheap champagne, it's as if they are at court, and the actors start to play new roles:

> The world of the theatre was re-creating the real world in a sort of solemn farce under the hot glare of the gas. . . . And nobody dreamed of smiling at the strange contrast presented by this real prince, this heir to a throne, drinking a barn-stormer's champagne, and very much at ease in this masquerade of royalty, surrounded by whores, buskers and pimps.[66]

General Knollys noted that the reports of Bertie's visit were "very unsatisfactory": "suppers after the Opera with some of the female

Paris notorieties etc etc."[67] Bertie's supposed infatuation with Hortense Schneider—she was known as Le Passage des Princes after the Paris arcade—was widely publicized.[68] Another of his Paris ladies was the courtesan Giulia Beneni, nicknamed La Barucci. She owned a luxurious house at 124 Avenue des Champs-Élysées, complete with liveried footmen, a grand white-carpeted staircase with velvet-covered banisters, and a tall cabinet stuffed with jewels. When Bertie met her, she arrived forty-five minutes late, having been strictly instructed by the Duc de Gramont to be punctual. "Your Royal Highness, may I present the most unpunctual woman in France?" said the duke. Whereupon La Barucci lifted her skirts to reveal nothing but "the white rotundities of her callipygian charms."

"Did I not tell you to behave properly to HRH?" Gramont rebuked her afterward.

"I showed him the best I have and it was free," was the reply.[69]

News of Bertie's adventures reached Vicky, who later blamed wicked Paris for corrupting him. "What mischief that very court and still more that very attractive Paris has done to English society," she wrote. "What harm to our two eldest brothers!"[70] Victoria agreed. "Your two elder brothers unfortunately were carried away by that horrid Paris, beautiful though you may think it, and that frivolous and immoral court did frightful harm to English Society . . . and was very bad for Bertie and Affie."[71]

Aged twenty-five, Bertie was too young and too spoiled to come to terms with the fact that his beautiful wife was now a deaf cripple. In denial, he threw himself headlong into the frenzied pursuit of pleasure and late nights. Victoria, for her part, was convinced that Alix was an invalid for life. "I fear very much that she will never be what she was." As for Bertie, she wrote, "Poor Boy, it is very sad to think of his whole existence changed and altered and *dérangé* by this lamentable illness."[72]

Bertie was blamed for his apparent lack of concern. Lady Macclesfield complained that "the Prince (childish as ever) does not see anything serious about it."[73] Bertie was certainly immature, but perhaps his behavior had deeper roots. In spite of his outward forbearance toward Victoria, he seethed with rage. He had grown to be genuinely fond of his wife, but he resented the way his mother and sister Vicky had conspired together to trap him into an arranged marriage. People commented on his ill looks. He spent much time away from home. He was driven by the impulse to revenge himself against his mother, but the person who suffered most from this behavior was his vulnerable wife, Alix.

At Ascot in June, Bertie received a "flat reception" from the crowd when he appeared at the races without Alix, but he insisted on inviting the "fashionable female celebrities of the day" to luncheon, a party that Knollys thought in questionable taste.[74] Some of these were harmless flirtations. He was spotted "spooning with Lady Filmer."[75] She was the wife of his friend Sir Edmund Filmer and a dancing partner of Bertie's; shooting deer at Invercauld in 1865, he wrote that "I had the good fortune to have Lady Filmer with me (who also had a small Whitworth rifle) and I enjoyed a very pleasant tête à tête with her."*[76]

In his diary, Lord Stanley reported, "Much talk in society about the P[rince] of Wales and his disreputable ways of going on. He is seen at theatres paying attention to the lowest class of women, visits them at their houses etc."[77] Bertie insisted on going to Paris again in July, in spite of the opposition of General Knollys, who saw the prime minister, Lord Derby, and stated his anxiety about the visit "after the scenes I had been led to believe had taken place at the former one" and with "the Princess in such a state."[78]

For Bertie, the summer of 1867 was a tipping point. He was unfaithful to Alix, not just with the "lowest class" of women, but with women in society. Perhaps to him it seemed the natural thing to do. Among the men of his set, debauchery was seen as a healthy amusement, which Bertie indulged in the same way that he drank and smoked. Alix's illness seemed to sanction his return to bachelor ways.[79] But if he expected that he could use women for sex and then discard them, he was to be disillusioned. Many of the women with

---

* Bertie wrote to Sir Edmund Filmer, enclosing photos for Lady Filmer, "for which I must apologise—as she will be quite bored possessing so many of me—but the waste paper basket is always useful." (Hibbert, *Edward VII,* p. 92.) This hardly suggests that Bertie was having a passionate affair with the wife.

whom he began relationships that summer refused to go quietly. Blackmail, pregnancy, even a court case were to return to haunt him. There was no such thing as a relationship without consequences.

Alix was not prepared to sink gracefully into social death as a sofa-bound invalid. While Bertie was in Paris, she drove out for the first time in the garden at Marlborough House. Accompanied by Princess Louise, her friend among Bertie's sisters, she had herself carried in a wheeled chair over a platform level with the carriage, and the chair placed where the carriage seat had been removed. Defying doctor's orders, she was determined to appear at a military review on Bertie's return; General Knollys was mightily relieved when the review was canceled, believing that if Alix had appeared alongside Victoria, "the Princess would have received an ovation but it would have been at the expense of the Q[ueen]."[80]

By mid-August, Alix was sufficiently recovered to travel with Bertie to Germany, to Wiesbaden, the capital of Dessau, the spa town recommended by the doctors. Accompanied by their three tiny children, twenty-five servants, and a retinue of courtiers and doctors, the Waleses steamed up the Rhine. Alix sat on the hot deck in her wheelchair in a specially constructed cabin and amused herself by drawing all day. The Prussian flag flying on the stern of the boat upset her, and she became agitated when a crowd gathered on shore to see her being carried out of the ship in a sedan chair and into a carriage: Knollys noted her extreme dislike of appearing in public as an invalid.[81]

At Wiesbaden, Alix took daily baths under the supervision of Paget, her doctor, and Bertie reported her progress to the Queen: "Every day she walks on crutches and can put her foot to the ground and swing it about."[82] Bertie itched to escape downriver to the fleshpots and gambling tables of Baden, a prospect that filled Knollys with horror, on account of the "disgraceful tone" of society there and especially Bertie's friend Marie of Baden, the wicked Duchess of Hamilton, and her scandalous son the duke, whose character was so "irretrievably lost" that there could only be "contamination" in associating with him.*[83] This was just the sort of company that Bertie most enjoyed and, ever the rebellious adolescent, he wrote to Victoria: "I know, dear Mama, so well what these German Baths are, and I think I know who to avoid and who not—and not to compromise myself in any way. I know that Vicky has written to you on the subject, but one would imagine that she thought me 10 or 12 years old and not nearly 26."[84]

Wiesbaden was within driving distance of Rumpenheim, the white-fronted, green-shuttered schloss set in dull, flat countryside on the banks of the River Main near Frankfurt where Alix's family spent their summer holidays. Here the relations greeted one another with affectionate kisses a dozen times over, astounding the prim, buttoned-up English; they spent long days out of doors, dined at five in an over-crowded dining room, and played rumbustious evening games.[85] This noisy, boisterous family life was oxygen to Alix, the sort of world she herself tried to re-create at Sandringham. Victoria thought the family party there "the very worst society for Bertie possible which my Angel . . . said he must be kept out of"; but she needn't have worried, as Bertie found the early dinners and healthy games deadly dull.[86]

The German royalty gathered at Rumpenheim inhabited a doomed world that was relentlessly hemorrhaging power to Prussia. Charles Carrington, who accompanied Bertie on a visit, found it a melancholy experience—"a huge building inhabited by Grand Dukes and Grand Duchesses who are in short street."[87] Alix's grandfather, the Landgrave of Hesse-Cassel, had grievously miscalculated by supporting Austria in the 1866 war against Prussia, and Bismarck now took his revenge. That September, the elector† was forced to sign an agreement whereby he surrendered political power over Hesse in exchange for keeping his personal fortune.[88] Little wonder that when Alix and Bertie visited, the anti-Prussian feeling was "most rabid."

---

* The Duchess of Hamilton was a daughter of the Grand Duke of Baden; her mother, Stephanie Beauharnais, was an adopted daughter of Napoléon I.
† Alix's grandfather died in September 1867 and was succeeded as Landgrave by his brother.

"They all seemed to have been bit by some Prussian mad dog," wrote Knollys, "the slightest allusion set the whole party[—]and we were 36 at dinner[—]into agitation, at which my friends the Russians seemed highly amused."[89] Nor was it surprising that Alix shared their feelings.

On 19 September 1867, only two days after her uncle signed away his power, a telegram arrived for Alix from the King of Prussia, who was Vicky's father-in-law, proposing to pay her a visit at Wiesbaden. Encouraged by her sister Minnie, Alix dictated a reply so uncivil that Knollys refused to send it. When Bertie returned at eleven p.m., he made excuses for his wife, telegraphing the King that Alix was too unwell to receive him.[90]

Victoria was enraged by her daughter-in-law's behavior. "I can't tell you how shocked I am at Alix's refusal," she told Vicky.[91] "If only she understood her duties better."[92] A very strong letter to Bertie followed, but he refused to dragoon his wife, guilty perhaps at his neglect of her, he defended her right to her own opinions. "I myself should have been glad if she had seen the King," he told his mother, "but a lady may have feelings wh[ich] she cannot repress, while a man must overcome them. If Coburg had been taken away—as Hanover, Hesse (Cassel) and Nassau have been—I don't think you would much care to see the King either."[93]

Alix's insult to the King of Prussia made Vicky's position difficult, and she and Alice both implored Bertie to induce Alix to change her mind. Bertie needed no persuading, but Alix refused to listen. He enlisted Queen Louise, who, he told Knollys, was "so sensible and could make her daughter do what was proper."[94] A few days later, the King of Prussia telegraphed again. Once more Alix declined to see him. Queen Louise, Knollys, and Bertie confronted her and begged her to compromise. But Alix was adamant. Louise gave up and left the room, while Knollys watched as Bertie "used every argument but in vain to persuade the Princess. It was a question of feeling with the Princess and she would not listen to reason of any kind," he wrote. "After a long discussion the Princess ended it by getting up and walking out of the room by the aid of her stick saying that she would not talk any more about it."[95] Eventually, on Knollys's advice, Bertie wrote a telegram inviting the King to visit and showed it to Alix. Shortly afterward, Queen Louise packed her bags and scuttled off to Rumpenheim.

On the morning of the King's visit, Knollys remarked that Alix looked pale. "Yes, she said, I may be pale but it is from anger at being obliged to see this King of Prussia and not from cold—and what I mind most is that it is [in] consequence of [Bertie's] two sisters interfering (I am afraid she said these two old women tho not much older than herself) or I should not have been obliged to do so."[96]

Surprisingly, the visit was a success. Alix was "very <u>civil</u>" to the King, who was satisfied with his reception.[97] But the moral victory belonged to Alix; she had defied both her mother and her mother-in-law and made it plain that she was not a passive invalid who could be ignored.

It was one thing for Alix to thumb her nose at the King of Prussia; quite another for her to keep her restless, easily bored husband amused. She worried that Bertie found it "terribly dull" to have an invalid wife who could no longer accompany him everywhere.[98] Bertie wrote from Wiesbaden to his friend Carrington: "This place has become frightfully dreary, it rains nearly every day and it is awfully cold. . . . Our Trente et Quarante table has been suppressed, and the second roulette table moved into another room. I have had two or three lucky coups. . . . On Saturday we leave here (thank God)."[99]

By the time they returned home, Alix was once again pregnant. She could now walk upstairs on two sticks, but her knee was still completely stiff. At Windsor for Bertie's twenty-sixth birthday, she was frail and thin but very pretty, and Victoria commented, "It is a sad sight to see her thus and to those who did not see her so ill as we did, when one really did not dare to hope she would get better, it is sad and touching to see." Victoria found Bertie full of amiable qualities, which "makes one forget and overlook much that one would wish different."[100] This new pregnancy so soon after he and Alix had resumed marital relations imposed yet more strain on their ailing relationship.

Bertie busied himself writing letters. One of his correspondents was a woman named Madame Didier. She seems to have been a French countess; he may have met her in Petersburg, and he certainly saw her that summer in Germany.* *"Je vous envoie les boutons Marius que je vous ai promis a Wiesbach [sic], et j'espère que vous avez l'occasion de les porter bien souvent et bien longtemps."*†101

Letters such as this, enclosing tokens of buttons, were harmless enough, one might think; elaborate exercises in a platonic game of courtly love. When Bertie visited Russia in 1874 for the wedding of his brother Alfred to the sister of the czarevitch, he wrote to Madame Didier from the Anitchkoff Palace, where he was staying. *"J'espère de pouvoir vous rendre une visite entre 4 et 5 heures cet après midi si cela vous conviens."*‡102A harmless afternoon call, perhaps; but afternoon calls were the prince's time for flirtation. Ten days later, on the eve of his departure, Bertie wrote again, bidding the countess farewell, regretting that they had not met at the balls of the past week, and enclosing a photograph of himself.103

Nearly half a century later, after the Russian Revolution had destroyed the glitzy, over-the-top St. Petersburg court, Madame Didier was an old lady in Monte Carlo, living in one small room in an apartment near the station. She wrote to Lord Stamfordham, private secretary to George V, asking whether the royal family would be interested in buying three letters from Edward VII together with a signed photograph.104 The palace dispatched an emissary named Dr. Pryce Mitchell, who reported that Madame Didier was "refined, dignified and must have been a very beautiful woman, poorly dressed but clean and tidy. Her surroundings denote abject poverty, even privation, yet she is treated with marked respect by the woman who owns the apartment.

---

* Madame Didier is a mystery woman who has eluded genealogical research. She always wrote in French, and she was probably Herminie Julian de Rascas, the wife of one Marie François Calixte Emmanuel Pina de St. Didier (1814–87), *officier armée russe,* but we cannot be sure.

† "I am sending you the Marius buttons which I promised you at Wiesbach, and I hope that you will have occasion to wear them often."

‡ "I hope to be able to pay you a visit between 4 and 5 this afternoon if that is convenient for you."

She attributes her present misfortune to the unhappy state of affairs in Russia."[105] She claimed that unless she could produce the sum of 2,600 francs, her few personal belongings would be seized. Pryce Mitchell and the royal advisers worried that Madame Didier was being advised by a third party intent on blackmail, and after protracted negotiations the old lady agreed to part with her precious letters for £20. Pryce Mitchell refused to pay more, pointing out that the letters were of no importance or value.[106]

But in that case why had Madame Didier treasured them for fifty years and smuggled them out of Russia when she fled the revolution? The story of Bertie's letters to Madame Didier encapsulates the puzzle for historians of knowing what his relations with women really were. He had only to look at a woman for her to be branded his mistress. He wrote a great many letters to women. It was often assumed—as the advisers of George V imagined—that these letters were evidence of passionate affairs that might damage the monarchy. Usually they turn out to be bland, formal, and, frankly, dull. It is hard to infer anything but a social relationship from these missives, but the question remains: Why did he write them? And why did so many of the women keep them? These were private letters, written in his own hand, not invitations dictated to an equerry. They were often to arrange a private meeting—just the two of them, the prince and the lady. The husbands were not present. But was this any more than flirtation? It would be a leap in the dark to imagine that Bertie's brief, discreet letters were the last remaining souvenirs of the glorious moment when Madame Didier, so impoverished and faded, had been mistress to a prince.

CHAPTER 8

Marlborough House and
Harriett Mordaunt

1868–70

In 1867, Walter Bagehot, editor of *The Economist,* published his famous
book on the *English Constitution,* which, like most books, seems to have
passed Bertie by. One of the fallacies Bagehot skewered was the idea
that it was the function of the Crown to give a moral example to the
nation. Queen Victoria's domestic virtues were admirable, but not an
essential part of her role, claimed Bagehot, and it was unfair to criti-
cize her son for not following her example. "All the world, whatever is
most attractive, whatever is most seductive, has always been offered to
the Prince of Wales of the day, and always will be. It is not rational to
expect the best virtue where temptation is applied in the most trying
form at the frailest time of human life."[1]

Queen Victoria did not agree. She bombarded Bertie with letters,
warning about "the frivolity, the love of pleasure, self-indulgence, luxury and idleness" of the aristocracy which, she thought, "resembles
the time before the French Revolution. . . . It is, dear Child, in <u>your</u>

power to do <u>much</u> to check this," she wrote. "It is for this reason that I always <u>urge you so</u> <u>strongly</u> <u>not</u> to <u>frequent Races</u>, for they <u>lead</u> to every species of evil, gambling etc."[2]

Victoria envisaged Bertie acting as "social sovereign," giving a moral example to the nation, as she and Albert had done before. As she told Knollys: "The respectability of the Queen's and Prince's Court, without its ever having tended to austerity or exclusion of amusement,—but quite the contrary,—was universally acknowledged to be a great safeguard to the Throne and Country—and it is therefore so absolutely necessary that the P[rince] and P[rince]ss, who are too young themselves to know of the effect of all these things, sh[oul]d be very <u>particular</u> in distinguishing People whose characters are <u>not</u> respected—by wh[ich] she means, not asking them to dinner—not down to Sandringham—and above all, not going to their houses."[3]

If Victoria really expected Bertie to provide moral leadership, she was being utterly unrealistic. She knew it, too; as she confided to one of her ladies, she felt it her duty to write to Bertie about the state of society, but "I fear it will be of little use, as he is far too weak and self-indulgent, but <u>still</u> it is a <u>duty</u> wh[ich] I must do,—and I trust <u>some</u> of the <u>advice</u> may <u>still</u> remain <u>dinning</u> in his ears."[4]

Many of the members of Bertie's court of whom Victoria most disapproved had, in fact, defected to Marlborough House from Windsor. One defector especially frowned upon by Victoria was Louise, Duchess of Manchester.

Nine years older than Bertie, Louise von Alten was the daughter of a Hanoverian count. Her husband, the Duke of Manchester, was a B-list duke of little brain, but Louise was a social climber with a nose for power. Her ambition was to command the very pinnacle of society by gaining appointment as Mistress of the Robes. The highest court position open to a woman, this was always held by a duchess, whose role it was to control the Queen's ladies-in-waiting and organize state ceremonies. The office had been monopolized by Harriet, Duchess of Sutherland, Queen Victoria's close friend, throughout the long ascendancy of the Whigs;* but in 1858 the Tory prime minister Lord Derby appointed Louise Mistress of the Robes. For the twenty-six-year-old German girl to leapfrog to the peak of London society was an astonishing coup. When the government fell and she resigned in June 1859, Victoria took leave of her with regret, "for she is really a very pleasant, nice, sensible person."[5] By 1863, the Queen had changed her mind. Louise received no invitation to Bertie's wedding, a slashing snub. Perhaps the Queen had learned that Louise had gained her appointment as Mistress of the Robes as a result of a deal she made with Derby before he became prime minister.[6] More likely she was put off by stories about Louise's wild behavior. Playing a boisterous game of hare and hounds, Louise fell over in a ditch to reveal a shocking pair of scarlet tartan knickerbockers beneath her crinoline.[7] Victoria complained that "the D[uche]ss of Manchester is become very fast—flirts, and coquets and is much talked about. I cannot take her again as Mistress of the Robes."[8]

Realizing that social leadership had passed from the Queen to Marlborough House, the duchess now threw herself at the Prince of Wales. "No one knows how gloriously beautiful a woman can be who did not see the Duchess of Manchester when she was thirty," old gentlemen would later recall.[9] Photographs of a short, affectedly posed woman turning her profile to the camera make this hard to credit, but being a "beauty" in the 1860s was as much a matter of playing a social role as possessing regular features. Beauty was a cult, and men competed to pay homage. When Bertie made an afternoon call on the Duchess of Manchester, he noted in his diary: "Found her well and looking lovely. I stayed there about 45 minutes."[10]

Bertie's admiration for Louise's looks was inflated by the gossips into scandal. There was talk that the duchess was trying to seduce the Prince of Wales, and it was rumored that she had been warned off and ordered to leave Bertie alone.[11]

But Louise was never Bertie's mistress. On the contrary, she took care to befriend Alix as well, creating a role for herself as social mentor

* Harriet, Duchess of Sutherland, was Mistress of the Robes 1837–41, 1846–58, and again in 1859–61.

and confidante to Marlborough House.[12] This infuriated the Queen, who told Knollys that Louise was "not respected"; people avoided her "in every way," and it was the duty of the prince and princess to "let her feel that her conduct has obliged them to be distant towards her."[13] What Louise had done to deserve this latest explosion was to conduct an affair with another friend of Bertie's: Lord Hartington, rising Whig politician and heir to the Duke of Devonshire. The affair was discreetly managed—she always addressed him as Lord Hartington, and he called her Duchess. Louise was heard to let slip her guard only once, when she remarked, "Harty darling, stand me a stamp."[14] But it was an open secret—they were treated like an engaged couple and asked together to dinner parties—and it meant that the doors of Victoria's court slammed firmly shut on her.

Bertie remained loyal. In February 1868, he stayed a week with Louise at Kimbolton, the Manchesters' seat in Huntingdonshire. Victoria tried to stop him going, but Bertie insisted, staunchly defending Louise ("I do not like to hear her abused").[15] It was his first visit in six years—he had previously stayed with them when at Cambridge—and it marked Louise's full endorsement by Marlborough House.

Alix remained behind at Sandringham, unable to face the journey. "I hate when he is away," she wrote; without "my darling husband" the house seemed "empty and desolate and lonely."[16] At Kimbolton there was hunting all day and dancing all night. Carrington, who was a fellow guest, found it "a very hard week." "We scarcely got to bed at all."[17] They posed on the steps, dressed for riding to hounds; Louise, imperious in top hat, veil, and wasp-waisted riding habit, stands beside Bertie, looking jaunty in his pink hunting coat. The duchess had "arrived." Her closeness to the prince underlined her position at the very heart of society. As the "Double Duchess" of Devonshire (she married Hartington in 1892), installed at Chatsworth, heavily rouged and addicted to gambling and bridge, Louise clung on until 1911.

Bertie's household at the time of his marriage consisted largely of men who had served him before 1863. General Knollys headed the household as comptroller and treasurer. One of Bertie's equerries, Major Teesdale, had been picked by Albert to attend him at White Lodge in 1858; another, Captain Charles Grey, had accompanied him as equerry on his trip to Italy. Bertie's old tutor at Oxford, Herbert Fisher, became his private secretary.[18] This was a household of which even Albert would have approved, and Bertie set about changing it as soon as he was settled in Marlborough House. By 1867, General Knollys was in a perpetual panic at his inability to control his royal master or persuade him to comply with the Queen's commands. The Queen implored Bertie to gather around him "really good" people, as Albert had done, but he insisted on surrounding himself with cronies.[19] His friend Arthur Ellis, whom he made equerry in 1867, belonged to the much-intermarried Ellis/Hardinge dynasty of courtiers, and Victoria raised no objection to his appointment. But she complained about the appointment as equerry of Captain Oliver Montagu, a younger son of the Earl of Sandwich and a "rollicking" officer in the Blues, whom Bertie called a "wicked boy."[20] Another friend of Bertie's to whom the Queen objected was Charles Carrington. Bertie wished to make him an equerry, but Carrington declined the offer after consulting his father, who said: "You are his friend now, if you are a member of his household you will be his servant—he may get tired of you; and your position as equerry would not be a pleasant one."[21]

Bertie's masterstroke was the appointment of General Knollys's son Francis as his private secretary in 1870. A dapper little man with shiny black hair and a beard cut into a strip down his chin, Francis Knollys resembled an Italian waiter. The Queen thought he was not fit for the post. "You ought to have a clever, able man, capable of being of use to you, and of giving you advice," she told Bertie. Though "very good natured," Francis Knollys was "not considered clever by anyone."[22] He was too deeply involved with Bertie's circle for the Queen's liking; worse, he was a Liberal in politics. Bertie mollified his mother by keeping on the seventy-three-year-old general, and pretending that Francis was merely sharing the work; the general, said Bertie, was "delighted" and felt that the thirty-three-year-old Francis was now "perfectly qualified" for the post.[23] The appointment marked a decisive shift. All important correspondence at Marlborough House crossed the desk of Francis Knollys. Bertie had at last emancipated himself from Victoria's court.

The rule of the Knollys family over Marlborough House was completed when Francis's sister, Charlotte, became bedchamber woman to Alexandra in 1872. The Ellis family were almost as deeply entrenched: Arthur Ellis's sister, Mary, who was married to Sir Arthur Hardinge, an equerry to Queen Victoria, was lady-in-waiting to Alexandra.

Smoking, which the Queen abhorred, was the badge of Bertie's court. Bertie smoked constantly; photographs from this date invariably show him with a cigar or cigarette in hand. He tried to introduce smoking in the morning room at White's Club, then the smartest club in London, and when the older members voted against it, the prince and his friends seceded in protest to found the Marlborough Club.*[24] At 52 Pall Mall, just across the road from Marlborough House, the club was an annex to the Wales court. Bertie, who visited daily, and personally selected the four hundred members, commissioned *Vanity Fair's* Carlo Pellegrini ("Ape") to draw caricatures of the twenty-two founder members. The satirist Samuel Beeton sketched the club in verse in 1874:

A fragrant odour of the choicest weeds,
A hum of voices, pitched in high-born tones;
A score of fellows, some of our best breeds,
The Heir-apparent to the British throne[25]

Once Bertie offered Pellegrini a drink in the morning room, and the artist, emboldened by his success, replied, "Ring the bell." "The Prince

---

* The Marlborough Club was funded, according to Carrington, by "an old snob called Mackenzie; the son of an Aberdeenshire hatter, who made a fortune in indigo and got a baronetcy." (Bodleian, Lincolnshire Papers, MS Film 1120, "King Edward as I Knew Him.") For Mackenzie, see pp. 328–29. The freehold was bought for £18,000 in May 1868, and the club, which was housed in an undistinguished building (now destroyed) designed by the architect David Brandon, opened the following year.

of Wales, without a word, rang the bell. To the servant who entered, he said, 'Please show Mr. Pellegrini out,' and never spoke to him again."[26] For all his affability, Bertie knew how to pull rank, perhaps the least attractive of royal characteristics. His informality was neatly encapsulated by a courtier who remarked: "Yes, His Royal Highness is always ready to forget his rank, as long as everyone else remembers it."[27]

Several Rothschilds were among the original club members. They received the seal of royal approval in 1868, when Bertie went stag hunting at Mentmore. He traveled down on the train with Natty Rothschild, smoking all the way; at Mentmore he devoured a breakfast so enormous that it seemed "as if he did not mean to go out," and then rode very well all day. Natty noted admiringly that the prince was "marvellously strong," in spite of the fact that for the past week he had been "sitting up night after night smoking etc and has never had more than 4 hours' sleep."[28] Natty was a Cambridge friend of Bertie, but even so, the immensely successful Jewish Rothschilds had had to struggle to gain admission to the top set. When Bertie was invited to a Rothschild ball in 1865, Lord Spencer, who was Groom of the Stole to the Prince of Wales, strongly advised him to refuse: The Rothschilds, he said, "are very worthy people but they essentially hold their position from wealth and perhaps the accidental beauty of the first daughter they brought out in the world."[29] The snobbish Spencer failed to see that the Rothschilds were valuable to Bertie precisely because of their wealth. Bertie—to do him justice—invited a number of Jews to join his inner circle, and recognized that their cosmopolitan networks abroad were indispensable when he traveled.[30] Lacking the anti-Semitic prejudices of many Victorian Englishmen, he was more than happy to trade social recognition for Rothschild cash and company.

Bertie's court fool was an elongated dandy named Christopher Sykes. Ten years Bertie's senior, he was the bachelor second son of Sir Tatton Sykes, a boorish hunting squire who owned vast tracts of northeast England. Bertie first stayed with Sykes at Brantingham Thorpe, his house in Yorkshire, in 1869, and soon "the great Christopher," as the prince called him, was to be spotted unfolding his giant frame in the inevitable house-party photographs, "the head always at the characteristic tilt, the clothes always a little more beautiful than the imagination would evoke."[31]

At the Marlborough Club one night Bertie emptied a glass of brandy over his friend's head. As the liquor trickled down his face and golden beard, Sykes moved not a muscle. There was an anxious silence, and then he gravely bowed and said: "As your Royal Highness pleases." Sykes, who was a sycophantic snob, probably saw no humor in his performance. Bertie, like a child, couldn't repeat the joke too often; every time Sykes dutifully obliged. And always the courtiers guffawed until their sides ached.[32] Sykes had been beaten by his brutish father as a boy, and he was complicit in Bertie's rituals of humiliation. But Bertie's treatment of him was not simple bullying. The reason he tipped brandy over Sykes was that his friend was drunk. Most of the stories about Christopher Sykes revolve around his alcoholism, and drunkenness was the one vice Bertie abhorred.

Marlborough House was not just about such manly things as smoking and practical jokes. Alix made the new court the leader of fashion. Whatever she wore, other women rushed to follow. Her image was endlessly replicated in *cartes de visite*—the photographs pasted onto cards that started to appear in the 1860s. A study of photographs registered for copyright shows that royalty tops the list, and Alexandra was the most frequently photographed, with more images than either Bertie or Victoria.*[33]

Madame Elise, the Regent Street dressmaker and one of the pioneers of haute couture, became royal warrant holder to the princess in 1867, and Alix's patronage assured the house's success.[34] Alix had a dress allowance of £10,000, but she also had to contend with the disapproval of her mother-in-law. When Alix visited Paris, the Queen implored her not to spend too much on clothes. "There is . . . a very strong feeling in the country against the luxuriousness, extravagance and frivolity of society and everyone points to my simplicity," wrote

* Between 1862 and 1901, 676 photographs of Alexandra were registered, 655 of Bertie, and 428 of Queen Victoria.

Victoria. Rather than vie with the fine London ladies, Alix should be "as <u>different</u> as <u>possible</u> by <u>great</u> <u>simplicity</u> which is more <u>elegant</u>."[35] Bertie bought Alix only two frocks in Paris, "simple ones, as they make them far better here than in London, but if there is anything I dislike it is extravagance on outré dresses—at any rate in my wife," he told Victoria.[36] The Empress Eugénie wore crinolines and enormous dresses designed by Charles Frederick Worth that were heavily satirized in *Punch,* but by 1869 the imperial court was sinking into decadence, and Worth's work was perhaps too strongly identified with the regime for Alix to buy his clothes.[37] Not until 1878 did Alix visit the shop of the great couturier Worth.

Alix developed her own distinctive style—not cutting-edge, but always right for every occasion. Conscious of her beauty—how could she not be?—she thrived on the admiring glances she attracted in glittering ballrooms. She walked with a limp, carried an elegant cane, and perfected a technique on the dance floor known as the "Alexandra glide." She learned to ride sidesaddle again, crooking her left leg rather than the customary right one, and keeping her stiff right leg straight—she thought it "[looked] ugly!!!"[38] She concealed the scar on her neck with high collars of lace or velvet, and many-rowed collars of pearls.*

On an average of twenty seven days a year in the late 1860s, Bertie cut ribbons, ate luncheons and dinners, adorned fetes, opened bazaars, planted trees, and laid foundation stones.[39] His good works attracted little attention at the time, partly because charity was seen as belonging to the female sphere; it wasn't real work of the sort Prince Albert had done; but, in fact, Bertie pioneered the role of "welfare monarch."[40] He took his role as president or patron of charities seriously, chairing meetings and speaking at dinners. As president of St. Bartholomew's Hospital, for instance, he made a point of visiting the vic-

---

* Alix's neck was slightly scarred when she married: Vicky mentions a botched childhood operation that left a mark. But marriage photographs show a swan-necked princess. Only after her illness did she invariably appear in high collars or pearl chokers.

tims of the Irish Fenians' Clerkenwell bombing (13 December 1867), telling the Queen: "I am so glad now to have an excuse of going as often as I can. . . . A kind word or cheerful look, I think, helps and cheers them in their sufferings."[41]

In 1868, he paid an official visit to Ireland. To appease the Irish nationalist Fenians, Prime Minister Disraeli proposed a royal visit, "as during two centuries, the Sovereign has only passed twenty-one days in Ireland."[42] Victoria agreed, though she grumbled to Bertie that the highlight of the visit was the Punchestown races, which would strengthen the belief, "already far too prevalent, that your chief object is amusement."[43]

Everyone assumed that the prince would visit Ireland alone, but Alix had other ideas. Though almost six months pregnant, and still convalescent from her knee, she wrote an appeal to Victoria that was as emotional as it was unpunctuated: "I have a sort of very strong wish and feeling, if I may say so, to go with my Bertie this time to Ireland, and as three medical men don't see any objection I feel I [would] much rather go (although I must say it won't be very amusing for me) than be left behind in a state of fever about him the whole time which I don't think can be very good for me now and as I really feel so well and my leg is so much stronger I feel I can as well go to balls etc there than here and as for the journey I don't really much mind that."[44]

This was an appeal the Queen could not resist; she always found it hard to refuse Alix. Thus began what *The Times* described as "the Danish conquest of Ireland." Attended by Mrs. Stonor, her closest confidante among her ladies, the pregnant princess charmed the crowds, all the more because they knew (as the papers put it) that "she struggled against temporary indisposition and some influences of no slight weight in order to accompany her husband."[45] Alix the suffering, wronged princess personified the romance of monarchy in a way that Bertie never could—even in London, cheers for the princess were always given with "extraordinary vigour." A hundred thousand people turned out at the Punchestown races to catch a sight of prince and princess. But the success of the Irish tour was, as Victoria cynically wrote, "of no real use."[46]

Victoria fretted about Alix's "miserable, puny" children. "I can't tell you how these poor, frail, little fairies distress me," she told Vicky.[47] But when she suggested to Bertie that he and Alix should spend the summer with the children in the country, he was indignant. "It would doubtless be far pleasanter for us to live more in the country," he replied tartly, "but as you know we have certain duties to fulfil here. . . . Your absence from London, renders it more necessary that we should do all we can."[48]

Bertie urged Victoria to appear in public. He regretted her refusal to open Parliament. No doubt she disapproved of William Gladstone, the incoming prime minister, for introducing a bill disestablishing the Irish Church—as it happened, so did Bertie: but "I fear that the people do not know your reason, and will feel much disappointed and vexed to miss the pageant and the éclat which your opening Parlmt [sic] always gives."[49] Victoria protested that the noise of the London traffic gave her headaches, but Bertie insisted: "I feel sure that if you were to drive in the Parks and be seen occasionally there . . . the people would be overjoyed beyond measure. It is all very well for Alix and me to drive or ride in the Park—it has not the same effect as when you do it, and I say thank God! that such is the case, as we live in radical times, and [the] more the people see the Sovereign, the better it is for the people and the country."[50]

Bertie had touched Victoria's weak spot. Her stubborn refusal to appear after seven years of widowhood was increasingly criticized. In 1868 she published *Leaves of Our Life in the Highlands,* a collection of extracts from her Balmoral journal in Albert's time, which was a surprise bestseller: The cheap edition sold eighty thousand copies within weeks, to the delight of the Queen, who thought she had discovered a way of reaching her people without appearing in public.[51] But in May 1868 she was savaged in the press for neglecting her duty, leaving Windsor, and traveling six hundred miles to Balmoral just as the Conservative government seemed about to fall. The "cruel" press criticism caused her pain and shattered nerves, which, in turn, dictated rest in order to avoid a breakdown.[52] No doubt the forty-nine-year-old Queen's frequent headaches and swollen feet were signs, as Vicky wrote, that she was approaching "the most trying and unpleasant" stage in a woman's life.[53] The menopausal monarch was no slouch, as a glance at her voluminous correspondence reveals. Each day she spent many hours at her desk, often writing letters and in her journal until well after midnight. It has been estimated that she wrote 2,500 words every day of her adult life, penning a total of sixty million in the course of her reign.[54] But her neurotic unwillingness to come out of widowly seclusion meant that she depended on Bertie to perform public duties, and he seemed strangely lacking in any sense of the limits on a prince's behavior. Locked into a dysfunctional relationship that made them oblivious to the world outside the palace, mother and son drifted toward catastrophe.

A photograph of Bertie in June 1868 shows him jauntily dressed in a double-breasted coat edged with braid, and soft checked-tweed trousers. Not for the fashion-conscious prince the formal Victorian male uniform of frock coat and sober black. He wears a flower in his buttonhole and patent leather boots. He carries gloves, cane, and top hat: essential kit for the man about town paying calls.

While Alix awaited her confinement at Marlborough House, Bertie was at liberty to make calls on ladies as he pleased. The women of his household must sometimes have felt that he considered them to be his personal harem. Once he asked Alix's lady-in-waiting Mary Hardinge if he might visit her in her private apartments:

Without coyness or embarrassment . . . [she] looked at him calmly and agreed, saying she would await him. Later, she went into her rooms, changed into her very grandest dress and put on her finest jewels as though she were to attend a great state occasion. In due course the Prince came to her apartment, knocked and she called for him to come in. He saw how magnificently she was dressed and was surprised and taken aback; for a moment or two he didn't speak—and he then asked her if it was necessary to dress so splendidly for a private conversation? To which [she] replied "If your Royal Highness does me the honour of paying me a visit, I wear the clothes that are suitable for such an occasion." With that he bade her "goodnight" and departed—and she breathed a sigh of relief.[55]

One address that Bertie visited often that summer of 1868 was number 6, Chesham Place, off Belgrave Square. This was the house that Lady Mordaunt had taken for the season. Harriett Mordaunt was the twenty-year-old wife of Sir Charles Mordaunt, a Warwickshire MP. She was the daughter of Sir Thomas Moncreiffe, a well-connected Perthshire baronet, and two of her sisters—Helen, who married Sir Charles Forbes, and Georgie, the wife of the fabulously rich Lord Dudley—were friends of Bertie's. Harriett had known Bertie since she was seventeen, when he asked her to stay at Sandringham, and an exchange of photographs and letters took place.

The eighteen or so letters that Bertie wrote to Harriett over the next few years are so innocuous that it is hard to believe that this was anything more than a social friendship. For example, he wrote on 7 May 1867:

> My dear Lady Mordaunt,
>   Many thanks for your letter, and I am very sorry that I should have given you so much trouble looking for the ladies' *umbrella* for me at Paris. I am very glad to hear that you enjoyed your stay there. I shall be going on Friday next and as the Princess is so much better, shall hope to remain a week there. If there is any commission I can do for you there it will give me the greatest pleasure to carry it out. I regret very much not to have been able to call upon you since your return, but hope to do so when I come back from Paris, and have an opportunity of making the acquaintance of your husband.[56]
>   Believe me yours very sincerely,
>   Albert Edward

A lady's umbrella could perhaps be construed as a metaphor for male impotence, and Bertie's letter could be read as a coded reference to Harriett's husband, but Bertie could equally well have meant exactly what he said without intending any double meaning.[57] There was gossip, nonetheless. When Harriett became engaged to Sir Charles Mordaunt, Lord Dudley took his future brother-in-law aside and warned him of the dangerous intimacy that Harriett's parents had allowed to exist between her and the prince. And Harriett, who was a bubbly girl, prone to hysterics, sometimes behaved in a strange manner. Young men were startled (or charmed) to find her giving them passionate embraces. Soon after she was married, sharp-eyed servants started to keep diaries recording the behavior of Lady Mordaunt.

Once or twice a week at about four o'clock, Bertie would drive up to the house in Chesham Place in an anonymous hansom cab. In the hall he would hand his hat, gloves, and cane to Bird, the butler. This was a sign that the meeting was prearranged, as etiquette dictated that the gentleman who made an uninvited call should sit with hat, gloves, and cane on the floor beside his chair, signifying the fleeting and casual nature of the visit. The prince would enter the drawing room, where Harriett waited for him alone. Her husband was never at home when Bertie called; he was busy in the House of Commons, or competing in pigeon-shooting matches at the newly established Hurlingham Club in Fulham.* Bird received instructions from Lady Mordaunt that "no one else was to be admitted after his Royal Highness came."[58]

Afternoons were the accepted time for adultery, rushed and uncomfortable though it must have been in crinoline and stays on a sofa. But what took place in the hour and a half or so when Bertie was alone in the drawing room with Harriett was not witnessed. The servants had their suspicions, but nothing improper was ever reported.

On 15 June 1868, Sir Charles Mordaunt departed on a fishing holiday to Norway, leaving his wife behind. While he was away, Harriett saw a great deal of a friend named Lord Cole. One night Cole dined with her, and stayed on alone after the guests had left until one a.m. Meanwhile, on 6 July, Princess Alexandra gave birth to her fourth child,

---

* Rock doves imported by train from Scotland were released from cages and shot at twenty-five yards' range.

a daughter, wisely named Victoria. The Queen thought the baby a "mere little red lump," and joked that her grandchildren were being born at the rate of rabbits in Windsor Park.[59]

The following week, Sir Charles returned unexpectedly to Walton Hall, his Warwickshire home, having cut short his fishing holiday. It was a blazing hot summer's day, and in front of the house he saw his wife in her pony carriage. She was showing off the two white driving ponies she had bought a few months before from the Sandringham stables. On the steps of the house, admiring her, stood a man—none other than the Prince of Wales.

Bertie hurriedly departed. Shortly afterward, Sir Charles ordered the groom to bring the two ponies round onto the lawn. Dragging Harriett down the steps, he shot the animals dead in front of her.

The whispered scandal was misery for Alix, who clung obsessively to "my Bertie." Her leg was still sore—Bertie reported that she had at last been able to "valse" with him—and now her husband decided to take her away to spend the winter abroad, beginning with Denmark.[60]

By running away from the gossip and pleasing Alix, Bertie annoyed the Queen. There was the usual tug-of-war about taking the children out of the country. Alix wanted the three eldest, Eddy, Georgie, and Louise, to spend Christmas with her parents at Fredensborg, leaving baby Victoria behind at home, but the Queen forbade the one-year-old Louise to travel. She gave a grudging assent for the two boys, but only if the doctors agreed: "They are the Children of the Country and I shall be blamed for allowing any risk to be run."[61]

Alix implored Victoria to relent over Louise, who was a sickly child: "I would prefer to give up the trip rather than leave the little darling behind. You will understand this best, my angel mother, and therefore I speak so openly to you."[62] No one, not even Vicky, dared to appeal to Victoria's feelings in this way, but for once the Queen resisted Alix's charms and accused her of being "very selfish" and "unreasonable." This provoked a furious outburst from Bertie. "Alix has made herself nearly quite ill with worry of all this," he told the Queen, "but what she has felt most are the words you have used regarding her. Ever since she has been your daughter in law, I think she has tried to meet your wishes in every way—and you have never said an unkind word to or of her." Selfish she most certainly was not, "and her whole life is wrapt up in her Children." Was it not inconsistent, he demanded, to forbid Alix to travel home to her parents with her children when Vicky and Alice regularly brought their babies with them to England?[63]

At this Victoria wisely gave way, as she always did in an unwinnable situation. Little Louise accompanied her parents to Fredensborg.

Six weeks with Alix's family bored Bertie. The weather on Denmark's windswept sands made it almost impossible to go out, and there was nothing to shoot except foxes.[64] A bear-shooting expedition with the King of Sweden was spoiled by fog, though the King inducted Bertie as a freemason, which annoyed Victoria.[65] Alix wept bitterly when the time came to leave her parents and the "children of the nation" were sent home. They were packed off to stay with Queen Victoria, who grumbled about having the house at Osborne "crammed full" of grandchildren and complained that they were spoiled.[66] Irked by his mother's remarks, Bertie wrote a tart letter warning her not to be too strict with the grandchildren lest they should grow to dislike her, "and we should naturally wish them to be very fond of you, as they were in Denmark of Alix's parents."[67]

From Denmark, Bertie and Alix proceeded to Berlin, dreading the meeting with Vicky, who, said Bertie, had become "so elated and proud" since Prussia's victories.[68] Bertie was invested with the order of the Black Eagle, but it was Alix who took Berlin by storm, captivating the King of Prussia, in spite of the spat of the previous summer. The popularity of the Danish Rose with the people of Berlin was such that the Queen of Prussia became quite jealous and picked a quarrel. When Alix said, "I thank your Majesty for all your kindness and friendship," the Queen, who wanted Alix to call her Aunt Augusta, although she was not, in fact, her aunt, snapped: "It is very impolite of you. By the way, you may call me as you wish, it doesn't make any difference to me." Whereupon she turned her back on Alix and stalked off.[69]

From Berlin, the party traveled to Vienna, and then from Trieste they sailed to Alexandria for a cruise down the Nile. Letters from Victoria pursued Bertie throughout the journey, complaining about the "quantities of extraordinary people" he had invited to meet them in Cairo.[70] One of these was the Queen's bête noire, the Duke of Sutherland, "whose style is not a good one in any way."[71] Even worse was Samuel Baker, the explorer who had discovered the source of the Nile, invited by Bertie to act as a guide, abhorred by Victoria because it was said that he had bought his wife in a slave auction and lived with her before he married her.[72]

The Nile cruise was one of the happiest times of Alix's life. A procession of barges towed by five steamers glided in a floating court. Bertie and Alix lived on the *Alexandra* dahabeah with a lady-in-waiting (Mrs. Grey) and three maids. Bertie's friend Carrington and Alix's admirer Oliver Montagu traveled on a luxurious steamer. The Duke of Sutherland and his party, including the naturalist Richard Owen and journalist W. H. Russell, who published an account of the journey, sailed behind in another steamer, as did the Egyptian khedive. "You will doubtless think we have too many ships," Bertie told Victoria, "but . . . in the East so much is thought of show that it became almost a necessity."[73]

For Alix, having Bertie to herself was paradise. As for Bertie, Samuel Baker, who excelled as a big-game hunter, was the ideal companion. "I cannot say how glad I am to have asked him to accompany us here," Bertie told Victoria.[74] Theirs was a different age. Bertie shot a crocodile with eighty eggs inside it, and Alix adopted a ten-year-old Nubian boy named Ali Achmet, who, in spite of his subsequent baptism at Sandringham, turned out to be a compulsive thief, loathed by all the servants.

From Paris, where they stayed on the journey home, Bertie wrote: "Sad stories have indeed reached our ears from London of 'scandals in high life'—which is indeed much to be deplored—and still more so, the way in which (to use a common Proverb) they 'wash their dirty linen in public!' "[75]

The dirty linen belonged to Harriett Mordaunt. At the end of February she had given birth to a premature daughter, probably an eight-months baby. Soon afterward, she started to say strange things. She asked the midwife whether the baby was "diseased." She said that the baby came from the time when her husband Sir Charles was away in Norway. She was sure the father of the child was Lord Cole. Harriett seemed indifferent toward her baby, but when she noticed a discharge coming from her eyes, she became distraught. She told the midwife that Sir Frederick Johnstone, Bertie's old Oxford friend, was a "fearfully diseased man."*[76]

Convinced that the child was infected with venereal disease, Harriett insisted on making a confession to her husband. "Charlie you are not the father of that child," she declared. "Lord Cole is the father of it and I am the cause of its blindness." She told him that she had been very wicked. "With who?" asked her startled husband. "With Lord Cole, Sir Frederick Johnstone and the Prince of Wales, and with others, often and in open day."[77] Harriett confidently expected her husband to forgive her, but she had misread him badly. Sir Charles was a proud man, rigid and insecure. The shock and humiliation of being cuckolded was more than he could bear. He determined on revenge. He wanted a divorce, and he wanted to see his wife's lovers, especially the Prince of Wales, in the witness box.

At the Mordaunts' Warwickshire home, an appalling tragedy was now enacted. Harriett found herself deserted by her husband, bullied by his family, surrounded by spying servants, and repeatedly examined by doctors. Sir Charles interrogated the servants and ransacked her desk, finding the eighteen letters from the Prince of Wales. Soon the lawyers became involved, as he prepared to sue for divorce.

Harriett's family were hardly more sympathetic, being determined above all to protect the family honor and save themselves from dis-

---

* This seemed baffling, but it later transpired that Harriett had slept with Johnstone after she became pregnant—and that her husband told her that Johnstone suffered from a "disease" that might be conveyed to his children.

grace. The Moncreiffes had a great deal to lose. Their tentacles extended deep into the aristocracy surrounding the court.* When her sister Helen Forbes heard of Harriett's confession, she immediately responded: "Tell me is there one name mentioned? I mean the Prince?" She added, "He has ruined the happiness of many families." Helen was rumored to be a mistress of Bertie's herself, and it was whispered (probably wrongly) that her daughter Evelyn, born in March 1868, was a royal love child.

"Our great object," wrote Helen Forbes, "is to prevent anything being brought before the public."[78] The Matrimonial Causes Act of 1857 made divorce easier, but Parliament's decision against allowing cases to be heard in secret meant that proceedings could be freely reported in the newspapers.[79] Advised by his lawyers, Sir Thomas Moncreiffe knew that the only hope of keeping the scandal out of the press was for Harriett to plead insanity. It was vital to show that she had not been in her right mind when she made her "confession" to Sir Charles, and that she had been mad ever since.

Harriett's behavior was increasingly strange. She rarely spoke, but sat silent and dumbly unresponsive. She stood motionless with a fixed stare, as though playing "statues." Sometimes she burst out into a fit of mad laughter. The Mordaunt family and the servants at Walton were convinced that she was shamming, faking madness on the instructions of her father. Sir Charles's doctors examined her and reported that she was sane. But the doctors sent to inspect Harriett on the instructions of the Moncreiffe lawyers diagnosed puerperal mania.[80]

Bertie and Alix, meanwhile, seemed a devoted couple. Egypt had been a second honeymoon, and Alix returned pregnant with her fifth child. But she looked ill and thin, while Bertie was overweight and balding.

---

* Harriett's sister Louisa was married to the Duke of Atholl. Her mother-in-law the duchess was a friend of Queen Victoria and served as Mistress of the Robes in 1852.

The baby—another girl, named Maud—was born in November. Alix told Minnie that she had telegraphed for "my Bertie," who was away when her pains began, and he arrived just in time to be with her in the bad hours, "for without him the angel I would certainly not have been able to stand them—they gave me a little chloroform, but only so little that I felt everything and went off into fits of laughter into the bargain."[81]

Building work made Sandringham uninhabitable that winter, and the Waleses rented Gunton, Lord Suffield's house nearby. They spent six weeks there after Christmas, entertaining relays of rowdy shooting parties. In one period of just four days, 3,207 head of game were shot. The bill of fare gives a glimpse of the menus composed by French chefs for the royal nursery, the little princesses, the stewards' room, the servants' hall, and the royal kitchen, climaxing in the Royal Dinner. Shooting breakfast typically consisted of *Poulet sauté aux champignons*, rump steaks *pommes, saucisson de dore* (browned) and *oeufs brouillés aux truffes* (scrambled eggs with truffles). Shooting lunch was Don Pedro sherry, curry of rabbits, *ronde de boeuf,* partridges, roast beef, galantine foie gras, wild boar, apple pudding, and rum baba. Dinner reads like a restaurant menu:

Tortue Claire. Purée de gibier.
Turbot sauce homard. Eperlans frits sauces anchois.
Foies gras à la Financière.
Filets de phaisant à la Maréchel. Doits asperges.
Roastbeef. Dindes braisés purée de céleris.
Jambon Braisé.
Wild ducks. *Asperges.*
Macédoines de fruits. D'artois crème.
Pailles au fromage.
Abricots ice.[82]

At least the Prince of Wales had not lost his appetite from worry.

One night Christopher Sykes, who had just introduced a bill for the preservation of seagulls, his sole achievement in a parliamentary ca-

reer of twenty-seven years, had a dead seagull put in his bed for a joke.*
Sykes was "so tipsy that leaning against the wall of the ballroom his
feet slipped from under him; and he fell and lay flat on his back—so we
carried him to bed, and he lay on the seagull all night."[83] Little wonder
Alix found it exhausting, though she liked some of Bertie's friends,
"now that I know them all so well, though only being *intime* with very
few."[84] As for Lord Suffield, when a fire destroyed Gunton ten years
later, it was rumored that he had taken desperate measures, as he could
no longer afford to entertain the prince.

Sir Charles Mordaunt petitioned for divorce on 27 April 1869, accusing
Lord Cole, Sir Frederick Johnstone, and "some other person" of committing adultery with his wife. Bertie was not named, but behind the
scenes he tried to hush the scandal up. Harriett was bundled off to a
villa in Worthing, where she was kept under virtual house arrest, an
act of dubious legality which was sanctioned by Bertie's doctor William Gull.

If Harriett had been feigning insanity at first, the keepers who
watched her in Worthing thought that she really did go mad. She was
unable to carry on a conversation. She was apathetic and restless by
turns, with a strange, vacant look.[85] Doctors visited often, but rather
than attempt to help the poor demented woman, they filed reports for
the lawyers.

"My dearest Mama," wrote Bertie on 10 February 1870: "It is my
painful duty (I call it painful, because it must be so to you to know that
y[ou]r eldest son is obliged to appear as a witness in a court of justice)
to inform you that I have been subpoened [*sic*] by Sir C. Mordaunt's
Counsel to appear as a Witness on Saturday next at Lord Penzance's
Court."

Sir Charles Mordaunt, who "has shown such a spirit of vindictiveness ag[ain]st me—& such a bad spirit," was determined to make him

---

* The bird (a young kittiwake) was afterward stuffed and given an inscription: "To the Gull's
Friend."

appear in court. Bertie added: "Alix has been informed by me of everything concerning this unfortunate case."[86]

The Queen's response was instinctive and definitive. Though deeply regretting his involvement, she never for one moment doubted his innocence. "I cannot sufficiently thank you," wrote Bertie, "for the dear and kind words."[87] Her support was crucial, both for its own sake, and because it meant that the government backed him. Both the prime minister, Gladstone, and the Lord Chancellor were on his side.

As for Alix, she was in no doubt that her angel had been wronged. Her newly discovered letters to her sister reveal that she remained fiercely loyal. "Imagine only my feelings my Minny! To see one's husband being accused in such a scandalous mean way was nearly more than I could bear, and we were both of us nearly ill at it . . . imagine that he, my angelic Bertie, in his high position, was trumped [sic], that is to say those brutes accused him in the face of the whole world in such a mean way that everybody naturally believed the worst."[88]

Bertie and his lawyers had done everything possible to prevent the case from coming to court. They were careful to operate in a clandestine way, which has made it difficult for historians to learn the truth, but it seems that Harriett Mordaunt's father, Sir Thomas Moncreiffe, was in league with Marlborough House to ensure that Harriett was declared insane and not fit to appear in court. In November 1869, the royal doctor William Gull visited her and declared her mentally incapable. Harriett's condition had, in fact, been improving, but after her father paid a visit she became madder by the day. She laughed uncontrollably, she spat, she finger-painted excrement, she ate fluff off the carpet. Did Moncreiffe put her up to this, as the Mordaunts suspected? And how come Sir Thomas, who was notoriously short of money, was willing to risk crippling legal expenses unless he had a guarantee of finance from "somebody" if the case went against him?[89]

The case came on in Westminster Hall on Wednesday, 16 February 1870. The courtroom was packed, and the verbatim report of the proceedings filled a whole page of the newspapers. The nation was agog. "Reading the Mordaunt Warwickshire Scandal case," wrote Reverend

Kilvert in his remote vicarage on the Welsh marches. "Horrible disclosures of the depravity of the best London society."[90] Queen Victoria ordered the newspapers to be hidden from her younger children, as the details were "such as hardly to be readable for any one and make everyone shudder that the world sh[oul]d be fed with such scandal!"[91]

Harriett was declared unfit to appear. The Moncreiffes claimed that she had been mad ever since her baby was born. Sir Charles Mordaunt, on the other hand, insisted that she was feigning and, in order to establish her motive for this, the judge, Lord Penzance, allowed the facts of her past life to be put before the jury. This was a turning point in the trial, and it came as a blow for Bertie and the Moncreiffes. As Carrington wrote, Sir Charles seemed "determined to make everybody he possibly can share the disgrace with him and on his wife's confession drags in the Prince of Wales." It was a "terrible thing," thought Carrington, and "will do an awful lot of harm."[92]

Sir Charles appeared in the witness box on day three of the trial (Friday, 18 February), and did his best to involve Bertie. His counsel, Serjeant Ballantine, examined him:

—Were you also aware that the Prince of Wales was an acquaintance of your wife?—I was.

—I believe you had not personal acquaintance with his Royal Highness?—I cannot say that I knew him well. I had a slight acquaintance, and had spoken to him, but he was not a friend of mine. I was not intimate with him.

—You were aware that he was acquainted with your wife's family, and was on intimate terms with them?—Certainly.

—Did he ever come to your house upon any invitation of yours?—Never.

—Did you ever have any conversation with your wife about him? Did you ever express your desire as to her not continuing her acquaintance with his Royal Highness?—I did. I warned her against continuing her acquaintance with him.

—Lord Penzance: What was it that you said to her about not continuing this acquaintance with his Royal Highness?

—Sir C. Mordaunt: I said I had heard in various quarters certain circumstances connected with his previous career which caused me to make the remark.[93]

Bertie was not actually cited as corespondent, but Sir Charles's evidence forced him into the witness box. As Bertie told the Queen: "He took care to mention my name so often,—& in order to compromise me in every possible way—that I fear I have now no other alternative but to come forward and clear myself of the imputations wh[ich] he has cast upon me."[94]

The Lord Chancellor, Lord Hatherley, considered that by expressing his willingness to appear in court, Bertie would silence the rumors about him.[95] Sir William Knollys agreed, convinced as he was that Bertie was "innocent of anything beyond thoughtlessness."[96] Bertie's letters to Harriett appeared in *The Times* on 21 February, a leak that certainly benefited Bertie even if his advisers did not inspire it. As the Lord Chancellor wrote, the publication of the letters "has really been of great service, though probably intended for annoyance, for persons have been surprized [sic] to find them so simple and free from impropriety."[97]

The danger, as Lord Chief Justice Sir Alexander Cockburn warned, was that by going into the witness box, Bertie would expose himself to hostile cross-examination.[98] Behind the scenes, Prime Minister Gladstone worked to prevent this.*

On "Saturday evening" (19 February), Bertie scrawled a note to

* As Francis Knollys wrote in 1891, at the time of Bertie's second court appearance, over the Tranby Croft gambling scandal: "HRH remembers that in 1869 [sic] when he was called upon as a witness in the Mordaunt case, Mr. Gladstone, who was the Prime Minister, took all the indirect means in his power (and successfully) to prevent anything being brought out in the court of the trial that could prove to be injurious to the Prince or the crown." (Hatfield House, Salisbury Papers, 3M/E, Knollys to Schomberg McDonnell, 11 June 1891: cited in Magnus, *Edward VII*, p. 229.)

Francis Knollys from Marlborough House. "I saw Sir Thomas Moncreiffe this evening and had a most satisfactory interview with him. He is coming here tomorrow at 3 to your room." Also summoned were Bertie's doctor, Oscar Clayton, and his solicitor, Arnold White. "They had better each be in a separate room." It sounds like a drawing-room farce, but the purpose of this conference was to prepare for Bertie's appearance in the witness box. "I am in great hopes that this horrid business will now end very well," he told Knollys.[99]

Bertie was scheduled to give evidence on day five of the case (Wednesday, 23 February). He entered the witness box at around three p.m., coming in from a door at the back of the box, and when he appeared, the court, which was packed, fell silent. Dr. Deane, counsel for the Moncreiffes, examined him:

—Were you acquainted with Lady Mordaunt before her marriage?

—I was.

The prince's calm, assured manner breathed patrician honesty as Dr. Deane bowled soft questions at him.

—We have heard in the course of this case that your Royal Highness used hansom cabs occasionally. I do not know whether this is so.—It is so.*

—I have only one more question to trouble your Royal Highness with. Has there ever been any improper familiarity or criminal act between yourself and Lady Mordaunt?—There has not.[100]

---

* That the prince should use a hansom cab was especially shocking to the Victorians. There was something unpleasantly sly and furtive about a prince hiring a public carriage to drive anonymously through gaslit streets. (Roger Fulford, "The King," in *Edwardian England*, ed. Simon Nowell-Smith [Oxford University Press, 1964], p. 9.)

Bertie pronounced this answer in a firm, manly tone, and clapping burst out in the court, but it was instantly checked. To Bertie's relief, Serjeant Ballantine, the formidable counsel for Sir Charles, whose cross-examination Bertie had been dreading, declined to question him. This was presumably Gladstone's doing.

The ordeal lasted seven minutes, and Bertie received an ovation as he left the court. Later that day he wrote a relieved letter to the Queen: "I trust that by what I have said today the public at large will be satisfied that the gross imputations wh[ich] have so wantonly been cast upon me are now cleared up."[101] That night Bertie and Alix dined with Mr. and Mrs. Gladstone. "Extremely gracious and kind," wrote Gladstone in his diary. "It is a critical time."[102] The next day *The Times* printed a long leading article defending the prince, whose sole error was that he had been too careless of his reputation. As the editor Delane told the palace, "the whole British nation was relieved and rejoiced by the Prince's evidence."[103] The jury's verdict, delivered the same day, was that Harriett Mordaunt had never been in a mental state to answer Sir Charles's suit. Her confession was the raving of a madwoman. Sir Charles did not get his divorce.

No one claimed that Bertie was the father of Harriett's child. But few agreed with Alix that he stood "white as snow in the face of the world."[104] Tradition among the family of Sir Charles Mordaunt maintains that Bertie committed adultery with Harriett.[105] On the other hand, Harriett's great-nephew, Iain Moncreiffe, family historian and genealogist, was convinced that Bertie was innocent, and had not "tampered with Aunt Harriett."[106] Queen Victoria shrewdly wrote: "He did not know more of, or admire, the unfortunate, crazy, Lady Mordaunt any more than he does or did other ladies."[107] Even if he was innocent, he was damned. The republican *Reynolds's Newspaper* considered that his "childish and ungrammatical letters" revealed the heir to the throne as being a dunderhead, uneducated and unintelligent.[108]

Victoria urged Bertie to change his ways. "B feels now," she told Vicky, "that these visits to ladies and letter writing are a mistake."[109] Prompted by the Queen, Gladstone wrote warning Bertie that his reputation "with respect to whatever touches the sanctity of family relations" was a matter of national importance, crucial to the security of the throne.[110] But Bertie saw no reason to act differently. He continued to visit ladies, he still wrote letters, and he still saw his "fast" friends. We shall never know whether or not he had sex with the women he visited in the afternoons. Most probably an abrupt lunge would be followed by a kiss smelling of tobacco and a hasty grope, all over in a few minutes.

Soon after the trial, Bertie and Alix attended a house party with Louise Manchester at Kimbolton. Victoria begged Alix to avoid Louise: "the Duchess of Manchester is not a fit companion for you. She has done more harm to Society from her tone, her love of admiration & 'fast' style than almost anyone, & what will people say if they see you & Bertie going on a visit to her House, just after all that has happened?"[111] They went all the same. Carrington described a drunken scene on Sunday night when, after a very merry dinner, the entire party marched off to chapel to hear their host read prayers. "Hartington pushed over the front of the pew a huge prayer book which struck an enormous powdered footman on the head, who was sitting below. He fell on his face with a groan and a loud crash and was dragged away insensible—thus completing the success of the party, which was very great. We hardly went to bed at all."[112]

Meanwhile, in a villa in Seaford, poor crazed Harriett Mordaunt threw a cup of tea at a likeness of the Prince of Wales: "That has been the ruin of me. You have been the curse of my life, damn you." But perhaps the real villain was Harriett's proud, unforgiving husband Sir Charles, who had refused to do the gentlemanly thing and accept the child as his own—as Rosa Lewis, the Duchess of Duke Street, expressed it: "No letters, no lawyers and kiss my baby's bottom."[113]

Harriett was later incarcerated in Dr. Tuke's asylum in Chiswick, where she grew rapidly worse. For the rest of her life, she was a certified lunatic. She died aged fifty-eight in 1906.

CHAPTER 9

Annus Horribilis

1870–71

When Bertie attended Royal Ascot and processed up the course in the state carriage, the crowd hissed. His horse won the last race, and a cheering mob collected in front of the royal stand. He turned to Carrington and said, "They are in a better temper than they were this morning."[1] But the truth was that the Mordaunt case had made Bertie deeply unpopular. He was booed at the theater, and a letter appeared in *Indépendence Belge,* purportedly written by Bertie to Affie, relating how *"la mère"* had done a deal with Sir Charles Mordaunt before the trial, and complaining that Victoria was always telling him to be good like Albert.[2] It turned out to be a clever hoax, denied by Bertie "absolutely and indignantly," but it was written by someone with inside knowledge.

Fresh scandal threatened when a Sheffield paper carried a report that Lord Sefton, a racing friend of Bertie's, was bringing an action for divorce citing the prince as corespondent. Bertie signed an affidavit, denying the "slightest impropriety" with Lady Sefton.[3] Sefton sued for libel and won, but not before Lord Stanley had noted the rumors in his diary: "Another trial like that of last year would most likely create, which does not exist, an acknowledged Republican party, bent on putting an end to the Monarchy after the Queen's death. His folly almost amounts to insanity in this one respect: no warning seems to have any effect."[4]

The sleaze was symptomatic of a deeper malaise. For the first time since the reign of George IV, the monarchy was facing a crisis of legitimacy. Not just the Prince of Wales but the Queen herself was under attack, drowning in a tide of gossip and innuendo. Even more toxic than the revelations of the Mordaunt case were the rumors concerning Victoria and her relationship with her Highland servant, John Brown.

John Brown, the Highland gillie, had been summoned from Balmoral to Osborne back in 1864. He soon became a privileged favorite. Promoted from leading her pony to personal servant, he enjoyed unique access to the Queen; he came to her room each day after breakfast and after lunch. Rumors soon spread. In 1866, the *Lausanne Gazette* printed a story that the Queen had secretly married Brown and was expecting his child. This was a fabrication, and a libel. But the rumors refused to die and, as the Queen's unpopularity grew, the sleaze about "Mrs. Brown" thickened.[5] It was whispered that "there was actual sexual intercourse between John Brown and the Queen."[6] The Liberal politician Loulou Harcourt recorded in his diary for 1885 a story about Dr. Norman Macleod, the Scottish Presbyterian minister to whom the Queen looked for spiritual guidance. According to his sister, Macleod confessed on his deathbed in 1872 that "he had married the Queen to John Brown, and added that he had always bitterly regretted it."*[7]

For the widow Queen to have a sexual relationship with anyone—let alone a servant—was almost, but not quite, unthinkable, and the stories still persist today. The tales of Victoria's secret marriage to

---

* In the 1950s, Harold Nicolson claimed that while researching at Balmoral, he came across the "marriage lines" of Queen Victoria and John Brown in a game book. He allegedly replaced the document where he found it, for fear that it would be destroyed. (Christopher Tyerman, letter to *The Times*, 21 December 2004.) It has never been seen since.

Brown are hard to credit, unwitnessed as they are. No marriage certifi-
cate for Queen Victoria and John Brown has ever been found. Victoria's attachment to Brown was strongly emotional, nonetheless.
Throughout her life she depended upon the support of dominant
men, and the rough, plain-speaking Brown, who addressed her as
"wumman" at a time when she craved intimacy and no one called her
Victoria anymore, went some way to filling the gap in her life left by
Albert.

Brown was a drunkard and a bully, and he terrorized the household, who nicknamed him the Queen's Stallion. Victoria's children
hated him. His cruelty toward the hemophiliac Prince Leopold is documented; he hit Leopold, scolded him from morning till night, and
kept him in isolation, banishing his favorite dog.[8] The children came to
dread holidays at Balmoral, where Brown reigned supreme.[9]

Among the guests at Balmoral in September 1869 was the Austrian
sculptor Edgar Boehm, who had been commissioned by the Queen to
model John Brown, as well as to teach sculpture to Victoria's fourth
daughter, the artistically talented Princess Louise. At twenty-one, Louise was pretty, flirtatious, and rebellious. As Bertie diplomatically told
his mother: "I must candidly confess that [from] what I know of her
character she would not be happy if she remained too long unmarried."[10] She soon became intimate with the blue eyed, long-legged
Boehm.

John Brown complained about Boehm to the Queen, claiming that
the sculptor was overfamiliar with Princess Louise. Brown and Victoria burst into Boehm's studio and found Louise there. "The Queen
asked her what she was doing, and the girl got angry and said if she
was to be chased about and spied on she would leave home. The
Queen ordered her to her room but as she (the Princess) was going out
she took John Brown by the shoulders and said, 'Look here, John
Brown, this is your doing. Either you or I leave this house.' She then
shut herself up in her room."*

---

* Boehm related this story to Catherine Walters, the courtesan also known as Skittles, who
told it to the diarist Wilfrid Blunt in 1885.

The Prince of Wales was summoned, as he "was very fond of his sister and had most influence over her," and they set about finding a husband for Louise.[11] Louise was Bertie's ally among his sisters, and he sympathized with her over John Brown. "I am sorry to hear that that brute JB made himself disagreeable during your stay at B[almoral]. I wish you would tell me what he did," he wrote in 1871.[12] Bertie also supported Louise in the negotiations over her marriage, asserting his position as eldest brother and challenging Victoria's control over her daughters. "You know dearest Louise," he wrote, "how fond I am of you, & would do anything to serve you—& can have but <u>one</u> wish & that is y[ou]r happiness but I trust I shall be informed <u>before</u> it is <u>actually</u> settled what future Mama intends f[o]r you—& not like Lenchen's marriage, when <u>everything</u> was settled before I had even a suspicion. That is all I ask."[13]

The first candidate for Louise's hand was a Prussian prince, whom no one much liked, least of all Louise, so he was dropped. The next suitor found by Victoria was Lord Lorne, eldest son of the Duke of Argyll. Though Louise preferred the blond-haired Highland chief to the Prussian, she told the Queen that she "did not like Lorne enough."[14]

Finding a mate for the strong-willed princess was becoming a matter of urgency. In 1870, the Reverend Robinson Duckworth, a handsome, dark-eyed man with a soft voice, was dismissed from his post as governor to Prince Leopold. He was suspected of flirting with Louise, and she had become overfond of him.[15] At Balmoral that summer, the matchmaking was resumed in earnest. Two more German princes were summoned and, to the "utter astonishment" of the Queen, Louise also insisted on inviting Lorne, her spurned suitor of the previous summer.[16] In October, she became engaged to him. Louise later bitterly regretted her marriage, and she blamed Victoria for forcing her into it, writing in 1884: "It was y[ou]r wish for two years, that I sh[oul]d marry Lorne, & because I saw how much it bothered & worried you, that I said I w[oul]d see him again. You asked me to choose between him & another, all I answered was that I thought Lorne was the best of those two, if you remember."[17]

Bertie opposed the marriage. "I always liked Lorne," he told Louise, "but his position will require tact & discretion, which cleverer men than him would find difficult to maintain."[18] To Victoria he wrote more bluntly. "I decidedly maintain that a marriage with a subject is lowering the position of the Royal Family, & in the instance of Lorne—he is excessively poor, & Louise's position will naturally be less good."[19] Louise was the first member of Victoria's family to marry a commoner, and this set a historic precedent. But the real reason why Lorne was a bad choice was that Louise was not in love with him. Alexandra, who was close to Louise, wrote, "She resents him like the devil, the poor man, I am sorry for both of them, and he is going to suffer for that! He is in love with her *voilà tout*."[20]

Relations between Bertie and Victoria were made worse by the war of 1870 between France and Germany. Once again, mother and son were divided. The Queen sympathized with Germany, claiming that this was a war of aggression by France. Bertie shared none of her pro-German feeling. Vicky addressed emotional appeals to the Queen— "Oh that England could help us!"—but Bertie refused to forget the past, commenting tartly, "Nobody could express feelings more touchingly or simply than dear Vicky—I only wish to call to her recollection what the feelings of unfortunate little Denmark must have been when they heard that the Armies of Prussia and Austria were ag[ain]st them. Everybody must confess that that campaign was a war of aggression."[21]

When the German armies with Fritz at their head smashed the French at Sedan (1 September 1870) and the Emperor Napoléon III surrendered, Bertie made no attempt to disguise his sympathies. He predicted "fearful carnage" in Paris, with "revolution the final and inevitable result. It is a sad business and so unnecessary. France will not recover from this shock and humiliation for years to come."[22]

The Queen's loyalty to her German relations made her unpopular at home when the victorious Prussian armies laid siege to defenseless Paris. But, on the other hand, Bertie's French sympathies did him little good. The fall of the French monarchy boosted English republicanism, and Bertie's identification with the decadent French court exposed him to criticism. When the Empress Eugénie fled to exile in England, Bertie impulsively dispatched a letter offering her the loan of Chiswick, the house he rented from the Duke of Devonshire. But his failure to consult either the Queen or the government beforehand meant that his generous offer was a political embarrassment, and gave yet another example of his lack of judgment.[23] Bertie lent a horse to the Prince Imperial, the son of Louis-Napoléon, who had joined his parents in exile. Out hunting, the Prince Imperial had a fall trying to jump some iron railings. As "the hope of Imperial France lay on the ground with all the wind knocked out of him," all the Prince of Wales could say was, "Oh my poor horse, what has happened to my poor horse!"[24]

Exiles from the imperial court were royally entertained at Marlborough House. Among them was Blanche, the half-American Duchess of Caracciolo, who scandalized London society that winter, going out shooting in a kilt and smoking cigarettes. Her ailing husband was cruelly teased by a prankster who dressed up as a doctor and told him he was dying, while his valet disguised himself as a priest and heard his last confession.[25] Soon the duchess was pregnant, and she gave birth to a daughter named Alberta Olga, in honor of Bertie, who was the baby's godfather and rumored—probably falsely—to be her father, too.*[26]

For three years Bertie and Alix had spent little time at Sandringham while the house was being rebuilt. Alix worked hard to arrange "everything" herself, and the house reflected her idiosyncratic taste.[27] There were no ancestral portraits or old masters and no antiques. The furniture came from Maples store on Tottenham Court Road. Visitors walked straight into the hall, where Alix presided at tea over a narrow

---

* Bertie was rumored to have fathered numerous children, but most of these "bastards" were apocryphal (see pp. 179–80). Olga Caracciolo was probably not Bertie's daughter. It was the duke himself who registered her birth in August 1871.The story of her royal paternity was local gossip in Dieppe, however, where she was brought up in the 1880s. The duchess was a dedicated Anglophile, who dressed in the tailored style of Princess Alexandra. Occasionally Bertie would visit her in Dieppe, always arriving in a yacht.

oblong table. Upstairs was a "truly sinister warren" of small rooms and narrow passages—children's bedrooms, guest rooms, rooms for ladies-in-waiting and equerries.[28]

The new house was ready in time for Alix's twenty-sixth birthday on 1 December 1870. One of the guests was Oliver Montagu, whom Bertie had appointed equerry. Alix described him to Minnie as "my good friend O."[29] She was still endearingly loyal to "my Bertie," but she had come to depend on Montagu's companionship. Outwardly loud and bumptious, Montagu had a softer, religious side, and he became Alix's devoted admirer. To conduct a platonic flirtation with a gallant officer, a cavalier with whom she always danced the first after-dinner waltz, made her feel adored without being threatened.

Alix's sixth pregnancy was different from the others. She was always tired. She suffered irregular bleeding, so she was unsure whether she was pregnant or not.[30] At six months she felt depressed and listless, but "still not showing it much, and still dancing."[31] She fell heavily out skating on the ice, crashing down on her bad knee, and her mouth filled with blood.[32] At seven months she fell again, tumbling out of her carriage at the wedding of Princess Louise to Lord Lorne.[33]

Back at Sandringham for Easter 1871, Alix woke early on 6 April with pains. At twenty minutes to seven Bertie knocked on the door of the lady-in-waiting Mrs. Stonor. She realized at once that the princess was going into premature labor, and telegraphed the royal obstetrician, Arthur Farre, and monthly nurse, Mrs. Clarke. Bertie stayed with Alix as the pains grew more severe until the baby was born at half past two. Only the local doctor was present—Dr. Farre arrived from London almost an hour later.[34] The six-weeks-premature baby was very small—even smaller than Eddy had been—but beautifully formed, with fingernails. His head was "quite black" and Bertie thought him "very ugly"; Farre assured them that this was because he was born facing downward, and was of no consequence.[35] The baby's hands and feet were cold and his circulation was feeble.[36]

Mrs. Clarke rubbed the infant with brandy, but by eight p.m. he was sinking fast and the clergyman was hastily summoned to perform the baptism.[37] Alix asked for this to take place at her bedside, but when she saw her son for the first time, she broke down and pressed him to her. She was (said Mrs. Stonor) "dreadfully affected and the Prince was so overcome that he cried most bitterly."[38] Bertie held a small Russian cup containing holy water, and as the sick baby was baptized with the names "Alexander John Charles Albert," it gave such signs of life that "we all hoped there was still a faint hope."[39]

The next morning, Good Friday, the baby was a blue-livid color and Dr. Farre said it couldn't live.[40] Alix insisted on having him with her in bed. Prince John died after twenty-four hours, and "so calmly that we never knew the exact moment when it drew its last breath."[41] Alix lay next to the dead child until eight in the evening, sobbing as she held his hand, which was warm though his head was cold and his limbs were stiffening.[42]

The next day, Bertie placed his baby son, dressed in a frock tied with white satin bows and a cross of bog oak round his neck, in a little wooden shell. While Alix wept in her bedroom next door, the prince and Mrs. Clarke snipped tiny wisps of baby hair and screwed down the wooden lid.[43]

The day before the funeral, Bertie placed the little shell in a lead and mahogany coffin, which he covered with white satin and arranged with white flowers, camellias, and banksia roses. Mrs. Stonor found him "so much affected, the tears were rolling down his cheeks."[44]

On Easter Tuesday (11 April) Bertie walked hand in hand with Eddy and Georgie, both wearing kilts and black gloves, behind the tiny coffin, which was carried by three grooms and the coachman, across the park to the church. From her bedroom upstairs, Alix called to Mrs. Clarke to draw the curtain so she could watch the procession. Sobbing bitterly, she took her prayer book and asked to be left alone.

Inside the church, the Dean of Windsor, Gerald Wellesley, intoned the service inaudibly, croaking with a hoarse voice, and Bertie wept throughout. Afterward, he and the young princes laid white wreaths on the coffin, and when it was lowered into the ground, the children threw primroses and anemones into the grave.[45]

Infant mortality was a fact of Victorian life, and Bertie's grief seems perhaps excessive, but he had good reason to weep. The death of

Prince John marked a watershed in his marriage. The day before the funeral, Dr. Farre had had a "very long and serious" talk with him about "the Future and perfect rest." Mrs. Stonor reported to the Queen that Dr. Farre "says the Prince quite agreed with him in all he said," and it was "a most satisfactory conversation."[46] Farre seems to have warned Bertie to desist from conjugal relations as Alix's health was in danger. A letter from the Dean of Windsor to Victoria suggests that the doctor had not summoned up the courage to speak as plainly as the Queen had hoped. Wellesley urged her to speak to her son herself, as "many who might speak to him with authority, with respect to the health and moral welfare, both of the Princess and himself, shrink from doing so directly, so that he loses hearing the truth, which might perhaps be a little disagreeable to him."[47]

The harsh truth was that there were to be no more babies. Alix was only twenty-six, but repeated pregnancies and premature births had worn her out. She was very ill, spitting blood.[48] Six births in eight years of marriage meant that she had spent forty-eight months, half of her married life, pregnant.* With the exception of Louise, whose arrival was precipitated by Alix's illness, the girls' births were relatively straightforward. As Bertie explained, "There is always more risk with a boy of its being born before the proper time."[49] Eddy was born at seven months, Georgie at eight months, and now John, born too early to live. Alix ached for more children, and it was a permanent sadness in her life that she was unable to have the large Victorian family of her fantasies.

For a man as sexually rampant as Bertie, a celibate marriage might seem a cruel mockery. But, as the dean perceived, Bertie was "deeply attached to the Princess, despite all the flattering distractions that beset him in society"; he genuinely wanted to "be more careful about her."[50] At first, the death of their baby son strengthened the marriage. "What my angelic blessed Bertie was to me all this time no words can describe, a true angel!" wrote Alix. "If anything could have bound us closer together, it is this, our first great sorrow."[51]

* Eddy was born on 6 January 1864; Georgie on 3 June 1865. Louise was next, on 20 February 1867, then Victoria (6 June 1868) and Maud (26 November 1869).

———

The court went into mourning for ten days for the infant Prince John. Ladies were ordered to wear black silk dresses trimmed with crêpe, black shoes and gloves, and black fans, feathers, and ornaments. Gentlemen wore black court dress, with black swords and buckles and plain linen.[52] When Victoria suggested that Bertie and Alix should retire into prolonged mourning, her son snapped back: "Want of feeling I never could show, but I think it's one's duty not to nurse one's sorrow, however much one may feel it." Alix must resume her social duties, "else she will get into a low and morbid state which I am certain will be very injurious to her. You have . . . no conception of the quantity of applications we get . . . to open this place, lay a stone, public dinners, luncheons, fetes without end and sometimes people will not take <u>no</u> for an answer . . . and all these things have increased tenfold since the last 10 years. . . . It is however gratifying that this wish exists in these Democratic days, as one must show oneself in public however irksome it may be—and sometimes it is indeed so.[53]

Out of private tragedy, Bertie endeavored to redefine the monarchy. "Showing oneself in public" was to be central to the survival of the institution in the democratic age. In 1871, however, there was reason to doubt whether even that would be sufficient.

Far from engaging public sympathy, the death of Prince John was greeted with republican catcalls. Ever since the Mordaunt case, the radical *Reynolds's Newspaper* had voiced a strident republicanism. The paper was the publication of G. W. M. Reynolds, an ex-Chartist dedicated to fighting the class war and exposing royalty as an undeserving burden on the taxpayer. It cruelly recorded the death of the baby Prince John thus:

We have much satisfaction in announcing that the newly born child of the Prince and Princess of Wales died shortly after its birth, thus relieving the working men of England from having to support hereafter another addition to the long roll of State beggars they at present maintain.

Reynolds was equally savage about:

the miserable mockery of interring with royal funereal ceremony a shrivelled piece of skin and bone, grandiloquently entitled "prince," not 24 hours old . . . and to augment the folly the
Court goes into mourning for the loss of the wretched abortion
which . . . was carried to the grave by four stout men.[54]

Grumbling about the extravagance of the publicly funded Prince of
Wales swelled into a vicious personal campaign. *Reynolds's* ridiculed
Bertie's speeches as "tautological twaddle," "slip-slop stuff" that was
evidence of intelligence "of a very low order."[55] *The New York Times*
pronounced that the Prince of Wales was totally unable to understand
the "questions of the day, the temper of the people or the times in
which he lives."[56] Fired by the example of the socialist Paris Commune, republicanism surged.

The Queen came under attack as well. Her demand for an annuity
from Parliament for Louise on her marriage sparked a storm of republican agitation, objecting to semi-royals leeching on the taxpayer.[57]
Walter Bagehot, who had penned an apology for the monarchy in his
English Constitution in 1867, wrote a stern leader in *The Economist*: "The
Queen has done almost as much injury to the popularity of the monarchy by her long retirement from public life as the most unworthy of
her predecessors did by his profligacy and frivolity."[58] *What Does She Do
with It?* demanded a pseudonymous pamphlet that claimed that the
tight-fisted Queen was hoarding money from the £385,000 voted by
Parliament in the Civil List.[59]

The Queen complained vigorously that she was overworked, but
her unofficial private secretary General Grey advised Prime Minister
Gladstone: "Pray dismiss from your mind any ideas of there being any
'weight of work' upon the Queen." Encouraged by her sycophantic
doctor, Jenner, Victoria had become entrenched in a "long unchecked
habit of self-indulgence." Her workload consisted of "very short
notes" and a "shorter interview" when she ordered Grey to "'write

fully' on this or that subject" and subsequently to "approve of the draft which I submit to her."[60]

Gladstone, though a Liberal, was dedicated to preserving the monarchy, and he judged that the moment had come to grasp the "burning issue" that he had been "continually revolving" for the past year: "To speak in rude and general terms, the Queen is invisible and the Prince of Wales is not respected."[61]

A grim-faced Gladstone traveled by train to Balmoral on 25 September. He wrote to Lord Granville: "Send for and read *Reynolds's Newspaper* of last Sunday on the gambling at Homburg. These things go from bad to worse. I saw 'What Does She Do With It' advertised on the walls of the station at Birkenhead."[62] The copy of *Reynolds's Newspaper* Gladstone carried in his pocket revealed that the Prince of Wales had been spotted in a crowded casino at Homburg gambling away the gold that had been wrung from the toil and sweat of the working man—and this at a time when gambling in England was illegal.[63]

At Balmoral, Gladstone found the Queen more invisible than ever. She had succumbed to a mysterious illness and stayed in her room for much of the day.[64] She communicated by sending written notes. Not until day four of his stay did she see the prime minister, and then only for half an hour, during which she exercised what he called "the repellent power which she knows so well how to use."[65] She would hear no criticism of herself, but Gladstone reported that she was "much vexed" by Bertie's gambling. "That part of the case, poor soul, she can discern well enough."[66]

The Queen's newly appointed private secretary was in attendance. Shrewd and clearheaded, with a nice sense of irony, the thirty-six-year-old Henry Ponsonby was a surprising choice.* Ponsonby went for a walk in the rain with Gladstone, and held conspiratorial conversations with Princess Alice, who was also at Balmoral.[67] Alice undertook to speak to Bertie about his gambling, but she dared not approach her mother. "I long to be able to ask her to say she will do something but I

---

* He was a Liberal in politics, he disliked dressing up in court uniform, and he was devoted to his wife. The letters he wrote from Balmoral give unrivaled glimpses of Victoria's Highland court.

really am afraid and have been advised not," she told Ponsonby, dropping her voice dramatically so that she was barely audible. The Queen saw no one and heard nothing; Ponsonby marked the newspapers for her, but she seemed not to read their criticisms. "Yet," said Alice, "she knows all that is said against the Prince of Wales she thinks he has become so unpopular that it is useless to expect he will come to the throne. She thinks the monarchy will last her time and that it is no use thinking of what will come after if the principal person himself does not, & so she lets the torrent come on."[68]

Après moi le déluge was Victoria's excuse for doing nothing.

The stories of Bertie's gambling at Homburg and Baden were exaggerated. Francis Knollys told Ponsonby that the prince had entered the casino and thrown a few gold pieces on the table, and that was all; he lost very little money.[69] But Knollys must have been biting his tongue. He knew that Bertie was sitting on one, if not two, explosive sexual scandals, which he was busily trying to defuse.

A letter had arrived at Abergeldie.* The envelope was addressed to Francis Knollys, but there was no doubt who the contents were for:

My dear Sir,

I cannot tell Your Royal Highness how <u>utterly miserable</u> I am that You should have left London without coming to see me. You have shewn me <u>so much</u> kindness for the last four years that I cannot understand Your having twice been in London for two days without coming to see me. What have I done to offend You? I did my best to obey the orders Your Royal Highness gave me the last time I had the happiness of seeing You but the answer was, <u>too late</u> and <u>too dangerous</u>. I was anxious to avoid <u>writing</u> on such a painful subject but You have forced me to it. I cannot describe to you <u>how</u> wretched I am—and Life is so uncertain and

---

* Abergeldie Castle, a tower house on the south bank of the Dee, three miles from Balmoral, was leased by the Queen from its owner and lent to Bertie after he married.

I am far from strong and I felt I may perhaps never see You again, therefore You may imagine my feelings when I received your letter yesterday and knew that You were really off to Scotland!!

Forgive this wretched letter and wishing Your Royal Highness every blessing this world can bestow.

I remain as ever

Y[our]r Royal Highness's obed[ien]t servant

SV-T[70]

SV-T was Lady Susan Vane-Tempest, a mistress whom Bertie was anxious to discard. Before traveling to Scotland, he had spent a few days in London after attending the maneuvers at Aldershot. He was photographed by the society photographer Alexander Bassano in a Piccadilly studio, dressed in his uniform as colonel commanding the 10th Hussars.*[71] But he made no effort to visit Susan, who had begged him to see her before he left London.

Susan was the wayward daughter of the red-bearded Duke of Newcastle who had taken Bertie to America. The duke had been one of Gladstone's closest friends, and when, twenty years before, Susan's scandalous mother had left him and bolted to Italy with her lover, Gladstone had followed in hot pursuit, in a vain attempt to rescue her. Susan had been Vicky's bridesmaid, but she then disgraced herself by making a runaway marriage to Lord Adolphus Vane-Tempest, a son of Lord Londonderry, who, Queen Victoria told Vicky, "drinks and has twice been shut up for delirium tremens." The Duke of Newcastle refused to give his consent; there were "no settlements, no trousseau, nothing," and because he wouldn't allow her to use his carriage, Susan walked to church with her governess. The Queen joked that there was a bet about which of the two, Susan or Adolphus, would be confined first. Within days, it was Adolphus who had gone mad and been locked up.[72] He tried to kill Susan, and according to the Queen, he died in 1864 in a struggle with his four keepers when he burst a vein in his throat.[73]

---

* Bassano's glamorous photograph, which shows the prince smoking a cigar, was a study for a painting he commissioned by Alfred Sheldon Williams.

Bertie's relationship with Susan had begun in 1867, and he was a frequent visitor to her house in Chapel Street, Westminster.[74] In 1871, she became pregnant. Her baby was conceived in March, shortly before the birth of Alix's dead son.[75]

Susan delayed telling Bertie about the pregnancy, she later explained, because "I hoped to the last that my efforts might be successful and that then I need never have told You of the anxiety I had gone through." She evidently understood that it was her responsibility to prevent pregnancy, and if her precautions failed, it was then her duty to abort the baby. She saw her own doctor, who did "everything he could for me as long as it was possible to do so with safety." Susan admitted that "Perhaps I was wrong in keeping silence but I did it to save you annoyance—so please forgive me for You little know how sad and unhappy I am."[76]

She at last summoned the courage to confess her condition to Bertie in early September, when she was already five or six months pregnant.[77] Bertie ordered her to consult his doctor, Oscar Clayton.* Susan delayed, and felt compelled to explain: "Your Royal Highness blames me for not at once going to Dr. C[layton] as You desired me, but You can understand it was most painful to go to an utter stranger under such sad circumstances."[78]

She eventually agreed to consult the sinister Dr. Clayton, but Bertie now refused to see her. Instead, she was interviewed by Francis Knollys. Not surprisingly, she found it hard to speak freely to him. "I was so confused today that I hardly knew what I was saying to you," she told him.[79] Knollys arranged for her to see Dr. Clayton the following day. Susan never used the word, but Clayton's role was plainly to perform an abortion. His verdict, however, as she told Bertie, was that it was "too late and too dangerous."[80]

Bertie ordered Susan to leave London and have the baby secretly in the country. She reluctantly concurred. "I am ready to obey Your orders in everything and it grieves me more than I can say to feel that You

---

* Oscar Clayton was described by Ponsonby as "a dreadful little snob and Jenner says not a good doctor. But he is most attentive and that is everything." (RA VIC/Add A 36/1340, Henry Ponsonby to Mary Ponsonby, 24 October 1877.)

are annoyed with me," she wrote, adding pathetically, "Don't please be angry if I <u>entreat</u> you to come and see me before I go away. . . . <u>Please</u> don't let me leave without saying '<u>Goodbye</u>.' "[81] Desperate to avoid a scandal, he still refused to meet her.

Susan needed money, but by now she lacked the courage to ask. Her friend Harriet Whatman wrote a thinly disguised blackmail letter to Bertie, telling him that if "the event" was to be kept a secret, he must pay her at least £250.[82] Susan settled into 26 Wellington Crescent, Ramsgate, a large Regency terraced house looking out over the sea, to await the birth of her child, which was due in early December.

After Christmas 1871—presumably after the baby was born—Susan wrote to Dr. Clayton asking for an appointment: "The same symptoms still continue and for the last three weeks I have had a white discharge. My back aches dreadfully and I feel altogether <u>very</u> unwell."[83] A few weeks later she wrote to Knollys asking for more money, as Dr. Clayton had ordered her to return to London. "He has not allowed me to leave my Room since I returned & I may not even put my foot to the ground. . . . I cannot enter into particulars but Mr. Clayton will explain all to Him when he sees Him."[84] She had an ulcer on her foot—"I am a cripple on two sticks and cannot move about!!!!"[85]

Nothing is ever said of the baby. No birth was registered in Susan's name in the Ramsgate (Thanet) area. Nor was any infant death recorded.[86] Perhaps the child was handed over to someone else, or perhaps it was stillborn. It is conceivable that the obliging Dr. Clayton performed a dangerously late termination. The distressing symptoms related by Susan seem to hint at a venereal disease. The gumma or leg ulcer is a symptom of tertiary syphilis, and so is spinal pain. But tertiary syphilis develops five years after the initial infection, and it's unlikely that Susan would have been Bertie's mistress if she had been suffering throughout their affair from the disease.*[87]

Four years later Susan Vane-Tempest was dead.

---

* Susan's symptoms may well have been caused by complications or infection after childbirth or a possible termination.

———

Susan's story is an unsettling reminder of the human cost of Bertie's pleasure. Like Harriett Mordaunt, she was a victim, cast away once she became an embarrassment to the prince. His ruthlessness is chilling. Susan's letters were preserved not because Bertie felt sentimental about her, but because they landed on Knollys's desk—all her communications to HRH were sent under cover to his secretary. Once Bertie sniffed the terrible scandal of a pregnancy, he left Knollys to deal with Susan. His refusal to see her in spite of her very real distress can only be described as cruel. Coldly and efficiently, he saved his princely skin from contamination.

Susan's letters are the only ones from a mistress that are known to have survived. Other letters from women with whom he became entangled were destroyed, either by Bertie himself or by Knollys. Plenty of Bertie's letters exist, as most of his female correspondents kept them. Susan's howls of pain could hardly be further removed from the polite gossip and mildly flirtatious small talk that Bertie usually wrote to his women friends. Perhaps Knollys chose to keep her letters because they were exceptional, or it may have been an accident that they escaped the bonfire; it's impossible to tell whether other women wrote to him in this way. But her anguished letters give a glimpse of the abyss—of the reality of disgraceful pregnancies and life-threatening abortions that lay behind the carefully crafted world of afternoon visits and discreet notes.

Susan's is the only illegitimate pregnancy that can be credited with certainty to Bertie—and even so, the child cannot be traced. The destruction of the women's letters means that there is no way of knowing for certain whether other mistresses bore his children. Had it not been for the fact that her letters happened to be preserved, Susan herself would have vanished from the record; there is no other evidence of her relationship with the prince.

Of course, there were rumors of Bertie's bastards, and the villages around Sandringham and Balmoral are alleged to be thickly populated with cousins of the Queen. But genealogical research, meticulously establishing birth dates and checking them against Bertie's movements and social connections, which are exceptionally well documented, has revealed that most of the alleged illegitimate children are mythical.[88] This has led to speculation that his "preferred sexual techniques excluded penetrative sex."[89] Susan Vane-Tempest's letters suggest another explanation: birth control.

Contraception was not unknown in England, but it was far more widespread in France. The French, it seems, practiced birth control without writing about it, while the English talked about it but rarely used it. Contraception was a professional necessity for prostitutes, and the Paris sex industry could hardly have functioned without it. Barrier methods such as the condom and the diaphragm were available, and prostitutes also relied on vaginal sponges and douching.[90] Bertie's visits to Paris courtesans meant that he was far better educated about sex and contraception than his disapproving compatriots. It was part of a courtesan's job to protect herself against pregnancy and disease, and Bertie expected his mistresses to do the same. Married women could pass off illegitimate children as belonging to their husbands, but this was not possible for a widow such as Susan Vane-Tempest. If contraception failed, abortion was available as a second line of defense. It was illegal and considered morally abhorrent, but men like the suave and silky Dr. Clayton would always oblige.*

"I fear fresh bothers are brewing—from abroad—in which my brother and myself are concerned," Bertie admitted to Knollys in July.[91] Among the documents preserved by Knollys is a small, fat, brown-stained envelope labeled "Beneni," stuffed with tightly folded letters written on thick paper. Someone has endorsed the packet: "Re Barucci—treat with care."[92]

La Barucci, the courtesan Giulia Beneni, who four years before had

---

* Gladstone's gossipy secretary Edward Hamilton wrote in his diary in 1881: "In deference to the Prince of Wales, Oscar Clayton has been submitted for knighthood. It is to be hoped that no disagreeable stories will come out about him." (*Diary of Sir Edward Hamilton 1880–1885*, ed. Dudley Bahlman [Clarendon Press, 1972], vol.1, p. 355 [2 November 1881].)

entertained Bertie in her Champs-Élysées mansion with its white velvet staircase, died of consumption during the Siege of Paris in a house on the rue de la Baume.* Her brother, a failed Italian tenor named Piro Beneni, moved in to claw her legacy and blackmail her royal clients.

La Barucci had accumulated a valuable trove. She possessed twenty or so letters from Bertie. He had been careful not to sign them, but they were evidently genuine and most were of a "delicate" nature.[93] La Barucci had also stashed away a hoard of photographs. They included *cartes de visite* signed "Albert Edward"; a large photograph of his brother Affie, the Duke of Edinburgh, wearing Highland costume in a crimson velvet frame signed "Alfred"; an album of the whole royal family inscribed "Alfred to Giulia 1868"; and several photographs of Alix's brother Frederick, Crown Prince of Denmark, one of which was signed *"de votre ami dévoué,* Frederik."[94]

In September 1871, Bertie received a blackmail letter from "that scoundrel Beneni," demanding £1,500.[95] He forwarded it to Knollys, and instructed him to consult Kanné, the royal courier and agent. The royal advisers agreed that paying the blackmailer would be a mistake, and they planned instead to seize Bertie's incriminating letters.

When Beneni wrote again, threatening to put the letters up for sale, Kanné was sent on an undercover mission to La Barucci's house on the rue de la Baume. On 9 November he found Piro Beneni very ill, conducting an informal auction of his sister's things from his bed. "The wretch" took a liking to him and showed him Bertie's letters. Beneni wanted £400, and Kanné offered £240, which was rejected. Kanné then pretended to lose his temper and became very angry. He laid the money on the table and accused Beneni of blackmail, claiming that two policemen were waiting outside to make an arrest if everything was not handed over in ten minutes. The bluff succeeded. Beneni crumpled: *"Prenez tout, mais laissez moi l'argent, je suis si pauvre."* (Take everything, but leave me the money, I am so poor.) Kanné went to the cupboard in the drawers of which the letters were kept, took the bundles, counted them, and put them in his pocket. Pretending to go out-

* See p. 127.

side and talk to the policemen (who did not exist), he returned five minutes later and demanded everything Beneni possessed belonging to the Prince of Wales and his brother. Beneni, who was by now white and trembling with fear, handed over the key to a black cupboard, which contained the cache of letters and photographs.[96]

Kanné wired Knollys, who cabled back: "Your prompt action highly approved of."[97] The letters were destroyed. As Kanné warned, the prince "can not be too careful in his writing. Every scrape [sic] of his writing becomes every day of more value and importance."[98] Writing "delicate" letters to a courtesan was political suicide at a time when the tide of republicanism seemed unstoppable. When the Liberal MP Sir Charles Dilke addressed meetings on republicanism, loud groans were given for the Prince of Wales.[99]

That autumn, Bertie and Alix were guests of Lord Londesborough for a week's grouse shooting near Scarborough. The house party included Louise Manchester and Lord Chesterfield, and twenty-seven people were crammed into the small, boxlike rooms of Londesborough Lodge, perched high on the clifftop above the town. Bertie's valet slept in a cubbyhole six feet high. Three maids shared an unventilated attic, and the sewage backed up whenever the tide rose. The house, as *The Lancet* later reported, was in effect "a vessel inverted over the mouth of a pipe, through which rises continually, sometimes with violence, a deadly vapour."[100] Lady Londesborough "was quite the queen" at Scarborough, holding court in a gilt chair with Bertie sitting at her side, while one by one her guests fell ill with diarrhea, Alix among them.[101]

Back at Sandringham for his thirtieth birthday. Bertie complained of a chill and a whitlow or blister on his finger, and called for cherry brandy and a hot bath, but still insisted on traveling to Buckinghamshire to shoot with his friend Carrington.[102] He arrived by train at Woburn Sands in a howling gale, and Carrington, who drove the coach himself, nearly crashed on the way back from the station; dinner was ruined and the nine royal servants somehow managed to lose Bertie's luggage. The next morning Bertie tried to shoot, but he felt so ill that he gave up and sent for the doctor, the inevitable Oscar Clayton. Long white whitlows had appeared on the palms of his hands, and Clayton ordered him home at once.[103]

Bertie developed fever, rose-colored spots, and a severe headache. Alix summoned "nice" Dr. Gull, "whom he likes and in whom we have the greatest confidence" (this was the same Dr. Gull who had confined Harriett Mordaunt to a madhouse).[104] She also sent for Sir William Jenner. Bertie's symptoms now allowed a diagnosis: typhoid fever.[105] No attempt was made to cover up his illness or conceal it from the public, and the doctors issued regular daily bulletins. Among William Gull's papers is a diagram charting the course of HRH's illness and calibrating the days as the infection progressed through its classic stages. First, headache, vomiting, fever; then the telltale rose spots and diarrhea, high fever, and delirium, followed by a critical stage when the lungs became congested.[106] There was no treatment, just minute expert observation by the physicians and skilled nursing.

Bertie lay behind a screen in a darkened room, breathing very rapidly and loudly. Alix watched him devotedly, refusing to leave his bedside. "No words of mine can EVER fully express to you how fearful and MISERABLE these days of AGONY have been to me," she told her sister-in-law Louise.[107] Gull's doctor's notes read: "mind wanders constantly. State to cause great anxiety but not at present alarm."[108] At one point Bertie was too ill to recognize Alix, when she told him she was his wife, he replied, "That was once but is no more, you have broken your vows!"[109] His raving became so candid—"all sorts of revelations and names of people mentioned"—that the doctors ordered Alix to leave the room.[110]

Alix's love of nursing brought her close to Bertie; for once, he was dependent on her, and he couldn't escape. But she wasn't allowed to have him to herself. Princess Alice, who happened to be staying in the house, bossily tried to take charge. "We are all furious at seeing our Princess [Alix] sat upon and spoken of as if she had not sense enough to act for herself," wrote Lady Macclesfield.[111]

By now the doctors were issuing several bulletins a day, each more alarming than the last: 26 November 1871, 6:00 p.m.: "The course of the fever today has been rather severe but regular. The Prince's strength continues good"; 27 November, 9:00 a.m.: "His Royal Highness the Prince of Wales has passed a sleepless night. The course of the fever is marked by increasing intensity, but the strength does not fail."[112] The doctors' drafts, preserved in Gull's papers, are crossed through and re-worded; they show a striving for medical accuracy, rather than political spin, but in their artless attempts to state the truth, the doctors were the unwitting agents of a resurgence of loyalty to the monarchy. The nation was gripped. "The alarm in London very great," noted the Queen. "Immense sympathy all over the country."[113]

Queen Victoria, who was always energized by illness, yearned to be at Bertie's bedside, but she needed to be asked. She had never visited Sandringham before, and Alice opposed her coming now. For once Alix overruled her domineering sister-in-law, and wrote on her own initiative inviting her mother-in-law. The drama of the widow Queen, who herself had been ill, rushing by special train (the details of the route were printed in the paper) to visit her wayward son on his sick-bed, almost exactly ten years after the death of her beloved Albert, transfixed the nation.

The Queen slept badly before her journey to Sandringham on 29 November. Alice and Alix, thin and tearful, met her at the door. Peep-ing in at Bertie's darkened room, she saw him lying on his back, breath-ing loudly as he dozed with one lamp burning, and Albert's illness came flooding back to her.[114] What they didn't tell her was that Bertie now thought he had succeeded as king, and raved of reforms in the household that "set all their hair straight on end."[115] He gave orders that all gentlemen were to wear tights, "because I'm very particular about dress and General Knollys must kneel down and give me a glass of water, it was always done in former days."[116]

The next evening, when Victoria went to Bertie's dressing room after dinner, a tearful Alice rushed in, saying that his temperature had suddenly fallen (from 105°) and his breathing seemed all wrong. The Queen went into the bedroom. "What I saw reminded me terribly of December '61!" She followed Alix out into the dressing room, and "when [Alix] completely broke down I tried to reassure her, although my heart was heavy with fear, and held her dear little slight frame in my arms." Dr. Jenner told Victoria that Bertie had a threatening of the congestion of the lungs or pneumonia that had killed Albert. "Went sadly to my room, very, very anxious," she wrote.[117]

In fact, Bertie had turned a corner toward recovery. The next morning he was sufficiently robust to ask for an egg, and the Queen returned to Windsor.[118] The doctors' bulletins on 1 December signaled cautious optimism.[119] But the same day brought news of the death from typhoid of Lord Chesterfield, another guest at Londesborough Lodge. This was apparently proof that the fetid drains of Scarborough had caused the prince's illness, which had hitherto been hotly denied by Lord Londesborough, but it was a shock that, said Lady Macclesfield, "came like ice upon all our hearts."[120] On 5 December, Gull wrote in his private notes that the prince's breathing was easier and all his symptoms had improved, though "there remains the liability to relapse and reduplication of the attack."[121]

Gull was right to fear a double dip. On 7 December, the twenty-sixth day of the illness, the ominous rose spots returned. Soon Bertie's breathing became rapid, he began to clutch at his sheets (a symptom that particularly worried the doctors), and his mind wandered in a constant state of delirium.[122] Bulletins were issued every four hours.[123] For the first time, *The Times* openly discussed the possibility of the prince's death.

The Queen was advised that if she wished to see her son before he died, she should leave immediately, and she set off for Sandringham at once that afternoon.[124] She was expected at four, and at two o'clock Gull and Jenner took a few minutes' walk in the garden. Jenner said: "Well, if he lives until Her Majesty comes I shall be satisfied." Gull replied: "That will not satisfy me. Now we shall see if Shakespeare's *signa mortis* are right, for they are marked enough here"—and he quoted *Henry V,* on the death of Falstaff: "After I saw him fumble with the sheets and play with flowers and smile upon his fingers' ends, I knew there was but one way; for his nose was as sharp as a pen and a' babbled of green fields."[125]

The Queen arrived at seven thirty p.m. in deep snow and was met by Lady Macclesfield, who told her Bertie was "very bad." She rushed up to his room, where Alix and Alice sat on either side of the bed. Bertie lay breathing rapidly.[126] Telegrams were sent summoning Arthur, Leopold, and Beatrice. Both Helena and Vicky were refused, partly because there was no room, even though Vicky begged her mother to be allowed to come.[127] The house was so crowded that the princesses Louise and Beatrice were obliged to share a bed.

Bertie's illness had called forth a general expression of sympathy, which, said *The Graphic,* "in its quiet earnestness is a satisfactory proof of the loyalty of the nation."[128] On Sunday, thinking that Bertie had rallied, Alix slipped out from the sickroom to church. She passed a note to the vicar: "My husband being thank God somewhat better, I am coming to Church. I must leave, I fear, before the service is concluded, that I may watch by his bedside. Can you not say a few words in prayer in the early part of the service that I may join with you in prayer before I return to him?" Trembling with emotion, the vicar prayed while Alix stood in the royal pew alone.[129] Reported in *The Times,* this poignant image stirred the public's heart.

Bertie passed a tranquil morning, but by Sunday evening the bulletins were grave.[130] Gull's notes describe a "paroxysm" or spasm of coughing, and the short, guttural, suffocative cough baffled and worried him.[131]

On Monday, the Queen was woken at five thirty a.m. with a message from Jenner that Bertie had suffered a severe spasm and might at any minute "go off," so she put on her dressing gown and hurried to the bedroom. She found Alix and Alice sitting in vigil in the dreary light beside Bertie, who was breathing as if he would choke at any moment. He raved continually, talking on and on, whistling and singing. "This has been a terrible day," wrote Victoria, who went back and forth continually to the sickroom, and took her meals upstairs.[132]

Downstairs, the family and household waited for news, talking in whispers in the great hall, pacing the slippery floors, trying not to trip over the skins and enormous protruding heads of the animals that Bertie had shot.[133] Bertie's brothers Affie and Arthur giggled at his ravings, earning stern reproofs from Victoria.[134] Alice snubbed the devout Alix for praying, and briskly declared: "*Providence,* there is no Providence, no nothing, and I can't think how anyone can talk such rubbish."[135] In London, Gladstone found the suspense painful, and trembled when he opened the telegrams from Sandringham.[136]

Wednesday, 13 December 1871, the day before the anniversary of beloved Albert's death, was, said Victoria, "the worst day of all." Yet another fit of suffocating coughing nearly killed Bertie. The Queen and Alice said to each other in tears: "There can be no hope."[137] Alix was so desperate to stay by his side that when the doctors told her that it would distress him to know that she was in the sickroom, she crawled in on hands and knees so as to be out of sight.[138] She scarcely ate, and the exhaustion of sitting up night after night had made her so deaf that she was not easy to wake when asleep. "How she will bear the final blow when it comes, one cannot imagine," groaned Lady Maccles-field, who confidently expected the prince to die.[139]

On the morning of 14 December, the Queen crept into the sick-room and stood behind the screen. Bertie asked the nurse if the Queen was in the room. Victoria went to the bed, and he kissed her hand and smiled and said, "So kind of you to come; it is the kindest thing you could do."[140]

So, on the anniversary of his father's death, Bertie's recovery began.

The following Sunday, at Clyro church in Radnorshire, the vicar read out the bulletin from the paper: "The Prince has passed a tranquil day and the symptoms continue to be favourable." The Reverend Kilvert commented in his diary: "I love that man now, and always will love him. I will never say a word against him. . . . God bless him and keep him, the Child of England." A little girl in Sunday school was asked who had died for us on the cross. "Lord Chesterfield," was the reply.[141] This was Bertie's apotheosis: He had become a holy prince. Among the best things he did was nearly to die.

PART TWO

Expanding Middle

CHAPTER 10

Resurrection?

1871–75

The day after Bertie's fever passed the crisis, Francis Knollys and Henry Ponsonby went for a ride at Sandringham. They cantered over some jumps and both fell off their horses. In between, the private secretaries discussed the future. The prince, said Knollys, had reached the turning point in his life. "If after the illness and the great sympathy for him he takes up some line of work it will save him from frivolous idleness and the follies he has been accused of and may make something of him." The only question was what he should do. Philanthropy or science and art, suggested Ponsonby.[1] No, said Knollys; he had "never shown any inclination whatsoever" for social work, and as for the South Kensington Albertopolis, as the Albert Hall and Victoria and Albert Museum were called, he only did the bare minimum.[2] Knollys's solution was foreign affairs. In a memo to Ponsonby, he proposed that the Queen should forward dispatches for the prince.[3] But, as Ponsonby objected, "writing empty minutes which will not be read" was a waste of time and could hardly be called employment.[4]

William Gladstone, meanwhile, proposed to stage a grand thanksgiving ceremony at St. Paul's Cathedral. On 21 December 1871 he had a long audience with the Queen at Windsor. Victoria's journal breezily records: "After discussion it was agreed that I should send [Gladstone] a letter."[5] Gladstone gives a different version. His lengthy memorandum records a furious argument with the Queen, who violently resisted the public thanksgiving. Treating her rather as he did his sister Helen, who was mad, the prime minister laboriously explained that the feeling in the country had been "wrought up to the highest point, and nothing short of a great public act of this kind can form an adequate answer to it." The prince's illness had "worked in an extraordinary degree to the effect of putting down that disagreeable movement with which the name of Sir C. Dilke had been connected": the aim now must be to get rid of it altogether, "for it could never be satisfactory that there should exist even a fraction of the nation republican in its views." Reluctantly, the Queen agreed to a public thanksgiving, but when Gladstone mentioned giving employment to the Prince of Wales, "this brought out no direct response" but an icy vagueness.[6]

Bertie's recovery was distressingly slow. He developed agonizing pain in his left leg, especially in the hip. His fever climbed, his mind wandered, and he fancied himself in an American hotel, unable to realize that the aching leg actually belonged to him. The leg gave him violent spasms that baffled the doctors and prevented him from sleeping.[7] He had frightening attacks of breathlessness, too, and the doctors feared a deep-seated inflammation.[8] He was tortured by toothache. Later, the leg periodically became swollen, as the circulation was obstructed—the result, said the doctors, of the "narrowing of the veins caused by their inflammation"; his bad left leg troubled him for the rest of his life.[9] Having become emaciated during the fever, he now put on weight too quickly.* Victoria thought he was looking "so aged

* Poole's Archive shows his chest and waist measurements increasing from 33¾ inches and 29½ inches in 1860 to 43 inches and 39½ inches in 1876.

and shaken and so deathly pale—and very lame."[10] Leopold, too, found him "much aged—the top of his head is quite bald."[11] At thirty, Bertie had become middle-aged.

His enfeebled state brought him closer to Alix. "You can hardly think HOW happy I am," she told her sister-in-law Louise. "We are never apart, and are now enjoying our second 'Honey Moon.'"[12] Later, she would look back on Bertie's convalescence as the time "when I could do everything for him and be of use and pleasure to him—and never were we so close to each other before!!"[13] When Bertie came to Osborne to convalesce, even Victoria noticed "something different" about him, "which I can't exactly express. It is like a new life—all the trees and flowers give him pleasure as they never used to do. . . . He is constantly with Alix and they seem hardly ever apart."[14] Photographs show them standing close together, Alix resting her head on his shoulder or putting her arm through his; they seem touchingly devoted, where before they had avoided any form of contact before the camera.[15]

Alix looked "more lovely," according to Prince Leopold, "and I might say angelic, than ever."[16] Nursing suited her. She told William Gull, the doctor whom she credited with saving Bertie's life, how she rubbed him to keep him warm after he took his first bath: "You cannot think how happy and thankful I am to see him so fully restored."[17]

The national thanksgiving on 27 February 1872 was an extraordinary outpouring of public loyalty and affection. How strange it was, mused Bagehot in *The Economist,* that "a middle-aged lady is about to drive, with a few little-known attendants, through part of London, to return thanks in St. Paul's for the recovery of her eldest son from fever, and the drive has assumed the proportions of a national event."[18]

Victoria dreaded the day and bickered furiously with Gladstone beforehand. The prime minister supervised the organization of the ceremony down to the last detail, following the precedent of George III's thanksgiving at St. Paul's after his recovery from illness in 1789. Credit for the revival of the late-Victorian monarchy is usually given to Disraeli, but Gladstone's insistence on making a ceremonial occasion of Bertie's recovery was crucial.[19] Indeed, so successful was Gladstone in burying republicanism and silencing critics of the monarchy that he undercut his second aim: to devise a useful employment for the Prince of Wales.

Gladstone wanted the Queen to process in formal robes and state coaches, but Victoria insisted on semi-state and open coaches, in order that the people should see her.[20] The family squabbled for weeks beforehand about who was to travel in which coach. Bertie and Alix annoyed the Queen by requesting a separate carriage, a request she refused.[21] Whether Bertie would, in fact, be well enough to go was uncertain until the day before.

Early in the morning of 27 February, surging crowds massed outside Buckingham Palace and blocked the Mall. Bertie was so lame that Victoria took his arm as they walked slowly down the Grand Entrance and entered an open state landau, in which they rode together with Alix, Beatrice, and Prince Eddy. The Queen's landau was preceded by a sovereign's escort of seven open carriages, and in front of them came the Lord Chancellor. At the head of the procession the Speaker set the pace in his quaint old carriage that could only advance at a walk. This was Gladstone's idea, to stop the Queen dashing through the crowds at a brisk trot. "Dear Alix," in blue and sable, "was not looking well," thought Victoria, and Bertie seemed even iller; but John Brown, who sat behind, was splendid "in his very fullest and very handsome full dress."[22]

"We seemed to be passing through a sea of people as we went along the Mall," wrote Victoria.[23] At Temple Bar, the Lord Mayor presented the Queen with the sword of the City, and when she "took dear Bertie's hand and pressed it—people cried." This was the gesture the crowd was waiting for, a demonstration of affection; in spite of her dread of public appearances, Victoria was a great actor when she needed to be. Bertie's hat was constantly off his head and, wrote Victoria, "I often felt a lump in my throat."[24] St. Paul's was packed. Bertie walked slowly and painfully up the aisle on his mother's arm, holding the eight-year-old Eddy by the hand. The Queen, who had complained vigorously about mixing monarchy up with religion, grumbled that St.

Paul's was a dreary, dingy place and the service was "cold and too long."[25]

Lying on a sofa that evening at Marlborough House, in great pain from his leg, Bertie scrawled a hurried note to his mother: "I cannot tell you how gratified and touched I was by the feeling that was displayed in those crowded streets today towards you and also to myself."[26] He had made the intoxicating discovery that he was the most popular man in the country.

Monarchy was projected as a narrative shared by the nation, a story in which all could participate. As Alix explained to Victoria: "The whole nation has taken such a public share in our sorrow, it has been so entirely one with us in our grief, that it may perhaps feel it has a kind of claim to join with us now in a public and universal thanksgiving."[27]

The question was what role Bertie should play in this royal narrative: prodigal son or playboy prince.

For Gladstone, the thanksgiving was only a beginning, the first phase of his mission to reform the monarchy. He had a bigger plan. Convinced that this was an opportunity not to be missed, he thought the prince should be given "a central aim and purpose" that would shape his entire life.[28]

In July 1872, the prime minister sat down to pen a thirty-four-page letter to the Queen. "Began the formidable letter to H.M.," he wrote in his diary, "by which I am willing to live or die."[29] He proposed to send Bertie to Ireland, where he would act as the Queen's representative during the winter months. In the summer, the Waleses should return to London, where they would deputize for the Queen on occasions of court and public ceremonial.[30]

The Queen read Gladstone's paper with "a good deal of irritation." She minuted to Ponsonby: "Whoever knows the Prince of Wales' character well must know that he will always lean to a Party—and in Ireland he would be unable to withstand this and would be beset by people who would force him into one extreme or the other." As for the training business, "any preparation of this kind is quite useless; and the P. of Wales will not do it and unless you are absolutely forced to do it you never will try." Not that she blamed him for this: She confessed that she herself "never could before her accession take the slightest interest in Public affairs," but the moment she had to, she worked hard "tho she hates it all as much now as she did as a girl."[31]

Snubbing Gladstone with a three-line scrawl ("The Queen has so much to write and to do"), she instructed Ponsonby to compose a memo, coolly rejecting the proposal.[32]

Buried in Gladstone's long-winded obfuscation was an unpleasant threat. The Queen's recent illness had shown, he wrote, "that it is neither just nor possible to expect from Your Majesty what was once so freely and beneficially rendered; so that he will be very careful to guide his own future conduct by this consideration."[33] This was Gladstone's way of telling the Queen that she was no longer up to the job. By promoting the Waleses, he planned to make the Queen redundant and ease her into premature retirement—a plot he referred to euphemistically as "the kindred matter" or the "comprehensive" solution.[34] Little wonder that the Queen disliked Mr. Gladstone. True, he was a devoted monarchist, determined to save the monarchy by reforming it, and he did more than Disraeli to reinvent the crown as a visible, decorative symbol. But the principal reform he proposed was virtually to force the Queen to abdicate.

Victoria genuinely believed that Bertie was incapable of filling her place. She complained to Vicky that she was overworked and longed to retire to a cottage in the hills, "if only our dear Bertie was fit to replace me! Alas! Alas! I feel very anxious for the future."[35]

Gladstone refused to take no for an answer. Insisting that "bitter fruit will be reaped hereafter" and "retrospective judgement" passed upon him for neglecting this "golden" opportunity, he continued to bombard the Queen with lengthy memoranda.[36] What he failed to realize was that Bertie himself had no wish to go to Ireland. Gladstone demanded to see Bertie face-to-face. He was disappointed to learn that the prince had, in fact, "implored the Queen to take the matter upon herself," fearing that a direct refusal would annoy the prime minister and make him angry.[37] For once, mother and son were in agreement.

In answer to Gladstone's third lengthy five-point memo urging the Irish plan, the Queen crisply replied that she thought it "useless" to prolong the discussion.[38] When he suggested that Bertie should prepare himself for ruling by a course of reading, Victoria was not encouraging. The prince, she said, "has <u>never</u> been fond of reading and . . . from his earliest years it was <u>impossible</u> to get him to do so. Newspapers and <u>very rarely</u>, a novel are all he ever reads."[39]

When Gladstone stayed at Sandringham in November 1872, he found Alix "most kind and simple as usual," and "none of the stiffness of a court."[40] But though he had every opportunity, he "did not even mention" the subject of employment to the prince, much to Francis Knollys's annoyance, and Bertie "said nothing to him."[41]

Meanwhile, a truce developed between Windsor and Marlborough House. This was largely the work of Francis Knollys and Henry Ponsonby. Unlike former private secretaries such as Sir Charles Phipps or old Sir William Knollys, neither Ponsonby nor Francis Knollys saw his role as being to tell tales to the Queen about the prince. Rather than divide mother and son, Ponsonby endeavored to strengthen the monarchy by patching up a common front. Writing in bold black ink in a voice of ironic detachment, he smoothed over rows, gently punctured inflated egos, and outwitted the interference of meddling politicians.

Lord Granville, the foreign secretary, began to send the Prince of Wales selected dispatches from the Foreign Office. At first Granville was skeptical, complaining that when he supplied confidential information during the Franco-Prussian War, Bertie handed around his notes at a dinner party.[42] To everyone's surprise, however, Bertie really read the dispatches and took "a deal of interest."[43] Gladstone admired Bertie's love of movement and excitement, and his genuine good nature and empathy; but complained of his "total want of political judgement, either inherited or acquired."[44] Perhaps for this reason the dispatches dried up.

So the problem of how Bertie was to occupy himself was not solved, and the opportunities were lost to engage him after his illness, to cash in on his new popularity, and to build on his more serious frame of mind. Queen Victoria observed that "if this great warning is not taken, and the wonderful sympathy and devotion of the whole nation does not make a great change in him, it will be worse than before and his utter ruin."[45] After the defeat of Gladstone's plan, however, "the prince's life continued in its former rut."[46]

Heinrich von Angeli, the Austrian artist, made a portrait of Bertie and Alix with their children Eddy and Maud in 1875. Queen Victoria, who had also been painted by von Angeli, claimed that he was her favorite artist. "What I like is his honesty, total want of flattery and appreciation of character," she wrote, and his portrait of the Wales family can be read as a psychological commentary.[47] Bertie stands behind his family. The iconography of rule—a pillar behind him, his heir, Eddy, in tartan at his side—gives him authority; yet his costume is not that of a royal person but of a masterful mid-Victorian father. He wears a black coat, and his white cuffs seem to escape from his sleeves as though he has dressed rather hastily. These are clothes suitable for the Victorian public sphere, and he seems to have come in from somewhere outside the picture. Alix, seated with the six-year-old Maud on her knee, wears the sideways skittish look for which she was famous. There is no eye contact between husband and wife, and Bertie's folded arms form a barrier. The focal point of the painting is Alix's hand, which rests on her daughter's lap. The emotional bond between mother and daughter seems stronger than that between husband and wife.

Insulated from the world by her growing deafness, Alix became unknowable, and few people penetrated behind the mask. As Victoria perceived, in spite of her disability, Alix was incapable of leading a domestic life or staying quiet at home for long. Neither she nor Bertie could live without excitement. Alix never read a book, telling Victoria that "she had been promised that she should have no more lessons after she married!"[48]

The Waleses stayed at Chatsworth in December 1872. The serious-minded Lady Frederick Cavendish, who kept a diary, was not impressed by the fat prince; he was kind and amiable but only got on with "chaffy, fast people." She was captivated, however, by Alix's "perfect charm." After dinner, Alix was a sight never to be forgotten, "as she whisked around the billiard-table like any dragon-fly, playing at 'pockets'; punishing the table when she missed, and finally breaking her mace across Lady Cowper's* back with a sudden little whack. Likewise at bed-time, high-jinks with all the ladies in the corridors; and yet through all one has a sense of perfect womanly dignity, and a certainty that no one could ever go an inch too far with her."[49]

Her ladies-in-waiting would have cheerfully laid down their lives for Alix. Francis Knollys's sister, Charlotte, followed her with a doglike devotion for more than fifty years. Alix was perfectly attuned to the "feminization" of monarchy that occurred during Victoria's reign. A decorative monarchy was essentially a female one—a matter of appearance, rather than power, of philanthropy rather than foreign affairs, and here the radiant Alix could shine. Bertie, on the other hand, was marginalized and emasculated.

Bertie had no desire to play the part that his father, Albert, had played at the center of domestic family life. Styles of parenting had changed. Mid-Victorian fathers were often absent, and no longer expected to provide the moral authority within the family. Bertie's parenting conformed not to the "bourgeois" model of Albert, but to the pattern of his aristocratic contemporaries. To his children he was a benevolent figure, often absent, but affectionate. He belonged to the male spaces of the billiard room and the shooting party; he ran Sandringham as an aristocratic estate. He was no domestic tyrant. Nor is there any evidence that he beat his sons as Albert had beaten him.[50]

Over in Berlin, Vicky agonized about the education of her boys, and fought a losing battle to control the schooling of William, her eldest son.[51] She told Victoria how much she envied Bertie, who could bring up his children as he pleased.[52] But Bertie did not bother to involve himself. Like many aristocratic fathers, he delegated this role to tutors. Perhaps because his own education had failed so dismally, he was oddly indifferent to the schooling of his sons.

---

* Katrine Countess Cowper, wife of the 7th Earl.

Alix insisted that the children were brought up simply, as she had been in Denmark. They were conscious, of course, of being a race apart, but they had battered toys and rickety old dolls. Queen Victoria approved of the "absence of all pride."[53] But she also complained that Alix spoiled them terribly.[54] "They are such ill-bred, ill-trained children. I can't fancy them at all."[55] The Wales children were not brought up as Bertie had been, paraded before the nation as the "royal family," and expected to behave as little paragons. At Sandringham, they were liberated from the formality of court life. Alix encouraged boisterous practical jokes and the noisy, knockabout games beloved by her own Danish royal family. When Disraeli stayed at Sandringham, the little princesses appeared at lunch. "What do you think," he wrote, "of these young ladies, in their glittering costumes being sent on their hands and feet under the table, at which there were 30 guests, to pinch Mr. Sykes's legs? They had to count the guests on each side to secure the right man; but made the mistake of one and as Mr. Sykes was sitting next to me they began to pinch me instead. I thought it was a dog and gave a kick."[56]

Alix was especially protective of Eddy, who was a delicate child, quiet, apathetic, and a slow developer. Georgie, who was brighter, was strictly forbidden to quarrel with his brother. Bertie, however, had no patience with Eddy, and he was rumored to snub him "uncommonly"— as Ponsonby wrote, "his jealousy (or whatever it is all the family have always had) of his eldest son is showing itself already."[57] In 1871, when Eddy was seven, a tutor was engaged for him and Georgie: the Reverend John Dalton, a thirty-two-year-old curate from Whippingham, near Osborne, who had been spotted by Queen Victoria. Dalton was more concerned with imposing a strict schoolroom routine and correcting the princes' moral character than encouraging learning.[58] Like most little princes, Eddy and Georgie were shielded from competition or comparison with other children, but when Canon Duckworth, Leopold's tutor, took charge of them one holiday, he found they knew nothing: At the ages of eight and nine the boys could neither speak nor understand French, "which is a serious drawback for a Prince."[59]

It suited Dalton to blame Alexandra as a frivolous flibbertigibbet who disrupted the schoolroom routine. But the letters she wrote to Dalton show a perceptive understanding of her sons' education. Even after they were removed from their mother's influence, the princes continued to underperform. Word got out that they were stupid, especially Eddy, who was often described as half-witted. This was a myth. The chief reason the princes were so poorly educated was because Dalton, a rotten teacher but a feline intriguer, managed to insinuate himself into the confidence of the Queen and prey on the insecurity of Bertie and Alix, making everyone believe that he was indispensable and the only hope for the survival of poor dull Eddy and his brother.

In his *Christmas Annual* for 1872, Samuel Beeton published a long poem entitled "The Coming K" that lampoons the court of the Prince of Wales alias Guelpho (Guelph was the family name of the Hanoverian kings). Three copies were said to be at Sandringham.[60]

The satire shows how the Prince of Wales's debauched court is the very mirror image of Arthurian chivalry. At Guelpho's court, the modern knight is described thus:

Marriage he must eschew; but still maintain
Expensive villas in the Fulham Road . . .
Smoke like a furnace; gamble, if needs be;
Know all the dyed-haired, painted queans who leer
Upon the stage or from the window-pane;
. . . Moreover, he must make inane remarks;
Be bored at everything; affect a lisp;
Profess he's steeped with silly cynicism;
And ever try to hide what brain he has.
And never once pronounce the letter "R."[61]

Alix doesn't feature in the poem, and there is no queen at Guelpho's court. This is a man's world, and Guelpho's women friends are courtesans, such as Gettarre, a loud-voiced whore with a painted face who drives her ponies in the park. This was Catherine Walters, also known as Skittles, a quick-witted Liverpudlian horsebreaker, who Bertie first met in the early 1860s when she caused a sensation riding in a skintight habit on Rotten Row as the *poule de luxe* of Lord Hartington, the Devonshire heir. She made the prince laugh with her sharp repartee. There's a smutty story, which Bertie never tired of telling, about her umbrella (many of Bertie's risqué jokes involved umbrellas). It happened to be shabby. Prince of Wales: "It wants re-covering." Skittles: "I have had it covered twice, but there has been no produce."*[62]

Hartington threw Skittles over (he left her for Louise Manchester), and Skittles retreated to Paris. After the Commune, she returned to London and, bankrolled by the genial Hartington, who gave her a generous allowance for life, set up house on South Street in Mayfair. A blue plaque commemorates the home of "the last Victorian courtesan" at number 15.† It was in the early seventies, probably in 1872, but Skittles was always vague about dates, that she recalled encountering Bertie, who said: " 'You always promised we should be friends some day.' And so it began."[63] Exactly what "it" consisted of can never be fully established. Skittles claimed that she possessed a drawer full of letters from Bertie, which were in her house at the time of his death, but these have long since vanished.[64]

Perhaps the real story about Bertie's relationship with Skittles can be glimpsed from the marble statuette he kept in his library at Marlborough House. "On a kind of shrine at the angle of a bookcase" there stood a half-sized classical nude posed as the Venus de Milo, with her arms flung back behind her head. Bertie had commissioned this nude from Boehm; it is a superb piece of English erotic sculpture, unrivaled for its date. He showed the statuette to the aesthete Lord Ronald Gower in 1878. "And who do you think sat for this figure?" he asked.

---

* On a visit to Coventry in 1874, Bertie told his equerry to arrange for a bowling alley to be included in the itinerary. When the bemused Hartington made no attempt to conceal his boredom, the mayor uttered the line in which he had been coached: "HRH especially asked for its inclusion in tribute to your lordship's love of Skittles."

† Florence Nightingale, a chronic invalid, lived opposite at number 35, also commemorated with a blue plaque. Both women did much of their work in bed.

"Of course I could not guess," wrote Gower in his diary. "'Skittles,' said HRH with delight."[65] A courtesan such as Skittles, who understood the rules and knew the boundaries, posed no threat to Alix. On the contrary, Alix was happy to ask her to find suitable horses for her to ride.[66]

Bertie was beginning to be gossiped about again. The future Liberal prime minister Lord Rosebery was asked by Knollys to lend his London house as a place for Bertie and Affie to meet their "actress friends" in 1873. Rosebery refused.*[67] Different from actresses were married women, such as the Canadian Mrs. Sloane-Stanley. Would Lord Granville be so good as to ask her to his ball? asked Francis Knollys; the prince would like it very much. To which the cynical Granville replied: "I am much obliged for your hint and shall be still more obliged if you will not tell the Prince of Wales you have given it to me."[68] When Captain Haig, an equerry, innocently asked Mrs. Sloane-Stanley to go in with him to supper at a ball, Bertie rushed after her and tried to stop her; Mrs. Stanley at length went off for supper with the captain, and Bertie called out after her, "I hope you will like your new man."[69]

More lasting was Bertie's relationship with the nineteen-year-old Mary (Patsy) Cornwallis-West. The daughter of Lady Olivia Fitzpatrick, who had (allegedly) been expelled from court for flirting with Prince Albert, Patsy married at sixteen and had produced three children by the time she was twenty-one. "The loveliest woman I have ever set eyes on," according to Lord Rossmore (who had a conflict of interest, being one of her lovers), Patsy was known as the Irish Savage, combining professional beauty with startling feistiness.[70] Her son, George Cornwallis-West (born 14 November 1874), was widely believed to have been fathered by Bertie; indeed, his alleged royal descent shaped his life. It is possible that Patsy and Bertie had a love affair, and the story gives an indication of the dates, but there are no known letters, and at the time of the conception, which must have been around

---

* On a visit to Vienna with Bertie, Knollys slept with "about as low a woman" as he could find, before learning that all the ladies of the town were poxed. He confessed to being "in a horrible fright." (Rosebery's diary, April 1873, in Hibbert, *Edward VII*, p. 305.)

mid-February 1874, Bertie was safely out of the country in Russia. It is a biological impossibility that George Cornwallis-West was his son.

Alix's sister Minnie and her husband the czarevitch visited London in the summer of 1873. Alix pretended that the "unbearable dress non-sense" was "boring me beyond description," but she and Minnie had planned their wardrobe meticulously beforehand. "I will order the 9 dresses you want," Alix told her sister, "but I think that it will be better to wait with the décolleté toilettes until you come they sew so quickly and some dresses at least we must have exactly alike."[71] These identical frocks led the fashion for double dressing: Minnie and Alix wore the same costumes on at least thirteen occasions that summer—a caprice that may have been meant to signal the closeness of relations between the Russian and English royal families.[72] One of their outfits was a dress of plain white tulle, decorated with gold, loaded with diamonds, and incongruously crowned with wreaths of straw and ivy. In spite of her unconventional dresses, Alix's "marvellous feminine tact" and "wondrous talent at conciliating adverse tempers and binding family affection" meant (according to one columnist) that having been first seen as a "mere adjunct to the Royal Family," she had grown to be the "gentle guide and ruler of them all."[73]

The letters that Alix wrote to her sister, dashed off in her indecipherable loopy handwriting that has been likened to crochet work or loose knitting, and written in Danish, were impenetrable to anyone but Minnie. "We must be twins," she wrote, "only you forgot to come to the world until three years after me!"[74] Each parting brought dreadful weeping—days and days of it—so much so that Queen Victoria urged Alix to pull herself together—"I had to think of her who had lost all her relations and her husband!!!"[75] Alix understood very well that the close bonds between the sisters made them stronger as a force in dynastic politics. "We all of us know each other too well and are too intimate to let others come between us with intrigues."[76] Clinging to Minnie was perhaps a sign of Alix's emotional neediness. She still shared a bed with Bertie—she thought at one point that she was pregnant again—but even she could no longer pretend to herself that "my angelic Bertie" was always faithful.[77]

Bertie and Alix traveled to Russia in January 1874 for the grand state wedding of Bertie's brother Affie to Marie, the only daughter of the czar, Alexander II. Bertie was disappointed because Victoria would not allow him to accept the colonelcy of the Russian regiment that he had been offered by the czar. "He had set his heart upon it," wrote Knollys.[78] The new Russian uniform, which had already been stitched by Poole the tailor, was never worn.

After the Russian celebrations, Affie and Marie arrived at Windsor. Victoria held a grand dinner in St. George's Hall, the first since Bertie's wedding, and when she walked around the ladies after dinner, she asked Alix to whisper the names in her ear; the Queen knew no one because she never went out.

When Marie and Affie and the royal family stood on the balcony at Buckingham Palace to show themselves to the people, none of the dust sheets had been taken off the furniture. "My Bertie was so angry, but that did not help of course," wrote Alix, so she herself set to tearing off the covers and arranging the sitting room—"my gloves . . . were as black as coal at the reception!" At the drawing room afterward, Marie, in spite of being a Romanov and the daughter of an emperor, was given a rank below all of Victoria's daughters, even the unmarried Beatrice—a snub that did lasting damage to her relations with her new family.[79] In spite of her grandeur, Marie, like all the Romanovs, was startlingly earthy. At the christening of her first child, she breast-fed the baby, regardless of Queen Victoria finding it "indecent and dégoûtent [disgusting]!!!" When the child puked over her fine dress, Marie was quite unembarrassed: "She stood up and the Empress [of Russia] took the little one and Marie ran about with her big breast hanging down in front of everyone and wiped the dress clean!!!"[80]

At Marlborough House that summer, the Fancy Dress Ball (22 July 1874) was the grandest royal ball for decades. The décor and costumes were designed by Sir Frederic Leighton. Bertie led the Van Dyck quadrille dressed, somewhat incongruously, as the slender, chaste King Charles I and wearing a large wig of yellow curls.

Bertie was widely reported to have debts of £600,000.[81] Francis Knollys, who was on good terms with Delane, the editor of *The Times*, inspired an editorial in the newspaper that authoritatively contradicted the story and explained the "true" state of his finances. If the prince occasionally spent more than his income, said the article, there were very good reasons. His income of £100,000 was less than that of many peers; and yet he was expected to perform the Queen's work, entertaining foreign royalties, representing the Queen abroad, and leading London society.[82]

The *Times* article enraged Victoria. She denounced the claim that Bertie did her work as an "abominable falsehood."[83] Relations with Marlborough House became frayed once again. Ponsonby wrote to Knollys complaining at the article "firing a broadside at us."[84]

In October 1874, Bertie visited France for the first time since the war with Prussia and the formation of the Third Republic. Victoria deplored the trip. Bertie had accepted an invitation to stay with the Duc de La Rochefoucauld-Bisaccia, who had just been sacked as French ambassador in London for demanding the restoration of the monarchy, and the visit was seen as a signal of English support.

Victoria appealed to the new prime minister, Disraeli, whom she found infinitely more sympathetic than Gladstone, and Disraeli wrote Bertie a flowery letter of discouragement ("whether a visit to France at all is, at this moment, desirable; [is a question] on which I will not presume to offer an opinion. . . . No living man is more competent to form a correct judgement . . . than Your Royal Highness"), and suggested that the prince call upon the president in order to demonstrate his support for the Republic.[85] This Bertie agreed to do—in future years he always made a point of calling on the president whenever he visited Paris—and he assured Disraeli that he intended to travel incognito as the Earl of Chester.[86]

The *Times* printed an editorial, inspired again by Francis Knollys, that denied that the visit had any political significance; but the real worry was less about the politics of Bertie's trip than the fact that he proposed to visit France alone, leaving Alix with her family in Denmark.[87] Old Sir William Knollys warned that Paris was "the most dangerous place in Europe, and it would be well if it were never revisited. In fact remaining on the Continent whenever it involves a separation of the Prince and Princess—whether Her Royal Highness is in Denmark or elsewhere"—was "most undesirable" and should be as brief as possible in the interests of both.[88] Alix herself was blissfully, some might say naïvely, unaware of the dangers. "Deaf as a post," she refused to listen to what she didn't want to hear.[89] Each morning at her parents' house in Denmark she rose at seven to write to "my angelic little husband." In place of Bertie, she shared her bed with her youngest sister, the twenty-one-year-old Princess Thyra.[90]

Bertie stayed first with the Duc de La Rochefoucauld-Bisaccia at Esclimont, his Renaissance chateau on the Loire. Assembled at Esclimont was a party of grandees—indeed this was the very world that Proust romanticized and fictionalized.[91] Bertie himself was a character in Proust's work, haunting *In Search of Lost Time* as the epitome of grandeur and sophistication.

To entertain the Prince de Galles, La Rochefoucauld arranged an English *chasse*. The French reporters, who were bemused by this Anglo Saxon activity, noted that 500 shots were fired, and 400 missed; the prince, however, "fires with rare precision; at least 80 of his shots were well aimed."[92] Fortunately, the duke had taken precautions, having placed an order for five hundred pheasants with the London poulterer Mr. Bayly—presumably the birds were already safely dead, ensuring a respectable bag in spite of the wildly inaccurate marksmanship of the blue-blooded French dukes.[93]

Among the guests at Esclimont were Monsieur and Madame Standish. Henry Standish, in spite of his English name, was a grandson of the Duc de Mouchy. As for his wife, Hélène, wrote Proust, "It would take a whole lecture to explain to certain foolish young men why Madame Standish is at least as great a lady as Duchesse de Doudeauville."[94] She had made a sensation in London the year before and was said to have captivated Bertie; Robert Lytton, the Paris attaché, was surprised to find her "instead of fast and flippant very quiet, well bred and womanly."[95] In Paris, the prying police followed Bertie wherever he went, and tracked him to the house of Madame Standish, where he spent many hours.[96] The liaison between "Missis," as the Parisians called her, and the Prince of Wales was soon common knowledge. Proust noted that Madame Standish dressed with tailor-made austerity, and wore gowns that "moulded her figure with a precision that was positively British."[97] In fact, she dressed like Alix, with a wasp waist, curled false fringe, and high dog collar—this was her way of advertising the fact that she was a mistress of the prince.

Next came a visit to Chantilly, where Bertie hunted stags with the Duc d'Aumale. Among the ladies who followed the hounds on horseback was the Princesse de Sagan.[98] The daughter of a rich banker, with a nose too large to be beautiful, the princess was estranged from her much older husband, Boson de Talleyrand-Périgord, Prince de Sagan, a frightening, monocled dandy, who was also the original of a character in Proust. She soon became one of Bertie's regular Paris dates. Bertie later visited de Sagan's lavishly luxurious Château de Mello. Robert Lytton, who accompanied him, thought Mello "furnished with a mixture of splendour and comfort I have never seen equalled in any English country-house." Madame Standish was among the guests. A band played throughout dinner "the most animating not to say amative strains," making the company (thought Lytton) "so 'jolly' that I really know not what might have happened in the course of the evening" had Bertie not been obliged to return to Paris at midnight by special train.[99] It was allegedly on this visit that the princess's fifteen-year-old son, looking into his mother's boudoir and spotting Bertie's clothes, was seized by a fit of rage and threw the clothes into the water fountains. For this, he was apparently banished to a monastic reformatory.*[100]

---

* The second son of the Princesse de Sagan, who was born in Paris on 20 July 1867, was alleged to be Bertie's bastard, but Bertie's relationship with the princess seems to have begun sometime after the child was born. In late October/early November 1866, he was not in France. He left England for St. Petersburg on 1 November 1866, traveling via Brussels and Potsdam, where he stayed with Vicky. (Leslie, *Edwardians in Love,* pp.70–72; Camp, *Royal Mistresses,* pp. 350–51.)

Bertie's next project was truly ambitious: a visit to India. In March 1875 he asked the Queen for her permission, and to his and everyone else's surprise, she agreed. An editorial appeared at once in *The Times,* proclaiming the prince's forthcoming visit as a great historical pageant that would visibly link East and West.[101]

Victoria instantly regretted giving her consent. She claimed that Bertie had tricked her into agreeing by telling her that the trip had been approved by Disraeli and the Cabinet when, according to Disraeli, the prince had merely mentioned it casually "at table after dinner."[102] Disraeli blamed Bertie for taking his name in vain; but Disraeli was more economical than most with the truth, and Bertie grumbled that he was "beginning to think him a humbug."[103] He far preferred dealing with Gladstone.

Victoria protested that Bertie's health would not stand the trip. Not only did she worry that he would get into some scrape, but, Ponsonby suspected, she was envious of the prestige he would gain if the visit succeeded.[104] Soon open war broke out between mother and son, and Disraeli found himself in the middle of it. Victoria objected to some of the people Bertie proposed to take with him, especially her bête noire Carrington and the rollicking naval officer Lord Charles Beresford, who she complained was half-cracked and addicted to practical jokes. She appealed to Disraeli to intervene, and wrote a furious letter for him to read to the Cabinet that made ministers snigger; it was written, said foreign secretary Derby, "with so much violence and so little dignity that to hear it read with gravity was impossible."[105] Bertie stormed off to Downing Street and demanded an interview with Disraeli, at which he "manifested extraordinary excitement."[106] He was thirty-three, objected the prince, and the Queen had no right to exercise a sort of guardianship over him.[107] Disraeli counseled the Queen to drop the matter and, on Ponsonby's advice, she agreed.[108]

Urged on by "the toadies who hang about him," such as the Duke of Sutherland and Carrington, Bertie's Indian plans became increasingly ambitious.[109] As the tour built momentum in the press, he gained popularity by attacking the parsimony of the Cabinet.*[110]

To Alix's fury, Bertie refused to take her with him to India. She had dreamed of repeating the success of her Egyptian tour, and being left behind rankled for the rest of her life. She appealed to the Queen, who forbade her to go, and then she approached Disraeli. "You believe in sympathy," she told him. "*I want to go.* I trust to you to manage it for me!"[111] Even this was unavailing, which, thought Lord Derby, was just as well, as "whether she goes or not, the prince is sure to run after women, and the scandal will be less if he does so in his wife's absence than if she were there." Derby picked up gossip that Bertie had skipped off to Menton on the Mediterranean for Easter with the notorious Mrs. Murrieta, the wife of a wealthy Spanish merchant. "The thing is so openly done that it cannot fail to make a scandal," he wrote hopefully.[112] Alix, however, was unaware, and believed that Bertie had fled to Menton for the sun, which relieved the pain in his leg.[113]

Shortly before Bertie was due to depart, Victoria wrote forbidding Alix from traveling to Copenhagen with the children for Christmas while he was away. Bertie, who was finding the parting from Alix trying enough as it was, appealed in desperation to Disraeli. "I have not had the heart to tell [Alix]," he wrote, "as I know it would pain her, and I am naturally anxious that the few days left for me to be with her should be happy ones."[114]

Disraeli obliged with a letter to the Queen, pointing out that forcing the princess to "live in seclusion" for six months while Bertie was away seemed somewhat "harsh."[115] Victoria relented, and Disraeli was rewarded with an invitation to Sandringham. Royalty to Disraeli was irresistible. Now he was flattered to be admitted to the confidence of Prince Hal, as he called Bertie. Bertie talked alone with him at midnight for over an hour, and at one a.m. "tried to seduce me to the bowling room and its attendant fumes, but I was firm and retired, and he went to begin his day." Disraeli sat next to Alix at dinner. Conversation,

---

* Bertie demanded £100,000 from the government, and eventually the Cabinet agreed to ask Parliament for £60,000.

never easy with the deaf princess, was made harder by her misery at the impending separation, and (wrote Disraeli) "while with strained attention I devoured her words instead of my dinner, there was always an entrée or a sauce interposed or offered at the critical moment." She began by saying: "When you were here two years ago, you said you would write a book for me about sympathy—now I want sympathy indeed." That, wrote Disraeli, "was not a bad beginning—but . . . she is no fool."[116]

Bertie's parting from Alix on 12 October 1875 was drawn out and emotional. Alix broke down repeatedly; Princess Helena told the Queen, "She looks so worn and tired and pale and so sad. Really it makes one's heart ache to see them both."[117] Alix accompanied Bertie on the steamer to Calais, and the final farewell was a passionate embrace on deck. Both of them were weeping, and (Alix told Minnie) "had to tear ourselves away from each other, and I saw him disappear over the dark landing bridge, and there on the ship stood poor Alexandra alone, so totally alone, with her bursting heart."[118]

Alix wired the Queen from Sandringham two days later: "Everything seems sad and dreary without him."[119] Her devotion to her Bertie, in spite or perhaps because of his philandering, was more intense than ever.

CHAPTER 11

India

1875–76

The tearful parting left Bertie feeling low.[1] To Alix he wrote "the most beautiful, loving letters you can imagine, so like himself."[2] He told Lord Granville that he felt so depressed that he contemplated turning back.[3] He looked terrible, too. Alexander Bassano, the society photographer who had snapped him as a jaunty man-about-town before his illness, took a photograph that summer that, in spite of studio airbrushing, shows him looking puffy, overweight, and middle-aged: As Victoria wrote, "He is grown so large, and nearly quite bald."[4]

From Paris he traveled overland to Brindisi, where he boarded the HMS *Serapis*. Here he was united with his suite. The eighteen men he had picked to accompany him included the inner circle of the Marlborough House set: His friends "Sporting Joe" Aylesford and Charles Carrington came as personal guests, Lord Suffield and Owen Williams were equerries, and Lord Charles Beresford was an aide-de-camp. The leader was silver-haired Bartle Frere, an old India hand, who was charged by the Queen with speaking plainly to the prince. A "dear old *patapouf*" (according to Ponsonby), Frere probably lacked the authority to influence the prince. The Queen sent Lord Alfred Paget as her representative, much to Bertie's annoyance.[5] A member of the family which had monopolized so many posts at Victoria's early court that it was known as the "Paget clubhouse," the fifty-nine-year-old Lord Alfred made himself unpopular by bagging the best cabin and by constant grumbling.[6] W. H. Russell of *The Times* was appointed historian and given exclusive reporting rights, provoking complaints from the rest of the press. To keep his rivals happy, it was agreed that Russell should report nothing until they reached Bombay.*[7]

There were no women on board the *Serapis*. This was perhaps the only time in his adult life that Bertie was surrounded entirely by men. It was also his first experience of political responsibility and a real job that he had worked hard to get. The Indian trip, which had begun as a bachelor spree, had turned into a royal progress, but the men he picked to accompany him were not qualified for the work. Cronies, drinking companions, and practical jokers, they had left behind in England a trail of adultery and scrapes. One of the functions of a court is to promote talent, but Bertie had filled his court with wastrels and socialites, uneducated philistines who could no more rule an empire than write a book.

On board the *Serapis*, Bertie and his floating court of men lived in spartan luxury. The extreme heat and early hours agreed with him; he played energetic lawn tennis on deck and he looked "wonderfully well in the face."[8] He was provided with duplicate sets of private apartments, one running each side of the vessel, so that he could use whichever was least sunny. His plain metal bedstead was not fixed to the floor but suspended from brass uprights, so that it swung freely to neutralize the rolling of the ship.[9] In HRH's drawing room, which was

---

* Russell had accompanied the prince on his visit to the Middle East, and he published the story of HRH's journey to Egypt and the Crimea in 1869. Sidney Hall was the official artist. As well as Francis Knollys and the equerries Dighton Probyn and Arthur Ellis, the suite included Prince Louis of Battenberg as aide-de-camp and Canon Duckworth as chaplain. Russell's reports to *The Times* were published in 1877 as *The Prince of Wales's Tour*, with engravings by Sidney Hall.

furnished like a gentleman's club, with heavy leather-upholstered mahogany furniture bolted to the floor, the party was unusually subdued. As Carrington wrote, "We are more like a lot of monks than anything else—no jokes or any approach to it." Aylesford and Beresford were quietness itself: no rows, no whist, no bear fights.*[10]

Bertie had been shocked to discover that the Indian Civil Service (ICS) had no official uniform to wear in order to receive him, and he was disappointed when his proposal for a brass-buttoned blue coat was rejected. On board the *Serapis,* however, he devised his very own dress uniform of black trousers, short blue jacket with silk facings and gilt buttons, and black tie.[11] Sweating in their uniforms in temperatures of well over 100 degrees, the all-male suite dined each night at seven thirty prompt, serenaded by a band that played throughout the meal as they chaffed the rubicund Lord Alfred Paget, known as Beetroot, who declared he never ate at sea and then devoured more than anyone else. After dinner, Bertie would rise and propose a toast to Her Majesty the Queen, and all stood while the band played the national anthem.[12]

Security in India was tight. One of the suite sat up all night outside the prince's door, while another slept in his room.[13] Lord Suffield, who acted as chief of the household, went everywhere with Bertie, ready to leap in front of him should an attack be made on his life.[14] More effective perhaps was Colonel Edward Bradford, the stern head of the Indian secret police, who had lost an arm after being mauled by a tiger.†Victoria worried about her son's health and bombarded him with anxious letters and telegrams warning him not to do too much.[15] To please his mother, Bertie wore a white pith helmet.

The *Serapis* reached Bombay on 8 November 1875. The Prince of Wales drove through six miles of streets lined with silent crowds. Lord

* Or so they said. A report reached the London press of two members of the suite playing a practical joke on W. H. Russell and emptying everything out of his cabin. Russell demanded an apology, and Bertie forced them to comply; the captain was furious and threatened to drop them at the nearest port. (*Reynolds's Newspaper,* 26 December 1875.)
† Bradford served as chief commissioner of the Metropolitan Police, 1890–1903.

Northbrook, the viceroy, hastened to assure the Queen that cheering was not the Indian way.[16] The following day, his birthday, Bertie held his first royal audience. One by one the chiefs and princes were taken firmly by the hand and led, as if in custody, to meet the Prince of Wales, who advanced from his silver chair to an appointed spot on the carpet, took each Indian's hand, and conducted him back to the chair. Bertie wore a field marshal's uniform, which contrasted with the bejeweled magnificence of the turbaned rajas, and played his part to perfection, listening to the princes, looking them in the eye, and treating them as royal equals.[17] Instinctively he grasped the essence of the Raj; he himself was the embodiment of the alliance between the Queen and the native princes that had been forged after the Mutiny of 1857. As W. H. Russell wrote in *The Times,* Bertie had grown with the greatness of the occasion and elevated a royal visit into a historic event.[18] This was royalty as theater, and he excelled in his role. His passion for uniforms and dressing up coupled with his addiction to the London stage meant that he knew his lines perfectly and understood instinctively how the role of prince-emperor should be played.

At Baroda, Bertie paid a state visit to the thirteen-year-old ruler, known as the Gaekwar. The boy Gaekwar had recently been adopted heir to Baroda, and the prince's visit helped legitimize a new regime.[19] Russell's account in *The Times* reads like an Eastern fable:

> There was an elephant of extraordinary size, on which there was a howdah which shone like burnished gold. . . . It was covered with a golden canopy, and it was shining in the morning sun with surpassing splendour. This exquisitely burnished carriage was placed on cushions covered with cloth of gold and velvet, which were fastened upon the embroidered tissue which almost concealed the outline of the beast which stood swaying his painted proboscis to and fro as if he kept time to the music of the bands outside. . . .
>
> The golden ladder was placed against the howdah step, the Guikwar [*sic*] stepped up, helped carefully, and the Prince followed and sat by his side. . . . Then as the elephant made its first

stride on-wards, the clamour of voices and of sound deepened
and grew and spread.[20]

Queen Victoria (according to the Indian secretary Lord Salisbury)
had visions of Bertie escalading "zenanas [harems] on ladders of
ropes," and to avoid scandal Salisbury arranged for the party to be kept
constantly on the move.[21] Bertie was indefatigable. Carrington thought
the viceroy's staff asked far too much of him, especially as he was
more than willing to oblige.[22] His reward was an elephant shoot in
Ceylon.

The elephant shoot was organized like a military campaign. Fifteen
hundred men labored for two weeks in the Ceylonese jungle to prepare a stockade and nets for the royal party. Wearing his solar topee
and special gaiters to protect his legs from bloodsucking leeches, Bertie set off in torrential rain at six a.m. for his high stand, where he
waited for five hours without firing a shot. Eventually the beaters lit a
forest fire, and the terrified elephants came crashing out of the jungle.
Bertie wounded one and shot another, which fell as if it were dead, but
when his artist Sidney Hall tried to sketch it, the beast struggled to its
feet and lumbered off. Crawling through the jungle, streaming with
sweat and tearing his clothes, Bertie eventually crept close enough to
kill an elephant, which toppled over and dammed a stream. Surrounded by a cheering crowd of natives, he jumped on top of the
mountain of inert flesh and cut off the tail, as was the custom. Sidney
Hall sketched the primitive scene, as the elephant's blood oozed into
the swamp.[23]

The image of the prince standing victorious on the dead beast
seemed to radicals and republicans back home morally repulsive; it
epitomized in a disgusting way the rule of the white conqueror over
the subject Indians. Shooting an elephant was an affirmation of man's
dominance over the animal kingdom, which to radicals was as offensive as the British subjugation of the Indian peasant.[24] Elephant hunting, however, was part of the feudal, traditional India, and it legitimized
the prince's status as greatest prince of all. Shooting an elephant was a

public act, a performance where the prince was the principal actor: He must be seen to kill the great beast.*

From Ceylon, Bertie steamed in the *Serapis* north to Calcutta, where he began a ceremonial progress to Delhi. Sport was an essential part of the program. Radicals back home dubbed him the pigsticking prince, and complained that he was wasting public money making brutal war against animals.[25] "It were best had the Prince of Wales stopped at home," wrote *Reynolds's Newspaper*.[26] Pigsticking, which involved galloping after ferocious wild boar with a spear, Bertie, in fact, declined, perhaps sensibly, as four members of his suite were injured.† Tiger shooting, however, was mandatory. Staying with the Maharaja of Jaipur, Bertie shot his first tiger—a pregnant female with three cubs. It took four shots to kill her.

The Queen confessed herself bored with Bertie's progresses, which she dismissed as a wearying repetition of "elephants—trappings—jewels—illuminations and fireworks," but Bertie was in his element.[27] As Bartle Frere told Victoria, he outworked everyone on his staff, and "showed less susceptibility to heat and exposure to the sun than any of us."[28] He could remember every name, every firework display and every banquet; as Russell put it, his memory "holds every fact in a vice."[29] He knew more chiefs than all the viceroys and governors put together. His ability to connect with the rulers of the princely states helped to legitimize the Raj as a neo-feudal alliance between the Indian princes and the English Queen. Indian Civil Service officer Sir

---

* Sixty years later, George Orwell wrote an essay about shooting an elephant that was on the rampage in Burma. Orwell had all sorts of doubts about killing the beast, but when he stood in front of an expectant crowd of natives, he realized that he had no choice but to shoot. This to him exposed the hollowness of imperial dominion in the East: The white man with his gun, seemingly the lead actor in the piece, was, in reality, "an absurd puppet pushed to and fro by the will of those yellow faces behind." (George Orwell, "Shooting an Elephant" [1936], in *Inside the Whale* [Penguin, 1962], p. 95.)

† Prince Louis of Battenberg broke a collarbone and so did Carrington; Lord Charles Beresford broke his teeth, and Lord Suffield was injured by his own spear.

Henry Daly commented, "The effect of the Prince on the Chiefs is miraculous. There is a sentiment in their feudalism which has been touched. . . . His manner and air to them is perfect."[30]

At Benares, Sir John Strachey, governor of the North-West Provinces, received Bertie in a camp that resembled a dream city in canvas, luxuriously fitted out with double-lined tents furnished with fireplaces.[31] Bertie and his suite drank almost eighty dozen bottles of Strachey's champagne in a fortnight and fourteen dozen bottles of soda a day.[32] After visiting Delhi, Bertie was entertained again by Strachey at Agra. Watched by a crowd of seven thousand people, and serenaded by a band playing music from *Don Giovanni,* he paid a visit by moonlight to the Taj Mahal, which had been recently restored by the energetic Strachey. As Bertie left, he observed a European official, wearing a white hat and morning dress, rudely push an Indian raja to clear the way. He at once dispatched Knollys to express his displeasure, and when the European failed to get the point, sent the Duke of Sutherland, who made it still more forcefully.[33]

Reported in the English press, the incident dramatized Bertie's disapproval of the bullying racism of the British rulers. "Because a man has a black face and a different religion from our own, there is no reason why he should be treated as a brute," he told Lord Granville.[34] To Salisbury he grumbled about British officers speaking of Indians, "many of them sprung from the great races," as "niggers."[35] When he complained to Queen Victoria about the brutality and contempt with which English political officers treated the native chiefs, she entirely agreed with him. "I believe it is dreadful how they treat these poor creatures," she wrote, and forwarded his letter to Salisbury.[36] Mr. Saunders, the resident in Hyderabad, was dismissed in consequence.[37]

Among the Stracheys' party at Agra was the nineteen-year-old Mabel Batten. She had auburn hair and a mezzo-soprano voice, and she was used to being admired. Her father was the judge advocate general of North-West India, George Hatch. A few months before, she had married George Batten, a forty-three-year-old Indian officer, who was the brother of Lady Strachey.

Lady Strachey was not impressed by Bertie. "The Prince's tastes are low and childish," she wrote. "He has a perfect mania on the subject of dress . . . fresh orders come nearly every hour about what the suite are to wear and if a button is wrong it is noticed at once and remarked upon. His other tastes are for eating and drinking. He is at times thoroughly selfish and inconsiderate. . . . As for his moral character, it is as bad as possible and the respectable part of his suite are always in agony lest he misbehave."[38]

On closer acquaintance, Lady Strachey changed her mind. "He is so goodnatured and polite and likeable that one can't help liking him," she wrote.[39] She could hardly have guessed that the person with whom Bertie would misbehave would be her own sister-in-law. In the camp at Agra, Bertie saw a great deal of Mabel Batten. He arranged to meet her a few weeks later, when he reached Allahabad, but Mabel did not appear. Bertie wrote her a letter, enclosing photographs that had been taken at Agra: "I was very much disappointed not to meet you last Tuesday [7 March] as I had hoped, 'mais l'homme propose et la femme dispose.'" He ended: "Hoping that you may soon come to England and will let me know of your arrival."[40]

What happened at Agra can never be known, but it was probably no more than a flirtation. Bertie remained loyal to Mabel, however. Two decades later, when she returned to England, she resumed contact. Illegible letters from "AE," written on tiny cards and stuffed into even smaller envelopes, proposing himself for a cup of tea at five o'clock or a chat between twelve and one, began to plop fatly through the letter box of her Chelsea home.[41]

Back in London, on 8 February 1876, in bleak, wintry sleet and snow, a truculent Alix sat with the Queen in the semi-state carriage as they processed in slow time from Buckingham Palace to Westminster for the state opening of Parliament. Alix had been furious when Victoria insisted that she should cut short her visit to her family to attend the ceremony, provoking the "biggest and the best" of the rows over the princess's trips to Denmark.[42] "Her not returning and being with me on these occasions when you were absent," the Queen told Bertie, "would have been misunderstood and have done her harm."[43] The coach windows were closed, but the crowd outside hissed until they reached Westminster, where the schoolboys raised a loud cheer.[44] The House of Lords was packed with scarlet-robed peers sitting in deep gloom, until promptly at two p.m. the gaslights flared, a low hum of voices broke out, and the whole house rose as the Queen entered. She took her place on the throne with Alix sitting opposite on the woolsack, and her speech was read by the Lord Chamberlain.[45]

This was only the fourth time the Queen had opened Parliament in person since Albert's death fourteen years before. She stubbornly refused to go through with this part of her duty unless she wanted something out of her ministers. Usually it was money for her children: She attended in 1866 in order to persuade Parliament to grant annuities for Alfred's coming of age and Helena's marriage, and her appearance in 1871 was prompted by the need for a dowry for Louise and an annuity for the twenty-one-year-old Arthur.*[46] Now she needed Parliament's support for something different: the Royal Titles Bill, creating her new title of Empress of India.

Victoria had persuaded Disraeli to capitalize on the goodwill sparked by Bertie's visit and rebrand her Queen Empress as she had long wished to do. On 18 February she told Bertie: "The title of Empress of India is now to be really and legally adopted, which I am sure you will be pleased with."[47] She was annoyed by the Liberals' opposition to the bill. "Considering that I was always called [Empress] in India and by many people here, it seems very extraordinary that they should have got up a cry as though I was going to change my <u>English name</u>."[48]

Bertie had not been consulted, and the English mail took a month to reach him, but when he heard about the Royal Titles Bill, he was furious. He wrote a stinging letter to Disraeli, complaining that he had only learned of the Queen's plan from the newspapers, having received

---

* In 1867 she had opened Parliament as a gesture of support for the Conservative government. She favored Disraeli by opening Parliament three times during his second ministry, in 1876, 1877, and 1880.

no intimation from the prime minister.[49] He was right to object that he hadn't been formally consulted, and he worried that his own title was to be changed to a foreign-sounding "Imperial Highness."

"I must frankly tell you," he informed Disraeli, "that I could never consent to the word 'Imperial' being added to my name."*[50] The open criticism of the bill in Parliament was bound to damage British authority in India, he thought, and if the news leaked out that he opposed the change of title, it would "through increasing his popularity, damage that of the Queen."[51] Disraeli had indeed handled the bill badly by failing to bargain for opposition support beforehand, and Bertie had good reason to feel ill-used by the Queen. Victoria had strenuously opposed his plan to travel to India, but when the trip succeeded, she executed a spectacular U-turn and, without consulting him, stole his glory by upstaging him with this coup de théâtre. The Queen, who took a close interest in India, which she saw as her special fief, had no intention of leaving all the kudos to her son.

By now, Bertie and his party had reached the foothills of the Himalayas. The uniforms, the gold lace, and the cocked hats were packed away, and Bertie enjoyed an orgy of sport, organized by the cheroot-smoking Sir Henry Ramsay, the King of Kumaon. Never had tiger shooting been more luxurious. Bertie's camp consisted of 2,500 men, 119 elephants, and 500 camels. Lunch was cooked by French chefs, brought out on elephants, and served by German waiters. In the evenings, as they sat around campfires burning logs as big as tree trunks, Gurkha military bands played Mozart and Offenbach. The prince notched up a total of twenty-eight tigers. His sporting exploits were reported not only by Russell in *The Times* but also by Mr. Simpson of *The Illustrated London News* and Mr. Johnson of *The Graphic*, who shared an elephant, lurching and bumping along behind the shooters.[52]

---

* In fact, he succeeded his mother as Emperor of India. But unlike Victoria, who now began to sign herself "VR&I" (*Victoria Regina et Imperatrix*), Bertie as king usually used the two initials "ER."

The Queen was not amused. "I am compelled to mention to you that there is a very strong feeling amongst <u>all</u> classes. . . . The minute description of the unavoidable <u>sport</u> in India has not made a good impression."[53] *Reynolds's* deplored the "sickening and disgusting, nay, barbarous and sanguinary account of the special correspondents."[54]

Bertie's diary for 20 February 1876 contains the cryptic entry: "Letters!!!"[55] Next day, he went out and shot six tigers—and, he told the nine-year-old Georgie, "some were very savage—two were 'man eaters.'"[56]

CHAPTER 12

The Aylesford Scandal

1876

One of the letters that reached the prince's camp in Nepal on 20 February 1876 was from Edith Aylesford to her husband Sporting Joe, Earl of Aylesford, Bertie's friend who had accompanied him to India. She announced that she had been unfaithful with Lord Blandford. Would Joe prefer her to leave home at once, she asked, or should she wait until he returned, as "she was willing to live as his wife before the world but no more"?[1]

In Bertie's circle, adultery was a sport that had to be played according to strict rules. The first of these was Never Divorce. Not only did divorce bring social disgrace, but court cases risked public exposure, which could be horribly damaging, as Bertie had discovered during the Mordaunt case.

Edith Aylesford's defection did more than humiliate her husband. She triggered a social scandal that tore apart the Marlborough House set. Coming as it did when Bertie had at last justified his existence by touring India, the timing could hardly have been more unfortunate.

Edith Aylesford was a sister of Bertie's equerry Owen Williams. Photographs show a plump woman with a long face and heavy chin accentuated by the fashionable bonnets that she wore perched on the front of her head. She was evidently amusing; certainly Queen Victoria thought it must be Edith whom Bertie admired rather than Sporting Joe, as "Lord A. was too great a fool to be really agreeable to the P. of W."[2]

To understand the explosive impact of Edith's letter, we need to track back to November 1874, when Joe and Edith Aylesford entertained Bertie and Alix at Packington Hall, their Warwickshire home near Birmingham. This was one of those defining house parties that shaped Bertie's life as Prince of Wales. He and Alix stayed for five nights at Packington. Sporting Joe could ill afford it, but he spared no expense. A lake was created in the center of the vast dining room table (this unfortunately leaked, spoiling the dresses of ladies sitting at dinner), and a temporary wooden ballroom was constructed on the terrace. Fireworks rocketed money into the air, and adorning every room were wreaths of flowers and exotic plants, grown in the luxurious new conservatories that were specially admired by Alix. The chief entertainment was shooting in the Capability Brown park. After every second drive, each gun would shout "Boy!" and there would appear a bottle of champagne, curiously shaped like a "retort," which must be drained instantly.* Luncheon, which the ladies attended, was held in a tent, and throughout the meal the party was serenaded by the band of the Warwickshire Yeomanry Cavalry. Afterward, Edith and Alix sat together in the pony carriage for an elaborately posed photograph, and

---

* A retort is a long-necked glass container. HRH once visited Joe in the hospital with a broken leg. He brought two "boy" champagne bottles. "Joe, have a drink," said Bertie. "Oh, after you, Sir," replied Joe, whereupon HRH opened a bottle and drank the lot (no mean feat). After more chat the episode was repeated, and the prince quaffed the second bottle, too. (Author interview, Lord Aylesford, November 2006.)

then went driving together. Edith had four ponies, known as "rats," which she drove at speed around the estate.*[3]

The guest of honor was the czarevitch, Bertie's brother-in-law, who arrived in time for the climax of the visit, a grand ball on the last night. Six hundred guests thronged the temporary ballroom, which was decorated in crimson and hung with gold coronets. In the center stood an alpine grotto, constructed of rough virgin cork, flanked by pines, decorated with ferns, and containing a fountain that spouted sprays of water in the shape of the Prince of Wales's feathers. One guest who is listed as staying in the house on the night of the ball, but not earlier in the week, was Lord Blandford.[4] He was the eldest son of the Duke of Marlborough and a long-standing friend of Bertie's.[5] Clever and attention seeking, his aim in life was to wreak as much havoc as possible and achieve fame as a rakehell.

The last dance ended at two o'clock. Upstairs in the darkened house, lights still burned as ladies' maids dismantled their mistresses' elaborately pinned and padded hair, unlaced their stays, and arranged them for bed. Long afterward, the passages continued to creak. For the faster members of the Marlborough House set, corridor creeping was the dangerous sport of house party entertainment, and to signpost their nightly wanderings hostesses posted helpful names into brass plates screwed to bedroom doors.

The story, which is still told in Warwickshire today, goes like this. Padding along the passage toward the bedroom of Edith Aylesford came not one but two predator males. Putting out his hand in the dark, one of the men felt a beard: the only bearded man in the house (apart from Lord Hartington) was the Prince of Wales.† "Sir," murmured the first man, and beat a hasty retreat, leaving Edith's bedroom

---

* Edith gave birth to a daughter the following year, and Alix stood as godmother. At the baptism at the Chapel Royal on 24 July 1875, Alix held the baby over the font, and it was christened Alexandra.

† This is corroborated by the photograph of the party posed on the balustrade beside the conservatory. Bertie in the center is flanked by Alix and Edith, who stands next to Joe Aylesford and Louise Manchester. The czarevitch is on Alix's right. Apart from Hartington, who was Louise Manchester's acknowledged lover, Bertie is the only bearded man.

to his rival. The man stumbling back along the corridor was not Sporting Joe, owner of the house, host, and the lady's husband. It was Lord Blandford. Edith Aylesford was entertaining both Bertie and Blandford.[6]

The suggestion is that the two men had reached an understanding. Blandford agreed that for now Bertie would have his way with Edith. In exchange, Bertie would arrange to take Joe with him to India, leaving Blandford to conduct an affair with Edith while her husband was thousands of miles away.

This theory—that Edith was Bertie's mistress, and that he colluded with Blandford—rests largely on hearsay and is incapable of proof. Many people believed it at the time, however, and it was this that made the Aylesford affair so scandalous.

Joe knew that Bertie admired Edith, because he had seen the prince's letters to her, written in December 1873. These letters (as Blandford later related) "had been shown to Lord Aylesford by Lady Aylesford when she received them, but had been taken no notice of by her husband."[7] It would not be surprising if Joe took the view that the letters were not incriminating. Possibly he chose to ignore them because it was to his advantage to allow the prince to flirt with his wife. His reward was admission to the inner circle of Marlborough House. He and Edith were invited to travel with Bertie to Russia for the wedding of Prince Alfred to the czar's daughter in 1874, he was allowed the dubious privilege of bankrupting himself by entertaining the Waleses at his Packington estate, and he was taken by Bertie to India.

Joe was four years younger than Edith, who was convinced that he had long ceased to care for her. "You do not know, you never can know," she told her mother-in-law, "how hard I have tried to win his love and without success."[8] Later, in court, it emerged that he was in the habit of going after dinner to Cremorne Gardens and forming "vulgar amours" with prostitutes, then drinking at his club and returning home intoxicated at three or four a.m.[9]

Joe knew about Blandford, too.

When Joe traveled to India with HRH, Edith stayed behind at Packington. The servants were puzzled each morning to find a pool of candle wax outside the door of the white drawing room on the garden front. This door was rarely used, so one night the house steward sat up to keep watch. The man he spotted being let into the sleeping house by Edith was Blandford. He frequently visited in the day as well, arriving about midday and remaining alone with her until ten or eleven at night. All this was reported by the servants to Joe in India.[10]

From India, Joe had written chatty, affectionate letters to Edith, complaining forlornly, "I have not had a letter from you for a very long time in fact I should hardly know your handwriting HRH says that I am the only one that hardly has any letters when the bag is opened."[11] When Edith wrote announcing her affair with Blandford, something snapped inside good-natured Joe Aylesford. Two days after receiving Edith's letter, he wired: "By your letter you have decided for yourself about your future and have no other alternative but to leave at once."[12] The same day, he telegraphed his mother: "Send for the children and keep them until my return. A great misfortune has happened."[13] On 28 February 1876, he left the prince's camp in an elephant howdah. "He is gone home broken-hearted at the disgrace," wrote Carrington.[14]

In Nepal, the telegraph wires were buzzing. In England, news of the scandal spread like fire, and Alix soon heard of her friend Edith's defection. She telegrammed Bertie, imploring him to prevent Joe suing for divorce. "Tell Joe not to take rash steps," she wired. "Mother done nothing yet."[15]

A few days later she wired again. "I know all about E, but things look a little better. There is a chance. Pray try your utmost to smooth matters with Joe. Hope to God all may come right yet."[16] Bertie was adamant. "It can never come right. If you had seen letter you would say the same. Joe left us today. Take my advice and do not mix yourself up in the matter or you will regret it."*[17]

Louise Manchester telegraphed Bertie. "Entreat you persuade A[ylesford] bid her stay till his return. Not too late—you can prevent much misery. Essential you exert influence."[18]

"It is too late," replied Bertie. "After letter A received a week ago reconciliation is impossible. He will not allow her to remain under his roof, and returns to England at once."[19]

Louise Manchester visited Edith at Packington. As soon as she saw her, she knew the case was hopeless. "I might just as much have talked to a stone," she told Bertie. "She is an altered woman—speaks, thinks and talks like Lord Blandford who seems completely to have bewitched her." Louise blamed Blandford, who was determined to get Edith into his power and "create as much scandal and notoriety as he could in imitation of a bad 4th rate French novel." He had given Edith a box of poisonous pills to take in case anything happened to him, and she kept rattling them about in her pocket.[20]

Blandford reveled in the attention and the drama. Heedless of the fact that he was himself still married, and his wife, Bertha, refused to divorce him, he demanded that Aylesford divorce Edith. If he refused, raved Blandford, "I shall only wait till HRH comes back to appear on the scene and then if A tries to lick me I shall do my damnedest to defend myself & afterwards if I am all right, I shall lick HRH within an inch of his life for his conduct generally, and we will have the whole thing up in the Police Court!!"[21] His wife's response was apt: When Blandford came down to breakfast one morning, he lifted the silver chafing dish to find a pink doll, instead of the customary poached egg.

Blandford's family tried frantically to prevent the disgrace of a divorce. Their only hope was to persuade Bertie to forbid Joe from leaving Edith. When persuasion failed, they tried to threaten him. Lord Lansdowne, a Whig grandee who was married to a sister of Bertha

* These brief messages are the only known communications between Bertie and Alix that have survived the bonfires of letters after their deaths.

Blandford, warned the prince that "Lady Aylesford, anticipating the danger to which she would be exposed in her husband's absence, had used every effort to prevent him from going to India, but . . . you had insisted on his accompanying you."[22] This veiled threat that he had engineered the scandal and colluded in Blandford's affair with Edith infuriated Bertie, who reprimanded Lansdowne for the "objectionable" to⌐

F⌐ ⌐s Blandford's younger brother, Lord

r ¹ of Bertie and a member of his

⌐s begging him to intervene.

final decision of Ayles-

February.[24]

[RH. "Had you seen cer-

gret that such should be

ke advise Aylesford . . . to

ness will be held respon-

is adopted and is already

ived today has caused me

ve not advised A though

)lph Churchill tried black-

her sisters to think again

et weapon: the packet of

)f 1873. She gave copies of

)m a play. Edith went to see

npanied by her friend Lord

) made himself exceedingly

re on Bertie to dissuade Joe

)ut "means at his disposal"

t the case from coming to

aid Randolph, "of the most

1em to the solicitor general,

who had given his opinion that if they ever came before the public, the Prince of Wales "would never sit on the throne of England."[*28]

A shaken Alix confided in Bertie's former comptroller, old Sir William Knollys. While she was discussing the bruising interview she had endured with Randolph, her friend and cousin Mary, Duchess of Teck, was announced.[†] Quick as a flash, Alix invented a white lie, telling Mary that she had misheard when the footman announced that Edith Aylesford had called, and agreed to see her under the impression that it was her friend Lady Ailesbury.[29] Though this story gained credence, it seems likely that Alix, in defiance of Bertie's command, had in fact prearranged Edith's visit.[‡]

Meanwhile, Alix's subterfuge succeeded. She asked her cousin for advice as to how to limit the damage, and Mary knew exactly what to do: "Order your carriage at once, go straight to the Queen and tell her precisely what has happened. She will understand and entirely excuse you from any indiscretion. It will be in the Court Circular that you were with the Queen today and any comment will be silenced."[30] Sir William Knollys agreed. "Her Royal Highness is giving very good advice. Pray follow it at once."[31]

---

* It was not true that the solicitor general had seen Edith's letters, as Randolph claimed. The opinion that Bertie would never sit upon the throne of England if the letters came out in court was based on a hypothetical case. (St. Aubyn, *Edward VII*, p. 183.)

† Mary, Duchess of Teck, was related to both Bertie and Alix. Her father was the Duke of Cambridge, Bertie's great-uncle, and her mother, Augusta of Hesse-Cassel, was a first cousin of Alix's mother, Queen Louise. Alix wrote to her sister when the duchess was pregnant with the future Queen Mary: "Mary of Teck is here—you probably know that she is in a certain condition!!! Can you imagine her so—she is enormously big but we do not really see yet as she is so fat above, and thereby is hiding the lower part of her body!!" (Copenhagen Letters, Box 102, Alix to Minnie, 21 January 1867.)

‡ Bertie had strictly forbidden Alix from becoming involved in the Aylesford divorce, and she knew that receiving a woman as tarnished as Edith might damage her reputation. Edith told Louise Manchester on the day of the interview that "the Princess had sent for her to go to Marlborough House at 6." According to Louise, "It was that busy body Mr. Sturt [Lord Alington] who most improperly went to the Princess and urged an interview, and . . . her kindness of heart prompted her to see what she could do to save misery to so many people." (RA VIC/Add C07/1/1090, Duchess of Manchester to B, 27 March 1876; see Henry Ponsonby to Francis Knollys, n.d., in Randolph Churchill, *Churchill: Companion*, vol. 1, part 1, pp. 30–31.)

So Alix ordered a carriage for Buckingham Palace and told the Queen the story of her interview with the odious Randolph. The visit to the palace was duly reported in the *Times* Court Circular.[32] Victoria was sympathetic. She knew all about the scandal already, and she thought it "unpardonable" to drag Alix into it. "Her dear name should never have been mixed up with such people. . . . Those Williamses are a bad family."[33]

Bertie, meanwhile, was steaming home from India on board the *Serapis*. By the time the news of Randolph's bursting in on Alix reached him (28 March), he was staying at Cairo in the khedive's palace. In a rage, he dispatched Lord Charles Beresford in the royal yacht *Osborne* to England with a letter to Lord Hardwicke, the Master of the Buck Hounds. Evidently "written under great excitement," the prince's letter called for "a hostile meeting" with Randolph—in other words, a duel.[34] Churchill's response was superbly insolent. He apologized for approaching the princess on so painful a subject, but "this is the only apology which circumstances warrant my offering." He refused to apologize to the prince; and with regard to Bertie's challenge to a duel, he was crushing: "No one knows better than HRH the P[rince] of Wales that a meeting between himself and L[or]d R. C. is definitely out of the question. Please convey this to HRH."[35]

The idea that Alix had hitherto been sheltered from all unpleasantness was a romantic fiction; it cannot have come as surprise to her to learn that Bertie had conducted a flirtation with Edith Aylesford. But by confronting her with evidence in the shape of Bertie's letters, Randolph Churchill had torn away the veil and forced her to confront the painful fact that her husband was repeatedly and publicly unfaithful. With brutal accuracy, Randolph had skewered the web of lies and deceit that Bertie had woven around his marriage. While her husband was away in India, Alix had poured out page after page of longing for "my angel Bertie" in her letters to Minnie, and no doubt she wrote like that to Bertie, too.[36] Now not even Alix, whose capacity for self-deception seems almost unlimited, could still cling to the belief that her Bertie really was an angel.

By refusing to apologize, Randolph was committing social suicide. He blamed Bertie for his brother Blandford getting involved with Edith in the first place, alleging (so Hardwicke reported to Bertie) that it was "through your influence that Aylesford left his wife to accompany Your Royal Highness to India, that you knew of Blandford's intimacy with Lady Aylesford before you left . . . that you rejected an imploring letter from Lady Aylesford begging of you not to take her husband away, that in fact there was collusion between Your Royal Highness and Aylesford to throw Lady Aylesford into the arms of Blandford."[37]

Randolph's claim that Aylesford wanted to throw his wife into the arms of Lord Blandford seems bizarre, and his allegation that Bertie forced Joe to go to India against Edith's will was untrue. Afterward, Bertie found letters from Edith (which he showed to the Queen), in which she gave up her opposition to Joe's visit to India, agreeing with Bertie that "it would be greatly to Lord Aylesford's advantage that he should accompany HRH."[38]

When Bertie received a fifty-page letter from Hardwicke reporting Randolph's threats, he appealed immediately to the Queen. Victoria was staying at Coburg. She unhesitatingly believed his claim that the letters to Edith were innocent. That Bertie said so was enough—true, it was unfortunate that there were any letters at all, but writing letters, said the Queen with a smile, was a family failing.[39]

The letters that Bertie wrote to Edith Aylesford in December 1873 were preserved by Francis Knollys, tightly folded in a sealed envelope.* The first, dated 11 December 1873, was written from Blenheim, where Bertie was staying for a shooting party.

---

* Queen Victoria forbade publication of the letters, as (Ponsonby wrote) "colouring might be easily given & injurious inference deduced from hasty expressions." (Henry Ponsonby to Francis Knollys, 18 April 1876, in Randolph Churchill, *Churchill: Companion*, vol. 1, part 1, p. 38.) Not publishing gave rise to wild speculation about the lurid contents of the letters (see, for example, Mary S. Lovell, *The Churchills* [Little, Brown, 2011], p. 57). These extracts from the letters that Randolph Churchill used in his attempt to blackmail the Prince of Wales have never before been revealed.

My dear Lady Joe,

I hope you won't think me very impertinent for addressing you "as above," but it is so much shorter. I cannot resist writing you a few lines to thank you for y[ou]r very kind letter—& how glad I am to hear that you liked y[ou]r stay at Sandringham.

. . . Y[ou]r sixpence is on my watch chain and will I am sure bring me luck. I am so glad to hear fr[om] Joe that you have decided to go to St. Petersburg next month, although I advised him at first not to go, so that we shall I trust meet very often there, and I trust I shall be able to be of some use to you.

I thought I should puzzle you by the mysterious way in which I mentioned the "discretion" I intended asking of you but it may perhaps astonish you still more when I really ask it. But I am in no hurry—you kindly ask me (for your "discretion") anything that belongs to me. I fear I have nothing worth offering you, but if you could give me some idea I should be much obliged to you.[40]

Much of this seems a flirtatious code. Edith's correct title was of course Lady Aylesford, not Lady Joe, and Joe's first name was actually Heneage. Bertie was a stickler for correctness, so calling Edith Lady Joe was a form of intimate joshing, as presumably was the sixpence.

In his second letter, written a week later from another house party, Bertie enlarges on the theme of "discretions."

My Dear Lady Joe,

Many thanks for your letter, which I received this afternoon, and it is very kind of you having ordered a harmonic-flute and American organ at Chappells to be sent to Marlborough House and I hope to find them there on our return on Saturday and I am quite sure that one of the two is sure to suit.

I cannot allow you to consider our bets or "discretions" as quits, and as you have no preference, you must allow me to choose something and send it [to] you for Christmas.

My "discretion" must keep as I have something in view, but

would rather <u>not</u> ask you for it <u>yet</u>. You have never told me whether you did not consider my letter from Blenheim rather a cool one. I was afraid afterwards you would.

After discussing arrangements, he ends:

> Believe me, my dear Lady Joe,
> Yours very sincerely,
> Albert Edward

> PS The "discretion" you owe me I shall never dare ask of you, and I fear you will never grant it if I did. Am I not mysterious?[41]

The PS is the closest Bertie came to showing his hand, but even this is arch and playful. Letter number three, written from Sandringham on 26 December 1873, firmly closes the correspondence.

> You must be sick of my handwriting but after the kind letter received from you this morning I cannot help writing you a few lines to thank you for it.
> I am so glad you like the vases—although they are mere trifles and not worth thanking me for. . . .
> Now goodbye my dear Lady Joe—I look forward to our journey together and our sojourn in Russia.[42]

Lord Hartington, to whom the letters were later referred for his opinion, considered that they contained expressions which "are imprudent and which, though possibly meaning nothing, are capable of a construction injurious to the character of HRH."[43] The journey to Russia was of course with Joe, not Edith on her own. The sixpence on Bertie's chain, and the talk of "discretions" and gifts and secrets: None of this is actually incriminating—just as Bertie's letters to Harriett Mordaunt had been apparently innocent. But it's hard to believe that Edith sent him a sixpence for his chain without some sentimental reason; and the talk about discretions, innocent though it may have been, can be construed as flirtatious, if not sexual. The very fact that he wrote the letters at all was damning. Queen Victoria summed up with pithy acuteness. "She quite believes there was no harm in the letters as she always believed what he says, but a chance expression may be twisted and even the fact of the existence of the letters—harmless as they may be—would create a bad effect."[44] But Randolph's claim that the letters were dynamite that could rock the monarchy seems laughable.

In 1876, Lord Randolph Churchill was twenty-seven and MP for Woodstock. He wore a bristling waxed moustache and he had inherited the gooseberry eyes of the Churchill family, along with their bad temper. Thin, with an electric, restless sort of energy, he looked younger than he was, and people often remarked on his schoolboy charm. He suffered from mood swings, when he became depressed and paranoid, and he could be brutally rude.*

Randolph claimed that his motive in blackmailing Bertie was to protect the honor of the Marlboroughs by preventing Blandford from divorcing and thus disgracing the family name. As the younger, favorite son, he saw it as his duty, or so he said, to save the family from his dissolute brother. He was envious of Blandford and never ceased to complain that he was a "horrid bore," "heartless," "selfish," and "very bad."[45] It was no coincidence that for Randolph, protecting the family honor involved preventing Blandford from getting his way. At once dutiful and rebellious about his background, Randolph was nonetheless closer to Blandford than he was to his distant father the duke or his overbearing mother, at the rustle of whose silk dress the household trembled.[46]

---

* In later life his moods were exacerbated, possibly by syphilis; but Lord Derby for one believed that Randolph had inherited mental illness through his mother. (John Vincent, ed., *Later Derby Diaries*, [Bristol, 1981], pp. 74, 88.) The Duchess of Marlborough was a daughter of the formidable Frances Anne, Lady Londonderry, and a sister of Lord Adolphus Vane-Tempest, mad husband of Bertie's former mistress, the unhappy Susan Vane-Tempest—odd to think that she was Winston Churchill's great-aunt.

In September 1873, Randolph had become engaged to the nineteen-year-old American beauty Jennie Jerome after a whirlwind three-day romance. They had met at Cowes, at a reception given by the Prince of Wales. Randolph's parents opposed the match, especially as Jennie's father, the New York entrepreneur Leonard Jerome, had just lost his fortune in the 1873 financial crash. Randolph's brother Blandford did his best to stop the marriage, too. He told Randolph that he was crazy to marry at twenty-five, and Randolph discovered that he "had been talking . . . most tremendously against me and telling all sorts of lies about me and entreating my father not to allow it."[47] Desperate to obtain his parents' consent, as the Jeromes would not allow the marriage unless the Marlboroughs agreed to it, Randolph appealed to his friend Francis Knollys to use his influence with the Prince of Wales. Nudged by Knollys, Bertie wrote to Blandford entreating him to support the match. A copy of the correspondence was sent to Randolph, who described it as "quite the most quiet, sensible and altogether the most gentlemanlike letter I ever read."[48] Randolph showed the letter to his parents, and "it produced a good effect and showed them there are two sides to the question. They are in a much more reasonable humour."[49] Soon afterward, they relented and gave their consent.

At the wedding in Paris in April 1874, Francis Knollys was best man. Bertie gave Randolph a silver cigarette box from Moscow; Randolph told Jennie that HRH was "very cordial and nice, asked much after you and said that . . . he was very glad that everything was so pleasantly settled at last."[50]

Not without reason, Bertie considered that Randolph owed him a debt of gratitude. Thirty-five years later, he remarked of Winston Churchill: "If it had not been for me and the Queen, that young man would never have been in existence." How so? "The Duke and Duchess [of Marlborough] both objected to Randolph's marriage, and it was entirely owing to us that they gave way."[51]

Jennie's first child was born at Blenheim in November 1874 after only seven months of marriage. The family insisted that the baby Winston was premature, though it is often suggested that Jennie was already pregnant when she married.[52] No suspicions were raised, however, about the baby's paternity.

Shortly after the birth, the Churchills returned to their London house on Charles Street. Jennie's sister Clara, who stayed for six months, wrote: "I don't know why it is but people always seem to ask us when HRH goes to them. I suppose it is because Jennie is so pretty, and you have no idea how charming Randolph can be."[53] HRH's engagement diary for 1875 reveals that he dined with the Randolph Churchills on 21 March; they dined with him in Paris on 4 April; he drank tea with Jennie at her house on Charles Street on 15 August.[54] The young Lady Randolph had entered Bertie's life, and would remain his friend on and off for thirty-five years.

Jennie Churchill wrote an autobiography. Published in 1908, this volume of society memoirs is predictably discreet. Bertie's name barely features, but if, as her great-niece Anita Leslie suggests, he was "toying with the idea" of an affair with her in 1875, her memoirs give a good idea as to what attracted him.[55] An American in London, Jennie found herself cold-shouldered as a cross between a "Red Indian" and a Gaiety Girl. She had spent her teenage years in Paris, growing up in the scented hothouse of the imperial court, where her mother was a friend of the Empress Eugénie. As Lady Randolph Churchill, Jennie found herself plunged into the chilly, Old World stateliness of Blenheim Palace. At luncheon, massive silver covers were placed in front of both the duke and the duchess, each of whom carved a vast joint to feed the entire household. Every night at eleven, the family trooped out to an anteroom and, lighting candles, each in turn kissed the duke and duchess good night.[56]

Jennie scorned the strict etiquette that dictated that Englishwomen, even when married, must always travel chaperoned by a maid. Her "pantherine" style, Native American bone structure, and Paris fashions made her conspicuous among the dowdy Englishwomen in their muslin and sealskin. One of the first of the American women whose inva-

sion of London society caused a minor social revolution, Jennie had a
New World energy and brio that Bertie found irresistible.[57]

Randolph's extraordinary anger against Bertie is more understandable if it was fueled by sexual jealousy. If Bertie really was flirting with
his wife, then social suicide was perhaps not too high a price to pay.[58]

Bertie was still fond of Randolph, but Randolph's ungrateful insolence
and his bullying of Alix enraged him. When Lord Charles Beresford
returned bearing Randolph's non-apology, the *Serapis* was at Malta.
Bertie decided on a sudden change of plan, delaying his return by an
impromptu visit to Spain.

Queen Victoria worried that Bertie would make himself unpopular
with the animal-loving English by witnessing a bullfight in Spain.[59]
The prince refused all bullfight invitations, but his actual destination
was far more compromising. He spent three days sightseeing at Seville. Here, as the foreign secretary, Lord Derby, related, he had arranged to meet "a certain Madame Murieta [*sic*], well known in
London society."[60]

Jesusa Murrieta was the Spanish wife of José de Murrieta, a South
American merchant living in London.[61] Bertie had scandalized the Foreign Office by traveling to France with Madame Murrieta before he
left for India.[62] The Murrietas belonged to the London smart set and
entertained lavishly at their houses in Kensington Place and Wadhurst
in Sussex. They were friends of Jennie Churchill's, and if Bertie intended by his visit to Madame Murrieta to put Jennie's nose out of
joint, he certainly succeeded. "I have no doubt [HRH] will abuse me,"
she told Randolph when she heard about the visit, "as most likely she
will talk about me."[63]

"Pray be careful your Royal Highness is not taken prisoner like
Coeur de Lion on your return from your Crusade," wired Disraeli to
Bertie in Seville.

"Much amused by your telegram," telegraphed Bertie in reply, but
he perhaps did not appreciate the joke.[64] Disraeli's mocking irony al-

ways set him on edge, especially as he suspected the prime minister was laughing behind his hand about the Randolph Churchill affair.

Equally infuriating, someone had leaked the Aylesford affair to the press. *Vanity Fair* carried a titillating paragraph: "With reference to the return from the East there is much talk of the three letters which are said to have been dispatched." This seems harmless innuendo by comparison with the savage satire of Regency cartoonists or the vile comments in *Reynolds's Newspaper* about the death of the baby Prince John, but Bertie exacted his revenge. The following year, he refused to meet the connoisseur Lord Ronald Gower, brother of the Duke of Sutherland, on the grounds that he contributed to *Vanity Fair*. When Gibson Bowles, the editor, asked for an explanation, HRH refused to give one; and he had Bowles kicked out of his club, having first checked with his solicitor Arnold White, who gave his opinion that Bowles had "abused the hospitality extended to him, and made public matters which came to his knowledge through a courteous admission into a private society."[65] Bertie's social sovereignty gave him extraordinary powers to cut, snub, and ostracize.

Meanwhile, the prince made careful diary plans, choreographing a triumphant return home. He wrote Alix "a very dear letter," telling her that on his return to English waters, he wished to see her "first and alone."[66] The *Serapis* arrived off Yarmouth, Isle of Wight, at eleven a.m. on 11 May 1876, where Bertie boarded the *Enchantress* and was reunited with Alix and his children.[67] In London, Bertie and Alix visited the Queen at Buckingham Palace, where a large crowd had gathered. Victoria, jealous of her own popularity, noticed that when Bertie and Alix drove away, and she appeared alone at the palace window, the crowd "turned round and cheered"—the enthusiasm for herself was greater than for Bertie, she thought.[68]

Arriving at Marlborough House at eight, Bertie and Alix paused briefly to change, and then drove to Covent Garden. They made their carefully planned entry during *Un Ballo in Maschera*, Verdi's opera about regicide, but the irony was perhaps lost on them. The Queen thought going straight to the opera a "great mistake," but Bertie in-

sisted that, though he would have far preferred to dine quietly at Buckingham Palace with his mother, this would be "impolitic" at the present
moment, when "the friendly feeling which exists towards him should
[not] in any way be damped."[69]

By the time of Verdi's second act, the opera house was packed.
Women glittering with diamonds waited and whispered with anticipation until at last the prince and princess arrived. The whole assembly
rose, and it seemed the cheers would never cease. Bertie bowed and
bowed repeatedly, and then, in accordance with his instructions, the
soloist Mme. Albani sang "God Bless the Prince of Wales," with such
vigor that renewed cheering broke out.[70]

The following evening at seven thirty, Lord Hardwicke called on
Bertie at Marlborough House. He had just come from seeing Lord
Aylesford, and he brought the news that Sporting Joe had decided not
to divorce Edith, but to arrange a private legal separation.[71] The scandal had been averted.

There is at Packington Hall a large silver cigar box in the shape of a log
cabin, designed for handing round cigars after dinner.[72] The Packington log cabin was a present from Bertie to Sporting Joe.

Bertie had much to be thankful for. Joe had returned from India in
a confused and reckless state of mind, determined to fight a duel with
Blandford. On discovering that under the rules of dueling "if I call him
out . . . he is not allowed to shoot at me . . . but I have a cool shot at
him," and considering this unfair, Joe agreed instead to hire a lawyer.[73]
He was advised by friends such as Hardwicke to agree to a legal separation, as in a divorce case all his past misdeeds would come out in
court.[74] But Joe's real reason for deciding against divorce was perhaps
to protect the Prince of Wales. When someone mentioned that Bertie
had written letters to Edith, he threatened to horsewhip the tale-teller
for propagating "a scandalous falsehood," even though he already
knew all about the correspondence.[75] Blindly loyal to his prince, Joe
was willing to give up all he had—his wife, his fortune, even his
home—to serve him.

Joe shut up Packington Hall and rented a house in Bognor, where he lived with a woman named Mrs. Dilke and consorted with "negro minstrels" and ladies who danced around the room in smoking caps. Bertie kept in touch. He visited Joe when he was ill, and he invited him to Sandringham.[76] We catch a glimpse of Joe at New Year 1882, playing "Snapdragon" before dinner: "the P[rince]ss of Wales' lace tea gown caught fire. L[or]d Aylesford caught her in his arms, and pressed her very tight, and put out the flames and saved a bad accident."[77]

Later he immigrated to Texas—hence the log cabin cigar box. Installing himself and his retinue in the only hotel of a shanty town named Big Spring, he bought twenty-two thousand acres. The cowboys set about separating him from his cash, but it's good to learn that he won their respect and "they would spill their blood for him as quickly as he would open another bottle for them."[78] Joe died of drink at age thirty-six. Bertie's note in his diary signifies that he still considered Joe one of his court: "Receive sad news of death of L[or]d Aylesford in Texas USA."[79] The curmudgeonly Lord Derby commented: "He had run through his whole fortune by gambling, racing and extravagance generally; and was one of the very worst examples of the English peerage. Naturally he belonged to the Marlborough House Set."[80] This was a harsh verdict. Joe had inherited debts, and he spent a good deal of his fortune serving the Prince of Wales.[81]

Edith, by contrast, was ostracized. Leaving her children at Packington forever ("It is like being dead and yet alive," she told her mother-in-law), she fled to Paris, where she and Blandford lived together under the names Mr. and Mrs. Spencer.[82] In 1881 she produced a son, named Guy Bertrand.* Blandford's wife divorced him two years later, but though he claimed that Guy Bertrand was the child he loved most, he didn't marry Edith. After a scandalous affair with Lady Colin Campbell, he married a rich American widow. Edith died in Paris in 1897, two days before the great Devonshire House Ball. Her death con-

---

* Many years later, at Dunkirk, Michael, the 9th Earl of Aylesford, who was Joe's nephew, allegedly met a French officer who introduced himself as Guy Bertrand's son. Michael Aylesford invited the Frenchman into his tank to shelter from the bullets, but both men were killed when it was hit by a shell. (Author email from Lord Aylesford, 3 December 2006.)

demned the relatives who had shunned her for more than twenty years to observe mourning, which meant that they were unable to attend the ball and their elaborate outfits were never worn. Her sister-in-law Mrs. Hywfa Williams watched the festivities from an upstairs skylight. "How I longed to be down in the room!" she wrote, "but very sad was Edith's death for all her sisters."[83]

As for Randolph Churchill, he got his way and stopped the Aylesford divorce, but he had broken all the rules of courtly behavior and for this he had to be punished. Nothing if not stubborn, Randolph refused to grovel. Bertie appealed to Prime Minister Disraeli, Lord Chancellor Lord Cairns, and Hartington to arbitrate. Arrangements were made for the entire Churchill family to go into exile. The Duke of Marlborough reluctantly accepted Disraeli's offer to become Viceroy of Ireland. The royal connection had already cost him dear—in 1875, shortly after entertaining the Prince of Wales at Blenheim, he had disposed of the Marlborough gem collection for thirty-five thousand guineas. The duke grimly sold off more land, and arranged to take Randolph with him as unpaid private secretary.

Randolph first skipped off to America. As Jennie breezily put it, having had "serious differences of opinion with various influential people," Randolph felt in need of "a little solace and distraction."[84] A form of apology drafted by the Lord Chancellor was sent for him to sign, and he succeeded in doing this in what the Lord Chancellor thought was "the most ungracious and undignified way that was possible."[85]

However ungracious, the apology had been extracted, and Bertie had seemingly won his point. The Queen entertained the Duke and Duchess of Marlborough at Windsor in December 1876, and Bertie grudgingly agreed that he would bow to Randolph. However, he let it be known that he would not speak to him and would boycott any house that entertained the Randolph Churchills. This was not mere spite. No one mentioned the fact, but Randolph still had Bertie's letters to Edith in his possession. Being a social exile was the making of

Randolph as a politician, as he no longer wasted his time partying at Marlborough House.

In July 1885, a mysterious locked box was delivered to Lord Cairns. On opening it, he found a sealed envelope addressed to the Prince of Wales. Cairns forwarded the box to Marlborough House. Inside the sealed box were the three letters that Bertie had written to Edith.[86]

CHAPTER 13

Lillie Langtry

1877–78

A photograph taken of Alix in the summer of 1876 shows her wearing a skintight tailored jacket buttoned up to her throat. Her wasp waist is fiercely corseted and belted, making her look abnormally thin. The photo is a fashion plate, and it shows the princess modeling the new style of figure-hugging tailored day clothes that she popularized. These dresses liberated women from the voluminous skirts that restricted physical activity, subjecting their wearers instead to the tyranny of tightly laced corsets.[1] She carries a jaunty umbrella and wears an unflattering round hat, but her eyes are heavy and dark-rimmed, her face is pale, her mouth set, and her glance avoids the camera.[2]

That winter she became ill. The official version, as conveyed to the Queen by woman of the bedchamber Charlotte Knollys, was that Alix was "dreadfully pulled down" by a "severe cold."[3] But her illness was more serious than that. The Queen of Denmark wrote in strictest confidence to Victoria, telling her of Alix's "indisposition." Victoria forwarded a translation of the letter to Dr. Gull, urgently asking for his advice. "She is too dear and precious to us all to let her be sacrificed to others. It is on them or rather on him that we must work and act. . . . What is to be done?"[4] Evidently the Queen was referring to Bertie, but exactly what she meant by Alix being sacrificed isn't clear. Perhaps it was the old complaint about the frenetic pace of Bertie's life wearing Alix out, but this had been said so often before that it's hard to see why the Queen of Denmark needed to write in strictest confidence. Perhaps conjugal relations had been resumed and Alix had suffered a miscarriage. There are references to neuralgia and fatigue.[5] Three years before she had complained of pain in her eyes, which was so severe that she was unable to write.[6] Whatever it was, Dr. Gull was alarmed and ordered her to stay for six weeks in Athens with her brother Willie, the King of Greece, for a "complete change"—something Victoria would never have normally allowed.[7]

Bertie, meanwhile, had developed an abscess on his bad leg. The surgeon Sir James Paget was obliged to cut it twice. For the second operation Bertie was given laughing gas and ether, which, Alix told the Queen, "made him fight with the doctors and being so strong he fell off the sofa and I saw him and the doctors rolling together on the floor!! This brought him to and he had no idea where he was. They had then to begin it all over again—and strapped him down poor boy! And then Paget cut it about 4 inches long and deep." The pain afterward was torture.[8]

For ten days after his operation, Bertie dined alone with Alix. He entered this methodically in his diary.[9] He had never been alone with her for so long, and though he was convalescent, it was also perhaps a sort of penance. Bertie was not well enough to escort Alix when she left for Greece on 4 April 1877. "Will write so sorry to leave dearest Bertie although he is very nearly well but both he and doctors insist upon it," Alix wired the Queen.[10] The next day she telegraphed from Paris after a rough crossing ("very ill"): "miss my poor Bertie dreadfully."[11]

———

In *The Times* classified section throughout May 1877 there appeared the following advertisement:

EFFIE DEANS
BY J. E. MILLAIS R.A.
On view daily at the King-Street Galleries,
9 King-Street, St. James's, S.W.

On 9 May, Bertie dined with Sir Coutts Lindsay at his newly opened Grosvenor Gallery on New Bond Street, where he saw James McNeill Whistler's painting of fireworks, *Nocturne in Black and Gold,* which Ruskin rubbished as "flinging a pot of paint in the public's face."[12] No doubt Bertie agreed. Certainly he bought no Whistlers for the royal collection. Unlike Albert, who had been an eager collector and patron, Bertie showed little interest in art. He has been accused of an "inborn philistinism"; not a single important contemporary British or French picture was acquired by him for the royal collection.[13]

Two days after the Grosvenor Gallery dinner, accompanied by his artistic sister Princess Louise, Bertie again visited a gallery: He went to King Street to view John Everett Millais's *Effie Deans.*[14] Whistler contended that art should stand alone, regardless of its subject matter, but *Effie Deans* was a virtuoso exercise in narrative art. Effie was the tragic heroine of Sir Walter Scott's novel *Old Mortality,* and Millais's painting shamelessly milked the pathos, showing the beautiful country girl parting from her seducer, holding her maiden "snood," the hair ribbon worn by Scots virgins, to which she had forfeited the right. Millais's model was an unknown woman named Lillie Langtry.

Millais had met Lillie at an at home held by Lady Sebright, a hostess who collected artists and writers. Mrs. Edward Langtry's entry that evening had caused a sensation. Among the "rush of cavaliers" who jostled to take her in to supper, it was Millais who won.[15] Frank Miles, another fashionable artist, sketched her there and then, and the image was reproduced as a penny postcard that was sold on street corners. Frank Miles specialized in drawing society beauties for magazines, and Lillie came to his studio on Salisbury Street for her sittings. While she posed, Prince Leopold often called, and he bought Miles's drawing of her sleepy features on a background of lilies and hung it above his bed at Buckingham Palace. One day when he was ill his mother the Queen came to visit him in bed, and (according to Lillie) the picture shocked her so much that she took it down at once, standing on a chair to reach.[16]

Bertie, who was no slouch where professional beauties were concerned, let it be known that he wanted to meet Mrs. Langtry, too. The intermediary was Sir Allen Young. "Alleno" was a wealthy bachelor, a yachting acquaintance of Bertie's who had earned fame as a polar adventurer; he spoke rarely and in monosyllables, and, as Mrs. Langtry tactfully put it, his gray eyes had the "curious, far-away look which one associates with a great explorer."[17]

A dinner was fixed for 24 May 1877. Bertie's diary that day was, even by his standards, unusually packed. He returned from Portsmouth where the previous day he had inspected Lord Charles Beresford's battleship *Thunderer*, arriving back in London at 1:30; lunched with his sister-in-law Marie, Affie's wife, the Duchess of Edinburgh; chaired a committee meeting at the Marlborough Club, and then took leave of Marie at Charing Cross at 8:15.[18]

The dinner party of ten assembled at Alleno's Stratton Street home was kept waiting. "I am afraid I am a little late," boomed a "deep and cheery voice," and Mrs. Langtry noticed an expectant hush. According to her own account, which is frankly unbelievable unless she was strangely dense, she was quite unaware that the Prince of Wales was expected. Alleno presented her to Bertie, whose chest was apparently adorned with glittering orders and a blue Garter ribbon, and she became panic-stricken and longed to escape. At dinner she "found herself" seated next to him and was struck silent.[19] Her ordeal was brief. At 11:30 the prince departed for Lady Dudley's dance.

In her memoirs, *The Days I Knew*, written in 1925, Lillie created a myth about herself. Brought up in Jersey, the only daughter of William Le Breton, the philandering Dean of Jersey, she ran wild as a girl with her six brothers, and married impulsively a seemingly wealthy Irish widower named Ned Langtry. After recovering from a dangerous illness, said to be typhoid, she came to live in London with Ned, who took lodgings on Eaton Place. In the spring of 1877 she was in mourning for her younger brother, and she appeared at Lady Sebright's feeling shy and countrified, wearing a plain black dress and no jewels because she had none, with her hair twisted in a simple knot on the nape of her neck. "Fancy my surprise when I immediately became the centre of attention," wrote Lillie.[20] The next morning her table was heaped with invitations, and she and her reluctant husband found themselves attending two or three parties a night. Everywhere she went she wore the little black dress, which was the only evening gown she possessed.

Lillie's narrative of herself as an innocent country girl to whom success just happened is disingenuous. Her assault on London society, though far more spectacular than she could ever have dreamed, was carefully planned. She admitted as much in an interview she gave to *The New York Herald* in 1882. Wearing a loose red robe and drying her waist-length hair before the fire, she told the reporter that the Le Breton family had a "prescriptive right" to the deanery of Jersey, which they had held for generations. "My pedigree being good and my position in Jersey society being assured, it was not surprising that I should be well-received." She was introduced to London society, she claimed, by Lord Ranelagh, whose daughter had married her brother Clement. She was no adventuress.

Langtry denied that she had ever set herself up as a beauty. "I never thought I was one, and I don't think I am now. I am never in the least surprised when I hear people say they are very much disappointed about my beauty."[21] Her modesty is engaging. Photographs show rather heavy features, a wide nose and a square jaw, but to the London of 1877 she was the epitome of classical beauty. Her admirers raved over her Greek profile; she was a portrait on a Greek coin, the lost Venus of Praxiteles, Venus Annodomini, the modern Helen. Millais, Frank Miles, Edward Poynter, and George Frederic Watts vied to idealize her low forehead, her chiseled mouth, and the feature they admired most of all, her column-like neck, the "augustly pillared throat" with its three *"plis de Venus"* or creases of skin at the angle of the jaw.[22]

A portrait of Lillie by James Sant, which belonged to Bertie and seems to have been commissioned by him, shows her Grecian profile.[23] Her hair is simply knotted on her neck, her throat is bare, her skin innocent of makeup, and she wears a loose muslin blouse. Sant's image breathes health and country freshness; Lillie epitomized the new fashion for ample beauty, which was the antithesis of slim Alix with her false fringe, her tightly laced wasp waist, and her scarred throat concealed by pearl chokers and lace collars.

This was the season of the Professional Beauties. "Do come, the P.B.s will be here," hostesses would scribble on their invitation cards.[24] PBs were paraded as trophies at parties; like horseflesh their merits were compared and discussed. Artists in search of bestselling soft-porn pinups competed to paint them; their photographs were sold as postcards by the thousands; women stood on benches to spy them over the crowds in the park, and their dresses were instantly copied. Lillie's chief rivals that season were Mrs. "Patsy" Cornwallis-West and Mrs. Luke Wheeler. Mrs. Wheeler she damned with faint praise ("Her beauty was of line and expression rather than colour, and, while disappointing to some people when first seen, its charm grew on acquaintance"); Patsy Cornwallis-West, an old flame of Bertie's and a far tougher proposition, she befriended. The two women lived on the same London street, Eaton Place, and they competed for Bertie's attentions.[25]

According to Anita Leslie, whose grandfather was one of Lillie's lovers, her seduction technique was to fix her admirer with her huge blue eyes and "appear to swoon, the idea being that the charm of his person had rendered her senseless. A lady in this state has to be held, supported on the sofa and perhaps her clothes loosened." However, "she did not have to faint to get the Prince of Wales, of course. He was never bashful."[26]

Alix was not completely recovered, and Dr. Gull ordered her to "limit fatigue and keep early hours."[27] This gave Lillie the opportunity to blossom as ruling favorite. According to her own account, she rode with the prince on Rotten Row each evening—in spite of the fact that she had barely ridden sidesaddle before, and when one admirer put her on his horse she fell off in a dead faint.[28] The prince's daily parade at seven p.m. on his horse with its red brow band was one of the rituals of the season, eagerly scrutinized by royal watchers. Accompanying HRH would have been a public affirmation of Lillie's status. Bertie apparently made no attempt to conceal his new mistress or keep the affair secret—but we have only Lillie's mythmaking and her own account to go on.

Alix, meanwhile, now recovered, involved herself with Eddy. The thirteen-year-old prince had become ill with typhoid, caused, so Alix believed, by drinking bad water at Sandringham. She nursed him devotedly, but she found the "constant fear" engendered by the dreaded typhoid almost unendurable.[29] "I am with him all day long, and only take a short drive in the evening, and he continues as good a patient as possible—but what a long and dreary time it has been," she told Victoria.[30] A flare-up of Eddy's illness kept Alix a willing prisoner at Marlborough House, while Bertie escaped to Cowes, where he spent most of August on board the *Osborne* with the younger children, avoiding the typhoid in London.[31]

Under the prince's patronage, Cowes Week had ballooned from a family yachting party, where the royals could walk about freely without ceremony, into a crowded regatta with a perpetual garden party on the lawn of the Royal Yacht Club. Bertie raced his yacht the *Hildegarde* in a half gale and won his first Queen's Cup; ladies rushed onto the platform to see the finish in defiance of the rules of the Royal Yacht Squadron, and Bertie received a stirring ovation that "will be one of the brightest dreams of his life."[32]

Lillie Langtry was there, too, staying with her husband as guests of Sir Allen Young on his yacht *Helen*. Alix's absence did not go unnoticed. Soon stories of an estrangement were circulating in London.[33]

It is often claimed that Alix felt no jealousy for Lillie Langtry, but her behavior hardly suggests a happy princess. That autumn at Abergeldie, her woman of the bedchamber Charlotte Knollys fell ill, apparently yet another victim of typhoid. The "inevitable" Charlotte was unpopular with the household but devoted to her mistress, and Alix dropped everything to nurse her, refusing to leave her while she remained ill. Her care for "my poor dear Charlotte" earned the approval of Victoria ("her unselfishness is indeed beautiful"), but Alix found comfort in martyrdom; nursing had perhaps become an emotional necessity to her.[34] Alone at Abergeldie, without Bertie, she drew close to "Beloved Mama" as she called the Queen (behind her back, she referred to her as "Mutter"),* telling her that "you quite spoil me with all the <u>kind words</u> but you may rest assured that I appreciate them all <u>very very</u> deeply—but I am sure you know how happy it makes me to think that we should have understood each other so very well."[35]

Not until late November was Charlotte well enough to move; still very weak, she was lifted into the train by Alix's Highland piper and traveled in a special carriage that had been carefully heated to sixty degrees (this was the temperature that Queen Victoria ordained for the rooms of her palaces) by hot-water pans.[36]

Sometime in 1877, Lillie acquired a plot of land in Bournemouth from Lord Derby and began to build a house. The foundation stone reads: "ELL 1877," for Emilie Le Breton Langtry, and the house was a red-brick seaside villa, many gabled, half-timbered, and sprawling. Inside it was emblazoned with mottoes. "They say—What say they? Let them say." "And yours, my friends." Legend has it that Bertie bought the land for her through an intermediary and paid for the house to be built, and that he stayed there and played at domesticity with Lillie. No evidence has ever been produced to support this.[37]

Nonetheless, 1878 was Lillie's year of triumph. She and her husband, Ned, moved into a house at 17 Norfolk Street, off Park Lane, early in the New Year. Money was tight—when her furniture was sold a few years later, "the only thing at all nice was a low Chippendale

---

* She may have used the name in letters to Minnie to distinguish Victoria from her own mother Queen Louise; more likely, it was a disparaging reference to Victoria's pro-German sympathies.

wardrobe"—but Lillie by now was earning a little.[38] *Cartes de visite* of her photographs filled the shop windows, and the society papers fed their readers with titillating crumbs of gossip about her. Her portraits by Millais and Poynter were the star attractions of the Royal Academy summer exhibition, and Lillie was mobbed by admirers as she walked through the rooms on the night of the opening banquet.[39]

One of her admirers was Bertie's friend Rudolf, the eighteen-year-old Austrian Crown Prince. He had come to England to see his mother, the Empress Elizabeth of Austria, who was spending the winter riding to hounds in Northamptonshire, much to the annoyance of Queen Victoria, who thought it "very unbecoming": "It <u>lowers</u> Royalty, and female Royalty above all to have an Empress coming over to hunt."*[40] The callow prince danced with Lillie at a ball given by Ferdinand de Rothschild. Lillie, who was wearing an expensive gown of pale pink crêpe de Chine, suddenly realized that Rudolf had become unpleasantly hot, and his sweaty hands were making marks on her new dress. When she asked him to put his gloves on, he ungallantly replied, *"C'est vous qui suez, madame"* ("It's you who sweats, madam").† Rudolf had misread the signals. He had called often at Lillie's Norfolk Street house, presumably under the impression that Mrs. Langtry was a royal *poule de luxe,* but he was unwelcome.[41]

Lillie claimed in her memoirs (and her biographers have repeated it) that she went everywhere with Bertie in the season of 1878. Their friendship has often been described as a domesticated love affair, but there is a hole—a silence—at the center of the narrative. No letters from this time survive. Many of the stories seem to be exaggerated or

* The fitness-obsessed empress ruined the shoes of her ladies-in-waiting by walking each morning twice around Hyde Park (about eight miles). Though a skilled haute école rider, she lacked the hunting woman's ability to make a horse gallop. "Come on, madam, come on!" her exasperated pilot, Bay Middleton, would yell; her trail across country could be followed like a paper chase from the throwaway squares of Japanese rice paper that she used as handkerchiefs. (Cornwallis-West, *Reminiscences,* pp. 76–78.)
† Men dancing with sweaty hands is a trope of royal stories. My father as a young man once danced with Princess Margaret, who was wearing a sequinned dress. He was nervous and hot, and afterward he noticed that his right hand was covered with sequins. To his horror, he saw an imprint of his hand on the princess's waist.

wrong. Lillie is alleged to have consummated her relationship with Bertie when Alix refused an invitation to accompany him to a royal house party at Crichel, Dorset, with Lord Alington in January 1878. In fact, Alix *was* there, playing a central role in the ball and festivities, which lasted a week. Louise Manchester reported to Disraeli that Bertie was "very snappish" throughout the whole visit; the Langtrys are not mentioned.[42]

Lillie was presented to Queen Victoria in May. Her husband had been presented by Bertie a few weeks earlier, and Lillie's presentation validated her ambivalent social status.[43] She was low down the list of ladies, but the Queen, who usually left her drawing rooms well before the end, stayed on purpose to see her, or so Lillie believed. Victoria, dressed in black satin with the blue Garter ribbon across her bosom, looked straight in front of her and put out her hand, Lillie thought, in "rather a perfunctory way." Lillie worried that her headdress, of three ostentatiously large ostrich feathers, cheekily aping the Prince of Wales's crest, had annoyed the Queen. According to her own account, she went on to curtsey to the waiting row of royalties, beginning with the Prince and Princess of Wales; and later that evening, while dancing at Marlborough House, Bertie chaffed her on her feathers. Most of this anecdote seems to have been make-believe on Lillie's part. Bertie was not present at Lillie's drawing room. He was in Paris. So was Alix. Lillie's presentation had been arranged in order to avoid embarrassment to the Princess of Wales.[44]

We can glimpse Bertie's relationship with Lillie in a gossipy letter written by Disraeli, newly ennobled as Earl of Beaconsfield. One night his private secretary, Monty Corry, dined with Prince Hal, as Beaconsfield called Bertie. Afterward, Bertie took Monty to supper with a friend, and there he found "Mr. Standish and Mrs. [Sloane-] Stanley and the Jersey beauty whose name begins with an L; and what with oysters and champagne and so on it was getting very late and very late it was when they broke up. And then Prince Hal said, 'I shall go to the Turf now and play whist!' Even Monty could not stand that and escaped, having had a real day with Prince Hal!"[45] Perhaps, like Shakespeare's Hal, Bertie was a prince who roistered and drank until the small hours, and Lillie was his wench. Perhaps their relationship was not a grand passion, but a matter of companionship, of low life and late nights.

Bertie was taking risks, nevertheless. He had become the first modern gossip-column prince, keenly spied on by the new society papers such as *Truth, Vanity Fair,* and *The World* that mushroomed in the 1870s, competing for royal scoops and syndicating their columns to the provincial press. Everything he said or did was commented upon and often distorted. *The World* hinted at adultery, and warned Prince Hal, as it also called him, of the "gathering disfavour with which his widely conspicuous life is beginning to be watched."[46] The Queen's private secretary Henry Ponsonby reported "an undefined feeling" against Bertie, as he "does not treat the Princess fairly." Because Alix was more popular, any suspicion of unfaithfulness created indignation against him. He was accused of leading a frivolous life, but this, thought Ponsonby, was "hard on him for what is he to do."[47]

The week before Lillie was presented at court, Bertie made a speech in Paris at the opening of the great Exposition. He chaired the British section, and in his speech he declared, "I am convinced that the *entente cordiale* which exists between this country and our own is one which is not likely to change."[48] His words were welcomed by the French as signaling a thaw in relations with England, which had frozen into a cold war ever since the birth of the Third Republic. On 6 May 1878, Bertie met Léon Gambetta, the architect of the Republic, and the two men agreed in their distrust of Germany and Chancellor Bismarck. The visit had turned into a state event, and Bertie was followed by reporters wherever he went. When *"Vive la République!"* was cried and Bertie was seen to put his hat on his head, a gesture of sympathy that he didn't intend, he remarked, "I thought they were going to say 'Vive la France!'" The *Times* reporter insisted that Bertie had put his hat on simply because it was raining.[49]

Never before had Bertie been taken so seriously as a diplomatic figure. The experience went to his head. He confided in Carrington that when he became king, he intended to act as his own foreign secretary. Carrington repeated this to Gladstone, who was horrified, and growled that in that case, the prince would "probably find his Foreign Office in foreign parts."[50] In England, anyone who disagreed with Bertie's politics instantly declared that he was exceeding his constitutional powers. Abroad it was different. When he spoke to the Russians or the French, he was taken seriously; foreigners assumed that the British heir apparent carried the same weight at home as his counterparts abroad. This was the secret of his lifelong involvement in foreign politics. He had discovered that, in a Europe of monarchical great powers, his position gave him far more freedom and power to influence events abroad than those at home.

Bertie's biographers, trying to give shape and purpose to the life of the future king, picture him taking an active interest in the Balkan Crisis of 1876–78.* His views on the 1876 revolt of Serbs and Bulgarians against Turkish rule were certainly forthright. He staunchly supported the Ottoman Empire and blamed Russia for encouraging and promoting the Slavs. This brought him into line with Queen Victoria, who was fiercely anti-Russian, but caused a split with Affie, whose wife, Marie, was the daughter of the czar Alexander II. Alix's loyalties were also pro-Russian. Not only was her sister Minnie the wife of the czarevitch, but her brother Willie, King George I of Greece, depended on Russian support for his throne. But though the Balkan Crisis made fault lines in British politics, its impact on the royal family was far less seismic and divisive than the wars of German unification had been.

Bertie agreed with the pro-Turk Beaconsfield, who stubbornly refused to declare his sympathy for the Bulgarian Christians massacred by the Turks in the summer of 1876. When Gladstone launched a moral crusade against the Bulgarian atrocities and published a bestselling pamphlet, *The Bulgarian Horrors and the Question of the East,* Bertie wrote to prime minister Beaconsfield giving his support. "I deeply deplore the present agitation over the so-called Bulgarian atrocities. . . . It

---

* Sidney Lee titled his chapter on Bertie's life in 1876–78, "Political Estrangement from Russia," writing as if foreign policy was the prince's chief occupation. (Lee, *Edward VII.*)

must, I fear, weaken the hands of the government, who are so anxious to do all in their power to obtain peace."[51]

But the Foreign Office no longer sent Bertie dispatches. Beaconsfield grumbled that Bertie talked indiscreetly to his friends about government secrets, and Victoria ordered that dispatches should not be sent.[52] Her refusal to confide in Bertie contrasted starkly with her confidence in Leopold, twelve years Bertie's junior, who acted as her private secretary on Beaconsfield's recommendation (this was a move to block the influence of the Liberal Ponsonby, as Leopold was a staunch Tory). For his twenty-fourth birthday in April 1877, Leopold received a Cabinet key to the government red boxes, the coveted symbol of admission to the Queen's confidence, which had always been denied to Bertie. To avoid trouble with Leopold's "Royal Brothers," Beaconsfield advised the Queen to ask for a second Cabinet key for her own convenience, rather than mentioning Leopold by name.[53] Such matters were not discussed between Bertie and Victoria.

As Ponsonby wrote: "It is true that the Queen does communicate all unpleasant matters with the Prince of Wales through third persons—but so does he. They dread personal meetings on these controversies. Whenever they take place the Queen has always the best of it and he gives way on all points and throws any blame off himself quickly. But they write a great deal to each other—but even then avoid controversial subjects."[54]

Bertie's judgment on foreign affairs was worryingly naïve. His chief source of information on the military position in Turkey was his friend Colonel Valentine Baker, who had been dismissed from the 10th Hussars, of which Bertie was colonel in chief. Baker had been accused of attacking a girl in a railway carriage, and though he was acquitted of rape (but convicted of indecent assault), Victoria, who considered that he was a disgrace to the British Army, insisted on cashiering him. Bertie stood loyally by his friend, helping to get him appointed as a military adviser to the Turks, and as Pasha Baker, he became a military hero.[55] Bertie pestered Beaconsfield to see Baker, but the prime minister, who was no doubt fearful of annoying the Queen, declined to take his advice.[56] Ponsonby despaired at Bertie's inability to concentrate.

"Nothing can be more genial and pleasant than he is for a few minutes. But he does not endure. He can't keep up the interest for any length of time. And I don't think he ever will settle down to business."[57] To the suggestion that he should follow up his Indian tour by becoming a member of the Indian Council, Bertie was indifferent. (He did, however, lend his collection of Indian animals to London Zoo, which probably did more good, as visitor numbers soared, increasing the zoo's takings by over £6,000.)[58] Knollys complained of the difficulty of getting him to enter into any subject and decide on it. "They have to catch snap answers from him as he goes shooting etc."[59]

Just how much of a loose cannon the prince could be became evident in the winter of 1877–78, when Russia invaded Turkey and advanced toward Constantinople. Bertie now spoke openly about war with Russia; Lord Derby, the foreign secretary, who was a dove, complained that the hawk prince "talks loudly and foolishly in all companies."[60] English politicians dismissed Bertie's violent language as out of order, but, as Derby discovered, in Russia his explosions were taken seriously and created the impression that England was bent on war. Count Schouvaloff, the Russian ambassador in London, who knew better, "in vain tried to explain the position of the Prince of Wales, and the little importance that attaches to his words: but that is not easily understood in Petersburgh."[61]

Russia was eventually brought to book at the Congress of Berlin (13 June–13 July 1878). This was a personal triumph for Beaconsfield; Turkey regained its independence, and Britain gained Cyprus. The Congress alarmed the French, who feared a threat to their influence in Egypt, and made Britain so unpopular that the ambassador in Paris advised Bertie to postpone the visit he was due to make in July. Bertie did the opposite. He went to Paris; and he held mediation talks with Gambetta, which helped win around the French. Salisbury, newly appointed foreign secretary, wrote to thank him "very earnestly."[62] When Bertie did what his foreign ministers wanted, they were all smiles, but his position at home was always vulnerable.

At a reception that summer (Lillie related), the parchment-faced Beaconsfield sat wearing his newly awarded Garter ribbon. He was introduced to Lillie. "What can I do for you?" asked the prime minister. "Four new gowns for Ascot," came the pert reply, at which he laughed, patted her hand, and said, "You are a sensible young woman. Many a woman would have asked to have been made a duchess in her own right."[63]

Lillie's own story (which is unsubstantiated) implies that she was now recognized as royal mistress, like Charles II's Nell Gwyn. As her biographer has observed, however, her career was one of invention. She excelled at self-fashioning, carefully constructing an image of herself as royal mistress to project to the world.[64]

Historians will probably never know the intimate truth about Bertie and Lillie, but Bertie certainly pulled strings to advance her family. He asked Lord Lytton, the Indian viceroy, to promote her brother in the Indian Civil Service; Lytton, however, replied that Le Breton had only recently been promoted to chief inspector of post offices in Rajputana, and "to put him over the heads of all his seniors . . . would I fear be too rapid promotion even for Mrs. Langtree's [sic] brother."[65]

The Murrietas were rumored to have created a love nest for Lillie on their estate at Wadhurst, the new house that the two bachelor brothers, Christobel and Adriano de Murrieta, had built with the profits of their Argentinian trade. Here Bertie's friend Jesusa and her husband José de Murrieta, now ennobled by the King of Spain as the Marquess of Santurce, created fashion history by seating guests at separate tables in the dining room, arranged like a restaurant.*[66]

Members of the Marlborough House set attempted to curry favor by dotting the countryside with cottages ornées where the prince could conduct secret assignations. At Gunton, near Sandringham, it is well authenticated that Lord Suffield, who was Lillie's friend, lent her a shooting box, Elderton Lodge, where she could meet the prince.[67] The

* Wadhurst Park was built by E. J. Tarver in 1872–75, and another wing was added to entertain the Prince of Wales in 1881. It is now demolished. The Murrietas, who invested heavily in Argentinian railways, lost their fortune in the Barings crash of 1890, when Argentina defaulted on bond payments.

stories about royal love nests always feature Lillie, and never the other mistresses.[68] By keeping Lillie in secret houses, Bertie hoped to live a double life and shield Alix from embarrassment. The tales are revealing, too, about Lillie's ambivalent social status—in spite of her friendship with the prince, she was not considered a suitable house party guest.

Alix seems to have found some consolation in the support of Oliver Montagu. As Lady Antrim, later Alix's lady-in-waiting, recalled, the gallant Montagu "shielded her in every way, not least from his own great love, and managed to defeat gossip. Oliver Montagu was looked upon with awe by the young as he sauntered into a ballroom, regardless of anything but his beautiful Princess, who as a matter of course always danced the first after-supper waltz with him. But she remained marvellously circumspect."[69] An enigmatic letter that Montagu wrote to his father, Lord Sandwich, in October 1878 can be read as evidence of his tortured relationship with the princess:*

Yes, believe me, that though I says it as shouldn't, the cock child is not a bad'un at bottom. I know he has faults as others have, and perhaps even more of them, but his heart is in the right place. Outwardly he is a noisy crowing brute, but if everyone knew what his inward feelings are and what he has had to go through, they would not envy him his existence. I know not nor have I read of anyone put in the unfortunate position that I have been and yet, thank God, to have got through the worst without much damage to others.[70]

He could be talking about anything. But the words about his feelings and the position into which he has been put suggest that the unspoken subject of this letter is his painfully platonic relationship with his princess. Loyal cavalier that he was, he could hardly mention her by name.

* Montagu made frantic attempts to obtain a post in the royal household, but the Queen disliked his free and easy manners. (Richard Davenport-Hines, "A Radical Lord Chamberlain at a Tory Court," *Court Historian*, vol.16 [2011], p. 224.)

CHAPTER 14

Prince Hal

1878–81

The fourteenth of December 1878 was the seventeenth anniversary of Prince Albert's death. Bertie and Alix went to Windsor for the customary service in the mausoleum, but this year the melancholy occasion was clouded by impending tragedy. The previous day had been punctuated by alarming telegrams from Darmstadt, where Bertie's sister Alice lay desperately ill with diphtheria. Sir William Jenner, dispatched by the Queen, wired that the disease had spread to her windpipe; she had great difficulty in breathing, high fever, exhaustion, and restlessness.[1] The glands in her throat were so swollen that her neck was as thick as her cheeks. Her tonsils were coated with patches of false membrane, and the danger was that she would die of suffocation, as they obstructed her windpipe. Throttling by membrane had been the cause of the death of her four-year-old daughter, May, four weeks earlier.[2] At two thirty a.m., Alice became unconscious, and she died at 7:30 on the morning of the fourteenth. The cause of death of the thirty-five-year-old princess was given as exhaustion and cardiac failure.[3]

As soon as the Queen received the dreaded telegram, she went to Beatrice, returned to her room and spoke to Leopold, and only then went to Bertie's sitting room. She wrote in her journal:

He was not ready for a few minutes, but soon came out in his dressing gown, having received the same dreadful news from Sir William [Jenner], looking dreadfully pale and haggard, trying to repress his violent emotion, quite choked with it. His despair was great, *and he could hardly speak.* As I kissed him he said, "The good are always taken and the bad remain."[4]

The words in italics were cut from the 1926 edition of the Queen's letters, presumably because they showed a lack of manliness; but they give a glimpse of the most sympathetic side of Bertie's character— unguarded, emotional, and self-deprecatory.[5] As for Alix, when the Queen went in to see her while she dressed and took her in her arms, she said simply: "I wish I had died instead of her."[6]

The tragedy at Darmstadt had all the makings of a Victorian melodrama—except that it was genuinely heartbreaking. Apart from one daughter, Elizabeth (Ella), Alice's entire family, including her husband, Louis, had been infected with diphtheria within eight days. When little May died, her body was placed in a coffin covered with white flowers, and Alice was the only member of the family present at the funeral service in the castle. After it was over, she left the room and walked slowly upstairs. "At the top of the stairs she knelt down, and taking hold of the golden balustrade, looked into the mirror opposite to her to watch the little coffin being taken out of the house."[7]

Medical reports remarked on the unusual fact that none of the sixty members of the Hesse-Darmstadt household had been infected, and deduced that the infection was spread by kissing.[8] Alice herself allegedly caught the disease when she broke the news of May's death to her ten-year-old son, Ernie, who was so overcome that she embraced him—and thus her own death. Disraeli used his novelist's skills to paint a pathetic picture of this tragic kiss in his speech in the House of Lords, which "greatly moved" Bertie.[9]

As Victoria remarked, Alice had expected to die early and had been talking about it for years.[10] A family portrait made by Heinrich von Angeli in 1878 shows a paunchy, bearded Louis; Alice, wearing a strange nunlike garb, looks haggard and unhappy. Ever since the trauma of nursing her father, Albert, on his deathbed as an eighteen-year-old, she had suffered from depression.[11] For years she complained of failing vision, neuralgia, and "rheumatism," but her symptoms were so vague as to defy diagnosis. In 1876 she described herself as "absurdly" wanting in strength, dull, tired, and useless. "I have never in my life been like this before. I live on my sofa."[12] Queen Victoria, who saw her in the summer of 1878, thought she looked "very weak and delicate and is up to nothing," and when she heard of the diphtheria she dreaded that her semi-invalid daughter would be too frail to survive.[13]

Alice's son Frittie had inherited the hemophilia gene, and in 1873 the two-year-old had fallen from a window in Alice's bedroom and died soon after from internal bleeding on the brain. For months—years even—Alice could think of little else but the horror of his sudden death. It brought her exceptionally close to her surviving son, Ernie. "Seldom a mother and child so understood each other," she wrote. "It requires no words; he reads it in my eyes."[14] Alice was unfulfilled in her marriage to the amiable but bovine Louis. She was estranged from her mother, whose unfair letters made her cry with rage. "I wish I were dead," she wrote in 1877, "and it will probably not be too long before I give Mama that pleasure."[15] Morbid foreboding was always in the air at Darmstadt. Ernie, too, was profoundly affected by Frittie's death, and as a mawkish little boy he would say to Alice: "When I die, you must die too, and all the others; why can't [we] all die together? I don't like to die alone like Frittie."[16] Five years later, Alice and May did indeed die together.*

---

* Nor was this the last of the Hesses' tragedies. Alice's daughter, the czarina Alexandra, was murdered with all her family at Ekaterinburg in 1918. Ernie's eldest son, the Grand Duke

At Windsor on 14 December 1878, the dark blinds came down, and a fall of snow blanketed the castle in silent stillness. The Lord Chamberlain ordered the court to wear deep mourning for six weeks: black dresses, white gloves, pearls, and diamonds.[17] Victoria's reaction to Alice's death was strangely muted; for her, perhaps, nothing could ever be so bad again as Albert's death. It was Bertie who was overcome. "My Bertie . . . is <u>so</u> sad," wrote Alix.[18] "She was my favourite sister," Bertie told Lord Granville, "so good, so kind, so clever; we had gone through much together—my father's illness, then my own."[19]

Late on Monday, 16 December, Bertie, Leopold, and Helena's husband, Prince Christian, crossed to Flushing and traveled all the next day by train to Frankfurt. After the service in Darmstadt, Alice's coffin was drawn through thick snow to the mausoleum at Rosenhohe, where Frittie and May already lay. The mourners followed on foot; chief among them was Bertie. Alice's husband, Louis, though recovering from diphtheria, was not yet strong enough to walk through the snow. At ten thirty that night, an exhausted Bertie wrote to Knollys: "This has been a terribly trying day, and I hardly like to think of it, the interview with the poor G[ran]d Duke and the children was also inexpressibly painful. All was conducted with the greatest respect and quickly as was possible—but it was simply dreadful. I still feel as if I was under the impression of a horrid dream."[20]

Back at Windsor, a memorial service was held at the time that Alice's coffin was taken to the Rosenhohe. Alix, "who has been a real devoted sympathising daughter to me," gave her arm to the Queen as they walked into the private chapel, which was draped with black. Victoria bore up to the end, when the Dead March from *Saul* was played; then, in floods of tears, she retreated to Albert's Blue Room and knelt in prayer.[21]

George, was killed in 1937 along with his wife, Cecile, who was Prince Philip's sister, and their two young sons, in an air crash. Earl Mountbatten, who was the son of Alice's daughter Victoria, was assassinated in 1979 by a bomb planted by the Irish Republican Army that also killed his grandson. (see David Duff, *Hessian Tapestry* [Muller, 1967].)

After the funeral at Darmstadt, Bertie rejoined his mother at Windsor. Victoria went to see him as he sat writing in his room with Fossy, his little dog, lying beside him.[22] They talked of Alice's younger days, and Bertie was "so dear and nice."[23] "It has brought all so close together," wrote Victoria.[24] Later, he wrote her "a very dear kind [letter], speaking of Alix being 'much too good for him' and so delighted at my great praise of her."[25]

Alix's youngest sister, Thyra, was not a beauty like her sisters. At twenty-five she was considered an old maid, and her teeth stuck out. She was taller than Alix, and (according to Queen Victoria's adviser Howard Elphinstone) "decidedly clever and most sensible and agreeable."[26] Gossips whispered that she had given birth to an illegitimate child in 1871 when, at the age of eighteen, she disappeared abroad for eleven months; the father was supposed to be a Danish hussar named Marcher, who committed suicide shortly afterward. The Danish royal family claimed that the rumor was a smear story started by Bismarck, and that Thyra had, in fact, been ill, first with jaundice, and then with typhoid in Italy. In Rome, visiting Bertie and Alix, she met Ernest, Crown Prince of Hanover.[27] Ernest had an abnormally long neck, a nose so flat that it was almost nonexistent, narrow shoulders, and thick pebble spectacles. Alix thought him "the ugliest man there ever was made!!! But I like him so much."[28] Thyra fell in love with him at once.

Ernest's father, the blind King George V of Hanover, Queen Victoria's first cousin, had sided with the Austrians in the Austro-Prussian War of 1866, with catastrophic results. Prussia dethroned him, annexed Hanover, and sequestrated his immense hereditary fortune, which was known as the *Welfenfond*. Bismarck paid the income into his "reptile fund," the slush money he used to bribe the reptiles, as he called the liberal press. George V died in 1878, and Ernest wrote an ill-advised letter to the German emperor, laying claim to his title as King of Hanover. This destroyed any chance he had of getting his fortune back. He became locked into a quarrel with Prussia. Queen Victoria, who was his father's executrix, tried in vain to persuade him to drop

The royal family at Osborne, 1857. From left: Affie, Albert, Helena, Arthur, Alice, Victoria with baby Beatrice on her lap, Vicky, Leopold, Bertie.

Bertie at Oxford, 1859 (center). In solitary confinement with his keepers: his tutor Herbert Fisher (left), and his governor, General Bruce (right).

Bertie and Alix on their wedding day, 10 March 1863. Queen Victoria insisted on inviting the entire household to the ceremony in St. George's Chapel. Bertie was allowed only four friends.

The young Prince and Princess of Wales with baby Eddy.

Queen Victoria in mourning. Staring—glaring—straight into the camera.

Bertie's entry in the measure book of tailor Henry Poole. When he was first measured at Oxford in 1860, his chest was 33¾ inches; his waist 29¼. In 1905 his chest was 47 inches; his waist 46½. Alix's minuscule measurements (waist 21 inches, bust 31½ inches) are on the bottom line. Scrawled across the entry in pencil is: "Dead 6/5/10."

Bertie's brother Affie, Duke of Edinburgh, wearing the dress uniform of a naval officer.

Louise, Bertie's artistic sister.

Alice, Bertie's favorite sister, with her husband, Louis, Grand Duke of Hesse.

House party, 1860s. Lady-in-waiting Lady Macclesfield, the "precise little stick" who
delivered Eddy, looks up at Alix. Oliver Montagu, equerry and "wicked boy,"
lies on the grass at Alix's feet. Bertie stands behind holding his hat.

Goodwood party, 1860s. Bertie poses in a white suit (left).
Alix, fourth left, appears to ignore him.

Alix, with her hair down,
convalescing from her illness
with a seedy-looking Bertie
at her side, 1867. Georgie
and Eddy in frocks.

Hunting party at Kimbolton, 1868. Bertie stands
on the balcony (middle). Beside him is Lord
Hartington, and next to Hartington is his
mistress Louise, Duchess of Manchester.
Below, hatless, is Louise's husband,
the Duke of Manchester.

The Prince of Wales, c. 1867: Known for
his womanizing and gambling, Bertie was
an unpopular figure at this time.

Susan Vane-Tempest, Bertie's discarded
mistress. "I cannot describe to you <u>how</u>
wretched I am," she wrote him.

John Brown. Adored by Victoria but hated by the household, who called him "The Queen's stallion."

Danish sisters: Alix (right) and Minnie "double dressing."

Minnie's Russian family. The czar, Alexander II (seated) in front of his daughter, the Grand Duchess Marie, who married Affie in 1874. Alix's sister Minnie sits with her baby, the future Nicholas II, on her knee. Her bearlike husband, the czarevitch Sasha, later Alexander III, stands behind her.

Alix (left) and (right) Oliver Montagu, her close friend
and admirer. His support helped her survive Bertie's
unfaithfulness and Eddy's death.

Bertie in Ceylon, 1875.

Lillie Langtry, the Professional Beauty
(PB) whose Grecian profile took
London—and Bertie—by storm.

Alix, photographed by Alexander Bassano in
1881. Note the collar of pearls concealing
the scar on her neck.

Jennie Churchill, Bertie's *chère amie*.
"Had Lady Randolph Churchill
been like her face she would've
governed the world."

his claim to the throne of Hanover. Dreading Victoria's wrath if he married a wife of whom she disapproved, Ernest distanced himself from Princess Thyra.

The deadlock was broken by Alix. She wrote to Ernest telling him that Thyra much wished to see him, and suggested a secret meeting in Frankfurt. Fearing a trap, Ernest hesitated, but Alix insisted, and accordingly, one day in September 1878, Queen Louise of Denmark and her daughters Alix and Thyra drove into Frankfurt, pretending that they needed to see an ear doctor. Ernest duly appeared at the appointed rendezvous. First Alix talked to him, and then Queen Louise, while Thyra waited anxiously in the water closet. At last Thyra was allowed to see Ernest alone. She wasted no time. As soon as he had kissed her hand, she proposed to him herself. Waiting outside the door, Queen Louise became agitated and, fearing that the meeting was a mistake and Ernest was indifferent, pushed Alix into the room. Alix saw at once that the radiant Thyra had been accepted and all was settled, but this made Queen Louise even more flustered. "My God, then *she* has proposed," she declared, and tried to intervene, but it was too late; the couple were locked in an embrace. When the time came to leave, the Queen had to force them apart. "I stood behind the door," Alix told Minnie, "and saw their parting kiss!!!"[29]

By marrying Thyra, Ernest leapfrogged from being a sacked ruler at the bottom of the royal heap, and positioned himself at the center of the anti-Prussian dynastic bloc, becoming brother-in-law to the Prince of Wales, the Russian czarevitch, *and* the King of Greece.[30]

At the wedding in Copenhagen, a large party of Hanoverians appeared, which gave Berlin an excuse to denounce the Danish king for harboring conspirators against the German Empire. The German ambassador was conspicuously absent. The deterioration of Denmark's relations with Berlin worried Bertie, and he worked behind the scenes to help Ernest and protect the Danes from Bismarck's anger. "I foresee troubles ahead for my excellent brother-in-law," he told Sir Charles Wyke, the British ambassador in Copenhagen. "If he had only not irritated the German Emperor by that injudicious letter all the bullying which has since taken place would not have occurred and he might now have had his fortune."[31] Bertie appealed to Vicky, who explained that though she sympathized with Ernest and Thyra, private intervention by Victoria or Bertie could do no good unless Ernest formally rescinded his letter to the German emperor. "The question does not only resolve itself into what is 'right' or 'wrong.' I wish it were as simple as that!" she told Bertie, and warned, "I . . . think it a pity that political questions should step in to disturb the peace and harmony of the family and be treated as personal ones!"[32] But of course the personal *was* political—that is the essence of dynastic diplomacy—and the German emperor's bullying of Ernest served only to tighten the links of the anti-Berlin dynastic bloc.

Bertie had wanted to educate Eddy at a public school, preferably Wellington, of which he was a governor. When Eddy was thirteen, this plan was abruptly abandoned. His tutor Dalton wrote darkly of the young prince's backwardness, and warned against separating the brothers. "Prince Albert Victor [Eddy] requires the stimulus of Prince George's company to induce him to work at all. If Prince George left Prince Albert Victor, the education of the latter, even now extremely difficult, would be rendered still more so."[33] He proposed sending Eddy to Dartmouth as a naval cadet, along with Prince George; the unspoken advantage of this arrangement was that it ensured that he remained their tutor.

Dalton had no trouble in convincing Bertie of the wisdom of his plan. But Queen Victoria, who was the ultimate arbiter in matters of her grandsons' education, objected strongly to Dartmouth, on the somewhat surprising grounds that the navy would "make them think that their own Country is superior to any other," which was undesirable in a king, who needed to be free from all national prejudices.[34] Dalton, who showed more talent for intrigue than he did for teaching, managed to overcome the Queen's objections, and in October 1877 the two boys were dispatched to the *Britannia,* the training ship at Dartmouth, accompanied by Dalton. For Alix, the parting from her sons was "a great wrench": "poor little boys, they cried so bitterly."[35]

For Eddy, Dartmouth was a disaster. In December 1878, Lord Ramsay, the commander of the *Britannia,* nerved himself to write to the Prince of Wales about the boy's progress: "It is <u>very</u>, <u>very</u> unsatisfactory, indeed so unsatisfactory that I really think Your Royal Highness should reconsider the advisability of his remaining in the *Britannia.* . . . Prince Edward is learning nothing. . . . And this is not the worst. It is still more discouraging that every master and tutor who has had to do with him seems to despair of being able to teach him anything. . . . The experiment . . . has failed."[36] Prince George, on the other hand, was making excellent progress, doing better every day.

After this bombshell, it can have come as no surprise when Eddy failed the passing-out examination. Dalton, however, emerged unscathed. He took no responsibility for sending Eddy to Dartmouth. Instead, he blamed the boy's inadequacy. Eddy's problem was "that extreme inability . . . to fix his attention to any given subject for more than a few minutes consecutively." According to Dalton, "it is to physical causes that one must look for an explanation of the abnormally dormant condition of his mental powers." The prognosis was hopeful, as the prince would improve with time; meanwhile, competition with boys of his own age must be avoided. Dalton proposed a solution that could hardly have been more extreme: Eddy and George should be launched together on a world cruise for two years. Naturally, their tutor would accompany them.[37]

Once again, Dalton easily persuaded the royal parents of his bizarre proposal. When Victoria first heard of the idea, she "did not like it all," but Dalton succeeded in changing her mind.[38] The plan was condemned by the Cabinet, which objected that it would "agitate and distress the country."[39] But this intervention backfired, as Bertie and the Queen joined forces in their annoyance at the politicians' unwarranted interference.*[40]

---

* When Dalton heard that the *Bacchante,* a new ironclad corvette, had been chosen, he objected that it was not safe and demanded that the two princes should be separated. Bertie was "very much put out" by Dalton's change of mind, and after much toing and froing Dalton eventually agreed to the *Bacchante.* (RA VIC/Add C07/1, Francis Knollys to Henry Ponsonby, n.d. See Ponsonby's Memo, n.d., in Arthur Ponsonby, *Henry Ponsonby,* p. 105.)

Bertie accompanied Eddy and Georgie to Portsmouth and saw them depart for a six-month cruise to the West Indies. On board the *Bacchante,* the two boys shared a plainly furnished cabin, which was connected with Dalton's cabin by a door cut through the bulkhead.[41] "Felt parting from dear boys dreadfully," Bertie wired Victoria.[42] He told Georgie: "I shall never forget what I felt wishing you goodbye on the 19th."[43] No one could accuse him of being hard-hearted toward his sons.

The shocking thing about the sorry tale of the education of the princes, especially Eddy, is the unquestioning trust that both Bertie and Alix placed in Dalton. "He has my total confidence," wrote Alix, "he is such an upright man whose aim <u>totally</u> is the good of the boys!"[44] Dalton had contrived to make himself indispensable by preying on the parents' fears. His talk of the "physical causes" of Eddy's backwardness has given rise to all sorts of speculation. Some say that Eddy had inherited Alix's deafness, others that his two-month-premature birth caused "neuro-developmental impairments," which meant that he was educationally subnormal, or that he suffered from petit mal epilepsy.[45] Banishing him on a world cruise was not helpful. Anything better calculated to encourage speculation that he was abnormal can hardly be imagined. The truth was that Eddy was lazy and a slow developer, and today he might be diagnosed with attention deficit disorder. But the letters he wrote as a young man show a lively intelligence. It's hard to avoid the conclusion that his problems were made worse by Dalton and his system of shutting him up for years in isolation on a ship.

Sarah Bernhardt, the Divine Sarah, took London by storm in the summer of 1879 with her passionate performance in the Comédie-Française's *Phèdre.* It left her so shattered that she vomited blood all night as her doctor pressed crushed ice to her lips. The illegitimate child of a Jewish courtesan, Sarah Bernhardt had frizzy red hair, a white face, and an unfashionably waif-like figure. She possessed a very modern genius for publicity. At the house she rented in Chester Square, she posed for photographers wearing the suit of white *pantalons* and jacket that she used for painting, and she bought a cheetah and a wolf-hound to add to the menagerie of a monkey and a parrot that she kept in the garden.[46] Naturally, Bertie was captivated. He watched her perform night after night, and he visited her gallery in Piccadilly.[47] Sarah was introduced to the prince. "I've just come back from the P of W," she scrawled to director Edmond Got. "It is 1:20 and I cannot rehearse at this hour. The Prince has kept me since 11. . . . I shall make amends tomorrow by knowing my part."[48] There were rumors, there always were, of an affair, but this was a flirtation, beneficial not only to Bertie, who was addicted to celebrity—a craving he shared with Oscar Wilde, passionate admirer of both Lillie Langtry and Sarah—but also to Bernhardt herself, who gained social validation from his approval. She was lionized, much to the chagrin of Lady Frederick Cavendish, who thought it "outrageous" that an actress, and a "shameless" one at that, should be invited to the houses of respectable people.*[49]

Lillie Langtry found herself eclipsed. She was never in love with Bertie; in old age she remarked that she was always a little afraid of him, and "he always smelt so very strongly of cigars."[50] For her, what mattered was her status as royal favorite, and here the warning signs were plain to see. The names of Mr. and Mrs. Langtry first appear in the guest list for a Marlborough House Sunday dinner in Bertie's diary in April 1879.[51] The fact that Bertie invited Lillie to dine with Alix indicates that he no longer considered her to be his mistress. An exchange at a charity bazaar at the Albert Hall in July neatly encapsulates her declining stock. Bertie bought a cup of tea from Mrs. Langtry's stall. Before handing it to him, she put it to her lips. "I should like a clean one please," snapped Bertie.[52] The public snub is the closest we can get to Bertie's feelings, which are, as ever, unrecorded. Lillie, for her part,

* When Bernhardt came to London in 1881, Bertie asked some English ladies to be invited to a supper that he directed to be given for her at the wish of the Duc d'Aumale. The party was not a success. "It was one thing to get [the English women] to go, and another thing to get them to talk when they were there; and the result was that, as they would not talk to Sarah Bernhardt and she would not talk to them, and as the Duc d'Aumale was deaf and not inclined to make conversation on his own account, nobody talked at all, and an absolute reign of the most dismal silence ensued." (Stephen Gwynn and Gertrude Tuckwell, *Life of Sir Charles Dilke* [John Murray, 1917], vol. 1, p. 414.)

embarked on an affair with a younger man—the teenage Lord Shrewsbury, who was just nineteen. One afternoon Bertie called unexpectedly (Lillie had tried to put him off, but he didn't receive her note) and
found her with Shrewsbury. According to the story Lord Derby heard,
the lovers were discovered in flagrante, and a terrible row ensued.[53]
Lillie even thought of marrying Shrewsbury, but decided against it, as
she found him "quite as uneducated and much more jealous than
Ned . . . and he gets worse every day—In fact I should despise him in a
month."[54]

The new breed of scurrilous gossip papers, which had created Lillie
Langtry, now threatened to destroy her, and burn Bertie in the process.
Town Talk was a weekly London society paper edited and published by
the twenty-seven-year-old Adolphus Rosenberg. Throughout September, it ran a story that Ned Langtry had filed a petition for divorce, and
that the Prince of Wales was named as corespondent.

Rosenberg then claimed that Patsy Cornwallis-West used her house
at 49 Eaton Place as a photography studio, running from one camera
to another in order to mass-produce the *cartes de visite* that she sold on
commission in a Victorian version of *Hello!* magazine. Patsy's husband
sued for libel at once. When the court case opened, Rosenberg was
surprised to find himself further indicted for publishing libels against
the Langtrys.[55] How the notoriously hard up Ned Langtry paid the
lawyer's fees has never been explained.

Neither Lillie nor Patsy was present in court. Ned Langtry testified:
"I have read these articles and there is not one single word of truth in
them. . . . I am now living at home with my wife."[56] Rosenberg was
sentenced to eighteen months in prison. But the silencing of *Town Talk*
was achieved at a cost. Day after day throughout October 1879, *The
Times* had printed column inches repeating the paper's allegations
against the Prince of Wales.

Queen Victoria, who was always generous when Bertie was in trouble, blamed his love of country house parties. "It is what has done dear
Bertie so much harm," she told Vicky. "That visiting is . . . the worst
thing I know and such a bore. The gentlemen go out shooting and the

ladies spend the whole day idling and gossiping together. Alix hardly ever goes now—she hates it so."[57]

The fact was that at thirty-eight, Bertie was a playboy Prince Hal, poised dangerously close to the edge of scandal. The London society press created a discourse of social slights and innuendo, of fashion and tittle-tattle, that reverberated nationally as it was reprinted in the gossip pages of local newspapers. Knollys's desk filled with letters about petty social disputes, gambling debts, and slanderous chitchat and quarrels with *Vanity Fair*. Bertie had become the chief of the aristocratic tribe, ruling over the atavistic honor culture of the Victorian nobility, but this was hardly a fit role for a modern prince. The problem—what was the Prince of Wales to *do*?—remained unsolved.

Or so it seemed. The Marlborough House mailbag for 1879 also includes business letters from Beaconsfield about matters such as Egypt.[58] There was correspondence with the Colonial Office about a Colonial Exhibition in New South Wales, with the Foreign Office about the Paris Universal Exhibition, with the Archbishop of Canterbury about the Society for Promoting Christian Knowledge and with the governors of Calcutta about the water supply in Dacca. Bertie's life had a serious side, which is too easily overlooked. He performed twenty public engagements in 1879, visiting schools and hospitals, laying foundation stones, and presiding at dinners; he made nineteen appearances in the House of Lords, and at Buckingham Palace he held four levees, two drawing rooms, and two state concerts.*[59] When the Queen retreated to the Italian lakes in March, "Prince Hal" told Beaconsfield that he wished to be in frequent communication with the prime minister. "This is all very well," commented Beaconsfield, "if it do not take, as threatened, the form of a rather protracted Sandringham visit."[60]

Bertie's diary for 1880 records at least seven visits from Prince Louis of Battenberg.[61] The handsome twenty-six-year-old naval officer was on

* In the same year, he attended the theater, opera, or concerts on eighty occasions.

leave and half-pay, and on his frequent visits to London he stayed at Marlborough House.

Louis was the eldest of four Battenberg sons, and like his brothers, Alexander (Sandro) and Henry (Liko), he shamelessly exploited his charm and royal family connections to promote his career. Since joining the Royal Navy at age fifteen, he had benefited greatly from the patronage and generosity of "Uncle Bertie." Louis's son, Lord Mountbatten, was later to devote much effort to elaborating a romantic version of his antecedents, insisting that the Battenbergs were equal members of the German royal family. Louis was the son of a cousin of Princess Alice's husband, the Grand Duke of Hesse, by a morganatic marriage—that is, a marriage to a woman who was not of royal rank.[62] Provincial German courts were obsessed with the blood royal, the magic elixir that empowered toy-town princesses to marry kings, and in the snobbish world of the *Almanac de Gotha* the Battenbergs were looked down upon as "half-castes." As Vicky's husband, Fritz, remarked, they were "not . . . of the blood—a little like . . . animals"—a comment that perhaps says as much about Fritz as it does about them.[63]

In 1880, Louis Battenberg began an affair with Lillie Langtry. Whether Bertie knew about this and was complicit, as some have suggested, or whether he was irked by his good-looking young cousin stealing Lillie away from him can only be surmised; we have no real evidence either way.[64] At a ball in May or June 1880, so the story goes, Lillie is supposed to have angered the prince by drinking too much champagne and slipping a spoonful of strawberry ice down the back of his neck. This was lèse-majesté indeed; Bertie could never bear to be teased.[65] Lillie denied the incident, claiming that it was actually Patsy Cornwallis-West who was responsible; true or not, the story can be read as a measure of her falling stock with Bertie.[66] There is no doubt that the prince wanted to distance himself from the scandal of the court case involving Lillie and Patsy Cornwallis-West.

At a Sunday dinner at Marlborough House (so Lillie related in her memoirs), she became suddenly ill with stomach pains, and Alix implored her to leave early. The royal physician Francis Laking followed her home to Norfolk Street. The next day, to Lillie's everlasting delight, Alix called at Norfolk Street, accompanied by Charlotte Knollys, and made tea for her.[67] Neither Bertie nor Alix mentions these events in their diaries, and this episode could easily be dismissed as yet another of Lillie's apocryphal stories. Being forgiven by Alix was the fantasy of every ex-mistress. It validated the mistress socially and gave closure to the affair. In this instance, however, there seems to be some truth in Lillie's story. She wrote a letter shortly afterward to her friend Lord Wharncliffe:

> I have been so seedy again lately. . . . I felt so unwell after dinner that Sunday at Marlborough House that I had to leave an hour before the rest. I tell you this because no doubt you will hear as I did that I fainted <u>at dinner</u> because the Prince wasn't civil enough!!!
>
> The Princess and Miss Knollys came to see me before they left town and had tea and stayed for an hour. I was so puffed up about it . . . more especially as she kissed me when she left.[68]

Lillie's letters to Lord Wharncliffe give edited highlights of her social career, but she would hardly have invented a dinner at Marlborough House, nor Alix's visit—though her later claim that Alix made her a cup of tea seems improbable, to say the least. (Did Alix know *how* to make tea?)

What Lillie chose not to reveal in her letter to Wharncliffe was the reason why she felt unwell. She was pregnant. Which of her many lovers was the father of the child was a puzzle, most likely even to Lillie herself. The one man who was not in the frame was her husband, Ned, as he had walked out after the *Town Talk* libel case. The obvious candidate was Louis Battenberg.[69] Lillie told him that he was the father, and he believed her. He confessed to his parents, who put paid to any foolish notions he might have had of marrying Lillie and arranged a financial settlement.[70] Bertie may have worried that the child was his—there is a story that he tossed for paternity with Battenberg and lost—but it's unlikely that he would have introduced Lillie to Alix and allowed his wife to become involved if he was sleeping with Lillie at the time.[71] Whoever the father was, hushing up the scandal was imperative. Lillie was lent £2,000 to pay her debts, and her husband, Ned, who often visited her unannounced, was prevented from seeing her, constantly occupied with invitations to shoot or fish. Keeping him in ignorance of the pregnancy was vital; he was angry and resentful, and the worry was that if he discovered that Lillie was pregnant by another man, he might sue for divorce, dragging Bertie into the law courts. Lillie spent the summer holiday in Jersey. One Friday in October, by now four months pregnant, she visited London briefly and saw Bertie.[72] On 17 October 1880, Bertie held a meeting with his doctor, Oscar Clayton, and saw Louis Battenberg.[73] The same day, Louis departed on a two-year voyage around the world on the aptly named *Inconstant*. Lillie herself was spirited away to France. Her baby was born on 18 March 1881—a girl named Jeanne Marie.

What Bertie did not know was that throughout her pregnancy Lillie clung passionately to another man. His name was Arthur Jones; a rakish Jersey sportsman, he was the illegitimate son of Lord Ranelagh. His sister Alice, another illegitimate child of Lord Ranelagh, had married Lillie's brother Clement Le Breton. Lillie's letters to Jones, discovered in 1978, make it clear that she preferred plain Mr. Jones to both the Prince of Wales and the glamorous Prince Louis Battenberg. She told Jones that he was the father of her child, and he bought the potions from the chemist that she took in fruitless efforts to precipitate an abortion. The love letters she wrote during her pregnancy suggest that she at least was convinced that the baby was his, and he was with her in Paris when the child was born.*[74]

---

* Society, on the other hand, believed that the child was Louis Battenberg's. Jeanne married the Conservative politician Ian Malcolm in 1902. Margot Asquith, crashingly tactless, told the unsuspecting bride on her wedding day that her real father was not Ned Langtry but Louis Battenberg, causing a lifelong rift between Lillie and her daughter. When Lillie's granddaughter Mary Malcolm died in 2010, her obituaries claimed that her grandfather was Edward VII.

Oscar Wilde wrote *Lady Windermere's Fan* in 1891. He offered Lillie the part of Mrs. Erlynne, which she refused. "Why he ever supposed it would have been . . . a suitable play for me I cannot imagine," she wrote, disingenuously.[75] In the play, Mrs. Erlynne is a professional beauty with a heart of gold. She is hated by the society ladies, one of whom quips, "Many a woman has a past, but I am told she had at least eleven, and they all fit."

"You whose whole life is a lie, could you speak the truth about anything?" asks another. But Wilde's play turns on the idea that it is London society that is morally corrupt, not Mrs. Erlynne, who has been redeemed through her suffering and disgrace. "You don't know," she says, "what it is to fall into the pit, to be despised, mocked, abandoned, sneered at—to be an outcast! To find the door shut against one, to have to creep in by hideous byways, afraid every moment lest the mask should be stripped from one's face."[76]

Bertie helped to pull Lillie out of the pit. After her baby was born, he did all he could to support her career as an actor, making a conspicuous appearance at her debut performance of *She Stoops to Conquer*.[77] Lillie was a moderate success on the stage; as the diarist Loulou Harcourt wrote, after seeing her in *School for Scandal* in 1885: "She is fairly good when she is simply acting the lady of fashion moving about in society but the moment she tries to show any passion or force of feeling she is a miserable failure and proves herself to be no actress but people will continue to go and see her because she is Mrs. Langtry and is dressed by Worth."[78] Thanks to Bertie's patronage, Lillie received a semi-royal welcome when she toured the United States, and she became a successful racehorse owner—she was the first woman owner to win the Cesarewitch.

Lillie's long-estranged husband, Ned, died of drink in Chester Asylum in 1897. Francis Knollys was kept closely informed by the solicitor George Lewis when Ned Langtry's landlord threatened blackmail, claiming to possess compromising letters Bertie had written to Lillie. "I was upon friendly terms with Mr. Langtry up to the last," wrote

Lewis. "I am sure he would sooner have sent me any letters than have given them to his landlord."[79] It seems that Ned Langtry used George Lewis as a broker, trading silence and cash in exchange for Bertie's love letters. Bertie, meanwhile, maintained a lifelong friendship with Lillie. "How I wish you were on board sailing with me now," he wrote from Cowes in 1885.[80] He attended her opening nights—"I count upon you to reserve the Box for me."[81] He helped arrange for her daughter, Jeanne, to be presented to the Queen.[82] He even gave Lillie a dog that had belonged to his current mistress, Lady Warwick: "Perhaps you would write Lady W[arwick] a line to W[arwick] Castle and tell her you like the dog and ask her the name."[83]

Alix spent the summer of 1879 in Denmark with her sister Minnie, staying with King Christian at Bernstorff, his summer residence. An unpretentious early-nineteenth-century building with whitewashed walls, Bernstorff stood in a romantic park beside the sea. It had been the childhood holiday retreat of Alix and Minnie, and that summer the two sisters insisted on staying there together, refusing to move to the grander and larger castle of Fredensborg. They even shared the bedroom they had used as girls.[84] The house was crammed with Romanovs and Waleses and their suites, and twenty or thirty people sat down to dinner each night at five o'clock, which, complained Charlotte Knollys, made the evenings "dreadfully long."[85] It rained every day, and Charlotte found that "one day here is so exactly like the other that there really is nothing to tell."[86]

Minnie's husband the czarevitch Alexander arrived, bringing with him four yachts. Charlotte Knollys thought him "much improved in manners (he used to be rather rough)."[87] Alix reported that he was "most amiable . . . sensible and by no means violent in politics."[88] When Bertie joined the party, arriving on board his own yacht *Osborne,* Queen Victoria worried that her indiscreet son would cause trouble with England's archenemy. Bertie replied diplomatically: "I shall of course avoid politics as much as possible but as he married dear Alix's sister whom I am very fond of, I am most anxious that our relations should not be strained."[89] The two brothers-in-law competed to entertain on their yachts. In Paris, on the journey home, they spent four days together, Bertie showing the czarevitch round the boulevards. Beaconsfield commented that Bertie had "come back very Russian, they say."[90]

Back in England, Alix missed "my own angelic little Minnie." Usually, she told Minnie, she could survive their separations, but this time, "I have been so miserable that everyone asks what is wrong with me, but it was only homesickness for you!!"[91] She found herself talking aloud, imagining that she could hear Minnie's voice speaking to her. "It is always a pleasure to me when somebody says our voices are alike and that we look like each other!"[92] It was as if Minnie was the other half of herself, wearing the same clothes, speaking in the same voice. Having a doppelgänger made her feel secure.

At Sandringham, she rode her six horses every day and indulged her passion for hunting. This had to be kept secret from the Queen, who disapproved almost as strongly of princesses riding to hounds as she did of them breast-feeding, but Alix found it more thrilling each time, in spite of bloodcurdling falls. On one occasion, the horse jumped and "I silly animal lost my balance and flew over the wrong side, head down, thinking my last moment had come—but I got my head out of the sand and picked myself half up, then I talked to the horse, and then it stopped, the sweet animal—then one of the gentlemen, [Dighton] Probyn, jumped off and pushed me into the saddle and then everything was well and I hurried on!!!" Another time the horse jumped over a wide, deep ditch, "but it jumped too short and put its head through a fence, getting so afraid that it went on its hind legs down into the ditch and there we walked up and down and I could not get it out." Eventually it rolled out, and fortunately both horse and rider were unharmed. She implored Minnie, "Do not tell!"[93]

At Sandringham, Alix was adored. Mrs. Louise Cresswell, the lady farmer and tenant of Appleton House on the estate, worshipped her. Alix would visit for tea, driving herself over in her four-pony carriage. Mrs. Cresswell was an occasional guest at the Big House, but she was terrified of the prince. He was frighteningly unpredictable—a jovial figure in the ballroom, but a tyrannical Henry VIII on the estate. His black looks spelled disaster.

Mrs. Cresswell fought a running war against the estate office, complaining that the royal pheasants and hares ruined her crops, and the clash sharpened as agricultural depression deepened after the wet summer of 1879. "Every proprietor of land is 'down in the mouth' at present," wrote Bertie, and Mrs. Cresswell complained that he showed her scant charity.[94] In 1880, the bank foreclosed on Mrs. Cresswell and called in its loans. She later wrote a book describing her battles, entitled *Eighteen Years on the Sandringham Estate* (1887), in which she failed to mention the fact that she owed more than two years' rent. As her debts grew, she became convinced that she was being persecuted by HRH. The estate was reluctant to evict her, but their offers to help were met by threats of lawsuits, wild accusations, and unreasonable demands for rent reductions.[95] Bertie emerges if anything with credit from the episode, but Mrs. Cresswell was able to write a one-sided account, presenting herself as the innocent victim of HRH's Germanic lust for shooting—an attack to which he was powerless to reply.

Bertie stayed at Hughenden with Beaconsfield for a night in January 1880. The court-loving prime minister fussed about the visit and the guest list for weeks beforehand. He threw a small dinner party, which was a triumph, and the next morning, while Bertie retired to write to Alix, dashed off an ecstatic report to Lady Bradford. Prince Hal had "praised the house, praised his dinner, praised the pictures; praised everything; was himself most agreeable in conversation, said some good things and told more." The prince went to bed no later than midnight, and Major Teesdale the equerry told Beaconsfield that "in regard to late hours, eating, drinking, everything, there is a great and hugely beneficial change in his life."[96]

Bertie's feelings toward Beaconsfield were ambivalent. On the whole, he sympathized with his politics, especially in foreign affairs. But he distrusted Beaconsfield's knowing irony, he bristled at his camp obsequiousness, and he despised his inability to say what he thought to his face. Above all, Bertie disliked Beaconsfield because he was Victoria's favorite. He worried that Victoria confided too much, and that, like John Brown, Beaconsfield knew too many family secrets.* With Gladstone, the opposite was the case. Bertie shared his mother's opposition to Gladstone's Liberal politics, though his views were less extreme. But he had no sympathy with Victoria's violent dislike of Gladstone himself. On the contrary, he found Gladstone personally agreeable.

In March 1880, Beaconsfield called a snap election and was unexpectedly and overwhelmingly defeated. Rather than wait to meet defeat in Parliament, as was customary, he made constitutional history by resigning immediately, and Queen Victoria found herself confronted with the inevitability of a hated Liberal government, with Gladstone as it its most likely prime minister. She told Ponsonby she would rather abdicate than appoint "that half-mad firebrand," and she endeavored to make the Whig Lord Hartington prime minister instead.[97]

For the first time in his life, Bertie attempted to play a part behind the scenes. He was a friend of Hartington's, and he was on good terms with Lord Granville, the third candidate for the premiership. He had several meetings with Hartington, which he reported to Ponsonby: "I think it right to let you know that I had a long conversation again with Hartington yesterday evening—and he is more anxious than ever that the Queen should send for Mr. Gladstone to form a government instead of sending either for Lord Granville or himself." Personally, Bertie was "strongly of the opinion that the Queen should send for Mr. Gladstone. Far better that she should take the initiative than that it should be forced on her."[98] When Ponsonby showed Bertie's letter to the Queen, she scrawled furiously across it: "The Prince of Wales . . . has no right to meddle and never has done so before. Lord Hartington must be told . . . that the Queen cannot allow any private and intimate communications to go on between them, or all confidence will be impossible."[99]

* See pp. 585–86.

The Prince of Wales had indeed no constitutional role, nor had the Queen asked him to intervene. But his advice was sensible, well meant, and correct—Gladstone was the inevitable prime minister, and for the Queen to block him would have been a dangerous mistake. By snubbing Bertie so brutally, Victoria could hardly fail to make trouble. Bertie blamed his youngest brother, Prince Leopold, who was a staunch Tory and Beaconsfield's pet. Leopold enjoyed the Queen's confidence and acted as her adviser during the ministerial crisis, and Bertie accused him of poisoning the Queen against Gladstone and persuading her that Gladstone was an enemy of the royal family.[100]

Soon the prince and his mother were quarreling again. The Queen proposed to make Bertie colonel in chief of the Household Cavalry, but in exchange she demanded that he should give up his colonelcy of the Rifle Brigade, which she desired to transfer to Prince Arthur. Bertie abandoned the Rifles with "extreme reluctance," and let it be known that he would have preferred to keep both regiments.[101] Without telling the Queen, like a small boy he persuaded Arthur to allow him to wear the Rifles' black buttons whenever he chose. Victoria wrote irritably to Arthur: "I wish Bertie would not meddle so much in everything concerning you brothers as he does now; for you are my children and you owe him no allegiance or obedience, which belongs only to me! Pray do not yield to him, for he has no right to do it. . . . He was most unkind to poor Leopold the other day, but he won't stand being treated like a little child."[102] Bertie, for his part, complained that Victoria did not consult him. "I do not think that I am prone to 'let the cat out of the bag' as a rule, or betray confidences, but I own that it is often with great regret that I either learn from others or see in the newspapers hints or facts stated with regard to members of our family," he told the Queen.[103]

"Receive sad intelligence of assassination of Emperor of Russia by explosive bomb!" noted Bertie on 13 March 1881.[104] The czar Alexander II had lived like a hunted animal in the last months of his life, repeatedly targeted by terrorists, and he was eventually murdered driving in his sleigh in St. Petersburg. In London, the Liberal politician Charles Dilke watched Bertie at the mass in the Russian chapel. The small room was packed and stifled with incense. Bertie wore a heavy uniform and carried a lighted taper, and Dilke saw him go to sleep standing, "his taper gradually turn round and gutter on the floor."[105]

The new czar, Alexander III, was Bertie's brother-in-law, and in spite of the security risks and hostility toward Russia, Bertie persuaded a reluctant Victoria to allow him and Alix to attend the funeral. This was his third visit to Russia. "There is very general surprise expressed at them being allowed to go there at all," commented Loulou Harcourt in his diary.[106]

On the day of the funeral, St. Petersburg was blotted out by thick snow raked by a bitter, swirling wind. The city buzzed with rumors of mines that had been timed to detonate during the service. Inside the heavily guarded Peter and Paul Cathedral, the atmosphere was overpoweringly hot and perfumed with flowers and incense. Bertie and Alix arrived after the interminable funeral mass had already begun, and watched as Minnie—now styled the Empress Marie Feodorovna—along with the rest of the czar's family, filed past and one by one kissed the mutilated hands of the blackened and putrefying corpse of Alexander II, which lay in its open coffin.[107] At least Alix was spared the kissing.

The next day Bertie invested his brother-in-law Alexander III with the Order of the Garter at the Anitchkoff Palace, where he and Alix were staying. The new czar had moved there from the Winter Palace, but even here he was a virtual prisoner, in constant danger of assassination, and confined for exercise to the palace backyard, which, Bertie declared, was an area unworthy of a London slum.[108] The Garter ceremony was performed privately. As Bertie marched into the throne room at the head of five members of his staff, carrying the insignia on narrow velvet cushions, Alix could be heard crying out to Minnie: "Oh! My dear! Do look at them! They look exactly like a row of wet-nurses carrying babies!"[109]

CHAPTER 15

Prince of Pleasure

1881–87

During the 1880s, the number of Bertie's openings, dinners, and other such public engagements climbed to a yearly average of forty-two; but his amusements grew in proportion.[1] Cowes Week swelled to fill a fortnight, or sometimes the entire month of August: to "get the sea breezes and yachting" was "an immense relaxation," he explained, "after the fatigues of the London season." From 1883 he escaped to Cannes for three weeks in February and March, which he found "very beneficial . . . at that somewhat trying time of year."[2] Keeping the prince amused was "a major social problem," and stratagems were devised to relieve the tedium of staying year after year with the same parties in the same great houses.[3]

The routine of his social season was reconfigured. Bertie stayed most years during the 1880s in mid-July at Waddesdon.[4] This brand-new French chateau in the Rothschild county of Buckinghamshire was the creation of Ferdinand de Rothschild. A member of the Austrian

family, he was a widower in his forties. Morose, depressive, and solip-
sistic, he disliked racing, took no interest in pretty women, and dined
on cold toast and water.[5] Though his priceless collections seemed to
give him little pleasure, he was a perfectionist. Once after a storm devastated the flower garden, an early rising guest noticed an army of
gardeners replanting the borders to their former glory in time for
breakfast.[6] The nervy-fingered "Ferdy" seemed an unlikely friend for
Bertie, but the connection suited both men. The novelist Henry James
found the "gilded bondage of that gorgeous place" oppressive, but
Bertie had always been drawn to Rothschilds, because he "relished
their sensible cosmopolitan outlook, public spirit, geniality and pa-
nache."[7] Waddesdon became a favorite place for the prince to entertain, effectively an alternative court. Guest lists were sent in advance to
Marlborough House for approval, and Bertie noted the names carefully in his diary, as he did whenever he stayed in a country house.[8] The
Rothschilds appealed all the more in the 1880s as, squeezed by agricultural depression, Bertie's English friends no longer vied so keenly for
the expensive honor of entertaining him.

Alix did not come to Waddesdon. But she accompanied Bertie, at
least at first, to another new social fixture: the Duke of Richmond's
house party for Goodwood races, which ended the summer season in
late July. The first of the huge royal Goodwood parties took place in
1881.[9] Dean Stanley, Queen Victoria's beloved friend who had accompanied the twenty-year-old prince to the Holy Land, had died a few
days before. The funeral was brought forward to suit HRH. Bertie's
diary notes: "Attend Dean of Westminster's funeral at Westminster
Abbey 4. Leave Victoria Station 6 for Chichester drive to Goodwood
House and stay there."[10] He was truly a railway prince. Victoria grieved
that Bertie refused to cancel his end-of-season ball at Marlborough
House out of respect for the dean.[11] People were even more shocked
when Alix opened the first quadrille dancing with King Kalakaua of
Hawaii. Bertie took the king with him everywhere that season, insisting that he should be given precedence. He wanted to persuade Kal-
akaua to agree to the annexation of his islands by Britain, rather than
America. At Lady Spencer's party, the King of Hawaii marched along

beside Alix, while Fritz, the German Crown Prince, trailed humbly behind. When the Germans objected, Bertie retorted: "Either the brute is a King or else he is an ordinary black nigger, and if he is not a King, why is he here at all?"[12]

Bertie's appetite was inexhaustible; after a dinner of many courses, he was said to retire with a cold chicken beside his bed, which, so the story went, was always bare in the morning.* His nickname was Tum Tum—though he was sensitive on the subject. When Sir Frederick Johnstone was behaving obstreperously in the billiard room at Sandringham, Bertie put his hand on his shoulder: "Freddy, Freddy, you're very drunk." Johnstone pointed at Bertie's expanding middle and, imitating his rolling *rrr's*, replied: "Tum Tum, you're *verrry* fat!" Bertie walked out of the room, and the friendship was terminated. Johnstone left the house before breakfast the next morning.[13] Carrington described a shooting party at Holkham with the Earl of Leicester in December 1881: "We fell at once to luncheon. Woodcock pie, mashed potatoes and champagne, curacao, cigarettes, and then fevered and restless sleep." Dinner (men only) followed at eight sharp, and by 9:15 they were in the smoking room for an evening of play for high stakes.[14]

When Bertie attended a party with Lord Stamford in Leicestershire, the shooting was ruined by the crowd of thousands of textile workers who crammed into the fields beside the woods and cheered lustily whenever Bertie appeared. They snatched at the dead pheasants as they fell to the ground and tore them to pieces in their enthusiasm, but nevertheless Bertie noted a tally of 8,463 pheasants over four days.[15]

Eating and shooting were not enough to keep boredom at bay. For amusement Bertie turned to the young women from the New World who invaded English society in the 1880s. One name that features often in the lists of guests at royal house parties is that of Lady Mandeville.

Consuelo Mandeville was the daughter of a Cuban landowner named Yznaga; she was born in 1858 on her mother's cotton plantation in Louisiana. As slave-owning Southerners whose fortunes fluctu-

---

* I have not been able to verify this story.

ated wildly, the Yznagas were excluded from the magic circle of New York society after the Civil War. At eighteen, Consuelo made a spectacular romantic marriage to the Duke of Manchester's son (she nursed him back to health after he fell ill from a fever while staying in her family house). The marriage turned out badly. Lord Mandeville was a weak-willed wastrel, and Consuelo's fabled millions did not materialize. Nevertheless, being Lady Mandeville gave her the kudos she needed to launch herself on the social scene in both London and New York.[16]

Consuelo Mandeville had tiny feet that uneasily supported her plump body; she told funny stories in a slow southern drawl, and she sang Spanish songs as she strummed her banjo. Later, Edith Wharton drew a sympathetic portrait of her in *The Buccaneers,* where she features as Conchita Closson, the dusky-skinned, cigarette-smoking southern beauty who leads the American invasion of England.[17] Consuelo and her two sisters, Nantica (who married Sir John Lister-Kaye) and Emily Yznaga, were often at Marlborough House. When Bertie and Alix took Consuelo and her two-and-a-half-year-old twin daughters to visit Queen Victoria, the children disobeyed instructions to kiss her hand, and rushed toward her, climbed into her lap, and flung their chubby arms around her neck, covering her with kisses and chanting, "Nice Queen! Nice Queen!" To the relief of all, Victoria was delighted, returned their kisses, and asked them to stay for luncheon.[18] A favorite of Bertie's ("He's crazy about her Spanish songs"), Consuelo was rumored to be his mistress. She was so short of money that when the prince came to dinner, she had to ask her friends to send around the French cuisine.[19]

More than three hundred American women married into peers' or baronets' families between 1870 and 1914, and by 1914 as many as 17 percent of such families had American connections. Only a few of these marriages were straight financial transactions, trading American dollars for English titles. It was not so much the Americans' cash as their style that appealed: their fearlessness, their talkativeness, and their lack of respect for rank.[20] How to know whether an American girl came from a good family was a puzzle for English hostesses; as the fictional Lady Brightlingsea remarks in *The Buccaneers,* "I don't see how they can tell each other apart, all herded together, without any titles or distinctions."[21] Consuelo knew exactly which American was which, and she acted as social gatekeeper. When Bertie asked her advice, she would habitually reply: "Oh, Sir, she has no position at home; out there she would be just dirt under our feet."[22]

From 1882, Bertie retired each year to Homburg, where he spent several weeks taking the cure. Homburg was an island of Englishness in Germany.* Here, each morning at seven, Bertie drank the waters from the Elisabeth-Brunnen, the spring named after his great-aunt, Elizabeth, Princess of Hesse-Homburg: three beakers of the salt-rich and gaseous waters were supposed to relax the bowels within an hour. Between each glass of water, Bertie joined spa visitors in walking as fast as he could up and down the avenue.[23] He played lawn tennis for weight-reducing exercise, and in the evenings he dined at the Kursaal, the grand conversation house of the spa with its marble columns and ballroom.[24] He pretended to lead the simple life, but Homburg was hardly a quiet retreat; Bertie's arrival made it instantly fashionable and the English competed to hold grand balls in his honor.[25]

At Homburg in 1882, Bertie's list of dinner guests included an American family: Mr., Mrs., and Miss Chamberlain. Nineteen-year-old Jane (Jeannie) Chamberlain, whom Bertie admired, was the daughter of William Selah Chamberlain, millionaire heir to a Cleveland railroad fortune. A shrewd American debutante, she refused to see Bertie without her parents being present. Chamberpots, as Alix called her, remained in favor for a couple of years. Whether she was really as innocent and virtuous as she pretended is debatable. In 1884, the Paris police watched Bertie paying visits to Jane Chamberlain (among many other women) at the Hotel Balmoral, and according to them, she was his *maîtresse en titre.*[26] In July that year, Edward Hamilton, Gladstone's secretary, saw Bertie at a dinner party and noted that "as usual, he oc-

---

* Elizabeth (d. 1840), the third daughter of George III, had married the hereditary Prince of Hesse-Homburg, and spent her fortune paying off the debts of this miniature principality and laying out English gardens. The spa was frequented largely by English visitors. (Flora Fraser, *Princesses: The Six Daughters of George III* [John Murray, 2004], pp. 305–8, 351–55, 367.)

cupied himself entirely with Miss Chamberlain," and in August, Bertie asked for the de Falbes, the Danish minister and his wife, to invite the Chamberlains to their ball.*[27]

John Brown died of erysipelas in March 1883. Queen Victoria was utterly crushed. The shock left her unable to walk.[28] Bertie detested Brown, but the death of the favorite brought him no closer to his mother. Alix wrote sympathizing tactfully with the Queen's grief: "I can quite understand how every day and hour at Balmoral must remind you of one who was ever near you."[29] It might do some good, she told the grieving Queen, "to put one's Sorrow into words and confide the almost intolerable <u>loneliness of suffering</u> to a sympathising soul! And that you know dearest Mama you have indeed in poor me!"[30]

Bertie was appalled by the Queen's plan to commemorate Brown by publishing a volume of *More Leaves from the Journal of a Life in the Highlands,* which she dedicated to "the Memory of my devoted personal attendant and faithful friend," John Brown. "I have grave doubts," he told the Queen, "whether your private life, which ought to be considered as sacred as that of your humblest subjects, should be as it were exposed to the world."[31] This was a fundamental clash over the role of monarchy, and Victoria's response indicates a startlingly modern approach. "I certainly <u>cannot</u> agree," she wrote. "In these days of Radicalism," she considered that publications of this sort, sold in cheap editions to the humblest of her subjects, could only strengthen the monarchy. "I <u>know</u> that the publication of my first book did me more good than anything else."[32]

In *More Leaves,* Victoria described a life at Balmoral of nice breakfasts, pony-riding expeditions, and Highland weather. "It is innocence itself," commented the prime minister on reading the Queen's book. But, as the editor of his diaries remarked, the innocence in this case was Gladstone's, not the Queen's.[33] By reinventing herself as a nonpo-

---

* Jane Chamberlain married Captain Herbert Naylor-Leyland in September 1889. Their son, born 6 December 1890, was named Albert Edward.

litical, out-of-doors person, the Queen effectively disarmed her radical critics, who had previously complained, with good reason, that she was politically partisan and interfering.

"It might create surprize," Bertie told the Queen, "that the name of your eldest son never occurred in it."[34] Victoria could not resist telling him that his name was mentioned five times: "I fear you have not read the book if you overlooked this."[35] She inserted into the new edition a lengthy account of Bertie's leave-taking before his visit to India in 1875. "I can't deny that your remarks about my book pained me very much," she told him, "as I was particularly anxious to hurt no one's feelings, and I thought I had succeeded."[36]

Bertie tried, as he had tried before, to persuade his mother to open Parliament; as before, he failed. Victoria refused to appear to give support to the hated Gladstone, though she had opened Parliament three times during Disraeli's 1874–80 government.[37] The prince claimed to be neutral: "It is . . . well known that I have always favoured no party side in politics."[38] But he found Gladstone easy to deal with—in fact, Bertie was "the only friend among members of the Royal family whom Mr. Gladstone has got."[39] He understood that Gladstone's fierceness toward the Queen masked a thin skin. Staying at Sandringham, Gladstone weighed himself at the prince's request (165 pounds), and he was charmed by Alix, who told him sweetly, "You will have your favourite hymn Rock of Ages."*[40]

Bertie's contacts kept him well informed about Gladstone's night walks, when he prowled the London streets for prostitutes, whom he attempted to redeem. Gladstone was fascinated by Lillie Langtry, who wrote so often, enclosing her letters in double envelopes to protect them from prying eyes, that his private secretary Edward Hamilton had to warn the prime minister against seeing her, as her reputation "is in such bad odour that, despite all the endeavours of HRH, nobody

---

* Lady Geraldine Somerset, Tory lady-in-waiting to the Duchess of Cambridge, wrote that Gladstone's invitation to Sandringham made her "blood boil": If Gladstone died, she wrote, Bertie would no doubt run at once "with ten special trains and twenty extra engines, and enveloped in yards and folds of crepe, to do honour to his funeral!" (Lady Geraldine Somerset's diary, in Giles St. Aubyn, *The Royal George* [Constable, 1963], p. 268.)

will receive her in their houses."[41] Catherine Walters (Skittles) was another of Bertie's friends who attracted Gladstone. He read to her, gave her gifts of tea, and measured the size of her waist by putting his hands around it. Skittles reported all this back to Bertie, who advised her "not to trouble [Gladstone] about politics at first, but when he has got into the habit of coming then I mean to let him have it."[42]

"Receive news of successful bombardment of Alexandria by Adm[iral Sir Beauchamp Seymour's squadron!" Bertie wrote in his diary on 11 July 1882.[43] Britain's intervention to suppress the revolt of Arabi Pasha against the pro-Western khedive in Egypt thrilled him, and he implored the Queen and the government to let him join the military expedition. Reasonably enough, Victoria refused permission; the forty-year-old heir to the throne lacked military training, and his sole qualification was the honorary colonelcy of regiments. For once, she found Gladstone in agreement.[44]

Blocked by his mother from seeing the telegrams about the British expedition to Egypt, Bertie appealed to his friend in the Liberal government, the Foreign Office minister Sir Charles Dilke. Dilke owed him a favor. It was thanks to Bertie that Victoria had consented to his appointment to government office. Victoria had wished to exclude him as a republican, but Bertie preempted her by asking to meet Dilke at dinner with Lord Fife in 1880. The meeting was a success. As Ponsonby wrote: "The Republican had drunk in the honeyed words of Royalty, had written his name down at Marlborough House and had enquired when the next Levee was to take place."[45]

It was largely due to Dilke, now promoted to president of the Local Government Board, that Bertie was appointed in 1884 to the Royal Commission on the Housing of the Working Class. Accompanied by Carrington (who was also a member of the commission), and trailed by a Scotland Yard detective, Bertie disguised himself in rough clothes to explore the worst and poorest courts in St. Pancras and Holborn. In one room a half-starved woman lived with three children lying naked in a heap of rags. The landlord asked her where her fourth child was.

"I don't know," replied the woman, "it went down into the court some days ago and I haven't seen it since." When the landlord commented, "What can I do with her, she can't pay any rent and she won't go?" the prince was so horrified that he had to be restrained from giving her a five-pound note.[46] Bertie's concern was genuine, but this did not stop him returning to Marlborough House in time for luncheon at two o'clock.[47]

A few days later, the prince spoke in the House of Lords—the only full speech he gave there—in which he described his visit: "I can assure your Lordships that the condition of the poor, or rather of their dwellings, was perfectly disgraceful."[48] He attended sixteen of the commission's thirty-eight meetings; as Dilke wrote, he showed "a devotion to the work of my Commission which was quite unusual with him."[49]

Dilke was the rising star of the Liberal government, but his career was dramatically destroyed by a sex scandal in the summer of 1885. Twenty-two-year-old Mrs. Virginia Crawford, the wife of a Liberal MP, publicly accused him of seducing her. Her husband sued for divorce, naming Dilke as corespondent. Shortly after the scandal broke, Bertie proposed a vote of thanks at the commission in "an extremely cordial speech" (20 July 1885). Dilke wrote thanking him for his support: "This foul charge, with which I have long been threatened in unsigned letters, was first made known to me on this day last week, and I was completely prostrated by it on the day on which I saw Your Royal Highness. . . . I write thus freely to Your Royal Highness because I can never cease to feel that Your Royal Highness is . . . one of my truest friends."[50] Bertie gossiped to Skittles that Dilke's method of seduction was "by bawdy books and tea parties in which the tea service has represented the various parts of generation."[51] Dilke's disgrace had one plus point, as Bertie explained: "It will at any rate show to the public in general and the radicals in particular that the latter are not more moral than the 'bloated aristocrats'!"[52]

On 28 March 1884, Bertie was at Aintree Racecourse for the Liverpool spring meeting. His horse, The Scot, was favorite to win the Grand

National, but fell at Becher's Brook. "After the race heard terrible news of the Duke of Albany's [Leopold] sudden death at Cannes," noted Bertie.[53] He returned immediately to London. The hemophiliac Leopold, only thirty years old, had fallen in Cannes and hurt his knee, causing bleeding. He died from sudden convulsions and "breaking of a blood-vessel in the head" the same night.[54] Bertie wrote at once to the Queen, asking permission to bring his brother's body back to England.[55] The following evening he left London by special train, traveling through the night to reach Cannes thirty hours later. A short service was held at the Villa Nervada, the house where Leopold had died. Bertie stood at the head of the coffin. "He was painfully affected," reported *The Times*, "his face bearing only too evident signs of his grief, and more than once during the ceremony he could not restrain his tears."[56] Bare-headed crowds lined the streets of Cannes to watch the funeral procession to the station, and Bertie broke down again when Leopold's coffin was placed in a black-draped railway carriage. His relationship with Leopold had not been easy, but he was genuinely moved, especially by the suddenness of his brother's death. "The more I think of our loss," he told his son Georgie, "the less can I bring myself to believe that it is true!"[57]

Victoria thought Leopold was the cleverest of her sons, but his Tory partisanship made him a liability and he gave advice that was often wrong. His insistence (contrary to constitutional practice) that the Speech from the Throne was the Queen's and not her ministers' caused a damaging row with the Gladstone government in January 1881.[58] Victoria was saddened by Leopold's death, but "not ill at all"; for him, perhaps, she thought it was best, as he had suffered so much and "there was such a restless longing for what he could not have."[59]

Eddy and Georgie had returned from their voyage on the *Bacchante* in May 1880. Georgie had flourished on board ship, but for Eddy the experiment was an utter failure; today we would say that he was depressed. The decision was made to separate them. George would train for a naval career; Eddy was to follow Bertie's example and study at

Cambridge. J. K. (Jem) Stephen, son of James Fitzjames Stephen and a first cousin of Virginia Woolf, was engaged as his tutor.

Stephen was a tall, muscular twenty-three-year-old, a star athlete and top scholar from Eton and King's College, Cambridge.[60] He reported that Eddy "hardly knows the meaning of the word to read." This was not because he was stupid, but his "one great difficulty is in keeping his attention fixed. . . . Sometimes he attends pretty well for a time, and then suddenly, for no apparent reason, his mind relapses almost into a state of torpor." Stephen was reasonably optimistic. If Eddy could only learn to concentrate, "I see no reason why he should not become a tolerable scholar of English history. The subject interests him: and he has a very fair memory for the more picturesque parts."*[61]

Bertie took Eddy up to Trinity, Cambridge, in October 1883. Determined to ensure that his son was not subjected to the solitary confinement that he had endured at Madingley, he arranged for him to live in college, chaperoned by Dalton, who, limpet-like, acted as governor, and Stephen, who directed his reading. Eddy attended lectures with Sir John Seeley, the Regius Professor of Modern History, and was excused from examinations.[62] It is sometimes claimed that at Cambridge Eddy lived a "dissipated and unstable life," but the truth was more prosaic: He enjoyed the freedom of a normal undergraduate.[63] He made his first public speech in support of the movement for a Cambridge settlement in the East End of London, declaring that "nothing is more necessary for building up a healthy commonwealth than that all classes and parties whether religious or political should unite together in the attempt to better, not only each other but the community."[64] Whether he wrote them himself or not, these were not the words of a fool. Austen Chamberlain, son of radical politician Joseph Chamberlain, seconded Eddy, and many years later he told Bertie, "I was struck by the fine simplicity of his character and by the strong sense of public duty which he showed even in those early days."†[65]

---

* Stephen's life ended tragically. After a head injury, he developed manic depression. While he was incarcerated in an asylum, he learned of Eddy's death, and allegedly the news so upset him that he refused to eat and died of starvation thirty days later.

† Bertie annotated this: "A charming letter."

In the summer, Eddy attended the University of Heidelberg, where he studied German for five hours a day. No correspondence survives between father and son, but one letter that Bertie wrote to Dalton in July 1884 gives a sense of his irritation.

> What you tell me about [Prince Eddy's] dawdling when he dresses in the morning is really too bad, as the most valuable time in the morning is lost. . . . Now I am determined that a stop must be put to this childishness. I take a <u>quarter</u> of an hour dressing but will let him have <u>half</u> an hour but not a minute more. . . .
>
> If he does not feel that he is 20 and half but more like 14 or 15 he must be treated as a boy and not as a man. . . . I had hoped that his younger brother's diligence and success in his recent exam would have stimulated him to work hard, but I fear this is not the case.
>
> It is really most annoying and makes one think very seriously of the future.[66]

Alix was unperturbed, believing Eddy to be "a very good boy at heart, though perhaps he is a little slow and dawdly, which I always attribute to his having grown so fast."[67] Georgie, on the other hand, was hardworking, bright, and affectionate. Bertie wrote him gruff, manly letters that barely mask his affection. "It gives me gr[ea]t satisfaction to hear that [you] are working so hard for your exam; remember it is of the <u>greatest</u> importance that you should pass with credit to yourself. Your whole future career in the service depends upon it."[68] Georgie, said Alix, was a "sweet clever boy and the life and soul of the house, always merry and so happy and so funny."[69]

At Sandringham, Alix filled the house with children, and the noise of laughter, piano playing, and horseplay made it almost impossible even to write a letter.[70] Her deafness made the noise worse, as people had to shout in order to be heard. A Russian grand duke recalled of this time that "a stranger walking into the dining room . . . would have thought he was witnessing a family quarrel."[71] Alix spent as much time as she could at Sandringham. A letter Bertie wrote to Knollys in May 1888 reveals his exasperation at her willfulness. "After having written twice to the P[rince]ss urging her to come to Town at latest today to go to the R[oyal] Academy this afternoon I got her telegram yesterday evening—'Thanks for letters am not going till Friday—children are anxious to stay one day longer!'" In spite of Bertie's urging that attending the Academy was almost a public duty, Alix refused to budge. "If the P[rince]ss will not even in a small matter like this sacrifice the pleasure it gives her to remain at Sandringham 24 hours longer I am powerless to do anything," he wrote ruefully.[72]

Unable to have the large family that she craved, Alix kept her children young, as did all the mothers of the Marlborough House set, "for the younger generation, we knew, would date us."[73] The princesses received almost no education at all.* Affie's daughter Marie (later Queen of Romania) remembered their habit of adding "dear little" or "poor little" to everyone they talked about. It gave the impression that "life would have been very wonderful . . . if it had not been so sad."[74]

In 1885, Princess Louise wrote to Knollys, enclosing drawings of the three sisters as animals. "Dear old Thingy," she wrote. "We hope that the pictures will put you in mind of your little friends, Toots [Louise], Gawks [Victoria] and Snipey [Maud]. You must notice that Toots is practising her steps for the tiresome Court ball, that Gawks is going to bed instead like Cinderella, and that Snipey is trying to console herself with a song instead of singing hymns in Church as she ought to do. . . . Now goodbye old thingy and hoping you will appreciate the works of art we send you. Your affectionate little friends: Toots, Gawks and Snipey."[75] Louise was then eighteen.

Bertie welcomed the Third Reform Bill, which gave the vote to two-thirds of the male population, and had to be dissuaded from voting for

---

* As the Duke of Windsor said of his aunts, "You might say that they could just read and write, period. That was all." (Quennell, *Lonely Business,* p. 214.)

it in the Lords.*[76] On 21 July 1884, a demonstration in support of the bill marched through London, and Bertie invited himself and Alix to watch the procession with his friend Carrington, who lived on Whitehall. As the crowd approached, singing "La Marseillaise," HRH said, "I don't think this looks like a pleasant afternoon!"

"Wait a bit," said Carrington, who had tipped off the organizers of the demonstration. "I think you are going to get the reception of your life." The prince's reception was "stupendous," equaled only by that given to the radical John Bright. After one and a half hours of standing at the window, Alix grew faint, but when she retired, the crowd shouted for her, and Carrington propped her up with a heap of cushions. When Bertie came and stood at the window, "A roar of applause went up that could have been heard at Windsor Castle."[77]

Encouraged by his popularity at home, Bertie agreed to visit Ireland in the spring of 1885. With the country on the brink of nationalist rebellion, the timing could hardly have been more risky. Accompanied by Eddy and Alix, the prince received an enthusiastic welcome in Dublin, but as the three traveled south, the crowds lining the roads grew ominously quiet, and sinister black flags appeared.[78] At Cork, they met a bitterly hostile crowd, though Bertie made light of it, explaining that the demonstration had been stirred up by the nationalist T. P. O'Connor, "who was so furious at the good reception we received in Dublin that he wished to counteract it."[79] Arthur Ellis sent the Queen a vivid account. "No one who went thro[ugh] this day will ever forget it," he wrote: The procession of seven carriages was assaulted by a storm of hisses and hoots, shouts of "No Prince but Parnell," an "angry, unwashed" crowd of 2,000 to 3,000 shaking fists and sticks and waving black flags. "The Prince and Princess showed the greatest calmness and courage," but "it was like a bad dream."[80]

"They ought really not to have gone there," was Victoria's verdict.[81] Bertie preserved a diplomatic silence, but Gladstone was impressed by his handling of the visit. He told his secretary Edward Hamilton that

* He had opposed reform in 1866.

he admired the prince's quickness of perception and happy knack of always saying the right thing. "He would make an excellent sovereign. He is far more fitted for that high place than her present Majesty now is. He would see both sides. He would always be open to argument. He would never domineer or dictate."[82]

Bertie still resented his exclusion from Cabinet secrets. At a dinner with Ferdinand de Rothschild, he complained to Edward Hamilton that he was "kept too much in the dark" by the government.[83] Hamilton approached Gladstone, who agreed, but insisted that the Queen must first be consulted. So Hamilton saw Ponsonby, who wrote a note to the Queen: "The Prince of Wales complains that the Govt tell him nothing. Mr. Hamilton thinks Mr. Gladstone would readily tell HRH anything of importance that takes place in the cabinet. . . . But first he asks would Y[ou]r Majesty sanction this?" Victoria scrawled over Ponsonby's note in bold mauve pencil: "The Queen thinks he should be told when things are no longer secrets . . . for he is not discreet."[84] Gladstone asked for clarification, and Ponsonby wrote another note: "Mr. Gladstone is anxious to obtain a direct authorization from Y[ou]r Majesty tomorrow, as to the cabinet reports which he is to furnish to the Prince of Wales." This time the purple pencil was even more emphatic. "Regular ones w[oul]d be quite irregular and improper. Only some g[rea]t decision or change of policy he might be let known of before it is publicly known."[85] That was the end of the matter. Before the purple pencil of the sixty-six-year-old widow Queen, strong men quailed.

In his forties, Bertie achieved a new maturity; people began to remark on the soundness of his judgment and his generosity and loyalty to his friends. Observers commented that he was a reformed character and had abandoned womanizing. According to an anonymous French commentator, the Prince of Wales "is very different in 1885 from what he was in 1878. The *vie orageuse* is over and forgotten, or remembered only and looked at through the mellowing medium of middle age."[86]

Not everyone agreed. Lady Geraldine Somerset, lady-in-waiting to

Bertie's Aunt Cambridge, wrote in her diary (1885) of the "reigning young ladies." The list included Margot Tennant (twenty-one) and Julie Stonor (twenty-six). How strange, mused Uncle George (Duke of Cambridge), was this new line of the prince's, "taking to young girls and discarding the married women."[87]

Julie Stonor was the daughter of Alix's "beloved" lady-in-waiting, Elise Stonor. She and her brothers were orphaned when their father suddenly died in 1881, quickly followed by their mother ("She loved him above everything in the world, she will probably die herself from despair," predicted Alix).[88] Alix brought the Stonor children up as if they were her own. The Stonors were an old Catholic family, and Alix encouraged them in their faith; Julie Stonor's Roman Catholic missal was a gift from the prince and princess. According to the waspish Lady Geraldine: "Dear papa and both sons are by way of being more or less in love with her."[89] Julie was certainly a close friend of Prince George, who even talked of marrying her, though her Catholicism was an insuperable impediment. But the implication that she was a mistress of Bertie's is groundless fabrication. Fiercely loyal to "Motherdear," as she called Alix, Julie Stonor was not the sort of girl to engage in flirtation with HRH, whom she saw as a father figure.*[90]

Margot Tennant was different. The daughter of the Glasgow industrialist Sir Charles Tennant, she prided herself on being fearless and outspoken. In her *Memoirs,* she related how one evening in 1887 her father sent the brougham with a last-minute message asking her to accompany him to dinner with Lady Randolph Churchill. Margot had no time to change, and she arrived wearing a white muslin dress with "transparent chemise sleeves, a fichu and a long skirt with a Nattier blue taffeta sash" (the detail is characteristic: Margot considered herself to be a fashion statement). To her horror, all the other ladies present wore off-the-shoulder ball gowns and tiaras. The prince arrived, came straight up to her (she had met him twice before), and told her

---

* In 1891 she married Bernard, Marquis d'Hautpoul, but continued to live in England and became a great friend of Queen Mary. Her brother Harry Stonor was a lifelong courtier and one of the best shots in England.

that she was to sit next to him at supper. "Oh no, Sir," said Margot, "I am not dressed at all for the part! I had better slip away, I had no notion that this was to be such a smart party. . . . I expect some of the ladies here think I have insulted them by coming in my night-gown!" Of course the prince admired her frock, and they ended the best of friends.[91]

Margot's story about her white muslin is strikingly similar to the story about Lillie Langtry and her plain black dress. Both are variants on the Cinderella myth, the young girl's fantasy that Prince Charming spots her in her homely frock and, ignoring the ugly older sisters of the court, dances with her all night.

In her diary for 1885, Margot wrote a single, unpunctuated sentence: "The Prince asked to be introduced to me and was rather taken and excessive and gave me a horseshoe and his photo wanted to meet me when he could but I refused twice to lunch and once at Waddesdon."[92] To the twenty-one-year-old Margot, the prince was a sexual predator, an older man to be kept at a safe distance. In April 1886, Margot's life was torn apart by the death of her sister Laura, to whom she was exceptionally close, and the prince wrote a sympathetic letter. "It is not many years ago that I lost my favourite and deeply beloved sister. I know what I then suffered, and I therefore know what you suffer!" Bertie could offer no consolation, he wrote, "beyond the privilidge [sic] of being looked upon as a friend and therefore truly sympathising with you."[93]

Margot seems to have taken up the offer of friendship. At Christmas she sent him a tortoiseshell cigar case: "Don't think me a brute for not having thanked you," wrote Bertie. "I shall always value it as your gift and still more for y[ou]r kind thoughts of me."[94] Soon he was proposing to call on her, but Margot, as an unmarried woman, in spite of her reputation for being fast, was oddly prudish, and she refused him. Bertie wrote tartly, "Very well—I shall not inflict my presence on you and when we meet . . . you shall explain the reasons to me."[95] Another time he invited himself to call, and reassured her: "I really do not think it would excite any remark and be considered quite natural."[96] Margot, however, seems to have won, and Bertie was rejected.

Bertie's new political friend in place of the disgraced Dilke was the equally disreputable Lord Randolph Churchill, who was now the rising hope of the Tory party. The prince had at last, after eight years of banishment, agreed to meet Jennie and Randolph Churchill at a dinner in March 1884. The formal reconciliation came on 16 May 1886, when Bertie dined with the Churchills at their house at 2 Connaught Place. He "thought it best to be on speaking terms though we can never be the same friends again."[97] In fact, the dinner turned out better than he expected, in spite of an electricity blackout caused by the breakdown of the dynamo that Randolph's brother Blandford had installed in the cellar. The Randolph Churchills were instantly restored to favor. They stayed at Sandringham for Bertie's birthday, and their names were included in the lists of Bertie's guests at Waddesdon.[98]

Randolph's letters often mention Bertie's kindness; it's plain that he valued the rekindling of their friendship.[99] As Chancellor of the Exchequer in Lord Salisbury's new Conservative government, the thirty-seven-year-old Randolph was a political star, famed for his modern style of Tory democracy. But his ministerial career turned out to be even briefer than Dilke's. In December 1886, after five months in office, he sent a resignation letter. The Queen was outraged because he had written his letter while staying as her guest, using Windsor Castle writing paper. Bertie came to the defense of his friend: "Lord Randolph is a poor man and a very ambitious one but he gave up £5000 a year in ceasing to be Ch[ancellor] of the Exchequer. . . . Should his life be spared (and he has not a good life) he is bound to play sooner or later a prominent part."[100]

"Should his life be spared." Randolph had been informed by his doctors that he was suffering from syphilis. His mood swings and violent rages, his growing deafness and cardiac weakness were made worse by the poisonous treatment he was prescribed: mercury and potassium iodide. Whether he actually had syphilis is controversial; his symptoms are consistent with a brain tumor or some other neurological condition; but the fact is that he believed he had it, his doctors diagnosed it, and he might as well have had it.[101] About this time he broke off physical relations with Jennie but didn't tell her the reason. Hurt and confused, Jennie needed a confidant, and perhaps she found one in the prince.

"Now we come to the suspicious events," wrote Jennie's great-niece Anita Leslie. "During the rest of that summer season [of 1886] Lady Randolph Churchill several times received the Prince for luncheon and <u>alone</u>. One might take it for granted that a physical affair had started."[102] Anita Leslie could find no evidence, as she readily admitted, to prove that after lunch the prince and Jennie walked upstairs to the drawing room and, after Jennie had ordered the footman to remove the coffee cups, the prince expertly unlaced her complicated clothing as she lay on a chaise longue. Bertie's letters give nothing away. What is one to make, for example, of a message like this: "Unless you are engaged I wonder if I may propose myself to luncheon on Monday next"?[103] Or, marginally more revealing: "Would it be very indiscreet if I proposed myself to luncheon?"[104] But this seems to have been the guarded language that Bertie used to conceal the fact that Lady Randolph Churchill had become his mistress.

At thirty-five, she *looked* the part: Margot, who met her at Punchestown races, couldn't take her eyes off her. Wearing a Black Watch tartan skirt, braided coat, and astrakhan hussar's cap, Jennie had "a forehead like a panther's and great wild eyes that looked through you."

"Had Lady Randolph Churchill been like her face she would have governed the world," was Margot's acid verdict.[105] None of Jennie's letters to Bertie survive. The scores of cards and notes he sent to her, and which she preserved, are mostly undated, and usually not postmarked either, as they were often hand-delivered by an orderly, but it's clear that Jennie had become an integral part of his life. In London she entertained for him. She joined him on his February visit to Cannes. She went sailing with him on the Riviera—"Will you dine with me afterwards? . . . Perhaps you would order a room at an hotel at Nice, where your maid could meet you and bring a change of dress, as we cannot tell when the race will be over."[106] Jennie Churchill was rumored—at the time—to have slept with two hundred men. It seems unlikely that she failed to consummate her relationship with the morally lax heir to the throne.

CHAPTER 16

William

1887–89

At eleven thirty on the morning of 21 June 1887, wearing a field marshal's uniform and mounted on a magnificent pale chestnut charger named Vivian, the Prince of Wales rode out of Buckingham Palace in the procession for the Queen's Jubilee. He was met by a roar from the crowd. An even louder cheer greeted the Queen, in an open landau drawn by six cream horses, with Alix and Vicky, the two most senior princesses, seated in the back. The guards' bands played as the carriages bearing Victoria's daughters and granddaughters followed by her sons and sons-in-law on horseback formed up behind the coaches of the Indian princes, the royal household, and various European royalties. The complex choreography had been revised the day before by Bertie, and the maneuver proceeded with machinelike precision as the glittering procession snaked along Piccadilly and Pall Mall through cheering crowds to Westminster Abbey.[1] Bertie rode in line with his brothers Affie and Arthur at the back of the cavalcade; just in front of him rode Bertie's brother-in-law Fritz, the German Crown Prince and husband of his sister Vicky, a towering figure in the magnificent white uniform of the Pomeranian Cuirassiers, with a silver breastplate and eagle-winged helmet. Cheered loudly by the crowd, Fritz was compared to Lohengrin, the legendary hero of Richard Wagner's opera—a sharp contrast with Lord Lorne, Bertie's other brother-in-law, husband of his sister Louise, who humiliatingly fell off his horse.[2]

In Westminster Abbey, which was packed with nine thousand people squeezed into specially constructed wooden galleries, the Queen sat alone in the Coronation Chair. She wore her usual black dress and bonnet trimmed with white point d'Alençon lace and the Garter ribbon strapped across her breast. The widow Queen's mourning was no doubt iconic, almost as much so as the Virgin Queen Elizabeth's pearl-embroidered white, but it made her family groan. She had resisted suggestions that she should wear her crown and robes of state; when Alix, as favorite daughter-in-law, was sent to persuade her, she had had her head bitten off—"I was never so snubbed in all my life."[3]

During the service, the Queen seemed "deeply affected" and the Prince of Wales, who stood near, "gazed tenderly and anxiously at her from time to time."[4] After it ended, Bertie was the first of the family to advance, bow, and kiss her hand. Defying protocol, the Queen leaned forward and kissed him on the cheek. Then, carried away by the impulse of the moment, she embraced all the princes and princesses with "manifest emotion." Calling back Fritz, she embraced him, too, with special affection.[5]

"How long will it last?" asked the radical journalist W. T. Stead in the *Pall Mall Gazette*: Will the Prince of Wales, "the fat little bald man in red," who looked so unimpressive beside his splendid German brother-in-law in white, ever reign over us? he wondered.[6]

Seated in the Abbey among the Queen's grandsons, seething with rage against his English relations, was Fritz's son William. William had asked his grandfather, the ninety-year-old Emperor William I, to appoint him as his representative at the Jubilee instead of Fritz. William's pushiness and disloyalty infuriated Victoria, and she pointedly ignored him throughout the event. In the procession he was denied the starring role that he considered his due as eldest grandson, and his wife complained that at court functions she was snubbed by being placed behind the "black" Queen of Hawaii.[7]

A week after the Jubilee ceremony, in a small, dark room at number 19, Harley Street, Fritz was operated on for a growth on his larynx. Whether he would outlive old William I and succeed as emperor was in doubt, and William plotted ruthlessly to oust his father from the succession.

William's quarrel with his English relations had begun three years earlier, in April 1884, at the wedding at Darmstadt of Louis Battenberg to Victoria of Hesse, Princess Alice's eldest daughter. Alice's four daughters were the most glamorous princesses in the dynastic marriage market. Cousins of the czar, cousins of the kaiser, and granddaughters of Queen Victoria, they were superbly well connected; though not rich, they were blondly pretty Valkyries with long thin noses and long fair hair. What no one knew was that some of them had inherited from their mother a genetic time bomb in the recessive gene for hemophilia.

For Louis Battenberg, the match was a brilliant coup. The letter he wrote to Prince George on his engagement reads less like a man in love than a cat who has got the cream. "I am nearly off my chump altogether with feeling so jolly. I hope you will be pleased to have me as a cousin. It makes me ten times happier to think I shall be the nephew of your dear parents and cousin to you all."[8] Being related to the English royal family perhaps mattered more to Louis than the happiness of his bride.

The Battenbergs were a family of dynastic social climbers, goodlooking minor royals who contrived to marry the heirs to the great powers or get themselves adopted as kings of new countries such as Bulgaria. The rise of these outsider families was hotly resented, especially by the blood-obsessed German royalty, who claimed that the Battenbergs' great-grandfather had been a valet. In the same way, they had gossiped in the past that Prince Albert was the illegitimate son of

a Jewish court chamberlain and that Alix's mother had conducted outrageous affairs.

The twenty-five-year-old William objected furiously to the Battenberg marriage. Outwardly a shy, fair-haired Guards officer with puffy
eyes and a wispy moustache, married to a dull, dutiful minor Protestant princess, William was angry and ambitious. He disapproved of his
cousin Victoria of Hesse's alliance with Louis, who was not "of the
blood." He was consumed with rage against the English relations who
marginalized him, and especially against his grandmother, Queen Victoria.[9]

William's hostility took Bertie completely unawares.[10] The Prince
of Wales was on more cordial terms with William's mother, Vicky,
than he had been for years. Alice's death had brought Bertie and Vicky
together, and he saw her when he took his annual cure at Homburg.
He attended every family event in Berlin. He was present at William's
wedding in 1881 to Princess Augusta Victoria of Schleswig-Holstein-
Sonderburg-Augustenburg, whose nickname was Dona.* He gave William a Highland costume in Royal Stuart tartan, knowing that his
nephew shared his own passion for dressing up.

Some say that William was brain-damaged at birth; others claim
that he was a textbook case of narcissistic personality disorder: a
grossly inflated sense of self, very quick to take offense, incapable of
learning from experience, and ultimately superficial. Because of his
withered arm and his intellectual mediocrity, he could never satisfy his
powerful mother, Vicky: "She wanted him to be a Prince Albert, and
yet used his limitations to keep him dependent and intensely involved
with her."[11] Already he exhibited some of the traits of a sociopath. He
had no sense of remorse and no empathy for the feelings of others. He
seemed incapable of feeling affection.[12]

To William's horror, his mother now proposed that his sister Victoria (Moretta) should marry the second Battenberg brother, Alexan-

---

* Dona was the niece of Prince Christian of Schleswig-Holstein-Sonderburg-Augustenburg.
Her father was the unsuccessful claimant to the duchies of Schleswig and Holstein in 1864,
which explains why Alix objected to her.

der (Sandro), the Prince of Bulgaria. Sandro was the star of the Battenberg family: He was parachuted into the newly created country of Bulgaria, becoming prince at age twenty-two in 1879. A romantic figure, tall and bearded, he flashes across the dynastic scene in 1884–85. Reams of coroneted and embossed royal writing paper were consumed by the Battenberg marriage project. To William it was contamination. The more Vicky urged it—and she grew almost hysterical in her support for Sandro—the more estranged mother and son became.

This quarrel caused a major shift in the fault lines of dynastic diplomacy. For almost twenty years, Europe's royals had been split between the Germans and their supporters, who included Queen Victoria, and the anti-German Danes and their allies, foremost among whom was Bertie. Now the Germans were split themselves. The conflict was not just about the romantic Sandro. At issue was the future of Germany. Vicky and her husband, Crown Prince Fritz, stood for a liberal, pro-English Germany. Against them, Vicky's son William and his allies, his grandfather the old emperor, and Bismarck, represented authoritarian, militaristic Germany. In this matter, Queen Victoria naturally sided with her daughter. Bertie supported Vicky, too, acting as a sort of unofficial envoy on her behalf in the Battenberg affair. As a result, William's hatred of him became almost obsessive. When Bertie visited Berlin for the kaiser's eighty-eighth birthday in March 1885, William wrote to Alexander III: "We shall see the Prince of Wales here in a few days. I am not at all delighted by this unexpected apparition, because— excuse me, he is Your brother-in-law—owing to his false and intriguing nature he will undoubtedly attempt in one way or another to push the Bulgarian business—may Allah send them both to hell, as the Turks would say!"[13]

Bertie spent several weeks in Austria-Hungary in the autumn of 1885. The Habsburg lands offered an intoxicating mixture of sport, realpolitik, and eroticism that was far more exciting than the stiffness and parochialism of the Danish or German courts. In Vienna, he had the misfortune to be spotted emerging from one of the city's "most infamous brothels in broad daylight at 12 noon," and his nephew William, who also happened to be staying in Vienna, wrote gleefully to his grandfather the kaiser about the "stupidity" of his libidinous uncle.*[14]

From Vienna, Bertie proceeded to Budapest. Here (according to William), "He led such a fast life . . . that even the Hungarians shook their heads."[15] William's innuendo hints at more brothels, but the main thing that Bertie did to shock the Hungarians was to challenge their anti-Semitic prejudices. Professor Arminius Vámbéry was a distinguished explorer and traveler whom Bertie had met in London twenty years before. Because he was a Jew of humble background, he was shunned by Hungarian society. So Bertie gave a dinner, and walked with Vámbéry on his arm into a room full of Hungarian grandees, who bowed deeply and were civil to the Jewish professor—for the moment at least.[16]

When William eventually arrived in Budapest, Bertie told him "in great embarrassment" that he had been forced to cancel his invitation to stay at Sandringham that year, as Queen Victoria did not wish to see him because of his attitude toward the Bulgarian marriage. William pretended to be glad that he had a weapon to use against his mother if she should reproach him for not being sufficiently well-disposed toward Queen Victoria ("the old hag").[17] In fact, this was a crushing snub, and one for which William, who never forgave an insult, was soon to seek revenge.

Bertie and Alix's twenty-fifth wedding anniversary fell on 10 March 1888. Celebrating a silver wedding was a German custom, hitherto unknown in England, and the Waleses were the first to popularize it.[18] But the ninety-one-year-old Emperor William I died the day before, and Fritz's serious illness was now public knowledge. Shops in the West End added black drapes to the silver decorations they had arranged for the Waleses. The family dinner went ahead nonetheless, and the Queen herself broke with habit and attended. The guests wore silver and white, the dining room was decorated with white flowers

---

* William's criticism of Bertie was hypocritical; while boasting of his faithfulness to Dona, he, too, consorted with Viennese prostitutes. (Rohl, *Young Wilhelm*, pp. 464–69, 489.)

and gleaming silver plate, and towering above all this stood a wedding cake six feet high and decorated with white roses. Everyone remarked how youthful Alix looked. "We all looked like old ladies," said one of her bridesmaids, who were invited to the celebrations, "but the Princess was as young and fresh as she was on her wedding day."[19] In a hint at her unpunctuality, Bertie gave her a silver clock engraved with the letters A—L—B—E—R—T—E—D—W—A—R—D in place of numbers.

Three days later, Bertie traveled to Berlin to attend the emperor's funeral. The journey by special train was bitterly cold, and Berlin was covered with deep snow. Fritz, who now became Emperor Frederick III, was too weak to walk in the procession behind his father's coffin. He watched the black-draped funeral cortège from an upstairs window, a frail figure standing at attention in a general's uniform. When the hearse passed beneath him, he broke down.

Bertie had feared the worst since November, when he told Georgie: "We are terribly anxious about poor dear Uncle Fritz, as a fresh growth has appeared in his throat, and we are all terribly afraid that it may be cancerous."[20] Vicky was in denial, but Bertie could no longer pretend to himself that Fritz was not a dying man. Arthur Ellis, who accompanied the prince, sent a stark report back to Knollys:

This place is too gloomy for words.
Emp[ero]r dead, the other surely dying.
Even the P[rince] of W[ales] sees it now. It is really a most terrible tragedy.
He [Fritz] received us.
He is quite dumb.
It was one of the saddest things I ever experienced.[21]

Bertie sent a message via Ellis to Ponsonby: "The Emperor [Fritz] is very very ill. The Queen should realise this. This is what the Prince of Wales bids me to say."[22]

———

Bertie was staying at Sunningdale for Ascot races on 14 June 1888 when he heard at noon that all was over, and returned immediately to London.[23] Fritz had ruled for ninety-nine days.

On 16 June, Bertie left once more for Berlin, accompanied by Alix, who had agreed to venture into the German "robber's den" as a special mark of sympathy for Vicky. "Greatly relieved to hear that dear Alix would go with Bertie to Berlin, as I begged her to," wrote Victoria.[24] Bertie found "darling Vicky" in a state of great distress: "She cried and sobbed like a child."[25] In the days after Fritz's funeral, he and Alix were with her all the time, and Bertie wrote afterward that "Ever since we parted on that lovely but sad Sunday afternoon my thoughts have continually been with you."[26]

Vicky's position was terrible indeed. Not only had she lost her husband, but she was at war with the entire Prussian court and especially with her son. On the night that Fritz lay dying, William had ordered his hussars to form a cordon around the Charlottenburg Palace to prevent his mother smuggling out her papers. (Vicky had anticipated him by locking them away at Windsor.) Once he became kaiser, William pointedly ignored and humiliated his mother, in spite of—or perhaps because of—a stream of telegrams and letters from Queen Victoria begging him to take care of the grieving widow. Vicky had been very briefly empress, ruling Germany from Fritz's sickroom. Now her influence was nil. William gave her a tightfisted allowance and evicted her from her palace in Berlin.

William's treatment of his mother was heartless, but her response made it worse. Her pain and anger rained down in a torrent on Windsor and on Marlborough House. Most of the things she wrote about William were true. He was indeed an atavistic, reactionary autocrat; he was putty in the hands of the devious Bismarck; he was ignorant of everything except military matters; he was nationalistic, xenophobic, and anti-Semitic. Vicky was correct to predict that William would lead Germany to nemesis. But for a woman of such intelligence and humanity, she was extraordinarily lacking in insight. Her grief was displaced into anger against her son, much as Victoria had turned against

Bertie and blamed him for Albert's death. She seemed unable to perceive that quarreling with William was ultimately self-destructive.

From Windsor, Victoria poured the oil of sympathy onto the flames of Vicky's anger. From Marlborough House, on the other hand, Bertie urged his sister to mend the quarrel. After he returned from Fritz's funeral, he wrote: "There will I know be endless difficulties with W[illiam] but you must not be disheartened dearest Vicky and try and surmount them. Above all if possible try and have some influence with him so that he may not be entirely at the mercy of those in whose political opinions you cannot agree."[27] And again: "Let no estrangement exist between you both, and remember he is his father's eldest son."[28] She must ignore the campaign against her. "If as you say there is a party who wish to get rid of you and drive you away from the country I hope you will not play their game—and show that you have only contempt for the abominable way they behave and let it fall back on them when they wish to crush a defenceless woman."[29]

For the rest of her life, Vicky dressed in black. She was becoming more and more like her mother, "not only in her appearance but in the way she 'moves.'"[*30] In her stubbornness, too, she resembled Victoria. She knew very well that her estrangement from William was no mere family quarrel, but threatened to destabilize Anglo-German relations. But she refused to listen to Bertie's good advice.

Mourning for Fritz canceled the London season of 1888 for Bertie, and after a party-free summer he retreated to Homburg. Here he lived on

---

* Mother and daughter were alike in their habits, too. Vicky's daughter Moretta (Victoria) traveled on a sleeper to Balmoral in the same compartment as Queen Victoria in 1889. She wrote to her mother: "I was just dozing off when Grandmama came to bed—and how it reminded me of you, my Mother. She looked so clean and dear—all in white—& it took some time before she was settled—the shawls, & cushions—then the lamps to put out—then again, it felt too hot—then not warm enough, & in the night—Annie was called many a time—to bring her something to drink etc. Oh! It did remind me so of our travels!" (*Queen Victoria at Windsor and Balmoral: Letters from Her Grand-daughter Princess Victoria of Prussia*, ed. James Pope-Hennessy [George Allen and Unwin, 1959], p. 51 [7 June 1889].)

a regime of spa water, tennis, and Wagner, traveling to Frankfurt to hear *Lohengrin, Die Walküre,* and *Tannhäuser,* and he saw Vicky who was staying at the palace.[31]

On 10 September 1888, Bertie arrived in Vienna on a month's visit. He drove to the Grand Hotel at 6:45 a.m., and the Austrian emperor Francis Joseph visited him at 11:00, followed by Crown Prince Rudolf at 12:45. Changing into his uniform as colonel of the 12th Austrian Hussars (gold-frogged tunic, red breeches, Hessian boots, and white shako—one of the few smart uniforms still remaining in the Austrian army), Bertie returned the emperor's call at the Hofburg.[32] Francis Joseph mentioned that William planned to arrive in Vienna after Bertie had left, on 3 October. Bertie, who had written twice to William asking the date of his arrival but received no answer, declared that he would change his program to be sure of being in Vienna to welcome his nephew. The next day, he learned from the British ambassador in Vienna, Sir Augustus Paget, that the German ambassador had informed him that the kaiser did not wish to meet his uncle in Vienna and, as Bertie put it, that he "preferred my room to my company!"[33] This ostentatious snub became known as the Vienna incident.[34]

At first, Bertie was angry and upset. He deliberately misunderstood the message to stay away, insisting that by welcoming William in Vienna he would signal friendly relations. This embarrassed Emperor Francis Joseph, who, as the subordinate partner in the Dual Alliance with Germany, felt under pressure to obey the kaiser's wishes. On 12 September, Bertie dictated a note for Colonel Swaine, the military attaché in Berlin, who was authorized to show it to William. The letter declared that the prince, who had "the greatest affection" for his nephew, had been looking forward to their meeting with pleasure, and the news that William would prefer not to meet had caused him great pain. "I have never seen the Prince of Wales so upset about anything and he is racking his brains in vain to discover the cause. . . . What is the meaning of all this?"[35]

Bertie was being disingenuous. It could hardly have escaped his notice that William had made a speech at Frankfurt on 16 August, the day after Bertie's arrival at Homburg, attacking those who claimed that

Fritz had intended to surrender Alsace-Lorraine. This was a coded broadside against Bertie, and after his speech William was heard to say, "I hope my uncle the Prince of Wales will understand that!"[36]

Bertie had asked Bismarck's son Herbert whether it was true that, if Fritz had lived, he would have wished to return Alsace-Lorraine to France.[37] He also asked about Alsace in an audience with old Bismarck, but because Alix was present, Bismarck had given a civil answer, and Bertie had taken advantage of this unwonted amiability to draw up a paper recording the conversation. The following day Herbert Bismarck had forced Sir Edward Malet, the British ambassador, to withdraw this document, claiming that it had not been sanctioned by Prime Minister Salisbury, and this apparently had hurt Bertie, as it was the first state paper he had ever written.[38]

Bertie was vulnerable because he was so closely identified with the hated Empress Vicky. Spies reported his unguarded private conversations to Bismarck. Every mistake that Vicky made was credited to Bertie's influence: "He was the scapegoat against which all Berlin hurled themselves."[39] Bertie's friendly relationship with his brother-in-law, Czar Alexander III, also made him a danger. The previous autumn the czar had spent his customary family holiday at Fredensborg, and Alix had used the opportunity to poison him against William, telling stories about his bad behavior toward his parents. The czar, who for all his autocratic politics was a devoted family man, was shocked, and Russia's commitment to the German alliance was compromised as a result.[40] No one could say that Alix lacked influence.

The incident at Vienna rapidly escalated into a standoff. Bertie received no reply to his message to the kaiser. Still huffing and puffing, he departed for Hungary on a shooting expedition with Crown Prince Rudolf. Spending time with the lively prince made Bertie even angrier with William. Rudolf was thirty and Bertie forty-six, but their friendship prospered.

Rudolf detested William. Clever and sardonic, he found William's heel-clicking arrogance intolerable. Politically liberal (in so far as such a thing was possible for a future Habsburg emperor), he bitterly resented Austria's dependence on Germany. He told Bertie that William had remarked that "if his uncle wrote him a very kind letter, he <u>might perhaps answer it</u>!!"⁴¹ Rudolf reported that "Wales" was "in great fettle, wants to see everything and will not allow himself to be left out in the cold. Nothing seems to tire the old boy. I long for a rest."⁴² Bertie always dismissed the rumors about Rudolf's dissolute habits—the visits to lowlife prostitutes and the drinking binges—but surely knew of Rudolf's quarrel with his father, Emperor Francis Joseph, and the young man's estrangement from his wife.

At the time that William made his state entry into Vienna on 3 October, Bertie was traveling to Bucharest to stay with the King and Queen of Romania; the queen, as Elizabeth of Wied, had been considered as a possible wife for Bertie twenty-seven years before. He wore his English field marshal's uniform with the Grand Cordon of the Star of Romania. Back in England, meanwhile, Lord Salisbury tried to patch up the damage. Bertie's spat with William threatened to upset the prime minister's carefully crafted European entente, balancing France by cultivating German friendship. Salisbury told Victoria that Bertie's blunder was that he had treated William "as an uncle treats a nephew, instead of recognising that he was an Emperor who, though young, had still been of age for some time."⁴³ Victoria agreed that personal quarrels should not be allowed to affect the foreign policy of the two nations, but pointed out that "with such a hot-headed, conceited and wrongheaded young man, devoid of all feeling, this may at ANY moment become <u>impossible</u>."⁴⁴ Alix told Georgie that William had been "most <u>frightfully rude</u>" toward Papa and refused to meet him in Vienna. "Oh he is mad and a conceited ass—who also says that Papa and Grandmama don't treat him with proper respect as the Emperor of all and mighty Germany! But my hope is that pride will have a fall some day!! Won't we rejoice then."⁴⁵

Bertie returned home on 22 October. Before his departure for the Newmarket races, the prime minister visited him at Marlborough House and explained his policy of appeasing Germany, warning Bertie not to allow a family quarrel to get in the way.⁴⁶ But Salisbury had failed to appreciate that, though foreign policy in Britain was controlled by politicians, in Germany family quarrels really did dictate foreign policy. And in Bertie's case, the quarrel with William had strengthened his position at home by ending his long rift with his mother.

Between 31 August and 30 September 1888, in the slums of Whitechapel, the sex killer Jack the Ripper strangled four poor prostitutes, then cut their throats, slashed their stomachs, and eviscerated them. His fifth and final victim, Mary Jane Kelly, had her throat slit and face and body horrifically mutilated on 9 November.[47]

The identity of the Ripper has never been conclusively established. Conspiracy theories continue to proliferate. One of the most far-fetched (published in the 1990s) claimed that Mary Jane Kelly was murdered because she was pregnant by the Prince of Wales. This theory lacks evidence or plausibility: No connection has ever been proved between the prince and the victim. On 9 November, Bertie was at Sandringham, celebrating his forty-seventh birthday with a dinner for three hundred estate laborers and a county ball.[48]

More enduring are the conspiracy theories linking Prince Eddy with the Ripper murders. The most sensational of these came to light in the 1970s; the source was a man named Joseph Gorman, who claimed that his grandmother, Annie Crook, who worked as a shopgirl on Cleveland Street, had made a clandestine marriage to Eddy, who was studying drawing with the artist Walter Sickert in his studio nearby, and in 1885 had a daughter by him. When Queen Victoria found out, she was horrified at the possibility of blackmail and, so the story goes, appealed to Lord Salisbury to put an end to the liaison. Salisbury ordered a raid on Cleveland Street, and Annie Crook was incarcerated in a madhouse. However, Annie's friend, the prostitute Mary Kelly, spread the story, so Salisbury enlisted the royal physician Sir William Gull to eliminate all Mary's friends: the Ripper victims Mary Anne Nichols, Annie Chapman, Elizabeth Stride and (mistakenly) Catherine Eddowes, and finally Mary herself. The murders were a cover-up, and once Gull had done his work the killings ceased. This explanation solves one of the puzzles about the Ripper: why the murders suddenly stopped if they were committed by a sexual psychopath who was never arrested.[49] However, it bears no relation to fact. There is not a shred of evidence to connect Eddy either to Annie Crook or to Sickert.[50]

A still more far-fetched theory proposes that Eddy himself was Jack the Ripper.[*][51] This version turns on the alleged "discovery" of the secret papers of Sir William Gull, which supposedly reveal that Eddy contracted syphilis while on a cruise in the West Indies, causing him to go insane, and committed the murders in a fit of mad rage. Gull then confined him to a private mental home near Sandringham, where he died of softening of the brain. This crackpot theory has been rightly demolished. Gull's secret papers are nowhere to be found. Eddy didn't suffer from syphilis. Far from being incarcerated, he was active and living a very public life between 1888 and 1891. Nor was he anywhere near Whitechapel on the date of any of the murders; his alibis can be verified from reading *The Times* Court and Social.[52] The Eddy/Ripper theory is interesting, however, because it is a classic royal myth. Like so many such stories, it builds a conspiracy theory, which is by definition almost impossible to prove or refute. Key ingredients in such narratives are syphilis and/or pregnancy, madness, sex, prostitutes, establishment cover-ups, and "missing" papers that seemingly contain the solution to the mystery. Our image today of Jack the Ripper is not that of an impoverished Jewish or Irish immigrant in the East End, but of a toff in a cloak, top hat, and elegant Edwardian evening clothes. In the popular imagination, the Ripper lives on as a figure like Eddy.

At seven o'clock on the evening of 13 December 1888, Bertie walked into the gloom of St. George's Chapel, Windsor. The choir was shrouded in darkness, and a small group of watchers stood beside the

---

* An even more fantastical variant claims that Eddy's former tutor Jem Stephen committed the murders. Devastated by the breakup of his alleged homosexual relationship with Eddy and driven insane by a blow to the head, Stephen is claimed to have sought revenge against Eddy by killing prostitutes. (Why?) (Casebook: Jack the Ripper, http://www.casebook.org/suspects/.)

hole that workmen had carefully made in the floor, revealing the royal vault below. The coffins of Henry VIII and Charles I could be dimly seen by the light of a single coil of magnesium wire. Bertie stooped down and silently lowered a small oak case, which he placed on the coffin of the martyr king Charles I. Inside the case was an ivory casket containing relics taken from Charles's coffin when the Prince Regent opened it in 1813: a chip of cervical vertebra cut with a sharp instrument, a piece of auburn hair from the king's head, and a tooth. Bertie withdrew, and the workmen immediately returned to close the vault.[53] His feelings are unrecorded, but this grim little ceremony surely gave a chilling reminder of the transience of princes.*

Bertie spent the morning shooting ducks at Sandringham on 30 January 1889, the day he received news of the sudden death of Crown Prince Rudolf.[54] He was shocked and "greatly upset."

"I knew him so well," he told Jennie Churchill, "and had seen so much of him last year that I cannot bring myself to believe that I shall never see him again."[55] Rudolf was found shot through the head at his hunting lodge at Mayerling. In his bed lay the dead body of his mistress, the eighteen-year-old Marie Vetsera. Official reports claimed that the Mayerling tragedy was a double suicide, the result of a lovers' pact, but Salisbury was convinced that Rudolf and Marie Vetsera had been assassinated.[56] Bertie made it his business to ascertain the true story.[57] He told the Queen on 12 February that Rudolf had killed Marie Vetsera and then himself.

> It seems poor Rudolf has had suicide on the brain for some time past—he wrote letters saying he was going to die—and the poor young lady wrote the same to her family. He shot her first—then decked her out with flowers—and then blew his brains out—and he had only half an hour for all this. . . . Nobody knew that the young lady was with him but his valet. The latter seems to have

---

* Staying at Newburgh Priory with Sir George Wombwell in 1877 or later, Bertie asked his host to break open the vault that allegedly contained Oliver Cromwell's bones. According to the local story, Bertie and the estate carpenter were caught in the act, trying to break into the coffin. (*The Times,* 18 October 1913.)

had orders from the Emperor not to leave him alone—but he peremptorily ordered him away—ag[ain]st the poor man's wishes before the deed was done.

According to Bertie's informant, there was "some unknown reason" why Rudolf committed suicide, and he didn't do it on account of Marie Vetsera. Bertie hinted at dark secrets: "There are details I could tell you—which I cannot write—which clearly show complete aberration of the mind for some time past—the whole story is like a bad dream and I can think of nothing else."[58]

Rudolf had plenty of reasons to blow his brains out. He suffered from syphilis, and he may well have inherited the Wittelsbach depression through his mother, the Empress Elizabeth, whose cousin, the mad King Ludwig II of Bavaria, died in mysterious circumstances in 1886. But what really happened at Mayerling is still a mystery, and the answer is said to lie in a locked archive in the Vatican. With its stories of secret papers that will reveal all and hints at an establishment cover-up, Mayerling mirrors the Eddy/Ripper myth—a tale of a flawed and mentally unbalanced heir to the throne, syphilis, sexual promiscuity, and murder.

Bertie attended the Catholic requiem mass for Rudolf at Farm Street Church of the Immaculate Conception, but he disappointed the Austrian court by staying away from the funeral in Vienna, though he sent a "beautiful" wreath—"the words were in black on white satin." By then tales were spreading of the "awful crime" that Rudolf had committed, and no one in Vienna regretted his death.[59] Bertie, however, remained loyal to his friend's memory. For him, the prince's death was more than a personal tragedy. Rudolf, who had also been a favorite of Vicky's, was the last link in Bertie's project of an Anglophile German bloc. First Fritz's death had ruled out the prospect of a good Germany. Now Rudolf's death ended the dream of a liberal Austria.

Bertie did gain one key contact in Austria through Rudolf: Baron Maurice de Hirsch, the Austrian railway magnate, who was descended from a family of Jewish financiers at the Bavarian court. Rudolf had agreed to give him an introduction to the Prince of Wales in exchange for a loan.[60] After Rudolf's death, Hirsch became Bertie's financial adviser, helping to fill the growing gap between the prince's income and his spending.

In February 1889, the kaiser let it be known that he wished to visit England in the summer. Still smoldering from the Vienna incident, Victoria was adamant that "William must <u>not</u> come this year," telling Bertie, "<u>you</u> could not meet him, and I could <u>not</u> after all he has done and said."[61] Bertie agreed, refusing to meet the kaiser unless he received an expression of regret for the incident at Vienna. But Bertie and his mother failed to reckon with Lord Salisbury. He insisted that Britain needed good relations with Germany, and William must be allowed to come. "It is your Majesty's interest," he told the Queen, "to make his penitential return as easy to him as possible."[62]

Pushed by Salisbury, Victoria reluctantly consented to invite her nephew, but only to Cowes and not to Windsor. Like a small child, the kaiser was ecstatic, and wired Victoria that he was "overjoyed to be allowed" to come to the "dear old Home."[63] This was strange language for a German emperor to use, but it hints at his confused sense of identity. For William (as one psycho-historian has suggested), England was identified with his mother, and though he resented the dominance of Vicky/England, at the same time he longed for her approval. Validation by Vicky/England was crucial to his sense of self-worth.[64] To Vicky, the news of William's impending visit came as a "<u>stab</u>."

"The thought that W[illiam] who has <u>so</u> trampled upon me, and on his beloved father's memory, should now be received . . . in my own dear home," she found unbearable, betraying by the violence of her language—"stab," "trampled"—the rawness of her emotions toward her son.[65]

Bertie's quarrel with the kaiser was still unresolved. Bertie was by now "sick . . . of the whole affair," and, guided perhaps by Knollys, who had thought all along that the Queen was the best person to reach a settlement, he decided in May to "leave the matter entirely in dear Mama's hands."[66] His relations with Victoria had never been better. At

Easter she granted him his "long looked for wish": She stayed at Sandringham.[67] Only once had she come before, in 1871–72, when she
thought Bertie was dying of typhoid. The Easter visit was a success;
she was "pleased with her reception" through the triumphal arches
escorted by the West Norfolk Hunt, and she enjoyed the theatrical performance that Bertie arranged with Ellen Terry and Henry Irving.[68]

Salisbury frightened the Queen by threatening that a rupture with
Germany caused by a personal quarrel within the royal family would
endanger the position of the monarchy at home.[69] He then drafted a
friendly letter to William for the Queen to sign.[70] Bertie considered the
letter was "too mild."

"My only fear," he told Vicky, "is that W[illiam] will consider the
matter as over and will not allude to it again."[71] He needn't have worried. William's reply to this innocuous document was as insulting as it
was postmodern. The whole Vienna incident, he now declared, "is
purely a fixed idea which originated either in Uncle Bertie's own imagination or in somebody else's, who put it into his head."[72]

The kaiser's mendacious reply "made matters worse than ever,"
wrote Ponsonby.[73] At Windsor and Marlborough House the Queen
and prince and their advisers feverishly wrote and rewrote angrier or
less angry letters to William deploring the insult and outrage to the
prince.[74] But it was no use. Salisbury insisted that their letters would
only worsen the quarrel, and none was sent. Knollys lamented that
"the Prince of Wales is sacrificed by Lord Salisbury to political expedi-
ency."[75] Bertie deplored what he saw as Salisbury's weakness and willingness to appease the bullying Bismarcks. Salisbury had given "the
worst possible advice, making us virtually 'eat humble pie'!"[76] In fact,
the episode was a triumph for Salisbury, who had skillfully finessed
both the Queen and the Prince of Wales into dropping their family
quarrels where these conflicted with the foreign policy of constitutionally elected ministers.

Salisbury was equally shrewd in dealing with the kaiser. On learning that William cared even more about uniforms than his uncle Bertie, he persuaded Victoria to offer William the rank of a British admiral.
The effect was electric. William was childishly grateful. "Fancy wear-

ing the same uniform as St. Vincent and Nelson," he gushed; "it is enough to make one quite giddy."[77] Soon he was writing gaily to "Dearest Grandmama" to say how glad he was that the Vienna incident was concluded, "and I shall be happy to meet Uncle Bertie in Osborne."[78]

The visit to Osborne in August was a triumph. Bertie was on board the royal yacht *Osborne* to welcome William, who arrived on the *Hohenzollern* wearing his new admiral's uniform, and William kissed the Queen affectionately on both cheeks. Bertie was constantly in attendance, and even Alix was present.[79] William was gratified when Victoria invited him to breakfast in her tent, "a rare honour."[80] He told the Queen afterward how delighted he was "to feel and take an interest in your fleet as if it were my own."[81]

William's honeymoon with England enabled Germany to adopt the liberal foreign policy urged by Vicky and Fritz. Soon the Bismarcks were sacked and their pro-Russian policies abandoned. Vicky watched with divided feelings. She approved of William's pro-English views, but she found his triumphalism and boasting about the way he had been feted by the English court a toxic pill to swallow. She deliberately refrained from interfering. "Wronged and persecuted as I have been, I could have appealed to you," she told her mother, "and all my brothers and sisters to seek redress for me. . . . But this I could not do in my position. England must appear to ignore what are affairs of the German court and see that relations between the two great countries be not disturbed or affected by family affairs."[82] Lord Salisbury could not have put it better himself.

But Salisbury's insistence on elected governments controlling foreign policy failed to allow for the dynastic marriages of Queen Victoria's extended family. Never before had the English royal family been so closely related to the rulers of the great powers. As the generation of Victoria's grandchildren succeeded to the thrones of Europe, the scope for the dynastic diplomacy at which Bertie excelled was to expand. But not yet: not while Salisbury and Victoria were in control.

CHAPTER 17

Scandal

1889–90

One day in February 1889, Bertie received a surprise visit from a member of the Marlborough House set: Lady Brooke. Daisy Brooke at twenty-eight had china-blue eyes, a tiny waist, a curvaceous figure of the type that delighted the prince, and the irresistible charm of manner that comes from always getting one's own way. Bertie found himself unable to decline an appeal for help from "Beauty in Distress."[1] Years later, Daisy recalled her conquest: "He was more than kind . . . and suddenly I saw him looking at me in a way all women understand. I knew I had won, so I asked him to come to tea. For ten years afterwards he came to tea with me every day when we were both in London."[2] This was Daisy's way of saying that she had become the prince's mistress.

Daisy's enemies alleged that she had barely met the prince at the time of her Beauty in Distress interview, but this was far from the case. Bertie had known her since she was a child. She was an heiress, inheriting a fortune and Easton Lodge, an estate in Essex, from her grandfather Viscount Maynard at the age of three; this gave her a confidence and sense of entitlement that was unusual among women of her class. She was a court insider, as her stepfather, Lord Rosslyn, a friend of Disraeli, was a favorite of Queen Victoria. The Queen chose Daisy as a suitable bride for Prince Leopold, but this project suited neither party. Determined to take possession of her inheritance at Easton Lodge, the nineteen-year-old Daisy infuriated her parents by marrying her childhood sweetheart, Lord Brooke, heir to the Earl of Warwick.* Bertie attended the wedding and signed the register at Westminster Abbey in 1881.[3] Daisy came into Bertie's life again in 1886, two children later, when she and "Brookey" stayed at Sandringham in January, and in June the prince paid his first visit to the Brookes at Easton Lodge. The names at that first royal house party are listed in Bertie's diary. The guests included the nucleus of the Marlborough House set: Lady Randolph Churchill, Lady Mandeville, and Lord and Lady Charles Beresford.[4] Together with Daisy herself, these people were to form the dramatis personae of the scandals that almost derailed Bertie's life in the years 1889–91.

Daisy Brooke was a fearless rider and dedicated fox hunter. Once, as she later related, while staying at Windsor, she defied etiquette by leaving before breakfast by the earliest train in order to go hunting, wearing the scarlet riding habit she had designed for herself (it was considered bad form for women to wear red). Peeping behind a curtain at an upstairs window, Victoria watched her go. "How fast!" said the Queen. "How very fast!"[5] This story is probably apocryphal, but it is revealing about Daisy's image of herself. Liberated by her marriage, and bored by Lord Brooke, whose passion was shooting, she began an affair with Lord Charles Beresford. The swashbuckling naval officer, who had won glory at the bombardment of Alexandria and then in the rescue operation after General Charles Gordon's death at Khartoum, was "a Regency figure trapped in a Victorian moral universe."[6] He was

---

* In 1883, the Maynard estates comprised 13,844 acres in Essex and Leicestershire, yielding an income of £20,000. Daisy was rich, but she was not one of the super-rich.

an old friend of Bertie's—he had commanded the royal yacht *Osborne,* and accompanied Bertie to India—and the Prince of Wales no doubt knew all about this liaison. Beresford's wife, Mina, was already forty; the couple were dubbed the Red Admiral and the Painted Lady, on account of Mina's frowned-upon habit of applying her makeup in public.[7] Daisy was merciless about the older woman, describing with cruel glee an occasion when Mina, caught out by a blast of wind, found her hat blown off on the grass, with her yellow hair attached.[8] So far as the nubile Daisy was concerned, Mina was no competition. Beresford was the father of Daisy's second child, Marjorie (born in 1884). When he announced that he must end the affair because Mina was pregnant, Daisy was furious.[9] In January 1889, she wrote him an absurdly indiscreet letter, demanding that he leave his wife and implying that Mina had no right to have a child by her husband. Unfortunately for Daisy, Beresford was abroad, inspecting Kaiser William's navy, and in his absence Mina opened the letter. Mina fought back tooth and claw. She consulted the solicitor George Lewis, giving him Daisy's letter for safekeeping, and he wrote to Daisy warning her off.

It was George Lewis's letter, effectively accusing her of sexual harassment, that prompted Daisy to seek an interview with Bertie. What happened next can be reconstructed with accuracy because Mina Beresford later wrote a detailed account for Lord Salisbury.[10] That same night, at two a.m., Bertie drove round to Lewis's home on Portland Place and demanded to see the letter Lady Brooke had written to Lord Charles Beresford. Flouting all professional etiquette, and without consulting his clients the Beresfords, the hapless lawyer "was prevailed upon" to obey the prince.[11] He drove with the prince to his office on Ely Place, took the letter out of the box in the strong room, and showed it to HRH, but refused to allow him to keep it.[12] It was the most controversial act in his entire career.

Bertie's next move was to call upon Mina Beresford. In her words, he "<u>ordered</u> me forthwith to give the letter up to <u>him</u>!!" which she refused to do. George Lewis wrote another letter on Mina's behalf to Daisy, telling her that if she stayed away from London that season, her letter would be returned. This was blackmail, and Daisy appealed again to the prince, who called on Mina a second time. On this occasion, she recalled, "he was anything but conciliatory in tone to me and even <u>hinted</u> that if I did not give him up the letter, my position in Society!! and Lord Charles's would become injured!!"[13]

Daisy swiftly dropped Beresford in order to become the prince's favorite. According to Mina: "Wherever he went, he desired she also should be invited, and invited she was, but to the disgust of everyone."[14]

When Mina was put down for a house party, Daisy recalled, Bertie "simply cut her name out and substituted mine for it and wrote to the hostess that he thought it would be better for her not to meet the angry woman till she had cooled off." Thenceforth, "my husband and I were down on the Prince's 'list.'"[15] Brookey always came along too, playing the role of complaisant husband.

In 1889, Bertie stayed at a house party at Easton for Daisy's birthday (10 December).[16] It seems likely that this was the occasion when they became lovers. "How well I remember spending your birthday with you just 10 years ago at your old home," he wrote in 1899, regretting that the "very warm feelings" they then shared had "cooled down."[17]

When Charles Beresford discovered that Bertie had moved in on his own mistress, he demanded an interview at Marlborough House in January 1890, before setting off to sea in HMS *Undaunted*. According to his account, he told the prince "in no measured sentences" that bullying George Lewis into allowing him to see Daisy's letter was "a most dishonourable and blackguard action." Bertie, "being somewhat excited," called Beresford a "blackguard" himself, whereupon the latter demonstrated "with some warmth and considerable clearness that there was only one blackguard in the case at all, and that was YRH who had dared to interfere in a private quarrel."[18] The two men—who had previously been intimate friends—came very close to blows. According to Daisy's later and doubtless somewhat colored account, Bertie told Beresford that he must stop Mina from blabbing and that he must give up Daisy. Beresford became very angry and declared that he would never give Daisy up.

" 'You're not her lover,' cried the Prince.

" 'I am,' the sea captain retorted, 'and I'm not going to stop.' "*[19]

Whereupon Bertie seized the inkstand from the table and hurled it at Beresford's head. Fortunately it missed, but Daisy claimed she saw the ink stain on the wall the next day.[20]

From then on, Bertie ostracized both Beresfords, Charlie and Mina, refusing to speak to them. The quarrel dragged on for another two years.

In July 1891, Alix invited Daisy to dinner at Marlborough House. Now that the Princess of Wales had received the "unabashed adventuress," Mina decided to take her revenge.[21] Her retaliation was deadly: She leaked the story.

She and her sister, Mrs. Gerald Paget, composed a pamphlet entitled "Lady River" (after Babbling Brooke, Daisy's nickname). This gave scurrilous and possibly libelous details about Daisy's various affairs, and reproduced her infamous letter to Charles Beresford. Throughout the summer of 1891, the typescript of "Lady River" circulated at country house parties, and readings from the pamphlet were eagerly attended.[22] Daisy Brooke herself seemed blissfully unaware. Rumors reached Vicky in Germany—"I suppose there is no truth in Lady Brooke having a divorce," she wrote.[23] Daisy sailed serenely on. Carrington was captivated by her at a dinner in July. "Lady Brooke has developed into a very beautiful woman," he wrote. "She has the great gift of appearing intensely interested in anything that concerns anyone she may be talking to: and though a desperate attempt has been made to 'knock her out' of Society, she will weather the storm yet: as she smiles on everybody and looks pleasant, and never abuses or says an unkind word of any human being."[24]

Lord Charles Beresford held the office of Fourth Lord of the Admiralty (an appointment he owed to Bertie's influence), and in July he appealed to the prime minister, Lord Salisbury. He sent Salisbury a draft letter he had written to the prince, accusing him of "instituting a

---

* These quotes are taken from the account of the interview that Daisy gave many years later to journalist Frank Harris, who published it in 1916.

species of social boycotting" against his wife. "The days of duelling are past but there is a more just way of getting right done in such cases than ever duelling supplied and that is publicity."[25] Salisbury, who regarded the affair as "sordid and pathetic," dissuaded Beresford from sending the letter and tried to prevent him from going public by appealing to his sense of honor. Beresford, wrote Salisbury, owed a duty of honor to Daisy as his former mistress—"It must not be your face or hand that brings her into any disgrace because she yielded to you."[26]

In December 1891, Beresford returned from the Mediterranean and dispatched another letter—even more furious—to the prince. Accusing Bertie of deliberately slighting his wife, he demanded a formal apology and blustered once again that he would make the scandal public.[27] In threatening publicity, Beresford broke the golden rule of Marlborough House: No Scandal. "Whenever there was a threat of impending trouble," Daisy later wrote, "pressure would be brought to bear, sometimes from the highest quarters, almost always successfully."[28] Mina Beresford wrote to the Queen. Alix now became involved, letting it be known that she was angry with Beresford, and she thought his letter to Bertie "disrespectful" and "improper."

"She warmly supports the prince in everything connected with the unfortunate affair, and is anxious to do all in her power to assist him," wrote Knollys.[29]

Arthur Balfour, Salisbury's nephew and political protégé, believed that Beresford was playing a deep game. "I still have faith in Charlie's acute perception of his own interests," he told Salisbury. "At the same time I admit that when you have to deal with one woman who is mad with jealousy [Mina], another who is mad with spite [Daisy], and a man who is mad with vanity [Bertie], anything may happen."[30] Salisbury disagreed, dismissing Beresford as "a mere tool" in the hands of his wife.[31] The quarrel reached deadlock because (as Schomberg McDonnell, Salisbury's private secretary, wrote) "Nobody could approach Lady Brooke because the Prince of Wales would not allow it," and, on the other hand, Mina Beresford "would agree to nothing which did not stipulate for the withdrawal of Lady Brooke from the Court and from London for at least a year."[32]

The crisis came on 21 December 1891, when Beresford wrote yet another violent letter to Bertie.[33] Salisbury proposed a compromise: Beresford should withdraw his letter in return for a letter of apology from Bertie. An exchange of letters took place on 24 December. A few weeks later, the "Lady River" pamphlet was ceremoniously burned.[34]

Bertie does not emerge from this tangled affair with much credit. He had protected Daisy Brooke, who had behaved outrageously, even by the standards of Marlborough House. By making her his mistress, he had himself behaved even more outrageously. As Beresford wrote: "Under our constitution Your Royal Highness's sole duty is to guide and direct what is named society," and this was compromised when the prince's mistress happened to be involved in the quarrels he tried to arbitrate.[35] Bertie pretended to be the injured party and refused to accept that he was in any way at fault. He blamed Beresford, writing to the latter's brother: "I can never forget, and shall never forgive, the conduct of your brother and his wife towards me. His base ingratitude, after a friendship of about 20 years, has hurt me more than words can say."[36] This seems a strangely one-sided view of friendship. The Beresfords were surely justified in retaliating when Bertie had interfered in their private affairs, almost broken their marriage, ostracized Mina, and stolen Charles Beresford's mistress. Bertie's talk of chivalry rings somewhat hollow.

Nor does his remorseless prosecution of the vendetta impress. He allowed the affair to split his court. Consuelo Mandeville was one of those who circulated the "Lady River" pamphlet, and this made Bertie extremely angry. He punished her by striking her name from the guest lists, refusing to speak to her for many years.*[37] "These American ladies talk too much," he wrote, "and their indiscretions and inaccuracies are most annoying. Those who profess to [be] Lady B[rookes]'s best friends have shown their friendship in a very doubtful manner."[38] As Knollys remarked, Daisy had "cleared out 'the American gang.'"[39]

---

* Consuelo's husband, Lord Mandeville, was declared bankrupt for £100,000 in 1889, which can't have helped. (Vincent, *Later Derby Diaries*, p. 855 [16 March 1889]; Vane, *Affair of State*, p. 186.)

Involving the prime minister in the quarrels of Marlborough House was not a good idea. A figure of immense physical bulk and massive intellectual authority, dreadfully badly dressed and contemptuous of fashion, Salisbury was a private man with strong family loyalties. Episodes such as this seemed to confirm his view that the Prince of Wales was inferior, both morally and intellectually.[40] The Marlborough House set epitomized all that he thought rotten within the aristocracy. Salisbury's Hatfield House was barred to Bertie except on official occasions; it was the only country house where he was not welcomed.[41]

By the end of the 1880s, Bertie's finances had reached a crisis point. He was pestered by moneylenders, and in Paris the ubiquitous French police reported that the hotels where he stayed were ringed by hucksters.[42] The Prince of Wales's annuity from Parliament was fixed at £39,000. The income from the Duchy of Cornwall grew from £59,000 in 1881 to £64,500 in 1890, in spite of agricultural depression, but the prince's gross income dropped from £122,000 in 1881 to £107,600 in 1890.[43] The deficit was evidently yawning.

Gladstone's secretary Edward Hamilton had urged his master as a matter of urgency to reform the prince's finances in 1884. He considered that Gladstone was the only person who could do it. "A Tory administration would have the greatest possible difficulty about bringing the matter forward." Gladstone, by contrast, "would be bound to be supported by the Opposition, would carry most of his own side with him, and would be able to stave off hostility from all but the very extremes."[44] Gladstone disagreed. Parliament, he warned, would be certain to insist on a commission of inquiry and would probably find "a total absence of economic management."[45] Bertie took the hint. He never asked for an increase in his allowance as Prince of Wales. He had no intention of inviting scrutiny of his affairs by Parliament.[46]

In 1889, the Queen appealed to Parliament for royal grants for the children of the Prince of Wales, in the light of the impending marriage of his eldest daughter and the coming-of-age of his sons. Parliament grudgingly voted the prince £36,000 per annum in trust for his children, as well as a capital sum of £60,000, but this came at a price: the most lengthy—and uninhibited—debate on the monarchy to take place during Victoria's reign, with 134 voting against the grants.[47] Bertie's income was freely discussed, and some argued that from his £112,000 per annum he could well afford to pay for his children himself.[48] Others declared that the Queen, whose Civil List income of £385,000 was topped up with £50,000 from the Duchy of Lancaster, ought to subsidize her son, as she had devolved upon him so many of the functions of the Crown.* What exactly did the prince's work consist of? asked Mr. Abraham, the radical MP for Glamorgan: On a typical day HRH held a levee, he unveiled a statue, he dined at the Mansion House, and he witnessed part of *Figaro* at Covent Garden—"And that, then, is a hard day's work!"[49]

Rather than risk parliamentary criticism, Bertie's solution was to borrow from financiers. "My dear Natty," he wrote to Lord Rothschild in 1883, "I cannot find words too extreme [in] gratitude for your great kindness and liberality, which you may be convinced will never be forgotten by me."[50] Documents in the Rothschild archive evidence a private advance of £100,000 made to the prince in 1889, paid in cash and secured against title deeds. A further loan of £60,000 advanced on the Sandringham estates was made in 1893.[51] Whether this money was ever repaid is not clear.

Another man who subsidized the Wales court was a self-made Scottish millionaire named James Mackenzie. The son of an Aberdeen stocking merchant who made one fortune in indigo in India and then another on Lombard Street, Mackenzie bought the Glenmuick estate (29,500 acres) bordering on Balmoral in 1869. Bertie and his sons nicknamed him MacTavish, and treated him as a cross between a factotum and a sugar daddy. The grouse shooting at Glenmuick was good, and

---

* Gladstone considered that the Queen ought to help him out. "Her Civil List had been fixed with a view to her keeping up full state; she now lived a life of comparative retirement: duties and expenses consequently devolved on him which would naturally fall on the Sovereign; and yet the Queen allowed him nothing." (*Diary of Edward Hamilton 1885–1906*, p. 98 [20 June 1889].)

Mackenzie was generous with invitations to Bertie's friends and relations.[52] Bertie wrote asking him to place bets for him on racehorses.[53] Mackenzie owned Sunningdale Park, which the prince borrowed for several years for Ascot races. An 1887 letter from Bertie to Mackenzie gives a sense of the relationship: "When I saw you a week ago did I understand you rightly when you said we might occupy Sunningdale Park for Ascot Races this year? as you did not intend entertaining. If so it would be most kind of you to lend it to us—as it is a charming house and such a pretty place, only pray do not hesitate to refuse if it is inconvenient to you."[54] Though not exactly a command, such a request was hardly possible to refuse. From at least 1884 Mackenzie lent the prince large amounts of money, secured against the title deeds of the Sandringham estate.[55] There is a family story that when Mackenzie died in 1890, having been created a baronet in the nick of time, Knollys appeared at his house, and the deeds were hastily handed over.[56] The money owed to Mackenzie was rumored to be a staggering £250,000, and the trustees were obliged to call in the debt, causing consternation at Marlborough House. Enter the Austrian Jewish financier Baron Maurice de Hirsch. According to Lord Derby: "Hirsch seized the opportunity to pay off the debt, make the Prince his debtor, and so secure for himself a social position."[57]

Hirsch was much richer than Mackenzie, whose will was proved at £694,731. No one knew for sure how rich Hirsch was, but his wealth was estimated at well over £20 million. Descended from a family of Bavarian court bankers, "Turkish Hirsch" had joined the Brussels banking house of Bischoffsheim, married the boss's daughter, and then made another fortune out of the Orient Express, punching a railway through the Balkans from Vienna to Istanbul.[58] Throughout 1890 Baron Hirsch, with his waxed Hercule Poirot–like mustaches, was constantly at Bertie's side. His influence over the Prince of Wales, wrote Derby, "was a puzzle to society, since he is neither a gentleman, nor reputed altogether honest."[59] Hirsch rented luxurious Bath House in Piccadilly, as well as a country house near Sandringham, and Grafton House near Newmarket. Egged on by the prince, he bought the racehorse La Fleche from the Royal Stud for a record price of 5,500 guineas. La Fleche went on to win £34,700 in prize money, all of which Hirsch gave to hospitals (Bertie, by contrast, tended to give his racing winnings to mistresses).[60] Bertie was *"dreadfully* annoyed" when Victoria refused to invite Hirsch to a state concert at Buckingham Palace, and the Queen remained suspicious of the baron, complaining that Bertie accepted too much of his hospitality.[61]

Hirsch entertained Bertie at St. Johann, his vast shooting estate in the sandy plains of Hungary. The anti-Semitic Austrian archdukes gasped when the prince became the guest of a Jew. Bertie thought St. Johann "an unpretentious house but most comfortable"—the more so as Jennie Churchill was among the guests.[62] The shooting was spectacular, though Bertie was as usual dissatisfied with his own performance. "I never saw so much game in my life," he wrote, "but there is nothing the least tame about it."[63] Six hundred beaters formed a circle seven miles in circumference, converging on the shooters, who stood sixty yards apart, each gun stationed in a box walled in with fir branches to ensure that shots were fired safely into the air.[64] The party killed an obscene total of twenty thousand head of game in ten days, mainly partridges. This, Bertie told Georgie, "certainly beats everything on record and will quite spoil one for any shooting at home."[65] At Sandringham, Bertie copied the design of Hirsch's game larder, which was the biggest in the world, capable of holding seven thousand birds.[66]

"We resented the introduction of Jews into the social set of the Prince of Wales," wrote Daisy Brooke, "not because we disliked them . . . but because they had brains and understood finance. As a class we did not like brains. As for money, our only understanding of it lay in the spending, not the making of it."[67] Reactionaries sneered at the prince's Jewish court, while Bertie's defenders praised his broadmindedness. But for Bertie, the munificence of men such as Rothschild and Hirsch was as much a matter of financial survival as social inclusiveness. Rewarding them with recognition was the very least he could do. These men had saved Marlborough House from disaster.

Bertie's admission of Jewish plutocrats to court was unique. In no other Western country were Jews accepted as leaders of society.*

On 27 July 1889 Bertie gave away his eldest daughter, Louise, who married his friend Lord Fife in the private chapel at Buckingham Palace. Marie Adeane, one of Queen Victoria's maids of honor, noted that Alix "looked as usual much younger than the bride, but rather tired." Lord Fife lost his way in the "Have and to hold" sentence so the archbishop had to repeat it, and there was "a good deal of fumbling with the ring but there were no tears and very little agitation."[68] When his sister Louise had married Lord Lorne in 1871, Bertie had objected that marriage with a subject was "lowering to the royal family," but he was delighted with his daughter's match, telling Vicky that "they have been devoted to one another for two years but he was too shy to propose."[69] The issues of protocol, however, caused Bertie concern, and at his insistence, Victoria reluctantly agreed to promote Fife from earl to duke.[70] Fife was well known to the Paris demimonde, who dubbed him *"le petit Ecossais roux qui a toujours la queue en l'air."*[71] That the twenty-two-year-old Louise, a shy, plain girl who had led a secluded life, was being married off to a dissipated man eighteen years her senior seemed not to weigh upon the prince's mind.

Bertie's concern that autumn was his son Eddy, now twenty-five. After leaving Cambridge, Eddy joined the fashionable cavalry regiment the 10th Hussars, but his military career was a farce. He was ig-

---

* The Jewish historian Cecil Roth considered that this was damaging to English Jews. Not only did their leaders withdraw from the Jewish community, seduced by society's glittering prizes, but the social prominence of rich Jews fueled anti-Semitism of the Hilaire Belloc and G. K. Chesterton variety. According to Roth, the people who paid the price for the social prominence of the Jewish plutocrats were the poor Jewish immigrants of the East End. Roth was writing in 1943. (Cecil Roth, "The Court Jews of Edwardian England," *Jewish Social Studies*, vol. 5, 1943, pp. 355–66.) Seen from the perspective of the twenty-first century, it is arguable that the openness of English society under Edward VII played a part in the assimilation of the Jews, and may be one reason why Britain escaped the anti-Semitic excesses of the twentieth century.

norant of the history of battles, and he detested drill and cavalry riding. ("One has to go jogging round and round the riding school in a very tight and uncomfortable garment called a stable jacket and very hot work it is I can assure you.")[72] His instructor at Aldershot found that Dalton had taught him *absolutely nothing!!*" But, according to Lady Geraldine Somerset, the instructor was "equally astonished how much he has got on with him, and thinks, under the circumstances his papers are infinitely better than he dared to expect. He has his father's dislike for a book and never looks into one, but learns all orally, and retains what he thus learns."[73]

The chain-smoking Eddy was aimless and lackadaisical and distressingly prone to put his foot in it. He was remarkably sweet-natured, however, and Alix's favorite. Bertie, though, was infuriated, and teased him for his dandified clothes and the tall "masher" collars he wore to hide his abnormally long neck ("Eddy-Collar-and-Cuffs"). To stiffen his son and keep him out of trouble, he resolved to send Eddy on a six-month tour of India.[74]

Bertie had a meeting with his equerry Lord Arthur Somerset, the superintendent of his stables, and instructed him to see that Eddy was properly equipped with saddlery for his Indian tour, arranging for him to meet the prince on 30 September 1889.[75] At the last minute, Somerset wired to excuse himself from the meeting, as he was obliged to leave "on urgent private affairs" for Dieppe.[76]

Lord Arthur Somerset was the third son of the Duke of Beaufort. Known as "Podge," he was a major in the Royal Horse Guards (the Blues), a tall bachelor with luxuriant ginger facial hair. "He was inclined to fat; his small eyes were on the watch."[77] No one would have guessed that he was in the habit of visiting a homosexual brothel on Cleveland Street. Podge's vice had come to the attention of the authorities in July 1889, when a postboy apprehended for theft had been found with the princely sum of eighteen shillings in his pocket. Questioned by police, the boy confessed that he and two others had received the money as payment for "indecent acts" with men at number 19, Cleveland Street, near Fitzroy Square. Under Section 11 of the 1885 Criminal Law Amendment Act, "gross indecency" between two men, whether public or private, was a criminal offense. Policemen kept watch on the house in Cleveland Street and spotted Lord Arthur, who was identified by the postboys and then interviewed by detectives. Podge waited uneasily during the summer, as the case against two men who had procured the boys came to court. He attempted to bribe a young male prostitute, a waiter from the Marlborough Club, but this led him straight into a police trap. By the end of September, the case against him was complete, but the government hesitated to issue a warrant. A homosexual scandal at Marlborough House was the last thing Lord Salisbury wanted.

Lord Arthur Somerset's movements and conversations are documented in the letters he wrote to his friend Reginald (Regy) Brett, later Lord Esher, a married man and closet homosexual. Brett preserved these letters and bound them into a volume he entitled "The Case of Lord Arthur Somerset." This forms one of the chief sources for the tangled events that ensued.[78]

In London on 5 October, Lord Arthur saw his commanding officer, Oliver Montagu. They agreed that the prince must be told, and Podge wrote a letter confessing his sins. Montagu undertook to go to Fredensborg, where Bertie was on holiday with Alix's extended family, to see the prince, "so as he may hear the right story first."[79]

"I don't believe it," Bertie told Dighton Probyn, the eccentrically bearded comptroller and treasurer of his household. "I won't believe it any more than if they had accused the Archbishop of Canterbury."*[80]

From Fredensborg, Bertie ordered Probyn in London to clear up Lord Arthur's case. "Go and see Monro [the police commissioner], go to the Treasury, see Lord Salisbury if necessary."[81] On the evening of 18 October, Probyn saw Lord Salisbury for a few minutes on King's Cross station before he caught the 7:30 train home to Hatfield. On the same night, Lord Arthur Somerset fled the country.

Later, in the House of Commons debate on 28 February 1890, Salisbury was accused of entering into a criminal conspiracy to pervert the

---

* No doubt Bertie was unaware, but Archbishop Benson was an unfortunate example to choose; his wife, Mary Benson, was a lesbian, and his three sons were homosexuals.

course of justice. The case against him turned on the fact that Arthur Somerset escaped to France on the same night as the King's Cross meeting.[82] Salisbury denied the charge, but doubts have always lingered. Might Probyn have hurried around to the Marlborough Club, where Somerset was staying, and tipped him off?[83] Salisbury's biographer considers that the prime minister felt justified in warning Somerset, out of a sense of class loyalty to his father the Duke of Beaufort.[84]

Bertie wrote to the PM to say how glad he was to learn that "no warrant is likely to be issued against the 'unfortunate Lunatic' (I can call him nothing else) as, for the sake of the Family and Society, the less one hears of such a filthy scandal the better."[85] On 12 November, however, the warrant was issued at last, charging Lord Arthur Somerset with "gross indecency" with other male persons contrary to the Criminal Law Amendment Act. By then, he was living in a villa in Monaco. He never returned to face charges.

Lord Arthur Somerset always maintained that his refusal to stand trial was more than a mere matter of saving his own skin. His real reason he explained in the letters he wrote from abroad to Brett. These documents reveal a sensational story: that Arthur Somerset was a scapegoat who went into exile in order to shield the name of Prince Eddy, who had also visited the Cleveland Street brothel.

Soon the rumors about Eddy's involvement in the scandal were circulating in London, and an article in *The New York Times* (10 November 1889) actually mentioned him by name. This caused a "great pother" in the Prince of Wales's household, and when Bertie returned to London in mid-November, Marlborough House swung into action to suppress the gossip. Oliver Montagu implored Lord Arthur Somerset to return and stand trial in order to clear Prince Eddy's name.[86] Somerset refused. Nor did he make any attempt to protest the prince's innocence. He explained his predicament in a letter to Brett:

I cannot see what good I could do P[rin]ce E[ddy] if I went into court. I might do harm because if I was asked if I had ever heard anything against him—whom from?—was any person mentioned with whom he went there etc?—the questions would be very awkward. I have never mentioned the boy's name except to Probyn, Montagu and Knollys when they were acting for me and I thought they ought to know. Had they been wise, hearing what I knew and therefore what others knew, they ought to have hushed the matter up, instead of stirring it up, as they did, with all the authorities. I have never . . . ever told <u>any one</u> with whom P[rin]ce E[ddy] was supposed to have gone there. I did not think it fair as I could not prove it & it must have been his ruin. I can quite understand the P[rince] of W[ales] being much annoyed at his son's name being coupled with this thing but . . . it had no more to do with me than the fact that we (that is P[rin]ce and I) must both perform bodily functions which we cannot do for each other. . . . If I went into Court and told all I know <u>no one</u> who called himself a man would <u>ever</u> speak to me again. Hence my infernal position.[87]

Bertie was furious with Arthur Somerset. He wrote to Carrington on 2 January 1890: "I hardly like to allude any more to the subject of AS as it is really a too painful one to write about—and his subsequent conduct makes me wish that he had never existed."[88]

It's possible, as one account suggests, that the rumors about Eddy visiting the Cleveland Street brothel caused such consternation to Marlborough House "not because they were false but because they were true."[89] An alternative scenario suggests that the rumors about Eddy and Cleveland Street were slanders that were deliberately spread and embroidered by Lord Arthur Somerset. In his letter to Brett, quoted above, Somerset concedes that he cannot *prove* the rumors about Eddy visiting Cleveland Street. After his ignominious flight, he needed to vindicate himself and show he was a man of honor. What better way than to claim that he had voluntarily gone into exile in a chivalrous bid to throw his cloak over the young prince?[90] Whether or not Prince Eddy did, in fact, frequent Cleveland Street—or whether he was gay or, more likely, bisexual—is perhaps not the issue. The real point is that Eddy had *become* the story, and that made him a liability.

Lord Arthur Somerset was exceptionally well placed to damage

Eddy because of his family connections. His sister, Blanche, with whom he kept in close contact throughout the drama, was married to the Marquess of Waterford, older brother of Lord Charles Beresford. In his attempt to damp down the scandal, Oliver Montagu wrote to Blanche Waterford complaining that some female members of her family had been "insinuating things about Prince Eddy."[91] The woman he had in mind was her sister-in-law: Mina Beresford. Mina had given Daisy Brooke's incriminating letter to Lord Waterford for safekeeping. She must have known about the Lord Arthur Somerset/Eddy story, and she had every motive to spread damaging rumors. The Cleveland Street scandal was intimately linked to the Beresford affair. Both were fueled by the fury of Mina Beresford.

As for Eddy, he seemed happily unaware. On 7 October, as the Cleveland scandal was about to break in London, he wrote a letter from Fredensborg to his cousin Louis Battenberg, confessing that he loved his first cousin Alexandra (Alicky) of Hesse, and asking Louis, who was married to her sister Victoria, to find out "if there is any real reason why Alicky does not care for me, and if I have ever offended her in any way." In a fluently written letter, which shows little sign that Eddy was the fool he is often supposed to be, the prince poured out a story of unrequited love. "I can't really believe that Alicky knows how much I really love, or she would not I think have treated me quite so cruelly. For I can't help considering it so, as she apparently gives me no chance at all, and little or no hope; although I shall continue loving her, and in the hope that some day she may think better of what she has said, and give me the chance of being one of the happiest beings in the world."[92]

Eddy was created Duke of Clarence and Avondale—"the poor boy seems to be destined to have two names, why can't you darling Motherdear try to get it altered and let him only be called Duke of Clarence," wailed Georgie to Alix.[93] Days later Eddy was rejected by Alicky. Her letter came as no surprise, as she had never pretended to like him, and she had set her mind on marrying his cousin Nicky, the czarevitch. Marriage between the weak-willed prince and his neurotic, controlling cousin would probably have been a disaster, but rejection by Alicky made finding a wife for Eddy a matter of urgency. "I am well aware how anxious the government are that Eddy should marry," Bertie told the Queen.*[94]

The choice was limited. Vicky's daughter Margaret (Mossy) was ruled out by Alix because of being Prussian.[95] The only eligible German princesses—a Mecklenburg and two Anhalts—were, according to Queen Victoria, "all three ugly, unhealthy and idiotic:—and if that be not enough, they are also penniless and narrow minded!"[96]

Meanwhile, Eddy made his own choice. He had fallen for Princess Hélène d'Orléans, the nineteen-year-old daughter of the Comte de Paris, the pretender to the throne of France. She was, however, a devout Roman Catholic. Such a marriage, said Queen Victoria, was "utterly impossible."[97]

Eddy's romance with Hélène had begun in the summer of 1889, at Sheen, Richmond, where the Fifes lived close to the Comte de Paris at Sheen House. While his sister Louise spent the summer recovering from a miscarriage, Eddy "got to like or rather love" Hélène.[98]

In July, he succumbed to a mysterious illness, possibly gout, and recuperated with the Fifes at Mar Lodge, where Hélène was staying, too. On 29 August, Eddy drove over to Balmoral and paid a surprise visit to Queen Victoria.[99] Holding Hélène by the hand, he told the Queen that she had loved him for years, and was prepared to make the sacrifice of changing her religion for his sake. Victoria, who was sentimental, was won over. She wrote in a memo to Lord Salisbury: "I have never seen him so eager, so earnest and she was touchingly pathetic in her equally earnest appeal. It was difficult not to say yes at once."[100]

In fact, as Arthur Balfour, the minister in attendance at Balmoral,

* In India, Eddy "had relations" with a certain Mrs. Haddon, the estranged wife of a railway engineer whom he met at a ball. In 1914, she created a disturbance outside Buckingham Palace, claiming that Eddy had fathered her son. She was promptly arrested and packed back off to India, but Eddy's putative son later assumed the name of Clarence and made a career out of his paternity claim, publishing a book and attempting to blackmail George V, for which he was imprisoned. Clarence Haddon was an impostor. He was born before Eddy met his mother, but his story had a basis in fact, as Eddy clearly had a relationship with Mrs. Haddon and wrote her letters. (Camp, *Royal Mistresses*, pp. 386–89.)

perceived, the idea of sending the young couple to the Queen was Alix's. The letter Alix wrote to the Queen the following day impressed even the cynical Balfour. "What astounding but <u>delightful</u> news are [*sic*] these. Dear Eddy has told me all that took place yesterday how he & dear Hélène went straight to you. . . . <u>Nothing</u> on earth could give me greater pleasure than to see these two dear children united. . . . I hardly dare allow myself to dwell on so blessed a prospect—Now however that you have so kindly promised your all powerful help let me thank you from the bottom of my heart."[101] Balfour commented, "My opinion of the Princess of Wales's diplomacy is raised to the highest point."[102] Hélène was intelligent—seemingly rather more so than Eddy—and stylish. And, more important than anything else so far as Alix was concerned, she was not German.

With the Queen in support, it remained only to overcome the resistance of Hélène's parents and of Lord Salisbury. Marriage to a Roman Catholic would have excluded Eddy from the succession under the Act of Settlement. Now that Hélène proposed to convert to Anglicanism, Eddy naïvely believed that this would satisfy Salisbury. He was wrong: Salisbury was dismayed. His reasons were chiefly diplomatic. Marriage to a French princess would annoy the Germans, jeopardizing his policy of cultivating the central powers in order to balance the threats posed to the British Empire by France and Russia. Nor would the marriage please the French Republic, as Hélène's father, the claimant to the French throne, was pledged to its destruction. As he had done over the Vienna incident, Salisbury cloaked his foreign policy objections in a lecture on the constitutional position of the monarchy, writing a memorandum in which he listed seventeen reasons why the marriage could not take place.[103]

Hélène's family were unhelpful, too. Her mother, a keen shot who preferred deer stalking to chaperoning her daughter, supported the match. But the Comte de Paris was a sick man, disillusioned by the failure of his bid for a monarchist restoration in France, and he was in no mood to allow his daughter to convert to Protestantism. Hélène appealed to Pope Leo XIII, but he predictably supported the count.

"This," said Bertie, "brings everything to a dead lock" and "makes poor Eddy quite wretched, as he is very devoted to H."[104]

By the autumn, it was plain that the Orleanist marriage was not to be. Ponsonby and Knollys heaved sighs of relief. Tampering with the Act of Settlement, worried Ponsonby, would raise debate in Parliament "as to whether there should be any succession at all," and might encourage "actual opposition to Prince Eddy coming to the throne."[105] Deep-seated anxiety as to the future of the monarchy meant that ultimately personal feelings must be sacrificed to preserving the institution—in the end the reason why Götterdämmerung was averted in England.

Hélène was devastated. Before her marriage to the Duc d'Aosta four years later, she told Margot Asquith* that she had resisted the match, considering it a desecration of Prince Eddy's memory. When Margot replied that she had always wondered at her devotion to someone "so much stupider" than her, Hélène's "eyes filled with tears as she explained to me the sweetness of his character."[106]

Hélène might well have been unhappy with Eddy. At the same time that he declared himself to be "in love" with her, he was flirting with Lady Sybil St. Clair Erskine, Daisy Brooke's half sister, penning her playful letters. "I thought it was impossible a short time ago to —— more than one person at the same time," he told her.[107] Meanwhile, he appealed to the solicitor George Lewis to help him pay off two ladies who were demanding money for the return of his letters. "I am very pleased you are able to settle with Miss Richardson," he told Lewis, "although £200 is rather expensive for letters."[108] It was only too reminiscent of his father's youth. So, too, was the fact that the illness from which Eddy was suffering turns out not to have been gout after all, but gonorrhea, as a prescription made out by the young doctor Alfred Fripp reveals.†[109]

---

* Margot Tennant married the Liberal politician H. H. Asquith in 1894.
† Theo Aronson speculates that the close friendship that grew up between Eddy and Fripp was homoerotic, but this seems gratuitous.

CHAPTER 18

Nemesis

1890–92

In the summer of 1890, Bertie gave up dancing. "I am getting too old and fat for these amusements," he told Georgie.[1] He had suffered the previous year from phlebitis, a painful swelling of the veins behind the knee, and the doctors ordered him to avoid exercise.[2] Instead of dancing he feasted on opera.

Driven by the dynamic Gladys de Grey, a member of the Marlborough House set who acted as a one-woman Arts Council, the Royal Opera House in Covent Garden was undergoing a revival, and Bertie's patronage was crucial. This was the season when Nellie Melba took London by storm, and Bertie saw her twice in *Roméo et Juliette*. He went to sixty-seven theater performances that year.[3] Attending the opera meant eating a short and early dinner; the shortness did not matter to him, but the earliness was a "real sacrifice."* Often he stayed

---

* On other occasions when he went to the opera he was preceded by a chef and six footmen

at the opera for only an hour or so before "going on" to an evening party. As Daisy wrote, the special achievement of Marlborough House was "to turn night into day."[4]

Bertie returned from his cure in Homburg in early September 1890 in time for the Doncaster races. For years he had stayed with "good old Xtopher" Sykes, but Sykes was ill and had dissipated much of his fortune on entertaining the prince. "I do not wish him—with his reduced income—to spend a farthing on my account—I shall be furious if he gives me a birthday present!" said Bertie in 1889.[5] Instead he stayed in 1890 with Arthur Wilson, a wealthy shipowner from Hull, at his house, Tranby Croft. On 8 September 1890 at twelve thirty, Bertie and his retinue boarded the special train from King's Cross. Daisy Brooke was on the list, but she canceled at the last minute on account of the death of her stepfather, Lord Rosslyn, two days before.[6] Traveling with the prince were Christopher Sykes and Sir William Gordon-Cumming. A lieutenant colonel in the Scots Guards, the forty-two-year-old Bill Cumming was a red-faced veteran of the Zulu War and Khartoum; caustic-tongued and arrogant, he was a bachelor who boasted of "perforating" (his word) large numbers of "the sex," including Lady Randolph Churchill and Lillie Langtry.[7] He had first stayed at Sandringham back in 1881, and Bertie allegedly borrowed his Belgravia house (2 Harriet Street) for secret assignations.[8]

The royal party reached the local station of Hessle near Hull at five fifteen. Bertie found the architecturally undistinguished Italianate mansion of Tranby Croft "new and comfortable," and the Wilsons "most kind and hospitable."[9] As well as courtiers such as Owen Williams, Lord Coventry, and Lord Edward Somerset, Podge's brother, the party included the Wilsons' twenty-two-year-old son, (Arthur) Stanley, his sister Ethel and her husband, Edward Lycett Green, and a young Scots Guards officer named Berkeley Levett.

After dinner, at about eleven p.m., someone suggested playing bac-

---

bearing hampers filled with silver and gold plates and food for the twelve-course dinner that was served during the interval in the room at the back of the royal box. (Hibbert, *Edward VII*, p. 197.)

carat. The game was Bertie's current craze, and it was the fashion at country house parties. It was also illegal, a recent High Court ruling having declared it a game of chance rather than skill.* That night at Tranby Croft, Bertie was the banker. There was no baccarat table in the house—old Arthur Wilson disliked the game—so one was improvised by placing three whist tables together and covering them with a piece of colored tapestry. Acting as croupier was Bertie's unofficial bookie, the pearl-studded Reuben Sassoon.[10] A member of the Jewish dynasty of Bombay bankers, Sassoon had not worn European clothes until adulthood; he often stayed at Sandringham, but it was unkindly remarked of him that he "never opened his mouth, except to put food into it."[11] He distributed the leather counters stamped with £2 or £5 and engraved on the reverse with the Prince of Wales feathers in gold that Bertie always carried when he traveled. The banker is the only player in baccarat who needs skill in calculating his risks, and he must watch carefully the stakes made by the players before deciding whether to deal another card and risk paying out.†

That night, Bertie noticed nothing unusual. Young Stanley Wilson, however, thought that he saw something odd about Gordon-Cumming's play. Gordon-Cumming had a piece of white paper with two columns marked B and P on which he made a dot with a pencil to record whether the bank or the player won. Sitting with one hand clasped over the back of the other on the table before him, he placed his stakes on the white paper. He played according to a system known as *coup de trois* or *masse en avant,* whereby if he won, say, £2, in a coup,

---

* The young Winifred Sturt had been shocked to see the royal family play this illegal game every night at Sandringham. "They have a real table, and rakes, and everything like the rooms at Monte Carlo." (Quoted in Magnus, *Edward VII,* pp. 222–23.)
† Bertie played a version of the game known as baccarat banque. Four packs are combined and shuffled to make 208 cards. The banker deals only to the two players sitting on his left and on his right. All the players sitting on the right of the banker make one tableau, and the ones on the left form another, and their role is simply to put out their stakes. The banker deals two cards facedown to the players on his left and right and to himself, and one card to each faceup. He then looks at his cards and offers one more card to the players on his left and right. The object is to get eight or nine. The player declares, and if the banker's cards are not equally good, the banker loses the whole of that side of the table.

he would leave his red £2 counter and add his winnings of £2 and another £2, thus tripling his stake.

Stanley Wilson, who was sitting next to Gordon-Cumming, saw, or thought he saw, Gordon-Cumming surreptitiously push out £5 counters to add to his £5 stake when the players' cards were good. When the players' cards were bad, Gordon-Cumming withdrew money from his stake. Wilson turned to his friend, the twenty-seven-year-old Berkeley Levett, who was sitting on his other side, and (as he related later in court) whispered, "My God, Berkeley, this is too hot!"

"What on earth do you mean?" said Levett.

"The man next to me is cheating."

Levett watched, too, and noticed that when the banker declared, Gordon-Cumming added two counters to his stake, and was paid £15. He turned to Wilson and said, "It is too hot."[12]

After the game was over and the party had retired to bed, Wilson followed Levett to his room. Levett threw himself down on the bed.

"My God!" he exclaimed. "To think of it—Lieutenant Colonel Sir William Gordon-Cumming Bart caught cheating at cards!"

"What on earth can we do?" said Wilson.

"For goodness' sake don't ask me!" said Levett. "He is in my regiment and was my captain for a year and a half. What can I do?"*[13]

This late-night conversation between two excited young men sounds like something out of a Flashman novel, but it was to have momentous consequences that rocked the monarchy.[14] Stanley Wilson was a young "masher" with a carefully tended black mustache, who had dropped out of Cambridge and prided himself on doing nothing very much.[15] Levett, as an officer in Gordon-Cumming's regiment, owed him loyalty, but he made no attempt to restrain or silence his young friend or protect his brother officer.

Stanley Wilson walked out of Levett's room and told his mother what he had seen. "For goodness' sake, don't let us have a scandal here," she exclaimed.[16] The next morning, Stanley told his brother-in-law Lycett Green, who told his wife. Already five people knew of the secret.

---

* The quotes are taken from the transcripts of the subsequent trial.

The following evening there was baccarat again. This time Gordon-Cumming was watched by five pairs of eyes. Once again the prince was banker, and once again the two young men saw, or thought they saw, Gordon-Cumming cheat, flicking out extra counters with a long, flat carpenter's pencil when the cards were favorable.

The next day, after the races, the Wilson family decided to say something. With Lycett Green acting as spokesman, they approached Lord Coventry and told their story. Owen Williams was called in. Lycett Green, who was very angry, threatened to denounce Gordon-Cumming at the races unless he signed a document admitting his guilt. Owen Williams, ramrod straight and mustached, insisted that the prince must be told at once. He made no attempt to investigate the Wilsons' story, in spite of the fact that they were unknown outsiders. Nor did he discuss the matter with Gordon-Cumming, an old friend and brother officer.

Much has been written about Tranby Croft, but much remains unexplained. For a start, the behavior of the Wilsons. If Mrs. Wilson really wanted to avoid a scandal, the obvious course was either to involve her husband (which she was oddly reluctant to do) or to confront Gordon-Cumming herself. As her friend Lady Middleton, who was Gordon-Cumming's sister, wrote: "Oh Mrs. Wilson if I had thought your son or husband was doing such a thing I would have warned him privately for your sake."[17] Going to the courtiers could only make matters worse. When Lycett Green saw Owen Williams, he burst out: "I will not be a party to letting Gordon-Cumming prey on society in future."[18] Perhaps this was Yorkshire puritanism speaking, but Lycett Green's anger seems to have been fired by Gordon-Cumming's reputation as a seducer of wives.

The behavior of Owen Williams is puzzling, too. Especially perplexing is his failure to find out for himself whether Gordon-Cumming had indeed cheated. The Wilson family had little experience of baccarat, their evidence was inconsistent, and they were expecting to see Gordon-Cumming cheat. The only one of them who had not been influenced by anyone else was Stanley.

After hearing the Wilsons tell their story, Owen Williams went straight to the prince before dinner and told him that the only way to prevent the scandal getting out the next day was to compel Gordon-Cumming to sign a paper agreeing never to play again. This was the first that Bertie had heard of the affair. Rather than question Gordon-Cumming's guilt, he, too, believed the charges. When someone asked him about this later, in court, he replied, "The charges appeared to be so unanimous that it was the proper course—no other course was open to me—than to believe them."[19] Williams and Lord Coventry then saw Gordon-Cumming and told him that he had been accused of foul play. Gordon-Cumming hotly denied the charges. "Do you believe the statements of a parcel of inexperienced boys?" he asked, and demanded to see the prince.[20]

After dinner, the Wilsons told their story to Bertie, who listened without saying much. Then it was Gordon-Cumming's turn. Once again he denied the charge, but all Bertie said was "What can you do? There are five accusers against you."[21] After a few minutes, Gordon-Cumming was asked to leave the room. Half an hour later, Owen Williams summoned him back and, in his oddly mincing voice, asked him to sign a document. In exchange for a promise from the prince, the courtiers, and the Wilson family to preserve silence, Gordon-Cumming was to undertake "never to play cards again as long as I live."* When Gordon-Cumming objected that signing would be tantamount to an admission of guilt, they agreed, but asked him to sign all the same, as it was the only way to prevent Lycett Green from telling everyone at the racecourse the next day. Under pressure, Gordon-Cumming agreed to sign, and early the following morning he left the house on foot and made his way to London.

---

* The paper was signed by the Prince of Wales, Lord Coventry, Owen Williams, Arthur Wilson, the Hon. Arthur Somerset (not Podge, but a relative who was an equerry), Lord Edward Somerset, Edward Lycett Green, Stanley Wilson, Berkeley Levett, and Reuben Sassoon. The one courtier who avoided signing and kept a low profile throughout was Christopher Sykes. As Carrington wrote: "The only man who has kept his head is the supposed ass Christopher Sykes; though he was present his name has never been mentioned, nor was he called as a witness." (Bodleian Library, Lincolnshire Papers, MS Film 1120, Carrington Diary, 17 May 1891.) Perhaps Sykes was not such a fool after all.

Why did Bertie put his name to the paper? As Queen Victoria later wrote, "The incredible and shameful thing is that others dragged him into it and urged him to sign this paper, which of course he should never have done."[22] Bertie was indeed foolish to sign. He dropped his old friend Gordon-Cumming and went along with the Wilsons, whom he barely knew, accepting their story without asking any questions. By signing, he also made it clear that he was playing an illegal gambling game.

A lawyer who reexamined the case in 1977 concluded that Gordon-Cumming was innocent, on the grounds that no man who intended to cheat would deliberately place his counters on a white paper where they were clearly visible.[23] There seems good reason to argue quite the opposite: that Gordon-Cumming was guilty. In fact, everyone cheated. Bertie's insistence on high play at country house parties was widely resisted. Lord Derby heard stories that the prince "tries to induce young men to play, and is angry when they will not. . . . It is added, which if true is worst of all, that he resents refusals to play when, as often happens, they tell him they cannot afford it."[24] Being pressured to play validated cheating; it was a legitimate way of defying the spoiled and bullying prince. Anita Leslie once asked an old courtier whether Gordon-Cumming had, in fact, cheated. "Of course he cheated," was the reply. "We all did. It was such a nuisance being made to play and lose money . . . and the young men longed to be dancing instead. But Cumming cheated *too much* and he had a lot of enemies."[25] And the witnesses, Stanley Wilson and Berkeley Levett, were too young and naïve to realize what was going on.

Gordon-Cumming was a long-standing member of the Marlborough House set. The owner of thirty-eight thousand barren Scottish acres, he could trace his pedigree back to Charlemagne. The Wilson and Lycett Green families were second-generation nouveaux riches. If cheating was widespread and usually overlooked, why did Bertie side with the Wilsons' new money and throw his friend Gordon-Cumming to the Yorkshire wolves? A legend persists that Gordon-Cumming was a scapegoat for Bertie, who had himself cheated. But no one suggested this at the time, and there's nothing to support it.[26] It's possible that Bertie wanted to make an example of Gordon-Cumming, who had insolently won £225 off him in two nights.* Or perhaps he wanted revenge. Two days before the Tranby Croft party, Bertie had walked into Gordon-Cumming's London house, so the story went, and discovered Daisy Brooke in his arms.[27] Whether or not he was guilty of cheating, Gordon-Cumming had humiliated Bertie and had to be dropped into outer darkness. The trouble was, he refused to go quietly.

Bertie made haste to leave Tranby Croft. The death of Mrs. Wilson's brother gave him a welcome excuse to depart, and he stayed after the races in York at Eddy's quarters in the Cavalry Barracks (10th Hussars).[28] On 12 September 1890, his diary records: "Return to York 5. Take tea with Lord and Lady Brooke at Station Hotel, then return to Barracks."[29] The teatime conversation with Lady Brooke, who was traveling north to her stepfather's funeral, was not recorded, but it seems unlikely that Bertie said nothing about the events of the past week. He was conscious, however, of his gentleman's promise to keep the secret, and he sealed Gordon-Cumming's signed paper, together with an account of the events by Owen Williams, and placed both documents in a packet that he sent to Knollys for safekeeping.[30] On the same day he received a pathetic appeal from Gordon-Cumming, imploring him not to cut him; "the forfeiture of your esteem," said Gordon-Cumming, is "the cruellest blow of all."[31] This remained unanswered.

Early in January 1891, Bertie heard that the Tranby Croft secret was out, and Gordon-Cumming was preparing to bring an action for slander against the Wilson family. The American press had published Dai-

---

* Gordon-Cumming had "cuckolded so many husbands; been witty at the expense of so many fools." (Gordon-Cumming's daughter Elma, in Havers, *Baccarat Scandal*, p. 270.) He had attempted to seduce the newly wedded Leonie Leslie, who pushed him away, prompting him to say, "Silly little fool, all the married women try me." Stories such as this did him no favors. (Leslie, *Edwardians in Love*, p. 143.)

sy's portrait beneath the headline "The Babbling Brook(e)," accusing her of having leaked the scandal and claiming that, but for her indiscretion, the cheating episode might have been kept secret. When Daisy wrote to the American editors pointing out that she had not been present at Tranby Croft that weekend, she was informed that the story had been sent by their London correspondent, "a lady moving in the best society."[32] Was this lady correspondent Daisy's sworn enemy Mina Beresford, seizing the chance to aim yet another blow at her rival? In a letter to *The Times* in 1911, Daisy tried to clear her name, alleging that mourning for her stepfather meant that she was the last to hear of the scandal at Tranby Croft; but this rings hollow, as she chose to overlook the teatime meeting on York station.

Determined to avoid a damaging court case that would drag the prince into the witness box, the courtiers now tried frantically to silence Gordon-Cumming. They demanded an inquiry by a secret military tribunal, which would effectively preempt a court case. Gordon-Cumming tried to dodge this by resigning from the army, but the courtiers obstructed him. Owen Williams and Coventry then appealed to the adjutant general, Sir Redvers Buller, to order a military inquiry. To the fury of Marlborough House, Buller first agreed and then changed his mind, having been persuaded that a military inquiry would prejudice a civil action.[33] Bertie's brother Arthur, Duke of Connaught, who was colonel in chief of Gordon-Cumming's regiment, refused either to intervene or to travel from Portsmouth to discuss the matter. "Being the Prince's brother it was more than ever incumbent on me not to allow myself to be used in a way that might cause the world to think that Cumming was to be sacrificed to the Prince," he explained. Putting "undue pressure" on the regiment with the aim of "smashing" Gordon-Cumming would only damage Bertie.[34] This enraged Bertie, but Connaught was right. Quashing the court case would have been unconstitutional. It implied that the army was a state within the state, immune from and above the law. If the courtiers at Marlborough House had got their way, Gordon-Cumming might have become England's Alfred Dreyfus—an officer wrongfully denied a civil trial whose case became a cause célèbre, raising deep issues about the position of the army, and the monarchy, too.

Bertie's attempt to block the court case was a public relations disaster. He was attacked in the press for plotting a royal cover-up, and Gordon-Cumming was portrayed as a martyr.[35] Bertie worried especially about what his mother would think. "I know that the Queen has been shown every newspaper that attacks me about this affair," he told Ponsonby.[36] No matter that Victoria scrawled over Ponsonby's note that she had seen none but the *Strand* and the *Pall Mall Gazette,* which ran a pro-Wales story written by the ubiquitous lawyer George Lewis. "Who tells the Prince of Wales these lies," she wrote. "Would to God he would listen as little to tales as I do."[37] Bertie dreaded Victoria's harsh words, and let it be known that he would refuse to go to Windsor if she intended to speak to him about gambling. The Queen's friend Monty Corry intervened, imploring the Queen to speak gently to the prince ("He is sensitive and hard words will do harm") and assuring Ponsonby that baccarat was a thing of the past.[38] Bertie now took up whist. Victoria was well aware that Bertie was "in a dreadful state," for "he has been dreadfully attacked."[39] Once she had given him her views about gambling, Knollys and Ponsonby agreed that "there was no use in the subject being pursued any further," as it "would only irritate him and it might even cause a temporary breach."[40]

"The whole thing has caused me the most serious annoyance & vexation," wrote Bertie.[41] He canceled his spring trip to the South of France. The veins in his leg flared up; the doctors diagnosed "gouty muscular rheumatism" and once again forbade exercise.[42] He put on weight. When equerry Arthur Somerset saw the forty-nine-year-old prince coming out of the Marlborough Club, he noticed that one side of his beard had gone gray.[43]

The management of the case for the defense was entrusted to George Lewis. Wearing a monocle and a fur coat even on hot days, Lewis was the inevitable society lawyer, a man of Mephistophelean cunning who knew all London's secrets and excelled at keeping disputes out of the courts. "Whatever is going on, not merely before but behind the footlights, is an open scroll to this astute, terrible, and within certain limits, very nearly omnipotent gentleman."[44] He had advised Bertie over the Mordaunt case in 1870, but it was his "lickerish servility" over the Beresford scandal, when he betrayed his clients, defied professional protocol, and showed Daisy Brooke's infamous letter to Bertie, that earned him an invitation to Sandringham.[45] Partly perhaps because he was Jewish and self-made, Lewis was resented by some members of Bertie's court, and his handling of the Tranby Croft case was much criticized. Carrington thought he was out of his depth. "His sphere lay in the police courts and he was known in the legal profession for being dishonest and a blackmailer." Lewis was so ambitious, claimed Carrington, that he refused to settle out of court with Gordon-Cumming: "He cannot resist the splendid advertisement of this miserable baccarat business."[46]

The trial began at eleven a.m. on 1 June 1891. By ten thirty, the court was packed. The event was more like a society wedding than a trial. Women in smart summer dresses and fashionable bonnets peered through their opera glasses as Bertie entered the courtroom and positioned himself in a red morocco chair placed at the front of the court, on the left of the judge's seat. Sitting where he was, and being who he was, he could hardly fail to influence proceedings.

Wearing a black frock coat, arms folded and smiling broadly, the prince listened to the opening speech on behalf of the plaintiff, Gordon-Cumming, by Sir Edward Clarke, solicitor general in the Salisbury government. After a mild and cautious beginning, Clarke, who was feeling his way, examined Gordon-Cumming. His lengthy questions were intended to show that Gordon-Cumming was innocent: He was a man of honor who had been sacrificed to save the courtiers. That evening, Ponsonby found Bertie "rather tired" from six hours in court, but relieved, "saying the case was going strongly against Cumming." Clarke, Bertie told Ponsonby, "did not speak with any assurance as if he believed in his client's innocence," and Cumming's evidence was "extraordinarily weak."[47]

Tuesday, 2 June, was the day appointed for Bertie to give evidence. He betrayed no obvious nerves beforehand, though one of the journalists timed him stroking his beard for seven minutes, and another thought he looked "anxious and worn."[48] Francis Knollys sat directly behind him. In the witness box, Bertie was dignified and noncommittal. Clarke dealt courteously with him, and his answers were brief and given in a hoarse voice with great rapidity. When the lawyers had finished, a man from the jury stood up and asked the two questions the lawyers had not dared to ask but everyone thirsted to know. As banker, had the prince seen any cheating on the part of Gordon-Cumming? No, replied Bertie, and explained that it was not usual for the banker to look for cheating among friends. To the second question, whether at the time he believed the charges against Gordon-Cumming, he replied that he had had no choice but to believe them.[49]

Sir Charles Russell, the barrister appointed by Lewis, needed to show that Gordon-Cumming was guilty of cheating and that he had thereby wickedly abused the Wilsons' hospitality. This was not easy, as the Wilsons' evidence was neither consistent nor convincing. Lycett Green was "deplorable in every way; voice, manner and matter."[50] Under cross-examination he broke down and could remember barely anything, admitting that he had never heard of the system of *masse en avant* that Gordon-Cumming had used—a critical point in Gordon-Cumming's favor. Knollys thought that Lycett Green "completely lost his head" out of nerves.[51] Refusing to remember may, however, have been a deliberate ploy on the advice of George Lewis, who considered that Lycett Green's role at Tranby Croft had been "so unsympathetic that the less he remembered the better."[52] His incoherence was redeemed by his wife, Ethel, an assured witness who looked pretty in black, and on 4 June, Knollys reported to Ponsonby that Lewis had told him that "the general opinion in Court was that Cumming had not a chance."[53]

The sensation came with Sir Edward Clarke's speech on Monday, 8 June. With the Prince of Wales sitting in court before him, Clarke demolished the Wilsons' case against Gordon-Cumming. "Nobody except Stanley Wilson saw any foul play except a person who was expecting to see it."[54] If Gordon-Cumming had intended to cheat he would never have placed his counters on white paper. As Bertie shifted uneasily in his seat, Clarke declared that Lord Coventry and Owen Williams had acted as false friends toward Gordon-Cumming, whom they had thrown over in order to shield the prince. "There is a strong and subtle influence of royalty," urged Clarke, "a personal influence—which has adorned our history with chivalrous deeds; and has perplexed the historian with unknightly and dishonouring deeds done by men of character, and done by them . . . to save the interests of a dynasty or to conceal the foibles of a prince. This is what was in the minds of Lord Coventry and General Owen Williams."[55]

"HRH is very greatly annoyed," wrote Knollys that evening. Clarke's swipes were gratuitous: "without any apparent object [he] brought in the Prince's name as often and as offensively as possible."[56] Bertie resented Clarke's "spiteful" attack: Clarke, however, was reported to be "quite unconscious" of having been severe or causing offense.[57]

Bertie was not in court on 9 June to hear the four-hour summing-up by Lord Coleridge, the Lord Chief Justice, virtually ordering the jury to decide against Gordon-Cumming. The jury retired for only thirteen minutes before returning with a unanimous verdict for the defendants. In court this was greeted with booing and hissing, and the Wilson family were mobbed as they left. Bertie, who was at Ascot, was hooted by the crowd. On the last day, his horse, The Imp, won a race and he received a tremendous ovation, which, he wrote, was "most gratifying especially after the way the Papers have abused and vilified me after the Cumming trial."[58] The toffs remained silent, however, as "dumb as fishes," prompting Carrington, himself a Liberal, to reflect that "the people and the Liberals are far more loyal supporters of the Crown than 'Society' and the Tories—when Royalty is in real difficulty."[59]

Clarke's speech left a bitter taste. Queen Victoria thought it a "fearful humiliation" to see the future king dragged "through the dirt just like anyone else, in a Court of Justice."[60]

But that was the point, really. The monarchy was not above the law. Public opinion considered the verdict unfair, and Gordon-Cumming became a hero. The day after the verdict he was dismissed from the army and married a twenty-two-year-old American heiress, Florence Garner, usually known as Flip. He was received on his return to his native Forres with an address from the provost and "great rejoicings."

"Such is <u>Scotch</u> morality and piety!" commented Bertie.[61]

Bertie, meanwhile, plumbed new depths of unpopularity. Bishops deplored his gambling from the pulpit, the postbag at Marlborough House bulged with angry resolutions from Nonconformist churches denouncing his wickedness, and the press poured a torrent of moralizing upon his head.[62] As *The New York Herald*'s L. J. Jennings wrote to Knollys, "anybody would think that he had broken all the ten commandments at once, and murdered the Archbishop of Canterbury."[63] The republican *Reynolds's Newspaper* gloated that royalty was revealed as rotten to the core: Bertie had brought the monarchy to the verge of destruction.[64] Queen Victoria worried about the damage, but, as Vicky pointed out, much though she abhorred gambling, the press campaign was hypocritical and exaggerated.[65] In the *Pall Mall Gazette*, George Lewis tried to stop the stampede by deploring the double standards that led the press to vilify the nonpolitical Prince of Wales for committing a minor sin while turning a blind eye to adultery by politicians.[66] Though gambling was abhorred by Nonconformists and sections of the middle and upper classes, its growing popularity among the working classes meant that Tranby Croft probably did little serious damage to Bertie's standing.[67]

The lesson of Tranby Croft, however, was, as *The Times* pointed out, that the prince was not entitled to a private life. No matter how hard he worked at his public duties, the people still had a right to know what he did in private and a right to deplore his gambling, because he was "the visible embodiment of the Monarchical principle."[68] The court case, which was reported at length in the newspapers, offered a vivid, intimate snapshot of Bertie's social life, zooming in on such details as the gambling counters he brought with him in his luggage, and marked a landmark in the development of a democratic monarchy open to public scrutiny.

Bertie resented his inability to answer his critics, and refused to bow to the pressure.[69] The Nonconformist churchmen went unanswered. Victoria urged him to write an open letter to the Archbishop of Canterbury, but he resisted, declining to write anything hypocritical.[70] In this affair at least, Bertie knew that he had acted "perfectly straightforwardly and honourably."[71] Honor was the key to the whole thing, and for Bertie and his court it counted for far more than middle-class morality. Gordon-Cumming was a "d——d blackguard."[72] He "has no sense of wrong or right."[73] By going to the law, he had broken the code of honor and "done his utmost to mix my name up in the matter in endeavouring to cloak his iniquities."[74] Alix, who was always seen as the ultimate arbiter in matters of chivalry, agreed. Gordon-Cumming, she told Georgie, was a "brute" and a "vile snob" who had "behaved too abominably to them all."[75]

The punishment was social disgrace. Gordon-Cumming and his wife went to live in lonely exile on their barren Scottish estates. The neighbors never called, no invitations ever came. His friends refused to speak to him. But at least he had Flip's $80,000 a year, and he used her money to renovate his castle at Gordonstoun.

Bertie had at last concluded that Eddy's army career was "simply a waste of time."[76] Eddy was worryingly lacking in energy and self-esteem. Carrington watched him visit Wycombe and make a speech: "When he sat down he turned round and said to me, 'I have made a rare ass of myself.' It is pathetic to see how little confidence he has in himself."[77] Bertie suggested three alternatives.[78] Plan number one was to send Eddy on a long sea voyage to the colonies, out of reach of temptation. Queen Victoria put her foot down. Eddy, she said, had been "dosed" with the Colonies. She urged Bertie's option two: a European tour.

He has been . . . nowhere but to <u>Denmark</u> in <u>Europe</u>. He is only
able to speak French badly and German equally so. He has <u>never</u>,
like <u>every</u> <u>other</u> Prince . . . been in contact with any other court
but Berlin or seen fine works of Art . . . [He ought] not merely
go to young colonies, with no history, no art and nothing but
middle class English speaking people . . . If the Prince of Wales
is afraid of his making a *mesalliance* which the Queen is not
afraid of, Australia, Canada etc. would be worse in its dangers in
this respect.[79]

Bertie, however, was concerned not with Eddy's education, or lack
of it, but with his dissipated behavior, a subject he dared not mention
to his mother, as Knollys explained in a note to Salisbury: "Unfortunately [the Queen's] views on certain social subjects are so strong that
the Prince of Wales does not like to tell her the real reasons for sending
Prince Eddy away, which is intended as a punishment and as a means
of keeping him out of harm's way, and I am afraid that neither of these
objects will be attained by his simply travelling about Europe."[80]

Bertie's third option was a surprise: to marry Eddy off to Princess
May of Teck. Princess May was the daughter of Queen Victoria's first
cousin Mary, the Duchess of Teck, known to many as Fat Mary. The
Duke of Teck was the son of Duke Alexander of Württemberg, who
made a morganatic marriage to a Hungarian countess. The blight of
"commoner's" blood meant that, instead of succeeding to the throne
of Württemberg, the Duke of Teck was reduced to "vegetating incon-
spicuously in England, pruning roses."[81] Incapable of living within
their means, the Tecks ran up large debts; they were pursued by their
creditors, and, after the humiliation of auctioning their possessions in
1883, spent two years in exile in Florence.[82]

Princess May's nonroyal blood ruled out marriage to a German
prince, and even the Wales princesses looked down on "poor May!
with her Württemberg hands!"[83] Yet, her father's lack of funds dis-
qualified her from marrying an English duke. Her marriage prospects
seemed dim: "She was too Royal to marry an ordinary English gentle-

man, and not Royal enough to marry Royalty."[84] Better educated than
the Wales children, Princess May was a studious girl with a phenomenal memory for objects and faces and a passion for lists. Had she not
been a princess, she would have made an excellent museum curator.[85]
In Alix's eyes, she had the great advantage of not being German. May's
mother, Alix's friend and cousin the Duchess of Teck, gushing, good-
hearted, extravagant, and chronically unpunctual, drove Bertie crazy,
while Princess May, who was frightened of him, annoyed him. Only
the year before, she had been rejected as a possible wife for Eddy because the "vision of P[rince]ss May haunting Marlborough House
makes the Prince of Wales ill."[86]

Meanwhile, Alix, who was not at the time on good terms with Bertie,
departed for Fredensborg. Here, outwardly at least, the Glücksburg
family party was rumbustious as ever. Oliver Montagu arrived to find
himself "in a room with an Emperor, Empress, 3 Kings, 3 Queens and
Grand Dukes, Grand Duchesses, princes and princesses to the number
of 30 or 40!" Three hundred beds were occupied in the palace, but the
royal families saw nothing of their suites, and lived in each other's
rooms, "running in and out like rabbits." In the hall, Montagu found
the czar of all the Russias and persecutor of the Jews, Alexander III,
"running around after the children with a huge whip which he was
cracking, dogs barking and children howling." Alix seemed "perfectly
happy," or so thought her parfit knight Montagu; in truth, as news
reached her, brought perhaps by Montagu himself, of Bertie's indiscretions with Daisy Brooke, she felt angry and humiliated.[87]

Instead of coming home, Alix decamped to the Crimea, accompanying the czar and Minnie on their silver wedding anniversary trip.[88]
This sudden change of plan meant that she would not return until
after Bertie's fiftieth birthday party on 9 November 1891—the strongest signal of displeasure she could give.

In Alix's absence, arranging Eddy's marriage fell to Bertie. Eddy
could be dragooned and told "he must do it—that it is for the good of
the country etc etc," but Princess May's acceptance was by no means

certain.[89] With staggering tactlessness, Bertie commanded Daisy Brooke to invite May and her parents to a house party at Easton, and here the preliminaries were settled.[90] The Duchess of Teck was in seventh heaven; after a life spent on the fringes of royalty, always short of money, she was now transported to within spitting distance of "the greatest position there is."

It was while he was staying at Easton that news reached Bertie of a fire at Sandringham.[91] From the pine-clad slopes of Livadia, Alix cabled laconically to Victoria: "Arrived safely beautiful easy journey . . . lovely place. In despair at dreadful fire at Sandringham cannot conceive cause."[92]

By dint of keeping the gas blazing for a week, Sandringham dried out in time for Bertie's birthday, and he held his party almost as if nothing had happened.[93] Alix was conspicuous by her absence.

No sooner was the party over than disaster struck again. Georgie succumbed to a bilious chill, which turned out to be typhoid. Frightened of being stuck at Sandringham with a critically ill son, Bertie rushed him up to Marlborough House. Here, as the doctors posted twice-daily bulletins on the gates charting the alarming course of the fever, Bertie was confined with his son. He seldom left the house; he was the only family member allowed to visit the sickroom. He attended the doctors' consultations and wrote telegrams to the Queen and Alix.[94] "I deeply regret Alix's absence . . . at this moment," he told Vicky.[95]

Alix regretted it even more, and her anger with her husband melted as she hastened home from the Crimea: "terrible [sic] anxious about poor darling Georgie such a shock on top of fire. Travelling night and day to get home," she wired the Queen.[96] By the time she reached London on 22 November, Georgie was over the crisis.

Taking everyone by surprise—the engagement had been expected in the New Year—Eddy proposed to May while staying with the de Falbes at Luton Hoo.* "Of course I said yes," wrote May in her diary.[97] At last Eddy had done something right, and Bertie was overjoyed. May,

* Christian de Falbe, the Danish minister, acquired Luton Hoo, near Bedford, when he married the widow of the previous owner, Mrs. John Shaw Leigh. Bertie visited Luton Hoo in 1886; thereafter it became a regular fixture. Bertie described it as "one of the most comfortable houses I know of." (*The Times*, 30 November 1886; Lee, *Edward VII*, vol. 1, p. 573.)

he told Vicky (who was not thrilled by the news, as she still had hopes that Eddy would choose one of her own daughters), was "very well brought up with a good head on her shoulders."[98] Not everyone was taken in by Bertie's newly discovered enthusiasm for the charms of the Teck princess. "Considering he has known her intimately since birth, it has taken him some considerable time to find it out, nearly one quarter of a century!!!" wrote Lady Geraldine Somerset in her diary.[99] Alix was in no doubt that Eddy had found the right bride: "Thank God we all know and love darling May so many years that she will be one of us at once and the fact of her being English will make all the difference and carry the whole nation with them—particularly as dear May has always been one of the most popular members of the family."[100]

For Eddy's twenty-eighth birthday on 8 January 1892, a shooting party was arranged at Sandringham. There was talk of appointing him after his marriage as Viceroy of Ireland—the post that Bertie had rejected with contempt twenty years before—and Bertie, who supported the plan, arranged to discuss it with Salisbury in London the following Monday.[101] Meanwhile, out shooting on 6 January, Eddy felt ill and walked back after lunch to the house. Influenza was rampant that winter—*The Times* carried daily reports detailing the progress of the epidemic—and at Sandringham Francis Knollys was ill and so was one of the equerries. On the eighth, Eddy struggled downstairs to see his presents, but felt too ill to appear at his birthday dinner. Alix cabled Victoria: "Poor Eddy got influenza, cannot dine, so tiresome."[102] The next day, Saturday, Dr. Laking was summoned from London. Bertie cabled Victoria on Sunday: "Eddy's attack of influenza very sharp now developed some pneumonia in left lung, restless night, strength well maintained, Laking here, Broadbent coming today."[103]

On Monday the first announcement appeared in *The Times*. The medical bulletins were now posted not once but twice daily outside Marlborough House, and Bertie canceled his meeting with the prime minister in order to stay at Sandringham. At 9:30 a.m. on Wednesday, 13 January, a new bulletin was posted that startled the knot of onlookers: "Symptoms of great gravity have supervened, and the condition of his Royal Highness the Duke of Clarence is critical."[104] Bertie sent a heartfelt message to his mother: "Our darling Eddy is in God's hands, human skill seems unavailable, there could not be a question of your coming here."[105] Snow was falling at Sandringham as the reporters watching the house spotted Bertie emerge and pace briefly up and down. Shortly after, Georgie and May appeared. Some said later that they were holding hands.[106]

Inside the house, in his small, high-ceilinged bedroom, Eddy lay delirious with fever on his brass bed. As he raved wildly, crying out "Hélène! Hélène!"* his fingernails turned blue and his lips were livid. At eight that morning, Alix, who had spent the night at Eddy's bedside, had woken Bertie to tell him that she thought their son was dying. All day Alix sat beside the bed as the three doctors and a nurse squeezed noiselessly past her in the narrow room. Bertie paced back and forth from the cramped sitting room next door, where the family waited in shocked horror. At midnight Alix was reluctantly persuaded to take some sleep on a sofa. At two a.m., the doctors woke her. The death agony had begun. For seven hours Eddy lay, a terrible rattle in his throat, with his mother holding his hand. Suddenly he said, quite clearly, "Something too awful has happened—my darling brother George is dead." And then: "Who is that? Who is that?" He died at nine a.m. on 14 January.[107]

"Our darling Eddy has been taken from us, We are broken hearted," Bertie wired Victoria.[108] Shortly afterward he put pen to paper: "What we went through for 8 hours watching poor dear Eddy from 2 to 10 this morning I shall <u>never</u> forget," he wrote to his mother. "Dear Eddy looks so peaceful lying on his bed with his hands crossed . . . and covered with flowers. . . . I cannot write more, as I am too upset and my nerves completely unstrung."[109] George echoed his despair: "I shall never forget that awful moment with us all sobbing round his bed where we had been watching for nearly six hours without being able to help him as long as I live."[110]

---

* In his delirium he called for Hélène d'Orléans, and not his fiancée, May of Teck.

The funeral was at Windsor, and Bertie begged his seventy-two-year-old mother, who was at Osborne, not to attend, because of the cold weather and the risk of illness.[111] Victoria, who had wished to be present, replied: "I have rec[eive]d your letter which has distressed me very much. You have stopped my going. . . . I feel quite ill at not going. Everybody expects me to go."[112]

Bertie hastened to heal the breach, protesting that he had stopped her coming not because he didn't want her, but to protect her health: "Your telegram has deeply pained us as you have misunderstood the motive which urges us to beg you not to undertake a journey for so painful a ceremony on account of incurring considerable risk while this illness is flying about."[113] As a sop to the Queen, he agreed to her request that his sisters Princesses Beatrice and Helena should attend the service at Windsor. Victoria's reply was hurt: "I am _very_ sorry that my telegram pained you, as my only wish is to save you all the pain I can."[114]

Alix wrote consolingly to Victoria: "Your dear words did my poor bleeding and crushed heart good. I feel I cannot stay away. My darling Eddy would have wished me to take him to his last resting place, so I shall hide upon the staircase in a corner, unknown to the world."[115]

Eddy's body was taken from the church at Sandringham to Windsor. Alix and her daughters watched the funeral from Catherine of Aragon's closet, looking down on the coffin as it lay in the choir. It was a damp, raw day, and Bertie "broke down terribly" and wept throughout the service.*[116]

Telegrams of condolence poured in, averaging a thousand a day. It was the saddest moment of Bertie's life.

---

* After the service, Princess Beatrice sent a message via Ponsonby, complaining that she had been locked into her pew. Arthur Ellis replied: "The Prince of Wales desires me to say that—the harem of Princesses was *not* locked into the . . . pew closet but the door got jambed [sic], and adds that none of them were wanted at all. No ladies were to attend, and the Princess of Wales especially requested privacy—and to avoid meeting her Osborne relations. So they all came. If Princess Beatrice was annoyed it cannot be helped and she must get over it—as she likes." (Arthur Ellis to Henry Ponsonby, 22 January 1892, in Arthur Ponsonby, _Henry Ponsonby_, p. 359.)

CHAPTER 19

Daisy Warwick*

1892–96

Alix was crushed by Eddy's death. At Sandringham she preserved his room as a shrine and visited it daily, strewing fresh flowers on the bed. His uniforms and clothes were kept in a glass cabinet, and his soap and hairbrushes were laid out exactly as they had been on the day he died.[1] Never again did Alix stay at Abergeldie. "Last time we were there," she wrote in 1902, "was with darling Eddy—& since then I c[ou]ld not bear to stay there again!"[2] Mourning brought her closer to Queen Victoria, who understood grief all too well. She leaned also on Oliver Montagu, whom she found "such a comfort and help"; despite his bluff manner, Montagu could relate to her religious feelings. "We often talked over

---

* Daisy was known by her husband's courtesy title as Lady Brooke until he succeeded his father as Earl of Warwick in 1893, when she became Countess of Warwick. To avoid confusion, I have called her Daisy Warwick throughout this chapter.

sacred things together," Alix wrote; something one can hardly imagine Bertie doing with his wife.[3]

Mourning emasculated Bertie. The Duchess of Mecklenburg-Strelitz* thought him "very fat and puffed, not knowing well what to do with himself now, during the mourning, it gave me a painful impression."[4] Forbidden social life, theaters, and races, he was condemned to accompany Alix as she wandered restlessly in search of peace, looking "lovelier than ever" in her long black veil.[5] Escaping Sandringham, with its sad memories, Alix brought Bertie to stay at Compton Place, the Duke of Devonshire's house in Eastbourne, for the day Eddy was to have married in February. "Hope beautiful fresh air may do us all good though our hearts remain sad wherever we are," she wired the Queen.[6] In the spring, the family fled to Cap Martin on the Riviera. For Bertie, incarcerated with a tearful, insomniac wife, the enforced domesticity and inactivity of a year's mourning was almost unendurable.

The newspapers were filled with respectful eulogies for the dead Eddy—all except *Reynolds's,* which declared that his mental faculties were "extremely limited" and he made "the poorest possible appearance" in public.[7] Eddy was no fool, but he seemed strangely vulnerable to scandal and lacking in common sense—a quality his brother, George, possessed in abundance. Bertie, however, was changed. There is no evidence that he considered Eddy's death a blessing. He was genuinely saddened.

Bertie's relations with the Queen reverted to their former coolness. He complained that "he is not of the slightest use to the Queen; that everything he says or suggests is poohed poohed [*sic*]."[8] Victoria had been quick to sympathize over Eddy's death, but she found Bertie's gambling and adultery hard to forgive. The Tranby Croft scandal was bad enough. Far worse was his affair with Daisy Warwick, which she knew all about thanks to a spiteful letter from Mina Beresford. In the

---

* Augusta, Grand Duchess of Mecklenburg-Strelitz, was the sister of George, Duke of Cambridge, and great-aunt of Princess May of Teck.

new era of moral politics and intrusive newspapers, Bertie's infidelity was a liability.

Salisbury's government fell in August 1892, and when Gladstone took office once again, he told the Queen that the Cabinet had agreed to communicate its proceedings to the Prince of Wales, "as has been in action for several years past." Victoria was horrified.[9] She consulted Salisbury, who confirmed that he had never sent a report of Cabinet proceedings to the prince.[10] Victoria scrawled triumphantly in purple pencil to Ponsonby: "The Queen is quite sure what Lord Salisbury says is the fact, for she is certain nothing of the kind was ever done or ought to be done."[11] Algernon West, Gladstone's private secretary, hastened to reassure her that the intention was merely to let the prince know "generally what was going on," and not to send him a copy of the prime minister's letter to the Queen, which was at that time the only formal record of Cabinet proceedings.[12] Gladstone was always more willing than Lord Salisbury to keep the Prince of Wales informed, which was one of the reasons why Bertie liked and respected him. Salisbury's attitude was strictly correct, but "there was a quality in it that was humiliating to him."[13]

Lord Rosebery, the foreign secretary in the Gladstone government, agreed to send Bertie the information he really wanted: confidential foreign dispatches. The most secret documents were enclosed in red leather boxes locked with a special key. Only the sovereign, the prime minister, and the head of the Foreign Office possessed copies of this key. Rosebery discovered in the Foreign Office the gold key that had once belonged to Prince Albert, and forwarded it to Bertie.[14] Unfortunately, it seemed not to work. Knollys thought Bertie had been tricked and given a key that "would open nothing," but the fact was, "that particular Cabinet key has to be pushed in a certain distance and then given a turn before it can go right home."[15] Even when he got his gold key to work, Bertie complained that the red boxes often contained little of interest. "The game is not to let me see any interesting or important Despatches! This has been going on for years under successive governments and it would be far better if FO sent me no more, which is preferable to the rubbish they send!"[16]

The years after Eddy's death were a strangely meaningless interlude. Not that Bertie was idle. In March 1893, when the year of mourning was at last over, he told George, "I don't think I have been more busy in my life."[17] In December 1892, he was appointed to the Royal Commission on the Aged Poor, and he conscientiously attended twice-weekly meetings from twelve to four p.m. during the parliamentary session. He was present for thirty-five out of the forty-eight meetings. His diary is crowded with a thicket of names, and each day bristles with appointments—public dinners, charitable events, theatergoing, entertaining royalty.

Bertie's diary, seemingly the most impenetrable and impersonal of documents, contains a code. Cracking the code gives the key to his preoccupations—the double life and the secret narrative that made his constant performance bearable. At intervals in the diary Bertie inscribed small symbols or initials in the left-hand margin. He frequently wrote the letters "VR," "G," or "Vy." Checking the dates when these initials occur against his correspondence confirms that "G," "VR" and "Vy" denote days when he wrote to George, the Queen, or Vicky. The diary for 1891 and 1892 is missing, but in the volume for 1893 the pages are scattered with a small symbol that resembles a capital D in reverse. This is inscribed not in the margin but at the top of the box headed "morning" or "evening."

The D in Bertie's life was Daisy Warwick. Anecdotal accounts stress the intensity of the affair during the early 1890s. Puzzlingly, however, the name of Lady Warwick occurs less and less frequently in his diary from 1893. He made a habit of staying with Lord and Lady Warwick in October each year at Easton Lodge, and sometimes in March as well. But her name seems to have dropped out of the Marlborough House parties held by Ferdinand Rothschild or Baron Hirsch. There is tantalizingly little evidence, as the letters that do survive from Bertie to Daisy date mainly from 1898 or later, when the affair was burned out. Daisy's letters were presumably destroyed after Bertie's death.

Poring over the foolscap volumes of Bertie's diary, sitting high up in the Round Tower at Windsor, I suddenly realized that the secret was staring me in the face. Whenever Bertie stayed with the Brookes at Easton Lodge, he invariably inscribed D twice, both in the morning and the evening. He surely would not write to Daisy twice a day when he was sleeping under her roof. Unlike the other symbols, which note when Bertie wrote a letter, the D records a meeting, carefully positioned in his diary to show the time it took place. In 1893, "D" is written on an astonishing sixty-nine days, sometimes twice or even three times a day. A year or so later, Daisy complained that "the worst of London is that [the prince] claims so much of my time during the rare visits I pay there now, and I see him so seldom that I feel generally obliged to fall in with his leisure time."[18]

Daisy had been the center of his life; more than his mistress, she had become "my little Daisywife." Whenever they were both in London, he took tea with her at her house at 50 South Audley Street, or they met for late-night suppers in a house placed at his disposal by a member of his household.[19] What took place at these assignations can only be surmised; the important thing was that no one else was present, not even servants. Daisy tells a story of one of these meetings. She arrived in a cab at the appointed house after the opera. Bertie had been given a latch key, and there were no servants in the house, just a supper waiting of lobster and champagne to be eaten in perfect privacy. On reaching the house, "what was my alarm to find my admirer on his knees on the pavement groping for a lost latch key." She hurriedly dismissed her cab and helped the search. But to no avail. "There was nothing left for us to do but—supperless—to go arm-in-arm for a midnight stroll in the empty, echoing streets before seeking our respective, lawful dwelling-places."[20] More than any of his earlier mistresses, Bertie was emotionally involved with Daisy Warwick. She was Anne Boleyn to his Henry VIII: She was the commoner with whom the middle-aged prince fell in love. By contrast with Tudor England, however, a royal divorce was never considered or even discussed. Bertie remained loyal—in his own way—to Alix. "She is my brood mare," he used to say. "The others are my hacks."[21]

Bertie had to meet Daisy in secret partly because she was a scandal-ous woman. Mina Beresford's campaign to drum her out of society meant that she could not be paraded as the favorite. As Bertie wrote to her in 1899: "You were persecuted by my family—society—and the press—to an extent that was never known before—and, alas! with my family, matters will I am afraid <u>never</u> come straight. . . . Society is al-ways jealous of a pretty woman if I have the misfortune to think her so—then there are certain women I don't like—and do not disguise my feelings towards them—who are sure to attack her and me."[22]

Undaunted, Daisy retreated to her Essex estates, where she enter-tained with louche luxury. "The most coveted invitations in England were those to house parties at Easton Lodge marked: 'To meet the Prince of Wales.' "[23] Her friend the novelist Elinor Glyn fondly recalled arriving on a winter's evening; the women dressed in velvet sable-trimmed tea gowns, the tea table laden with scones and cream, the footmen all the same height at six feet, the luxurious bedrooms with hot baths and writing tables equipped with pens from Asprey and bou-quets of flowers for wearing at dinner. Instead of the usual country-house sport of shooting, which Daisy disliked, weekends at Easton revolved around a game of adultery: a carefully choreographed flirta-tion that took place between the married women and their admirers—little notes would appear on a lady's breakfast tray from her admirer, and there were lovers' walks to the Stone House, an Elizabethan folly in the grounds, all orchestrated with velvety charm by Daisy. Most of the men fell hopelessly in love with her; she possessed what Elinor Glyn, coining a phrase, described as "It," the supreme personal charm which is "quite indefinable" and "does not depend upon beauty or wit, although she possessed both in the highest degree."[24]

But there was another side to Daisy's character, a social conscience and searching for purpose that sat uneasily with the royal mistress. Looking back on her life, she reflected that though at the beginning she worshipped the same gods as others of her class, she was changed when she met the journalist W. T. Stead in 1892. With his rough north-ern voice, his strong beard and mesmeric eyes, Stead became her Sven-gali. Daisy now entered what she called her "middle-class period"—her

"Board of Guardians, philanthropic, educational, lady-gardening period."[25] Stead had won fame as editor of the *Pall Mall Gazette*, forcing the government to raise the age of consent in 1885 through the "Maiden Tribute of Modern Babylon" revelations, and as editor of the *Review of Reviews* from 1890 he was the scourge of adulterers such as Charles Dilke and Charles Parnell. But he did not denounce the adulteress Daisy. On the contrary, he became her confidant and adviser.

Daisy was already tiring of Bertie. Not that she disliked him. As she later told the journalist Frank Harris: "He was very considerate, and from a woman's point of view that's a great deal. . . . I grew to like him very much; I think anybody would have been won by him."[26] But she confessed that when guests at Easton house parties left her alone with the prince, she found it "boresome as he sat on a sofa holding my hand and goggling at me."[27] In London, she became resentful of his constant demands, which monopolized her time. When they were apart, he wrote letters twice or thrice a week, which she must answer "or he used to say I had hurt him."[28]

Stead suggested that Daisy should use her influence to educate and improve the prince. In August 1893, he advised her that she must be "the priest of the parish" and Bertie the "parishioner."[29] A triangular relationship developed, Daisy regularly reporting on her relations with the "parishioner" to Stead.

Influencing the prince gave Daisy a kind of power. "Being a woman and thus cut off from public life which is open to men—worse luck—one's power is only in personal influence," she wrote.[30] This sort of power had always been the prerogative of the royal mistress. With the language of parishioner/priest, Daisy and Stead gave it a moral spin. Not only would the priest redeem the parishioner, and thus legitimize her adultery, but also, as priest, she was the dominant partner within the relationship. Supremely self-confident, Daisy could see that the prince was no different from other men. Because he read so little, he learned not from books but, "like a woman," from meeting people.* It

---

* What she meant was that women, lacking formal education, had to learn from their own observation.

now became Daisy's mission to show the prince "things as they really were," to teach him about the lives of the poor. She was well aware that her ability to do this depended upon his "extraordinary appreciation of physical beauty"—that is, her own beauty.[31] When Bertie stayed at Easton for Easter 1893, the visits to the Stone House and thoroughbred studs were interspersed with tea with the vicar and a tour of the workhouse. After the prince's visit in October, Daisy reported to Stead: "My 'parishioner' was very glad to spend these few quiet days at Easton, but I think he is rather jealous of your influence on my life and thoughts."[32]

Daisy's philanthropic activities are often dismissed as disorganized and impulsive, but she was right to urge Bertie to do good works. Thanks to Daisy Warwick, "the great womanizer was womanized."[33] Alix later told Lord Rosebery that at this time she "hated Lady Warwick."[34]

The death of Oliver Montagu was another blow to Alix. Eight years earlier Montagu had lost an eye, which had been injured in a shooting accident. Alix described the operation in gruesome detail: In order to stop the blood, sponges were stuck into the cavity where the eye had been; but OM's sufferings endeared him to her all the more. "I cannot really think of anything else," she wrote, "and he, poor one, had the loveliest eyes—I have never seen anyone as little vain as him."[35] Now, the forty-nine-year-old Montagu was mortally ill with cancer. He insisted on traveling to Cairo, and, after undergoing two operations, he died there in January 1893.[36] Alix was grief stricken. According to Skittles (who loved a good story), the princess went to bed and cried for three days. She confessed her feeling for Montagu to Bertie, but he "found nothing to object in it. He knew all about it." Skittles once received an anonymous letter complaining about Alix's relationship with Montagu; she showed it to Bertie, who remarked that he, too, received letters on the subject, usually from the wives of clergymen. When Skittles suggested that he ought to speak to the princess about it, Bertie "said he could not do that, as it would be an insult to her. He knew there was nothing in it."[37]

Alix depended upon Montagu emotionally and in religious matters, too. "I was so touched by your saying that you thought I have had some good influence on your dear nephew's spiritual life," she told his aunt Lady Sydney.[38] Montagu's body was embalmed and shipped back from Cairo in a sealed lead coffin. Bertie was chief mourner, but Alix did not attend the funeral at Hinchingbrooke. She and the young princesses visited the coffin the day before. "Please keep it strictly private as we settled," she told Lord Sandwich, Montagu's brother, "and might we quite quietly go in without anybody seeing us. I have sent a tiny cross to you begging you to be so kind as to <u>let it rest over him tonight!</u> and that I might take it away again with me tomorrow as a sad remembrance of my faithful friend."[39] Every year on the anniversary of Montagu's death she sent a wreath or a flower.

Alix was sentimental. This was the woman who had erected a tombstone in the pets' graveyard that still survives in the shrubbery at Marlborough House:

Bonny
Favourite Rabbit
Of HRH the
Princess of Wales
Died 8 June 1881

Bereft of Montagu, Alix was thrown on to the companionship of her woman of the bedchamber, the devoted Charlotte Knollys. As the princess's constant attendant and amanuensis, Charlotte gained an unhealthy influence over her mistress.[40] Isolated by her deafness, Motherdear clung, too, to her unmarried children, Victoria, Maud, and especially George. Her relations with "Georgie boy" had always been possessive, and she is often blamed for infantilizing her son, "holding him back in a mental playground where she could reign supreme."[41] She held all the tighter after Eddy's death. "Thank God dear Georgie the only one left is looking well I always feel that pang wherever [sic] I look at him now," she wired the Queen.[42]

Eddy's death meant that George's marriage had become a matter of urgency. As the heir presumptive, his life was all that stood between Bertie and the succession of his eldest daughter Louise, with the Duke of Fife as consort. The press clamored for Prince George to marry May of Teck, the tragic princess. So, too, to May's embarrassment, did her pushy parents. As Eddy lay dying, the stroke-disabled Duke of Teck had been heard to mutter, "It must be a tsarevich, it must be a tsarevich," referring to the marriage of Alix's sister Minnie to the czarevitch Alexander after the death of his older brother Nicholas, to whom she had been engaged.[43] (No one mentioned the less happy example of Henry VIII marrying his dead brother's widow, Catherine of Aragon.) Queen Victoria urged George to choose May, and was (Bertie told George) "in a terrible fuss about your marrying."[44] George himself had other ideas; he wished to marry his seventeen-year-old first cousin Marie, known as Missy, the daughter of the Duke of Edinburgh. Only after the headstrong Missy had turned him down in favor of the adopted heir of the King of Romania did George consider May of Teck.

The Duke of York, as George now became, had Eddy's allowance from Parliament, a house in St. James's Palace, and York Cottage at Sandringham. A life of ease was hard to resist. He spent two months improving his German at Heidelberg, and then marriage to May was all that remained to be done. Alix took him on a cruise to Athens to prepare; she told him that she was "worried to death" about his marrying. "Nothing and nobody can or shall ever come between me and my darling Georgie boy," she wrote.[45]

George returned home ahead of Alix, who remained abroad on purpose. He visited his sister Louise at Sheen Lodge; Princess May was invited over from nearby White Lodge, and the diffident prince was pushed by his sister into the garden, where he proposed to May and was accepted.*

"Melampus!" he wired to Bertie that evening. *Melampus* was the name of the ship he had taken in the summer, and the code word they

---

* More percipient than it could have known at the time, *Reynolds's* asked: "Is she in love with the Crown, irrespective of whose head wears it?" (Williams, *Contentious Crown,* p. 68.)

had agreed for an acceptance by May.[46] There was nothing spontaneous about this proposal, though it happened a day or two earlier than expected. Bertie was delighted. "What a relief it must be to your mind that all is now satisfactorily settled and you can easily understand that I have the same feelings," he told George.[47] Alix's emotions were more complicated. "You know what mixed feelings mine are," she wired Victoria from Malta.[48] To May she wrote a congratulatory letter that was affectionate but suffocating: "I hope that my sweet May will always come straight to me for everything," signing herself, "ever your most loving and devoted old Motherdear."[49]

The wedding took place in boiling heat on 6 July 1893 at the Chapel Royal. Between the wedding breakfast and a family dinner, Bertie somehow managed to squeeze in a clandestine meeting with Daisy Warwick—a D symbol is written in the diary.[50] George's first cousin Nicky, the czarevitch, stayed at Marlborough House and noted a shade reproachfully, "Uncle Bertie is in very good spirits and very friendly, almost too much so." Alix, lovelier than ever—and much more lovely than the bride—in ethereal white satin and diamonds, looked "rather sad" in church. "One can quite understand the reason why," wrote Nicky.[51]

The couple spent their honeymoon at York Cottage, Sandringham, where it poured with rain. After ten days, the entire Wales family joined them. York Cottage had formerly been the Bachelor's Cottage; it was unpretentious and cramped and only five minutes' walk away from Sandringham House. To the growing annoyance of her new daughter-in-law, Alix could never resist dropping in for tea or to rearrange the furniture.[52]

Many years later, King George V allegedly declared: "My father was frightened of his mother; I was frightened of my father, and I am damned well going to see to it that my children are frightened of me."[53] The remark was probably apocryphal; it was untrue, at least so far as Bertie's relationship with George is concerned. Of all the Hanoverian/Saxe-Coburg-Gotha monarchs, Bertie was the only one who never quarreled with his heir, an achievement for which he has not received the credit he deserves. Four days after the wedding, he wrote to Prince George: "I hope you will always look upon me as your elder brother and ask my advice always. . . . You are quite right in saying that we have not lost a son but you have brought us another daughter."[54] The relationship between father and son was, however, an unequal one. George's first cousin, who disliked Bertie, considered that "King Edward's affection for Prince George was due to the fact that the latter was prepared to be his complete slave."[55]

May never quite became another daughter to Bertie. The serious-minded princess disliked his "fast set" and disapproved of his habits of racing and gambling. George was not part of the Marlborough House set either. In many ways he seemed the antithesis of his fat, philander-ing father: devotedly uxorious, and thin, he disliked London society. Perhaps it was because George seemed his ideal alter ego that Bertie found him so congenial, unlike Eddy, who reminded him of his dissi-pated younger self.* Father and son had much in common, too: an obsession with punctuality, an addiction to smoking, a passion for uni-forms, and a devotion to the competitive slaughter of game birds. The happy result was that Prince George as Duke of York and heir pre-sumptive did much less in the way of public work than Bertie had done in his twenties, and his father never pushed him to undertake official

---

* Not that George was untouched by scandal. In May 1893, the *Star* printed a rumor that he had secretly married the daughter of a British naval officer at Malta. Ponsonby annotated the cutting: "The power of imagination among newspapers is extraordinary." (RA VIC/ Z476/28, 29 Cutting from the *Star*.) In the autumn of 1893, W. T. Stead wrote to Ponsonby informing him of an anonymous correspondent who alleged that George had two children by this marriage. (RA VIC/Add A12/2106a, Henry Ponsonby to Francis Knollys [1893].) Bertie was at first inclined to issue a contradiction. He consulted Gladstone, who advised taking no notice of the rumors, "which are equally scandalous and ridiculous." (RA VIC/ Add C07/1, Algernon West to Knollys, 26 October 1893.) So no denial was published, though the Queen thought this was a mistake, arguing as follows: "No one cares about it today. But in fifty years time when some young prince ascends the throne there will be a cry that he is illegitimate or his father committed bigamy. . . . Now—a simple denial will clear the clouds away." (RA VIC/Add C07/1, Ponsonby to Knollys, 27 October 1893.) This was prophetic. In 1911, E. F. Mylius printed a story that George V had married a daughter of Sir Michael Culme-Seymour in Malta and had two children. He was prosecuted for criminal libel and found guilty.

duties. "For seventeen years," as Harold Nicolson wrote, "he did nothing at all but kill animals and stick in stamps."[56]

Bertie's new toy was the royal yacht *Britannia*. Commissioned by him in 1892 and built on the Clyde, *Britannia* was both a state-of-the-art racing cutter and a luxury yacht. She won races in 1893, but 1894 was her most exciting season, as she battled race after race with her American rival *Vigilant*. The prince's coolness gained the admiration of his crew, who watched as *Britannia* heeled from side to side, maneuvering at the start of a race, while Bertie sat on deck reading the newspapers, his deck chair rolling violently. At length he stood up and held on to the rail of the ship, and both chair and papers fell overboard. Asked whether the chair should be retrieved, Bertie merely remarked, "Yes, pick up the papers," and a dinghy was dispatched to recover the royal *Times*.[57]

When Bertie went to the South of France in the spring, he stayed on board *Britannia*, cruising from one regatta to another. On 3 March 1894, the day that *Britannia* arrived at Marseille, Bertie noted, "Mr. Gladstone resigns premiership is succeeded by Lord Rosebery."[58] Victoria was delighted; half blind and deaf, the eighty-five-year-old Gladstone noted her "cheerfulness" when he tendered his resignation at Windsor, and he was hurt that she expressed no regret but made small talk, allegedly remarking: "I hear your daughter has been bitten by a mad cat. Is that true?"[59] To the prince, however, Gladstone wrote a sad little farewell letter ("the devotion of an old man is [of] little worth") conveying his "fervent thanks" for his "unbounded kindness" and that of the "beloved Princess."[60] Bertie reciprocated the old man's affection, and acted as a pallbearer at his funeral three years later.

Rosebery, Gladstone's successor, was welcomed by both Bertie and Victoria. The Queen liked the forty-six-year-old aristocrat personally and thought she could control him politically (she couldn't), and Rosebery was a good friend of Bertie's.

A letter writer with the lightest of touches, unstuffy, civilized, and sympathetic, the widower Rosebery was sufficiently close to the Wale-ses to write beguilingly to Alexandra imploring her to put aside her grief for Eddy and appear in public. ("I am half inclined to tear this letter up, but I leave that to Your Royal Highness.")[61] Bertie stayed with Rosebery at Dalmeny, where he grumbled about the all-male party, but he enjoyed slipping down to the Durdans, Rosebery's Epsom re-treat ("Rosebery was in great form and chaffed R. Churchill unmerci-fully").[62]

Perhaps Bertie knew too much about Rosebery. In August 1893, at Homburg, he had helped to rescue him from the mad Marquess of Queensberry. The homophobic marquess, who was the father of Lord Alfred Douglas (Bosie), the lover of Oscar Wilde, was convinced that his eldest son, Lord Drumlanrig, private secretary to Rosebery, was having a homosexual affair with Rosebery. He arrived in Homburg de-termined to "out" "that boy pimp and boy lover Rosebery." He was met by the police and interviewed by the Prince of Wales, who told him, "We are quiet people at Homburg and don't like disturbance." The scandal took another turn in October 1894, when Drumlanrig was found dead during a shoot. The official verdict was accidental death, but dark rumors circulated of suicide and homosexual cover-up, and Rosebery lived in terror that the vicious marquess would denounce him.[63]

When Rosebery offered himself as a suitor for Princess Victoria, he was sharply rebuffed by Alix. Toria, as she was known, was intelligent—not as pretty as Maud, but very "light in hand" according to Car-rington.[64] Years later, as an old lady, Anita Leslie recalled Toria reflecting that "there had been someone perfect for her but they would not let her marry him—'And we could have been so happy.'" The man, Anita later discovered, was Rosebery.[65] At the time, the millionaire widower prime minister seemed far from ideal. Not only did his involvement in politics rule him out,[66] but he was nineteen years older than Toria, painfully insomniac, and dogged by damaging rumors of homosexual-ity. And the fact was that Alix did not want her daughters to marry.

The husbandless state of Princesses Victoria (twenty-five) and Maud (twenty-four), unkindly known as "the Hags," was beginning to excite comment. "I cannot understand their not being married," wrote Vicky, "they would be such charming wives."[67] When the Queen taxed Bertie about it, he told her that "Alix found them such companions that she would not encourage their marrying, and that they themselves had no inclination for it (in which I think he is mistaken as regards Maud). He said that he was 'powerless,' which I cannot understand."[68] The reason why Bertie was "powerless" was because of the rift between him and Alix over Daisy Warwick.

The Queen was right about Maud. Known as Harry, Maud was the most attractive of Bertie's daughters; as her collection of designer dresses reveals, she was a size zero with an eighteen-inch waist. She admired Princess May's brother, Prince Frank of Teck, but her feelings were not reciprocated. In the autumn of 1895, on a Danish family holiday at Bernstorff, she became engaged to her first cousin Prince Charles, the second son of Alix's brother the King of Denmark and an officer in the Danish navy. Alix had hoped that Maud might marry the older brother. The Duchess of Teck thought Charles charming, but remarked that he looked "*fully 3 years younger* than Maud and has *no money*"[69] Charlotte Knollys declared that it was a love match: "He has cared for her for three years and she certainly seems extremely fond of him."[70] Maud was "very much in love," but everyone doubted whether she would be prepared to live "in a cottage in Denmark with a lady in-waiting" while her sailor prince was away at sea.[71] They were right. After her marriage in July 1896, she never ceased to grumble about her Danish exile, and was only happy at Appleton, the house that Bertie gave her on the Sandringham estate (it had previously been the home of the bad-tempered Mrs. Cresswell). Though Maud was supposed to be his favorite daughter, Bertie seemed oddly indifferent.

"Receive very bad accounts of Emperor of Russia's health," wrote Bertie on 30 October 1894.[72] His forty-nine-year-old brother-in-law, Alexander III, was terminally ill with nephritis (kidney disease) and had gone to Livadia, his palace in the Crimea, to die. The next day, Bertie and Alix, accompanied by Arthur Ellis and Charlotte Knollys, left Charing Cross on a special train. At Vienna they heard that the czar was dead. "Poor Mama is terribly upset," Bertie told George. Bertie was moved, too; he was genuinely fond of his brother-in-law. This was his fourth visit to Russia, and he found it "the most trying and sad journey I have ever undertaken, and 3 days and 3 nights in the train with a sea voyage to follow is a great undertaking."[73]

An hour after his arrival at the white-stuccoed imperial palace in the Crimea, Bertie found himself attending mass in the black-draped chapel, where the putrefying body of Alexander III lay in an open coffin. Twice daily he knelt with the royal families and their suites, wearing full uniform and holding a lighted taper while singers chanted mournful dirges in a language he could not understand.[74]

Alix never left her sister's side. Livadia was a palace-village of small houses, and Alix stayed in the imperial house with Minnie and her family.[75] The two sisters even shared a room, and Minnie was in consequence "able to sleep better than she has done for a long time." Bertie was ensconced in another house "on my comfortable own."[76]

Bertie was charged by Prime Minister Rosebery to win the sympathy of the new czar, his nephew Nicky. At twenty-six, Nicky had a childlike simplicity that portended disaster in the autocrat of all the Russians. "I know nothing of the business of ruling," said he. "I have no idea of even how to talk to the ministers."[77]

Bertie threw himself into the funeral arrangements. He summoned George to St. Petersburg, ordering his reluctant son to arrive in frock coat, cap, and sword. "Aiguil[l]ette* in <u>thin</u> crape excepting the points . . . cocked hat and epaulettes covered with crape and white gloves would be the mourning," he wrote.[78] He spent hours closeted with Count Vorontzov-Dashkov, the minister of the imperial court, who was too deferential to protest when the young czar's uncle dictated the arrangements for the journey to Moscow and even the funeral itself. "I wonder what his tiresome old mother would have said," remarked Nicky's sister the Grand Duchess Olga many years later, "if she had seen everybody accept uncle Bertie's authority. In Russia of all

* The tagged point hanging from the shoulder to the breast of a uniform.

places!"[79] Livadia was overcrowded and chaotic; one thousand people slept in the palaces, and Charlotte Knollys complained that she had to use her dressing table as a desk and keep her washing things in a piano.[80] Arthur Ellis thought the "confusion, indecision and bustle" was worse even than the "masterly inactivity and fussiness" of Windsor Castle.[81] Bertie impressed everyone: "He is never in the way and is so kind and civil to all the suite and even to the servants whom he recognises," wrote Charlotte Knollys.[82]

Bertie spent his fifty-third birthday traveling with the czar's remains on the imperial train to Moscow. The royal party wore full court dress for the entire five-day journey—"first-class purgatory!" groaned Arthur Ellis.[83] After the czar's body had lain in state for twenty hours in the cathedral in Moscow, the train crawled on to St. Petersburg. From the station, Bertie walked in the four-hour procession that followed the funeral car to the church in the fortress of St. Peter and St. Paul, where the coffin was deposited for the lying in state. The funeral took place on 19 November 1894, which was none too soon, as the body, which had been imperfectly embalmed, was rotting, the face looked a "dreadful colour," and the stench was "awful."[84] Leaning heavily on Alix, Minnie advanced to the open coffin and for the last time kissed the shrunken lips of her dead husband.

The wedding of the new czar Nicholas II and Queen Victoria's granddaughter Alexandra of Hesse (Alicky) took place a week later. Alix, who was suffering from a heavy cold, once again supported her red-eyed sister Minnie. Both sisters were dressed identically in simple white—a sign that their old intimacy had been restored. Bertie wore his Russian dragoon uniform, a birthday gift from Nicky, which was distinctly unflattering. Carrington was shocked to see "a fat man in a huge shaggy great coat looking like a huge Polar bear," who turned out to be the Prince of Wales.[85] After the service, the enthusiasm of the crowds was so great that Nicholas for once forgot his fear of assassination, and ordered the soldiers lining the route of the imperial procession to be removed. This spontaneous gesture prompted Bertie to predict a new dawn. "The people," he told Queen Victoria, "only wish to be trusted by him; and if Nicky is liberal in his views and tolerant to his subjects, a more popular Ruler of this country could not exist."[86] He was too optimistic. In May 1896 at the Imperial Coronation, a crowd stampeded, crushing thousands of peasants to death. Nicky refused to cancel or alter the ceremonies, heartlessly dancing while outside carts were piled high with corpses.[87] Queen Victoria had dreaded Alicky's marriage to Nicky: "My blood runs cold," she wrote, "when I think of her . . . placed on that very unsafe throne."[88] Already the signs were ominous.

Bertie traveled home with George, leaving Alix behind with Minnie in the Anitchkoff Palace. In the deep cold of the Russian winter, Minnie clung pathetically to her sister. Alexander III had been a double-dyed reactionary, but he was a devoted husband, and his death left Minnie alone and dependent on her son. "I am all right and darling Minnie too we lead a very quiet life together now," Alix wired the Queen.[89] She had little reason to return home; the "only magnet," wrote Arthur Ellis, "is the girls at Sandringham alone."[90]

Daisy had by now become Countess of Warwick, her husband having succeeded as Earl of Warwick and inherited Warwick Castle. In February 1895, she gave a spectacular white and gold *bal poudre* (powdered wig ball). Bertie was tactfully absent, at Sandringham. Daisy ordered her guests to dress in the fashion of the court of Versailles under Louis XVI: She herself appeared as Marie Antoinette. Two weeks later, an article in a socialist paper, *The Clarion,* contrasted the lavish luxury and glitter of the Warwick ball with the shivering poor crowded in their hovels, and concluded: "I deeply pity the poor rich Countess of Warwick." Stung by this personal attack, the philanthropic Daisy rushed up to London by the first train, sought out the dingy offices of *The Clarion,* and explained to the shabbily dressed editor Robert Blatchford that her ball had given work to half the county. Blatchford dismissed this as unproductive labor, and proceeded to give Daisy a lecture on socialist economics. Daisy left the office stunned; later, in her autobiography, she described this in quasi-religious terms as her conversion experience to socialism.[91] At the time, it hardly seemed so. True, she was elected to the Warwick Board of Guardians; but her chief concern seemed to be to spend her fortune as speedily as she could.

In May 1895, Bertie stayed at Warwick Castle. This was his first visit, and he must have noticed the reckless spending that struck Margot Asquith so forcefully when she stayed there in 1897. By contrast with Waddesdon, where every picture or objet d'art represented an investment, at Warwick, wrote Margot, all was waste: "Some rare book or picture goes up to Christies annually, and the proceeds of this and Daisy's private fortune goes to pay the florists, fruits, table linen, towels, hot water pipes, coiffeur etc—breakfasts like ball suppers, hot and renewed from 9:30 till 11:30, small scented notes with button holes on the table of the men at dressing time telling them the lady they are to take in to dinner." As Margot cruelly noted, there was "something of the kindness and all the impulses of the cocotte" about Daisy.[92] She would have been an easy victim for the French Revolutionists. Truly she seemed a latter-day Marie Antoinette.

As well as pouring money into her husband's Warwick Castle, Daisy lavished her fortune on her own property at Easton Lodge. When Bertie came to stay in October 1895, he arrived in his special train at Easton Lodge station, on a private railway that Daisy had paid for out of her own pocket.[93] Within six months, the Countess of Warwick was selling three thousand acres of her Essex estates.[94] Such spending seemed only natural to Bertie, and it did not occur to him that Daisy might need financial help. In many ways, Daisy and Bertie were similar characters: socially confident extroverts, used to gratifying every appetite, compulsive spenders, and voracious eaters. Daisy's granddaughter remembered Daisy in old age taking a bath, huge and devoid of her wig; she still wore Edwardian false hair and feather boas, and she wolfed pats of cheese and butter in the dairy.[95]

But Daisy claimed descent from Oliver Cromwell as well as Nell Gwyn. She had a puritanical streak, and she disapproved of drunkenness and gambling. She taught the prince to lead a better life; according to Knollys, she "terminated all the late hours and generally fast living that had prevailed before."[96] Perhaps Bertie grew tired of Daisy's do-gooding—her needlework circles and schools for poor children, her quixotic attempt to finance a welfare state out of her own personal fortune. The reverse D symbol still marched through his diary—it occurs on forty-odd days in both 1895 and 1896—but there were hints that their relationship was changing.

Daisy combined a social conscience with a commitment to sexual freedom; this very modern moral code was to be her undoing. Among the guests at the Warwick ball was a millionaire Durham coal owner named Joe Laycock. He was known as one of the ugliest men in England but also one of the most attractive—"ugly in that special way with eyes set very far apart, very lithe and very powerfully built and with such *vitality!*"[97] At some point in 1894–95 Daisy began an affair with him. That she should fall for such a man was not surprising; what was remarkable was that Bertie seemed prepared to accept her defection.

Bertie and Daisy both claimed in 1898 that their relationship had been "platonic" for "some years."*[98] This may have been a matter of necessity rather than choice. There were rumors that Bertie was impotent, possibly since 1895.[99] Often on "D" days the prince noted a morning appointment with his doctor, Laking. In January 1896, he underwent a course of "electrical treatment." This was the new wonder therapy of the day, and electric shocks were administered for impotence— though electricity was also used for many other ailments. At fifty-five, Bertie was overweight and threatened with heart trouble and possibly diabetes. His daughter Victoria noticed him panting when he walked upstairs.[100]

These were the years when the prince was often seen in Paris. In Montmartre, at the Moulin Rouge (opened in 1889), he was accosted

---

* Carrington noted that Daisy was due to be presented on Tuesday, 5 March 1895, by Lady Salisbury at a drawing room. "This fact has been privately notified to the Princess and there is a good deal of conversation in London on a paragraph in the Central News telegrams that 'the Princess of Wales' arrangements will not permit her to be present.' Spencer Ponsonby let Francis Knollys know that Lady Warwick was going to the Drawing Room by the <u>Princess's special orders.</u>" (Bodleian Library, Carrington Diary, MS Film 1120, 3 March 1895.) In the end, the presentation didn't take place, allegedly because Daisy had the flu; but if it was true that Alix approved, it is a sign that Bertie's relationship with Daisy was no longer physical. (*The Times*, 5 March 1895.)

by the cancan dancer Louise Weber, who jeered, *"Ullo, Wales! Est-ce que tu vas payer mon champagne?" (Will you pay for my champagne?)*[101]

Le Chabanais, founded in 1878, was a palace of sex decorated lavishly in a variety of styles, including Moorish, Japanese, and Louis XVI. The room Bertie used was known as the Hindu chamber; emblazoned above the bed was his coat of arms. The prostitutes with their frizzed black hair, long drawers, corsets, and bare breasts, seem to twenty-first-century (female) eyes strangely lacking in allure, but Bertie undoubtedly visited. He was watched by the Paris police, who kept files on his movements.[102] The copper bath that was filled with champagne while he consorted with prostitutes (anything less erotic than sitting in a cold and sticky champagne bath seems hard to imagine) still exists. Appropriately, it was bought by Salvador Dalí. The prize artifact in Bertie's room was the seat of love, which he allegedly commissioned in about 1890.[103] Exactly what permutations the complicated design of stirrups and supports was designed for is hard to see, but when it was later exhibited to visitors, they were told: "He stepped in there as if he were going to a stall."[104]

In 1894, Bertie's friend Randolph Churchill became alarmingly ill. Bertie asked royal physician Sir Richard Quain to seek a report from Randolph's doctor, Thomas Buzzard. This disregard for professional ethics caused lasting resentment among some of the Churchill family, as Buzzard's report on Randolph's "General Paralysis" seemed to confirm that he was suffering from the tertiary stage of syphilis. Buzzard's diagnosis was later challenged by Randolph's grandson, Peregrine Churchill, who maintained that Randolph died of a brain tumor; but Bertie now believed his friend was terminally ill with syphilis, and so did Jennie.[105] Bertie was all the more solicitous. On Christmas Day 1894, Jennie wrote the prince "a kind but dreadfully sad letter."

"I cannot describe," replied Bertie, "how much I feel for you. . . . You have indeed had a fearful time of it, but you have done your duty by him most nobly."[106] Randolph died at age forty-five on 24 January 1895, and Bertie wrote at once to Jennie: "There was a cloud in our friendship," but that was long forgotten: "Be assured that I shall always deeply regard him."[107]

After Randolph's death, Bertie saw a lot of Jennie. Her name appears often in his diary.[108] But even if their friendship now developed into a physical affair, renewing their relationship of a few years back, this was not an exclusive romance.* Also, Jennie invited Alix to dinner and consulted her about the guest list, something that would never have happened if Jennie had posed a threat to the Wales marriage.[109] Equally, Jennie was on friendly terms with Daisy, and often stayed at Easton. Indeed, Daisy later wrote that "one never thought of giving a party without her"—something she surely would not have said if Jennie had been a rival for the prince's affections.[110]

"Dearest Daisy," wrote Jennie, "I hear you look lovely and about 16!" "Will you be an angel," she asked, "and send me the recipe for Cumberland Sauce for the 'Wench' in my kitchen?"[111] Jennie's cuisine was notoriously good; she was one of the first hostesses to employ Rosa Lewis, expertly trained in French cooking in the kitchen of the Comtesse de Paris at Sheen. Rosa was a favorite of the gourmet Bertie, who enjoyed her cockney wit almost as much as her quails stuffed with foie gras. Hiring the freelance Rosa soon became essential for hostesses entertaining the greedy prince, who let it be known that she was his favorite cook.†[112]

"May I have a 'geisha' tea with you on Wednesday at 5?" Bertie wrote to Jennie Churchill.[113] And again: "You once said you would give me tea in your Japanese dress—I wonder if you could appear in it at 5:30 this evening? A bientot."‡[114] He now addressed her as *ma chère amie,* signing off, "*Tout à vous,* AE." Between February 1896 and 1897,

---

* See p. 300.

† The story goes that Bertie spotted Rosa standing in the dining room at a shooting party and, seeing they were alone, snatched a kiss. At lunch, he asked his hostess what had become of the guest with the white dress and wonderful complexion. "Sir, you mean Rosa the cook?" After that her career was assured. (Leslie, *Edwardians in Love,* p. 319.)

‡ "Geisha" was not a word the prince used lightly. He saw the West End play *The Geisha* on the day he wrote to Jennie. (RA EVIID/1897: 2 February.) Though a geisha might flirt, nineteenth-century geisha culture often banned sex.

he sent a flood of notes proposing himself to tea or lunch. It seems that he visited her in her new, tall house at 35a Great Cumberland Street almost once a week.[115] He included her name on the lists he sent in advance of house parties: She was at Chatsworth, at Waddesdon, at Welbeck, at Cowes. He teased her about her love life, which was lurid. When she broke up with Major Caryl Ramsden, fourteen years younger than her, after a spectacular row in Egypt, Bertie wrote: "You had better have stuck to your old friends than gone on your expedition of the Nile! Old friends are best!"[116]

An undated pencil-written card from Bertie, sent from the Ritz in Paris in the spring of 1899 (the Ritz opened in June 1898), is ambiguous but suggestive:

Delighted to call on you at 3:45
AE
And you shall have your enjoyments
Our dinner should be at 7.[117]

But the letters to *ma chère amie* come abruptly to a halt in 1900 when the forty-six-year-old Jennie announced her intention to marry George Cornwallis-West. Not only was he twenty years younger than her, but he was also rumored to be Bertie's son by Patsy Cornwallis-West.* The gossip was scurrilous and unfounded, but it made Lady Randolph look ridiculous, and Bertie told her so. Jennie was not amused. Bertie replied: "It has been my privilege to enjoy your friendship for upwards of quarter of a century, therefore why do you think it necessary to write me a rude letter simply because I have expressed strongly my regret at the marriage you are about to make?"[118]

---

* At a house party where a band was playing, Bertie met George Cornwallis-West on the landing on the way down to dinner. "What are you going to play tonight?" asked Bertie. "Bridge, I suppose, sir," replied George. Bertie looked around and burst out laughing: "I took you for the man who conducts the band." (Ruffer, *Big Shots*, pp. 96–97.) This hardly suggests that he recognized Cornwallis-West as his son.

So much is known about the detail of Bertie's daily life—what time he caught a train, whom he saw and when, all recorded in his diary and often published in the Court and Social. But what went on behind the mask—his thoughts, his talk, his laugh—is carefully concealed. One glimpse of the real Bertie exists. It is a record of an interview by Daisy's mentor, W. T. Stead. In spite of his hurtful gibe at "the fat little bald man in red," Stead managed to persuade Daisy to arrange a lunch for him to meet the prince. This was in December 1896, and it took place in her sister's house on South Audley Street.

Stead noticed that when Bertie arrived, Daisy made him a graceful curtsey, "prettier than any I had seen before." (Did she curtsey to him when they were alone?) The prince "does not shake hands nicely, only about half his hand he puts in and there is no grip in it." Daisy led the way into the dining room, Bertie followed, and Stead came last. Bertie sat at the head of the table, with Stead and Daisy on either side. The prince was slightly under the middle height (he was, in fact, five foot nine)[119] and not as fat as Stead expected, but "he had at first a look—I don't know whether it was his moustache or in his eyes—which made you have a half impression that he had either a slight squint, or that one of his front teeth was awry."

He ate everything very rapidly. When Daisy was in the room his conversation was society small talk, reminding Stead of a hostess who gives the impression of being interested but forgets all about it five minutes later. But after she had left the table, Bertie smoked two cigars and they talked about Russia, and Bertie revealed that he disliked its system of government and thought the persecution of the Jews "deplorable." Whenever Stead tried to draw him out, Bertie good-naturedly refused to engage. When Stead asked him about his relations with the Queen, or his own position, he would only say that it was "very difficult." "I cannot take any part in politics."[120]

After lunch, the two men walked upstairs to the drawing room. Daisy, who had concussed herself out hunting, was lying on a sofa with a quilt over her head. Few women did that in front of the Prince of Wales. The charm of Daisy was that she was so self-confident that she could always be herself. She was still "my little Daisywife."

Bertie lost his greatest political ally when Rosebery resigned from the premiership in June 1895. Salisbury, who returned to office with a Unionist majority, had little time for the Prince of Wales. Schomberg McDonnell, the prime minister's private secretary, promised to send Bertie when abroad a résumé of anything interesting going on at home. "Need I say I have never had a line from him!" complained Bertie.[121] In dynastic politics, too, the prince was marginalized. The uncle of the two most powerful men in the world, the czar of Russia and the kaiser of Germany, seemed condemned to a life of frivolity. When the kaiser invited him to the opening of the Kiel Canal in 1895, Bertie replied asking him to postpone the ceremony as the date clashed with the Ascot races.[122] The kaiser visited Cowes in August 1895 and the German diplomat Alfred von Kiderlen-Wächter complained that "Fat old Wales" had been "inconceivably rude" by keeping him waiting for three-quarters of an hour and butting into his conversation with Lord Salisbury.[123]

One doesn't need to be a Freudian to see the link between Bertie's powerlessness in politics, his impotence in the bedroom, and his new passion: horse racing. He had kept horses in training since 1885 (before then he raced his horses under other people's names, as the Queen objected to him using the royal colors).[124] In eight years he had won very little: His total prize money amounted to £5,904, an annual average of only £250 if one freak good year of 1891 is excluded.[125] In 1893, he moved his horses from stables at Kingsclere in Hampshire to Newmarket, and confounding all expectations, he bred a really good horse: Persimmon.

On Derby Day, 3 June 1896, Bertie arrived at Epsom with customary punctuality in time for the first race. Few people expected him to win. The odds on Persimmon were 5 to 1 against, and the favorite was Leo de Rothschild's St. Frusquin at 13 to 8. Persimmon was behind for most of the race, but drew level in the last hundred yards, striding ahead of St. Frusquin (whose jockey broke a stirrup leather) to win by a neck. The effect was extraordinary. A hurricane of spontaneous cheering was prolonged for a quarter of an hour. Crowds flooded onto the course as the prince led his horse into the winners' enclosure. "The scene of enthusiasm after the Derby was a most remarkable and satisfying sight," Bertie wired the Queen, with characteristic dryness: racing was the football of the age, and the win had restored him to a sense of connectedness with the public that he had lost since Tranby Croft.[126] Victoria remained stonily unimpressed. "Bertie has won the Derby," she told Princess Beatrice. "I cannot rejoice as I know what dear Papa felt & as it sets an example to so many who get ruined and break their Parents' hearts. Of course I congratulated him."[127]

In 1896, Victoria was seventy-seven. She had sat longer on the throne than any English monarch, beating her grandfather George III's record of fifty-nine years.[128] She was very lame, relying on her Indian servant to support her walking, and she was nearly blind from cataracts. She could no longer read, pathetically complaining that the candles gave no light and she could not find glasses to suit.[129] During the course of her long widowhood, the way her staff worked had been organized to ensure that she was seen as little as possible by the household. All communications took place in writing. Reprimands were written out and delivered in special boxes, marked "The Queen."[130] If a member of the household needed to tell her something, they had to pen a proper letter, beginning, "—— presents humble duty to Your Majesty," and place it in an envelope addressed to the Queen, which must be sealed but not licked.[131] No one was allowed to go outside until the Queen went. It was frowned on to meet her in the grounds when she was in her carriage, so any courtier who accidentally came across her was obliged to hide behind a bush.[132] She practiced bizarre economies, such as having newspaper cut into squares and used as lavatory paper.[133]

Sir Henry Ponsonby, who had served Victoria as private secretary for twenty-five years, saving her from herself and rescuing the monarchy in the process, suffered a stroke in January 1895, dying ten months later. The Ponsonbys and the Greys were an intermarried dynasty of royal servants—Henry Ponsonby had succeeded his wife's uncle, General Grey, as private secretary in 1870—and it seemed entirely natural that Henry's son Fritz, who had been an equerry, should become assistant private secretary. Sir Arthur Bigge was now the private secretary. The Queen relied increasingly on Princess Beatrice, especially after the death of Beatrice's husband, Prince Henry of Battenberg (January 1896), to read her correspondence and take dictation. Fritz Ponsonby despaired of Beatrice, who was hopelessly unprofessional about her secretarial duties, often neglecting to read important documents if she was in a hurry to develop a photograph or paint a flower for a bazaar.[134]

But the old Queen was reluctant as ever to share work with her heir. Only when it suited her did Victoria fall in with Bertie's suggestions. Nicholas and Alexandra had been invited to pay a private visit to Balmoral in September 1896. When Bertie proposed a ceremonial welcome, the Queen agreed, but only because Salisbury urged the need to cultivate Russian support.

Balmoral, where the Queen's regime of seclusion, silence, thirty-minute meals, nonsmoking, and open windows was at its strictest, was purgatory to the sybaritic Bertie, but he stayed for a week. Nothing ever changed; the same chairs were in the same places, the same biscuits on the plates—only the dogs were replaced when they died.[135] Bertie traveled to Leith in pouring rain to welcome the czar and czarina on their arrival from Denmark. He wore his Russian uniform with a splendid red and gray greatcoat, "not the least tight," noted lady-in-waiting Edith Lytton. Bertie was "very nice all day to everyone," and Edith (whose husband had been a clever diplomat) was struck by the absurdity of expecting the small and very young czar to solve the Eastern Question.[136] The visit was not a success. It rained constantly. Nicky had an abscess on his tooth, but his uncle Bertie took him out shooting all day long. He was put in the best place, but missed everything. On 25 September, Bertie noted the results of a deer drive:

Emperor of Russia. 0
Duke of Connaught . . . . 4 stags

Duke of York . . . . 5 stags

. . . .

Prince of Wales . . . . 0 (no shot)[137]

Lord Salisbury arrived, having insisted on a bedroom heated to a minimum temperature of sixty degrees, which was the hottest the Queen would allow.[138] Bertie was excluded from the "VERY SECRET" discussions between Salisbury and the czar, and he left Balmoral before the Russians.[139] Nicky breathed a sigh of relief. "After he left I had an easier time, because I could at least do what I wanted to, and was not obliged to go out shooting every day in the cold and rain."[140] Victoria, on the other hand, was annoyed. Bertie had departed to Newmarket, where Persimmon won the Jockey Stakes. The Queen made no secret of her disapproval.[141] As she remarked, *"Il faut payer pour être Prince." (One has to pay a price to be a prince.)*[142]

CHAPTER 20

"We Are All in God's Hands"*

1897–1901

Beatrice Webb watched the Prince of Wales presenting prizes to the students of the London County Council in 1897. She thought he "acted like a well-oiled automaton, saying exactly the words he was expected to say, noticing the right persons on the platform, maintaining his own dignity, whilst setting others at ease and otherwise acting with per- fectly polished discretion":

> Not an English gentleman, essentially a foreigner and yet an al- most perfect constitutional sovereign. From a political point of view, his vices and foibles, his lack of intellectual refinement or moral distinction, are as nothing compared to his complete de- tachment from all party prejudice and class interests and his ge- nius for political *discretion*. But one sighs to think that this

---

* RA VIC/Add A4/172, Bertie to Vicky, 5 August 1900.

unutterably commonplace person should set the tone to London Society. There is something comic in the great British nation with its infinite variety of talents, having this undistinguished
and limited-minded German bourgeois to be its social sovereign.[1]

The "unutterably commonplace person" had annoyed Beatrice
Webb because of his plan to commemorate the Queen's Diamond Jubilee. He proposed to endow the hospitals of London, creating the
Prince of Wales's Hospital Fund. The Fabian socialist Webb sneered at
this charitable project as the sort of proposal one would expect from
"a committee of village grocers."

Bertie's committee, which met at Marlborough House, included
the head of Anglo-Jewry, Lord Rothschild; the Chief Rabbi; the Bishop
of London; and millionaires such as Julius Wernher and Ernest Cassel.
Bertie was no figurehead; minutes show that he was "informed, involved and strong-minded."[2] It was he who drove the project.[3] On his
insistence, the fund created a sizable endowment: He gave a standing
order, and invited his City friends, many of them Jewish financiers, to
make generous subscriptions. King Edward's Hospital Fund, as it became, was at that time the most ambitious hospital fund ever conceived, and it survives today as the King's Fund, "arguably Edward
VII's most significant permanent memorial."[4]

The fund was the brainchild of Sir Henry Burdett, Bertie's adviser
on charitable projects. A hospital administrator and stockbroker, Burdett had come to Bertie's notice in 1889 when he published a book
entitled *Prince, Princess and People*. In it, he gave an exhaustive account
of the Waleses' philanthropic activities, which until then had gone
largely unnoticed. The charitable duties performed by the Prince of
Wales, wrote Burdett, "probably exceed those of any other single man
in the country." Burdett listed eighty-four hospitals that Bertie opened
or contributed money to.[5] He saw that the charitable work of the royals could be put to use more effectively. His book won favor at Marlborough House, and he was quick to ingratiate himself there. The
prince's charitable activities became more focused. In 1896, on Bur-

dett's advice, Bertie agreed to become president of Guy's Hospital, and head its fund-raising appeal, culminating in a festival dinner for four thousand guests. This raised £150,000, making it to date allegedly the most profitable dinner ever.[6]

Alix had a role as a champion of nurses. Her influence was phenomenal, if erratic. Brass plaques can still be seen in London hospitals that commemorate the Waleses laying a stone or opening a wing, bearing witness to their tireless activity: the Great Ormond Street Hospital for Sick Children; the Albany Wing of the National Hospital, opened by Alix as a memorial to Leopold (1885); the New Hospital for Women, later renamed the Elizabeth Garrett Anderson Hospital (1889); the London Hospital, Whitechapel (1887); Soho Square Hospital for Women; the Brompton Hospital (1879); the Putney Hospital for Incurables; the London Fever Hospital; the Royal Hospital for Women and Children at Waterloo Bridge . . . the list goes on and on.

Bertie provided the vital link between Burdett's world of hospitals and charities, and the new plutocracy. Contemporaries deplored the "social sovereignty of wealth over every class" in Bertie's court, and commentators complained that financiers, self-made millionaires, and South African randlords thronged the drawing rooms of Marlborough House.[7] When Thomas Lipton, child of the Glasgow Gorbals turned tea tycoon, raced his yacht *Shamrock* against Bertie's *Britannia*, the kaiser commented sarcastically that his uncle Bertie was "going yachting with his grocer."[8] What he didn't realize was that Lipton had made a donation of £25,000 to Princess Alexandra's fund to feed the London poor in 1897, followed by a further £100,000 for a poor people's restaurant. The social sovereignty of wealth was not unconditional; the plutocrat must be validated by charitable giving before he was rewarded at court. "The millionaire's quickest and surest route to royal favour is a big cheque for a necessitous hospital."[9]

Bertie spent the spring of 1897 in the French Riviera on board *Britannia,* as was his custom. Queen Victoria was at Cimiez, near Nice, and Bertie visited her there several times.[10] A crisis had erupted in the

Queen's household, and her ladies and gentlemen were threatening to resign.

Abdul Karim, the Queen's Indian servant, had joined the household at the time of the Golden Jubilee. Victoria, like Bertie, was genuinely free of racial prejudice, and her Indian servants symbolized the special connection with her Indian empire. They were also decorative. Abdul Karim, who was clever and manipulative, became Victoria's favorite. He gave her lessons in Hindustani, and he was promoted to be her teacher (Munshi); next she made him her Indian secretary. The Munshi's intimacy with the Queen outraged the household, not merely on racial grounds but also because he was revealed to be low class, the barely literate son of an apothecary. When the Queen's doctor, Sir James Reid, diagnosed him with "gleet" (gonorrhea), and the Queen insisted that he accompany her to Cimiez nonetheless, the household mutinied. Harriet Phipps, the woman of the bedchamber, was deputed to tell the Queen that they refused to go if the Munshi was of the party. The furious monarch responded by sweeping all the clutter off her desk onto the floor. They went.

Sir James Reid had been charged by the Queen with the Munshi's welfare, and in Cimiez he held endless talks with the household, with the Queen, and with Bertie. The Queen insisted that the Munshi was the victim of the snobbery and racism of the court, and demanded that they associate more with him. Reid countered by telling the Queen that her obsession with the Munshi made her seem insane. The Prince of Wales, said Reid, had "quite made up his mind to come forward if necessary, because quite apart from all consequences to the Queen, it affects *himself* most vitally. . . . Because it affects the throne."[11] Victoria broke down and admitted that she had played the fool. But Bertie did not come forward and speak to his mother—he failed to confront her, even on an issue where she was plainly in the wrong. The Queen continued to pander to the Munshi, who bullied her abominably. Perhaps, as some thought, Victoria had succeeded in making her widow's life so dreary that she needed the emotional excitement of the drama.[12] As with John Brown, she had allowed a favorite servant to monopolize access and disrupt the functioning of her court.

Bertie and his family, 1884. From left: Georgie; Maud; Alix, looking thinner and prettier than her daughters; Eddy, breaking sartorial convention by wearing a wing collar, flamboyant tie, and spats with a kilt; Louise, Victoria.

Bertie's daughters. From left: Maud, Victoria, and Louise, 1887. Unkindly known as "the Hags," they still wore identical dresses though Louise was already twenty.

Crown Prince Rudolf of Austria, shortly before the Mayerling tragedy.

Daisy Brooke entertains the Prince of Wales at Easton Lodge, November 1891. From right: "Fat Mary," Duchess of Teck; Princess May; the Marquis de Soveral, "the Blue Monkey" (seated); Daisy. Lord Brooke sits in front of Bertie.

Daisy with her son Maynard shortly after her "abdication" as Bertie's mistress.

Queen Victoria, photographed by Alexander Bassano in 1882 wearing her crown made of one thousand diamonds. She refused to share power with Bertie.

May of Teck: engagement photo, 1891. Just over six weeks later her fiancé, Eddy, was dead; in 1893 she married his brother George.

Britain's German family: Queen Victoria and Bertie at Coburg, 1894. From left: Arthur, Duke of Connaught; Affie, now Duke of Saxe-Coburg and Gotha; Kaiser William II; his mother, Vicky, the Empress Frederick. The kaiser's quarrel with his mother, his uncle Bertie, and his grandmother transformed dynastic diplomacy.

Invitation to the Coronation that was postponed
because of Bertie's operation.

House party at Rufford with the Saviles, 1899. Consuelo Marlborough is on Bertie's left. Mrs. Keppel sits, far right; as in all photographs, her gaze his firmly fixed on Bertie.

The King in his study in 1901. Overwork made him ill in the first year of his reign.

Bertie recuperating after the Coronation with Alix on a cruise aboard the *Victoria and Albert*.

Charlotte Knollys (left), woman of the bedchamber to Alix for more than fifty years, and Francis Knollys (right), her brother, Bertie's private secretary. After forty years with Bertie, he went on to serve George V.

Alix in the midst of her family in Denmark: her father (King Christian IX), her sister Minnie (Dowager Empress of Russia), and (with her back to the camera) her sister Thyra (Crown Princess of Hanover).

The kaiser (back row, fourth left) stays at Windsor, November 1907. There are five queens and four kings in this photograph.

The King photographed by
Baron de Meyer in 1904.

Dighton Probyn, court
comptroller and honorary
Sikh, with his "Blessed
Lady," Queen Alexandra,
in 1920.

Bertie spent a few days in Paris on his way home from the Riviera. Here he found Daisy Warwick, holidaying with her sisters. After sitting for the painter Carolus-Duran, Daisy would mount her bicycle and (so she archly told her friend W. T. Stead), "speed away" for "all sorts of adventures."[13] These included five assignations with Bertie, whose new toy was a four-cylinder motor car, supplied by Monsieur Panhard et Levassor's establishment, in which, like Mr. Toad, he drove to the Hotel Bristol.[14] Thanks to Bertie's patronage, the motor car was soon to become "as much a part of the courtier's baggage as is the cigarette case."[15]

Daisy's old enemy Lord Charles Beresford had returned from the Mediterranean, but he was powerless to harm her now. Bertie spotted him at Ascot in 1896, and was enraged when he "purposely passed close to me without bowing but he bowed shortly afterwards to my son and went up to the Duke and Duchess of Devonshire with a 'hail fellow well met' kind of manner and said how glad he was to see them again."[16] Eventually Beresford was made naval aide-de-camp, which "allowed the poor beast to get into Society again," but unfinished business remained.[17] In June 1897, the Duke of Portland forwarded a letter from Beresford expressing his regret for the angry letters he had written to Bertie and his wife's regret for the letter she wrote to the Queen.[18] The prince accepted the apology, and Beresford's letter was forwarded to Daisy, who wrote: "It is a great triumph to have received the apologies, and a great relief that the episode is closed."[19]

At Ascot in 1897, Bertie's horse Persimmon won the Gold Cup at a canter by eight lengths, and the entire crowd turned "as with one accord to the royal Enclosure, cheering for several minutes."[20] The cup, appropriately enough, was a replica of the famous Warwick Vase. "Lady Warwick was in very high favour," noted Carrington.[21] After Daisy had left, Bertie's racing manager Lord Marcus Beresford came up and asked him a favor. With tears running down his face, he begged the prince to allow him to bring his brother Charlie to offer his congratulations. "I had no alternative but to say yes," Bertie told Daisy later that day. "He came up with his hat off, and would not put it on till I told him, and shook hands. . . . My loved one," he wrote anxiously, "I hope you won't be annoyed at what has happened, and exonerate me from blame as that is all I care about!"[22]

Daisy by now cared not a jot about Charlie Beresford. All her attentions were taken up with Joe Laycock, who had been her lover for the past two years. Nor was Bertie faithful to Daisy. As well as Jennie Churchill, there was the beautiful Lady Dudley, sister of poor mad Harriett Mordaunt. "Midnight supper with Lady Dudley," Bertie had noted on the day he won the Derby in 1896.[23] But it was to Daisy that he wrote the long, confiding letters—letters that "contained some very candid criticisms of persons and events of the day," as well as political secrets.[24]

The morning of 22 June 1897 was close and dull, but when Queen Victoria was helped into her open state landau—an intricate operation involving her Indian servant and a sloping green baize plank—the sun came out. Bertie, wearing a scarlet field marshal's uniform, rode beside the Queen—a small figure in black silk embroidered with silver, sitting opposite Alix in mauve—at the end of the royal procession of seventeen carriages that formed up for the Diamond Jubilee.

The planning of the ceremony had occupied the committee that Bertie chaired at Marlborough House since January. Entertaining the royal families of Europe had cost the Queen exorbitant sums at her Golden Jubilee in 1887, and she threatened to boycott her Diamond Jubilee if she was asked to contribute to the costs.[25] The Treasury paid the bill, and the committee planned to economize and please the politicians by celebrating the empire. Bertie has been credited with organizing the event, but in fact his role was to facilitate the innovations of Reginald Brett (later Lord Esher), permanent secretary to the Office of Works.[26] The Queen was too lame to dismount from her coach, and Brett proposed to make the focal point an open-air celebration outside the west front of St. Paul's Cathedral. The support of Bertie as chairman for this controversial innovation was crucial. "Has one ever heard of such a thing! After 60 years Reign, to thank God in the Street!!! Who can have started such an idea, and how could the Queen adopt it?" exclaimed Augusta, Grand Duchess of Mecklenburg-Strelitz.[27]

As the royal procession crawled toward St. Paul's, the cheering was deafening. Women wept, men shouted themselves hoarse. "No one . . . has ever met with such an ovation as was given to me," wrote the Queen.[28] When she neared St. Paul's, where the colonial troops were assembled, the crowd burst out singing "God Save the Queen." The Archbishop of Canterbury cried, "Three cheers for the Queen," and a thunderous roar broke out. The small black figure was "much moved." As the tears streamed down Victoria's face, Alix gently held her hand.[29] The procession returned via London Bridge and the streets of south London, showing the Queen to the London poor, another innovation proposed by Brett and promoted by Bertie.[30]

Bertie played his part to perfection. In spite of all the long years of being put down and rejected, he made no attempt to upstage his mother and showed no trace of envy. How different from Kaiser William, whom the Queen refused to invite, and who wrote bitterly to his grandmother: "To be the first and eldest of your grandchildren and yet to be precluded from taking part in this unique fete, while cousins and far relations will have the privilege of surrounding You . . . is deeply mortifying."[31]

The climax of the Jubilee season was the fancy dress ball given at Devonshire House by Louise, Duchess of Devonshire. The sixty-five-year-old Louise's features had coarsened with age, not helped by her brown wig and gash of red lipstick; now stout and apparently incapable of showing emotion, she was feared and respected but not loved.*

Heading the list of seven hundred guests, Bertie came dressed as Grand Master of the Knights Hospitaller of Malta, wearing a black velvet tunic embroidered with jet. His costume celebrated his charita-

---

* Louise's weakness was gambling, which Bertie found unacceptable in a woman: He encountered her at Monte Carlo, squired by a Mr. Holden, "an awful little snob who looks like a stud groom—whilst her husband is making important political speeches at home—I can't understand at her age that she should come out to Monte Carlo to gamble! and go about with third rate men!" (RA VIC/Add C07/1, B to Knollys, 10 March 1894.)

ble work as Grand Prior of the Order of St. John of Jerusalem; with his fat legs poured into thigh-length boots, and a tall black hat, he resembled a prosperous vole. Alix was dressed in cream satin and cascades of pearls as Marguerite de Valois, the promiscuous and unhappily married French queen who was imprisoned by her husband. She was "horribly bored" on account of the crush, which must have made it impossible for her to hear.[32] Her friend Gladys de Grey, who came as Cleopatra, wore £6,000 worth of gold and orchids and was attended by an Arab slave; some considered that she was upstaged by a rival Cleopatra, the American beauty Minnie Paget, a favorite of Bertie's, whose Worth dress was encrusted with emeralds, rubies, and diamonds. (After her death in 1911, the dress fetched a mere £9 at auction.)[33] It was a good night for Charles Frederick Worth. Jennie Churchill appeared in another of his creations, dressed, appropriately perhaps, as the Byzantine empress Theodora, the sexually voracious barbarian courtesan who married the emperor Justinian. She wore a crown and carried a sovereign's orb. Daisy Warwick flaunted her quasi-royal status as Marie Antoinette—or perhaps she was economizing for once by wearing the same gown of turquoise velvet embroidered with silver fleur-de-lis that she had worn at her own Warwick ball.

Walking home through Green Park at dawn, Consuelo, the young American Duchess of Marlborough, was dismayed to find the "dregs of humanity" lying on the grass. "Human beings too dispirited or sunk to find work or favour, they sprawled in sodden stupor, pitiful representatives of the submerged tenth."[34] Like all historic parties, the Devonshire House ball was a tipping point: the beginning of the end of the great London houses—Devonshire House was destroyed in 1924—and the swan song of Louise, the Double Duchess.

After the season, Bertie and Alix escaped together to Bayreuth. In spite of being so deaf, Alix shared Bertie's love of opera. Bertie was gripped by *Parsifal*, which lasted six hours—from four until ten—but it "could be given nowhere but here. The stage is dark the whole time—and not a sound is heard. The orchestra is invisible as it plays under the stage."[35]

From Bayreuth, Alix traveled to Denmark, while Bertie headed for Marienbad to take his cure. This was his first visit to the Bohemian spa, two thousand feet above sea level, which was to become his favorite retreat. He stayed at the Hotel Weimar, rose at six, drank the waters, and walked for two hours. It rained incessantly, but, he told Georgie, "I manage to get through the day somehow."[36] His regime as he described it was that of an abstemious monk, but in fact he entertained often three times a day (including teatime). To the strains of a band, he dined on grouse (specially mailed from Britain), *aubergines frites* (his favorite vegetable), and peaches. His impeccably cut dark blue coat or gray striped suit with trousers precisely creased sometimes down the side, sometimes down the front, turned heads on the promenade. Sigmund Muntz, the contemporary chronicler of Bertie's days at Marienbad, noted that any study would "lack its most vital element," if it "prudishly" avoided HRH's relations with women.[37] In the afternoons, the prince took damp drives through the thickly wooded hillsides with a new friend: Mrs. Eddy Bourke.

Emma Bourke was the sister of Mabel Batten, the girl with whom Bertie had had a flirtation many years before in India. Emma, in her early forties, was manipulative, with a history of sending poison-pen letters.* Her husband, who was twenty years older than her, was a son of Lord Mayo, the assassinated Viceroy of India, though a stockbroker, he was often short of money. Bertie wrote to Emma shortly after leaving Marienbad, thanking her for her letter, written in French ("I can speak it fluently enough but have not your gift of writing it"), and apologizing for his execrable handwriting ("It comes partly from my writing so much. You imagine I get no end of 'billets doux' but I assure I have never had less from the fair sex than since I have been abroad this time. It is a case of 'out of sight out of mind' ").

"Let me at once dispel from your mind an erroneous impression," he wrote, "about being your best friend if not your lover! Indeed I did

---

* She allegedly sent anonymous letters about her ex-lover George Binning to his fiancée, accusing him of being a libertine. The case against her was never proved, but there seems little doubt that she "behaved in a contemptible manner." (Lees-Milne, *Esher*, pp. 89–90.)

not mean to imply that I wished to cease from being the latter. Far from it I can assure you but I meant to imply that the latter depended upon you my dear child but the former I always claimed to be."[38] Bertie's distinction between friend and lover hints at a physical relationship, but whether this was more than a brief embrace on a wet afternoon carriage drive is impossible to tell. The following spring, Emma received a summons to dine at a restaurant in Nice, and Bertie gave typically precise directions about dress: She and her daughter were ordered to wear a "high dress" and hats, "your husband in evening jacket and black tie as is the custom abroad."[*39] He took a paternalistic interest in Emma's precarious finances, addressing her as "My dearest little Friend." In 1899, he wrote, "I have . . . not forgotten the happy days I spent with you two years ago," and enclosed a hundred-pound note from his winnings at Ascot and Newmarket. "You are the kindest and best little woman in the world. I only wish there were more like you."[40]

By September 1897, Bertie probably knew that Daisy Warwick was three months pregnant. He continued to meet her through the autumn, but Daisy's pregnancy meant that he could no longer be seen with her in public.[41] It also brought Alix into the equation at last.

In January 1898, Alix accompanied Bertie when he attended a house party at Chatsworth.† Daisy took this opportunity to write him a "beautiful letter," which he gave to Alix to read, and she was "moved to tears." She, too, had received a letter from Daisy. "She begged me to

---

* Bertie's fussiness about dress extended to his mistresses. Skittles told a story about a lady who agreed, after some time, to gratify his wishes: "As soon as she had signified her willingness, he drew up a programme of her reception, the principal feature of which was that as the interview was to take place in the drawing room of a private house . . . 'we shall not,' he explained, 'be quite secure against interruption. But I will have screens put up. You must be sure to come in a small round hat and without a veil.'" (Fitzwilliam Museum, Wilfrid Blunt Papers, MS 10, Diary, 5 October 1910.)

† "Everybody seems gone mad about acting here," he told Daisy. "It is however a welcome change from the gambling." (Caroline Spurrier Archive, B to Daisy Warwick, 7 January 1898, Daisy's transcript.)

tell you," Bertie wrote, "that you had no enemies that she was aware of who were friends of hers, and that your name was not mentioned to her—or by her. I know, my darling, that she will now meet you with pleasure so that your position is, thank God! better now than it ever was since we have been such friends."

> She really quite forgives and condones the past, as I have cor-roborated what you wrote about our friendship having been pla-tonic for some years; you could not help, my loved one, writing to me as you did—though it gave me a pang—after the letters I have received from you for nearly nine years! But I think I could read "between the lines" everything you wished to convey. The end of your beautiful letter touched me more than anything—but how could you, my loved one, for a moment imagine that I should withdraw my friendship from you? On the contrary I mean to befriend you more than ever, and you cannot prevent my giving you the same love as the friendship I have always felt for you. Certainly the Princess has been an angel of goodness throughout all this, but then she is a lady![42]

This letter was written for Alix's eyes, and Alix responded on cue. She wrote no letter to Daisy, but sent her a crucifix wrapped in a piece of paper on which was written the barbed words: "From one who has suffered much and forgives all."[43]

Daisy had abdicated as *maîtresse en titre*. In exchange, she was granted forgiveness by Alix, which meant that she was reinstated at court. Daisy was triumphant, and wrote crowing to her friend W. T. Stead about her "complete reconciliation with the Princess of W[ales], and all estrangement on that score at an end."[44] Many years later, Daisy claimed that she would have remained with Bertie to the end, "but for an appeal made to her by Queen Alexandra to renounce him."[45] She remained friends with Bertie, who still addressed her as "my own adored little Daisywife."

There are hints that Daisy's pregnancy prompted Alix to confront Bertie. Of all Bertie's mistresses, Daisy Warwick posed the greatest threat to Alix and caused her the most unhappiness. Skittles, unreliable but well informed, related that after Bertie's death in 1910, Alix remarked: "Twelve years ago when I was so angry about Lady Warwick and the King expostulated and said I should get him into the divorce courts, I told him once and for all that he might have any woman he wished and I would not say a word."[46] It had taken Alix many years to come to terms with Bertie's philandering. As she later remarked: "But I thought I was *so-o-o* beautiful."[47] With Daisy's defection, some sort of truce had been reached between the prince and princess.

Daisy's son was born on 21 March 1898. The child was christened with only one name, Maynard, which was Daisy's maiden name, and the godfathers were Cecil Rhodes and Lord Rosebery, both sexually ambivalent men rumored to be homosexuals. The child was passed off as Lord Warwick's, but plenty of clues pointed to another father of this baby born after a gap of thirteen years. Bertie's name was sometimes mentioned, and the "D" symbol does indeed cluster around the Diamond Jubilee in June 1897, when the baby was presumably conceived.[48] Bertie took an interest in the "Diamond Jubilee" baby, as he called it in the letters he wrote to Daisy, but this need not imply paternity.[49] Daisy herself was in no doubt that the father was Joe Laycock.[50] Having a child by another man was the exit route that Lillie Langtry had chosen from her relationship with the prince, and in Daisy's case, as with Lillie, Bertie behaved generously, showing no sexual jealousy. Daisy by now had three children by three different men. No wonder that she made a virtue of sexual freedom, telling Lord Rosebery, whom she fruitlessly pursued, that "Far too much fuss, in my opinion, is made by women about personal morality which, after all, is entirely a matter for the individual."[51] Of the damage done to her children or other people's marriages, Daisy seemed unaware.

The "D" symbol recurs in Bertie's diary a decent interval after the birth of her son.[52] In June 1898, the prince stayed at Warwick Castle once more. Joe Laycock was also in the party, and Daisy took Bertie on a visit to Joseph Arch, the agricultural trade unionist, whose autobiog-

raphy she had edited. Bertie described the visit as "very interesting"—
Arch "remains what he always was—a working man, and does not
wish to be considered anything else!"[53] Daisy, however, found the occasion
excruciatingly embarrassing, as the prince sat beside the open
stove, prepared to listen sympathetically, while Arch harangued him
about class injustice.[54]

A flood of letters to "My own lovely little Daisy" continued to pour
from Bertie's pen. These letters only survive because, many years later,
Daisy disobeyed the orders of the royal advisers and made transcripts
of Bertie's correspondence before returning the originals. But they
give a glimpse of what the relationship was really like.

In spite of the Chatsworth agreement, the prince's feelings toward
Daisy seemed unaltered. "Though we do not see as much of one another
as formerly," he told her, "be assured that the sentiments and attachment
I have for you are in no wise diminished though the 'very
warm' feelings have under force of circumstances and by your own
wish, cooled down."[55] When she reproached him for neglecting her, he
replied: "Has it been my fault that we have not met so often lately as of
yore? Especially in the evenings?! Will you not try and consider me still
your best and most devoted friend? Have I deserved to forfeit it all?"

It is just 10 years since we became the great friends which I
hoped we were still. . . . Time and circumstances have doubtless
produced changes, but they should be faced, and not change a
friendship—may I say a devotion—which should last till "death
us do part." I do not blame you, and you should not blame me,
but how can we "kick against the pricks"? If I thought you did
not care for me any more even as a true friend, I should indeed
be the unhappiest and most miserable of men! My life seems an
easy and a happy one, but though I have no right to complain as
I receive so many benefits for which I cannot be grateful
enough—it is not always "a bed of roses" at home![56]

He told her: "You have become more serious, more independent
and I have felt for some time that I cannot be of much use to you in

your life. . . . Your continued devotion to me in spite of my many short-comings has astonished as well as pleased and touched me!"[57]

Daisy abdicated as mistress in January 1898. Alice Keppel was on the scene in February 1898. She makes her first appearance in Bertie's diary thus: "27 February 1898. Dine with Hon G. and Mrs. Keppel at 2 Wilton Crescent 8:45."[58] Mrs. Keppel was twenty-nine. She had thick chestnut hair, alabaster Scottish skin, wide shoulders, and a large bust. She was not photogenic. She had a deep throaty voice and she was very funny.

There are several stories about Bertie's first meeting with Alice. According to one version, related by Anita Leslie, it was at Sandown races where Bertie accosted Anita's grandfather John Leslie, who had Alice on his arm, demanded an introduction, and then strolled off with the lady.[59] Another story claims that they met at dinner with Lady Howe, and the prince spent the whole evening talking with Alice on the top landing "which rather shocked people, especially when they sat for a short time on two steps."[60] Others related that they met through Clarissa Bischoffsheim, society hostess wife of the German Jewish financier.[61] It was characteristic of Mrs. Keppel not to circulate her own version. She wrote no memoirs, and very few letters have survived; she was as clamlike as Daisy Warwick was gushingly indiscreet.

That Mrs. George Keppel should have become acquainted with the prince was hardly surprising. Through her marriage in 1891 to a younger son of the Earl of Albemarle, she had joined the outer circle of Marlborough House. Dutch by descent, the Keppels had been a dynasty of generals, admirals, and court officials. George Keppel's great-uncle, the five-foot-tall Admiral "Harry" Keppel, was a favorite at Marlborough House, and the tiny Princess Maud was nicknamed "Harry" after him. George's brother Derek was equerry to the Duke of York.*

---

* Another member of the York household was Daisy Warwick's sister-in-law Lady Eva ("Little Bird") Greville, who was lady-in-waiting to Princess Mary. Daisy's brother-in-law Sidney

Alice's family, the Edmonstones, were old established Scots land-owners. Her father was an admiral who inherited the baronetcy in 1871, and she was brought up at Duntreath Castle, fifteen miles from Glasgow. Money from coal and railways had paid for the rebuilding of the ancient castle in the Scots baronial style. Alice's daughter Violet remembered it smelling of cedar wood, tuberoses, gunpowder, and, oddly, minced meat.

At heart, Alice Keppel was a Scots gentry woman: "Intelligent, downright, devoid of pettiness or prejudice," as Violet wrote, "she loved a good argument, especially a political one."[62] She spoke clipped English, she was brisk and shrewd, and her feet were planted firmly on the ground. The youngest in a family of nine, as a child she was inseparable from her brother, Archie, the only boy. He was a year older than her and, according to Violet, they were like twins; "they seemed to complete one another." Archie detested shooting and "winced" through the Glorious Twelfth of August, the opening day of the grouse shooting season, while Alice swung sure-footedly across the moors, adored by all the keepers. "My mother all dynamism, initiative and, yes, virility, my uncle all gentleness, acquiescence, sensibility."[63] Masculinity was a characteristic of all Bertie's favorites. Lillie Langtry grew mannish in old age, and the hard-riding Daisy Warwick often lamented that she was not born a man.

Alice Keppel was modern. She smoked cigarettes, and she was very interested in money and how to make it, the more so as George Keppel was a third son and had very little. The Albemarles were grander than the Edmonstones but not as rich, and George and Alice started married life with only £20,000 of capital. George left the army and went into business, attempting to capitalize on his name. He did not prosper. In 1898, he was sued by a company promoter named Richard Prior for breach of contract when he resigned as director of the Grand Hotel and Theatre of Varieties in Ipswich. George won the case. The judge ruled it "a monstrous thing" if a gentleman "should be liable to a suit

---

Greville was an equerry to Bertie. Mistresses came and went, but the courtiers kept their jobs.

at the hands of the company promoter for all the losses which he said he had made because this gentleman had withdrawn his name."[64]

It was George, as Rebecca West once wrote, who was "the real beauty of the two."[65] He was six foot three and almost too immaculately dressed, with a curled mustache. Some said he was sexually cold. Perhaps this was what Violet meant when she said that "he never really grew up."[66]

Violet, the Keppels' first child, was born in June 1894. In adult life she fantasized that the king was her father. She claimed to be "Fitz Edward," and demanded to be addressed as Highness. But Violet was a mythomane and there is no reason to believe that Bertie knew Alice Keppel in 1893, let alone made love to her. Rumor, however, alleged that George Keppel was not Violet's father. Her biological father was supposed to be a Yorkshire banker and MP named Ernest Beckett. He was a glamorous widower, his American wife having died in 1891, and he allegedly had an affair with Alice Keppel. Whether Violet was the result, as is sometimes suggested, is impossible to tell.[67] Beckett was at the same time involved with another woman, a voluptuous South African divorcée, by whom he had a son who was born eight months after Violet.[68] For a married woman to have an affair before the birth of her first child was to defy social convention, and Mrs. Keppel was a conventional woman. Violet in later life never mentioned Ernest Beckett,[69] but she spoke of him when she was young; as for Alice Keppel, having committed this one indiscretion, she perhaps became super-discreet as a reaction. We shall probably never know.[70]

In July 1898, Bertie stayed at Waddesdon with Ferdinand de Rothschild. He wrote in his diary: "Prince of Wales falls downstairs . . . and fractures kneecap. Leave Waddesdon 3:30. . . . Dine in sitting room at Marlborough House."[71] Daisy, who was also a guest, related how she was running down a spiral staircase to breakfast when she heard a groan and discovered the heir to the throne lying at the bottom of the stairs unable to move. He had heard a bone crack. Daisy's husband appeared and tied the leg straight out onto one of the carrying poles of an invalid chair. The local doctor was called; he allowed the prince to eat breakfast with his leg down, which he did in excruciating pain: "He was ghastly white with beads of perspiration running down his forehead."[72] Some thought that the doctor's failure to splint the leg worsened the injury. Bertie insisted on returning to London, and at Aylesbury station his invalid chair broke and he was dropped humiliatingly and painfully onto the passenger bridge.[73]

Back at Marlborough House, the leg was placed in splints, and Bertie showed "wonderful pluck" in spite of the doctors' prognosis that his knee would always be stiff. Alix nursed him, and when Carrington visited, he thought the fifty-three-year-old princess, who was wearing a black-and-white-striped silk gown, looked about thirty-five. "Do you remember dining with us in this very room years ago," Alix asked Carrington, "when I was so ill and laid up?"[74]

Bertie raged at his enforced inactivity. "All my plans are upset, and I can make no future ones, nor can I at present form any idea when I shall be on my legs again."[75] For almost three months his diary is a painful blank.

Bertie was moved to Cowes, to recuperate on board the *Osborne*. Queen Victoria visited in her wheelchair, finding the prince lying on a couch under a tent that took up the entire stern of the ship.[76] Early in August, Alix was summoned to Denmark, where her mother lay dying. She left her daughter Victoria behind to nurse her father. On board the *Osborne*, Bertie became alarmingly ill with pleurisy, and Victoria was forced to send for Laking to apply a blister. Bertie for the first time in his life grew close to his daughter. Alix summoned her to join the family at the Queen of Denmark's funeral, but Victoria hated Denmark, and Bertie refused to allow her to travel.[77] He made no secret of his irritation with Alix, who dawdled in Denmark after her mother's death. "Surely," he told George, "dear Mama might for once in her life settle a definite date for her departure. . . . It is most inconvenient being kept in the dark for so long." Communication between husband and wife was nonexistent. "I have given up writing to her as she never writes to me now, not even a line to give me an indication when she thinks of leaving."[78]

Desperate to avoid the boredom of empty days, Bertie summoned old friends to visit. Daisy arrived, and found him ill-tempered: "His liver is bad and the enforced idleness is not making him look out pleasantly on the world."[79] Bertie wired Christopher Sykes, who was in Homburg recovering from a stroke. Unable even in extremis to say no, Sykes obeyed the summons. The journey nearly killed him. For Sykes's nephew, also Christopher, who wrote a brilliant, angry essay about his uncle and the prince, this was the climax of a long career of royal selfishness and bullying. The "great Xtopher" had almost bankrupted himself in entertaining the prince. But if Sykes was a victim, Bertie was an unwitting oppressor; he had nothing but pity for his old friend, he visited him in London, and he wrote to Sir Tatton Sykes imploring him to provide for his brother.[80]

At Marlborough House, a new court was taking shape. Francis Knollys, standing at his tall desk writing letters in a bold black hand, had by now served Bertie for almost thirty years. He was never quite comfortable in the twentieth century. There were three people who were to form an inner clique. One was Ernest Cassel. The others were the Marquis de Soveral and Mrs. George Keppel. All three were already in place by 1899.

Soveral, the Portuguese minister in London, was known as the Blue Monkey. His blue-black hair, jet-black imperial beard and heavy eyebrows, and the white flower in his buttonhole make him instantly recognizable among the faces lined up for the innumerable royal photographs. Bertie had known him since he was first posted to London in 1884, but it was after 1897 that Soveral became a central figure at Marlborough House. In August 1899, he accompanied the prince to Marienbad for his cure, and Bertie found him a "charming" traveling companion and "a great resource."[81] Soveral's clowning belied a sharp mind, and he was exceptionally well informed on European politics. He was flirtatious and liked to pose as a lady-killer. Being infinitely discreet, he conducted several flirtations at the same time.

He was Alix's favorite, filling the place in her affections left by Oliver Montagu; he always danced the first waltz at every ball with her, and he knew how to pitch his voice in a way that made it possible for her to hear.*[82]

Have you seen *The Importance of Being Ernest?* Bertie asked Soveral. "No, Sir," came the answer, "but I have seen the importance of being Ernest Cassel."[83]

The important Cassel filled the place left by Baron Hirsch, Bertie's financial adviser, who died suddenly in 1896. Cassel, a forty-five-year-old financial superstar, had been Hirsch's protégé. Hirsch allegedly left instructions to Cassel, his executor, that all Bertie's debts to him, which were rumored to amount to well over £300,000, should be written off.[84] Cassel took over the management of Bertie's investments, but on the astonishing understanding that he himself would absorb any losses.

Bertie and Cassel looked so similar—both bearded, cigar-smoking endomorphs dressed in double-breasted suits with rings on their fingers—that they were often mistaken for each other. It was even rumored that they were related—hence the joke about "Windsor Cassel."† Cassel was born in Cologne in 1852, the son of a Jewish banker, and came to England at seventeen. He was engaged as confidential clerk to the London house of the bankers Bischoffsheim and Goldschmidt, and, backed by Hirsch, whose wife was a Bischoffsheim, he amassed a massive fortune, speculating in railways. After the early death from tuberculosis of his wife, he secretly converted to Catholicism—an emotional act for a proud and humorless Jew who disdained small talk. He was greedy for honors, collected orders, and spent money on racehorses.

---

* According to Jim Lees-Milne (almost as unreliable as Skittles), the historian Gordon Brook-Shepherd came across some passionate letters at Windsor from Soveral to Queen Alexandra, "with whom he had an affair." (James Lees-Milne, *Holy Dread* [John Murray, 2001], p. 205 [1 December 1984].)

† Cassel was said to be the son of an illegitimate daughter of Prince Albert's brother, Duke Ernest of Saxe-Coburg, by an actress who married a Frankfurt Jew named Cassel. This story, sadly, lacks any foundation in fact. (Fitzwilliam Museum, Wilfrid Blunt Papers, MS 9, Diary, 27 June 1909; Camp, *Royal Mistresses*, pp. 355–56.)

Better than anyone, he understood the uses to which money could be put; he made himself indispensable to the prince's charitable projects.

Cassel became Bertie's most intimate male friend. From 1899, Bertie dined regularly with him either at 48 Grosvenor Square or at Moulton Paddocks, Cassel's opulent home near Newmarket. The prince was witness at the wedding of Cassel's only daughter, Maud, to the MP Wilfrid Ashley in 1901, and godfather to their daughter, asking for the child to be christened Edwardina (fortunately for her, perhaps, this was contracted to Edwina). Bertie bombarded Cassel with indecipherable notes about his investments.[85] The symbol *Ec,* presumably for Ernest Cassel, starts to appear in his diaries in 1899. By 1901, *Ec* is his most frequent correspondent of those noted in the diary, and the initials appear sixty-three times that year. In 1904, the King wrote forty-five letters to *Ec,* the same number in 1905, and fifty in 1906.

Finding his accommodation on Grosvenor Square too cramped, Cassel bought Brook House on Park Lane in 1905. He decorated the vast mansion with the rarest Italian marble. At the head of the staircase hung a portrait of King Edward. This was disconcertingly lifelike, causing guests to straighten themselves, and it proved a hazard, as some slipped and fell. Daisy Warwick considered that it was almost impossible to distinguish whether the portrait was of Bertie or of Cassel himself.[86]

The third new name that features regularly is the Hon. Mrs. George Keppel.

Bertie didn't pretend to be in love with Alice Keppel: "It is rather hard that I may not prefer the society of one lady to others without being supposed to be infatuated with her!"[87] Given his growing ill health and possible impotence, it's likely that he rarely if ever slept with her. But he was determined that his new favorite should not be persecuted in the way that Daisy had been. She must be accepted by society, and even by Alix.

That season, the word went out that wherever the prince was invited, the Hon. George and Mrs. Keppel must be asked, too. In September, Bertie paid a visit to the Edmonstone castle of Duntreath. "Mrs. GK was as usual the life and soul of the party," he told Emma Bourke.[88]

In 1899, the Keppels moved to the fashionable address of 30 Portman Square (now demolished). This was a square much favored by the Marlborough House set; indeed, it was almost an enclave of Bertie's court. The Keppels' neighbors included the Dukes of Fife and Manchester and (after 1901) Mrs. Eddy Bourke. It seems unlikely that George Keppel could have paid the rent out of his earnings. His business dealings were by that point an embarrassment. In 1900, a fraudulent company of which he was director wound up with debts of £4,000 and no assets, having tried to promote three companies, each of which failed.[89] George was found a job by Sir Thomas Lipton as wine manager in New York, "so he is provided for and got out of the way."[90] On the night of the 1901 census, Mrs. Keppel was alone at 30 Portman Square with two children, seven female servants, and three manservants—a substantial household. In December 1899, Alice Keppel paid her first visit to a Sandringham house party—unaccompanied by George.[91] On the day Bertie returned to London, he dined for the first time at 30 Portman Square.[92]

The people who invited the prince to house parties changed, too. Waddesdon was no longer an option: Ferdinand de Rothschild died suddenly in 1898. Often, however, when the people changed, the houses remained the same. The de Falbes died, but Bertie continued to stay at their house, Luton Hoo, which was bought by Sir Julius Wernher, the German financier and randlord.[93] Elveden, in Norfolk, was another house that was itself almost a royal subject. When Bertie's friend the Maharaja Duleep Singh died, it was bought by Lord Iveagh. Bertie once again slotted it into his shooting calendar. Glenmuick, near Balmoral, the estate that had once belonged to Sir James (MacTavish) Mackenzie, was bought by Lord Glenesk, who, as Algernon Borthwick, had founded *The Morning Post,* and Bertie became his guest of honor.

War was declared against the Boer republics in South Africa in October 1899. At first it barely impinged on Bertie's stately autumn progress of house parties and shooting. But the defeats of December 1899, known

as Black Week, jolted the monarchy into action. The Queen was stirred
to an unwonted display of leadership. "Please understand that there is
no one depressed in <u>this</u> house," she told Balfour. "We are not interested in the possibilities of defeat; they do not exist."[94] She canceled
her plan of spending Christmas at Osborne and remained at Windsor,
where she entertained the wives and children of soldiers at tea. "The
Queen is so right," wrote Bertie.[95]

    "I am very despondent and can think of nothing else," wrote the
prince in January.[96] The war gave him a new purpose. Day after day,
as the government poured more and more men into South Africa,
Bertie inspected detachments of troops before they sailed.[97] Tire-
lessly, he visited military hospitals and barracks, and he chaired the
Prince of Wales's Committee to coordinate the volunteer agencies
that proliferated to help the war effort.[98] With Alix, he traveled to
Southampton to receive a hospital ship returning full of wounded
soldiers. "Oh! this terrible war!" Alix kept saying as she made the
round of each man's bed. A burly six-foot Highlander was addressed
as "Poor little fellow."[99]

    The British reverses delighted the kaiser. He visited Sandringham in
November 1899 for the first time since 1880, restoring relations with
Bertie after the Vienna incident—though the German foreign minister
Bernhard von Bülow likened uncle and nephew to "a fat malicious
tom-cat, playing with a shrew-mouse," and Alix giggled at the special
barber William brought to curl his mustache.[100] But the kaiser was unable to resist rubbing salt in the wounds of Britain's humiliations in
South Africa. To Bertie he wrote after Black Week: "Instead of the
Angels' song 'Peace on earth and Goodwill to Men' the new century
will be greeted by shrieks of dying men killed and maimed by lyddite
shells. . . . Truly fin de siècle!"[101] He appended his own military obser-
vations and plan of campaign. On 4 February he wrote again, observing that the British were good losers, which was just as well. "Last year
in the great cricket match of England v Australia, the former took the
latter's victory quietly, with chivalrous acknowledgement of her op-
ponent."[102] This was too much. Bertie exploded that the war was nothing like a cricket match. "The British Empire is now fighting for its

very existence, as you know full well."[103] When Lord Roberts's strategy in South Africa succeeded, William claimed the credit. Little did Bertie know that his nephew was, meanwhile, intriguing with the Russians to invade India.

The war made Britain acutely unpopular in France. The government wanted Bertie to attend the opening of the 1900 Paris Exhibition, but he refused. For him to go, he said, "would be a positive slight to the Queen, and would be regarded by Frenchmen as a proof that he was indifferent to the vile caricatures and lampooning of his own mother by their Press."[104] Victoria supported him. The war effort brought Bertie and Victoria politically close. There was no more squabbling over secret dispatches: They both had too much to do. In March, when the relief of the Siege of Ladysmith brought a turning point in the war, Victoria drove around London, doing what Bertie had urged her to do all those years ago, and the spontaneous effect was electric—"as if a great wave of devotion and sympathy had passed over the capital. . . . Your Majesty does not much admire Queen Elizabeth," wrote Lord Rosebery, "but the visit to London was in the Elizabethan spirit."[105]

"I have no plans at present," wrote Bertie in March. "How can one have any when the war is going on?"[106] That Boer War winter, confined to London, Bertie dined out most nights. There were three London houses where he ate dinner so often that in his diary he wrote only the address. One was 30 Portman Square: Mrs. Keppel. The second was 17 Grosvenor Crescent, and the third was 35 Belgrave Square.

Number 17 Grosvenor Crescent was a large, heavy mansion off Hyde Park Corner, just behind St. George's Hospital, the home of two wealthy unmarried sisters, Agnes and Fanny Keyser. Bertie's first dinner with the Keyser sisters is always said to have taken place in 1898, but in fact he dined with Agnes Keyser back in 1895.[107] Agnes's money came from stockbroking; her family was linked to the Bischoffsheims, which may have been how Bertie came to know her. She was the least glamorous of his mistresses—if indeed she was one: a middle-aged spinster, controlling and governess-like, who fed him plain food. But in the winter of 1900, Bertie's regular visits to 17 Grosvenor Crescent had a purpose. Though untrained, Agnes had a vocation for nursing, and at Grosvenor Crescent she and Fanny started a private hospital for officers wounded in South Africa. As well as eating rice pudding, Bertie visited "Sister Agnes" in her starched uniform in the private ward. After the war, he persuaded his rich friends to subscribe, and Agnes Keyser's ward grew into King Edward VII's Hospital for Officers.*[108]

Number 35 Belgrave Square was the home of Mrs. Arthur Paget, the wife of General Paget, a friend of Bertie's, who was serving in South Africa. Minnie Paget, now in her midforties, was an heiress, the daughter of a New York hotel owner, the self-made millionaire Paran Stevens. Her ambitious mother had driven her up and down Manhattan with a coach waiting outside every venue so that the young girl didn't miss a single party. One of Edith Wharton's original Buccaneers—her brother was briefly engaged to Wharton—Minnie had come to London in search of a husband, had stayed at Sandringham, and had knitted Bertie a waistcoat. The Boer War was her finest hour. She raised £7,000 for war widows and orphans with a masque at the Haymarket Theatre, and she funded a hospital ship.

Minnie was not well liked. She was sharp and brittle; some people said that she was incapable of telling the truth.[109] When the seventeen-year-old American Consuelo Vanderbilt came to London (she later married the Duke of Marlborough), she was introduced to Minnie, who agreed to bring her out. "She was considered handsome," wrote Consuelo: "to me, with her quick wit and worldly standards, she was Becky Sharpe incarnate. . . . I realised with a sense of acute discomfort that I was being appraised by a pair of hard green eyes."[110] During Daisy's reign, the Americans had fallen out of favor at Marlborough House. Now, with the rise of Mrs. Keppel, they were back. When Minnie entertained the prince with dinner and cards, she could sense the sweet smell of social power. "Let us be either four or eight at dinner," he wrote, "but they should all be bridge players."[111]

* The 1901 census reveals six young officers described as "visitors" at 17 Grosvenor Crescent. The two sisters each deducted ten years from their age.

Brussels Nord station, 4 April 1900, 5:30 p.m. After strolling about the platform for thirty minutes, Bertie boarded the special train heading for Copenhagen on a visit to the King of Denmark. He sat down beside Alix opposite an open window, and a servant handed him tea. As the train pulled out of the station, a young man mounted the carriage step, put his gloved hand through the window, and fired two shots at a range of two yards. Alix felt a bullet whizz past and bounce off the woodwork just above Bertie's head. "If he had not been so bad a shot I don't see how he could possibly have missed me," wrote Bertie.[112]

The round-faced young man was hurled to the ground by the station manager and arrested. He was only fifteen, an anarchist named Jean Baptiste Sipido, and he had bought the revolver for three francs in a market and loaded it in a lavatory before making the assassination attempt. He claimed he was avenging the deaths Bertie had caused in South Africa.[113] It was Bertie's first—and only—near-assassination experience at a time when Europe teemed with anarchists, such as the man who had killed Elizabeth, Empress of Austria, eighteen months before, stabbing her with a shoemaker's awl ("that poor charming inoffensive woman," wrote Bertie).[114] According to Charlotte Knollys, who was in the carriage, Bertie "never even changed colour, and the Princess behaved equally well."[115] As the train steamed out of the station, the crowd on the platform cheered, and the prince and princess bowed from the open window.[116]

Bertie displayed considerable courage, and he was justifiably miffed when Salisbury refused to move a parliamentary vote of congratulation. Such a vote would have involved calling a special sitting of the House of Lords, wrote Salisbury, who was a master of the crushing putdown: "It was thought better not to take that course, as it was not then known that the pistol contained a bullet, which the extreme youth of the culprit rendered doubtful."[117] Bertie cursed his cousin King Leopold II for failing to make an example of Sipido, who was acquitted by the Belgian courts on account of being underage.[118] Afterward, the prince always took with him an *Agent de Sûreté,* or detective, when he traveled abroad.[119] The incident gave him a sharp reminder that "we are all in God's hands! in no one else's!"[120]

In South Africa, the war at last turned to victory. News of the relief of the Siege of Mafeking reached London on 18 May. Bertie and Alix were at Covent Garden for Wagner's *Lohengrin*. After the second act, someone shouted the news from the gallery, and everyone rose to their feet cheering wildly. The singer Madame Marchesi, who was in the stalls, started "God Save the Queen," which was sung by the entire house.[121]

Later that month, Bertie's horse Diamond Jubilee won the Derby. That year he also won the Grand National with Ambush II. But God's hands were never far away, and in July came the "terribly sad news" of the death of his fifty-five-year-old brother Alfred in Coburg.[122] Affie had been Prince Albert's favorite son; so much cleverer than Bertie as a boy, in middle age he was a friendless alcoholic.* In 1898, he collapsed on a visit to Egypt. "I don't believe Aunt Marie has the faintest idea of the gravity of his case," wrote Bertie; "every year his health gets worse."[123] Affie's only son, Alfred, committed suicide in 1899, and Affie himself was diagnosed with cancer of the throat, though he died of heart failure.

Victoria was devastated. "Oh God! My poor darling Affie gone too!"[124] Bertie told Vicky that he could "never remember being so upset before," but he had grown apart from Affie.[125] In truth, he was far more upset by Vicky's condition.

Bertie had known that Vicky was suffering from breast cancer for almost two years. She complained of "lumbago" as the cancer metastasized into her spine. In August 1900, Bertie traveled from Homburg

---

* Succeeding his uncle Ernest as Duke of Coburg in 1893 had not made things easier for him. His wealthy wife, Marie, the sister of Czar Alexander III, paid off Duke Ernest's debts, in addition to lavishing money on Clarence House, and by 1899 the Edinburghs were almost bankrupt. Affie appealed to Victoria for financial help, and she paid £95,000 toward his debts. Bertie was kept informed. (RA VIC/Add C07/1, Arthur Bigge to Francis Knollys, 3 April 1899. RA VIC/Add C07/1, Alfred to QV, 14 August 1899 [copy]. RA VIC/Add C07/1, Arthur Ellis to Alfred, 15 August 1899. RA VIC/Add C07/1, Fleetwood Edwards to Francis Knollys, 23 August 1899. RA VIC/Add C07/1, Fleetwood Edwards to B, 26 August 1899. RA VIC/Add C07/1, Lord Monson to Bigge, 23 August 1899.)

to be close to his sister at Friedrichshof. By now she was in constant pain. Bertie's "dear kind face" was always a comfort, but there was little he could do to help.[126] He consulted Laking, who advised injections of morphine rather than strychnine or arsenic, but the kaiser refused to allow the English doctor to attend his mother. "It would create a most deplorable feeling here," he told Victoria.[127] By October, Vicky reported that the morphine only dulled the pain for ten minutes. "The terrible nights of agony are worse than ever, no rest, no peace. The tears rush down my cheeks when I am not shouting with pain."[128] The doctors alerted Bertie to be in "constant anxiety" about her.[129] Her letters were so harrowing that Helena and Beatrice stopped reading them aloud to the Queen.

"Poor dear Mama was not looking well," Bertie wrote to Vicky on 19 November 1900.[130] He had been summoned to Windsor by the Queen's doctor, Sir James Reid, who was concerned about her symptoms. Victoria, who had risen so splendidly to the war, was suddenly older and shrunken. For months she had complained of insomnia, lack of appetite, disordered digestion, and depression.

Reid found it hard to persuade the prince to take his warnings seriously. Bertie seemed to think his mother was merely out of sorts, and he cheerfully expected that Christmas at Osborne would "take her out of herself."[131] This was wishful thinking. From the day she arrived at Osborne (18 December), Victoria was an invalid, confined to her bedroom. Most of the time she was "childish"—drowsy, incoherent, and confused. She had lost her royal rage, and she apathetically accepted things that had formerly irritated her. Reid suspected "cerebral degeneration," or dementia, and his diagnosis was confirmed by two other physicians.[132]

Beatrice shut her eyes to her mother's descent into childishness. Like an unmarried daughter whose status depended on an aged parent, the widowed youngest child continued to deal with the Queen's correspondence and write her journal each night as if nothing had changed. Few dared whisper the possibility of a regency, but the fact was, the Queen was now incapable.[133]

Helena telegraphed Bertie with a cheerful report each day, omitting all the worrying symptoms. She freely admitted that she did not want Bertie and Alix in the house. Bertie, for his part, was only too willing to believe her. He still discounted Reid's gloomy prognostications, encouraged by Laking, who reported back from Osborne that the Queen was her normal self. In fact, Victoria put on a special effort when she saw Laking. When Reid asked Bertie to approve a bulletin in the Court Circular about the Queen's poor health, he refused to give consent. The death of his mother was somehow unimaginable. Victoria herself, in spite of her confusion, seemed dimly aware that she was dying. "Is there anyone in the house?" she asked Reid one afternoon. "Is the Prince of Wales here?" Reid asked if she wanted him. "I do not advise it at present," she replied, lapsing back into drowsy dementia.[134]

The pretense that the Queen was in normal health continued until 19 January, when Reid happened to walk into the room of private secretary Arthur Bigge as he was shouting down the mouthpiece of the newfangled telephone to Francis Knollys at Marlborough House. Reid told Bigge to advise the Prince of Wales that the Queen might die at any time. He then confronted Helena and persuaded her to write an accurate telegram to Bertie. By five o'clock that afternoon, Bertie had arrived at Osborne.

The first medical bulletin was issued that day: "The Queen is suffering from great physical prostration accompanied by symptoms that cause anxiety."[135] Victoria rallied in the evening, and in a brief moment of lucidity she told Reid: "I think the Prince of Wales should be told I have been very ill, as I am sure he would feel it." When Reid asked if she would like the prince to come, she replied, "Certainly, but he needn't stay."[136] But Bertie didn't see her. He agreed with Reid that it was better not to tell the Queen that he was in the house. He even declined to look into the bedroom while she slept. He had never seen his mother in bed. Victoria was confused, and so ill that she needed oxygen in the night, but Bertie returned to London the next day to receive the kaiser.

None of the royal family wanted the kaiser there. He had, in fact, been summoned by the doctor, Reid, who was in collusion with him.

Without informing any of the family—"I knew the Princesses would disapprove"—Reid had telegrammed William, aware that he wanted to be present at the death.[137]

From Buckingham Palace, Bertie kept in contact by telephone. The doctors expected the Queen's death imminently. The next morning at eight a.m., Bertie and William left for Osborne.

That evening, for the first time, Bertie sat by his mother's bedside. She had been lifted from the grand mahogany marital bed and lay in a small bed in the center of the room, a tiny, huddled figure. After he had left, the semiconscious Queen took Reid's hand and kissed it repeatedly. Mrs. Tuck, the Queen's dresser, more alert or more sensitive to Victoria's needs, asked her if it was the Prince of Wales she wanted. "Yes," said the Queen.

Bertie returned to her bedside, and she said, "Kiss my face."[138] Then she put out her arms and said, "Bertie," whereupon "he embraced her and broke down completely."[139]

The next morning, the Queen was unconscious and clearly dying. The family was summoned to her bedside. Beatrice, Helena, and Louise told the blind Queen the names of the people in the room. The only name they omitted to mention was that of the kaiser, who was standing at her bedside. Reid asked Bertie why the kaiser was not named. Bertie replied, "It would excite her too much." Later, when the Queen was alone, Reid went to Bertie and asked if he could take the kaiser to see her. Bertie relented. "Certainly, and tell her that the Prince of Wales wishes it," he replied.[140]

In the afternoon, the family was summoned once more. Bertie sat at one side of the bed, behind Reid, who knelt supporting the Queen in a semi-upright position on her pillows. The kaiser knelt opposite supporting her with his good arm.

"At 6:30 she breathes her last," wrote Bertie in his diary.[141] That was all. Not even a hint of the turmoil this intensely emotional man felt at the death of the most powerful woman in his life.

PART THREE

King

CHAPTER 21

King Edward the Caresser

1901–2

At fifty-nine, Bertie was a reluctant heir. "I would have liked it 20 years ago," he said. The story circulated among the courtiers that, the moment Victoria died, Alix knelt before her husband and kissed his hand in homage. "Sire!" she said. Bertie replied, in German, "It has come too late."[1]

When the news of Queen Victoria's death reached the journalists waiting at the gates of Osborne, a mad crowd in carriages and on bicycles raced down the hill to the post office, whooping, "Queen dead!"[2] Victoria died at 6:30 p.m. on 22 January 1901, and it was not until 10:30 the next morning that the Prince of Wales, as he still was, left Osborne for London, accompanied by the royal dukes, to hold the Accession Council at 3 p.m. and take the oaths of sovereignty.[3] The prime minister, Salisbury, who saw him before the council, found him "very much upset. We had a long talk alone. He broke down."[4] Speaking in a room crowded ten deep with jostling privy councillors, the new King's voice cracked as he announced the death of his "beloved" mother. He declared his wish to be styled Edward, desiring that the name Albert should stand alone for his great and wise father, Albert the Good. Afterward, to the consternation of the clerks, who had neglected to bring a shorthand writer, it was discovered that he had made this definitive eight-minute speech entirely without notes.[5] Then the royal dukes kissed his hand on bended knee, followed by Lord Salisbury (who was annoyed when Bertie signaled the old man need not kneel if he did not wish), and the Duke of Devonshire. Though Bertie was now King, Alix refused to be called Queen or allow anyone to kiss her hand until Victoria was buried.

At Osborne the dead Queen's body was prepared for her coffin. In accordance with the "Instructions" that Victoria had written in 1897 for her dresser to open directly after her death, Sir James Reid arranged Albert's dressing gown beside her, together with a plaster cast of his hand and a long list of trinkets, photographs, and handkerchiefs. Victoria had lived for forty years in the borderlands between life and death and, like a barbarian queen (or perhaps a child), she desired to surround herself with keepsakes and mementos to take with her to the next world. Reid obeyed her instructions to the letter, keeping secret the orders that he knew would enrage her heir. At the last minute, he placed a favorite photograph of John Brown together with a case containing his hair in her left hand, which he concealed behind Alix's flowers.[6] On her finger was Albert's wedding ring, and in accordance with her instructions, she also wore the plain gold ring that had belonged to John Brown's mother, and which she had worn every day since his death.[7]

No monarch had been buried for sixty-four years, and the precedents had been forgotten. The Duke of Norfolk as Earl Marshal claimed the hereditary right to organize the funeral, but when Fritz Ponsonby, assistant private secretary to Queen Victoria, arrived at the Earl Marshal's office and spoke to the heralds, he found "absolute chaos."[8] Ponsonby took charge himself.

"The Queen," as Bertie called his mother's coffin, left Osborne in the royal yacht *Alberta*. Bertie followed in the *Victoria and Albert*. He noticed that the yacht's royal standard was at half-mast. The captain told him, "The Queen is dead, Sir."

"The King of England lives," replied Bertie, and the standard was hoisted.[9] The procession of great warships that glided behind the tiny *Alberta* across the gleaming blue Solent, booming their salutes, was, said Princess Mary, "one of the saddest finest things I have ever seen, a mixture of great splendour and great simplicity."[10] The cortège arrived at Victoria station at 8:00 a.m. on 2 February 1901. Wearing plumed helmet and cloak, Bertie rode for the last time beside his mother. The kaiser was by his side in the procession to Paddington. The crowds with their heads uncovered in deepest mourning were a sight "never to be forgotten," he told Vicky.[11]

From Paddington, the funeral procession traveled by train to Windsor. When the Queen's coffin arrived, the horses drawing the gun carriage bolted, breaking the traces. Ponsonby hastily improvised, and the gun carriage was dragged up the steep hill by the men of the naval guard of honor.* In St. George's Chapel, the Earl Marshal had forgotten to seat anyone in the choir, and Sir Spencer Ponsonby-Fane, the seventy-seven-year-old blind and bumbling comptroller to the Lord Chamberlain, shuffled about moving royals into the empty stalls. By some oversight, the King's son-in-law the Duke of Fife had been left off the list of guests. Bertie loudly upbraided Fritz Ponsonby in front of Fife. Afterward he took Ponsonby by the arm and told him he had done wonders. "I had to say something strong, as Fife was so hurt," he confided.[12]

The accession of an overweight fifty-nine-year-old philanderer hardly thrilled the imagination. "We grovel before fat Edward—Edward the Caresser as he is privately named," wrote Henry James, who thought

---

* This last-minute change was enshrined in tradition: Nine years later, Bertie's coffin, too, was pulled from the station at Windsor by the naval guard of honor.

the new King was "quite particularly <u>vulgar</u>!"[13] Rudyard Kipling referred to him as a "corpulent voluptuary." Even *The Times* could not resist a breath of criticism, causing a sensation with a triple negative: "We shall not pretend that there is nothing in his long career which those who respect and admire him could not wish otherwise."[14] The most that could be said for him, thought Wilfrid Blunt, was that "he has certain good qualities of amiability and of philistine tolerance of other people's sins and vulgarities which endear him to rich and poor, to the Stock Exchange Jews, to the Turf Bookmakers and to the Man in the Street."*[15]

Few kings have come to the throne amid lower expectations. But Albert Edward turned out well. Like Shakespeare's Prince Hal, the dissipated prince evolved into a model king.

Bertie was a poor talker and worse letter writer. He was not witty and he was very easily bored. Yet he possessed charisma. Instantly recognizable in his curly brimmed top hat and frock coat or double-breasted suit, he combined warmth with dignity and a sense of occasion. People mocked his inability to pronounce his *r*'s, and some accused him of speaking with a guttural German accent. Others claimed that his diction was "perfectly modulated."[16] He had a deep, throaty smoker's voice and he never used notes; he had perfected the art of the impromptu speech.

The stories told about him stress his insistence on correctness and protocol. When the American Consuelo, Duchess of Marlborough, wore a diamond crescent in her hair instead of the regulation tiara at dinner, he remarked: "The Princess has taken the trouble to wear a tiara. Why have you not done so?"[17] Fortunately, Consuelo possessed a

---

* Max Beerbohm, who spent a lifetime caricaturing and mimicking Bertie, told a story about the dinner at the Carlton Hotel that Bertie attended in 1900 to launch the *Dictionary of National Biography*. Finding the company of Sidney Lee, Leslie Stephen, and forty writers heavy going, he looked around morosely. "Who is that little parson?" he asked Lee in his guttural English, pointing at a certain Canon Ainger. "Vy is <u>he</u> here? He is not a wr-ri-ter!" (Max always gave Bertie a German accent.) "He is a very great authority," said Lee, apologetically, "on Lamb." This was too much for Bertie. "He put down his knife and fork in stupefaction; a pained outcry of protest heaved from him: 'On lamb!'" (S. N. Behrman, *Conversation with Max* [Hamish Hamilton, 1960], p. 85.)

tiara of her own, but the King could be merciless. To Fritz Ponsonby, who appeared dressed in a tail coat for a picture exhibition before lunch, he said: "I thought everyone must know that a short jacket is always worn with a silk hat at a private view in the morning."[18]

"My dear fellow," he remarked to a groom-in-waiting accompanying him to a wedding, "where is your white waistcoat? Is it possible that you are thinking of going to a *wedding* in a black waistcoat?"[19] He insisted that all the gentlemen of his household stayed up until he went to bed, which was usually between 1 and 1:30. Once he noticed that someone had slipped off, and he ordered the page to fetch him back. It turned out to be the seventy-five-year-old Sir Dighton Probyn, who was feeling unwell. Bertie roared with laughter, but Sir Dighton was not amused.*[20] Ladies were expected to kiss the King's hand. The Duchess of Mecklenburg-Strelitz observed, "He always pokes it out for that, too funny, but never embraces in return! Altogether this is quite a new fashion for ladies, to have to do so."[21] Not just ladies, either. The King ordered that his grandchildren, of whom he was very fond, kiss his hand before being kissed on the cheek, and address him as sir. Even the Prince of Wales kissed hands. These things really mattered to Bertie. Daisy Warwick noticed that he would turn from discussing European politics to consider the buttons and tabs on a regimental uniform "with a gravity that seemed quite out of proportion to the matter in hand."[22] Perhaps his obsession with correctness reflected a need to impose order and control on a chaotic world; but it chimed perfectly with *fin de siècle* imperial Britain, a society fixated on hierarchy and rank, which were dramatized through elaborately graded honors and decorations.

"I regret the mystery and awe of the old court," wrote Lord Esher.†[23] Bertie was determined to sweep it away. The camarilla of women, headed by his sister Beatrice, who had dominated Victoria's court, was purged. The royal palaces, shrouded and secret in his mother's reign,

---

* As Colonel of Probyn's Horse, Probyn was an honorary Sikh, and he never cut his beard, which hid the Victoria Cross he had won in the Indian Mutiny.
† Reginald Brett succeeded his father as Viscount Esher in 1899. As permanent secretary of the Office of Works from 1895, he was responsible for the royal palaces.

were restored to their true glory and thrown open. The monarchy was based once more in London. Buckingham Palace, not occupied regularly for forty years, became the seat of the throne. All the old ceremonial was revived, reinvented, and made glamorous again.[24]

At Windsor, wearing a pot hat and swinging a walking stick, Bertie clumped around the rooms with his dog at his heels, followed by Sir Arthur Ellis and Lord Esher. Queen Alexandra wished to live in the state apartments, but Bertie insisted on occupying Queen Victoria's old rooms. "There was quite a smart difference of opinion," wrote Esher, but the King had his way.[25] Day after day he poked around the castle, installing electric light, moving furniture, rehanging pictures. "I don't know much about *A-rr-t* but I think I know something about *Arr-r-angement*," he growled.[26]

His iconoclasm was more than a matter of taste. It was a posthumous revenge against his mother. Victoria's mementos of Brown and Albert were ruthlessly swept aside. "Alas!" Alix told Vicky after a visit to Copenhagen, "during my absence Bertie has had all your Mother's rooms dismantled and all her precious things removed."[27] At Windsor, Victoria's Indian servants wandered like "uneasy spirits," no longer "immobile and statuesque" as of old.[28] On Bertie's orders, a bonfire of the Queen's letters to the Munshi was made at his home, Frogmore Cottage, solemnly watched by Alix, Beatrice, and the Munshi himself.[29] Soon the Munshi took his leave of the King and returned to India on a pension, shadowed by detectives who were worried that he had smuggled out compromising letters written by Victoria.[30] Beatrice, Victoria's widowed daughter, who had lived both at Buckingham Palace and Windsor, was politely advised to remove her furniture as soon as possible.[31]

For the opening of his first Parliament on 14 February 1901, Bertie planned every detail. "I wished it to be in as grand State as possible," he told Vicky.[32] Victoria had last attended the opening of Parliament fifteen years before, in 1886, and on the seven occasions when she opened it after Albert's death, she refused to appear in state.[33] Now, for the first time in forty years, the monarch drove to Parliament in the old state coach. Drawn by eight cream horses, the tall glass coach towered above the crowd, lumbering and swaying on its leather springs. The House of Lords was packed as Bertie walked in procession, wearing a flowing crimson robe and the Imperial State Crown, unused since 1861. Alix, clasping his left hand, wore a black mourning dress and the Koh-i-noor diamond beneath her scarlet robes, and Queen Victoria's small diamond crown with a flowing crepe veil.*[34] Both she and Bertie were "very alarmed & shy & *emotionné*," but her regal appearance created a sensation.[35]

With Alix at his side ("I . . . *heard* & felt my heart beating loud all the time we were seated on that very conspicuous place," she wrote), Bertie read the speech himself—unlike Victoria, who had ceased reading it in person after 1861.[36] Most novel of all, the King's women friends were seated in the Ladies' Gallery. There was speculation as to whether he would address them. During his speech he looked up twice, but managed to maintain his dignity.[37] As *The Times* commented, the present generation had seen nothing comparable in splendor and solemnity, not even the Jubilees of 1887 or 1897.[38] What they were witnessing was the reinvention of monarchy as spectacle.

By projecting monarchy as tradition, Bertie was, in fact, modernizing and reforming it. He considered Victoria's withdrawal and retreat into invisibility to be almost a dereliction of duty. The sovereign, in his view, must not just do the work, but *be seen* to do it. Bertie embraced state ceremonial with the expertise of a man whose experience of foreign courts, especially those of Germany and Russia, was unequalled. Not for nothing had he whiled away so many evenings on theatergoing. Historians have looked at the revival and invention of tradition and the pomp of the Jubilees of 1887 and 1897 and linked them to the resurgence of popularity for the Victorian monarchy.[39] The brief but significant reign of Edward VII, however, has been underestimated. It was he who made sure that ceremonial was intentionally shifted to the top of the Crown's agenda.

---

* Queen Victoria's tiny crown, set with one thousand diamonds, was constructed in 1870. Being colorless, it was thought appropriate for widowhood.

Victoria had lived as a reclusive widow, retreating into the private, domestic sphere. As queen, she was both "powerful and powerless."[40] Her retirement from the public sphere dramatized her powerlessness, facilitating a transition to a monarchy with a merely symbolic role. Behind the scenes, however, the apparently powerless Victoria clung tenaciously to her political authority: She demanded to be kept informed, she debated policy, and she approved ministerial appointments. With regard to her private, family life, she pursued a policy of transparency. She issued *Leaves from a Journal of Our Life in the Highlands,* she authorized revealing biographies of Albert and her daughter Alice, she published photographs, and she chronicled her daily routine in the Court and Social column of *The Times.* This created an illusion of intimacy that played into the narrative of the widow Queen.*

Bertie's program with respect to the private sphere was the opposite of his mother's. This most visible of monarchs was extraordinarily secretive about his private life. Less is known about his family than that of any other recent sovereign.[41] Victoria and Albert's invention of the "royal family" as being constantly on show—an idea that was revived later in the twentieth century—was quietly dropped.

The difference in style can be seen from the diaries kept by mother and son. Queen Victoria's journal is among the great documents of the nineteenth century—confessional, self-examining, and often devastating in its candor, sweeping judgments, and violent emotions. Bertie's diary, which he wrote each night before dinner, consists mainly of appointments and lists: names of guests and racehorses, times of trains, numbers of birds shot.[42] Often he refers to himself formally in the third person, as The King. There are no feelings, no reflections, no opinions. It is dry, even repellent, to read, but the diary is a remarkable document of kingship, mapping a life spent largely in the public eye.

---

* A 1970 survey of dreams about Queen Elizabeth II found that people continued to dream about Queen Victoria seventy years after her death, so deeply was her narrative encrypted in the subconscious of the British people. (Brian Masters, *Dreams About the Queen,* Blond and Briggs, 1972, pp. 83–84.)

"Will he sell his horses and scatter his Jews or will Reuben Sassoon be enshrined among the crown jewels and other regalia? Will he become desperately serious?" Winston Churchill asked his mother, Jennie. "Will he continue to be friendly to you? Will the Keppel be appointed 1st Lady of the Bedchamber?"[43]

The new King made it plain from the start that he had no intention of dropping his lady friends. When Emma Bourke wrote a letter of condolence on the Queen's death, Bertie cabled in reply: "Much touched by your kind and sympathetic letter; shall never forget any of my old friends."[44] He continued to shower Emma with notes, and still addressed her as *ma chère amie* or "My dearest little friend," but "My Dear Mrs. Bourke" appears more often, and he signs himself ER instead of the old AE.

For the first year of the reign of Edward VII, mourning for Queen Victoria imposed a ban on society. "Racing has no interest for me this year," Bertie told Emma Bourke, and his horses were leased to the Duke of Devonshire.[45] But within two months of his mother's death, he had resumed his habit of dining out in London. Dining out was something that Queen Victoria had never done; but the King "has been making a good many small 'Mrs. George' [Keppel] dinners lately," wrote Carrington.[46]

Every effort was made to keep the King's relationship with Mrs. Keppel out of the newspapers. In May, he was on board Sir Thomas Lipton's yacht *Shamrock* with her when the masts snapped and all the canvas fell over the side. For a moment it looked as though no one would escape alive. The accident was reported in the press; but instead of Mrs. Keppel, the name of Lady Londonderry was printed, and she allowed it to stand uncontradicted.[47]

Not all of Prince Hal's old companions were allowed to come to court, however. The person who played Falstaff to Bertie's Henry V was Daisy Warwick.

Daisy's relationship with Joe Laycock was spinning into melodrama.

When Laycock became involved with a younger woman, Kitty, the Marchioness of Downshire, Daisy lost all sense of proportion, stealing Kitty's love letters to Joe and sending them to Kitty's husband, Lord Downshire, who sued for divorce and was granted a decree nisi. Now that Kitty was free, Laycock felt that he was honor bound to marry her. Daisy, made frantic by the unintended consequences of her action, became pregnant once more. When Laycock responded with indifference, she had the pregnancy aborted. The operation was botched, and she nearly died of septicemia.[48]

Alix wrote Daisy a "very kind" letter asking her to avoid the King.[49] There was a real risk that she would drag Bertie once again into the divorce courts. Daisy also received a visit from Lord Esher. "He told me, with charming courtesy and frankness, that he thought it would be well for all concerned if my close association with great affairs were to cease, as it was giving rise to hostile comment which distressed Queen Alexandra."[50] Daisy blamed her dismissal on her socialist ideas. In fact, she was dropped because her scandalous behavior had become a liability.

Alix flatly refused to be known as Queen Consort, and insisted on being styled Queen.[51] Bertie demanded that she be treated with full dignity. Within a month of his accession, he made her a Lady of the Order of the Garter, and when the herald raised objections about placing her banner in St. George's Chapel, alleging that women were not admitted to the order, the King curtly ordered him to do it.[52]

Though he was generous with honors and titles, it's hard to escape the conclusion that Bertie marginalized Alix. She complained that he did not permit her to assume her position as Queen, as "he takes everything to himself, lets her do nothing in the way of carrying out her duties."[53] Even such things as giving Red Cross prizes, which Alix had done for years—the Red Cross was her particular charity—Bertie insisted on performing himself. He even took charge of the redecoration of the palaces.

It had been sixty-four years since England had had a king, and no one could remember what the queen should do. "Aunt Alix," wrote Princess Mary, "is quite ready to do what is right if only she is told, but just at present everyone is quite at sea."[54]

The seventy-nine-year-old Duchess of Mecklenburg-Strelitz, a granddaughter of George III who could recall the court of William IV and Queen Adelaide, was summoned from Germany to give advice. How "extraordinary" it was, she wrote, "that nobody knows anything more about the last Reign but one!"[55] She observed that Bertie, who was every bit as jealous of his prerogatives as Victoria had been, blithely assumed court duties that belonged properly to the Queen. Alix had been told "to stand bye, mute & still, no presentations at the Drawing-room but to him; I told her Queen Adelaide had them presented all, she having to kiss Duchesses, Marchionesses (Countss [Countesses] I don't know) with two kisses, then one kiss down to Earls daughters, after which giving her hand to be kissed, and the man kneeling on one knee."[56] When Bertie was informed that the Queen and not the King should kiss the young ladies, he objected strongly.[57]

Alix's charitable duties were considerable. She concentrated on her own particular interest, nursing. Some found this irritating. "She is the stupidest woman in England," said Lord Haldane, when the Queen was suggested for the Territorial Army nurses. "Can't we do without a royal President?"

"He could not," was the comment of one historian.[58]

Six nursing bodies carried her name, but, partly perhaps because she lacked advisers, Alix made no attempt to channel her charitable impulses into a larger role, in the way that Queen Mary was later to reach out to the poor.[59] Nor (to her credit) did she attempt to interfere in domestic politics. What political views she did have were personal. She was still haunted by the nightmare of Germany, the "robbers' den," overrunning poor little Denmark, and her distrust of Kaiser William was as strong as her loyalty for her siblings in Russia and Greece was deep.

On the first anniversary of Queen Victoria's death, a sparrow flew into the service in the mausoleum at Windsor. "Do you think that little bird could be Mama's spirit?" asked one of the princesses. No, shot back Alix, "or it would not have made a mess on Beatrice's bonnet."[60] Lord Esher, who was one of her favorites, partly because he spoke in a way that she could hear, thought that "it is this mixture of ragging and real feeling which is so attractive about the Queen." He perceived that "her cleverness has always been underestimated—partly because of her deafness. In point of fact, she says more original things, and has more unexpected ideas than any of the family."[61]

Handicapped by tinnitus as well as deafness, Alix began to withdraw. There were complaints about her refusal to leave Sandringham; her daughter-in-law wrote that "it does not look well . . . for her constantly to leave <u>him</u> alone as she does."[62]

Alix was tiresomely vague about her plans, and persistently late, exasperating the obsessively punctual Bertie. "Keep him waiting," she would say, "it will do him good."[63] On a day appointed for the King and Queen to receive addresses, she was due to appear at twelve, but as room after room filled with waiting deputations, there was no sign of her. Bertie sat in full uniform, drumming the table in the equerries' room. At last, at ten to one, Alix appeared, looking lovely. "Am I late?" was all she said. Bertie swallowed hard and walked out of the room.[64]

Alix shrieked like a mandrake when she was uprooted from Marlborough House, obstructing the move to Buckingham Palace. She complained that there was no room for her possessions or to lodge Charlotte Knollys, but her real objection to leaving Marlborough House was emotional.[65] As she told Georgie, "All my happiness & sorrows were here very nearly all you children born here all my reminiscences of my whole life are here—& I feel as if by taking me away from it a chord will be torn in my heart which <u>can</u> never be mended again!!"[66]

Alix, who was neither ambitious nor remotely feminist, used her position to project her personality: decorative, generous, and lighthearted.[67] The verdict of one historian that she was best known for her beauty, and "perhaps more than any other royal consort she embodied the importance of the image over the substance of royalty" is harsh but contains a truth.[68] The story of her life as queen dissolves into anecdotes.

Full mourning for Queen Victoria ended on 24 July 1901. The ladies of the court needed to know whether black was still to be worn on that day, but Alix was vague and offhand. After much discussion, the household decided to play it safe and remain in black. The Queen appeared, late for dinner as usual, radiant in white and sparkling with diamonds, all the more striking against the black dresses of her household.*

In order to set off her own slender figure, she ordered her tall ladies to attend when the court was in London. Short ladies had to make do with dull mausoleum days at Windsor.[69] She could be imperious. When the courtiers tried to advise her about what to wear at the Coronation, she replied: "I know better than all the milliners and antiquaries. I shall wear exactly what I like, and so shall all my ladies—*Basta!*"[70] As queen, thought Lord Esher, Alix's attitude was "Now I do as I like."[71]

She provided the background of dogs, Kodak photographs, and family jokes for Bertie's public life. A secret smoker, she once dropped an illicit cigarette into a teacup when caught smoking by Bishop Randall Davidson, then persuaded him to smoke one with her and to conduct an impromptu service at Osborne around the bed where Victoria had died.[72] The day before the Coronation, when Davidson helped Bertie try on his robes in his dressing room at Buckingham Palace, Alix burst in: "Oh, I must look at you, I must see what it looks like." Davidson thought they were "so friendly and jolly together—so unlike what is usually supposed—not at all stately."[73]

Vicky was too ill to attend Queen Victoria's funeral, and one of the first things Bertie did after he became king was to visit her at Friedrichs-

---

* The ladies-in-waiting were ruled with a rod of iron by the Duchess of Buccleuch, Mistress of the Robes and a formidable grande dame: "They are to be present at breakfast in the morning—to consider themselves chaperones of the Maids of Honour, who are not to go out walking with the gentlemen of the household or to go into Windsor alone!" The court grumbled that the edict was "more like the instructions of a lodging house keeper to maids of all work." The duchess was trying to control two especially independent maids of honor—the Vivian twins, one of whom married the future Field Marshal Haig. (Bodleian, Lincolnshire Papers, MS Film 1121, Carrington Diary, 29 September 1903.)

hof. "My great anxiety is to see you again," he told her.[74] "Dearest darling Vicky," he wrote, "we shall have so much to talk about."[75] He brought with him one equerry, Fritz Ponsonby, and Laking, who masqueraded as physician in attendance (in fact Laking was there for a purpose: to give Vicky doses of morphine larger than the German doctors allowed).

Vicky was terribly swollen, in constant pain, and made wretched by nausea and vomiting. The kaiser hovered officiously, pressing Bertie to stay with him, but Bertie was adamant that "my visit is only to you, dearest Vicky."[76] Laking had a particularly uncomfortable time, as he was shunned not only by the German doctors but also by the kaiser and his suite. The superstitious Bertie worried that thirteen guests were sitting down to dinner, until he realized with relief that all was well, as Vicky's daughter Margaret of Hesse was pregnant.

After three days, Vicky sent for Ponsonby. He found her propped up on cushions and looking "as if she had just been taken off the rack after undergoing torture."[77] She asked him to take charge of her letters and transport them back to England. Shortly after one a.m., there was a knock on his door and four stablemen entered bearing two large black boxes. These contained all the letters that Vicky had written to Queen Victoria since her marriage, which she had asked to be sent out to her from England to reread as she lay ill; she was anxious that the kaiser, who did not appear in a good light in his mother's correspondence, would destroy them if they remained in Germany after her death. To baffle the secret police who stalked the palace, Ponsonby labeled one box "China with care" and the other "Books," and succeeded in smuggling these conspicuously large items out in his luggage.

On his return, Ponsonby did not, as might have been expected, deposit the boxes in the archives at Windsor, but kept them in his own custody for an astonishing twenty-seven years. In 1927, he published an edition of the letters. This caused consternation among the royal family, most of whom agreed with Princess Victoria that *Letters of the Empress Frederick* was "one of the most dreadful books ever published."[78] Ponsonby believed, however, that Vicky gave him the letters because she meant him to publish. If she had merely wished to ensure that the letters reached England for safekeeping, she would have taken the simpler course and given them to Bertie.*[79]

Since succeeding as king, Bertie had become very close to Vicky, consulting her on such matters as the decoration of the palaces and relying on her encyclopedic memory of the paintings in the royal collection. Her hands too swollen to write, Vicky dictated letters to her daughters. Her screams of agony were so loud that the sentries asked to be moved farther away from her room, but the doctors still refused to give her more narcotics, and Bertie despaired at his inability to help.[80]

Vicky died at Friedrichshof on 4 August 1901. Bertie wrote sadly against the last "Vy" symbol in his diary: "My last letter to my beloved sister ER."[81] Helena, who was at the deathbed, wrote Bertie an account of Vicky's last hours. The cancer had spread to her liver and lungs. "She was altered beyond recognition it was terrible. The weakness was very great and she could only speak with difficulty and a few words at a time. Her breathing was very laboured. . . . She spoke much of Mama repeating over and over again, 'Oh how I miss her, she understood my sufferings.' "

Helena realized something of the bond between Vicky and Bertie. "Let me say how I feel for you to whom she was so dear, and who loved you with a devotion not to be expressed," she wrote.[82] "I could hardly have borne seeing her again," Bertie told Georgie, "as she was I hear so dreadfully altered."[83] Alice, Victoria, and now Vicky—all the closest members of his family were dead: the three women who had dominated his childhood. Vicky's death was especially painful because in the last years of her life they had become real friends, forgetting their childhood quarrels and the strain caused by Germany's treatment of Denmark.

---

* Queen Victoria's letters to Vicky remained with Vicky's daughter Margaret, the landgravine of Hesse, at Friedrichshof. In 1945, when the Americans evicted the landgravine, George VI sent his librarian Sir Owen Morshead to get the letters and bring them back to Windsor. Both sides of the correspondence—Queen Victoria's letters to Vicky and Vicky's to Victoria—were edited by Roger Fulford and published in the important series beginning with *Dearest Child* (1964).

Kaiser William threatened to exclude Bertie from Vicky's funeral. "I was so worried because William wanted you <u>not</u> to go to Potsdam," wrote Helena, "but that is <u>all right</u> now."[84] So Bertie returned to bury Vicky, sweltering beneath a hot sun as he walked in the funeral procession to the mausoleum at Potsdam dressed in full uniform swathed in crêpe. Bertie, said his brother Arthur, "is too stout and suffered tremendously from the heat."[85]

Bertie's style of monarchy cost money. Advised by Ernest Cassel, he knew exactly how much he needed: a parliamentary grant of £500,000, in addition to the Duchy of Lancaster income of £60,000. This was more than Queen Victoria's Civil List of £385,000, but Victoria had also enjoyed a private fortune, which she left to her younger children, and Bertie had little capital remaining. His outgoings included Balmoral (£20,000) and Osborne (£17,000) as well as Sandringham, which cost £40,000 a year to run. Gossip credited the King with sensational liabilities, but Bertie realized that his bargaining power with the government depended on not asking the nation to pay his debts. "Gentlemen," announced Knollys to the commission inquiring into the King's finances, "it is my happy duty to inform you that for the first time in English history, the heir-apparent comes forward . . . unencumbered by a single penny of debt."[86] It was not strictly true; Bertie's debts still lurked, and Knollys omitted to mention that he had no capital; but his assurances convinced the politicians that the King was solvent.

Bertie summoned Edward Hamilton, the assistant financial secretary to the Treasury, and told him that he must have enough to "do it with," and he must "do it" handsomely, and for that he needed £500,000.*[87] He agreed to pay income tax, as his mother had done, and instantly regretted it. He later told Lord Salisbury that the decision was

---

* Michael Hicks Beach, the Chancellor of the Exchequer, offered £450,000, and agreed to increase the figure to £470,000, but Hamilton contrived to juggle the expenses on the Civil List (for example, Prince George contributed £20,000 to the upkeep of Balmoral and Sandringham), so that in reality the King received the income of £500,000 he asked for. (*Diary of Edward Hamilton*, p. 400 [20 February 1901].)

made "when he had only just succeeded and was quite new to everything," and though it was too late to go back on it, he paid tax "under protest and he wishes this protest to be recorded."[88] Meanwhile, his debts were gradually paid off by a scheme of life insurance devised by the cunning Cassel, so that by 1907 the King was genuinely free of all encumbrances.[89]

Even £500,000 was barely enough. On the recommendation of a parliamentary select committee, economies in the household were introduced. Household officials such as the treasurer, the comptroller, and the vice chamberlain had to take a salary cut. The Royal Buckhounds were abolished.[90] In addition to Windsor and Buckingham Palace, Bertie inherited Balmoral, which was Victoria's private residence, and a share in Osborne, which Victoria left to all her children. If he was to keep Sandringham, he must give up one of these, and he chose to drop Osborne, which he disliked. "Were it not for Sandringham," he wrote, "I could maintain Osborne but I cannot live in and maintain five places!"[91] Setting aside his mother's will, and overcoming shrill protests from his sisters, especially Beatrice, whose life was based there, Bertie gave Osborne to the nation.*[92] The house was converted into a school for naval officers. The room where Victoria had died became a shrine, closed off by an iron grille.

Bertie made the right choice. Keeping a royal residence in Scotland was politically important. Victoria's regime of so-called Balmorality—indoors: gloom, cold rooms, and low living; on the hill: lavish whisky rations and drunken gillies—played into the ethos of Scots Presbyterianism, but Bertie found it intolerable. He cut the stalkers' whisky and banned drunkenness.[93]

On Alix's insistence, however, as little as possible of Victoria's decoration was changed. "I will not have any of her things and treasures touched here," she wrote. "All shall remain as she placed them herself."[94] Soon there could be felt "that curious electric element which pervaded the surroundings of King Edward."[95] This king, ethnically German, was more Scottish than the Scots, wearing a kilt day and

---

* Beatrice made Osborne Cottage on the estate her principal residence.

night (Balmoral or Hunting Stuart tartan in the daytime, Royal Stuart for evening).[96] At dinner, Highlanders pumping ear-piercing bagpipes marched three times round the table when game was served.[97] The King and Queen spent almost a month there each autumn. Alix, who had disliked "dear old melancholy Abergeldie," took a childlike pleasure in Balmoral, which, with its picnics and horseplay, became for her another Fredensborg.[98]

For relaxation, there was Sandringham. "It is altogether different here from Windsor," wrote Esher. "No ceremonial at all. Just a country home."[99] It was hardly a normal country house, however. Luncheon at two thirty (the clocks were half an hour fast) was followed by tea, when the King scoffed poached eggs, petits fours, cakes, and shortbread. A twelve-course dinner followed at nine, and the King would cheerfully swallow several dozen oysters in minutes, and then devour at high speed course after course of pheasant stuffed with truffles, chicken in aspic, sole poached in Chablis, or quails and boned snipe packed with foie gras, the richer and creamier the sauce the better.[100] After the ladies had gone to bed, Bertie led the men to the billiard room, where his small black bulldog bit anyone who moved.[101] On Sundays, he invariably attended church, but the sermon was strictly limited to fifteen minutes. If the preacher ran over, Bertie would ostentatiously check his watch.[102] Afternoons were spent trudging around the estate. Ladies changed into walking skirts and strong boots for a three-hour walk. Some guests were charmed by the sight of the Queen in overalls in her kennel, feeding her menagerie of fierce dogs, but Lady Antrim was less amused. "We went round the gardens, stud etc till I felt quite cold."[103]

At Buckingham Palace, every detail of the redecoration was supervised by Bertie. Albert's Italianate marbling in the grand entrance hall had become so dark and dirty that Bertie called it the sepulchre. Lionel Cust, newly appointed Surveyor of the King's Pictures, found the paintings coated in a thin, dark film of dirt. Bertie determined to bring light into Victoria's fusty "funeral parlours."[104] Side tables crowded with wax figures, Highlanders in kilts, favorite dogs and hands made of marble—all were thrown out.[105] Never an admirer of literature,

Bertie gave instructions to the Windsor librarian to "pack up" Albert's fine books, and "get rid of those which were not required."[106] He hired the theater designer Frank Verity, who transformed the palace into a sea of scarlet, white, and gold.[107] Critics carped that it was vulgar and reminiscent of an opera house or the Ritz Hotel, but it formed a fitting backdrop for the ceremonial of monarchy.

Bertie abolished Queen Victoria's joyless afternoon drawing rooms, when ladies wearing full evening dress and décolletage were presented to the Queen in the unforgiving light of day, and introduced evening courts instead. The King and Queen sat side by side on a dais in the ballroom, receiving curtseys from the ladies with their elaborate trains supported by pages. This new ritual was choreographed by Bertie, with Esher and Sir Arthur Ellis, comptroller in the Lord Chamberlain's department. The King, wrote Cust, was like a "highly trained actor" who understood mien and deportment, entrance and exit.[108] The theatrical formality of the new courts gave legitimacy to social change. The small aristocratic London society that Bertie had first presided over forty years before had swelled since the 1880s into a new elite, embracing celebrities and the nouveau riche. The number of presentations exploded. The new ceremonial confirmed the role of the monarch as leader of *national* society rather than the old exclusive aristocracy.[109]

The first new court was held on 14 March 1902, and Bertie and Alix moved into Buckingham Palace a month later.

CHAPTER 22

"Edward the Confessor Number Two"[1]

1902

A proclamation issued in June 1901 announced that the Coronation would take place on 26 June 1902. As the date approached, Bertie was more than ever swamped in work. Hours spent distributing Boer War medals—one day alone he handed out three thousand—or visiting the wounded left him exhausted and irritable. In his sixtieth year, he had a full-time job for the first time in his life. One night he summoned Lord Redesdale to Marlborough House, and sat for two hours talking after dinner. About midnight he got up and said, "Now I must bid you good night, for I must set to work," pointing to a huge pile of red boxes.

"Surely Your Majesty is not going to tackle all the work tonight!"

"Yes! I must! Besides it is all so interesting," said the King.[2]

Bertie's private apartments at Buckingham Palace consisted of four adjoining rooms on the first floor, looking out over the garden. The third room was his bedroom. His bed, massive and heavy, stood in the corner. The wall was hung high with paintings of his female relations.

Bertie spent most of his time in his private sitting room. His desk was immaculately neat and ordered, and a portrait of Vicky always stood on the table. His bad-tempered French bulldog lay in its basket ready to snap at any visitor. Two cages of canaries hung above the chair and burst into song whenever the visitor spoke.[3]

The King breakfasted alone, wearing a shabby old mess jacket. In his pocket was a silver cigar case, loaded the night before by his valet with his pre-breakfast ration—one small cigar and two cigarettes. Each day he smoked between eleven and thirteen cigars in addition to twenty or so Egyptian cigarettes. Some of the cigars were gargantuan Havanas with names such as Cornia y Corona, Henry Clay's "Tsar," or Upmann's.[4]

The doctor Frederick Treves visited the King in January 1902 to treat a ruptured Achilles tendon. He found him in a state of despair, lying in bed surrounded by papers and telegrams. A valet came to ask what tune the band outside should play. "Why cannot they leave me alone!" groaned the King; but he insisted on making even the smallest decision himself.[5] At Buckingham Palace, Lionel Cust, Surveyor of the King's Pictures, would be summoned by Bertie whenever he could snatch a few minutes, often in his dressing room. Sometimes Cust witnessed the King send for his servant, Mr. Chandler, the Superintendent of the Wardrobe, and scold him mercilessly. "I learned to understand that this was pent-up anger which had to be let out," wrote Cust. After such a scene, the King was his normal cheerful self.[6]

A game of bridge with the King had become a terrifying experience. Previously he had drunk moderately, a glass or two of wine at dinner and a little brandy afterward, but now he relied on alcohol in order to "get on" with the work. Arthur the brusher, the only man in the palace who dared contradict him, incurred even more wrath than usual. "I told you," said the King, "to have those clothes altered. Why have you not done it?"

"You did not," said Arthur.

"How dare you speak to me like that, I told you to do it."

"You did not," said Arthur, and banged the door behind him.

After he had gone, the King said with a smile, "I expect Arthur is right."[7]

Bertie's figure had ballooned. His abdomen grew alarmingly, and his waist swelled to forty-eight inches, the same as his chest. No longer did he allow himself to be weighed. His uniform tunics became too tight. "He had the hunger of the dyspeptic," wrote Treves. He "ate anything and everything and bolted his food." He confessed that "he could not be bothered to masticate what he ate." Alix complained that his appetite was "appalling, that she had never seen anything like it," but he paid no attention to her warnings.[8] It seems likely that he was suffering from an eating disorder brought on by overwork and stress. Insisting on making every decision himself, he was overwhelmed. He had a deep need for order, but he felt that he had lost control. His illness was as much psychological as it was physical.

Bertie's diary for 16 June 1902 reads: "The King taken ill with severe chill. Unable to dine."[9] After gorging a large quantity of tough lobster, he had got wet at a military review at Aldershot. He complained of abdominal pain, and sent for Laking in the night.[10] He retreated to bed at Windsor. Ominously, he made no appearance at Ascot races. His belly was grotesquely extended and acutely painful. Laking suspected appendicitis, but Bertie refused an operation and insisted on returning to London.[11] Canceling the Coronation was unthinkable.

Bertie traveled from Windsor to London on Monday, 23 June. He had a high fever and the pain in his stomach was excruciating, made worse by every jolt of the carriage, but he smiled and bowed to the cheering crowd.

Treves, who was a leader in the new field of stomach surgery, examined him, and found a hard swelling in his abdomen.[12] Laking told the King that he had an abdominal abscess that would cause death from blood poisoning unless an immediate operation was performed. Bertie refused. "The Coronation cannot be postponed. I won't hear of it. I cannot and will not disappoint the people. . . . I will go to the Abbey on Thursday if I die there." Laking replied: "If Your Majesty did go on Thursday to the Abbey in all human probability you would die there."[13]

———

News that the Coronation was indefinitely postponed was announced on Tuesday. Wild rumors spread that the King was dying of cancer.

At 12:25 that morning, the King walked to the operating table that had been erected in his dressing room. He wore an old gray dressing gown and he was bent double with pain. Alix, greatly perturbed, thought it was her duty to remain by his side throughout the operation. She became desperately agitated when his face went black from the anesthetic, and when he began to throw his arms about she tried to pin him down. Treves, who was embarrassed at rolling up his sleeves in order to operate in the presence of the Queen, asked her to leave the room.[14]

Treves cut deep into the fat of the King's abdomen, and at four and a half inches he reached a hard swelling. When he drove the knife in, a pint of pus escaped with a violent gush.[15] Not cancer, then, but a large abscess. The King might yet live. Treves drained it with tubes and packed the wound with gauze.

The story has gone down in history that Bertie's appendix was removed as he lay on a billiard table at Buckingham Palace. This is not correct. The problem was indeed an abscess, and contrary to what has often been said, Treves did not remove the King's appendix.*

When Bertie regained consciousness, his first words were: "Where's George?" Bertie called for his son from his sickbed, much as his own mother, Queen Victoria, had called for him on her deathbed.

After an interval, Bertie asked Treves, "What noise is that?" referring to the sound of distant hammering. Treves replied: "It is the carpenters putting up stands [for the Coronation] in Constitution Hill."

"Poor people! Poor people!" said the King. That night, as Bertie lay

---

* The medical term is perityphlitis, an inflammation of the area around the appendix. For his successful operation on the King, Treves received a baronetcy, and his practice became overwhelmingly popular. He retired early at age forty-five.

awake, restless and in pain, Treves kept watch. Outside the palace, as the sentry paced to and fro, he could see the "ghoulish crowd huddled about the shadows at the gate." They were waiting. Waiting for the news that the King was dead.[16]

The next day, Bertie was well enough to pencil a note to Alice Keppel, asking her to visit him at five that afternoon: "Sleep was not good owing to oppression on chest—and I was so restless but got some sleep later on in a chair—as lying down was so unpleasant," he told her.[17] He wrote again the following day: "Not much sleep complete loss of appetite. Feel wretched but make the best of it."[18]

He read novels, a sure sign that he was ill. He thought them all very poor, especially Arthur Conan Doyle's *Hound of the Baskervilles*. Alix visited often. A secret door in Bertie's dressing room led to her apartments, and when she left she would say, "Good bye. I am the lady who lives in a cupboard." Her deafness meant that he had to shout to be heard, which was an effort for him, so he pretended to be asleep. His favorite visitor was his daughter Victoria, to whom, said Treves, "he was devoted."[19]

Treves noticed that Bertie, "being a most orderly and methodical man . . . was very particular as to the exact position of everything around him." He never forgot his dignity or his royal rank. He had an extreme dislike of being seen by anyone—even a valet—in a position of helplessness, so screens were placed around him. Above his bed hung a portrait of his dead son Eddy. When the bed was wheeled back into place, he always asked, "Is it exactly under the portrait?"[20]

When César Ritz, the proprietor of the new and fashionable Carlton Hotel, heard the news of the postponement of the Coronation, he collapsed with a seizure. Strategically located on the Coronation route at the corner of Pall Mall, the Carlton was one of Bertie's favorite restaurants, and Ritz had planned a gala dinner for five hundred.[21]

Bitterly disappointed, too, was Arthur Benson, an Eton housemaster who had written the words to the Coronation ode composed by

Edward Elgar. It all seemed so much wasted work, as he was convinced that it would never be played.[22] It included the chorus:

Land of Hope and Glory, Mother of the Free,
How shall we extol thee, who are born of thee?

The song seemed an unconscious mockery of the fat king:

Wider still and wider shall thy bounds be set;
God who made thee mighty, make thee mightier yet

Most of the visiting ambassadors and royals who had come for the Coronation returned home, and only the colonials remained. When the Coronation eventually took place, six weeks later, it was an imperial celebration, featuring native soldiers from every part of the empire. This was the unintended consequence of Bertie's operation and the postponement of the ceremony. Royal propagandists such as John Bodley, author of the official history of the Coronation, made a virtue of it and solemnly eulogized the ceremony as the "consecration of the Imperial idea."*[23]

Meanwhile, Bertie recuperated on board the *Victoria and Albert*, lying in a bed on deck, wearing a blue flannel suit and puffing a cigar.

The King and Queen drove in the state coach from Buckingham Palace to Westminster Abbey at eleven a.m. on 9 August 1902. Alix for once was punctual.

When Alix crossed the abbey threshold, the Westminster schoolboys shouted *"Vivat Regina Alexandra! Vivat, vivat, vivat!"* No matter that their *vivats* were out of time with the anthem. The congregation

* As a reward for the book, Bertie offered Bodley the Royal Victorian Order. Bodley wrote a pompous letter declining the honor. This infuriated Bertie: "In future I don't think I could have anything more to do with him. His conceit and snobbishness surpasses his crassness." (RA VIC/X29/72, Note by B on Bodley's letter to Francis Knollys of 10 July 1903.)

of eight thousand* had been in their seats for more than three hours already, but the Queen, dressed in golden Indian gauze with a purple train, was worth waiting for. The six weeks' breathing space had given the Earl Marshal, the Duke of Norfolk, time to drill his courtiers and pages, and the processions, which would have been a shambles in June, were perfectly choreographed in August.[24] The King's procession followed, bearing royal regalia, the scepter, orb and crown, and at last the King. *"Vivat Rex Edwardus!"* shouted the boys, too early, so that they had to shout it twice. As Bertie walked briskly up the nave—so fast that he had to be told several times to slow down—people noticed a strange hush and extraordinary stillness come over the abbey.[25] Consuelo, Duchess of Marlborough, felt a lump in her throat and "realised I was more British than I knew."[26] When Bertie took the oath, a deep silence descended, and "many ladies began to cry."[27]

Archbishop Temple was eighty-one, doddery, and nearly blind, so his words had been written out in large letters on scrolls, which Bishop Davidson held up before him to read. The effect was ridiculous. Bertie was too weak to wear the traditional St. Edward's Crown he had wished for, and the lighter Imperial State Crown was used instead.[28] Temple blundered and placed the crown on Bertie's head back to front, and Bertie himself had to help him put it right. At that moment, with this most precarious of coronations safely consecrated at last, a wild thunderous cheer burst out of "God Save the King!"

The first to pay homage was Temple, who by now was so exhausted that his legs gave way as he tried to rise from his knees. Bertie put out his hands, and three bishops came to the rescue of the selfish old man, who had refused to delegate any part of the service. When Davidson asked in a whisper how he felt, Temple rasped, "Go away!" in a voice that was clearly audible to the congregation.

When Georgie paid homage, Bertie pulled his son back by his robe as he turned, and kissed him twice in a gesture of touching emotion.[29]

In a gallery above the chancel where the princesses sat were the

---

* Only two thousand guests attended the wedding at Westminster Abbey of Prince William to Catherine Middleton in 2011.

King's lady friends who, not being peeresses, would otherwise have been excluded. Wits quipped that this was the King's Loose Box. Mrs. Keppel, La Favorita, was conspicuous in the best place; Jennie Churchill was there, and so was her sister Leonie. Sarah Bernhardt wore tactless and conspicuous white, and some observers said that Minnie Paget did, too.[30]

But the Queen stole the show. Her coronation came after Bertie's, and was performed by the Archbishop of York. She was crowned kneeling before the altar, beneath a canopy supported by four tall duchesses, among them Consuelo Marlborough and Millicent, Duchess of Sutherland (who was Daisy Warwick's sister). Alix had requested that the archbishop anoint her forehead rather than her hair, which was a wig; being devout and superstitious, she believed that holy oil must actually touch her body. As Consuelo watched the archbishop anoint the Queen with trembling hands, she saw a trickle of oil run down the royal nose.[31] The moment Alix was crowned was the signal for the four hundred peeresses sitting together to put on their coronets. This for Bertie was the most impressive part of the ceremony.[32] The peeresses had insisted on wearing their tiaras, contrary to tradition, and in order to add their coronets they had to arch their gloved arms high above their heads in an almost balletic scene.* As Alix returned from the altar, wearing her newly commissioned crown set with the Koh-i-noor diamond, and carrying her scepter and ivory rod, she dropped a low bow when she passed the King.[33] She was fifty-six, heavily made up, allegedly bald, and almost stone deaf, but she seemed like a queen from a fairy tale.[34]

That night, at the Carlton Hotel, Auguste Escoffier the celebrity chef served a gala dinner. The menu of eighteen courses included *Mousseline de Sole Victoria,* which was followed by *Poularde Edward VII.* Escoffier had prepared his masterpiece, *Poularde Derby,* back in 1881 to

* Not everyone was impressed. Arthur Benson, sitting high up in the abbey, thought it looked "rather absurd and very shoddy." (Benson, *Edwardian Excursions,* p. 71.)

woo the then Prince of Wales when he first stayed at César Ritz's Grand Hotel in Monte Carlo. *Poularde Derby,* which Bertie declared a "truly royal dish," consisted of chicken stuffed with foie gras and truffles served on a bed of more truffles cooked in champagne and foie gras. *Poularde Edward VII* was a variation on this dish that Escoffier had devised especially for the Coronation. In recognition of Bertie's Indian empire, the chicken stuffed with foie gras and truffles was served with curry sauce. Escoffier commemorated the Queen with *Pêches Alexandra,* a variation on his signature dish of *Pêches Melba.* Peaches poached in syrup were laid on a bed of vanilla ice cream and coated with strawberry purée (*Pêches Melba* used raspberry purée), sprinkled with rose petals and veiled with spun sugar.[35]

"Francis Knollys is the most powerful man in England at this moment," wrote Carrington in 1901.[36] Knollys had served Bertie for forty years, and when he became King, Bertie rewarded his old retainer by keeping him on as his private secretary. (Arthur Bigge, who had been private secretary to Queen Victoria and might reasonably have expected the post, was sidelined.)* Before 1901, Knollys had dealt with all the Prince of Wales's business himself, and "made it a one-man job."[37] At first, he tried to do the same in the new reign, writing every letter himself in bold black ink (neither shorthand nor the typewriter had reached Marlborough House). Though he worked all day, however, he was unable to keep pace with the King's correspondence. To relieve him, Bertie appointed Fritz Ponsonby, who had previously been assistant private secretary to Queen Victoria, as Knollys's number two. This arrangement was not a success. Marlborough House had for years despised Queen Victoria's household as fuddy-duddy and inefficient, and Knollys was suspicious of Ponsonby, whom he saw as an emissary from the enemy camp. Ponsonby wrote a full and funny (though not always reliable) account of Bertie's court in his *Recollections of Three Reigns;* but as a colleague he was stubborn and tactless,

---

* Bigge was appointed private secretary to the Prince of Wales.

and he lacked the political skills of his father, old Henry Ponsonby.[38] Knollys, for his part, found it hard to share power, and suspected Ponsonby of "trying to cut him out and take his place."[39] To marginalize Ponsonby, he made him share his job with a second assistant private secretary, Arthur Davidson, cutting his salary and allowing him to work for only half the year.

It is sometimes claimed that Bertie loathed paperwork and neglected it, but this was not the case.[40] The new King worked through the documents in his red boxes punctually and efficiently. According to Esher, "He *never* leaves over anything until next day. All papers and letters of the day are dealt with within 24 hours."[41] Bertie would pencil a brief scrawl on a government document that Francis Knollys then drafted into a letter. His penciled "Approved ER" or "Seen ER" reveal him as working like a modern minister, rather than a Victorian statesman laboriously covering reams of paper in black-inked screeds. His businesslike methods earned him the gratitude of the Foreign Office, who commented that "the rapidity and regularity with which the King's boxes are returned is really remarkable"—and a marked contrast with Queen Victoria.[42] He corresponded less with ministers than Victoria had done, but living in London he was more accessible than she had been. In foreign policy, he exercised influence and powers that none of his predecessors had dreamed of. At home, he clung tenaciously to his prerogatives and the Crown's traditional powers.

Salisbury, who was Bertie's first prime minister, had been a devoted servant of Queen Victoria. Her death stood second only to the death of his wife as one of the great blows that broke his health, "so strong was his personal love and devotion to her."[43] Balfour's remark, that the King "had nothing in common with Lord Salisbury, and Salisbury had little sympathy with the King," was an understatement.[44] Bertie found Salisbury's buffoonish absentmindedness intolerable. When Salisbury appeared late for a Buckingham Palace drawing room in 1897 wearing the "tunic of an Elder Brother of Trinity House, the hose of a Privy Councillor, the Garter on the wrong shoulder and a sword," Bertie was "furious: literally in a passion. 'Here is our foreign minister dressed like a guy—Europe in a turmoil—twenty ministers and ambassadors looking on—what will they think,' he wheezed, 'what can they think of a premier who can't put on his clothes?' "*45

Once Bertie acceded, relations improved. Salisbury reported a grudging respect for the new King, whom he found easy to work with. "I think we shall have to call him Edward the Confessor Number Two," he wrote.46

Bertie objected to the wording of the declaration he was forced to read at the opening of his first Parliament, repudiating Roman Catholicism as "superstitious and idolatrous." He read the words in a low voice that was barely audible, and afterward he wrote to Salisbury asking for the "crude language" to be changed as it was "not in accordance with public policy of the present day."47 Salisbury agreed privately that the oath was "scurrilous" and a stain on the statute book, but he feared a Protestant backlash if the wording was tampered with.48

The most serious disagreement was over honors. Declaring that "the initiative in the matter should rest with himself rather than the Prime Minister!" Bertie proposed to give peerages at the Coronation to Sir Thomas Lipton and Sir Ernest Cassel. "You may laugh if you like," he told the PM's secretary, "but no more suitable men could be found."49 Salisbury was dismayed, especially by the Lipton nomination: "The man has no services, and his name and vocation are moreover ridiculous."50 Cassel was ruled out as a German and a Jew. Salisbury got his way. Cassel had to be content with a privy councillorship (and even that was contentious), while Lipton became a baronet. Little did Salisbury know how much the two men had given to charity, nor could he have imagined the debt the monarchy owed to Cassel. Once again it is Bertie who seems modern.

One loyal servant who received an uncontentious peerage was Francis Knollys. Bertie showered honors like confetti at the Coronation. The number of peerages, baronetcies, privy councillorships,

---

* On another occasion the prime minister appeared at a drawing room wearing "a levee coat with epaulettes!! (tied on with string and fastened with pins). No sword, the Garter ribbon, no star and the Jubilee medal fastened on to the band of his trousers!!" (Bodleian Library, Lincolnshire Papers, MS Film 1121, Carrington Diary, 26 February 1897.)

knighthoods, and decorations totaled 1,540. (In 1911, George V handed out a mere 515.)[51] The new King resisted giving peerages to party hacks, and there were two orders that he insisted on controlling: the Royal Victorian Order, founded in 1896, and the Royal Victorian Chain, which he inaugurated in 1902. By far the most distinguished royal order was the Order of Merit. This was Bertie's idea, acting on a suggestion made by Esher in 1900 and inspired by the Prussian Order Pour le Mérite.[52] Bertie's aim was to honor both "officers of the Army and Navy and Civilians distinguished in the Arts, Sciences and Literature." Numbers were strictly limited to twenty-four. Partly because the order was nonpolitical, it was to be "a decoration entirely vested in the Sovereign's hand."[53] Salisbury opposed the creation of yet another bauble, but history has proved the old cynic wrong. The OM was, and remains, the most distinguished order in British public life.*[54]

Following in the procession at the Coronation behind the Knights of the Garter with their gorgeous purple cloaks and wearing a plain diplomatic uniform was the new Conservative prime minister, Arthur Balfour. The most powerful man in the country seemed "strangely undressed."[55] He had written asking for permission for privy councillors and MPs to wear trousers, but the King insisted on court dress, and the prime minister's legs seemed sadly spindly in breeches and stockings.[56] Because the office of prime minister was unknown to the constitution, Balfour walked in the procession in his capacity as Lord Privy Seal.

Balfour had seamlessly succeeded his uncle Lord Salisbury in July 1902. Salisbury was too unwell to attend the Coronation.[57] But the truth was he disliked "flummery," and so did his nephew Balfour.

---

* In 1903, Balfour proposed that Florence Nightingale should be awarded the OM, but the King objected, as he was "reluctant to begin giving the Order of Merit to Women." (Bodleian Library, Sandars Papers, MS Eng. Hist. C. 718, ff. 242–43, Lord Knollys to J. S. Sandars, 6 November 1903.) The statutes of the OM referred to "persons," and this presumably did not exclude women; but the King insisted that women were not eligible for admittance to the order. In 1907, Prime Minister Sir Henry Campbell-Bannerman revived the suggestion, and the King agreed, so Florence Nightingale became OM. Not until 1965 was another woman honored: Dorothy Hodgkin.

Arthur Balfour had been one of Queen Victoria's favorites. He was the leader of the Souls, the clique of cultured aristocrats who defined themselves in antithesis to the Marlborough House set, despising Bertie and his friends as ignorant philistines.* Balfour was quick-witted and charming, but he combined a streak of Scots puritanism with intellectual arrogance and a talent for casuistry. Philosophy was his hobby, and no one was cleverer than he at arguing that black was white—a quality that did not endear him to the blunt-speaking King.

"The King will take up a good deal more of his ministers' time than did the Queen," sighed Balfour in 1901.[58] Bertie's first King's Speech, submitted to him by Balfour as Leader of the House in February 1901, was returned covered in significant alterations. Bertie wanted to include legislation on the housing of the poor and on old age pensions. Balfour replied (as he later related) that if the King "took to writing his own speech, he'd have to take all the blame of the measures and enter into party politics."[59] He was obliged to give Bertie a lecture on the constitution: "If . . . the legislative programme is supposed to be in any way due to the personal initiative of the Sovereign, I fear that a novel constitutional precedent will have been set up which may have a disastrous effect upon the comfort, and even the popularity of the King."[60] Balfour's argument was unanswerable, and Bertie at once withdrew. As the clerk to the Privy Council Almeric Fitzroy observed, the clash revealed that "the idea of inaugurating his reign with a list of popular measures" had "taken very firm possession of the royal mind."[61] Bertie learned his lesson. "Never did it again," was Balfour's comment.[62]

As prime minister, Balfour at first treated the King with barely disguised contempt, not bothering to write to him with a Cabinet report. This was a mistake. Shortly after his first Cabinet, Balfour received a sharp rebuke from the King. "As you know the Prime Minister from time immemorial has always communicated to the Sovereign a report of what has taken place at every Cabinet Council immediately after

* In 1896, Balfour dined with Bertie's friend Consuelo, Duchess of Manchester. "I mentioned . . . that I had seen H[enry] S[idgwick]. She had never heard of him. I said he was a philosopher. She asked me if I cared for philosophy. This gave me pleasure." (Arthur Balfour to Lady Elcho, 4 December 1896, in Ridley and Percy, *Letters*, p. 153.)

each meeting. Otherwise the King or Queen would be left in the dark as to what was going on in connection with public affairs."[63] Queen Victoria had always insisted on being kept informed by her prime minister of Cabinet discussions. If Balfour assumed that the new King would allow this to lapse, he was badly mistaken.

There were lines that the government crossed at its peril. One of these concerned the Garter.

The first real clash between Bertie and the Balfour government took place only days after the Coronation. To complete his recovery, Bertie embarked on a cruise on board the *Victoria and Albert*. While the King was going through the Foreign Office box, Fritz Ponsonby heard an explosion of rage. Bertie had opened a letter from the foreign secretary Lord Lansdowne, enclosing a design for the Garter Star that omitted the Christian cross in the center. Fritz was astonished (he later claimed) to see the furious monarch hurl the document across the cabin and out of a porthole apparently into the sea, where it happened to land on a passing steam pinnace.[64] (The story seems to have grown with the telling: In an earlier account, Fritz merely stated that the King flung the design to the other side of his cabin.)[65]

The Garter with cross omitted was commissioned by Lansdowne, who proposed to give it to the shah of Persia. Lansdowne claimed that he had mentioned the design to the King a few days before, but Bertie remembered nothing about it. The proposal to give the Garter to the shah enraged him; he objected that it could not be given to a non-Christian. The shah considered that he was entitled to the Garter as his father had had it before; but since then Queen Victoria had ruled that non-Christians were ineligible. The real point was that Bertie considered the Garter to be in the gift of the monarch, and he refused to be bullied by the Foreign Office into giving it away—in spite of the fact that he heartily approved of the aim, which was to win the friendship of the shah against Russia.

Lansdowne's clumsy attempt to compromise by removing the cross from the Garter could hardly have been better calculated to annoy Bertie, whose passion for correctness in such matters was notorious. Lansdowne refused to back down. He wrote to Balfour threatening to

resign if the King blocked the shah's Garter, and asking him to intervene.

Balfour stayed at Balmoral in September, but nothing was said
about the Garter. Soon afterward, however, the prime minister went
on the attack, writing letters to Knollys that have been described as
masterpieces of Balfour's "fundamentally dishonest" technique of "rewriting history as a means of conducting policy."[66] Balfour claimed
that the issue was not whether Lansdowne had the King's authority to
issue the Garter (though, of course, that *was* the issue) but whether
Lansdowne was to be "thrown over." If Lansdowne was forced to go
back on his word, he would lose all authority, and would be unable to
continue in office: "And if he resigned could the matter stop there in
these days of Government solidarity?" asked Balfour.*[67]

This was round one to Balfour. The shah got his Garter, and Balfour
concluded that the new King could easily be outmaneuvered or bullied. He was soon to be proved wrong.

* This vain and petty squabble left deep wounds. Lansdowne, wrote Fritz Ponsonby, "felt it
all very deeply," especially as the Cabinet thought he was wrong. Afterward, "he always
feared King Edward and disliked him in consequence." (RA GV/GG9/218, Fritz Ponsonby
to Arthur Davidson, 15 January 1913.) Years later, in 1921, Ponsonby had lunch with Lansdowne to discuss Sidney Lee's biography of the King, and Lansdowne "asked particularly
that the incident of the Shah's Garter should not be referred to" in the book. (British Library,
Sidney Lee Papers, Add. MS 56087A, f. 144, Fritz Ponsonby to Sidney Lee, 18 February 1921.)

CHAPTER 23

King Edward the Peacemaker

1903–5

Edward VII's reputation as king rests largely upon his role in foreign policy. He was Edward the Peacemaker, responsible for making possible the Entente Cordiale with France. His visit to Paris in May 1903 was perhaps the most important political intervention he ever made. It was certainly the most controversial.

Bertie controlled all the arrangements for the Paris trip himself. Fritz Ponsonby, his assistant private secretary, was surprised that his master should insist on organizing his own schedule; but Bertie had learned the advantages of keeping his own diary, and he had very good reasons for doing this now. No one was informed of the whole picture. Neither Alix nor Knollys knew of his intentions. People were told what they needed to know, but information was kept in watertight compartments: "Most of the suite had no idea where they were going."[1] Ignoring usual practice, Bertie informed neither the British ambassador in

Paris, Sir Edward Monson, nor Lord Lansdowne, the foreign secretary.[2]

The King's itinerary ostensibly consisted of a visit to the King of Portugal in Lisbon, followed by a Mediterranean trip to Rome. Bertie's real agenda, of visiting President Loubet in Paris, was kept strictly secret. Not until rumors of the royal visit had reached Ambassador Monson did the King reveal his plans to the foreign secretary. He avoided asking Lansdowne to join him as minister in attendance, as might have been expected. Nor did he choose a senior Foreign Office official to accompany him. Instead, he picked Charles Hardinge, the most junior of the four undersecretaries at the Foreign Office.*

The King had good reason for keeping Lansdowne in the dark. The foreign secretary had told him that the British government had no intention of reaching an understanding with France over Morocco, the outstanding colonial dispute that needed to be resolved if relations between the two countries were to improve.[3] By visiting Paris, the King was taking the initiative and making foreign policy himself. This was a dangerous thing for the monarch to do: If the mission failed, it could be seriously damaging.

On 30 March 1903, Alix embarked for Copenhagen, "furious" at having to entertain the kaiser, who was paying a state visit to Denmark.[4] William was thus safely out of the way, being lionized by the Danish court. "I could not help being much amused at Apapa [King Christian] having created him an Admiral!" Bertie wrote to Georgie, "as Uncle Sacha and I were only Colonels of regiments! I wonder if Mama and Aunt Minny suggested it!!!"[5]

Meanwhile Bertie sailed for Portugal on the *Victoria and Albert*, taking with him seventy pieces of luggage. In addition to Charles Hardinge and Fritz Ponsonby, he brought the Marquis de Soveral, the Portuguese minister. These men composed an inner court; but of the three,

---

* Bertie had noted Hardinge's talent when the young man was posted at St. Petersburg. Hardinge's wife, Winifred (Bina) Sturt, was the daughter of Bertie's old friend Lord Alington of Crichel, and a favorite of Alix's, who had engineered her marriage and made her a lady-in-waiting.

only Soveral was privy to Bertie's plans. Bertie made his entry into Lisbon wearing his uniform as colonel of a Portuguese cavalry regiment, an exceptionally short jacket that "was not becoming to a stout man," as it revealed a large expanse of breeches.[6] Etiquette dictated that only the two kings could sit while all others had to stand, enduring not only a pigeon-shooting competition but also the gala opera that followed. The King was not impressed by the Portuguese nobility, who he thought looked "like waiters at second-rate restaurants." They all had hopes of receiving the Royal Victorian Order, wrote Ponsonby, "but as the first three are said to be disloyal and it would be difficult to give it to No. 4, none of them were given it."[7]

Ponsonby sat on board the *Victoria and Albert* busily deciphering the telegrams that poured in. Eventually the King told him, "You know we are going to Paris," and swore him to strict secrecy.[8] When they reached Gibraltar, the King heard that President Loubet was at Algiers and sent four cruisers to salute him, and the president replied inviting the King to visit. It was at this point that Bertie finally told the government that he intended to return via Paris. "The government showed great hesitation for various reasons but the King insisted and the visit was arranged."[9]

First came the visit to Italy. Bertie insisted on going ashore incognito—though as Ponsonby observed, this was somewhat absurd, as "no other human being in the world could come with eight battleships, four cruisers, four destroyers and a dispatch vessel."[10] (Paying for the royal tour out of taxpayers' money was apparently not an issue.) Lunch with Rosebery at his villa in Posillipo, where caterers provided a revolting meal of twenty courses, was not a success. How could a man amuse himself alone in such a place for weeks on end? wondered the extrovert King. "He is a strange, weird man, Sir," replied Hardinge.[11]

Bertie's plan to visit the Pope had created alarm lest it enrage English Protestants, and he reluctantly agreed to abandon it.[12] But he still intended to stay with the King of Italy at the Quirinal in Rome, and the Duke of Norfolk, a leader among British Catholics, urged that not to visit Leo XIII would be "looked upon as a terrible slight to an old man," which would have a "deplorable effect" on Britain's Catholics.[13] The Cabinet, on the other hand, opposed the visit, fearful of the effect it would have on Lancashire's working-class Tories, who were strongly anti-Catholic. Joseph Chamberlain, speaking for the Nonconformists, breathed fire and brimstone, and Balfour was inclined to agree. Bertie had already made plain his views when he objected to the oath castigating Roman Catholics that he had been obliged to swear in 1901. Now he dictated an angry telegram to Balfour that could only have made matters worse and might have forced the PM to resign. Hardinge was shocked when Ponsonby toned down the royal words and rewrote the telegram. It was Ponsonby who suggested that the King should pay a private visit to the Pope entirely on his own responsibility and without consulting the Cabinet.[14] This compromise solved the conflict. Bertie got his way and spent fifteen minutes with the ninety-three-year-old Leo XIII, who looked the color of a dead man but talked lucidly of Venezuela and Somaliland.[15]

The King's special train steamed into the Bois de Boulogne station in Paris at 3:00 p.m. on 1 May. As the King rode to the British Embassy in the president's state carriage, the sullen crowd thronging the Champs-Élysées jeered *"Vivent les Boers!," "Vive Jeanne d'Arc!"*

"The French don't like us," said one of the suite.

"Why should they?" replied Bertie.[16]

That afternoon at the embassy the King received a deputation from the British Chamber of Commerce and read a speech, drafted by Hardinge, that declared Britain's friendship for France. Effectively a press release, it appeared in the French papers next morning. When the King attended the Théâtre-Français to see a new play, *L'Autre Danger,* the house was full but the audience was icy. To the consternation of the Paris police, the King insisted on mingling with the crowd in the foyer during the interval. Spotting the actress Jeanne Granier, he walked up, kissed her hand, and said, "Oh, Mademoiselle, I remember how I applauded you in London. You personified there all the grace, all the *esprit* of France."*[17] The effect was electric; he was cheered as he returned to his box. By morning the King's gesture was on everyone's lips.

The next day, at a military review at Varennes, the King stood beside the president. Bertie wore a plumed helmet and military overcoat over his scarlet field marshal's uniform, and he was scrupulous in saluting the French troops. At eleven forty-five he attended a reception at the Hôtel de Ville. Flinging off his gray overcoat, he gave the briefest of impromptu speeches, delivered in faultless French: *"Je n'oublierai jamais ma visite à votre charmante ville, et je puis vous assurer que c'est avec le plus grand plaisir que je reviens à Paris, ou je me trouve toujours comme si j'étais chez moi."*†

"Comme si j'étais chez moi." No British politician could have said those words. Neither Balfour nor Lansdowne could conceivably have taken Paris by storm as Bertie did. From that moment at the Hôtel de Ville, he was met everywhere by frenzied cheers. All those years of dissipation as Prince de Galles were not in vain. "It was his personal knowledge of French ways, his charming Parisian manner and his Parisian way of living in Paris that won influence for him," wrote George Saunders, the *Times'* Paris correspondent, diplomatically hinting at Bertie's career as an English milord.[18]

That afternoon, the King was entertained with a race meeting at Longchamps. He found himself in a box sitting next to Madame Loubet, dowdy wife of the bourgeois French president. The prospect of spending the entire afternoon thus incarcerated was too painful, and after two races Bertie beckoned Ponsonby and whispered, "You must get me out of this. Go to the Jockey Club and ask someone to send me an invitation."[19] The Prince d'Arenberg came to the rescue and Bertie

---

* Or at least this was what Bertie was reported to have said by the French journalist Arthur Meyer, writing in *The Times* in 1922. Bertie first met Jeanne Granier in 1889, when the journalist Frank Harris brought her to his room at the Grand Hotel in Monte Carlo. Granier's racy stories of the French stage kept the prince and Randolph Churchill in fits of laughter until three a.m., and Bertie told Harris it was "one of the most charming evenings" he had ever spent.

† "I shall never forget my visit to your charming city, and I can assure you it is with the greatest pleasure that I return each time to Paris, where I am treated exactly as if I were at home."

escaped to the Jockey Club. The republican politicians began to murmur, but Bertie watched only one race from the Jockey Club stand, and he did not appear in the paddock where his friends from the *vieille noblesse* awaited him. He understood that the aristocracy were so deeply estranged from the politicians of the Third Republic that being seen to socialize with his old friends could only damage him and undo the good that his visit had done.

At dinner at the Élysée Palace, President Loubet mumbled a speech that he had written out and pinned to a candlestick. Bertie replied in fluent French without notes. Afterward, Jennie Churchill's nephew Shane Leslie watched him being driven to the Opéra "in a delirious struggling crowd. . . . The cry of *Vive le Roi* was raised, shouted down and raised again till it conquered."[20] Inside the Opéra, Daisy Pless, the glamorous daughter of Patsy Cornwallis-West, who was married to the Prince of Pless, saw the King sitting between the "monkey looking" Loubet and his wife, "who looks like a fat Jewess."[21] In fact, the King and the president were by now good friends. Bertie spotted in the audience the famous courtesan Liane de Pougy, one of the many women with whom he was rumored (falsely) to have had an affair. "Would you like her to be asked to leave?" asked Loubet.

"Not at all," replied Bertie, explaining that it pained him to think that the Parisians should find it necessary "to ignore the laws of gallantry in order to avoid offending my well-known taste for austerity."[22] In a little over twenty-four hours, the English milord had conquered Paris.

This was Bertie's defining intervention in foreign policy. The Boer War had left Britain beggared and beleaguered. Isolation was no longer tenable. The potential enemies of the empire included not only France and Russia but also Germany, as the kaiser had rushed to the support of the Boers. That Britain had to make a choice between the Germans and the Franco-Russian camp was widely acknowledged; that the decision should be a rapprochement with France was recognized by most of the Balfour government. But a diplomatic deal was impossible while opinion in France was so strongly anti-British. By his visit to Paris, Bertie defused this opposition. Acting without official support from the government, he upstaged the politicians; but he was not opposing government policy, he was facilitating it—or at least facilitating what he thought government policy ought to be. True, Bertie had his own motives for aligning England against Germany. These went back to William's quarrel with Vicky at the time of Fritz's death in 1888, and even further back to the rift within the family when Bertie sided with Alix against Queen Victoria and Vicky over Prussia's invasion of Schleswig-Holstein in 1864.

Bertie's Paris triumph was hailed by the English press. The government had no choice but to welcome it. At the time, no one was in any doubt as to the importance of the part played by the King in promoting the French entente. Lansdowne acknowledged his role when the agreement was negotiated the following year.[23] Eyre Crowe, the guru of the Edwardian Foreign Office, wrote a classic paper analyzing England's relations with France and Germany in 1907, in which he stressed the importance of the King's initiative in removing French suspicion and hostility toward Britain, and doing so almost overnight. "The French nation having come to look upon the King as personally attached to their country, saw in HM's words and actions a guarantee that the adjustment of political differences might well prepare the way for bringing about a genuine and lasting friendship."[24]

After Bertie's death, however, his role in the formation of the entente was downplayed. The politicians tried to write him out of diplomatic history. In an interview in 1911, Balfour assured the biographer Sidney Lee that the King "had nothing to do" with the entente. His visits to France were helpful, but "In no case did he go at the request of ministers: no political discussion that he held had much effect on policy."[25] Lee incorporated this version of events into the article he wrote about Edward VII in the *Dictionary of National Biography,* stating that "no direct responsibility" for the "initiation or conclusion" of the agreement belonged to the King. In 1915, Balfour was puzzled to read an account that credited Edward VII with the making of the entente. He wrote to Lansdowne: "During the years which you and I were his ministers, he never made an important suggestion of any sort on the larger questions of policy."[26] This view became orthodoxy, repeated by diplomatic historians, who dismissed the notion that the King had anything to do with the making of foreign policy.[27] What Balfour failed to acknowledge was that the King's visit to Paris was policy in itself.[28]

Strictly speaking, of course, it is true to say that the Anglo-French entente of 1904 was a settlement of outstanding colonial disputes, most importantly in North Africa. The British agreed to allow France control over Morocco in exchange for French recognition of British influence in Egypt. This barter of Egypt for Morocco was signed by Lord Lansdowne and Paul Cambon in April 1904. No one would claim that the King drew up state papers or negotiated a treaty.

But the orthodox account of the diplomatic revolution of 1903–4 is too narrow. It may have been true, as *Times* correspondent George Saunders wrote, that the French "greatly exaggerate King Edward's political part in arranging the Entente Cordiale and in working it"; but this in itself gave him influence.[29] French statesmen believed that the King personally directed British foreign policy. For them, his visit had the highest diplomatic importance. In his discussions with President Loubet and foreign minister Delcassé, Bertie exceeded his role as a constitutional monarch, warning the latter not to trust the kaiser, who he said was *"à la fois fou et méchant,"* (both mad and wicked) and stressing his personal desire for an agreement.[30] These conversations persuaded Théophile Delcassé to initiate negotiations with the British government.

England's embrace of the continental commitment plunged her into the world of European diplomacy that, as an isolationist, imperial power, she had discounted since the mid-nineteenth century. In the decade before 1914, England drew closer to the continent than she had been since 1815. This presented opportunities that Bertie was uniquely qualified to seize. Victoria's marriage policy meant that Britain, which had been for centuries on the dynastic periphery of Europe, was now at the center. As uncle of both Kaiser William and Czar Nicholas II, Bertie was head of the family. He spoke fluent French and German, practicing his languages on his Austrian valet, Meidinger, whom he employed for that purpose. As a result of his exclusion from politics as

Prince of Wales, he had spent many months each year in Germany and France; he had traveled several times to Russia and to Austria. His network of contacts and cousins meant that, unlike politicians such as Balfour or Lansdowne, he was a truly cosmopolitan figure. These links were important because, as Salisbury pointed out in 1896, Europe's future had come to depend upon the will of three or four men. "It is very remarkable that in spite of the progress of democratic ideas, the weight of individual personalities, for good or evil is greater than ever. Now every turn in the humours of the Emperor Nicholas or the Emperor William, or the Sultan of Turkey, is watched and interpreted—the fate of many thousands of lives depends on them."[31] After 1901, Bertie became one of those men.

The very success of Bertie's policy brought a down side. Britain's rapprochement with France led directly to her involvement in the Great War. If Bertie is to be credited with bringing about the entente, so, the argument goes, he must also be blamed for causing the war. It was summed up neatly with schoolboy humor in the spoof history of England *1066 and All That.* King Edward, who "smoked cigars, was addicted to entente cordials, married a Sea King's daughter and invented appendicitis," pursued a policy of peace that "was very successful and culminated in the Great War to End War."[32]

Bertie's popularity in France was resented by Kaiser William and added to his fears of the encirclement of Germany. No doubt, "if the king had stayed at home, occasionally inviting his nephew to shoot the pheasants of Sandringham, the *rapprochement* with France might have gone ahead without the exacerbation of Anglo-German relations."[33] By taking on William at his own game of royal tours abroad and effortlessly outdoing him, Bertie was bound to cause resentment and jealousy. He was well aware of this. In his dealings with William, he endeavored to use his influence to triangulate the French entente and contain German hostility. This was not an easy task.

On the morning of 31 March 1905, after dithering for two hours on board his steamer *Hamburg,* Kaiser William was bundled into an open

boat in the storm-swept Bay of Tangier and rowed, furious and terrified, through the breakers to the shore. On landing at Tangier, he
mounted an unfamiliar white horse that nearly threw him, and made
a speech at the sultan's palace, declaring that he had come to recognize
Morocco's independence. Having theatrically demonstrated his rejection of the Anglo-French colonial agreement of 1904—which gave
Morocco to France—and thus triggered an international crisis, the kaiser resumed his cruise on board the *Hamburg*. Steaming off to Gibraltar, he sent an April Fool's Day telegram to Uncle Bertie: "So happy to
be once more at Gibraltar and to send you from British soil expression
of my faithful friendship. Everybody so nice to me. Had a delightful
dinner and garden party with Sir George and Lady White and many
pretty ladies."[34]

William had been bullied into landing at Tangier by Bernhard von
Bülow, the German chancellor, but once the thing was done, he took
the credit and happily boasted about it.[35] His Morocco escapade was a
tipping point. It caused another rift in William's relationship with his
uncle, and this time it was never fully healed. A week later, at Marseille, Bertie embarked on a Mediterranean cruise on board the *Victoria and Albert*. From the royal yacht, he fulminated against his nephew.
The landing at Tangier was an "uncalled-for event." The kaiser "is no
more or less than a political 'enfant terrible,'" Bertie told foreign secretary Lord Lansdowne. "These annual cruises are deeply to be deplored and mischief is their only object."[36] To Louis Battenberg, the
King was even more unguarded. "I have tried to get on with him &
shall nominally do my best till the end—but trust him—never. He is
utterly false & the bitterest foe that E[ngland] possesses!"[37]

Each night after dinner on the *Victoria and Albert,* the King forced
Lord Salisbury,* the minister in attendance, to partner him at bridge.
How the unfortunate Salisbury must have regretted admitting that he
played. Whenever he made a mistake, which was often, the King
roared with rage. Eventually the scenes became so painful that Fritz

---

* Old Lord Salisbury died on 22 August 1903. This was his son.

Ponsonby and the equerry attempted to divert the royal wrath by pretending to quarrel furiously about each other's play.[38]

After a three-weeks' cruise, the *Victoria and Albert* returned to Marseille, and Alix and her daughters sailed on to Greece, while the King returned by special train via Paris. This was a private visit, but that did not stop him from doing all he could to repair the damage done by the kaiser. He dined with President Loubet, and he held two meetings with the pro-English foreign minister, Delcassé. Bertie could hardly have made a more ostentatious demonstration of his sympathy for France. Delcassé was the architect of the Entente Cordiale, and Bertie knew from the British ambassador that the kaiser was plotting to get him sacked.[39]

Bertie insisted that this visit should be incognito. Traveling as the Duke of Lancaster, he stayed at the Hotel Bristol rather than the British Embassy, and he declared his wish "to go about Paris . . . as he did when he was Prince of Wales."[40] Invitations flooded in, the Hotel Bristol was besieged by visitors signing their names, and Bertie packed his diary with engagements with old friends from the Faubourg Saint-Germain, such as the Standishes and the de Breteuils. At the table of the beautiful Madame de Pourtalès, he scandalized the party by threatening to land 150,000 men in Schleswig-Holstein.[41] Ponsonby endeavored to inform the police about the King's movements while ensuring that he was unconscious of their protection. When Bertie made a secret assignation with a noted beauty in the Jardin des Plantes, he was enraged to recognize the detective who was shadowing him. After that he tried to dodge the police by slipping out unnoticed in his car.[42] Throughout the visit, Mrs. Keppel was there, staying in Ernest Cassel's rooms at 2 rue de Cirque.[43] In his discreetly anecdotal memoir, Ponsonby gives a glimpse of her worrying for the King's safety in a restaurant when she noticed that the man sitting at the next table had a villainous face; he turned out to be yet another detective.[44]

The previous year, Bertie had delighted the kaiser by attending the annual regatta of the German navy at Kiel in June. This year he pointedly stayed away. William responded by publicly condemning Bertie's relationship with Mrs. Keppel. When this got back to London, Bertie was much annoyed.[45] Relations between uncle and nephew were deteriorating fast.

The King and Queen made a state visit to Ireland in July 1903. On his previous visit to Ireland in 1885, on the eve of Home Rule, Bertie had been greeted by sullen, hostile crowds, and this one began inauspiciously. After an overnight journey, he woke to pouring rain and the news that the Pope had died. No one was at ease, least of all the Irish chief secretary George Wyndham, who was minister in attendance. The King appeared dressed in uniform and consumed a substantial breakfast.[46] He told Wyndham to draft a speech for him, and soon they were smoking cigarettes together as the young man altered the address according to royal instructions. "The King vastly improved the draft and said exactly the right thing, so that Protestants and Catholics alike were pleased," Wyndham recalled.[47] In his speech, Bertie declared that the Pope's death had brought "a sadness which I share, remembering as I do the kindness with which his Holiness recently received me in Rome."[48] Wyndham noticed the King's relaxed professionalism, the "fat easy whisper" that put nervous Irishmen at ease. As the "Friend of Our Pope," Bertie received a rapturous welcome, especially in the Dublin slums.[49] "The King paced on and lit a cigarette, bowing and smiling and waving his hand to the ragamuffins in the branches. That finished me and now I love him," wrote Wyndham. As for Alix, she was "very naughty" and made Wyndham laugh as he gave his speech, but "did this in such a way as to make everyone, including the culprit, feel comfortable and witty." Standing beside her as she wore the Garter ribbon—which matched the blue of her eyes—ropes of pearls, and a breastplate of diamonds, Wyndham was in ecstasy: "She is an Angel."[50]

"Where's Alice?" heckled the crowd when they saw the King.[51] Mrs. Keppel's daughter Sonia (b. 1900) remembered "Kingy" coming to tea at their house on Portman Square and entertaining her by playing a game that consisted of racing pieces of bread and butter (butter side down) down the leg of his finely creased trousers.*[52] According to her sister Violet: "He had a rich German accent and smelt deliciously of eau de Portugal. He wore several rings set with small cabochon rubies and—true emblem of royalty—a Fabergé ribbed gold cigarette case."[53] At Queen Alexandra's children's garden party in 1904, the little Keppels caused raised eyebrows by climbing all over Kingy.[54]

Mrs. Keppel knew better than anyone how to entertain the King. Only she could avert that terrible moment, memorably described by Vita Sackville-West in her novel *The Edwardians,* when the King would "drum with irritable fingers upon the arm of his chair or upon the dinner-table. What a gulf there was between amusing the King and boring him! and for a woman all depended upon which side of the gulf she occupied. Life and death were in it."[55]

Gladys de Grey, Queen Alexandra's friend, finding herself sitting next to the King at dinner, whispered in desperation to Ponsonby: "For Heaven's sake suggest a topic for me to discuss with the King as I have sat next to him for three nights."

Ponsonby replied. "Give away your relations and friends and repeat any secrets about them."

She laughed. "But I did that the first night."[56]

Alice Keppel never bored the King. She always knew the latest scandal, the price of stocks, the last political move.[57] She understood that he preferred not to talk himself and liked to listen to general conversation. "King's Cross," she once ordered a cabbie.

"Not with you Ma'am," came the reply.[58]

Mrs. Keppel regularly stayed at Sandringham without her husband for the King's November birthday party. Lady Lytton reported in 1904 that the connection was "openly acknowledged at Court. The Queen does not like it but accepts the situation, being sometimes stiff with

---

* This much-repeated story seems improbable. George Lyttelton refused to believe it: "I mean, he may have been a fool about many things, but surely not about trousers?" (*The Lyttelton–Hart-Davis Letters,* vol. 3 [John Murray, 1981], pp.128–29.)

Mrs. Keppel, sometimes in appearance affectionate." Lady Lytton thought Mrs. Keppel "a rather coarse type of woman" but "very tactful, never putting herself forward or presuming on her position." When asked if any of Alice's children were the King's, she replied, "Oh no, they are very Jewish."[59]

In *The Edwardians,* Vita Sackville-West characterized Mrs. Keppel as Romola Chain, "a woman who erred and aspired with a certain magnificence": "She brought to everything the quality of the superlative. When she was worldly, it was on the grand scale. When she was mercenary, she challenged the richest fortunes. When she loved, it was in the highest quarters. When she admitted ambition, it was for the highest power." Alice Keppel was the sorely tried mother of Violet, the woman with whom Vita had a scandalous lesbian affair, but Vita could not resist a dig at "the one weakness" of Romola Chain: namely, that "she could not allow anyone to be better informed than herself. . . . The last word, the eventual bombshell of information, must proceed from her and no other."[60] Alice Keppel's thirst to be best informed was what equipped her to be Bertie's indispensable confidante, the guardian of his secrets. This was a role that Alix could never share.

After Bertie died, Alice Keppel told Lord Rosebery that for twelve years, "the King showed her every letter he received within minutes of receiving it." She claimed she had burned all her letters from him.[61] Barely a trace of this voluminous correspondence is to be found. The fact is that almost no evidence exists of Bertie's relationship with La Favorita.

In October 1903, much to the annoyance of clerk of the council Almeric Fitzroy, who was forced to make the journey specially from London, Bertie assembled the Privy Council at Lord Londonderry's Durham home, Wynyard. This was the first time the council had met in a country house since 1625, and Bertie insisted that it should be styled "At the Court at Wynyard."[62] Theresa Londonderry, once described as "a highwaywoman in a tiara, trampling on her enemies as if they had been a bed of nettles," was the queen of the Tory hostesses.[63] After the council, most of the party played poker except the King, who settled down to bridge with Louise, Duchess of Devonshire, heavily rouged and a fiend at the bridge table ("Ponte Vecchio," quipped the wags). Also playing bridge with him was Mrs. Keppel, who "behaved with great indiscretion," wrote Fitzroy, "for there is a self-consciousness about her which emphasises the equivoque of the situation. . . . She certainly retains great beauty, but her carriage suggests an uneven blend of pride and humiliation."[64] He might have been sketching Jezebel.

The Wynyard Privy Council illustrates the King's use of house parties for political purposes. To an extent often underestimated, Edwardian England was governed from its great country houses. The bachelor prime minister Balfour—"King Arthur" to the cultured clique of Souls—was, like Bertie, almost a professional house party guest. For the Souls and the Marlborough House set, such parties acted as a way of bonding and defining their identity. The house party was a feminized space; it was the sphere of the hostess, rather than her politically engaged husband. Great political hostesses such as Theresa Londonderry and Louise Devonshire used their social influence to bring opponents together and heal conflict; their role was inclusive and emollient, rather than partisan. The Souls were dedicated to cross-party friendships: at house parties Balfour would meet Liberals such as Asquith or Haldane on equal terms. Because it was neutral territory, the house party tapped into the role of the monarch as Bertie understood it—to act as a personal influence above politics and to smooth political differences. The rule at any social event where the King was a guest was that no one should talk politics, but Bertie's very presence gave a special political significance to the gathering.[65]

Bertie and Alix attended Louise Devonshire's Chatsworth Twelfth Night house party for the first time as King and Queen (they had stayed often as Prince and Princess of Wales) in 1904. Balfour was also present. While the King rode off to the shoot on his cob, the prime minister played golf. For the convenience of the King (but not, apparently, the prime minister), a telegraph wire was temporarily run into the house and a private office fitted up.[66] Alix was the party's life and soul. On the last evening she danced a waltz with Soveral, and then everyone took off their shoes to see what difference it made to their height. Daisy Pless, who excelled in the private theatricals, noted in her diary that "The Queen took, or rather kicked hers off, and then got into everyone else's, even into Willie Grenfell's old pumps. I never saw her so free and cheerful—but always graceful in everything she does." Mrs. Keppel was there, too: "The King has his bridge with Mrs. Keppel who is here—with lovely clothes and diamonds—in a separate room."[67]

Mrs. Keppel almost always accompanied the King on his house party visits. The Duchess of Portland made the mistake of leaving her off the list out of loyalty to Alix, and as a result incurred the royal wrath. Carrington recorded that "the King is reported to be more under Mrs. George's thumb than ever and the Portlands are in very bad odour because she was not asked to attend Welbeck. He looked on this as a slight to himself; and as she is asked by the Queen to Sandringham, her position is assured."[68] In the photographs that were invariably taken to commemorate the King's visits, Alice Keppel can be seen leaning back in her chair to display her bust-enlarging bodice, her eyes firmly fixed on her royal lover.

Each year in September the King stayed at Rufford, a famously haunted house, with Lord and Lady Savile for the Doncaster St. Leger. He brought a valet, a footman, a brusher, two equerries with valets, two telephonists, two chauffeurs, and an Arab boy to make coffee.[69] Mrs. Keppel was always there, and so were Mrs. Ronnie Greville and Lady Howe. "Lady Howe, who trots everywhere after the King like a little dog, is called the Kinki Bow Wow, and the Saviles and the Grevilles are called the Civils and Grovels."[*70]

The King was at Marienbad in August 1903, undergoing his cure and trying to escape the crowds who plagued him wherever he went,

---

* Mrs. Keppel's social-climbing friend Mrs. Ronnie Greville was a monster. The illegitimate daughter of Edinburgh brewer William McEwan by his cook, she resembled a Japanese pug dog. She entertained the King at Reigate Priory, and in 1906 she bought Polesden Lacey and decorated it in sumptuous red and gold. Bertie became a regular visitor. "I don't follow people to their bedrooms. It's what they do outside them that is important," she once remarked. "There is no one on earth quite so skilfully malicious as old Maggie," thought the diarist Chips Channon (*Chips: The Diaries of Sir Henry Channon* [Weidenfeld and Nicolson, 1967], pp. 208, 336.)

when he received reports from Prime Minister Balfour of a split in the Cabinet. Joseph Chamberlain had launched a campaign for imperial protection or tariff reform that shattered the Unionist party, and Balfour's equivocation and failure to give a lead only deepened the divisions, prompting five ministers to resign from the Cabinet. This was the first major political crisis of the reign. Though the details of the argument did not much concern him, Bertie thought tariff reform was a mistake.[71] "I am all in favour of taxing the *rich*," he declared, and when the Chancellor of the Exchequer asked whether he approved of taxing the food of the poor, he replied, "No . . . and I do not care who knows it!"[72] Mrs. Keppel was "a violent anti Chamberlainite, and a Free Fooder," which was probably significant.[73] Bertie's suggestion on 18 August that Balfour should refer the matter to a royal commission was politically naïve, and Balfour rightly dismissed it.[74] In September Bertie returned home, a stone lighter, sleek from his Marienbad diet of hock, no soup, and no puddings, to face his ministers.

The King wired Balfour asking him to delay announcing ministerial resignations until he had discussed matters at Balmoral. "This great haste is to be deprecated. . . . It would not look well in the eyes of the public that a matter of such importance should be settled without my having seen the Prime Minister."[75] Balfour claimed not to have received the telegram in time and released the resignations at once, but the breakup of the Cabinet and the hemorrhage of party support meant that he was a wounded prime minister and in no position to resist the King's demand to be consulted over the reshuffle. Not that Bertie was hostile to Balfour. If anything, he pitied him, regretting his lack of the "backbone" that "the distinguished uncle [Salisbury] he has lost possessed."[76]

The King's chief concern in the reshuffle was the appointment of the Secretary of State for War. St. John Brodrick, the incumbent, was tactless and self-important; Bertie later remarked that he found him "a most ridiculous personage" about whom he could never think "without bursting out laughing."[77] Since 1901, Brodrick had complained of the King's constant interference over issues such as uniform and promotions. During the Boer War, Brodrick was summoned so often to the palace that Sir Henry Campbell-Bannerman, the leader of the Liberal opposition, threatened to attack the King for trying to run the army himself. Brodrick in his memoirs charged the King with trying to emulate the kaiser, who decided army policy himself.[78] Bertie had no intention of behaving like the kaiser. His aim was to reform and modernize the army, which the Boer War had revealed to be alarmingly old-fashioned, rigid, and incompetent. His lifelong fascination with military matters went far beyond an addiction to uniforms. He was better equipped than many civilian ministers to push through reform, and he knew a great deal about European armies.

As part of the reshuffle, Balfour proposed to move Brodrick from the War Office to the India Office. The King was unexpectedly resistant to this. He had by now managed to tame Brodrick, and he thought he could rely upon him to introduce the much-needed army reform. Following the precedent of Queen Victoria, Bertie claimed a right to intervene over ministerial appointments. In place of Brodrick, he urged the appointment of Lord Esher to the War Office; and Balfour agreed.

Esher was a surprising choice. As permanent secretary at the Office of Works, his chief achievement to date had been the redecoration of the royal palaces. He was not a politician, and he had no military experience. In June 1902, at the end of the Boer War, Salisbury appointed a royal commission under Lord Elgin to investigate the organization of the army during the war, and the King nominated Esher as a member. Each day Esher filed incisive reports in beautiful handwriting to the King. This was just the sort of information that Bertie wanted, and Esher cleverly insinuated himself into the royal confidence. In 1902, Ernest Cassel offered him a job in the City with a salary of £5,000, and he resigned from the Office of Works; he was after bigger things.

Esher was summoned to Balmoral in September 1903, and the King (and later Balfour) offered him the War Office. He turned it down. This annoyed Bertie, but Esher was playing for high stakes. He had a reputation for refusing office, and this was the best refusal he ever made. Instead of taking office, he persuaded both Balfour and the King to appoint him to head a committee of three to carry out the reorganization of the War Office. "I am purely selfish in the matter," he wrote. Not only would political office mean sacrificing what he called his *intime* life,[79] but as a government minister he would be forced to leave the court, and he would no doubt quarrel with the King. Far better to exercise power without responsibility. As he explained to Balfour: "I <u>know</u> that as Secretary of State I should fail in the double capacity as a servant of the King and as your colleague."[80] Esher envisaged a system of double government, with the King's court operating in parallel with elected ministers. Rather than take office himself he preferred to operate backstairs at court. "It is the old story," he wrote. "Power and Place are not often synonymous."[81]

Esher was fifty-one, and his influence was at its height. His appointment as lieutenant and deputy governor of Windsor Castle gave him direct access to the King. He owed his entrée at Windsor to his wife, Nellie, who was a daughter of Queen Victoria's friend Madame Van de Weyer, the widow of the Belgian minister. Esher inherited his title from his father, a self-made lawyer, the son of a curate who became Master of the Rolls. His real emotional bond was to Eton. He was a protégé of the charismatic homosexual master William Johnson Cory, who encouraged him to have affairs with other boys, and even in adult life he never really grew away from his alma mater. At the time of his rise to favor at court, Esher was besotted with his own son, the unprepossessing Etonian Maurice (Molly), to whom he wrote adoring letters, pouring out all the secrets of the War Office. That Bertie knew of this infatuation is unlikely, but Esher was certainly running risks, living "on a knife edge." At Windsor Castle, he had a room that Maurice and other Eton boys visited, and which he called the Nest, where he kept blazers and photographs of boys.[82]

Esher understood the working of the King's mind. As he explained to Admiral Fisher, who complained that the King was unable to grasp details: "HM has two receptive plates in his mind. One retains lasting impressions. I have tested this over and over again. The other, only mostly fleeting ones. On the former are stamped his impressions of <u>people</u> and their relative value. On the latter, of <u>things</u>, and these are apt to fade or be removed by later ones. But, and this is the essential point, if you can stamp your image on number one . . . you can always rely on carrying your point."[83]

Esher's Committee on the War Office reported with impressive speed in January 1904. Esher proposed to establish an Army Council or General Staff. He was very clear that the army was to be run by politicians, not the King. "In Germany it is the emperor who co-ordinates the action of the German Navy and Army. In Britain it can only be the Prime Minister. That is a constitutional axiom."[84] By scrapping the commander-in-chief, the influence of the Crown was reduced. This was the price that Bertie had to pay to achieve his aim of reforming the army.[85] Not that royal influence was eliminated. The new office of inspector general was given to Bertie's brother Arthur, Duke of Connaught.*

The War Office loathed Esher for his meddling with appointments and for his "disgraceful" treatment of Lord Roberts, whom he had forced to resign as commander in chief.[86] The politicians loathed him, too, and with good reason. Esher did his best to undermine the Secretary of State for War, H. O. Arnold-Forster, a tactless but well-intentioned reformer. He interfered with Arnold-Forster's reforms by going behind his back to the King, and he purported to speak on the King's behalf. His palace intrigues "left a thread of mischief-making and bitterness woven into the reform movement" that jeopardized its success.[87]

The new Lord Salisbury told Balfour that Esher's relations with the King were "in the highest degree unsatisfactory. He ought either to be a responsible minister and defend his views in parliament or (at the very most) he should confine himself to intensely confidential conversations with yourself." Salisbury considered that Esher meddled far too much. "A person who is in confidential communication with the military chiefs and with the King and works against the Secretary of

---

* Esher saw Arthur at Balmoral in 1904 and was not impressed. The duke was a "very amiable but silly goose" and "very chancy in his kilt—sits in odd positions—and shows everything he has to show, which is not much." (Lees-Milne, *Esher*, p. 151.)

State is a dangerous individual."[88] If anyone abused the constitutional power of the Crown, it was Esher.

Esher was a liability, and yet Bertie seemed oblivious, such was Esher's skill in insinuating himself into the King's confidence. In December 1905, Carrington was in Francis Knollys's room when the door opened and in walked Esher. "He certainly is an extraordinary man and has a wonderful footing at Buckingham Palace. He seems to be able to run about as he likes—and must be a considerable nuisance to the household."[89] Early in 1906, the King told Esher (so Esher related), "Although you are not exactly a public servant, yet I always think you are the most valuable servant I have," and (Esher told his son, Molly) "then I kissed his hand as I sometimes do."[90] The coda, suppressed from the published version of this letter, is: "But in doing it I only thought how little all this meant including the kiss, compared with a kiss upon another hand, and a few words of affection or appreciation from other lips."[91] Bertie cannot be blamed for not knowing of Esher's secret life—he would surely have been horrified if he had known what was in Esher's mind at that moment; but his failure to see how dangerous Esher was must count as an error of judgment.

The tariff reform split of 1903 left the Balfour government mortally wounded. Balfour was in the unenviable position of John Major or Anthony Eden, the heir to a charismatic prime minister who inherits a government that is already sinking. Like Major or Eden, the qualities which made him a successful number two—administrative skill and a reputation for cleverness—did not equip him for leadership. Balfour's weakness made the King stronger. Bertie had grown into his job, while Balfour had failed in his. Balfour had begun the new reign by lecturing the King on the constitution, but the roles were soon reversed, and Bertie came to view his prime minister with a mixture of pity and exasperation. As part of the Entente Cordiale colonial barter with France, Britain relinquished fourteen thousand square miles in West Africa. Balfour invited Parliament to assent, heedless of the fact that the power to cede territory was a royal prerogative. Bertie considered that Balfour had treated him with "scant courtesy": "He is always so vague that probably he is wrong, but I must insist, if he is, and as a matter of principle, that he <u>admits</u> it."[92] The King was right, but he gave way, and the royal prerogative to cede territory passed to Parliament.

The power of the Crown is usually calibrated in terms of the monarch's power to resist his ministers, but the sovereign can equally play an important part in "putting his influence and authority behind the government, which is exactly what King Edward did."[93] So sorry did the King feel for his stricken prime minister, who, as a commoner, ranked below some members of his own Cabinet, that he wrote (through Knollys): "The King thinks it would be only decent and proper that the Prime Minister should have some precedency formally laid down for him. . . . After the Sovereign the Prime Minister is certainly the most important man in the Empire and he should therefore have a correspondingly important position."[94] Balfour replied (through his private secretary, J. S. Sandars) that he was "not a little touched by HM's condescension."[95] Accordingly, in 1905, a warrant was drawn up, based on a memorandum by Sandars, formally recognizing the prime minister as the King's fourth most important subject, after the Archbishops of Canterbury and York and the Lord Chancellor. This constitutional adjustment is usually credited to Balfour; but, as these documents reveal, the change was made on the initiative of the King.[96]

The King told Balfour in early 1905 (through Knollys) that "he is very sorry for you and for all that you have to go through, and he only trusts that you will not knock up."[97] Again, in July, after Balfour had received a mauling in the House of Commons, Knollys told him that "the King desires me to . . . say how much disgusted he feels at the crude and vulgar attacks" made especially by Winston Churchill and David Lloyd George, "and to add that he thinks your answer was an excellent one."[98]

One of Balfour's worst headaches was India, where George Curzon, the viceroy, was locked into a struggle with Lord Kitchener (the commander in chief). At issue was the question of whether the Indian army should remain subject to the dual control of viceroy and C in C, as Curzon insisted, or whether the C in C should take over the military administration, as Kitchener urged. The incompetent Brodrick, appointed Secretary of State for India in the reshuffle of 1903, mishandled the dispute badly and decided in favor of Kitchener. The King took Curzon's side during this controversy. Bertie and Curzon had little in common. Curzon despised the King, who he thought was not at all what a king should be.*[99] But when Curzon resigned, Bertie fired off a telegram to Balfour suggesting that, in order to soothe feelings, Curzon should be made an earl at once.[100] Balfour wired back the same day: "There are manifest difficulties in course proposed—GC has resigned because he differed from policy of Government. Under most favourable construction he cannot be said to have behaved well. To reward him would be equivalent to a public intimation that the sure road to honour was disobedience to instructions."[101]

The refusal of Curzon's earldom was urged by Brodrick, but it was Balfour who made the decision.[102] Francis Knollys complained to Sandars that "the position Mr. Balfour has taken up is a weak one. Are Curzon's five years' brilliant administration to be ignored and unrecognised for differing from the government and making difficulties about instructions, rather than disobeying them?"[103] Balfour replied with a twenty-five-page dictated letter splitting hairs but stubbornly justifying his position—a document that even today makes the heart sink.[104]

As usual, the King gave way. As usual, the King was right. Balfour's vindictiveness toward his old friend poisoned their relationship for life, and Curzon played a key role in breaking his leadership of the Unionist party in 1911. Self-indulgent philistine though he was, the King understood the art of management far better than Balfour the repressed intellectual.

* Bertie had annoyed the snobbish Curzon, who was a stickler for correctness, by telling him off for signing himself as plain Curzon, rather than using his formal title Curzon of Kedleston. The King's friend Earl Howe, whose family name was Curzon, had complained to the King that George Curzon had poached his courtesy title of Viscount Curzon. (Gilmour, *Curzon*, pp. 127–28.)

CHAPTER 24

Uncle of Europe

1905–7

Charles Stamper was engaged as motor engineer to the King in 1905. On every drive that Bertie made, Stamper sat in the front, next to the chauffeur, with his royal master in the backseat. Nattily dressed, with a waxed mustache, and a touch theatrical (his brother was an actor), the twenty-nine-year-old Stamper had begun his career as a coach builder, like his father before him.[1] It was his job to maintain the King's two 40 hp Mercedes cars, his Daimler and the Renault landaulet he used in London. The King's claret-colored cars had no license plate, which made them instantly recognizable. Only the Renault was fitted with a number, as the King used it when he wanted not to be seen. Like all HM's cars, it was emblazoned with the royal arms, so the disguise hardly made him invisible. Stamper arranged every itinerary, and he kept a record of his journeys, which he later published with some help from Dornford Yates.[2] Bertie timed his drives to the minute. "Fine run, Stamper. Fine run," he would say. When the King attended a house party, he traveled on the royal train, which was painted crimson and cream, and designed to resemble the royal yacht inside, with white enamel paint and polished brass.[3] At the nearest station, he would be met by Stamper, who had driven ahead, preceded by charabancs bearing the King's luggage.

In December 1905, Stamper drove the King to a house party at Crichel, where he was the guest of Lord and Lady Alington. They were second-generation members of the Marlborough House set and great friends of Mrs. Keppel, whose daughter Sonia Keppel remembered Lady Alington's "pale face and full lips and small alert eyes" as being somehow at variance with her large, lazy body, enveloped in "a billowing ocean of lace and ribbons."*[4] The King stayed at Crichel for five days, but if this disconcerted his hosts, they need not have worried, as Mrs. Keppel was also a guest, and "so long as Mrs. George is here, he is perfectly happy."[5] Over three days the party shot three thousand pheasants. The King's stand was marked by a red label on a stick (all the other places had white ones) so that the beaters could skillfully direct clouds of pheasants to fly over his head.[6]

Just before Bertie's visit to Crichel, a political crisis blew up. On the afternoon of Monday, 4 December, Prime Minister Balfour, had an audience at Buckingham Palace and offered his resignation. Balfour's government had been in a state of terminal decline for months, but he resigned without waiting to face the electorate. He insisted on going before Christmas 1905, earlier than expected, which, Bertie told Georgie, "I think is unnecessary and a mistake."[7] Pressed by the King to accept an honor, Balfour declined, but he agreed to accept the blue and red Windsor uniform. The following morning, at ten forty-five, Bertie summoned the Liberal leader Sir Henry Campbell-Bannerman and invited him to form a government. "Nothing could be nicer or more courteous than he was," Bertie told Georgie.[8] The sixty-nine-year-old CB was a round-faced, white-whiskered Scot. "We are not as young as

---

* The Alingtons' London house was 38 Portman Square, opposite Mrs. Keppel at number 30. Both of their parents had played minor parts in the Aylesford scandal. Feo Alington was the daughter of the Earl of Hardwicke, and Lord Alington's father was Henry Sturt (see pp. 229–30).

we were, Sir Henry!" said the King and shook him warmly by the hand. Whereupon (according to Margot Asquith's diary), "knowing that he ought to kneel and kiss hands, CB advanced and waited, but the King interrupted by some commonplace remark; when he had finished speaking, CB again advanced meaning to kneel, but the King only wrang his hand, at which he felt the interview was over, as to have had another try would have been grotesque."[9] After this, the King boarded the special train for Crichel.

Knollys regretted his master's absence from London: "Your Majesty would, I am sure, have had more direct control over the negotiations, and Sir H[enry] could then, without any difficulty, have referred to you from time to time the proposals which were made for the filling up of the various offices."[10] From Crichel, Bertie was accommodating. Knollys telephoned declaring: "The King agrees to everything."[11]

Bertie was back in London at five thirty on Sunday, 10 December, and an hour later he saw CB with the list of ministers. He wrote to his sister Princess Louise: "The new Gov[ernmen]t promises to be a strong one—and I find Sir H. Campbell-Bannerman charming to do business with."[12] CB was the first prime minister to receive formal constitutional recognition in accordance with the warrant drawn up by Sandars and Balfour at the King's suggestion. The next day, the outgoing ministers gave up their seals of office, and the new administration was sworn in at a meeting of the Privy Council. London was blanketed with thick black fog; the King's carriage was preceded by twelve running footmen bearing flaring torches, and the new government began, as Bertie quipped, "by losing their way!"[13] Esher noticed that the fog affected the King's breathing, and he was very unwell at dinner.[14]

By remaining at Crichel and distancing himself from the change of government, Bertie ensured that no one could accuse him of meddling. This has earned him the approval of some historians, who note that, unlike Queen Victoria, he allowed CB a free hand with appointments.[15] In point of fact, Bertie had been playing a cool game behind the scenes. By the time Balfour resigned, the King had done all he needed to do to ensure the outcome he wanted.

Campbell-Bannerman's succession as prime minister had not gone unchallenged. In the autumn of 1905, a plot had been hatched to banish CB to the House of Lords, thus making him a figurehead prime minister. This coup was planned by H. H. Asquith, R. B. Haldane, and Edward Grey, meeting at Relugas, a remote Scottish fishing lodge. The Relugas plot is remarkable because it hinged on an attempt to drag the Crown into party politics. Involving the King was the idea of Haldane, Scottish lawyer and German-loving intellectual, who had known Bertie for a couple of years. It was a dangerous game, especially for a Liberal politician. Even more extraordinary was the response of Knollys, whom Haldane approached. Acting with astonishing indiscretion for a man who had spent his life in the service of the court, Knollys wrote to Haldane giving guarded assurances of the King's support.[16]

Bertie knew about Haldane's intrigues, but he refused to be drawn in. In August, while undergoing his cure at Marienbad, he had met Campbell-Bannerman. It turned out that CB had spent his holidays at Marienbad for thirty years, bringing his invalid wife, Charlotte, to whom he was devoted. He disapproved of the King and the tainted ladies who buzzed around him like bluebottles. Bertie, for his part, expected the Scot, the son of a Glasgow merchant who looked like a grocer, to be "prosy and heavy," and distrusted him on account of the unpatriotic, "pro-Boer" line he had taken during the Boer War.[17] He asked CB to lunch, and was surprised to discover that he was a *bon viveur* with a sense of humor who shared his love of Austrian coffee and French food.* For two weeks, CB was constantly entertained by the King at the Hotel Weimar. Bertie told him that "he must soon be in office and very high office." CB thought this "most significant and very

---

* An illustrated paper printed a picture of the King talking earnestly to CB at Marienbad beneath the caption, "Is it Peace or War?" "Would you like to know what the King was saying to me?" CB asked his private secretary. "He wanted to have my opinion whether halibut is better baked or boiled." (Wilson, *CB*, p. 145.)

discreetly done."[18] Nothing was said by the King about CB's translation to the Lords.

So exhausted was CB by Bertie's "insatiable" energy and appetite, by the long evenings sitting out after dinner making sticky conversation while HM played bridge, that when the King departed he took to his bed for forty-eight hours. Bertie, on the other hand, considered Marienbad a rest cure.[19]

After Marienbad, he proceeded to Balmoral, where Haldane was summoned. Bertie told him that he had read his correspondence with Knollys "with much interest." He also told him that he had met CB, and liked him.[20] Haldane formed the impression that the King would cooperate in sidelining CB, but he was mistaken. Bertie's aim in all of this was to reconcile the Relugas conspirators to the leadership of CB—to smooth the rift in the Liberal party. CB, for his part, knew that he had the King's backing, and this made it possible for him to crush the Relugas rebels. He persuaded them to take office, and he refused to allow himself to be kicked upstairs to the House of Lords.

Bertie's chief concern in the change of government was to ensure continuity in foreign policy and uphold the entente with France. In the autumn of 1905, Esher was dispatched to consult Lansdowne as to his successor as foreign secretary. Lansdowne suggested Lord Spencer (who suffered a stroke) and, after him, Edward Grey—though he lacked experience and Lansdowne thought "his reputation has been rather cheaply earned."[21] The forty-three-year-old Grey was one of the Relugas three. He was also the King's godson; his father, General Grey, had been Bertie's equerry.

Grey got the job. "I shall do all I can to stem the impetuosity of the new Government but it will not be easy," Bertie told Georgie. "Fortunately in Sir E. Grey we have a sensible man who wishes as regards our foreign policy to walk in his predecessor's footsteps."[22]

A critical moment had been reached in Anglo-Russian relations. Because Russia was France's ally, the survival and strength of the Entente Cordiale depended on good relations between England and Russia. According to Charles Hardinge, who served in St. Petersburg between 1897 and 1902 and spoke to Bertie often at this time: "King Edward saw clearly what few others realised, that friendship with Russia was essential for us both in the Near East and Central Asia, and that this could only be obtained through the channel and by the cooperation of France."[23]

The friendship with Russia was strained to breaking point by the Russo-Japanese War of 1904. England agreed to stay out of the war, in spite of the fact that the Japanese had been their allies since 1902, but the Russians suspected them of lending secret support. When the Japanese confounded expectations and defeated the Russians, waves of Anglophobia swept through Russia. Urged on by Kaiser William, Czar Nicholas II blamed the English for Russia's humiliation. In Britain, anti-Russian opinion was inflamed by the Dogger Bank incident of October 1904, when the Russian fleet accidentally shot at British fishing boats, which they mistakenly thought were Japanese submarines.

It was here that Bertie's dynastic links had counted. Acting at the request of foreign secretary Lansdowne, he sought to reassure Nicholas II of England's friendly intentions.[24] "Nicky" was a small, conscientious man with velvety blue eyes who lived in isolation in a Fabergé-encrusted palace made unbearable by the neurosis of his wife, Alexandra. He was not an easy man to approach: "He will hardly ever see an ambassador." Stead, the journalist, was granted an interview and found the czar "absolutely like a child in the simplicity of his views and in the little knowledge of what is going on in the country"—Russia was at that time in the grip of the 1905 revolution.[25] Bertie had little respect for Nicky, whom he thought weak as water and unable to make up his mind to do anything.[26] But as uncle to both Nicky, who was uncannily like Prince George in looks, and Alexandra, Bertie enjoyed unequaled access. His role was to drive a wedge between his nephews, Czar Nicky and Kaiser William.* The kaiser cultivated the czar in indiscreet letters badmouthing their wicked uncle. The czar, as the kaiser

---

* Nicky was the son of Alix's sister Minnie; Alexandra was the daughter of Bertie's sister Alice; William was the son of Bertie's sister Vicky.

wrote, was "not treacherous but he is weak—weakness is not treachery but it fulfils all its functions."[27] Bertie's man in St. Petersburg was
Donald Mackenzie Wallace, a swarthy, cigar-smoking journalist, described by the kaiser as "very intelligent; a friend of King Edward's; a
Jew naturally."[28] Wallace had better access to the czar than the ambassador, and penned long, confidential reports to the King.

Bertie was fortunate in that both the Russian ambassador in London and the British ambassador in St. Petersburg were on his side.
Both were, in a way, Bertie's appointments. Count Benckendorff, who
became Russian ambassador in London in 1902, was a passionate Anglophile. A rich, easygoing aristocrat, he entertained more lavishly at
the Russian embassy than any of the ambassadors in London before
1914.[29] He took pride in behaving as a "private gentleman"; flouting
protocol about diplomatic tight lips, he freely expressed his own opinions.* Soon Benckendorff was asked to shoot at Windsor and to stay at
Balmoral. He was openly critical of Nicholas, whom he compared dis-
paragingly to Bertie, and thought Russia's only chance of salvation lay
in an entente with Britain.

In London, Bertie leaned on Lansdowne to accept his nominations
for key diplomatic posts.[30] Bertie was instrumental in shoehorning his
protégé Charles Hardinge into high office. As a reward for Hardinge's
work on the 1903 visit to France, Bertie pushed strongly for his appointment as ambassador to St. Petersburg in 1904. Lansdowne agreed,
though not without reservations—Hardinge was not yet due for this
senior promotion.[31] Hardinge wrote from St. Petersburg to Knollys:
"My appointment has been regarded as due entirely to the King's ini-

---

* Benckendorff was a favorite of Minnie's—he had been her dancing partner in the 1870s—
and it was due to her that he was appointed Russian minister in Copenhagen. This was
where Bertie first encountered him, and in 1902, when Baron de Staal, the Russian ambassador in London, retired, Bertie asked Nicholas II to appoint Benckendorff as a token of
friendship. On his arrival in London, he gave Benckendorff a private audience and told him
that he was touched by Nicholas's gesture in sending "the diplomat whom he had personally
mentioned." (Marina Soroka, "Debating Russia's Choice Between Great Britain and Germany: Count Benckendorff versus Count Lamsdorff, 1902–1906," *International History Review*, vol. 32 [2010], esp. pp. 3–7.)

tiative, and as a guarantee of peace and of more friendly relations between the two Governments."[32]

In the autumn of 1905, Bertie helped secure yet another promotion for Hardinge, who leapfrogged to the very top job of head of the Foreign Office. Hardinge wrote thanking Knollys for the part he had played in engineering the move: "I would be grateful . . . if you would seize a suitable opportunity to tell the King how thankful I am for His Majesty's gracious intervention on my behalf." When Benckendorff expressed a fear that Hardinge's recall implied a cooling of Britain's attitude toward Russia, Hardinge reassured him. "I explained to him the object and motives of my appointment to the FO at a moment when a change of government is imminent and I pointed out the advantage to the Russian government of having somebody at the FO who is friendly disposed towards them."[33]

Bertie wanted Hardinge in London because he needed someone to act as a handle on the incoming foreign secretary, the inexperienced Edward Grey. Hardinge benefited from the royal patronage, but he and his allies at the Foreign Office had an agenda of their own. With the help of the King's support, they levered themselves into key positions, purging the old guard that had controlled the FO in Lord Salisbury's day and creating a strongly anti-German climate.[34]

At the Foreign Office after 1906, Charles Hardinge dominated the inexperienced Edward Grey in a way that would have been unthinkable in the days of Salisbury or Lansdowne.[35] With the King, he made himself indispensable; he was effectively the King's minister. He corresponded frequently with Bertie and also with Knollys, short-circuiting Grey and giving the King detailed intelligence.

Hardinge insisted that all communication between the King and the Foreign Office should go through the "proper channels." This was code for cutting out the King's friend Esher, who was politically a Tory. When Esher on behalf of the King asked for information about the Baghdad Railway, Hardinge minuted Knollys: "We cannot possibly admit Esher's interference in our Foreign Office affairs." If the King wants information, "we look to receiving a request for it through the proper channel," that is, Knollys himself. "Sir Edward Grey feels very strongly that Esher is not the proper channel between him and the King."[36] Hardinge accompanied the King on all his meetings with the kaiser or other monarchs, filling the place of the foreign secretary as minister in attendance. He used the royal connection to gain access to the kaiser that would otherwise have been impossible for an official. Bertie discussed foreign questions with Hardinge in a way that he did with no one except Knollys. He would talk to ministers or ambassadors without admitting their argument. As his assistant private secretary Arthur Davidson wrote, "The King never allowed himself to go beyond generalities in either writing or speaking. . . . His mind and his brain took in everything although his lips were silent." The discussions came later with Knollys or Hardinge, but never with his informant. "That is why the King always scored, and therein his difference from the German Emperor who always answered, always discussed and always failed." The King's letters were "banal to a degree," but this was intentional; the only people to whom he opened up on paper were Hardinge and Knollys.[37]

The January 1906 election gave the Liberals a landslide victory, reducing the Conservatives to a rump of 157. "What a terribly radical speech the King had to make at the opening of Parliament," commented the Princess of Wales to her aunt Augusta. "How he must have hated it."[38] King Edward's correspondence with his prime minister reveals his attempts to apply the brakes. Like Queen Victoria, the King demanded to be kept informed, but in this respect Campbell-Bannerman turned out to be little better than Balfour. His Cabinet reports, penned in crabbed and shaky black ink, were perfunctory, sometimes only half a sheet of notepaper. The King's irritable comments, penciled on slips of paper, are bound beside them in the archive. "The information as usual is meagre."[39] CB's jottings were meant to forestall intervention by the King by preventing him from knowing what was going on; it is sobering to reflect that these scrappy notes form the sole official record of the 1906 Liberal Cabinet.

No doubt the seventy-year-old prime minister was feeling his years. As Esher wrote, "The influence of age is upon him. . . . He cannot bring himself to write. It thoroughly bores him."[40] But Bertie suspected that he was being deliberately kept in the dark. He was especially annoyed by the radical speeches of Lloyd George and Winston Churchill. When Lloyd George blustered about the creation of a minister for Wales, the King expostulated: "I have heard nothing on the subject from the Prime Minister! This proceeding is most unconstitutional, and I cannot pass over it in silence."[41] CB apologized and, smooth as ever, explained: "I ought to have been more on the spot," but his wife was seriously ill and he nursed her day and night.[42] The King was not mollified. "It seems inconceivable that the P. M. has so little control over the members of his Cabinet," he harrumphed. "The excuse he gives for Mr. L. G. is a very meagre one."[43]

Even more of a thorn in the royal flesh was Winston Churchill. Bertie watched with displeasure when the bumptious, self-seeking Churchill defected from the Tories and joined the Liberals in search of promotion, and he was "disgusted" by Churchill's "crude and vulgar" attacks on Balfour in 1905.[44] He was disgusted, too, by his behavior in office after 1905. Churchill behaved like a rebellious son, anxious for the King's approval and validation as well as his patronage, yet unable to resist pushing the boundaries and provoking a reaction. As colonial undersecretary, Churchill handled the granting of self-government to South Africa, and at the end of 1906 he wrote the King a thirty-five-page letter explaining his reasons for allowing the Boers the vote under the new constitution. Bertie's reply ended with a sentence drafted by Ponsonby but amended in pencil by Bertie (his words are given in italics): "His Majesty is glad to see that you are becoming a *reliable* Minister and above all a *serious* politician *which can only be attained by putting country above party.*"[45]

That winter of 1905–6, the King visited Agnew's Gallery on Bond Street, where he spent half an hour alone with Velázquez's painting of a nude Venus. Agnew's had bought the masterpiece from the cash-strapped owner of Rokeby Park in Teesside, and the newly founded National Art Collections Fund launched an appeal to buy it for the National Gallery. In early January 1906, the fund announced that they had failed to raise the £45,000 that Agnew's asked for, and the press reported that the Velázquez was lost to the nation. A few weeks later came the surprise announcement that, thanks to an anonymous donor, the painting had been saved. In spite of demands for transparency, the committee of the fund refused to reveal the identity of the last-minute savior of the *Rokeby Venus*. Not until 1996 was the secret uncovered. A letter was found, pasted into the committee's minute book, written on Buckingham Palace paper by the banker and collector Robert Benson, who was treasurer of the fund. It read as follows: "When you see Mr. Lockett Agnew at 11 a.m. about the Velasquez Venus with the Mirror you are at liberty to tell him that Major Holford mentioned the position to His Majesty who was much interested."[46] Holford was Benson's brother-in-law, also a collector and an equerry. On behalf of the King, Benson undertook to subscribe £8,000 and guarantee a further £5,000 for twelve months, making the purchase possible. In May 1906, the King became patron of the fund.

Velázquez's painting of the luscious back view of a fleshy nude lying on her side and holding a mirror excited a storm of controversy. Moralists attacked it as indecent; Lord Ronald Gower, art critic and homosexual, revolted perhaps by the female bottom, thundered against the folly of buying such a painting for a public gallery. Bertie, on the other hand, surely agreed with Lady Colin Campbell, who praised the "radiant warmth of the dimpled flesh."[47] Nowadays, perhaps, he preferred power to sex, but his secret gift of the Venus shows that he was indifferent neither to art nor to female beauty.

The *Rokeby Venus* had a life of its own. It became an icon of Edwardian sexuality, polarizing attitudes toward women. In May 1914, a suffragette named Mary Richardson slashed the canvas with a butcher's cleaver. She claimed she was protesting against the government's harsh treatment of the suffragette Mrs. Pankhurst, but as an old woman she admitted: "I didn't like the way men visitors gawped at it all day long."[48]

Bertie was vehemently opposed to women's suffrage. He ticked off the prime minister, Campbell-Bannerman, for supporting the Women's Franchise Bill in 1907, which he thought "undignified."[49] As for the suffragettes, their campaign was "outrageous and does their cause (for which I have no sympathy) much harm."[50] Yet this was the son of one of the most powerful women in British history, and the brother of an intellectual woman who was a key player in German politics. A man who despised his beautiful wife as bird-brained, respected his daughter-in-law Princess Mary for her intelligence, and relied heavily on the political advice of his shrewd mistress, Alice Keppel, could hardly be described as contemptuous of women's ability or education. But he had no time for the New Woman and remained firmly attached to the Victorian idea of separate spheres. When Daisy Warwick made speeches, he wrote: "Why on earth do you want women to be like men and copy their pursuits? God put you into the world to be different from us but you don't seem to see it!"[51]

In November 1905, Bertie fell down a rabbit hole while out shooting at Windsor and tore his Achilles tendon. Dr. Treves gave him an iron splint, and he hobbled painfully wearing this contraption. This did not stop him shooting. A specially constructed pony carriage conveyed him to his stand, where the pony was unharnessed, and the King shot sitting in the carriage.[52] He managed to kill 120 pheasants at Hall Barn in this way.[53] The royal physician Sir Felix Semon became concerned in February when an attack of bronchitis "threatened to involve the circulatory system," and on Semon's advice, the King traveled to Biarritz.[54]

The Hôtel du Palais at Biarritz was a brand-new French chateau poised on the very edge of the Atlantic coast. It was built on the site of the Empress Eugénie's palace, which had burned down in 1903. From his ground-floor rooms the King found the continual roll of the Atlantic "not unpleasant"; he worked on his government boxes in the sea air, beneath a striped canopy erected on the terrace.[55] Mrs. Keppel and her children stayed nearby as the guests of Ernest Cassel in the Villa Eugénie. Once the property of the Prince Imperial, the villa reminded Sonia

Keppel of "a large, uninhabited conservatory, with carpetless floors and glass doors, and with its inmates potted about in it like plants."[56] Assorted duchesses gathered nearby, providing bridge and entertainment; among them was Consuelo, Duchess of Manchester, who had been newly restored to favor. Her son had gone down on bended knee in the street to beg Bertie's forgiveness for his mother, who had been banished ever since Daisy Warwick had got rid of the Americans.[57]

Biarritz was perfectly positioned for Bertie's dynastic diplomacy. Princess Beatrice's daughter, Ena, had become engaged to King Alfonso of Spain, and Bertie did what he could to help place his niece on the Spanish throne. When Alfonso insisted that Ena should convert to Catholicism, Bertie ignored Protestant demands that he should withhold his consent, and appealed to the Lord Chancellor, Lord Loreburn, who ruled that the 1772 Royal Marriages Act, which required that marriages of descendants of George III receive the consent of the ruling monarch, did not apply to Princess Ena because she was a Battenberg.[58] Stamper, who had driven the royal cars out from England, accompanied the King on a visit to Alfonso at San Sebastián. The King laughed at the soldiers guarding the route, who lolled casually in the sun, smoking cigarettes. His car was mobbed by a hysterical crowd; at one point twenty people clung to the back, and Bertie had to be rescued by Sergeant Quin of the Criminal Investigation Department, who drove his car within a few inches of the King's.[59] The incompetence of Spanish security was shockingly revealed at Ena's wedding in Madrid in May, when a terrorist threw a bomb that missed the royal couple but killed people in the crowd, spattering the bride's dress with blood.

Only a week after Ena's wedding, Bertie's daughter Maud was crowned Queen of Norway, marking yet another success for Bertie's dynasty building. When the union of Norway and Sweden was peacefully dissolved in 1905, Bertie had pushed Maud's husband, Prince Charles of Denmark, to grasp the Norwegian throne, though the British government was strictly neutral. The Danish claim was opposed by Kaiser William, who wanted a pro-German Norway. Charles was a reluctant candidate, and Bertie had to bully him. "The moment has now come for you to act or lose the Crown of Norway," he wired. "I urge you to go at once to Norway, with or without the consent of the Danish government."[60] In November 1905, Prince Charles was elected King Haakon VII of Norway.

The kaiser, meanwhile, had held a secret meeting with the czar. In July, the two emperors arranged a yachting rendezvous at Björkö, in the Gulf of Finland. Giving their ministers the slip, Willy and Nicky were reunited like gleeful schoolboys. They grumbled about Uncle Bertie, who they agreed was the "arch-intriguer" and "mischief maker." Willy complained about Bertie's "absolute passion for making 'a little agreement' with every country, everywhere." Nicky replied, banging the table: "Well, I can only say, he shall not get one from me, and never in my life against Germany—my word of honour on it."[61] Whereupon Willy produced a paper from his pocket, and invited Nicky to sign a treaty with Germany.

Dismissed by the foreign ministers of both Russia and Germany, the treaty was never ratified, and Björkö has been described by one historian as a "fantasy of autocratic effectiveness."[62] Whether or not Bertie knew about it, he made no attempt to conceal his irritation with William. The Foreign Office quaked. Foreign secretary Lansdowne blamed the King for a worsening of relations with the kaiser: "He talks and writes about his Royal Brother in terms which makes one's flesh creep, and the official papers which go to him whenever they refer to H. I. M., come back with all sorts of accusations of a most incendiary character."[63]

Charles Hardinge, however, considered that King Edward "thoroughly understood" the emperor. "He knew his weaknesses, his vanity and his duplicity. He realised the Kaiser's jealousy of his own position and influence in Europe and the danger to be apprehended from the Kaiser's megalomania."[64] Touchy and volatile, lurching from grandiose swagger to kitsch homeliness and mawkish sentimentality, from bullying aggression to hypersensitive paranoia, the kaiser baffled his contemporaries and remains an enigma today.[65]

Like a fat old cat playing with an angry mouse, Bertie manipulated William and worked on his emotions. In January 1906, shortly after the

opening of the Algeciras Conference to resolve the dispute between
Germany and France over Morocco, Bertie wrote his nephew a birthday letter. "We are—my dear William—such old friends and near relations that I feel sure that the affectionate feelings which have always
existed may invariably continue. Most deeply do I deplore the uncalled-
for expressions made use of in the Press concerning our two countries
and most ardently do I trust that they will cease."[66] To Kaiser William
this appeal, however insincere, was impossible to resist. Assuring his
uncle that "my life's endeavour" was to achieve a mutual understanding between their two countries (which at one level was the truth),
William begged him to remember the "silent hours when we watched
and prayed" at the bedside of dear Grandmama, "when the spirit of
that great Sovereign-Lady passed away, as she drew her last breath in
my arms. I feel sure that from the home of Eternal Light she is now
looking down upon us and will rejoice when she sees our hands clasped
in cordial and loyal friendship."[67]

At Biarritz in the spring of 1906, Bertie received "concise and most
interesting" letters from Hardinge, updating him on the negotiations
at Algeciras.[68] William's designs to isolate France collapsed like a house
of cards as England and Russia stood by their ally. Germany suffered a
humiliating diplomatic defeat. William angrily blamed Bertie, as did
his ministers and the German press.[69] King Edward, sitting beside the
sea at Biarritz, going on motor picnics with Mrs. Keppel, had, in fact,
done nothing at Algeciras.[70]

Mrs. Keppel preserved the menu that the King wrote for dinner on the
last evening of his stay at Biarritz: scrambled eggs *aux fines herbes,* fillet
of sole, lamb chops, creamed spinach, chicken, roast woodcock, and
peach tart.[71] After this light meal, Bertie departed without his mistress
for a month's Mediterranean cruise with his wife. Alix was mourning
her father King Christian. Looking "very sad & tired after her great
sorrow," "Motherdear" was anxious to see her brother Willie, the King
of Greece, but this was no relaxing family holiday.[72] The Uncle of Europe was on a mission to sort out another errant nephew: Prince

George of Greece, whose arbitrary rule as High Commissioner of Crete had driven the people to the edge of rebellion.

The royal yacht *Victoria and Albert* was truly a floating court. The King insisted on the strict observance of protocol. At Corfu, Lord Charles Beresford, the Admiral of the Mediterranean Fleet, arrived with his fleet to escort the *Victoria and Albert* to Athens. When the King of Greece boarded his flagship, Beresford failed to change into full dress uniform. When Bertie heard of this solecism he ordered Charles Hardinge to make a formal complaint to the Admiralty. Whether or not it was a calculated insult, the uniform gaffe was badly timed. Charlie Beresford was embroiled in an ugly quarrel with Admiral John (Jackie) Fisher, and Bertie read his flouting of protocol as a challenge.

Fisher was a member of the King's inner group. He bombarded Esher and Knollys with letters written in a large, bold hand, often at four thirty a.m., and signed "Yours till hell freezes." Hardinge thought him a menace, "backbiting his opponents, full of self praise, avoiding points of criticism and distorting facts."[73] But Fisher was dedicated to building enough dreadnoughts to win the naval race with Germany. In 1905 he offered to resign and was dissuaded by the King, who gave him the Order of Merit. In January 1906, at age sixty-five, he was made an additional admiral, which allowed him to stay on as First Sea Lord—thus blasting Charlie Beresford's hopes of getting the top job. Bertie's objections to Beresford and championing of Fisher may well have ensured Britain's victory in the naval race with Germany. The Corfu incident in April was the first salvo in a quarrel that personalized and politicized the struggle between arms race reform, represented by Fisher, and naval orthodoxy, championed by Beresford.

Bertie at last agreed to visit the kaiser in August 1906. Grey was skeptical. He had made up his mind that compromise with Germany was impossible, and saw no reason to change this view.[74] The King was accompanied by Hardinge. In his memoirs, Hardinge denied that Grey was envious of his close relations with the King, but documents reveal that the opposite was the case.[75] Hardinge, as head of the Foreign Office and royal favorite, went behind the back of his boss, foreign secretary Grey, concealing his plan to accompany the King until it was too late for Grey to stop it. "I do not want him to know that I have said anything to anybody or to think that I know more than what he himself told me," he explained to Knollys.[76] He took elaborate precautions to avoid publicly upstaging the foreign secretary. He traveled out to Germany alone, and told Grey that he was accompanying the King privately rather than going as minister in attendance: "I think this is the best way of getting over any objections which Grey may have."[77]

The kaiser met his uncle's train at Cronberg station wearing the light green full dress uniform and steel helmet of the Posen Chasseurs. Bertie dressed in the suit and panama hat he had made fashionable at Goodwood races, conspicuously laying aside the uniform he usually sported when visiting another sovereign—a gesture intended to reassure the French by signaling the private character of the meeting.[78] Kaiser and King embraced cordially on the platform.[79] William greeted Fritz Ponsonby with heavy-handed chaff: "See you are getting grey like me. How old are you?"[80] There was "a feeling of thunder in the air," wrote Ponsonby.[81] Bertie was careful to avoid controversial subjects, and "very wisely," in Hardinge's view, talked only in general terms "of our policy."[82]

The real discussion at Cronberg took place between William and Hardinge. The kaiser was critical of the French ("a bundle of nerves and a female race not a male race like the Anglo-Saxons and the Teutons"). Though he claimed that he had been warmly welcomed at Tangier as the deliverer from French oppression, he expressed himself in favor of better relations with England.[83] Gaining access to the kaiser through the King was critical to Hardinge's diplomacy, and the meeting indicated an easing of the hostility of 1905.

Bertie's stay that summer at Marienbad was a dull one. No women were invited to his dinners owing to mourning for the King of Denmark. (Alice Keppel never came to Marienbad.) "What tiresome evenings we shall have," sighed Bertie.[84] Sometimes it seemed as if his closest companion was his dog, the white-haired terrier Caesar, who accompanied him on the long car drives he took with Stamper. The King always sat in the left rear seat, filling the car with smoke from the cigar that was constantly alight in his hand. Bertie never hit Caesar, but he would shake his stick at him: "You naughty dog," he would say very slowly. "You naughty, naughty dog." "And Caesar would wag his tail and 'smile' cheerfully up into his master's eyes, until His Majesty smiled back in spite of himself."[85]

Every other morning the King drove to the Rübezahl Hotel, where he remained for about an hour. The press, who followed his every move—when Ponsonby held a press conference, thirty-seven reporters attended—were curious, scenting scandal. In fact, the King was receiving electrical treatment, and he hired a room in the Rübezahl because it was the only place in the town with a sufficiently strong current. The press were told that the King suffered from rheumatism, but Bertie confided in his equerry that he was being treated for a "slight disease of the skin" and he wished this to be kept absolutely private.[86]

The truth was that the King had a rodent ulcer beside his nose. The Marienbad treatment with X-rays and Finsen light failed, and the ulcer was becoming distressingly large and difficult to hide. In 1907, it was cured by radium.[87] So delighted was the King that he persuaded Cassel to endow a Radium Institute in London, and declared: "My greatest ambition is not to quit this world till a real cure for cancer has been found, and I feel convinced that radium will be the means of doing so!"[88] This caused consternation in the household, as it fueled the persistent rumors that the King suffered from cancer, then a taboo disease.

In 1906 and 1907, the King spent fourteen or fifteen weeks abroad. Perhaps it was just as well. The cost of entertaining him—estimated at anything from £5,000 to £10,000 per house party—was becoming prohibitive. The "ordinary peer" who thirty or forty years before had played host to royalty was now too impoverished by agricultural depression to afford the expense.[89]

In July 1906, the King and Queen visited Newcastle to open Arm-
strong College at the university there. They stayed for two nights at
Alnwick with the Duke of Northumberland. Lists, instructions, and
questionnaires issued from the household for months before the visit
took place. The railway station must be closed, the entrance to the
castle decorated, the guests' names approved. Guards of honor sa-
luted, schoolchildren cheered at the castle gates, bands played before
dinner. The King brought two valets, a footman, a dresser, a lord-in-
waiting, a groom-in-waiting, a private secretary, two equerries and
their servants, as well as a minister in attendance. The Queen brought
two ladies-in-waiting, a gentleman-in-waiting, a hairdresser, and two
maids. In addition, there was an inspector, a sergeant and three con-
stables from the household police, and an inspector and a sergeant
from the Metropolitan Police, all mingling with the indoor servants
and wearing ordinary clothes.[90] The Percy family were reported to be
"very stiff," but Carrington noted, "We smoked after dinner, an un-
heard of thing, and everything was splendidly done."[91]

The King was more high-profile when he was abroad. Journalists
and detectives swarmed around him. Whatever the effect of his tours
on foreign policy, they certainly impacted on his position at home, as
column inches of newsprint detailed the enthusiasm with which King
Edward the international superstar was received.

In February 1907, Bertie visited Paris, bringing Alix. Traveling as
the Duke of Lancaster, he took over the entire British Embassy (the
ambassador moved out). When the King and Queen arrived at the
Gare du Nord in two feet of snow, they were loudly cheered by a crowd
of two thousand. Eyebrows were raised when Alix accompanied the
King to dinner with his old mistress Madame Standish ("This is all
thought a little odd," wrote Carrington) but the real love affair was
between Le Roi and the people of Paris.[92] Anarcho-syndicalist strikers
crippled the city that winter, and the officious Paris police were more
than ever vigilant. Bertie shrugged them off. "Who will hurt me in
Paris?"[93] King and Queen mixed happily with the crowd outside the
theater; what they did not know was that most of the people standing
near them were detectives. But the cheers that met the King wherever

he drove in his claret-colored motor were real, and Stamper found it hard to control his emotions as he sat in the front. "The knowledge that all the vast outburst of affection was focussed upon the one gentleman who was sitting behind me, was almost overpowering, and time and again I have found myself half way between laughter and tears."[94]

Living in the lonely bubble of a political leader, cocooned by his staff and detectives, with a mistress who was more political companion than lover and a deaf wife who shut herself away in Sandringham, Bertie craved the affirmation of crowds.

After his return from Paris, the King contracted a bronchial cough. The attack was more severe than previous ones.[95] When he reached Biarritz in March, he was still coughing. *The Times* printed two short paragraphs:

> King Edward did not return to the Hotel du Palais for dinner yesterday evening, as had been arranged, but stayed at the Villa Bellefontaine and dined with Sir Ernest Cassel, only returning to the Hotel at 11 o'clock.
>
> Bright sunny weather succeeded yesterday's rain, and his Majesty walked along the shore, where he sat for a long time on one of the benches. . . . After another short turn in the motor car, the King got back to the Hotel about 6 o'clock. He will dine in the town this evening, probably with Sir Ernest Cassel.[96]

This apparently innocuous report caused grave offense. The King's private secretary complained to Baron de Reuter, who gave instructions that Reuter's Agency was to publish no movements of the King except those of public interest.[97] The courtiers fussed because the report was unauthorized, and it implied that the King's cure was, in fact, a hedonistic holiday. But the image of the sick King sitting alone on a bench gazing sadly out to sea is infinitely more revealing than the dinners with Sir Ernest Cassel.

Winston Churchill, who stayed with Cassel at the Villa Bellefontaine, reported, "The King dines or lunches here <u>daily</u>!"[98] To those in the know, it was understood that Cassel's guest was Mrs. Keppel, so the newspaper paragraph was a coded reference to the King's dining each night with his mistress. Cassel's daughter Maudie, who was also at the Villa Eugénie, found the royal routine unbearably tedious. "We are his servants quite as much as the housemaid or the butler," she wrote.[99]

As Bertie's cough improved, he took longer drives in the afternoons, heading a procession of motors and announcing his arrival with a bugle, a practice he copied from the kaiser. Occasionally the claret-colored motor car with its overflowing ashtray would stop by the road-side for the King to drink coffee out of a giant Thermos.[100]

In Berlin, William grew paranoid about the plots he imagined his uncle was hatching. At a dinner he announced: "He is a Satan; you can hardly believe what a Satan he is."[101] Satan, meanwhile, steamed off on yet another Mediterranean cruise. This time the destination was Carta-gena, near Cadiz, where he had a yachting rendezvous with King Alfonso of Spain, now married to his niece Ena. As usual, he was accompanied by Hardinge. Grey made himself "disagreeable" to the King about Hardinge going to Spain, though Hardinge in the end "brought him round entirely to the King's views" as to the usefulness of the arrangement.[102] The meeting at Cartagena was the result of lengthy negotiations. King Alfonso was anxious for Uncle Bertie to pay a state visit to Madrid, but poor Spanish security meant that this was judged too dangerous. Grey, however, wished for closer relations with Spain. The meeting on board ship was a compromise proposed by Ber-tie, avoiding the danger and expense of a state visit while giving Al-fonso the validation that he needed.

The two royal yachts met at sea on 8 April, fired salutes, and, es-corted by twelve vessels, steamed to Cartagena. Here King Alfonso came on board the *Victoria and Albert* dressed in a British general's uni-form, and King Edward donned a Spanish admiral's uniform to return the call.[103] Between banquets and the firing of salutes, Hardinge nego-tiated an agreement with Spain over Morocco. Even Grey now accepted that the King's last two cruises in the Mediterranean had been "distinctly profitable from the Foreign Office point of view."[104] They had also been distinctly profitable in boosting the popularity of the monarchy at home.

The King's next assignation was with King Victor Emmanuel of Italy at Gaeta, near Naples. This yacht visit was purely social, but the press noted the cordial meeting between the two monarchs, who "embraced and kissed each other repeatedly."[105] Looking well and suntanned, Bertie was received enthusiastically by crowds on the shore, who cried "*Evviva Il Re Eduardo!*" as the Italian squadron boomed a twenty-one-gun salute.

Italy was Germany's ally, and Berlin went "stark staring raving mad" over Bertie's Gaeta meeting with Victor Emmanuel. The stock market fell six points.[106] Bertie asked Hardinge to make a formal protest against the German press, which had "imputed to His Majesty the most sinister motives and accused him of deep-laid plots" against Germany.[107]

The Germans had good reason to feel paranoid. The Anglo-Russian Convention was concluded in August 1907 and published the following month. Weakened by defeat in the war with Japan and then by revolution, Russia was unable to resist pressure to make terms with England—especially as their allies, the French, insisted on such an agreement as the price of a badly needed loan. The convention caused panic in Germany, where it was blamed on the Wicked King Edward.[108] In fact, his role, as at Algeciras, was very limited. He wrote letters to Nicky, but that was about all.

The family member who really could claim credit for the agreement with Russia was Alix's sister, the old dowager, the Empress Minnie. She visited London for the first time in more than thirty years in 1907, and her closeness with Alix was widely reported.

After the death of their father, King Christian of Denmark, the two sisters bought themselves a house. Hvidøre is a villa in wedding-cake stucco perched above a main road in the suburbs of Copenhagen, staring out over the gray sound, lashed by freezing Baltic winds. An inscription in Danish above the fireplace in the billiard room reads *Ost*

Vest Hiemme Bedst ("East West Home's Best"). "Queen Alexandra," wrote Bertie, "is so happy in her new little Danish house which she occupies with the Empress Marie Feodorovna."[109] Hvidore was not appreciated by all. "Her suite dread it," wrote Carrington.[110]

England's rapprochement with Russia meant that good relations with Germany were imperative, and Bertie's role was to make friendly noises to William. On Hardinge's suggestion, he invited the kaiser to pay a state visit. "I have already sown the good seed," wrote Hardinge on 6 April 1907, "and the King is quite ready to ask the German E[mperor] to Windsor in the autumn."[111]

Meanwhile, the kaiser invited his uncle to pay another visit on the journey to Marienbad in August. As at Cronberg the year before, the King brought with him Hardinge. Grey, who spoke no French, said "he preferred this arrangement to going himself, and that from a Foreign Office point of view it is very convenient as it is of distinct advantage to hear what Sovereigns and Foreign Ministers say at first hand."[112] Bertie signaled that the visit was a social one, and he was annoyed when he arrived at Cassel and William staged a military review, especially as it meant he got no luncheon until two thirty. Even worse, after dinner the kaiser made a formal speech to which Bertie felt bound to reply, speaking in fluent German—though there was an awkward silence when he stopped abruptly for want of a word and rapped his finger on the table. Hardinge commented: "I could not help seeing that there was no 'empressement' for each other's society and that there was no real intimacy between them."[113]

Edward VII was seen as the most powerful man in Europe. From Marienbad he fingered the pulse of the world's diplomacy. He watched the Hague Conference pass empty resolutions on world peace. Soveral, who was a delegate, sent him bulletins, which he found "not pleasant reading. . . . I wish you would write to Grey or Hardinge or to both telling them the real state of affairs."[114] His own visits to William "will I am led to believe be more conducive to the maintenance of peace than all the subjects being put forward at the Hague Conference."[115]

Stamper noticed that summer that the King's temper was worse than ever. In the car, he exploded with wrath when they got lost and were late for lunch. "I have never seen His Majesty so moved as he was that day," wrote Stamper.[116] Any slip could excite the royal rage. Emerald Cunard tried to amuse the table-drumming monarch by discussing the novels of Elinor Glyn, with their racy tales of Daisy Warwick's corridor-creeping house parties. The King glared and turned away; Emerald Cunard had forgotten that a *jeune fille* was present.*[117]

On 31 October 1907, ten days before the kaiser was due to visit England, he telegrammed to say that he was suffering from bronchitis and wished to cancel. Bertie suspected that the real reason was that Kaiser William feared a hostile welcome: "He dare not 'face the music' and has practically been told he will get a bad reception in England."[118] Bertie insisted that the visit should go ahead. It could hardly have come at a worse time for William. His court had been rocked by scandal when Count Eulenburg, his close friend, was exposed as the man at the center of a homosexual circle. There were hints that William's relations with Eulenburg were homoerotic—he was known as "sweetie" or *Liebchen*—but when William was informed of the allegations, his reaction seems to have been one of genuine astonishment.[119]

Bertie knew of these scandals but he remained tight-lipped. He was now on excellent terms with Edward Grey. Grey had incurred his anger by attending a reception at Buckingham Palace wearing plain clothes not uniform.[120] But at Balmoral in the autumn of 1907, he was "very much touched" by the King and the "kind way" in which he recalled memories of the days when Colonel Grey, the foreign secretary's fa-

---

* The *jeune fille* in question was named Elsie Gill. She was then twenty-two. As an eighty-five-year-old, she told Anita Leslie a story that gives a glimpse into the King's secret life, now so carefully hidden. Mrs. Sophie Hall Walker was thirty-five, and married to an older man, a wealthy racehorse trainer; she was rich and athletic and often stayed at Marienbad, where she won the ladies' golf championship. Young Elsie Gill had watched open-eyed as the hotel maids prepared Mrs. Hall Walker's room for a teatime visit from the King. The room was filled with sweet-smelling flowers and sprayed with scent and the curtains were drawn. It was some years before Elsie realized what the preparations were *for;* she had innocently imagined that kings were always received in the afternoons in darkened, perfumed rooms. (Leslie, *Edwardians in Love,* p. 302.)

ther, had been with Bertie as equerry.[121] Grey needed the kaiser's visit to take place, as he wished to avoid accusations from the left of the Liberal party that William had canceled in protest at the agreement with Russia. He telegrammed Sir Frank Lascelles, the ambassador in Berlin, and told him to warn the kaiser that postponement "would be attributed to the recent scandals in Berlin and nothing we could do or say would alter the impression."[122] The hint of blackmail coupled with the promise of a favorable reception owing to the "sympathy" the public felt at "the pain which recent revelations have given him" worked.[123] William's bronchitis took a sudden turn for the better.

Grey worried not only that the visit would panic the French but also that something disastrous would happen, making relations with Germany worse rather than better.[124] For the smooth running of the visit he had the King to thank. It was he who laid on the banquets, entertaining twenty-four royals to luncheon, and lining up eight monarchs in a photograph, and he who took the kaiser shooting in the "dear old park I know so well."[125] Grey wrote a briefing document listing the topics the kaiser might raise, but Bertie studiously avoided entering into political discussions. When William mentioned the Berlin–Baghdad Railway, the King merely referred him to Haldane, who was staying at Windsor. Haldane was thrilled to be summoned by the kaiser at one a.m. to his private room to discuss the Baghdad railway, and he dictated an excited memorandum claiming that the emperor had agreed to a settlement that would satisfy Britain, France, and Russia. But Haldane has rightly been dubbed a bear of little brain; the deal turned out to be illusory, as William had spoken (as he did at Björkö) without consulting his chancellor, Bülow. As one historian has observed, "both sides used the state visit as a kind of benign cover under which to pursue essentially hostile policies."[126] The British staged the visit in parallel with negotiations for the Anglo-Russian Convention, while the Germans pressed ahead with an acceleration of their program of battleship building.

Elderly Campbell-Bannerman was so shattered by being kept standing at Windsor for two and a half hours that he suffered a "seizure." The sixty-four-year-old King was made of sterner stuff. Esher thought he made a better show than the forty-eight-year-old kaiser. "He has more graciousness and dignity. William is ungraceful, nervous and plain. There is no 'atmosphere' about him. He has not impressed Grey."[127] All the same, Grey thought the visit was a success. William was "genuinely pleased" by his reception, especially when he visited the City and cheering crowds lined the route, and he made a speech declaring that blood was thicker than water. In fact, concluded Grey, "The result has been to mollify Anglo-German relations—at any rate for the time."[128] Characteristically, however, Grey gave the King no credit for this result.

CHAPTER 25

King Canute

1908–9

Paris, 6 March 1908, 10:30 a.m. Between breakfast with Sir Ernest Cassel and lunch with President Fallières, the King squeezed in a visit to the studio of the sculptor Auguste Rodin.[1] He asked to see the bust that Rodin had made of Daisy Warwick, but the sculpture was away being cast at the foundry. Rodin wrote about the King to Lady Warwick afterward: *"Il a pensé que j'étais devant de grandes difficultés car il a parlé de vos traits si fins, et a décrit votre charmante figure comme s'il corrigeait mon buste absent, et je sens que si je l'avais laissé en terre je l'aurais montré."*[*][2]

Daisy had already given Rodin seven sittings. She was one of the four Englishwomen he agreed to sculpt, all with the wide-cheekboned, square-jawed "handsome" faces that were his ideal of female beauty,

---

[*] "He thought I was facing the greatest difficulties because he talked of your wonderful features, and described your charming face as if he was correcting the bust that wasn't there, and I feel that had I the clay model, I would have shown it to him."

inspired by Michelangelo's statues of young men. By 1908, Daisy was running short of money and she was unable to afford Rodin's hefty fee of £1,000. Three years later, Rodin sent her the marble bust, but there is no record in his papers of any payment by her or anyone else. The story of Daisy's portrait is still shrouded in mystery, but it has been suggested that the King's visit to the studio was followed by a check that settled the fee.[3]

"What do you think of that charming Lady Warwick mounting a wagon at the corner of the street and addressing her 'comrades,' the scum of the labourers, and then taking off her glove to shake and feel their horny hands!" Alix had exclaimed at the time of the 1906 election.[4] Daisy Warwick, now forty-six, overweight, and loudly socialist, was intent on "revenge."[5] The *Daily Mail* announced that she was about to produce her memoirs, and she approached Arthur Pearson, owner of the *Daily Express*, offering to sell Bertie's letters for publication and threatening to go to the Hearst press in America if he refused.[6] Her sister Blanche Gordon-Lennox acted as go-between. Blanche had a meeting with Knollys, and told him that Daisy was feeling sour and neglected, and the best way to buy her off was to stage a reconciliation. Bertie agreed to appear at dinner with a mutual friend, but it was not until the autumn or winter that a meeting took place.[7] Eventually Daisy promised to abstain from public speaking. She also wrote a letter in which she declared that she had decided that writing her memoirs would be unwise, and in consequence all her papers had been destroyed.[8] She put it about that it had taken her three hours to burn Bertie's letters one evening.[9]

If Bertie was indeed the secret purchaser of the Rodin bust, this was perhaps his way of thanking Daisy. He remained loyal to her, and continued to see her until shortly before his death.[10] Daisy had not, in fact, abandoned the idea of publishing, nor had she destroyed all the letters. As for the marble bust, this was sent by Rodin to Daisy's home, Easton Lodge, in 1912. Less than a year later, it was sold secretly, in defiance of an injunction imposed by Daisy's creditors that restrained her from selling any of the contents of her estate. It has never reappeared.[11]

At four thirty on the afternoon of 4 March 1908, the day before he left London for France, the King visited the prime minister at 10 Downing Street.[12] He stayed for twenty minutes. Campbell-Bannerman had been critically ill with heart failure, and Bertie wished to say goodbye; he thought he might never see him again. A few days earlier, Bertie had spoken to the man marked out as CB's successor, H. H. Asquith. Bertie considered CB a "great gentleman," and liked him best of all the prime ministers of his reign. Asquith, by contrast, he thought "deplorably common not to say vulgar," but he made no attempt to resist his succession.[13] Bertie now told Asquith that if a change of prime minister became necessary, he must come out to Biarritz. Asquith found the King "very agreeable." "He talked a little all over the place, smoking a cigar, about Roosevelt, Macedonia, Congo etc."[14]

At Biarritz, the King occupied rooms on the ground floor of the Hôtel du Palais to save the strain of wheezing as he climbed the stairs to his usual first-floor suite. The drains smelled so bad that he threatened never to return.[15] As usual, Alice Keppel was installed with her children in Ernest Cassel's Villa Eugénie. While the Keppel children's nanny fussed about ironing and goffering Violet and Sonia's frilly knickers, the gentleman Sonia called "Kingy" took long drives with Mama in the afternoons. Stamper, who always sat in the front seat, described these drives but, being a loyal member of the household, never mentioned Mrs. Keppel by name.[16] The King growled at the news from London, watching angrily as Asquith planned his Cabinet changes while CB was still in Downing Street and fighting for his life. "It reminds one of a dying animal with the vultures hovering about him," he wrote. The suggestion that he should return to London infuriated him. "I do not see the necessity of going over to England . . . merely to hold a council and receive and give seals of office."[17]

On 2 April, CB dictated a letter to the King asking permission to resign. The King telegraphed the next day that he had no choice but to accept.*[18] On 5 April, he wrote to Asquith inviting him to form a government.

Asquith arrived in Biarritz in vile, lashing rain on the night of 7 April. At ten a.m. the next morning, dressed in his frock coat, he went to see the King, who was also wearing a frock coat, and kissed hands.[19] Elated by his promotion, Asquith himself made no complaint at having to go all the way to Biarritz, but in London, *The Times* roundly criticized the King for not returning to his country at such a moment.[20] Most observers agreed.

Summoning Asquith to Biarritz was widely seen as the King's first constitutional blunder in the seven years of his reign.[21] True, the King (influenced, it seems, by Mrs. Keppel)[22] returned home in time to hold the Privy Council on 16 April, but by then the damage was done. The episode demonstrated, as Carrington wrote, that "the presence of the King in this country is not a necessity"; but perhaps this was no bad thing. In the same way, Bertie had ostentatiously distanced himself from Campbell-Bannerman's Cabinet-making back in 1905, when he stayed at Crichel during the crisis. By remaining at Biarritz in 1908, he demonstrated that the paranoid views of the German press about his omnipotence were wildly exaggerated. "It would be a serious danger," wrote Carrington, "if the King were supposed to be a more important and influential political person than he is. This is all the more necessary as there is a genuine belief abroad that Esher, Fisher, Cassel and others are attempting to form a sort of backstairs influence on HM. If this feeling grows it may be dangerous—the Emperor of Germany's 'camarilla' has done a great deal of harm already everywhere."[23]

Carrington's fears of a backstairs clique were not without foundation. Esher wrote frequently to Knollys ("My dear Francis") confiding "ev-

---

* Bertie considered offering CB a peerage, but decided against; not only was CB likely to refuse, but Bertie judged the measures he had introduced not "worthy of my reward." (RA VIC/Add C07/2/G, B to Francis Knollys, 3 April 1908.)

erything that comes into my head," while Fisher's letters to Esher were addressed "My beloved E."[24] The three men formed a habit of dining together. Esher and Knollys resented Ponsonby's closeness to the King. "Poor dear Fritz," Esher wrote patronizingly, "is inclined to a certain pomposity. . . . His most serious fault is an uncertainty of judgement."[25] According to Arthur Bigge, the King's household "are all at sixes and sevens, and all frantically jealous of each other."[26]

Esher's influence was waning. He had already been cut out of the Foreign Office loop by Charles Hardinge, and as a Tory he was suspected by the Liberal government. In February 1908, a letter written by Esher appeared in *The Times* defending Fisher's record on naval reform: "There is not a man in Germany, from the Emperor downwards, who would not welcome the fall of Sir John Fisher."[27] This sentence was picked up by the kaiser, who took the extraordinary step of writing to Lord Tweedmouth, First Lord of the Admiralty, denying Germany's intention of starting a naval race and dismissing Esher's claims to authority: "I am at a loss to tell whether the supervision of the foundations and drains of the Royal Palaces is apt to qualify somebody for the judgement of Naval Affairs."[28]

It was a shrewd hit. Bertie replied, standing on his dignity, that "Your writing to *my* [author italics] First Lord of the Admiralty is a 'new departure.'"[29] But the spat did not end here. Tweedmouth, who unfortunately turned out to be suffering from a brain tumor that affected his sanity, leaked the kaiser's letter, and an article appeared in *The Times* attacking the kaiser for seeking to influence Admiralty policy.

Bertie was furious. He wrote Esher a formal reprimand, and blasted him to Fisher.[30] Esher, who was supported throughout by Fisher and Knollys, breezily predicted that the affair would soon blow over, and within days he was kissing the King's hand. But, in fact, his standing at court was seriously compromised. Bertie no longer trusted him to be discreet.* On his return from Biarritz, the King summoned Fisher and

---

* After the King died, Alice Keppel told Rosebery that "for the last two years the King did not confide in Knollys for he was afraid that everything he told Knollys went straight to Esher, who was a good man in his way but not the repository of confidences." (McKinstry, *Rosebery*, p. 496.)

told him off for talking too freely in society and boasting that "the King would see me through anything! that it was bad for me and bad for him as being a Constitutional Monarch." Then the King "smoked a cigar as big as a capstan bar for really a good hour afterwards, talking of everything from China to Peru, not excluding the Times article on himself."[31]

On 5 June 1908, the King traveled to Epsom races for the Oaks, dined with the Waleses and the Fifes, and then caught a ten o'clock train to Port Victoria, where he boarded the royal yacht *Victoria and Albert*.[32] The crossing of the North Sea was so rough that he was ill, and the Queen, who was rarely seasick, was thrown off her chair into a corner of the cabin and then lay flat on the deck "like a corpse," vomiting continually.[33] On 9 June, the royal yacht reached Reval (now Tallinn) on the Baltic and anchored there, close to the czar's yacht *Standart*.

This yachting meeting with Czar Nicholas was the culmination of much patient diplomacy. Giving affirmation to the Anglo-Russian Convention of 1907 with a meeting of King and czar was fraught with difficulties.[34] Meeting at sea in the policed, neutral space of royal yachts solved the security issue—though the British were amazed by the paranoia of the Russians. No one was allowed on shore, and the police even threatened to strip-search the women members of a local choir who serenaded the royal party.[35] Public opinion at home was also a problem. Keir Hardie, the first Labour MP and a veteran republican, attacked the meeting as "condoning the atrocities" perpetrated by the czar.

At Reval at eleven a.m. on 9 June, the King summoned Sir Arthur Nicolson, the ambassador in St. Petersburg, to his cabin on the *Victoria and Albert*. Bertie was sitting in a chintz-covered chair wearing the uniform of the Kiev Dragoons. It was uncomfortably tight. He fired questions at Nicolson: "whether the Emperor would wear the uniform of the Scots Greys or whether he would appear as a Russian admiral. what decorations he would wear and in what order: what about the Russian railways? Whether M Stolypin [prime minister] spoke French or German, or even English: what exactly were the present relations between the Government and the Duma; was the Duma a thing one should mention? Or not?" And so on.

At eleven thirty, Czar Nicholas II and his family came on board the *Victoria and Albert*. It was contrary to protocol that the czar should pay the first visit, and it signified the nephew's respect for the uncle.

King Edward VII spoke with Peter Stolypin and Alexander Izvolsky, the foreign minister. He discussed the marvelous progress of the Russian railways and the gratifying collaboration with the Duma, and remarked on how well the czar looked in the uniform of the Scots Greys. Afterward Stolypin told Nicolson how amazed he was by the King's grasp of Russian policy. As Harold Nicolson wrote, the King was a "supreme diplomatist." Unlike the kaiser, who patronized and bullied the czar, Bertie made him feel a "highly successful nephew," the more so because he avoided all awkward political questions.[36] He made no attempt to meddle in Russia's affairs, and Nicky seemed for once at ease.

The next night, the Russians dined on board the *Victoria and Albert*. Bertie's suite had feared that the notoriously difficult Czarina Alexandra might refuse to attend the dinner if she was forced by protocol to take second place behind her mother-in-law, Minnie, who accompanied the Russian party and, as dowager empress, enjoyed precedence. Bertie solved the protocol issue and prevented a scene by taking Minnie and Alexandra each on one arm. "Tonight I am going to enjoy the unique honour of taking two Empresses in to dinner."[37] He told Alexandra that her daughters spoke English with a Scots accent. She fired their tutor at once.[38] To flatter the czar, Bertie made him an Admiral of the Fleet. This honor gave Nicky childlike pleasure. After dinner, Jackie Fisher danced the fashionable Merry Widow waltz with Nicky's sister, the Grand Duchess Olga, both with their hands folded behind their heads, and watched in a circle by the monarchs and their ministers.*[39]

---

* The bumptious Fisher, who enjoyed showing off his dancing, once pushed his luck by asking Queen Alexandra to dance: "She put him in his place, and said, 'Certainly not.'" (Bodleian Library, Lincolnshire Papers, MS Film 1121, Carrington Diary, 31 May 1905.)

Politicians in London carped that the King erred in raising the question of the Jews in his talks with Stolypin, but in retrospect, Bertie's willingness to respond to concerns about the czarist pogroms shows a moral courage decidedly lacking among his ministers. More doubtful was his mention to Nicky of Cassel's desire to participate in a new Russian loan. When Kaiser William got to hear of this, he hastened to describe his uncle as "a jobber in stocks in shares," who counted on making a "colossal" personal profit out of the Russian loan.[40] Reval infuriated William, who minuted his ambassador's report: "[King Edward] aims at war. I am to begin it, so that he does not get the odium."[41] At home, Esher and Balfour grumbled that the King had taken with him Charles Hardinge rather than foreign secretary Edward Grey. But no one could deny that Reval had achieved its diplomatic aim of strengthening the ties between Russia and Britain.[42]

Asquith complained that the King had acted unconstitutionally in making the czar an honorary admiral without consulting his government beforehand. Bertie instructed Knollys to write a letter of apology, explaining that the King was "totally unaware of the constitutional point," and "regretted that he had, without knowing it, acted irregularly." Mindful that the gesture had consolidated the success of the visit, Bertie added a dig: "The King deplores the attitude taken up by Mr. Asquith on the Women's Suffrage Bill."[43]

Bertie seems to have misunderstood the prime minister's attitude toward women's suffrage. Like the king, Asquith was implacably opposed to giving women the vote.

Back in England, Bertie refused to bow to criticism. The names of the MPs who spoke out against his visit to Reval—Victor Grayson, Keir Hardie, and Arthur Ponsonby—were removed from the list of guests at the royal garden party that he held at Windsor on 20 June 1908. Arthur Ponsonby, son of Henry and brother of Fritz, should have known better than to vote against the King's visit, but his exclusion from Windsor provoked a row. Liberal whip Alexander Murray, the Master of Elibank, warned that the story might leak into the press "and he will be held up as a martyr to principle, for these Fleet Street scribblers will gloat over his exclusion." He feared that "an incorrect impression might thus be given of His Majesty's character and disposition."[44] Murray managed to stop the *Daily News* from reporting the incident and prevent an agitation "for socialistic and sensational gutter press purposes."[45] Arthur Ponsonby apologized and the King accepted his explanation.[46] The garden party affair was a storm in a royal teacup, but Bertie's uncharacteristic irritability had needlessly inflamed his critics.[47] The incident showed how powerful and intrusive the press had become. As Lord Northcliffe, the owner of the *Daily Mail*, explained, "The King has become such an immense personality in England that . . . the space devoted to the movements of royalty has quintupled since His Majesty came to the Throne, and our difficulties have increased in proportion."*[48]

King Edward, meanwhile, played a King Canute–like grumpy old man against the modern world. His efforts to ban from Hyde Park women who had abandoned the side saddle were unsuccessful, but he "let it be known that ladies who ride astride in the Park will not be allowed to go to Court."[49] To the Lord Chamberlain's request that smoking should be permitted in theaters, the chain-smoking King replied that "he cannot consent to its adoption in London," as no other country allowed it.[50] When Guards officer Colonel Gathorne-Hardy attended a levee wearing the wrong stripes on his trousers, he was mortified to receive a royal reprimand. "I will at once replace the gold stripes on my trousers with red ones," he hastened to reply.[51] Dinner guests at Windsor were expected to wear evening dress with knee breeches. Those who opted for more informality risked being greeted by the King: "I see you have come in the suite of the American Ambassador."[52] Not even the Queen was exempt. When she appeared wearing the Garter star on the wrong side, explaining that it had clashed with her other jewels, Bertie ordered her back.[53] The Duke of Marl-

---

* What no one could have guessed in 1908 was that within a decade the world would have become such a different place that in 1917, King George V, in order to secure the survival of his own dynasty, would judge it necessary to refuse asylum to his Romanov cousins, who were murdered at Ekaterinburg in July 1918.

borough (Sunny), who separated from his wife, Consuelo, in 1906, received a message (through his kinsman Lord Churchill) that "until the Duke and Duchess of Marlborough live together again under the same roof, and are asked out together, neither of them can be invited to 'Court.'"[54] Like Randolph Churchill before him, Sunny Marlborough was banished by Bertie for defying the rules.

Margot Asquith had been one of Bertie's "young ladies" twenty years earlier (as Margot Tennant), and now, as the wife of the prime minister, she watched the King with fascination. She considered that his bark was worse than his bite, which was far less lethal than the Queen's:

> If I had to choose between the King and the Queen I should be more afraid ultimately of the Queen. She is the most unsnobby, refined, fascinating lovely creature in the whole world and gives one a thrill from her distinction and sweetness, but au fond she is stupid, childish, obstinate and incapable of making up her mind. She has never grown up and enjoys the most ridiculous trifles. She takes great likes and dislikes and I should think would be unpleasantly unforgiving. The King is much kinder—a better sort altogether—but he is common and vulgar compared to the Queen."

To his old mistresses Bertie was unfailingly generous. Emma Bourke appealed to him when the 1907 City panic caused financial ruin to her husband's firm. "Mon Roi," she wrote, "my husband's capital has all been swept away and here we are, he at 72 and a very sick man left without anything." Would you, she implored, "for the sake of a friend in great distress, use all your influence with Sir Ernest Cassel to help us all he can?"[56] Bertie forwarded Emma's letter to Cassel: "It would be more than kind of you if you could be induced to give them a helping hand."[57] Two months later, Eddie Bourke was dead. Within a year, Emma Bourke had become engaged to her old flame Lord Clarendon, and Bertie wrote: "I am sure you have acted wisely in marrying the man who has been devoted to you for so many years."[58] He was loyal, too, to her sister Mabel Batten, with whom he had dallied forty years before in India; she dedicated a song to him in 1902, and he still wrote occasionally to "Ladye"—though he might have been less than overjoyed to learn that in 1908 she became the lover of Radclyffe Hall.[59]

With Skittles, now sixty-nine and in poor health, the King was helpful, too. When the Duke of Devonshire died in 1908, Skittles's payments stopped, and she wrote to the King, who sent Knollys to see her. She showed him her correspondence with the duke, who had once proposed to her. Fortunately, the duke's letter "contained a distinct promise that the allowance should be continued as long as she lived and when the matter was explained to the present Duke by Knollys no difficulty was made about it."[60] Skittles continued to live cozily on South Street in Mayfair; she claimed that the blue satin decoration of her bedroom was a gift of the King, and she was supplied with regular presents of game from Sandringham.[61]

Nothing was allowed to interrupt the sacred routine of the King's social and sporting calendar. In August 1908, after racing at Goodwood and yachting at Cowes, came the cure at Marienbad, with a visit en route to Kaiser William at Friedrichshof, near Cronberg, Vicky's old home.

The meeting with the kaiser was carefully prepared. Edward Grey drafted two memoranda, warning that if Germany continued her shipbuilding program, Britain was bound to keep pace, whereas a slowdown would be met by a friendly response.[62] Bertie was annoyed by Grey's presumption in telling him what to say—"This is I believe the first occasion on which the Sovereign has received instruction from his government"—but he absorbed the message.[63] As he minuted: "If Germany ceases her extensive shipbuilding—we shall do the same and not otherwise. It is the only chance of a real peaceful solution of the present feeling existing between England and Germany."[64]

As usual, Grey did not accompany the King, who brought with him Hardinge. Grey abandoned the attempt to dictate the agenda, conceding that "this is a personal matter between the King and the Emperor in which the King's own knowledge and judgement of the Emperor's disposition is much superior to any of us."[65] On the journey, the King discussed with Hardinge what to do with Grey's memoranda, but nothing was decided. When he came face-to-face with the kaiser, on the morning of 11 August, the King found him in "very good humour," but though "we talked freely on international politics, the subject of our respective navies was not broached."[66] According to Hardinge, "the Emperor showed such reluctance to discuss naval matters that the King refrained from pushing the question."[67] He mentioned Grey's memorandum, but as William showed no desire to see it, he said no more.[68] Bertie had judged William's mood correctly.

After luncheon, as the kaiser smoked his cigar, Hardinge confronted him on the naval issue, and he became extremely angry. "I regret to say," wrote Bertie, "that he utterly declined to modify his ship building programme in any way! We must now build more than ever, and as quickly as ever. We have no other alternative."[69]

Cronberg brought European war a notch closer. It caused a hardening of anti-German feeling in London. "We now know the worst and should be prepared for it," wrote Hardinge; "our only course now open is a big programme."[70] Bertie's royal diplomacy had failed to bring Germany and England together. But no one had seriously expected that William would agree to call off the navy race; the most that could be hoped for was to keep open communications.

After the stress of Cronberg, Bertie's meeting the next day in the Alpine town of Bad Ischl with Emperor Francis Joseph of Austria came as a relief. Hardinge thought the seventy-eight-year-old emperor "the dearest and most courteous gentlemen that lives," and Bertie had a genuine affection for the old man.[71] He had visited Francis Joseph the year before in his (relatively) humble wooden shooting box, its walls bristling with the heads of dead animals, and as before, this was an informal occasion.[72] Bertie persuaded Francis Joseph to ride for the first time in a motor car, and on a two-hour drive they discussed the European situation. Hardinge, meanwhile, held "quite a satisfactory" conversation with the foreign minister, Count Aehrenthal.[73]

Such was the fame of King Edward that his visits to the Austrian emperor excited wild speculation. In Hungary, aristocrats pondered whether the King was pursuing a secret political agenda. At shooting parties in their castles, they conjectured that the great peacemaker was intent on detaching Austria from its Dual Alliance with Germany.[74] They were wrong. There was no political substance to the visit. But Bertie was duped. Not one hint was given that Aehrenthal at that very moment was planning the coup that was ultimately to trigger the outbreak of war in 1914: the annexation of Bosnia and Herzegovina.

At Balmoral that October, the royal routine was shattered by the arrival of Count Albert von Mensdorff, the Austrian ambassador, bearing a letter from Francis Joseph. It contained news of the proposed coup against Bosnia.[75]

Bertie received Mensdorff at six thirty on 5 October 1908.[76] Mensdorff was his second cousin, a Saxe-Coburg relation and a member of the King's set who was given privileged rank at court.[77] But not on this occasion. With a few curt words, Bertie dismissed him. "Never did I see [the King] so moved," wrote Lord Redesdale. "No one who was there can forget how terribly he was upset."[78] Bertie complained bitterly about the breach of faith at Ischl. Mensdorff tried to persuade him that no decision had been made at the time of the meeting there, but he was unconvinced. Bertie refused to believe ill of Francis Joseph—in spite of mounting evidence that the devious old emperor had known all about it—and instead blamed the even more treacherous Aehrenthal.[79] But the annexation of Bosnia was a turning point. It proved that the elaborate system of royal visits was no more than a façade behind which the powers continued to pursue their real agendas.

European war was now a real danger, and the King made every effort to prevent it. He returned to London from Balmoral on 10 October, and the next day saw Hardinge for breakfast, followed by Grey, then Izvolsky, the Russian foreign minister, and finally Asquith.[80] The King supported the Cabinet in demanding an international conference, and in his talks with Izvolsky, he backed Russia's demands for the opening of the Dardanelles to Russian warships in exchange for an agreement not to intervene against Austria.

Grave though the crisis was, there was no suggestion that it should be allowed to interfere with the King's social program. On 19 October, he left London for a week's visit to Mrs. Willie James at West Dean, near Goodwood House.

The *Times* reports suggested that this was a purely social house party. Guests included Consuelo Manchester, Lady Sarah Wilson,* and, of course, Mrs. George Keppel, and the King spent three days shooting rabbits and partridges.[81] In fact, Bertie was working, closeted in his room most of the time, dealing with the Bosnian crisis. Hardinge, who had also been invited, felt obliged to cancel, as he explained to the King: "I am sure Your Majesty will understand that, since Sir E. Grey will be away, it will be impossible for me to absent myself from London while this crisis is still going on."[82] From London, Hardinge fired off bulletins to West Dean. Would it be a good idea for the King to write a letter to Czar Nicholas, asking him to keep Izvolsky in office—though "Your Majesty is better able than I am to express an opinion on this point."[83] The King wanted Izvolsky to stay, in spite of his deceit over Bosnia, on the grounds that he might be succeeded by someone worse.[84] He wrote to Nicky, and Izvolsky was retained, holding office until Bertie's death.[85] Would the King use his influence with Sir Ernest Cassel, asked Hardinge—"I see from the papers that he will be one of the guests for the weekend at West Dean." In order to demonstrate England's support for Turkey, the Cabinet wanted a bank to make a loan of £500,000: "We hope very much that Your Majesty may be able to encourage Sir E. Cassel to consider favourably this proposal."[86]

The King's hostess at West Dean, Evie James, was a socialite. She reminded the architect Edwin Lutyens of a "roundabout barmaid": She was very nearsighted with thick pince-nez, "nose tipped and very

---

* Sometimes known as Mrs. Keppel's lady-in-waiting, Lady Sarah Wilson was a sister of Randolph Churchill. Her "prominent eyes, harsh voice and sarcastic laugh" made some people shudder. (Balsan, *Glitter and Gold,* p. 55.)

tilted, lovely hands, gay, thoughtless, extravagant."[87] A talented comic actress—her performance as a little girl in short petticoats at the Chatsworth theatricals had the King in stitches—she was rumored to be a royal mistress.*[88]

On the last day, the King paid his regular visit to the King Edward VII Sanatorium for Consumption at Midhurst, which had been founded with a £2 million donation from Sir Ernest Cassel. When the King's car began the long descent on the return journey, Stamper realized to his horror that all the brakes had failed. As the heavy vehicle gathered speed, the King remained quite unaware that anything was wrong, but for Stamper, sitting helpless in the front seat beside the driver, it was a terrible moment. He nerved himself to leap out of the car and grab the brake wire, but eventually he and the driver managed to swing the car off the road. Afterward, Stamper worked all through the night to clean the oil that had leaked into the brakes, and by the morning the car was safe.[89]

The King never knew how close he had been to a fatal accident that afternoon. He was far more concerned with the race to stop European war. But the stress of trying to keep the peace of Europe almost single-handed was quietly killing him.

Two days after the King returned from West Dean, on 28 October 1908, Hardinge wrote enclosing a "pernicious production" from *The*

---

* Once when the King arrived at West Dean, the butler came down with a very large cardboard box. "Mrs. James is indisposed," he said, "but she sent you this." The King was handed a large pair of scissors, and when he cut the ribbon and opened the box, there was Mrs. James disguised as a doll with a wind-up key. (Edward James, *Swans Reflecting Elephants*, p. 12.) Evie James was the daughter of Helen Forbes, one of Harriett Mordaunt's sisters. Her son, Edward James, claimed—probably wrongly—that she was Bertie's illegitimate daughter. Edward James himself was also rumored to be Bertie's son. Nine months before Edward's birth (16 August 1907), the King had stayed at West Dean for a house party (19–24 November 1906), and the gossips did their arithmetic. Edward James was probably not his father's biological son, and he did show a physical likeness to Bertie. However, another of the guests in November 1906 was John Brinton, the man who later became Evie's second husband, and he seems a more likely candidate for paternity.

Daily Telegraph: an interview with the German emperor.[90] "You English are mad, mad, mad as March hares," declared the kaiser, complaining with his characteristic blend of bombast, stilted slang, and paranoia that his good and peaceful intentions toward England had been willfully misunderstood. The article was based on the conversations William had held when he stayed with Colonel Stuart-Wortley at Highcliffe near Christchurch in Dorset in the autumn of 1907 (after his visit to Windsor), and as Hardinge reported to the King, "we have received absolutely reliable information from the office of the Daily Telegraph" that the interview "emanates from the German Emperor himself and that the Editor has a letter from His Majesty forwarding the article and mentioning improvements and alterations which he had made."[91] The article did indeed originate with William, and it represented a crass attempt to improve Anglo-German relations by removing misunderstandings.

In Germany, William found himself engulfed in a political crisis that almost destroyed his credibility. His indiscreet remarks and manifest lack of judgment caused howls of outrage and stoked anti-English hatred. Betrayed by his chancellor, Bülow, who lied about his own role in approving the draft of *The Daily Telegraph* interview, William was savaged in the Reichstag. By mid-November he was ill, suffering from crying fits, confined to bed, and contemplating abdication. When Alix wrote to inquire about his "cold," he replied, "I am not suffering from cold but from complete collapse."[92]

If Bertie was amazed by William's foolishness and surprised that the owner of the *Telegraph*, his friend Lord Burnham, who regularly entertained him shooting at Hall Barn, had agreed to publish the interview, he was horrified by a second interview by the kaiser that surfaced in November. It transpired that William had spoken in July to an American journalist named William Hale. Mistaking Hale for a clergyman, the kaiser gave vent to a tirade of anti-English hatred; he announced that King Edward was corrupt and his court was rotten and declared that war with England was inevitable and the sooner the better. The German government suppressed publication of the article in the American *Century Magazine*, but they were too late to stop it appearing in *The New York World*. The *World* issued a denial, but proofs of the ten-thousand-word article had already reached the *Daily Mirror* in London, and *The Observer* published a summary of the story.[93] At the Foreign Office, Hardinge did all he could to suppress the article. "Were it to appear the indignation against the Emperor would be general everywhere. We have no desire to see him so exasperated and a danger to Europe."[94]

Hardinge sent the King early intelligence of the Hale interview. Bertie minuted it with one word: "Curious."[95] He was unconvinced by the denials printed in *The New York World,* or by Count Metternich, the German ambassador, who assured him that the interview was a fabrication. "I know the German Emperor hates me and never loses an opportunity of saying so (behind my back) while I have always been kind and nice to him."[96] Hardinge urged that the Hale interview made a visit by the King to Berlin imperative. "It is the only possible step that I can see by which it might be possible to rehabilitate [William's] self-esteem and to show that we have not taken his indiscretions too seriously. So long as the German Emperor is in a sore state of mind, as at present, he is a positive danger to the peace of Europe."[97] Reluctantly, the King agreed. Not only did he consent to visit Berlin in the New Year, he personally intervened to stop publication of the Hale interview in *The Morning Post* and also the *National Review,* which was edited by the violently anti-German Leo Maxse. "Maxse must really be spoken to most seriously," minuted the King.[98]

The King and Queen of Sweden stayed at Windsor in November. Esher thought the Queen "a very unbrilliant person, fond of sport and lawn-tennis"; she was under the influence of her doctor, Axel Munthe, "a clever pushing rather pretentious man," who ordered her to retire to bed at five p.m. and remain there until noon next day.[99] The Asquiths stayed at Windsor for the state banquet (22 November), and Margot found that King Edward and Queen Alexandra could talk of little but the kaiser's folly. The King told her: "It is very serious—he is most unwise and unbalanced and this ought to be a severe lesson to him. My poor sister it would have been a great grief to her in fact it would have killed her I think. He was always so unkind to her too."

The Queen agreed. "I am glad his poor mother is dead. It would have broken her heart," she told Margot. "<u>Such</u> a man! <u>Such</u> things! The newspapers shocking!" Alix imitated the kaiser out shooting (he was an excellent shot, in spite of the withered arm), " 'throwing his guns to his loaders for them to catch on their <u>knees</u> poor things! Like that!' and she made a most amusing series of gestures."[100] Margot rocked with laughter, and so did Lady Lansdowne and the Queen of Sweden.

Also staying at Windsor was Lord Howard de Walden, super-rich medievalist and Olympic fencer. The castle made him "feel medieval"; the gorgeous pictures and arms made his mouth water, but he was grieved by the portraits of ancestors with "lined faces and mouths like vices which look down from the walls." A self-styled "philosophic anarchist," he found court life hard to take seriously. "I feel it is a sort of sad last transformation scene: in a moment the curtain will come down and the harlequinade of pure democracy will begin."[101]

Chief among the obstacles to pure democracy was the King himself, but he was a sick man. On the day the Swedes departed, he insisted on standing in the cold and wet, inspecting improvements in the park at Windsor; it was his practice personally to supervise all estate works. He then caught a train to Sandringham, where he fell ill with bronchitis.[102] After ten days in bed, he departed for Brighton to convalesce. Here he stayed with Arthur Sassoon and his Italian wife, Louise—a brilliant hostess blessed with "magnolia complexion and chestnut curls, magnificent diamonds and French chef."[103] Their house, number 8, King's Gardens, is a tall brick villa in the French style on the seafront at Hove.* The house was not big enough to accommodate the King's suite, who grumbled at having to stay in a hotel nearby.[104] The King tried to curb rumors about his health, refusing to hold a Privy Council for the prorogation of Parliament at Brighton, as it would have given the impression that he was too unwell to travel to London. Almeric Fitzroy heard a rumor that originated with the Duke of Fife

---

* Henry Labouchere described Brighton as "a sea-coast town, three miles long and three yards broad, with a Sassoon at each end and one in the middle." While Arthur Sassoon lived in King's Gardens, Albert was in Kemptown, and Reuben in Queen's Gardens. (Allfrey, *Jewish Court*, p. 54.)

that in addition to bronchitis, the King was suffering from "an acute pain in the region of the heart."[105] On the first days of the visit, Bertie spoke very little and, during his drives with Stamper, dozed in the car. Soon he was better, "talking all the time, as was his wont, to those who were with him," among them Alice Keppel.[106] Stamper drove him along the coast to Seaford or Worthing, where he was mobbed by jostling crowds, when all he wanted was to stroll slowly along the shore and sit gazing out to sea.

He recovered in time for Christmas at Sandringham, where he was a distant but thrillingly important figure to his grandchildren. The grandson who Stamper thought resembled the King most in character was the eldest, Prince Edward, known to the family as David.*[107]

Soon the King's great crocodile-skin dressing case was packed with his papers, his leather-bound foolscap diary, his jewelry, a miniature of Alix, and photographs of his family, and loaded into the backseat of the Daimler, as he embarked on his January round of shooting parties. He was slower to swing after birds than before, and he smoked cigars all the time, one after another.[108] At Hall Barn with Lord Burnham of the *Telegraph,* the King "ate the usual enormous lunch in the usual tent," feasting on turtle soup, Irish stew, cold truffled turkey, mince pie, and pâté de foie gras. He told Carrington "he had been very unwell and it had taken him a long time to throw the effects off."[109] Little wonder, when the most effective measure to alleviate chronic bronchitis and slow the progression of emphysema is to stop smoking.

In spite of the King's poor health, arrangements went ahead for the royal visit to Berlin. This was a diplomatic necessity, as Grey explained: "If the visit had not taken place, it would have been a cause of offence

---

* Within little more than a decade, David, by now Prince of Wales, would write that York Cottage, Sandringham, was "too dull and boring for words! Christ how any human beings can ever have got into this pompous secluded and monotonous groove I can't imagine." (Edward, Prince of Wales, to Mrs. Frida Dudley Ward, 26 December 1919, in *Letters from a Prince,* ed. Rupert Godfrey [Warner Books, 1999], pp. 286–87.)

and made all politics most difficult. For this reason I am glad it is arranged, but otherwise I do not expect much good from it. To please the Emperor does not carry so much weight in Germany as it did."[110] As before, the King was accompanied by Charles Hardinge, who did the diplomatic work.

For the German-hating Alix, who was recovering from an attack of influenza and neuralgia, the visit was a penance. She told Margot Asquith afterward, "I never wanted to go to Berlin. I was made to go—and it has been a complete failure!"[111] Outwardly, the visit seemed a success. Bertie melted the unfriendly Berlin crowd when he made an impromptu speech in German at the Rathaus, giving thanks to the little girl who presented him with a golden goblet of Rhine wine. Alix smiled serenely when the horses in her carriage took fright at the crowd and fell and, to the mortification of the German court, she and the Empress Dona had to make a hasty exit into another carriage.[112] "Oh! I was charming . . . of course," she told Margot; but she "hated" the emperor all the time. She sat next to him at every meal, and noticed that he ate nothing. "You must eat more!" she told him. "I will give you some of my excellent lozenges. Sir Francis Laking gave them to me—they will strengthen your brain!" When Margot interjected, "You didn't really say that?" the Queen replied, "Of course I did, he wants a little chaff. He just grunted and said, You find me stupid? I said, Certainly I do—making all this commotion about nothing and kidooodle [sic] about your navy." Then Alix "waved her arms round her head and roared with laughter continuing, 'The stupid man I believe showed my lozenges to his doctor he thought I was going to poison him and I should like to have!' "[113]

Bertie was far from well. Climbing upstairs left him breathless, and at the first family dinner, he fell asleep. After lunch the next day at the British Embassy, he had a coughing fit while smoking a cigar and talking to Daisy of Pless. Horrified, she watched as he fell against the back of the sofa, "his cigar dropped out of his fingers, his eyes stared, and he became pale and could not breathe. I thought: 'My God, he is dying; oh! Why not in his own country.' "[114] Daisy tried to undo the tight collar of his Prussian uniform, Alix rushed up and they both struggled with it, at last Bertie came to and unfastened it himself. He instantly lit another huge cigar.[115]

Later, the kaiser summoned Bertie's doctor, Sir James Reid, who acted as secret go-between with the English court (had Bertie known of Reid's role as William's spy, he would surely not have approved). He gave Reid a private cipher to use in case the King became seriously ill:

I   Radium most interesting in its effect (HM seriously ill)

II Radium cures can be reconed [sic] with (Please come at once).

III Institute of Radium cures great success (HM rapidly sinking).[116]

As this bizarre instruction shows, having managed to make a star appearance at Queen Victoria's deathbed, the kaiser was now determined to be in at the death of his uncle, which he evidently thought was imminent.

At the ball that night, the King sat quietly observing the dancers and did not walk about. Very likely he was bored; as Alix remarked, the balls were "awful": "All the ugly German women dancing so stiff, the ugly minuets." She asked William, " 'When have you time at your balls for flirtations?' And he just grunted and showed me the only pretty woman."[117] Bertie took no interest in distributing decorations among the German court; Ponsonby, who had to sit up until two a.m. allotting medals, thought this a sign that the King was seriously ill. During the ballet *Sardanapalus*, which the kaiser produced himself, Bertie fell asleep. He woke with a start in the last scene, when the monarch burns all his treasures, thinking that the opera house really was on fire. Bertie was too unwell to work the crowd during the interval, and Alix did it instead, charming everyone though she was unable to hear a word they said.[118]

The Berlin visit did little good. It failed to slow the German navy race. The fact that the visit took place at all, and that the two rulers were civil to each other, was perhaps important, but their hatred soon reasserted itself. The Bosnian crisis, which had rumbled on since the autumn, was resolved in Austria's favor in March 1909, humiliating

Russia at a time of military weakness and leaving Serbia hungry for a war of revenge. For this unstable and unfair settlement Bertie blamed Germany, whose backing gave Austria the confidence to threaten a war against Serbia. As he told Hardinge, "Ever since my visit to Berlin the German Government have done <u>nothing</u> but thwart and annoy us in every way. . . . We may safely look upon Germany as our bitterest foe, as she hardly attempts to conceal it."[119]

People noticed that the King, by nature cheerful and ebullient, was increasingly prone to depression, sitting brooding in silence. After eight years of striving for peace, the world could hardly be said to be a safer place. Closing the ring around Germany only made William more paranoid. Even if he could be contained in the west, eastern Europe was increasingly unstable. The Balkan crisis had proved that Francis Joseph, seemingly the greatest gentleman of all, could not be trusted. Britain's reaction was to draw closer to Russia, but Bertie knew only too well that the weak Nicky was hardly a reliable ally. Bertie's superb contacts had enabled him to lead and support the process of bringing Britain into closer relations with the continental powers, but tightening the links seemed only to ratchet up the pressure for war.

CHAPTER 26

King of Trumps

1909–10

The Cabinet was bitterly divided over the Admiralty's program of dreadnought building to rival Germany. For Bertie, who took his naval policy from Fisher, the position was simple: "As long as Germany persists in her present programme of ship building we have no alternative but to build double."[1] The chief opponents of this two-to-one naval race were Churchill and Lloyd George, who claimed (rightly as it turned out) that Fisher and the Admiralty exaggerated Germany's shipbuilding. As far as the King was concerned, these two ministers could do no right. As prime minister, Asquith seemed unwilling or unable to check them, and Knollys wrote to complain at "the uncompromising attitude Mr. Asquith generally takes when Your Majesty finds fault with any of his colleagues."[2]

Asquith was a self-made, raw-boned lawyer; an immensely able man whose mind "opened and shut smoothly and exactly, like the breech of a gun."[3] Bertie found him "deficient in manners but in nothing else."[4] He was certainly preferable to Arthur Balfour, the leader of the Unionist opposition, whom Bertie disliked as "an effeminate creature mixed up with the Souls." As he confided in Margot Asquith: "It is a great drawback to a man not to be able to love a woman"—to which Margot felt inclined to respond, "How many, Sir?"[5] No one could accuse Asquith of being effeminate. But the King now began to suspect that the prime minister's unshakable imperturbability masked a worrying lack of principle.

Asquith's was the last Cabinet to use neither agenda nor minutes, and the letter that he penned in his elegant handwriting to the King after each meeting formed the sole official record. To interest the King, he emphasized foreign and military policy rather than domestic politics; and to prevent royal interference, he played down Cabinet divisions and disagreements.[6] In the winter of 1908–9, Bertie suspected that he was being "kept in the dark" by Asquith, who was less than frank about the split in the Cabinet over the naval estimates.[7] Asquith adroitly steered Winston Churchill and Lloyd George to agree to the principle of eight dreadnoughts at a key Cabinet meeting (24 February), but even so, the King was critical. When the naval estimates were introduced in Parliament, and the attacks from the Tories sparked a naval scare in the press, the King blamed Asquith.

In April 1909, Bertie joined Alix on a three-week Mediterranean cruise. He was in a furious mood. He had expected to be received by the Mediterranean fleet on arriving at Malta, but the ships were ordered elsewhere. Ponsonby was summoned to the King's cabin. "I at once grasped that there was thunder in the air. 'What do you think of that?' the King shouted at me as he tossed me a telegram, and before I had time to answer he stormed away at the disgraceful way he had been treated."[8] It took all Ponsonby's skill to dissuade the irate monarch from ordering the entire fleet back to Malta at once.

At Naples, the King's temper was no better. Ponsonby (who was inclined to exaggerate) told a story of Alix and her sister the empress Minnie, who mounted donkeys and disappeared toward the top of

Mount Vesuvius.* The King stayed behind in the hired train, fuming at the wait and furiously ordering the whistle to be blown to summon them to turn back. When at length they appeared, the King was "boiling with rage" but unable to let off steam at the empress or the Queen, so the unfortunate Ponsonby once again incurred the full blast of his wrath.[9]

In spite of these volcanic explosions, the King dictated a letter to Asquith on the same day (1 May), giving the prime minister his comments on the so-called People's Budget that Lloyd George had introduced, which proposed to pay for increased naval costs and old age pensions by raising income tax and new land taxes: "His Majesty wishes me to ask you whether in framing the Budget the Cabinet took into account the possible (but the King hopes improbable) event of a European war. The income tax, which has always been regarded as a war tax, now stands so high for unearned incomes over a certain amount that any great increase would have a most disastrous effect on land generally more especially if the war lasted for a considerable time."[10]

It was a farsighted comment. Bertie possessed the vision to see domestic politics in a wider European context; what he did not foresee was the political storm that the budget would provoke in Britain.

The King returned on 8 May after two months abroad to face complaints in the press that he spent too much time out of the country. W. E. Grey of the *Daily Mail* wrote an article pointing out that on his cruise the King had been "far from idle." He assured Ponsonby that "in future nothing will appear in the paper which is not pleasing to His Majesty, and that you can make what use of its columns you will."[11] Ponsonby agreed in exchange to provide the *Mail* with information. The King's popularity that summer was such that he had little need of Mr. Grey and the *Daily Mail*. As Daisy Pless told the kaiser, "The whole country adores him; indeed the feeling of loyalty in England is extraordinary."[12] This made the kaiser feel rather sick.

---

* In Minnie's version, Alexandra was carried in a chair by three men, while she herself walked. (Battiscombe, *Queen Alexandra*, p. 260.)

"Well, Stamper, what about the new car?" were the King's first words to his mechanic on his return.[13] The motor that had just been delivered was a 65 hp Mercedes in which the monarch sped through his realm. He drove the fifty miles from Newmarket to Sandringham in a record-breaking one hour and twenty minutes, averaging 37½ mph.[14] Though he exceeded the speed limit of 20 mph the King's car was never stopped. Police alerted in advance of his route cleared the roads of slow horse-drawn traffic. Often when the King drove through a village the local brass band played "God Save the King." Constant repetition of the national anthem must surely be the bane of a musical monarch's life, and Bertie had strong views on the matter; he ordered military bands to speed up the timing and play at the rate of eighty beats to the minute. However excruciating the village band, he always raised his hat and bowed in acknowledgment, often bursting out laughing as soon as the village was passed.[15]

That summer, the King's horse Minoru won the Derby by a head, and ecstatic crowds surged on to the course as Bertie walked from the royal box to lead in his horse. It was his third Derby win, and a wag shouted from the crowd, "Now King you have won the Derby, go back home and dissolve this bloody Parliament!"[16]

Parliament was bogged down in the budget. The Liberal government battled to get the budget through the Commons, the bill didn't pass until November, and the Lords threatened to throw it out. As class war smoldered into flame between the Liberals and the peers, Bertie busied himself with house parties and visits to old mistresses. He stayed with Minnie Paget and saw Isadora Duncan dance; he called on Lillie Langtry, now Lady de Bathe and "an old tart of a girl with reddish hair and a flamboyant manner," and inspected her successful racing stables; he spent a weekend with Emma Bourke and her husband, Lord Clarendon.*[17] In July, after a royal visit to Manchester, the King

---

* "I am quite ready to go to Church . . . on Sunday," he told Emma, "if the Service is only the morning Service (without Litany and Communion Service) & a short Sermon." (Humphrey Whitbread Archive, B to Lady Clarendon, 26 June [1909].)

and Queen drove back through pouring rain to Knowsley, where they stayed with Lord Derby, and cheering crowds lined the entire route. For mile after mile the King and Queen acknowledged their welcome, sitting in a closed car perched forward on the edge of the seat so that they could be seen, Alix bowing and Bertie perpetually raising his hat.[18]

With the cheers of the Lancashire crowd still ringing in his ears, the King brought his motor to stay at Nuneham Park with the Liberal minister Loulou Harcourt. As usual, he played a lot of bridge. "Mrs. George (the Favorita) was in great good humour and very smart, winning over 1000 points at bridge from the King."[19] Bertie was an indifferent player. According to Frank Lascelles, who played often with him, when he had a good hand as well as a good dummy, "he knows how to make the best of it, but he has no knowledge of where the cards are."[20] He was alarmingly short-tempered with his partners, but Alice Keppel could tease him out of it, quipping, "Sir, I am afraid I cannot even tell a King from a Knave." Once, grumbling that he had no cards, he put her into a high-no-trump contract and laid his own hand down as dummy. "All I can say, Sir, is God save the King and preserve Mrs. Keppel," observed Alice.[21]

Only days after the Nuneham house party, Loulou Harcourt made a speech attacking the "black hand" of the Tory peers for "issuing edicts of assassination" against Liberal measures. He denied using the word "assassins" to describe the peers, but he received a tart reprimand from Bertie in the shape of a letter from Knollys, pointing out that the King would have expressed regret if Harcourt had used such words "immediately after he had been your guest."[22]

Lloyd George continued to needle the House of Lords. He made an inflammatory speech at Limehouse (30 July 1909), in which he attacked the dukes as selfish, pampered parasites. The palace objected strenuously. On the King's instruction, Knollys wrote to the Liberal minister Lord Crewe, protesting at LG's speech, "which can only have the effect of setting 'class' against 'class' and stirring up the worst passions of its audience." "The King cannot understand how Asquith can tacitly allow certain of his colleagues to make speeches that would not be tolerated by any Prime Minister until within the last few years." Such speeches, said Knollys, were seen by the King "as being an insult to the Sovereign when delivered by one of his confidential servants."[23]

On 2 August, the czar and his family visited Cowes in the yacht *Standart*. Radicals attacked the King for entertaining the autocrat. But Bertie was returning Nicholas's hospitality at Reval; and, as Grey pointed out: "The King's influence with the Czar and the friendship of the British Government are really a support to Stolypin . . . and to the Duma and all friends of constitutional progress in Russia."[24]

On board the royal yacht *Victoria and Albert* with the King and Queen was the prime minister, and in the intervals of the complex choreography of boarding the *Standart*, firing royal salutes, and changing in and out of uniform, Bertie made certain that he squeezed in an interview with Asquith, who found the experience a chastening one. The King was very angry indeed about Lloyd George's Limehouse speech. It was the last time in English history that the monarch tore strips off the prime minister. "I have never known him more irritated, or more difficult to appease," Asquith told Lloyd George. He urged LG to apologize, because "the King, of course, lives in an atmosphere which is full of hostility to us and to our proposals; but he is not himself unfriendly, and, so far, he has 'stood' the Budget very well—far better than I expected. It is important, therefore, to avoid raising his apprehensions and alienating his goodwill."[25] Lloyd George wrote a disingenuous letter (5 August) explaining about the Limehouse speech, which, he claimed, had been provoked by violent Tory attacks.[26]

Bertie departed for his three weeks' cure at Marienbad, as he always did. Here he was reunited with the ravishing American actress Maxine Elliott. A friend of the Keppels, she had traveled to Marienbad the year before and positioned herself on the bench where she knew the King always passed on his morning walk. Recognizing the forty-year-old beauty demurely reading a book as the actress he had seen in a play,

Bertie sent back one of his equerries to invite her to dinner. According to Chips Channon, who knew her in old age, Maxine Elliott was "an immense bulk of a woman with dark eyes, probably the most amazing eyes one has ever seen." She was "lovable, fat, oh so fat, witty and gracious"—he once saw her consuming pat after pat of butter without any bread (butter was Daisy Warwick's downfall, too).[27] Channon claimed that Edward VII, along with Lord Curzon and many others, had shared her "tempestuous" bed. Rosebery had proposed to her, too. The King had lunch with her at Marienbad four times; who knows what went on in the afternoons behind closed curtains in her scented hotel room.[28] Certainly she received encouragement enough to buy Hartsbourne Manor in Bushey Heath in order to entertain Bertie, for whom she expensively decorated what she called the King's suite.[29]

A few days before Bertie left Marienbad, Sigmund Muntz the journalist was drinking coffee at an inn in the pine forests high up above the town, when the "Duke of Lancaster" unexpectedly stepped from his car. Leaning on a stick and muffled in a shawl against the autumn chill, Bertie incognito seemed a lonely figure. Briefly glimpsing the man behind the mask, Muntz pondered whether power and popularity had brought the King happiness.[30]

Back in London, Bertie seemed to have thrown off his depression. Esher was summoned to breakfast alone at Buckingham Palace. "I waited in the little room lined with his Indian armour for a few minutes, when he came in, punctually, with his dog. He looked wonderfully well, thinner and younger. We sat down, each with our own small silver coffee pot and boiled egg."[31]

The King's chief concern that morning was Winston Churchill, who had ridiculed the dukes as ornamental creatures "like goldfish." "These unfortunate individuals, who ought to lead quiet, delicate, sheltered lives, far from the madding crowd's ignoble strife, have been dragged into the football scrimmage."[32] Winston's speech, said Bertie, was vulgar and "American," and Winston was a traitor to his class.[33]

Lloyd George caused less annoyance. This was partly due to Mrs.

Keppel, "who likes him."[34] Six months later, Esher was predicting that Lloyd George will "someday drift over to the Tories."[35] A man of his class, wrote Esher, "is always easier to deal with, when once he is '*arrivé,*' than a man sprung from the 'upper' class. He is less dangerous, in spite of his flaming language. Most of that is mere Celtic gas."[36] Churchill, a protégé of the King who was in the habit of spending his weekends at Blenheim, was a different matter. Both Esher and Knollys disliked him. "Churchill thinks solely of party exigencies," wrote Esher. "He has his eye fixed on the radical wing, and means to lead it. He is conceited and thinks no one is so clever as himself."[37]

Lord Knollys was so enraged by Churchill's speech that he wrote a letter to *The Times* effectively accusing him of lèse-majesté for failing to acknowledge that the creation of peers was a royal prerogative.[38] "He and the King must really have gone mad," was Churchill's comment. "This looks to me like a rather remarkable Royal intervention and shows the bitterness which is felt in these circles. I shall take no notice."[39] Winston was right about Knollys. Panicked by the threat that class war against the peers posed to the Crown, his judgment deserted him. The King, on the other hand, saw clearly what WC ("whose initials are so well-named!" as he remarked to Esher) was trying to achieve.[40] By attacking the peers, Churchill hoped to goad the House of Lords into rejecting the budget, thus provoking the constitutional crisis that the King was anxious to prevent.

The King reached Balmoral on 23 September. A day or so later, he learned (through Esher, whose intelligence sources with the opposition were excellent) that the Unionist leaders had almost certainly made up their minds, after months of uncertainty, to throw out the budget in the House of Lords.[41] Bertie was "strongly opposed" to rejection, anticipating that if the Lords threw out the budget, the crisis would inevitably escalate.[42]

At Balmoral, the Russian ambassador Benckendorff found Bertie in a stimulated mood: "It is the first time I have seen him very excited about politics and . . . he does not mince words."[43] Watching the King in the smoking room after dinner, surrounded by men such as Haldane, Rosebery, and Reginald McKenna, made Benckendorff feel that the English "fearing for the constitution are truly idiotic"; the contrast with the autocracy of Nicholas II could hardly be more marked. "All the conversation is conducted, encouraged, made natural and amusing by his skill, his tact. . . . Telegrams are pouring in and he is reading them aloud, with private comments as if alone in the room."[44]

The King summoned Asquith to Balmoral, to ask whether he would be acting constitutionally if he talked to the leaders of the opposition.[45] Bertie spoke frankly. "He still wants the Budget to pass (this is most private)," Asquith reported to Margot, "and is making determined efforts to influence the Lords." In his interview with Balfour and Lansdowne, "He will urge the gravity of the step they are taking and the disastrous consequences which he considers must ensue. . . . This he is doing wholly on his own initiative."[46] For his part, Asquith undertook to write to Lloyd George, and endeavor to gag him from attacking the peers.[47] Asquith's warning letter was ignored by Lloyd George, who made a rabble-rousing speech at Newcastle (9 October) ridiculing the peerage as "five hundred men, ordinary men chosen accidentally from among the unemployed," intended to provoke them into voting for rejection. The King was not pleased. The next time he saw Asquith, he "told him how highly I disapproved of L. George's speech! The former tried to defend it but it was a mild attempt!"[48]

Bertie then summoned the opposition—Balfour and Lansdowne—to Buckingham Palace on 12 October. The interview was not a success: As Bertie wrote drily to Georgie, "No results accrued from it."[49] According to Carrington, the two grandees were "very stiff and reserved and HM apparently got nothing out of them." They told him (untruthfully) that no decision had been taken with regard to the budget. The King's intervention was "generally supposed to have been a mistake," wrote Carrington, "the first of any importance he has made."*[50] Esher nevertheless thought it was "appreciated all over the

---

* The King had precedents on his side. Esher supplied him with a memorandum listing two occasions when Queen Victoria had approached the opposition, in 1869 over the Irish Church Bill and again in 1884 over the Reform and Redistribution Bill. But Victoria never saw the opposition leaders herself, and the negotiations were conducted through intermediaries. (Esher's memo, 7 October 1909, in Brett, *Journals and Letters*, vol. 2, p. 413.)

country. It was a very wise move: even though it bears no direct or immediate fruit."[51]

Asquith, who stayed at Windsor in November, was impressed by
the King's grasp of the situation. "He is a very good listener and quite
a clever man: a capital head. Very superior to the Prince of Wales, who
is a dunderhead. . . . The King isn't educated of course, but he thoroughly understands." The King told Asquith that he liked Lansdowne
but thought him "not a clever man, not a clever man at all." Balfour he
cordially disliked as "the greatest political shuffler of our day" with
"no sense of honour or truth: he doesn't trust his judgement."[52] Discussing his views of opposition leaders with the PM was no doubt indiscreet, but Balfour and Lansdowne had done little to earn the King's
confidence.

The King was at Sandringham on 30 November, the day the House of
Lords voted to reject the budget. Among the guests assembled for the
Queen's birthday was Sydney Holland, the hospital reformer. The
King came up to him and talked about the London Hospital, of which
Holland was chairman. He sat down, "cross-legged, on a sort of saddle-
shaped stool, and made one feel at ease at once."[53] Out shooting that
day, Sydney Holland fired almost seven hundred cartridges and had to
send away for more. The pheasants at Sandringham were plentiful—
the place crawled with them; they were also notoriously low and easy
to shoot.[54] The King joined the shoot late. He wore a thick brown suit,
a Tyrolean hat, and boldly striped stockings. At lunch, which was eaten
in a tent flying the royal standard, the Queen lit a cigarette and asked
the King if he approved of ladies stalking or smoking. "They might
smoke, but not shoot," said the King.[55] He left the shoot early. Some of
the peers who were staying caught the train to London to vote, but by
the King's wish none of the household voted. Lord Knollys, who was
anxious to prevent what he called "a disaster happening to the constitution and, incidentally, to the Monarchy," had to be restrained by the
King from voting in favor of the budget.[56]

Parliament was prorogued on 2 December, and Almeric Fitzroy, the clerk to the Privy Council, traveled down to Sandringham, where the King held the Prorogation Council. After lunch Lord Knollys told him "very gravely and emphatically" that he thought the Lords were mad.[57] Bertie complained that he had never had such a miserable day. Not only did the council stop him from joining the shoot, but he suffered from toothache all night and had to send for the dentist, who performed an extraction. Holland asked if he had gas. "Oh, no, I just had some cocaine. I can bear pain," said the King.[58]

The Queen spent the day writing eight hundred telegrams of thanks for her birthday greetings of the day before.[59] One of these was to Daisy Pless: "I thank you and your dear Hans for kind wire for my old birthday." Daisy Pless was amazed to discover that Alix was sixty-five. She looked no older than fifty. Daisy observed that, contrary to gossip, the Queen's lips were not painted, "as they are always moist," nor was her face enameled, as was often rumored: "I have seen her at Cowes in the pouring rain."*[60] She noticed that Alix always sat side by side with Soveral; "he speaks distinctly and she always hears him."[61] Like Alix, Soveral was fanatically anti-German.

The King came out shooting on the last day of the house party (4 December). Being a good host, he put himself in the worst place, at the end of the line. Sydney Holland, who was standing in the place next to him, nervously praying that he would not miss, counted seven people in the King's butt: a body servant, a loader, a man with a dog, a boy carrying cartridges, another with coats, the agent from Balmoral, and the agent from Sandringham. It was a bitterly cold day, driving snow, and the King, who was wearing two coats, put on a third. He went home after one drive and changed into a pink flannel shirt, Guards tie, and colored flannel waistcoat.[62] Standing behind the King out shooting was his racehorse trainer, Richard Marsh. Some instinct impelled him to pick up and put in his pocket the last two cartridges

---

* Enameling was a method of face painting used by aging Edwardian beauties: a thick white zinc-based paste was applied to conceal wrinkles, and then painted with rouge. Alexandra is reputed to have used this on occasion. Her sister Minnie was also rumored to enamel her face.

that Bertie fired. They were the last he ever discharged at Sandring-ham.[63]

The rejection of the budget by the Lords plunged the King into the political firing line. It made an immediate election inevitable. The election was fought on the budget, but the Liberals also wanted a mandate to limit the powers of the House of Lords. Asquith opened his campaign on 10 December with a speech demanding "safeguards" curbing the legislative powers of the upper chamber. The House of Lords, which was overwhelmingly Conservative, had no intention of voting for a bill limiting its powers, and Asquith plainly intended to ask the King for some sort of guarantee to create extra peers if the Lords rejected a veto bill. This placed the King in an acutely difficult position. On the one hand, he wanted to hang on to his power to create peers, but on the other, he was reluctant to create extra peers to further the political demands of one party. Nor did he want to commit in advance.

Esher, who was having an excellent crisis, having been restored to favor after languishing in the backwater of the archives, was sent out to spy on the Liberals. In a memo to Knollys, he reported alarming intelligence. According to Haldane, "The Prime Minister wishes to obtain a promise from the King before the General Election." Ministers were also considering a proposal to transfer the royal prerogative of peer creation to the prime minister.[64] This last, thought Knollys, would "weaken the Monarchy so considerably that it would be better that the King should abdicate than agree to it."[65] He considered these proposals so "outrageous" that he thought it best to conceal Esher's letter from the King "for the present," as it "would be a mistake to set him still more against his ministers."[66]

On the day Parliament was dissolved (15 December 1909), Knollys, acting on behalf of the King, summoned the prime minister's secretary. He disclosed that "the King had come to the conclusion that he would not be justified in creating new peers (say 300) until after a second general election." As Knollys explained, "The King regards the policy of the Government as tantamount to the destruction of the House of Lords," and in consequence this issue must be put to the electorate at a second election.[67]

By claiming a right not to create peers to pass the veto bill unless it had been sanctioned by a second election, the King seized the initiative. Some consider that he was "stretching his constitutional role."[*68] He was certainly taking a great gamble. If the Liberals won an overwhelming majority, he would be unable to resist the demand for the creation of peers.

On the day that Knollys was closeted with Asquith's private secretary, the King was conspicuously absent from the political scene, staying at yet another house party: with Bendor, the fabulously rich and spoiled Duke of Westminster, at Eaton. Whenever the King stayed anywhere for more than two nights, a private telegraph office was installed in one of the rooms of the house by post office engineers, and throughout his stay at Eaton a stream of cipher telegrams was received and dispatched by operators.[69] At dinner, however, Bertie refused to be drawn on the political situation, merely commenting, "Yes! Yes! Disgraceful, disgraceful!"[70] He seemed far more interested in accompanying Alice Keppel and Daisy Pless on a surprise visit to Daisy's grandmother, Lady Olivia Fitzpatrick, who lived nearby. The old lady was not pleased to see him, and the visit started badly when the King sat down in her favorite chair. However, "he made outrageous love" to her and "in a few minutes they were both flirting desperately."

"Is it true," asked the King, "that my Mother sent you away from Court for trying to flirt with my father?"[71]

---

* The precedent for the use of the royal prerogative to create—or threaten to create—peers was the crisis over the Reform Bill in 1831–32, but this was not exact. The Reform Bill was rejected by the Commons, and an election was called that the Whigs won. The Lords then threw out the bill, and Grey's government asked the King to create peers. The King refused, but after the Tories had failed to form a government, he capitulated and agreed to the Whigs' demand that he should create peers if necessary to pass the bill. He did not demand a second election. King Edward could argue, however, that Lords reform was not the issue at the January 1910 election, and a second election was therefore justified.

On New Year's Day 1910, the King wrote a letter to "My Dear Mrs. George" from Sandringham, one of the very few letters to Mrs. Keppel that has survived. "My first letter of this New Year must be written to you today and wish you again all possible happiness and prosperity," he wrote. "Oh! The telegrams and letters they surpass all human belief and do not leave one a spare moment. I am so looking forward to Monday— when I shall hope to [sic] our next meeting between 5 and 6. I shall motor over from here." And he signed himself, "Tout à vous ER."[72]

The King's rendezvous with his mistress was at Elveden, where they were both guests at the annual January shooting party with the Iveaghs. In the cavernous marble hall created by the previous owner, the Maharaja Duleep Singh, the house party assembled for shooting tea. The women shivered in their tea gowns, as—in spite of the Guinness millions—there was only one fire, and that was where the King sat.[73] The Iveaghs lived like royalty themselves, with thirty housemaids and fifty servants living in the house. When the King and Queen came, they brought a suite of twenty-two, including a postman and a man in red livery who stood outside Bertie's door.[74] Carrington found the King "anxious about the state of affairs" but "on a very even keel and there will be no political talk in his presence." He played bridge until twelve thirty every night and went shooting every day, and Carrington thought him "really very well indeed."[75]

Lady Fingall, a fey, witty Irishwoman, was given the room next to the King's.* A double door joined her room to the King's, concealed on his side by a large bookcase. Through the door, Daisy Fingall could hear the doctor giving oxygen at night, and the King's voice, with its curious vibration that (she wrote) "I recognise now when I turn on my wireless and the German voices push out the others."[76] When she sat next to the King at dinner, he growled at her for sympathizing with the suffragettes. After dinner, in a corner of the drawing room, he told her: "Your friend, Mrs. Jameson, has hurt me deeply."

---

* Fifteen years later, Chips Channon stayed in the King's Bed, and in the small hours had a humiliating accident—"I somehow smashed the royal Chamber pot." (Rhodes James, *Chips*, p. 21.)

Daisy Fingall was astonished. Mrs. Jameson was the sister of the cavalry officer Douglas Haig, and she possessed psychic powers, transcribing messages from her dead brother George. The King disclosed that she had written to him with a message from Alice, Bertie's favorite sister, who had died more than thirty years before. It ran: "The time is short. You must prepare." When Daisy asked if Mrs. Jameson had proof that the message was from Alice, he replied: "She said I was to remember a day when we were on Ben Nevis together and found white heather and divided it."[77]

Only that summer Bertie had driven past Ben Nevis and recalled the time he had climbed it; his sister Alice was much in his thoughts.[78] Bertie was superstitious. He believed, for example, that odd numbers of asparagus brought bad luck, and if he had an odd number of stalks on his plate, he always asked for another to make the numbers even.[79] That New Year's Eve at Sandringham, as was customary, the house was emptied of guests and servants so that the King and Queen could be the first to open the front door in the New Year. A grandchild ran around from the back and triumphantly flung the door open. "We shall have some very bad luck this year," said the King.[80] Mrs. Jameson's omens disturbed him deeply.

From Elveden, Bertie retreated once more to Brighton to nurse his health with Arthur and Louise Sassoon. On 14 January, the day the election campaign officially began, he wrote in his diary: "In the morning walk on the beach near Shoreham. In the afternoon motor to Worthing and walk on the Promenade."[81] In these short, slow walks with Alice Keppel by his side, pausing often to catch his breath, Bertie no doubt pondered gloomily the consequences of a Liberal election victory. Whether he could resist if Asquith then demanded guarantees to create peers was by no means certain. Esher was sent on an intelligence-gathering mission to Whittingehame, Arthur Balfour's country house, to sound out the views of the opposition. He reported that Balfour was "amazed" at the "impudence" of Asquith's request for guarantees. The veto bill had not been drafted, nor had it passed the Commons. "It would be a breach of the King's duty, if not of his Coronation oath," said Balfour, "to pledge himself to create peers to pass a bill which he has never seen."[82]

Back at Windsor, Bertie waited anxiously for the election news. As the results trickled through, it emerged that the Liberals had won, but they had lost their overall majority and were now dependent on the Irish.* The atmosphere palpably lightened. As Esher reported, the verdict made the King "less depressed than he was, because undoubtedly the fix in which Ministers find themselves makes it impossible for them to bully him."[83] There was no question of Asquith demanding guarantees at once, as the reduced majority could not be read as a clear mandate for Lords reform. The King discussed the political situation with Esher. "He is quite clear that he will not assent to any request to make peers."[84]

Bracing himself for an unpleasant meeting, Bertie invited Asquith to dine and sleep at Windsor. In a breach of etiquette that seemed to confirm Bertie's view that he had no manners, Asquith rushed off to France without even writing a letter.[85] When Margot realized what a blunder her husband had made, she hastened to explain to Knollys that Asquith was exhausted after sitting up for two nights with his daughter Violet, who was devastated by the death of her fiancé Archie Gordon in a car crash.[86] Margot demanded to see the King herself: "I would only say how deeply sorry I am and Henry [Asquith] will be when he knows he has vexed him," she told Knollys. "I would <u>much</u> like to do this in person if only to stop all the insufferable gossip and the joy my political enemies (few I think!) have in repeating that the King is angry with us."[87] This letter was shown to Bertie, and his response was stiffly correct: "I am sure you know that he is always glad to see you," Knollys told Margot, "but he thinks that in this instance, as the matter in question is an official one, it will perhaps be better, if anything is said to him on the subject, it should come from the Prime Minister himself."[88] In

---

* The final figure was 275 Liberals, 273 Unionists, 82 Irish Nationalists, and 40 Labour . The parties opposing the budget—Unionists and Irish—were stronger than its supporters, the Liberals and Labour.

truth, Bertie was fuming with Asquith for going AWOL. "My Prime Minister's place is in London," he declared.[89]

Bertie was scrupulously correct in his dealings with the new Liberal government. Winston Churchill, his bête noire, was promoted to Home Secretary, but he seemed to have changed his spots.* One of Churchill's new duties was to write the nightly letter to the monarch describing the day in Parliament, and in these communications Churchill reinvented himself as the loyal servant of the King. Margot played bridge with Bertie and "rubbed it in" that Winston had much improved. She teased Bertie, saying he would soon be playing bridge with the Tories, to which he replied "he would be very sorry if we went out of office, and that Henry [Asquith] had served him well."[90]

Asquith worried that the King might refuse to open Parliament, and he was greatly relieved when he agreed to do so, "as I have done on all previous occasions since my accession to the throne."[91] The King read his speech "pretty badly" in the Lords.[92] He was ill once more with bronchitis. He took short breathless walks in the garden at Buckingham Palace, and his doctors urged him to go abroad.[93] He refused to leave until the political crisis eased, and only made up his mind to travel to Biarritz when Asquith insisted that he must for the sake of his health.[94]

* Bertie liked Winston's wife, Clementine Hozier. According to Esher: "The King spoke very appreciatively of Mrs. Winston, and told me what I had never heard, that she was dear old Redesdale's daughter. (Niece as well as daughter!)" (Churchill Archives Centre, Esher Papers, 2/11, 26 September 1908.)

CHAPTER 27

The People's King

March–May 1910

The King left London on the evening of 6 March 1910. After dining at Buckingham Palace, he drove in a closed carriage to Victoria station. Crowds of people waited to watch him walk across the crimson-carpeted platform onto the royal train.[1] He reached Paris the following afternoon, and saw the play *Chantecler,* which he thought "stupid & childish—& more like a Pantomime!" The heat at the theater was "awful," he told Georgie, and "I contrived to get a chill with a threatening of bronchitis."[2]

In fact it was worse—"acute cardiac distress," which his doctor Sir James Reid treated throughout the night.[3] The next day he was well enough to exchange visits with President Fallières and attend a large luncheon party with Madame Waddington, the American widow of the French ambassador to London. He laughed until he was red in the face when her grandson greeted him, "How do you do, King Edward?"[4] At lunch was the Comtesse de Pourtalès, now a dictatorial grande dame of seventy-four and one of his oldest friends, and she walked with him in the Jardin des Plantes. He had tea with the sixty-three-year-old Madame Standish, who had once been a mistress, and he confided in the Comtesse de Greffuhle: "I have not long to live. And then my nephew will make war."[5]

From Paris, Bertie traveled to Biarritz, and there his health broke.

"Unable to go out owing to a cold in the head," he wrote laconically in his diary.[6] In his rooms in the Hôtel du Palais, Mrs. Keppel nursed him. She scrawled a note to Soveral: "The King's cold is so bad that he cannot dine out but he wants us all to dine with him at the Palais SO BE THERE. I am quite worried entre nous and have sent for the nurse."[7]

The Times reported on 14 March that, on his doctor's advice, "King Edward remained in his apartments today as a storm was raging. His Majesty's health, however, is excellent."[8] This was disinformation. Even the King accepted that he was ill. His diary for 14–18 March reads: "Severe cold and bronchial attack. Unable to leave the house. Dine in sitting room."[9] Reid, who noted that the King was breathing fast and coughing badly with a fever, sat up all night in the next room.[10] Nurse Fletcher, who had cared for the King previously, arrived from England. "Physical signs in the chest" that threatened a fatal attack of pneumonia, occasioned Reid "no little anxiety."[11] Alice Keppel was "much alarmed," and little wonder.[12] Watching the King struggle for breath, she knew that he was fighting for his life. That the King of England should die in a hotel room in Biarritz, with only his mistress at his bedside, was a terrifying scenario.

But Bertie turned the corner. By 22 March, he was well enough to write to Georgie: "I have really had a nasty & sharp bronchial attack with a horrible cough, but I am now getting daily better and stronger, still I must be careful for a time."[13] The big cigars lit up again. He read a novel—always a bad sign.[14]

Reid took a risk, and, in order to avoid scenes with the King, concealed the true facts from the Queen, who had always nursed her husband in the past. Had Alix realized how close Bertie was to death, she would undoubtedly have rushed to his bedside.[15]

The public knew nothing.[16] *The Times* reported on 17 March that the King was "recovering from his slight indisposition," and on 25 March, "His Majesty is now completely restored to health."[17] When Ponsonby traveled to Biarritz to relieve Arthur Davidson as private secretary, he was astonished to discover how ill the King had been. Mr. Grey of the *Daily Mail* had agreed to suppress details of the King's illness in exchange for being kept fully informed.[18]

Partly because of this conspiracy of silence, a myth grew up about that last spring in Biarritz. It was alleged that the King had indulged in a "hedonistic holiday," running away from the constitutional crisis at home.*[19] Indeed, after he recovered, the King resumed his Biarritz routine. His diary fills with motor drives and dinner parties: not only Alice Keppel, but also Agnes Keyser and even Jennie Churchill feature in the lists.[20] But as Davidson, his assistant private secretary, later wrote, it was wrong to think that "because the King dined out or had a dinner party that he was indifferent to politics." The fact was that "the King either dined out or had people to dinner every night of his life—it was his ordinary life."[21]

To Georgie, the King wrote: "I think I had best keep my views to myself"—discretion that turned out to be unfortunate, as it meant that he never discussed the constitutional crisis with his son, who was to be called upon to make decisions all too soon.[22] The veto resolutions that the Cabinet introduced into the Commons (21 March), reducing the Lords' absolute veto to a delaying power of no more than two years, annoyed the King. He was enraged by Winston Churchill and Lloyd George, who made inflammatory speeches dragging the

---

* Sidney Lee said as much in his *Dictionary of National Biography* article, and Davidson felt obliged to summon him and tell him how painful the visit had been: The sick King was oppressed by "the weight of anxiety on the political situation which never left him." At this, Lee became "very much disturbed—moved about, asked how I knew etc, and when I told him I was there, said, This is one of those things that is really important, it is eyewitness evidence which cannot be ignored. I am bound to tell you though that this is not what I have been told." (RA GV/GG9/189, Arthur Davidson to Dighton Probyn, 5 December 1912.)

Crown into party politics. "The way the government is going on is really a perfect scandal, and I am positively ashamed to have any dealings with them," he told Knollys on 26 March, before embarking on a motor drive to Lac d'Yrieux, where he walked in the woods on the shores of the lake and Stamper served tea.[23]

No one knew whether the government would succeed in making a deal with the Irish or whether they would be defeated, and as the uncertainty deepened, the King's temper worsened. In spite of a soothing visit to a convent of religious sisters who passed their days in silence, he fulminated against the socialistic tendencies of his government and Asquith's inability to "make up his mind or make a clear statement." He told Knollys: "I do not suppose the P.M. will suggest my making a quantity of peers, but should he do so I should certainly decline, as I would far sooner be unpopular than ridiculous!"[24]

Alix urged him to leave that "horrid Biarritz," and join her at Genoa on a Mediterranean cruise, but the King refused.[25] "I fear she is much disappointed at my not going with her," he told Knollys. Bertie claimed that "I could not go so far away fr. Home—as I always feel I might be wanted at any moment and I can be in London fr. here under 24 hours."[26]

Without waiting to see the sick King return, Alix and her daughter Victoria departed on a whim for a fortnight's Mediterranean cruise to Corfu—a curiously irresponsible thing to do.

Asquith wrote on 13 April confirming the King's worst fears. Bertie had already received advance warning from Esher that the government had struck a deal with the Irish. In exchange for the Irish allowing the budget to pass, the Cabinet proposed to demand guarantees from the Crown to ensure that the Veto Bill passed the Lords.[27] Pithily expressed by Esher, the policy was this: "(a) Bribe or blackmail (whichever you like) for the Irish. (b) The price—a menace to the Sovereign."[28]

The menace was contained in Asquith's letter. In cloudy mandarin prose he explained that when the Lords rejected the Veto Bill, the Cabinet proposed "at once to tender advice to the Crown as to the necessary steps—whether by exercising the Royal Prerogative or by a Referendum . . . to be taken to ensure that their policy, approved by the

House of Commons by large majorities, should be given statutory effect in this parliament." In other words, the government proposed to ask the King to create peers to pass the bill. However, "if they found that they were not in a position to accomplish that object," that is, if the King refused, "they would either resign office or advise a dissolution of parliament." But—and this was the sting—"in no case would they feel able to advise a dissolution except under such conditions as would secure that, in the new Parliament, the judgement of the people as expressed in the elections would be carried into law." In short, they would demand conditional guarantees from the King before the second election. To sweeten the pill, Asquith added that the Cabinet "were all of the opinion that, as far as possible, the name of the Crown should be kept out of the arena of party politics."[29]

The King's reply was brief and formal. He informed the PM that he expected to receive a telegram with the results of the critical vote in the Commons on the budget on 19 April, "so that he can make his plans accordingly."[30] In private, he was fuming. "It is simply disgusting," he wrote. "Thank God I am not in London."[31] Asquith had gone back on his word not to ask for guarantees until after a second election, and to keep the Crown out of politics. Now he told the Commons (14 April) that if the Lords rejected the Veto Bill, "we shall find it our duty immediately to tender advice to the Crown as to the steps which will have to be taken if that policy is to receive statutory effect in this Parliament."[32] In plain language, as the King told Knollys, this meant that "he is going to ask me to swamp the H of Lords by a quantity of peers. . . . I positively decline doing this—besides I have previously been given to understand that I should not be called upon to agree to this preposterous measure. Certainly the P.M. & many of his colleagues assured me so—but now that they are in the hands of [Irish leader] Redmond & Co. they do not seem to be their own master."[33]

The Tories accused Asquith of bullying the King, but this was not his intention. On the contrary, Asquith liked and respected the King far more than Balfour did. He was a clever strategist driving through a constitutional revolution, steering a course between the radicals of his own party on the one side and the King on the other. The last thing he wanted was to force the pace and drive the king into the arms of the aristocracy. "Wait and see" was his tactic; he judged that the moment was right to ask for guarantees, and the King knew that if he refused, he risked identifying the Crown with opposition to democracy.[34]

Asquith's defection made Lord Knollys hysterical. He ranted that the prime minister intended "to commit the greatest outrage on the King which has ever been committed since England became a Constitutional Monarchy; and, if I were the King, I would, should the elections be in favour of the radicals, rather abdicate than agree to it."[35] Fortunately, Lord Knollys was not the King, nor did the King listen to his wild talk. The word "abdication" did not cross Bertie's lips, but he was angered "by the way in which my Ministers have treated me in mentioning my Prerogative in such a casual way especially the Prime Minister and I wish them to understand that I look upon them with the greatest displeasure and can no more be on friendly terms with them. They are not only ruining the Country but maltreat me personally, and I can neither forgive nor forget it."[36]

One of the drives that Stamper arranged took Bertie to Lourdes. He was received by the Bishop of Lourdes, who escorted him to the Church of the Rosary. He then climbed the steps and entered the basilica, which is perched on the terrace above. A company of pilgrims appeared and knelt on the steps as they sought the bishop's blessing. Stamper watched the bishop raise his hands above the kneeling crowd in the setting afternoon sun. "There above them all, one figure stood out sharply against the background of white. It was the King, standing bare-headed in the sunlight, watching the scene below."[37]

Stamper's image of the King is almost apocalyptic. Perhaps the visit was a political gesture, designed to appeal to his Catholic subjects. Perhaps, conscious of the approach of death, Bertie sought comfort from the Catholic shrine. He visited the Lourdes grotto, but his contemplation must have been sorely tried by the crowd, which was so great that he had to leave through a side door.[38]

The King returned home on 26 April. "I shall be sorry to leave Biarritz," he said, as he looked out from his veranda, adding, after a pause, "perhaps for good."[39]

He traveled directly to London, without pausing in Paris. On the journey, Ponsonby had "quite an interesting conversation with him as to how far the Sovereign could rightly go in settling the differences between the two Houses of Parliament."[40] In order to signal his displeasure, the King had previously asked Knollys to prevent Asquith, Lloyd George, and Winston Churchill from meeting him at Victoria station, as was customary, but when his train arrived at five forty-five on 27 April, Asquith and Churchill were waiting on the platform to receive him.[41]

At three o'clock that afternoon, Knollys and Esher met Balfour with Randall Davidson, Archbishop of Canterbury, at Lambeth Palace. Knollys had summoned the meeting, which Esher pompously called "a Conference at Lambeth," in order to sound out Balfour. If the government asked the King to dissolve Parliament and give guarantees, and if the King refused this "advice," would Balfour be prepared to form a government? Balfour replied that he would "come to the King's assistance" by taking office and immediately asking for a dissolution.[42] Quoting the precedent of William IV in 1832, Esher argued that Balfour's willingness to take office meant that the King was not bound to accept the advice of his ministers to create peers.

Later, Esher's Lambeth Palace meeting became the subject of furious political controversy. Knollys, who had declared that the King should abdicate rather than give conditional guarantees, abruptly changed his mind, and six months later he counseled King George V to agree to Asquith's demand. Extraordinarily, he concealed Esher's memorandum from the new King. Believing that he had no choice in the matter, George agreed to give the conditional guarantees to create peers that Asquith demanded before a second election. Had he known that Balfour was prepared to take office, he might have acted differently, and he afterward considered that he had been bullied into acquiescing by Knollys and Asquith. Knollys "seriously misled" the King, according to one constitutional expert, and gave dangerous advice; by agreeing to hypothetical pledges and committing himself in advance, George potentially compromised the political neutrality of the monarchy.[43]

The memorandum of 3 May in which Esher advised King Edward to refuse his government's advice to create peers was probably never seen by him. We can only guess at what Bertie would have done, but he would not have been kept in the dark about Esher's talks with Balfour. Nor would Knollys—or even Asquith—have dared to bully him. It seems likely, that, had he lived, he would not have given Asquith hypothetical guarantees before a second election.

The King held a thirty-minute audience with Asquith at eleven thirty on 28 April. "I do not look forward to it," he wrote; but Asquith reported to Margot afterward, "I had a good talk with the King this evening [sic] and found him most reasonable."[44]

On the afternoon of Thursday, 28 April 1910, the King attended the private view at the Royal Academy. He looked "tired and a little pale."[45] That evening, he appeared at Covent Garden and sat through one act of *Siegfried* alone in the royal box, looking "very tired and worn." Redesdale, who was in a box nearby, saw him give a great sigh as he got up; he opened the door of the box, lingered for a little in the doorway, and "with a very sad expression in his face—so unlike himself—took a last look at the house, as if to bid it farewell, and then went out."[46]

Redesdale was writing with hindsight. Esher, who knew the King far better, saw him on the evening of Friday the twenty-ninth and thought him "in excellent spirits—and apparently in excellent health."[47] On Saturday, he traveled to Sandringham, not, as the papers later suggested, to "combat a threatened attack" by a change of air, but because he wanted to oversee the estate as he always did.[48]

The King and his suite left St. Pancras at nine fifteen on Saturday and ate breakfast on the train. The doctors' report later said he was "feeling a little unwell," but he walked about the grounds inspecting new planting, and at dinner Ponsonby thought he was "in his usual form," telling stories of "amusing incidents of former years" and playing bridge.[49] On Sunday, the King drove the short distance to church in a "clarence," but later he walked in the garden and inspected the farm and stud. The drawing rooms were shut up, as the Queen was away, and the King insisted on working in Knollys's room, which was chilly, without a fire.

Monday morning was cold and very wet. Bertie traveled back to London in the afternoon. He was "not in a talkative mood," but it never occurred to Ponsonby or anyone else that he was beginning a serious illness.[50] That evening, he went to 17 Grosvenor Crescent to play bridge with Agnes Keyser. She was concerned by his coughing, and sent a messenger with a penciled note to Sir James Reid: "The King is dining here. He would like to see you tonight at Buckingham Palace at 11:15, if you would kindly go there, as he has a cold, and a little cough and Nurse is not there."[51]

Reid found HM sitting in his dressing room in an easy chair, panting very fast and coughing, with a temperature of one hundred degrees and complaining of difficulty in breathing. Reid applied linseed and mustard poultices to the King's chest and back and prescribed a sleeping draught of chlorodyne and morphine. When he returned home at one a.m., he told his wife: "The King may recover, as he did at Biarritz, but if not he will be dead in three days."[52]

The next morning, the King dressed but agreed to remain upstairs, doing business as usual. Ponsonby, who saw him during the day with letters, never thought his condition was alarming, and nor did Esher.[53] Grey requested an audience to discuss the guarantees, but the King refused to see him. At dinner with Ponsonby and two members of the suite, the King complained that he was unable to eat anything and talking made him cough. After dinner they were joined by Alice Keppel and her friend Venetia James, and they played bridge, which, as Bertie explained, meant that he didn't need to talk. He smoked a huge cigar, which seemed to soothe him.[54]

On Wednesday, 4 May, after a wretched night, Bertie struggled into his clothes and forced himself through his program of interviews, but he looked terrible, with large black blotches under his skin.[55] At eleven, he saw Newton Moore, the prime minister of Western Australia. His lord-in-waiting wrongly briefed him that Moore was the PM of New Zealand. Sir Francis Hopwood, the civil servant, corrected the error, and the King lost his temper, which set off a frightening fit of violent coughing. When Hopwood suggested that he should go to bed, the King replied, "No, I shall work to the end. Of what use is it to be alive if one cannot work?"[56] (Prince Albert would surely have approved.) At one thirty, he saw Georgie. The Prince of Wales was so alarmed that he wrote to warn "darling Motherdear," who, spurred by a "providential instinct," was hurrying back from Corfu.[57] "Thank God you are coming home to look after him," wrote Georgie.[58]

That evening, the King felt so unwell that he noted in his diary: "The King dines alone."[59] It was the last entry he ever wrote. It was also the saddest. The man who had spent his entire life trying to ensure that he did not dine alone was at last forced to confront himself.

Ponsonby had expected to play bridge with the King after dinner that evening. Bertie canceled the game. He looked "wretched."[60] For the first time, Ponsonby was seriously worried.

On Thursday, Reid found the King worse after another bad night. He was a bluish color in the face, and Reid told Ponsonby that he worried lest his heart fail.[61] Undaunted, the King refused to cancel his engagements. Lord Islington, newly ennobled governor of New Zealand, commented after his audience: "I think I have been with a dying man today!"[62]

Alice Keppel stayed with the King throughout the day. The nurse administered oxygen from a huge metal cylinder, but this only relieved his breathing for a short while. Reid gave an injection of strychnine to stimulate his heart. When he returned at noon, he found the King was worse, so he remained there with Laking.[63]

Alix had failed to grasp how ill Bertie was until she received George's letter at Calais. The first really ominous sign was that he was not present to meet her at Victoria station. When she and Princess Victoria reached Buckingham Palace at five p.m., they found Bertie gray and sunken and unable to sit upright in his chair. "It was a great shock to them," wrote the understated Prince of Wales, "to see Papa in this state."[64] Bertie insisted, nonetheless, on signing the documents that Ponsonby gave him from the red boxes.

At six p.m., an announcement was issued that the King was suffering from a severe bronchial attack. This was followed at eight p.m. by a bulletin posted on the palace railings and signed by the doctors that warned that "His Majesty's condition causes some anxiety."[65] The bulletin, which was approved by the King, effectively gave notice that he was on his deathbed.

Bertie met death with courage. At one moment he said, "I am feeling better and intend to fight this, and I shall be about again in a day."[66] He refused to go to bed that night, but sat up in a chair, fighting for breath and unable to speak.[67]

In the morning he was worse, but he insisted on dressing. He rejected the informal clothes laid out for him by his valet, and asked for gray trousers.[*] He was angry when the doctors forbade him from having a bath. He tried to do business with Davidson and Knollys but his voice was faint and indistinct. He smoked half a cigar and had a violent coughing fit.

Davidson telephoned Ernest Cassel to cancel his appointment. Half an hour later, Knollys rang summoning Cassel to come at once. He arrived at twelve. The King was standing up and looked "as if he had suffered great pain" but seemed in good spirits.[68] Cassel brought with him an envelope containing £10,000 in banknotes, which he left beside the King.[69]

Outside Buckingham Palace, a crowd gathered waiting for news. Margot Asquith was one of the first to go to the palace to sign her

---

[*] The Oxford gray suit and flannel shirt he wore that day was auctioned in New York in 1937, slit in the back where it was cut away from his body. It was sold for $20. (Catalog of Royal Robes and State Gowns, American-Art Anderson Galleries, 5 May 1937, http://www.victoriana.com/library/queen.html.)

name. Feeling tearful, she returned home to find Charles Hardinge "looking very sad, he had seen poor Knollys in tears." She ordered a black dress and wired Asquith to return immediately from his Mediterranean cruise. "It is like a dream and all London is standing still with anxiety," she wrote.[70]

At one p.m., Bertie walked to his bedroom window to play with his canaries, and fainted. Now the oxygen was given almost continuously and so were the strychnine injections, but to less and less effect; he gradually lost consciousness during the afternoon, slumping forward in his chair.

At Great Cumberland Street, Jennie Churchill and her sister Leonie Leslie sat waiting for news all afternoon, talking in whispers so the servants would not hear. The telephone rang and Leonie came back into the drawing room with tears in her eyes. "They can't get him out of his armchair. Alice has been sent for."[71]

Mrs. Keppel had been banished from the palace when Alix returned on Thursday, and she spent Friday morning in hysterics. Now, it seems, she presented the Queen with a letter that Bertie had written back in 1901. It read as follows:

My dear Mrs. George,

Should I be taken very seriously ill I hope you will come and cheer me up but should there be no chance of my recovery you will I hope still come and see me—so that I may say farewell and thank you for all your kindness and friendship since it has been my good fortune to know you. I feel convinced that all those who have any affection for me will carry out the wishes which I have expressed in these lines.[72]

To her great credit, Alix obeyed her husband's wishes, painful though the instruction was, and summoned the mistress to the palace.

When Mrs. Keppel arrived at five, Bertie was slipping out of consciousness and barely recognized her. The Queen and Princess Victoria were both in the room. According to the story Mrs. Keppel later related to her friends, the King told the Queen to kiss her. The Queen obeyed, and told Mrs. Keppel that the royal family would "look after her."[73]

Reconciliation with the Queen was the dream of every mistress, from Lillie Langtry to Daisy Warwick, but Mrs. Keppel's story is hard to credit. Not only was the King barely conscious, but Mrs. Keppel was in a highly emotional state. She was later to become notorious as a woman who "cannot resist lying and inventing and saying anything that comes into her Roman head."[74]

The official version, as recorded by Esher, goes like this. The Queen shook hands with Mrs. Keppel and said, "I am sure you always had a good influence over him," then walked away to the window. When the King fell forward in his chair, surrounded by nurses, Mrs. Keppel became hysterical once more. She was bundled out of the room, shrieking, and "before the Pages and the Footmen in the passage kept on repeating, 'I never did any harm, there was nothing wrong between us,' and then 'what is to become of me?' She fell into a wild fit of hysterics, and had to be carried into [Ponsonby's] room, where she remained for some hours." Mrs. Keppel's insistence that there was "nothing wrong between us" can perhaps be read as an admission that she had never slept with the King after all.[75] "Altogether it was a painful and rather theatrical exhibition, and ought never to have happened," wrote Esher.[76]

But Esher was an unreliable witness, too, and he was especially jealous of Alice Keppel.

That Mrs. Keppel was overcome by hysterics seems certain. Laking, who was in the room, recalled the Queen taking him aside and whispering, "Get this woman away."[77] The two versions of the story—Esher's and Mrs. Keppel's—clearly reveal the conflict between the mistress, emotionally distraught and desperate for closure and validation, and the members of the household, who closed ranks to exclude her as soon as the King lost consciousness.

The person who remained silent and gave no version of the story was the Queen.

The last authentically recorded words that Bertie spoke were "I am so glad," when Georgie told him that his horse Witch of the Air had won the four fifteen at Kempton Park.*[78]

He then suffered an alarming heart attack. Alix watched as her husband drifted into a coma. At eleven, they lifted him out of his chair into bed, quite unconscious.

Downstairs, people had come and gone throughout the day. Winston Churchill had bustled into the palace, anxious to assert his right as Home Secretary to witness the demise of the Crown. He was kept downstairs and not admitted even to the antechamber.[79]

The Archbishop of Canterbury had visited twice. He left at about seven without having seen the King. Esher registered concern. "I was so anxious that the Archbishop should be in the Palace, that I ventured to ring up his chaplain at Lambeth and suggest his return. Apart from all reasons, convention to a Monarchy has such powerful meanings."[80]

Esher's worry is understandable, but his words about convention having such powerful meanings are somewhat elliptical. He may have had another motive for recalling the archbishop. There are hints that a Roman Catholic priest was summoned to the palace in Bertie's last hours. The priest was Father Cyril Forster, chaplain to the Irish Guards, who had often been called to Marlborough House in the past when Catholic guests required his ministrations. Even if Father Forster saw the King, this is not to say that Bertie underwent a dramatic deathbed conversion. Nor is there any reason to believe that "he was given the sacraments or more than the blessing which any priest could give."[81] It is conceivable, however, that if Bertie had been formally received into the Catholic Church while he was abroad—as was, and still is, sometimes suggested in Catholic circles—Father Forster "could have given

---

* This seems more believable than the version give by one biographer, who recorded that the King's last words were: "I have done my duty." (Holmes, *Edward VII*, vol. 2, p. 598.) Laking told Skittles that as Bertie's mind began to wander, he cried out, "I want to p—." "What is it he said?" asked the Queen. "He is asking Ma'am for a pencil," said Laking. (Fitzwilliam, Wilfrid Blunt Papers, MS 11–1975, Diary, 14 December 1910.)

the absolution over a handshake."[82] If a Catholic priest was indeed prowling the corridors of the palace, this surely explains Esher's urgent summons to the archbishop. This was the only way to get rid of the priest.[83]

Archbishop Davidson returned at nine p.m., and waited with Esher and Knollys downstairs, in the secretaries' room. The Prince of Wales called the archbishop into the King's bedroom at eleven thirty. Fifteen minutes later, the King was dead. "I have seldom or never seen a quieter passing of the river," wrote the archbishop.[84]

At exactly seventeen minutes past midnight, Georgie and May drove out of the palace. The crowd could see that May was weeping uncontrollably. Two minutes later, a low-voiced household official brought the news to the people outside: "The King is dead!"[85] At Number 10 Downing Street, Margot Asquith had gone to bed and the messenger knocked on her door with the news: "So the King is dead!" she said out loud, and burst into tears.[86] The next morning, the crowd outside the palace had thickened to thousands, many wearing black. Ernest Cassel called on Margot, and the two of them sat crying on her sofa together. "He really loved the King," she wrote.[87]

Rumors spread that the King had died of cancer of the throat, a taboo kind of cancer especially because of its link with syphilis. *The Times* printed a denial, claiming that though the King was attended by leading laryngologists St. Clair Thomson and Felix Semon, he suffered from "smoker's throat."[88] Perhaps there was more to the rumor than this. Skittles was on friendly terms with Laking, who told her that for the past three or four years the King had had a swelling in his throat that was sprayed twice a day and that "might develop at any time into cancer."[89] Laking also told Skittles that the King really died of "blood poisoning caused by the injection of serum for his throat—it had relieved the throat but resulted in poisoning the blood."[90] "Vaccination treatment" to prevent catarrhal attacks was mentioned in the official doctors' report on the King's death.[91] It was an "experimental treatment" recommended by Laking; according to Skittles, it "may have done more harm than good." Reid treated him with these injections in Biarritz. Soveral, who was with the King during his illness in Biarritz, was convinced that he was killed by his doctors.[92]

Others blamed the politicians. "They have killed him, they have killed him," wailed the Queen to her friend the Duchess of Abercorn.[93] She accused Asquith and Churchill, who had publicly threatened to put pressure on the King in spite of warnings not to drag the Crown into party politics. It suited the Tories to take up the cry, which was "widely prevalent" in "lower middle class circles" in London.[94] The ministers' response was to point to the doctors' warnings that the King might die suddenly at any time.[95]

The truth was that Bertie died of emphysema and heart failure.[96] It was not the doctors or Asquith and Churchill that killed him, but his cigars. Three years earlier, Semon and Laking had handed Knollys a report on the King's health. The King had already suffered three attacks of bronchitis in three years, and they were concerned that his violent coughing might cause blood vessels to burst. Though his health appeared robust to the world at large, it was in reality precarious, and they warned that "an acute complication of any kind may bring about, apparently suddenly, very serious results."[97] For three years the King had lived on borrowed time. His survival depended on spending winters in the sun. The irony was that the political crisis had hastened his death. As Sir Felix Semon wrote: "How I wish the King instead of going home direct from Biarritz had, as usual during the last few years, made a Mediterranean trip and returned much later than he did."[98]

For eight days the King's body lay at Buckingham Palace in the bedroom where he died, on his simple mahogany bed, dressed in a pink silk nightdress. Alix invited a stream of visitors to say goodbye—fifty-eight were listed in *The Times,* and there were many more.[99] Bertie's face seemed peaceful, even happy, and there was no sign of pain. When Ponsonby visited, Alix told him that "she had been turned into stone, unable to cry, unable to grasp the meaning of it all, and incapable of doing anything." All she wanted was to hide in the country, but there was a terrible state funeral to be endured.[100] When Esher saw her, she moved about the King's room, speaking quietly but naturally, as if Bertie were a child asleep. At last "she had got him there all to herself," and in a way, thought Esher, she was happy. "It is the womanly happiness of complete possession of the man who was the love of her youth and—as I fervently believe—of all her life."[101]

Mrs. Keppel thought she knew otherwise. She told Rosebery that the King complained that Alix "never addressed a word of endearment to him"; though he was flagrantly unfaithful, he claimed "he had always put the Queen first."[102] On the day the King died, Alice did not return home to Portman Square, but stayed with her friend Venetia James on Grafton Street. People gossiped that she was avoiding her creditors and the press who clustered around her door waiting for news. But Alice Keppel was in a state of nervous collapse. When Venetia James took her frightened children to see her in bed, she looked at them "blankly and without recognition and rather resentfully."[103]

The mysterious packet of £10,000 in banknotes was returned to Ernest Cassel. Knollys wrote: "I presume they belong to you and are not the result of any speculation you went into for him." Cassel sent the money back, saying that "it represented interest I gave to the King in financial matters I am undertaking."[104] But there is no reason to suppose that the £10,000 found its way to Mrs. Keppel, as the King had presumably intended.

When Alice Keppel called at Marlborough House to sign her name after the King's death, orders had been given by Georgie and May that she should not be allowed to do so.[105] The kaiser, who had once sought out her company, refused to see her when she asked for an audience.[106] Little wonder that she thought that life had "come to a full stop, at least for me."[107] But Mrs. Keppel was well provided for. That summer she moved into her new house in Mayfair at 16 Grosvenor Street, a Georgian mansion of immense size, "gorgeously furnished" with gifts from the King. Esher spat blood. "It is almost indecent in its splendour," he wrote. Even more galling, she was rumored to have a fortune of £400,000 made for her by Cassel.[108] But she was living in the style that Bertie had intended, and she honored her side of the bargain.

In spite of being snubbed at court, she burned almost all of the King's letters, though she was careful to preserve the letter that Bertie had written in 1901 asking her to his deathbed.[109]

Behind drawn blinds at Buckingham Palace, Alix clung to her Bertie. "I always knew the Queen was in love with him," wrote Jackie Fisher after visiting the corpse.[110] Unlike the hysterical Alice Keppel, the Queen Mother, as Motherdear was now styled,* was calm and clear-headed. Esher and Knollys spent hours trying unsuccessfully to compose a message to the nation from the Queen. Then Alix sent down her own word-perfect draft, written on four sides of paper without a crossing-out. They published it unaltered: "From the bottom of my poor broken heart I wish to express to the whole nation and our kind People we love so well my deep-felt thanks for all their touching sympathy in my overwhelming sorrow and unspeakable anguish." Give me a thought in your prayers, implored the Queen, "which will comfort and sustain me in all I still have to go through."[111] Almost instinctively, she knew how to communicate her emotions to the people and, like a great actor, she readied herself for the last performance of her career.

Four days after the King's death, arrangements were made to place him in his coffin, but Alix refused to part with him, and the doctors and undertakers were sent away.[112] Bertie's body, declared Alix, was "so wonderfully preserved": "it must have been the oxygen they gave him before he died."[113] The Dowager Empress Minnie arrived on 11 May, attended by a giant Cossack, who had exchanged his Russian tunic for black mourning clothes. That evening, Archbishop Davidson read a service as the family knelt round Bertie's bed and (wrote George) "we kissed him for the last time."[114] The body was dressed in a military greatcoat and encased in a massive oak coffin, but the coffin was not

---

* The idea of styling Queen Alexandra "Queen Mother" rather than "Queen Dowager" originated with Archbishop Davidson. The only precedent for this was Henrietta Maria, who was known as Queen Mother after 1660. (Kuhn, *Democratic Royalism*, pp.101–2; Bell, *Davidson*, p. 609.)

sealed and it lay open on the King's bed. The plan was to remove it to
the throne room in the palace, but Alix could not bear to lose her Bertie. Each day the arrangements were made and announced in *The
Times,* and each day the Queen canceled them.[115] Her apartments ad-
joined the King's, and she spent her time beside his body, clinging to
the marriage that had ended so abruptly and unexpectedly. "They want
to take him away," the tearful Queen told Schomberg McDonnell, the
official who was responsible for the arrangements, "but I can't bear to
part with him. Once they hide his face from me, everything is gone for
ever."[116]

At last, on Saturday morning (14 May), she gave her consent, and
the coffin was sealed and removed to the throne room. Here the King
lay in state draped in a magnificent embroidered pall; the throne was
replaced by an altar, but the room was a blaze of crimson and gold and
(noted *The Times*) "absolutely devoid of funereal trappings."[117] This
was not the Victorian way of death. The only sign of mourning was
the four guardsmen who stood at each corner of the coffin, heads
bowed and hands folded over the butts of their rifles. Each night at ten
p.m., Alix asked for a special service in the throne room, inspired perhaps by the Russian masses that had been said for Minnie's husband,
Alexander III. One night the family were so overcome that they were
unable to sing the final hymn and left the room in tears.[118]

Tuesday, 17 May, was a dull, gray morning, and a black-garbed crowd
had been packing the Mall since seven a.m. At eleven o'clock precisely,
the funeral procession left the palace, preceded by rolling drums and
brass intoning Beethoven's Funeral March. The King's coffin, placed
on a gun carriage and draped in a cream silk pall on which lay the
crown, the scepter, and the orb, was drawn by black horses. The new
King George V walked behind, heading a procession of the household,
and behind them came nine carriages bearing the royal ladies. Alexandra traveled in the first coach with her sister Minnie and her daughters
Victoria and Louise. Critics carped that the widowed Queen took precedence over May (now newly Queen Mary), who traveled in the

coach behind; but the wonder was that Alexandra was there at all. Queen Victoria had hidden away at Osborne when Albert was buried at Windsor, and there was no script for a royal widow to follow. From the start, Alix made it plain that she would follow the procession.[119]

She riveted the crowd. Riding in the scarlet and gold of the state coach, she wore deepest black mourning with a long drooping veil, and as she passed the silent people, men doffed their hats and women curtseyed and bent their heads. From her coach, Alix raised her veil, leaned forward, and bowed her head in recognition. "God bless you!" cried the crowd, and the women sobbed. "Moved by that communion with the people" that one writer thought her rarest gift, Alix made the human connection the crowd longed for.[120] By the time the procession reached Westminster Hall, heralded by the wailing pipers of the Scots Guards, London was overcome by tears.

"Words fail me to give a description of the solemnity and dignity of the sight in that beautiful old hall," wrote Queen Mary, "with the coffin in the centre, the guards, all too upsetting."[121] St. Stephen's Hall was filled with members of the Lords and Commons when the royal procession entered. The King's coffin was followed by King George, walking with his mother and the Empress Minnie. Minnie wept and Princess Victoria looked "hopelessly miserable." Bertie's sisters Louise, Helena and Beatrice were there, "all old women now." Alexandra, by contrast, in simple black, "scarcely looked forty, so slim and upright and trim."[122] She was pale but composed. At the end of the short service, there was a strange silence. Alix rose from her chair and knelt beside Bertie's coffin and, with uplifted hands, prayed. All eyes turned to her. For a moment, it seemed she would be overcome. But she got to her feet, and "with queenly dignity signalled her son to escort her to the door."[123]

The last king to lie in state had been George III, whose body lay at Windsor for one day in 1820. No king had ever lain in St. Stephen's Hall. As Esher, who was opposed to the idea, pointed out, it was hardly appropriate given that it was the scene of the trial of Charles I.[124] Gladstone, who lay in state there in 1898, was honored as a great commoner. But Edward VII's lying in state achieved precisely what Archbishop Davidson intended: It brought the King's funeral to the people. The democratic character of the lying in state was assisted by Schomberg McDonnell, who ruled that the doors should open to the public at six a.m., and that press photography should be permitted.[125] Messenger boys were forbidden to hold places for others, and no tickets were sold, so the wealthy were obliged to wait in line with the poor, and the queue itself became a symbol of social equality.[126]

After the royal party left, Westminster Hall was opened to the public. By four o'clock, when the doors opened, a line of people one mile stood along the Embankment, headed by three seamstresses, "very poorly dressed but very reverent."[127] "They're givin' 'im to us now," cried a white-faced work girl as the doors opened. "They're givin' 'im to us now!"[128] As the queue of working people, many of them women, filed past the catafalque, it seemed that King Edward had at last become the people's king. Carpets had been laid to muffle the footsteps, and no one spoke. This "mute stream always always passing" were extraordinarily impressive in their silent loyalty.[129] Some waited all through the night in eight hours of torrential rain, a forest of black umbrellas, for the doors to open the next morning at six. On Wednesday, the queue was four miles long and six abreast—an orderly, respectful human procession, snaking around the streets of Westminster like the black ink that bordered the nation's mourning newspapers.

Soveral made a late-night visit on Wednesday with the King of Portugal. Carrington received them as Lord Great Chamberlain and wrote that Soveral was "terribly pale and upset. He held my hand for quite two minutes saying over and over again, 'This is too awful.' "[130]

On Thursday, the last day, the queues were longer than ever; in spite of deluging rain, a crowd twelve people deep and seven miles long waited patiently. That afternoon Carrington received a message that the hall was to be closed while the German emperor visited. The police were aghast and refused to deny entry to the crowd. The kaiser appeared soon after three p.m., entering the hall through the Star Chamber Court, led in by King George. He placed a great wreath of white and purple flowers upon the coffin and, after kneeling in prayer, rose and firmly clasped the new King's hand.*[131]

That evening, Asquith came and stood in Westminster Hall watching the people pass. Schomberg McDonnell thought his attitude offensive: "I fear he had dined well: and he seemed to regard the occasion as a mere show."[132] After the doors closed for the last time at ten p.m., Queen Alexandra paid a final visit. Just as she was expected to arrive, a party in evening dress swooped into the peers' enclosure. One of them was Alice Keppel. Loulou Harcourt, First Commissioner of Works, persuaded her to return to the Speaker's House, tactfully avoiding "a very great difficulty." Alix, noted Carrington, "had her veil up and seemed perfectly calm; she looked beautiful."[133]

It was a hot night, and Schomberg McDonnell opened the doors of the hall because he feared that the officers guarding the coffin might faint. To his horror, he saw Lady Desborough hovering at the entrance, with Maurice Baring and Evan Charteris in attendance. The Queen had long since left, the coffin was resting in dignified silence. The socialites nevertheless demanded admittance. Ettie Desborough fixed McDonnell with a grin that (he ungallantly wrote) "had doubtless been effective 20 years ago," but her "blandishments" were all in vain. Carrington angrily told her he was ashamed of her and begged her to go away, "for the Queen would be hurt and amazed if she heard of their behaviour."[134]

Nor was she the last. No sooner had Ettie reluctantly retired than a procession of four motor cars swept into Palace Yard. From these alighted the entire Churchill family, headed by Winston. His mother, Jennie Churchill, was there, and so was the Duke of Marlborough. Led by Winston, they advanced to the door, but McDonnell refused to allow them to enter. Winston blustered that if anyone had a right, he

---

* Even in death, however, his uncle haunted William. In 1941, an old man living in exile, William declared of Edward VII: "It is he who is the corpse and I who live on, but it is he who is the victor." (Lamar Cecil, "History as Family Chronicle," in Rohl and Sombart, *Wilhelm II,* p. 111.)

had, but McDonnell replied that as Keeper of Westminster Hall he declined to let him in. After a heated argument, they departed. It was, wrote McDonnell, "an amazing instance of vulgarity and indecency, of which I should not have thought that even Churchill was capable."[135] No one could have predicted that Churchill himself was to lie in state in the same hall; fifty-five years later, the most unpopular man in England had become the greatest Englishman of all.

The police at the door estimated that people filed through Westminster Hall at the rate of ten thousand per hour. The number who paid their respects to the King was estimated at four hundred thousand or more.[136] No one had predicted so many. No one could explain it, either. Observers noticed that people "really are profoundly stricken, do firmly feel a personal as well as a State loss, and look upon the late King as a friend and protector."[137] Never in recorded history, boomed *The Times,* had the death of a sovereign caused such wide and impressive manifestations of sorrow.[138] The crowds were bigger than at Queen Victoria's funeral, and the public sorrow deeper. Bertie, the dissipated, self-indulgent Prince of Wales, had somehow transformed himself into the father of the nation.

In spite of his passion for ceremonial and correctness, Bertie left no instructions for his funeral. The Archbishop of Canterbury suggested burial at Westminster Abbey, a radical proposal intended to commemorate the King's unique relationship with his people—the fact that he was "the most 'popular,' in the true sense, of all England's sovereigns."[139] George V insisted, however, that his father should be buried with his ancestors at Windsor, not beside his parents at Frogmore but in St. George's Chapel.

All through the night of Thursday, 19 May, people hurried into London. Crowds waited for twelve hours in torrential rain along the processional route of the King's cortège on Friday, from Westminster Hall to Paddington station. Soon after nine a.m., the funeral procession began to assemble in New Palace Yard. Margot Asquith watched as the gun carriage, the King's charger, with boots and stirrups reversed, and a kilted Highlander leading the wire-haired terrier Caesar waited in the grilling sun.[140] Eight kings came to Edward VII's funeral, and at ten o'clock the glittering procession clattered into the yard, led by George V with the kaiser on his right. As soon as Alix's carriage drew up, the kaiser leaped from his horse and rushed officiously to the door, opening it before the servants could reach it, and ostentatiously planted a smacking kiss on her cheek.[141] Alix stepped out, "a vision of beauty," dressed from head to foot in black crêpe; Margot and the politicians' wives curtseyed to the ground with bowed heads as she swished past them and into Westminster Hall in order to pay her final respects to the coffin. The kings* remained seated on their horses; it was rumored that their poor horsemanship might cause complications if they attempted to dismount.[142] Soon afterward, the coffin emerged and the procession formed up. Alix was seen to bend and pat Caesar, the King's dog.

Eight kings and one emperor rode behind the King's coffin. Theodore Roosevelt, former president of the United States, traveled in a carriage wearing plain evening dress. But the sight that made everyone choke was small white Caesar, who walked behind his master's coffin, on the instructions of the Queen Mother.†[143]

In Whitehall, the pavement was black with people wedged so tight they could not move. Between 200,000 and 300,000 people crammed into Hyde Park; the crowd was a hundred yards deep and men climbed the trees, shinning up the barbed wire that had been wound around

---

* As well as George V, there were present the kings of Norway, Greece, Spain, Bulgaria, Denmark, Portugal, and Belgium. Of these the worst horseman was King Ferdinand of Bulgaria, "who sat his horse like a sack, holding tight to the pommel." (PRO Northern Ireland, D/4091/A/6/1, Schomberg McDonnell's journal, "Edward VII," May 1910, pp. 42–43.)

† Not that Alix was especially fond of the dog. When Margot Asquith visited her afterward and remarked on its touching devotion, Alix replied: "Horrid little dog! He never went near my poor husband when he was ill!" On Margot remarking that Asquith had seen the dog lying at the dead King's feet, Alix responded, "For warmth, my dear." (St. Aubyn, *Edward VII*, p. 477.) However, the inscription she wrote on the dog's grave at Marlborough House suggests a change of heart: "Caesar. The King's Faithful and Constant Companion until Death and My Greatest Comforter in My Loneliness and Sorrow for Four Years after. Died April 18th 1914."

the trunks to stop them.[144] Many had neither eaten nor slept since the day before, and 1,600 received medical attention.[145] An iron wall of soldiers lined the processional route, many of them mounted, so the crowd could see very little of the procession, but there was no pushing or shoving. "The behaviour of the crowd was worthy of a democracy; it governed itself," wrote *The Times*.[146] As the funeral procession crawled past, the crowd fell eerily silent. No one smoked. Bare-headed, black-coated, hushed and awed, the people mourned their King.

Who were they, these poorly dressed people with pale, pinched faces, known only collectively as the crowd? Their lives had never touched Bertie's, but his death awoke powerful emotions of mute loyalty. What made the Tory diarist Lord Balcarres gulp was not the kings and the military bands, nor the death marches, but a wreath from "some embroideresses of Bethnal Green" or a handful of lilies of the valley in an old cardboard box.[147] Thousands of plain laurel wreaths had been brought to decorate the funeral route. Six thousand policemen patrolled the streets, but not a single incident occurred. The presence of so many kings was an invitation to any anarchist, and Scotland Yard posted plainclothes detectives every twenty-two yards (the length of a cricket pitch) along the route. The crowd on the streets was wedged too tight for any man to raise his arm to throw a bomb; the commissioner of police Sir Edward Henry worried that an explosive might be dropped from a window above, but his fears proved needless.[148]

All political lives, Enoch Powell once observed, end in failure, unless they are cut off in midstream. The life of Edward VII ended at the height of his political influence, but in death he achieved apotheosis.

Bertie's funeral procession reached Paddington station at eleven o'clock. At precisely the same time, a memorial service for the King was held in Paris in the English church on the rue d'Aguesseau. In the body of the church there assembled the politicians of the Republic, led by President Fallières, the first president to attend an English service in France, and including Georges Clemenceau and Théophile Delcassé, the architects of the Entente Cordiale. The galleries upstairs were reserved for members of society "personally known" to the late King, and the contrast in dress and manners between the republican bourgeoisie downstairs and the faded aristocratic beauties of Bertie's Proustian Paris seated above was "very striking," noted George Saunders of *The Times*. Among those in the gallery was Madame de Pourtalès, "once beautiful and still charming," with whom the prince had once spent long afternoons on the rue Tronchet.[149] "So ridiculous to think that everyone considered I had an affair with him," she wrote in her diary after the service. *"On ne prête qu'aux riches."*[*][150]

Meanwhile, at Windsor, the royal train bearing the King's coffin and the members of the funeral procession glided into the station at twelve thirty. For the previous two hours, St. George's Chapel had filled with politicians, ambassadors, and generals. Organization of the service was in the hands of the Duke of Norfolk, the Earl Marshal; charming, but hopelessly "fogged," he was expected by all to "make a hash of it," and he did not disappoint.[151] He had deliberately avoided making a seating plan in order to prevent difficulties over precedence. The result was that the pew openers changed people's places again and again, shoving them about when someone grander appeared, and the seating was a "mosaic of indecision and confusion."[152] When the procession appeared at the west door, the minor canons assembled to receive them craned their necks to see what was happening, the choir formed a huddled mob, and the Dean of Windsor, instead of keeping order, sat down among the spectators and became absorbed in conversation with a lady.[153]

Mrs. Keppel and Agnes Keyser both attended on the invitation of the new King. Alice, wearing full widow's mourning, was ushered in by Schomberg McDonnell, who met her at the cloister door.[154]

As the ragged procession of splendidly robed clergy and heralds moved up the aisle, followed by the coffin, a whisper of surprise rippled through the congregation. The Queen Mother was walking behind the King's body. Alix had been expected to watch the service unseen from the King's Closet high above the north end of the altar. Yet here she was, deeply veiled, the blue of her Garter ribbon shining

---

* "He had such a reputation!"

against her black dress, her right hand leaning on a stick, her left clasping the hand of her son George.[155] Pedants hissed that she claimed a precedence that was not hers by right; Queen Mary's sharp-tongued Aunt Augusta blamed the "pernicious influence" of the Empress Minnie, who had persuaded the widow Queen to push herself in front of her daughter-in-law, following Russian custom, which gave the widowed czarina precedence.[156]

But protocol was no match for human sympathy. A wave of compassion swept through the church, heads bowed, and knees bent. "She has the finest carriage and walks better than anyone of our time," wrote Margot, "and not only has she grace, charm and real beauty but all the atmosphere of a fascinating female queen for whom men and women die."[157] A prie-dieu was placed behind the coffin, and Alix took her place next to it. George fell back, and Alix was left standing, erect and alone. When the coffin was lowered into the vault, she knelt down and covered her face with both her hands, and everyone wept. Margot watched from her seat in the choir nearby: "That single mourning figure, kneeling under the faded banners and coloured light, will always remain among the most beautiful memories of my life."[158]

CONCLUSION

Biographical hindsight can be misleading. There was, in fact, nothing inevitable about Bertie's story, which can be constructed as a narrative that follows the trajectory of Shakespeare's Prince Hal, the dissolute prince who reformed after his accession to become the model king. It is easy to forget how different things might have been.

Bertie might have predeceased his long-lived mother, dying young like his own son Eddy. He nearly succumbed to typhoid when he was thirty. He almost died before his coronation and only survived thanks to the most recent medical advances. The doctors warned in 1907 that his health was being seriously undermined by his lifestyle of smoking, overeating, and overwork, and he was lucky to live as long as he did.

This book has revealed the angry feelings—at times murderous—of Victoria toward her eldest son. It sometimes seemed that she could never forgive Bertie for his "Fall," which, she believed, had caused Albert's illness and death. Even by the standards of the Hanoverians, who, "like ducks, produce bad parents. They trample on their young," Victoria was a brutal mother to Bertie.[1] Throughout the eighteenth century, Hanoverian Princes of Wales had quarreled with their fathers and formed a rallying point for political opposition. What if Bertie had rebelled openly against Victoria?

Max Beerbohm drew a cartoon of the middle-aged Prince of Wales standing in the corner like a naughty child cowering from the terrifying figure of Queen Victoria. Victoria used Bertie's scrapes and his reputation for indiscretion as an excuse to deny him access to government secrets. But it was he who enabled her to behave as she wished and to live in seclusion, hiding from her people for forty years. Bertie and Alix together performed the ornamental public role that Victoria declined. Had Bertie refused to do this—had the social functions of monarchy fallen into disuse—Queen Victoria's position would have been barely tenable.

What if twenty-one-year-old Bertie had not colluded and agreed to his arranged marriage with Alexandra of Denmark? The consequences of his alliance with the Schleswig-Holstein-Sonderburg-Glücksburg princess were surprisingly far-reaching, especially in foreign policy. Without Alix, Bertie would surely not have sided with Denmark against the rest of his family—his sister Vicky and Victoria herself—who supported Prussia over the Schleswig-Holstein war of 1864. What began as a family rift eventually triggered a realignment of dynastic diplomacy that was ultimately to see Britain entering the First World War on the side of Russia and France.

Bertie was not defined by his marriage, in the way that Victoria and Albert were. In spite of his genuine affection for Alix, he neglected her during her illness and pregnancies, and seemed incapable of being faithful to her. He was Edward the Caresser, notorious for his philandering. Margot Asquith wrote: "Women have been the excitement and the joy, the achievement of his life."[2] As a young man, however, he treated women with a thoughtlessness that bordered on cruelty. His flirtation with Harriett Mordaunt landed him in court, but he showed no remorse for her subsequent descent into insanity. When his pregnant mistress Susan Vane-Tempest—the only woman by whom he is known definitely to have fathered an illegitimate child—implored him to see her, he broke off contact.

In middle age, however, Bertie changed. He grew up. His life splits into two parts, divided by the tragedy of the death of Prince Eddy. Bertie fell in love with Daisy Warwick at the age of forty-eight, and the intensity of that affair is revealed in this book. He enjoyed an on-again, off-again (and most likely physical) relationship with Jennie Churchill over several decades. He rewarded Alice Keppel for her discretion, political advice, and skill at the bridge table with the things that mattered to her—money and acceptance at court. To these women—and many more—Bertie was loyal and generous long after the end of any physical relationship.

Bertie's survival as serial adulterer depended partly on the silence of the press in an era when, outside the divorce court, sexual gossip was considered off-limits. More important, however, was a compliant wife. What if Alix had refused to tolerate his unfaithfulness? Public confrontation in the style of Queen Caroline, the estranged wife of George IV, was not in her nature, but unofficial separation was certainly an option. The truth can be found in Alix's newly discovered letters to her sister Minnie. These private and revealing documents give a picture of Alix's deep affection for Bertie and her devotion to family life; leaving Bertie would have been unthinkable to her. Her loyalty was his most precious asset.

The climax of King Edward's reign, as Lytton Strachey wrote, was "the unresolved drama of its tragic close."[3] Bertie died suddenly and dramatically at the height of a constitutional crisis. At the time he seemed the only man capable of resolving the political conflict. King Edward was somehow above party, the nation's savior. No one could have foreseen that the spoiled young prince of fifty years before—the son whose accession Queen Victoria dreaded—would have been universally mourned.

Money and sexual scandal have been the twin demons of monarchy since the twentieth century. Neither troubled Bertie while he was King, and this was largely due to the lessons he had learned as Prince of Wales. Victoria and Albert had projected an image of the "royal family" as the embodiment of bourgeois domestic values. Bertie, by contrast, was King alone. In paintings and photographs he appears by himself, wearing military uniform, Highland dress, or a double-breasted suit—the public face of the sovereign. He made no attempt to "market" his family or lay claim to domestic virtue. How could he, when as Prince of Wales his gambling and adultery had made him notorious, and now as King he was openly accompanied by his acknowledged favorite, Mrs. Keppel? If anything, his outrageous flouting of middle-class morality endeared him to his people. As Logan Pearsall Smith quipped: "A virtuous king is a king who has shirked his proper function: to embody for his subjects an ideal of illustrious misbehaviour absolutely beyond their reach."[4] Refusing to parade the "royal family" was politically wise, however. As Bertie's successors were to discover, projecting monarchy as the "family firm" placed an unreasonable pressure on its members to lead exemplary lives.

Bertie the debt-ridden prince turned into an unexpectedly wealthy King. This was largely due to Ernest Cassel. By paying off Bertie's debts as Prince of Wales, Cassel ensured that he seemed solvent on his accession. Like the court Jews who had propelled the absolutism of small German states in the eighteenth century, Cassel made the King stronger in his relations with Parliament. Edward VII's finances were not an issue during his reign. He had no need to ask the government for extra funds, and this ensured that he avoided the humiliation and annoyance of parliamentary inquiry and debate. The sum of money that Bertie owed to Ernest Cassel has never been fully calibrated, but Cassel's role in underpinning the Edwardian monarchy was incalculable.

Bertie's travels as Prince of Wales—his familiarity with Paris courtesans and German spas—made him the most cosmopolitan of British monarchs; fluent in German and French, even speaking English with the hint of a German accent, he possessed the best address book in Europe and his own superior sources of intelligence. As King, he acted as his country's roving ambassador. An amazing number of Victoria's descendants held power in Europe, and Bertie was head of this immensely influential family. The fact that both Germany and Russia were ruled by his nephews gave a unique opportunity for dynastic diplomacy. The reconfiguration of British foreign policy after 1902 meant that the making of the ententes would have taken place in any event, but Bertie played a key part in enabling the Entente Cordiale through his visit to Paris in 1903. Historians have been slow to recognize his contribution, however, because—as the evidence clearly shows—after his death the politicians attempted to write him out of diplomatic history.

In his relations with the emperor of Germany, his nephew Kaiser William, Bertie's achievement is more ambiguous. His aim was to triangulate the ententes with Russia and France by maintaining friendly relations with Germany. He promoted the naval race with Germany, but he was dedicated to preventing war—which by the end of his life he considered inevitable. His dynastic diplomacy was compromised, however, by the baggage of family quarrels. He could never forget how the kaiser had snubbed him in Vienna, nor could he forgive William for his treatment of his mother, Bertie's sister Vicky. The kaiser, for his part, was paranoid about his uncle, whom he called "Satan." Negotiation with a character such as Kaiser William was doomed. In 1914, he blamed Bertie for the outbreak of war, declaring: "Edward VII is stronger after his death than I am who am still alive."[5]

No king since has played the part that Bertie did in foreign policy. George V, who rarely traveled and who spoke poor German and worse French, made no attempt to emulate his father in this respect. Instead, he sought to identify the monarchy with the British Empire—with India and the "British Dominions beyond the Seas," to which Bertie paid relatively little attention.

———

Debate still smolders over Bertie's legacy. On the one hand, his detractors allege that he was "indolent and overfed," a man whose lack of interest in domestic politics and aversion to paperwork led him to take the line of least resistance and do what his prime ministers wanted.[6] The result, it is suggested, was that he was the first truly constitutional monarch in the modern sense of the term—that is, a king who is not openly partisan and plays no part in politics. On the other hand, he has been hailed as the last king to wield the political power of the Crown, pursuing his own policies and fighting constant battles with his ministers.[7]

Both sides in this controversy assume that being a constitutional monarch is a sign of failure. Edward VII was indeed the first constitutional king. But rather than weakening the monarchy, he modernized it and made it stronger.

The decline in the power of the Crown—the consequence of the rise of democracy, the growth of a robust two-party system, and the triumph of liberal ideas—took place during the second half of Victoria's reign. Paradoxically, Victoria herself never accepted it, and she continued to behave as though her powers were undiminished. In the last decades of her reign she was virulently pro-Conservative, pursuing a vendetta against the Liberal party in general and Gladstone in particular. Though the Crown lost its power, however, its influence— private and nonpartisan—grew. As the Crown became distanced from politics, its authority increased. At the end of her reign, Queen Victoria was less powerful than she had been at the beginning, but her popularity was far greater and so was respect for the institution of monarchy.[8]

Edward VII was the first monarch to come to terms with this shift. He did not debate policy with his ministers; he showed no party preferences, nor did he veto ministerial appointments. But this did not mean he was a weak king. He relinquished the powers of the Crown, but he greatly expanded its influence. In foreign policy and defense, which were traditionally seen as the special preserve of the sovereign, he intervened behind the scenes.* Acting as an enabler, he facilitated his ministers' policies and promoted what he considered to be the national interest. When the Liberal government was formed in 1905, for example, he ensured continuity in foreign policy through his contacts at the Foreign Office and through engineering the appointment as foreign secretary of the pro-French Edward Grey. But he was careful to avoid any appearance of meddling in Sir Henry Campbell-Bannerman's Cabinet making.

Bertie understood the need to project the authority of the Crown through ceremonial and public display. Hence his impatience with Victoria's gloomy court, secluded at Windsor and Osborne. In contrast to his mother, he opened Parliament in state every year of his reign. Based in London, the monarchy became glamorous again. Buckingham Palace, which Queen Victoria had barely used after Albert's death, was restored to splendor. Showering decorations and medals like confetti, Bertie insisted on strict protocol. If sartorial correctness seemed to take the place of personal morality, this was because outward display was essential to the image of authority.

As the power of the Crown declined, the monarch acquired a new role: the head of state became the head of the nation. When Admiral Fisher asked why on earth the King was inquiring after the health of the republican Keir Hardie, Bertie went for him "like a mad bull." "You don't understand me!" he roared. "I am King of ALL the People!"†[9] How successful he was in gaining acceptance for that role was shown during the constitutional crisis of 1910, when both sides turned to him as mediator. He had become the nation's head. This was the greatest achievement of his reign.

Standing in front of a fire with a fat cigar between his teeth, King Edward seemed to Esher "wonderfully like King Henry VIII, only better tempered."[10] The fact was that Bertie adored being King. Confounding the naysayers, he was very good at it.

---

* The exception to this was the visit to Paris in 1903, which was a political intervention.
† This was what Daisy Warwick meant when she described Bertie as "the most democratic monarch who ever sat on the throne of England." (Warwick, *Life's Ebb and Flow*, p. 154.)

———

Alix never fully adjusted to widowhood. She made no attempt to create a new role for herself as Dowager, as did Queen Mary and Queen Elizabeth the Queen Mother. By now almost stone deaf, she found it hard to come to terms with change. Each year she joined Minnie in Denmark on their yachts for "the same old life": sixteen or eighteen people for every meal, but the regal sisters would never decide until half an hour before where they wanted to eat. So the cook prepared vast quantities of food regardless, and the result was a massive bill and a very disgruntled cook, who complained at the Queen's thoughtlessness, "never receiving any praise at all or being told what the Queen likes, but every dislike is made known to him."[11] Superbly coiffed, straight-backed, and radiantly smiling, the two old queens sat at either end of a long table. Everything was always "fine" or "splendid"—the pain of Bertie's death was never mentioned.[12]

Alix stayed on at Sandringham in the big house, while George V and Queen Mary squashed into York Cottage. Some have blamed Alix for refusing to move, but this is unfair—Bertie had left the house to her for her lifetime, and the King and Queen could have found another place to live.[13] Alix's household remained unchanged. Charlotte Knollys, seventy-five in 1910, continued as her companion and private secretary, and the seventy-seven-year-old Dighton Probyn stuck to his post as her comptroller. With his neck bent double, his chin and long white beard nodding on his chest, he fought a losing battle against the compulsive extravagance of the "blessed Lady," as he called her.

In old age, Alix the ever-youthful high-spirited princess metamorphosed into a monster. The princess who perhaps had never fully grown up reverted to a spoiled and willful child. Lacking inner resources, Motherdear clung unreasonably to her family. "Mama, as I have always said, is one of the most selfish people I know," wrote George.[14] Victoria, her unmarried daughter, suffered the most. She was forced to live with her mother, who treated her like a glorified maid. When Alix rang her bell, Toria was obliged to run, often to discover that her mother had quite forgotten why she wanted her.

The 1914–18 war shattered Alix's world. She became a frail old woman, incoherent and confused. George, whom, in deference to Bertie, Alix insisted on calling "King George" rather than "the King," was very good to her.[15] He wrote often, and in church he would sit beside her, finding her place in the prayer book. She found comfort in the company of children, and toddlers would be selected to entertain her.[16] T. E. Lawrence, who met her in 1920, saw beneath the black net veil and wrote cruelly of a "mummified thing": "the red-rimmed eyes, the enamelled face, which the famous smile scissored across all angular and heart-rending."[17] But her mind still went back to Bertie, and how, sixty years before, walking in the gardens at Laeken, "he suddenly proposed to me! My surprise was great & I accepted him with greatest delight!"[18]

AFTERWORD

Bertie and the Biographers

Bertie was extraordinarily secretive about archives and resistant to any sort of biography. In this he differed sharply from Queen Victoria. He lived a far more public life than his reclusive mother, but he disliked intensely her habit of releasing publications about her private life such as *Leaves from Our Life in the Highlands*.

For Victoria, biography was a way of putting the record straight and connecting with her people. When her children complained that Theodore Martin's biography of Albert revealed too much about their family life, Victoria replied: "<u>endless false</u> and <u>untrue</u> things have been written and said about us, public and private, and . . . in these days people <u>will write</u> and <u>will</u> know, therefore the only way to counteract this, is to let the <u>real full</u> truth be <u>known</u>, and as much as <u>can be</u> with prudence and discretion, and then <u>no harm</u> but <u>good</u> will be done."[1] Modern biographers could hardly put the case better.

The tidy-minded Albert had used a cross-referenced filing system. This had been continued after his death, but documents were not sorted and filed as assiduously as before. Indeed, by the time Queen Victoria died, her papers were in chaos. Fritz Ponsonby was appalled to discover that forty years of political correspondence had been stuffed into cupboards, filling several rooms at Windsor.[2]

Victoria left all her private and family papers under the control of Princess Beatrice. These were in a strong room to which Beatrice had the key, "until such time as she is able to go through them in accordance with the Queen's directions."[3]

Beatrice spent thirty years transcribing a bowdlerized version of her mother's journal into hardcover lined notebooks in her legible blue-black ink, rewriting and destroying the originals as she went.* Her labors filled 111 books and earned her no thanks from posterity. She is routinely berated for mutilating the text of Victoria's journals and destroying the originals. This is understandable but not entirely fair. Beatrice was a dutiful daughter obeying her mother's instructions. If the Queen's journals had been bequeathed to Bertie, the likelihood is that he would have burned the lot.

Beatrice herself burned thirty volumes of letters from Prince Alfred and all of Princess Alice's letters. As royal archivist Robin Mackworth-Young wrote: "Queen Victoria was perfectly entitled to do what she chose with her most private and intimate writings, and we can count ourselves lucky that they have been left to posterity in any form at all."[4]

Victoria bequeathed her political papers to her successors, and Bertie appointed Esher, then Secretary of the Office of Works, to take

---

* A transcript of the original of the journal, covering the years between Victoria's accession and her marriage, has survived, and from this it can be seen that Beatrice discarded about two-thirds of the text, including material that "could cause nothing but interest and delight." (Robin Mackworth-Young, "The Royal Archives, Windsor Castle," Archives, vol. 13 (1978), p. 123.)

charge. Victoria had talked about a biography toward the end of her life, but this idea was quickly dropped.[5] Instead Esher decided to publish a selection of letters from the early part of her reign. The aim, as he explained, was to let the letters speak for themselves without comment, "thus avoiding the trap into which most biographers notably fall," while cutting anything which "could give offence or pain."[6] Esher had no experience as archivist or editor, and he appointed a collaborator, Arthur Benson, son of the archbishop and ex-Eton housemaster. The real work of selecting and editing Victoria's letters was done by Benson. He was installed in the Round Tower and received strict instructions from the King that "not a single paper must on any pretence whatever be taken from the Castle, even for half an hour."[7] He had scant respect for Bertie, whom he described in his diary as looking like a "little dwarf . . . (What a figure!)"[8]

Esher's proposal for a book of Queen Victoria's letters made Bertie uneasy. "Should it be published?" he asked in 1904. "Anyhow not without my sanction and having looked over it."[9] He was "nervous" and "fussy," telling Esher there must be "nothing private, nothing scandalous, nothing *intime,* nothing malicious."[10]

All personal matters and references to the Queen's children were omitted; the letters contain nothing relating to Bertie's agonizing education, even though Esher knew this material and had discussed it with him.[11] Esher forced Benson to shorten the book and cut anything that might annoy Bertie. The success of the enterprise depended, in Esher's view, on obeying the King's wishes. "I am all for the King having his way," he told Knollys. "If he does not, I am sure that there will be trouble hereafter, as all sorts of people will gossip to him and write to him about the deficiencies of the book. If he starts in an attitude of 'bien veilleur' all will be well."[12]

The King had insisted on reading everything himself. Or at least that was what Benson and the publisher, John Murray, believed.[13] In fact, Bertie probably did not see the first draft. The manuscript was read and censored on his behalf by Esher and Knollys, both of whom were driven by overpowering anxiety about the risk of incurring the King's displeasure. As Knollys warned Esher: "If when the work appears anything in it strikes the King as inappropriate or in bad taste . . . the first person he will blame and fall foul of will be you, then Benson while I shall probably make a poor third."[14] Invoking the name of the King (who was actually safely out of reach in Marienbad at the time), Knollys and Esher compiled a list of excisions that ran to nine foolscap pages, cutting every "objectionable and doubtful" passage. By striking out strong language, political bias, and references to living persons, they made the published letters as mild and bland as possible.[15] Only after this was the King shown the final proofs; and there is no evidence that he actually read them.[16]

Arthur Bigge, who also read the proofs, urged caution, not just to protect Queen Victoria's reputation but also to safeguard the monarchy. "If I were the King," he wrote, "both from the point of view of son to mother and also for the sake of the monarchical idea and 'culte' I would publish nothing which would shake the position of Queen Victoria in the minds of his subjects."[17]

The *Letters of Queen Victoria* were published in three volumes in 1907. So successful were they that Esher considered publishing a further two volumes, covering the twenty years after Albert's death. He eventually decided that the material was too controversial, especially the letters dealing with German unification. Bertie's sigh of relief is almost audible. "I entirely agree," he minuted. "A considerable time <u>must</u> elapse before it would be prudent to publish more of Queen Victoria's letters."[18]

Esher's work on the Queen's papers allowed him to carve out a new position for himself as Keeper of the King's Archives. He posed as a constitutional expert, producing plums from the papers on demand. As an archivist, he inclined toward a policy of burning. In making an "excellent" rearrangement, Ponsonby and Esher between them managed to destroy an estimated 50 percent of Queen Victoria's political papers.[19] In this Bertie was a willing accomplice; in fact, Esher seems to have seen burning as a way of pleasing the King, offering up ritual sacrifices of letters for incineration.* Bertie was especially concerned by the papers relating to his childhood and education, some of which (said Esher) "the King made me burn."[20]

Queen Victoria had written numerous frank letters to Disraeli. The copyright in these was, of course, the sovereign's, but the physical letters—the originals—were in the possession of Disraeli. This worried Bertie dreadfully. When Monty Corry, Disraeli's executor, died in 1903, Disraeli's papers passed to Lord Rothschild, but Queen Victoria's letters were referred to the King to vet.

Victoria had written to Disraeli at length and "on every conceivable subject," both personal and political; her correspondence revealed Prince Leopold as persistently interfering in politics, often causing trouble.[21] When the journalist William Monypenny was appointed as Disraeli's biographer in 1904, Bertie asked Rothschild to allow Esher and Knollys free access to Victoria's letters at Rothschild's bank, where they were held, "and they could then tell me if they consider there are any I should object to being published."[22] Three years later (these matters move slowly) Knollys formally requested Rothschild to send all of Queen Victoria's letters to Windsor for the King to "look over."[23] Rothschild explained that the archive was in a horrible state of confusion, but Victoria's letters had been arranged by a certain Mr. Scones, who was the head clerk of Disraeli's solicitor, Sir Philip Rose. Mr. Scones's brother had been "frequently employed at Windsor by Her Majesty's permission making copies of letters."[24] When Esher heard this story, he could scarcely contain himself. That the "most confidential documents which can be imagined" should have been read by a lawyer's clerk was an outrage. "I don't think any right or reasonable claim can be put forward by the [Beaconsfield] trustees to retain the Sovereign's

---

* Esher destroyed documents relating to the Lady Flora Hastings scandal of 1839, Victoria's letters to Lord Granville, and letters to George IV from Georgiana, Duchess of Devonshire and Mrs. Fitzherbert.

letters." The affair seemed to him to show the necessity for an Act of Parliament giving the Crown power to recall documents. "I am having a short bill drafted," he told Knollys.[25] Esher's bill was stillborn, but he had convention on his side. Queen Victoria had laid it down that letters written by the sovereign should be returned to the sovereign after the recipient's death. This was often done during her reign.[26]

Esher felt justified in extracting from the Rothschild archive four packets of confidential Disraeli letters, including one packet that contained almost all of Bertie's letters to Disraeli. He showed them to Bertie, who ordered them to be destroyed.[27]

The same happened when George Profeit, the son of Queen Victoria's agent at Balmoral, Dr. Profeit, attempted to blackmail Bertie over letters about John Brown. Bertie entrusted Sir James Reid with the job of retrieving the letters. Reid eventually succeeded in persuading Profeit to surrender a tin box containing more than three hundred letters from Queen Victoria concerning Brown, many of which were "most compromising," which he handed in person to the King.[28] These were presumably destroyed.

When the Munshi died in India in 1909, Bertie worried about Victoria's letters. He wrote to the viceroy: "I am not satisfied in my mind that there may not be still letters in Queen Victoria's handwriting in their possession—and I should be glad if further discreet investigations could be made, informing the Munshi's family that . . . they must at once return them or they will be the sufferers thereby!"[29]

Bertie had successfully destroyed many of Queen Victoria's papers, and he made certain that his own documents were similarly censored. In his will, he directed that all letters to him from his mother and from his wife, and all private letters and papers, should be destroyed by his private secretary immediately after his death.[30]

Knollys was seventy-four in 1910. He had served Bertie as private secretary for forty years. He was eventually asked by George V to retire in 1913, for political reasons—his strong Liberal sympathies clashed with the politics of the King and his advisers.[31] Knollys wrote that he had one task yet to complete: "It is necessary that I should first look over, sort and when advisable, destroy the great mass of letters and papers of all descriptions which accumulated at Marlborough House and which have since accumulated at Buckingham Palace—in fact from the year 1863 to the present day."[32]

Not only were the letters in what Esher described as a state of "dire confusion,"[33] but Knollys himself was becoming confused. Since King Edward's death his colleagues had complained about his "mental apathy."[34] Ponsonby observed that "his memory has completely gone," and by 1914 he was referring to him as "gaga."[35] Senile or not, Lord Knollys was undoubtedly disaffected as he set about obeying his dead master's last orders. Baron Hermann von Eckardstein, the German diplomat, found him "greatly aged" and "almost tired of life," sifting through the King's papers, deciding which to keep and which to burn. The papers contained much both of a political and a personal nature: "Owing to their political content they should be handed down to posterity," but "due to their very delicate private character they should be withheld from future generations and should be burned." Knollys erred on the side of caution and inclined to "destroy too many rather than too few of such papers."[36] It took him only one month to complete this work. He wrote to George V on 17 March 1913: "Sir I have finished the papers and am vacating my room here today."[37] How much he destroyed can never be known, but posterity has accused him of a bonfire.

Meanwhile, a fuse was lit in the unlikely form of the *Dictionary of National Biography*. The 1912 supplement carried an extended article on King Edward by the editor, Sidney Lee. Lee was a hollow-eyed Shakespeare scholar who had contributed 820 articles to the *DNB* by dint of working seven days a week and living as a recluse. His *DNB* article on Queen Victoria, which he expanded and published as a book, had pleased the royal family, so his article on King Edward came as a thunderbolt.[38]

Lee claimed that the King possessed neither statesmanship nor "originating political faculty" (in my view, untrue), that he read no books (true), "lacked the intellectual equipment of a thinker and showed unwillingness to exert his mental powers" (untrue), was a poor conversationalist (true), and had no responsibility for the Entente Cordiale (untrue).[39]

From Marlborough House, where he now worked for Queen Alexandra, Sir Arthur Davidson, Bertie's former assistant private secretary, began a campaign to clear his master's reputation. He consulted Knollys and Esher, but both were oddly opposed to taking action. Esher reluctantly agreed to write an article, but he claimed that it would be said that he was "a sycophant and a courtier" and his views would carry little weight. He did all he could to "wriggle out" of it.[40] Loftily declining to descend into the gutter of literary quarrels, he suggested that instead he should write an article on some grand theme such as the philosophy of kingship.[41]

The real reason for Esher's prevarication soon became apparent: He himself had supplied Lee with material for the *DNB* piece.[42] He was up to his usual tricks, hunting with both the hare and the hounds. "Oh! Esher! Esher!" wailed Davidson. "I am sick of Esher and the way he has behaved over this."[43] "Manly men," as the royal archivist Owen Morshead recalled, "did not like Lord Esher." He was like a "medicated tom cat," and honest men such as George V and Lord Stamfordham "felt their skin prickle when he entered the palace, as some people react to the unseen presence of a cat in the room."[44]

Esher's treachery seemed the more dishonorable because he owed a debt of gratitude to Bertie.[45] Meanwhile, Sidney Lee agreed to write a letter of apology to Queen Alexandra. Alix replied (via Esher himself) regretting the damage that Lee had done to her husband's reputation, but it was never clear how much she understood or how much she wanted to know.[46] She read the *DNB* article and it upset her, but she was oddly disengaged, and so dilatory that Davidson despaired of ever being able to persuade her to give her attention to the matter of Bertie's biography.[47]

When Davidson and Probyn, Alix's comptroller, cabled to warn her that Lee's *DNB* article was being published as a stand-alone book, she wired: "I regret extremely that the same wretched and untruthful author should be allowed to repeat himself on that to me sacred subject."[48] The courtiers, thinking she had misunderstood, wrote explaining at length that Lee was not composing a new work, merely issuing a cheap edition. The Queen Mother snapped back: "Very many thanks long letter understand everything perfectly have done so all the time—don't tire yourself writing so much . . . your Blessed Lady."[49]

Henceforth, it was Davidson, not Alix, who played the part of the wronged widow, while Alix was kept in the dark. As Davidson explained to Probyn, the Queen "would not take it in and would not appreciate it. . . . The Queen has absolutely no idea of logic, that if you say a thing is wrong, you must prove it so, and also the Queen has no sense of appreciation. I mean it's a constitutional deficiency, and she will only think—whatever she may say—a great deal of unnecessary fuss—'much better have told Lee he was mistaken and get him to alter his article.' All the paraphernalia of the means of getting him to do so will be so much Sanskrit to her."[50]

Davidson's next move was to interview some politicians and ask them to write contradictions of Lee's article. Most were helpful in conversation, but they all seemed "to get very cautious and disappointing on paper."[51] Asquith wrote a one-page letter which Davidson thought "rather in the style of a master's character to a servant than that of the Prime Minister to his late Sovereign."[52] As for Balfour, "nothing could be more sympathetic" than his manner, but he declared that he had not read the article.[53] His dictated letter was typically evasive, avoiding detail but criticizing the article for its failure to convey the King's personality.[54]

Armed with these letters from Balfour and Asquith, Davidson confronted Sidney Lee, who explained that he had interviewed fifty people for his article. He was "amazed" at the letters Davidson showed him. He "could not understand" Balfour's letter, as Balfour had clearly told him that "the King's influence was absurdly overrated."[55] He had notes to prove it. Lee's typed notes of his interview with Balfour still survive in his papers today. Entente Cordiale: "King had nothing to do with it . . . qualities not great."[56] Balfour's remarks went straight into the *DNB* article.

The duplicity of Balfour and Asquith made Davidson "feel rather sick."[57] Ponsonby agreed. "What [Lee] said about Asquith does not surprise me but Balfour beats me. I now see his reluctance to read the article or commit himself in any way."[58] Balfour protested that he had been "ill-used": He had given Lee an off-the-record interview and kept no notes, and now his remarks were quoted against him.[59]

Davidson's files give a fascinating glimpse of the way history is composed. Balfour, who had never got on with Bertie, had written him out of the historical narrative. Asquith had done the same. Lee revealed that it was Asquith who had "supplied all the material" for the section of the *DNB* article on the Parliament Bill crisis.[60] Asquith alleged that King Edward had played a passive part in the crisis, being "content to watch the passage of events without looking beyond the need of the moment."[61] No one reading the article would have realized how important the King's role had been during the crisis, nor how badly Asquith had needed his support.

History, once written, proved unexpectedly difficult to unpick. Lee refused point blank to revise his article. To do so, he claimed, would "discredit the Dictionary, and would ruin its publication and myself."[62] The reality, as Lee knew very well, was that a revision of a single article in a volume of more than seven hundred pages would be ruinously uneconomic.

After consulting King George V, Davidson enlisted the support of Lord Morley, Gladstone's biographer, a minister and Grand Old Man of Letters. Lee was summoned to a meeting in Morley's office. Davidson listed the passages the King wanted expunged from the article. Morley asked: "You mean to say that if these were left out, it would satisfy you." Davidson replied: "Certainly not. We want a new work." Lee was appalled. The last thing he wanted was to write an official life of Edward VII. He became "very sulky" and tried to back out, protesting that he had just been appointed professor of English literature at the East End College of London University—"very hard work." Morley was relentless; according to Davidson, he "behaved like a <u>trump,</u> too <u>beautifully.</u>" He told Lee "it was no good him saying that he had not written depreciatory things, because he had."[63] Lee was too frightened of Morley to say no. "His <u>only</u> fear is that if he ignores Lord Morley's advice (which was the strongest I ever heard given on any subject from a man in his position) that Lord Morley will have done with him for ever."[64]

Lee was cornered. He agreed to write the biography, and arranged an advance of £300 from Smith, Elder, the publishers of the *DNB*.[65] It soon became apparent that his ideas about biography were very different from the courtiers'. Brandishing a copy of his 1911 lecture *The Principles of Biography*, he demanded access to all the available letters and papers.[66] King Edward's papers were in the hands of Esher and Knollys, and they had both initially refused to have anything to do with Lee and his book. Once the biography was agreed to, however, Esher was all smiles. Collared by the King, he agreed to supply Lee with the papers at Windsor.[67]

Lee spent a day reading documents at Windsor in June 1914. He arrived with a swollen face from toothache and kept looking at himself in the mirror. At teatime, Esher appeared. "He talked vaguely about the difficulties of Biography and then gave Lee a rough account of the part he had played in Army Reform. It was very good. He praised King Edward and made out he was the *fons et origo* [source and origin] of all army reform. Brodrick, Arnold-Forster, and Haldane were puppets but the person who pulled the strings was himself!" Ponsonby could see that Esher was playing a part, but he had no objection so long as King Edward "got his full share of credit."[68] Once again, history was being written.

Lee was only given access to carefully selected documents. He was allowed to see papers relating to Bertie's early life, but little thereafter. This was partly because the archive was still in a state of confusion. Ponsonby claimed that "With regard to 1875 to 1900 no papers appear to exist. Knollys burned everything."[69] This was not, in fact, the case, but the story of Knollys's holocaust proved very useful as a way of fobbing off the biographer. Lee was sent on wild goose chases, to work through the Granville papers, for instance, or the Foreign Office dispatches (uninformative and "deadly dull").[70] Ponsonby allowed Lee to work only once at Windsor. He worried that Lee would "be tempted to write up early incidents in too full detail." Worse, if Lee got into Esher's clutches, "there would be no saying what might happen." Esher selected papers from the archive at Windsor that Ponsonby vetted before giving them to Lee to work on at Buckingham Palace.[71]

Little wonder that Lee became discouraged and threatened to abandon the project. He was dismayed when Rosebery mischievously told him that he must bring Bertie's women into the book. A "threatening letter" that he received from Lady Warwick "greatly disturbed him."[72] For a confirmed bachelor such as Lee, sexual scandal was toxic, and gossip was a biographical sin. The outbreak of war in August 1914 came as a relief to all concerned. Lee opined that the publication of the biography was not advisable, as the King's anti-German feeling would doubtless be twisted into showing that he had always intended to go to war against Germany. As for Davidson, he was more than willing to agree to Lee's request to suspend work on the book until the war was over.[73]

Meanwhile, a furious tornado burst upon the royal advisers in the shape of Daisy Warwick, whose finances were once again in crisis, ruined by a company promoter who had swindled her out of £50,000. Her last remaining asset was her affair with the Prince of Wales. In the time-honored fashion of the courtesan, she proposed to cash in and reveal all in her memoirs.

In March 1914, she met the unsavory charlatan Frank Harris in France, and together they concocted a plot. Harris would help Daisy write her kiss-and-tell autobiography and publish it in the United States, where he assured her she stood to make the £100,000 she needed to pay off her debts.* But Daisy was playing a double game.

---

* One hundred thousand pounds was a wildly inflated sum to ask for Daisy's memoirs. Prime Minister Lloyd George received an offer of £90,000 for his war memoirs in 1922, which was dubbed "the biggest deal in the history of publishing." (David Reynolds, *In Command of History* [Penguin, 2005], p. 24.)

Her plan was to use the threat of publishing her memoirs to blackmail King George V. Back in 1908, she had promised Bertie that she had destroyed all his letters. Now it turned out that she still possessed a bundle of thirty, which she claimed had turned up when the bailiffs were ransacking her possessions. This was probably fiction; but by now the distinction between true and false was blurred. Daisy planned to offer the letters to George V for a price of £80,000; in return she would call off publication of her memoirs.[74]

Daisy's sister Blanche Gordon-Lennox considered that Daisy's mind was deranged; there could be no other explanation for her wicked behavior.[75] But Daisy did have some justification. She claimed that she had exhausted her inheritance in entertaining the Prince of Wales, and that she had received no reward for her nine years as royal mistress—unlike Alice Keppel, who was known to have made a fortune, largely thanks to Ernest Cassel's dealings on her behalf. Daisy's mistake was to imagine that George V could be blackmailed.

As her intermediary, Daisy chose Arthur du Cros, millionaire founder of the Dunlop Rubber company and one of her creditors. Calculating that du Cros was ambitious for recognition at court and a title, she confided her plan to him at a meeting in June 1914. Genuinely shocked, du Cros reported back to the palace. The courtiers were aghast. Ponsonby considered that publication of the letters would not only "blast" King Edward's reputation, but have a "far graver effect on the monarchy."[76] He urged paying her off, but George V was determined not to give in to blackmail, nor to allow Lady Warwick to humiliate his mother. Sir Charles Russell, the King's solicitor, was appointed, and he laid an elaborate trap.

On Russell's request, du Cros agreed to join Daisy on a trip to Paris (13 July 1914), where she met with Frank Harris to discuss the sale of the letters. Russell sent a detective, Mr. Littlechild, to follow Daisy to Paris and shadow her movements. Peeping through the window of her hotel, Littlechild saw Daisy produce several documents, like letters, one of which she gave to Frank Harris. "The lady did most of the talking, and appeared, by her gestures, to be very much in earnest."[77]

Instead of the six-figure check from the King that she was expecting, Daisy returned to London to find an injunction served upon her, forbidding her from publishing, circulating, or divulging letters received from Edward VII. "She was all smiles and politeness," wrote Russell, "but of rather an artificial kind." She declared that she would tell her story in court.[78]

Daisy was not silenced by the injunction. Quite the contrary. In the autumn of 1914, Frank Harris fled wartime France and sought refuge with her at Easton Lodge. Here he dabbled with her memoirs, composing a chapter or two, and she allowed him to rummage among the letters she kept in her room. In the winter, Harris sailed to America, taking with him some of Bertie's letters. Daisy claimed that he had stolen them, which may or may not have been true. Daisy was watched by spies and visited by Russell. Sir John Simon, the Attorney General, saw three of the letters and pronounced them to be "very bad," particularly the references to Queen Alexandra. In February 1915, Prime Minister Asquith wrote, "there is now proof that she has been disobeying the injunction and is again hawking some of [the letters]. So the Impeccable"—Asquith's name for Simon—"proposes to go to a Judge and ask him to 'commit' her—in vulgar language to send her to prison till she amends her ways."[79]

This was a serious threat. "You will remember," Russell wrote, "I was going to apply to commit Lady Warwick to Holloway."[80] The specter of prison was enough. Daisy promised to surrender all the letters she possessed and appealed for time to recover the letters from America as well as the manuscript of her memoirs. At length in June, and after renewed threats of committal, Daisy secured the material. She demanded to hand it over in person to George V, but the King declined to meet her, so her brother-in-law, the courtier Sidney Greville, delivered a packet of letters to Lord Stamfordham.[81]

Daisy salvaged as much credit from her humiliation as she could. Glossing over her attempt to blackmail George V, she wrote in a fury of indignation at the way she had been treated: "I am handing back with splendid generosity the letters King Edward wrote me of his great love, and which belong to me absolutely. I . . . have never dreamed of publishing . . . such things." But (and here was the sting), "My memoirs are my own affair, and every incident of those ten years of close friendship with King Edward are in my own brain and memory."[82]

Nightmares about Daisy's memoirs continued to haunt the royal advisers. Mrs. Keppel heard a rumor in 1921 that "a certain lady" planned to publish an autobiography based on her own diary, "where I believe, she put in <u>everything</u>, however sacred, this may mean that she can get out of actually using <u>letters</u>, by saying, in this beastly diary, what was in them."[83] "Sacred" is an odd word to use for adultery with a prince. The rumors about Daisy's diary turned out (unfortunately for historians) to be unfounded.

Daisy received no money from George V, but du Cros agreed to pay £64,000 toward her debts. This was what she had wanted all along. For his generosity and public service in paying off Lady Warwick, du Cros received a baronetcy in 1916.[84] Daisy made copies of Bertie's letters, and these have recently resurfaced in a private collection; they hardly seem "very bad," as Sir John Simon considered. Dating from the end of her affair with Bertie in 1898, they are not passionate love letters but the usual mixture of gossip and affectionate banter.

The royal advisers panicked again in 1928. The conditions by which Daisy had been saved from imprisonment in Holloway stipulated that if and when she published her memoir, "she undertook to submit it to a literary man."[85] She now sent an autobiographical manuscript to Esher, who insisted on cuts.[86] Daisy's daughter Lady Marjorie Beckett thought the book so vulgar that she could only describe it as "muck," which was a somewhat harsh judgment on one of the best-written Edwardian society memoirs, still often cited today.[87] Harmless extracts from Bertie's letters were quoted in her book, *Life's Ebb and Flow*, in which the narrative of Daisy's relationship with Bertie is related in a code that only insiders could see through.

"Don't you think that the time has now come when we might once more consider the question of Sidney Lee and King Edward's Life," wrote Davidson to Ponsonby in 1920. To contradict the view that King Edward was responsible for causing the war and to vindicate him in the war-origins controversy, Davidson wanted the book to show that he had foreseen the conflict and done what he could to prevent it—"hence the Entente."[88]

Sidney Lee's reappointment as biographer was confirmed by King George V in July 1920. The courtiers found Lee more insufferable than ever—"more important, more official and perhaps more difficult to deal with," and "eaten up with self concentration and self conceit."[89] Lee needed to find a new publisher, as Smith, Elder had gone out of business. The *DNB* had been sold to Oxford University Press, but the delegates had dropped Lee as editor and the snub rankled. The dons of the press disliked Lee, whom they described as "an obstinate old pig": "He will always be the Cad—he cannot help it."[90] The feeling against Lee was charged by anti-Semitism. It was widely known that he had changed his name from Solomon Lazarus to Sidney while an undergraduate at Balliol. Davidson thought he looked as though he "ought to be behind a Hokey Pokey wheelbarrow in Petticoat Lane."[91] Bertie's friend Admiral Fisher was even blunter and more horrible. "Levi is a liar! . . . This Jew who is out for money isn't my horse!"[92]

Lee eventually signed an agreement with Macmillan, and the game of hide-and-seek-the-letters began again. Ponsonby and Davidson solemnly assured Lee that very little material survived, as Knollys had burned "cartloads of papers and has only kept the official papers."[93] In fact, the courtiers were deliberately concealing material from Lee. Contrary to what they told him, the letters of King Edward had not all been destroyed. Davidson wrote to Ponsonby in 1922: "It is absolutely impossible to let [Lee] run riot amongst this chaos of the late King's letters. I cannot tell exactly how many there are, and there may or may not be interesting ones amongst them; but in any case the difficulties surrounding these letters—whose very existence has to be kept a dead secret—hedges the whole situation with a bristling fence of difficulties."[94] The letters were stored at Marlborough House, and Davidson considered it quite impossible for Lee to see them until he himself had gone through them. He died a few months later, so Lee probably never did see them.

When Lee visited the archives at Windsor, he went "fawning up" to

Sir John Fortescue, the Keeper of the Archives, who "cut him short" and did his best to be unhelpful, refusing to let him see the private and family papers. "I have always treated Queen V's papers," wrote Fortescue, "at any rate during her later years—as sacred and not to be pried into."[95] Lee was given carefully vetted selections of letters relating to Bertie's early life. The tempestuous correspondence between mother and son was deliberately withheld. Lee was assured that the letters contained little of interest, merely remarks about the weather and references to "trivial" family squabbles that blew over in a few days, and "ought to have been destroyed at the time."[96] Bertie's relationship with his mother gives the main narrative to his early life as Prince of Wales, but this was closed to Lee.

He was steered away from "rummaging about" in the Randolph Churchill papers at Blenheim, for fear he might discover too much about the Aylesford scandal, especially Bertie's challenging Randolph to a duel. Sir Henry Ponsonby's often acid letters were withheld; as Davidson wrote, "Lee has no idea of things as we see and know them."[97] Charles Hardinge refused to show his letters from King Edward. "They are far too confidential."[98] When Lee asked to see Bertie's diaries, Stamfordham responded with exasperation: "There are no diaries and if there were the King said no one should see them! Surely Sidney Lee has been very well done by us—and I trusted we had seen the last of him in the Round Tower at Windsor. He cannot have the volumes he asks for as they contain heap of letters which he ought not to see and we have not the staff to make any more copies."[99]

The courtiers did their best to shape Lee's interpretation. Ponsonby fed him the line that King Edward "always took an intense interest in politics, and that it was simply because he was not allowed by Queen Victoria to do so, that he turned his energies to less important matters."[100] In Lee's book, the motif of Bertie's long years as Prince of Wales became his struggle to obtain the key to the Cabinet boxes—not just the ordinary boxes, but also the special key to the top-secret ones.[101]

The portrait of Albert Edward, Prince of Wales, that Lee painted in his first volume, published in 1925, was almost unrecognizable. Gone was the playboy prince of the *DNB*. The picture of Bertie as a boy, complained Ponsonby, was "a mere effigy": "stilted phrases from letters probably written by his tutor or by the Prince Consort give one no idea of what manner of youth he was."[102]

The young prince was constructed as a prodigy of statesmanship, playing a central role in European politics and earnestly advising ministers on his frequent visits abroad. George V read the book and remarked that any reader would imagine that his father as Prince of Wales interfered with almost every department of state.[103]

Lee had sent Lytton Strachey a copy of his article on biography in 1918, and Strachey had replied that biography, like portrait painting, depended on "the curious and indefinable combination of truth and aesthetic arrangement. Perhaps, too, an *advocatus diaboli* might put in a word for the caricaturist."[104] There was little aesthetic arrangement and even less caricature in Lee's leaden prose. The courtiers, however, still complained that he had been too critical of Queen Victoria, and for that reason he was dissuaded from making a personal presentation of his book to George V.[105] But Ponsonby and Stamfordham had achieved their aim in turning Lee around and making him write a hagiography. They had only themselves to blame if the book was dull, because it was they who had supplied the materials and censored the documents that Lee was allowed to see. Lee, who was probably a suppressed homosexual, felt uneasy writing about the prince's relations with women; "it worried him very much" that "he had not found time to satisfy himself upon this aspect of his biography."[106]

Violating his own *Principles of Biography*, which called for brevity, Lee felt compelled to write not one but two fat volumes. His health broke down from overwork while he was writing the first. He developed heart strain, which prevented him from walking up the eighty-nine steps of the Round Tower at Windsor to the archives, and documents had to be brought down to him.[107] Writing the second volume, on the reign of King Edward, killed Sidney Lee. The publisher Frederick Macmillan assured Ponsonby that the book was "practically written," but this was not, in fact, the case.[108] When Lee died, he left only five chapters completed, together with drafts and outlines for others. The task of completing the book was given to his secretary, S. F. Markham, with whom his relationship had been strained.[109]

Volume two, published in 1927, is actually a much better book than volume one. The story of the reign presented far fewer problems for the authorized biographer than the scandalous life of the Prince of Wales, and Markham published an important selection of political documents. This volume contains the understatement for which Lee (or is it Markham?) is famous: The King "never toyed with his food."[110] But the unreal portrait of Bertie that Lee constructed in volume one sabotaged the project. Volume two did not receive the credit it deserved. Though it sold fifteen thousand copies, Lee's biography failed to deconstruct the picture of King Edward that he himself had drawn in the *DNB*.

After the publication of Lee's two volumes, official royal biography was effectively embargoed until after the Second World War.[111] Sir Alan (Tommy) Lascelles, private secretary to George V, had a conversation with Queen Mary in 1942 about the publication of Henry Ponsonby's letters to his wife. Queen Mary took the line that the letters ought never to have been written, let alone published, and that a private secretary had no business to mention his work in his letters to his wife. Tommy Lascelles disagreed. "That attitude is typical of the ostrich technique which this family so often adopts."[112] Unconsciously echoing Queen Victoria, he argued that the publication of a biography revealing ordinary human shortcomings actually enhanced the reputation of the monarch. As Keeper of the Royal Archives (1943–53), Lascelles sanctioned official biographies of George V by Harold Nicolson, Queen Mary by James Pope-Hennessy, and George VI by John Wheeler-Bennett. These authors were allowed considerable freedom but were instructed to write nothing embarrassing to the institution of monarchy. As Wheeler-Bennett quipped, royal biography was like matrimony; an enterprise "not to be entered into inadvisedly or lightly; but reverently, discreetly, advisedly, soberly and in the fear of God."[113]

The Royal Archives were not opened to another biographer of Edward VII until 1958, when Sir Philip Magnus began work on a new life. Magnus, who had already published lives of Kitchener and Gladstone, was a professional biographer and private scholar. He enjoyed friendly relations with Robin Mackworth-Young, the Assistant Keeper of the Royal Archives and a deft promoter of royal biographies. Magnus asked Mackworth-Young to lunch, and soon Mackworth-Young had dropped the "Sir Philip" and was addressing Magnus as "My dear Philip."[114] Magnus was given special privileges, such as a photocopy of Bertie's diary (admittedly, he was charged the substantial sum of £60, and asked to return it afterward). He was allowed to bring a typist to speed his transcribing, and Mackworth-Young even gave him permission to eat apples in the Round Tower, "since no one else will be working in the archives at the time, so that no one need know of the precedent."[115]

For the author of a bestselling biography of Gladstone, Magnus was oddly lacking in confidence about the historical context of his book, and he worried about what academic historians might say. He sought reassurance and validation by consulting the leading historians of the day, such as Lewis Namier and A. J. P. Taylor. Robert Blake, who was then contemplating writing a life of Queen Victoria (which never happened), acted as historical adviser and read the typescript.[116] While he was working on the book, Magnus was invited to deliver the prestigious Ford Lectures in English history at Oxford, on the theme "Biography and History—George III to George V." He accepted but withdrew shortly before the titles were published, frightened by A. L. Rowse, who warned him that he would be "torn to pieces by 3rd-rate dons."[117]

"I am working very hard on Edward VII," Magnus told his mother in 1959, "but have not yet completed the first chapter which I have actually rewritten at least a dozen times."[118] As each chapter was typed, he sent it for his mother to read. She had strong views. "My darling Boy," she advised (Magnus was then in his midfifties), do not "prolong the scandalous part" more than necessary: "After all it is not a woman's magazine darling, but a book by a splendid author!"[119] Magnus was pressed by his American publisher, Elliott B. Macrae of E. P. Dutton, to tell the full story of Edward VII and put in "all of the salt, pepper and spice."[120] Old Mrs. Magnus did all she could to keep it bland and cut out the pepper and spice. "Substitute another word for <u>murky</u> past," she wrote. "'For attempting to rape a governess in a railway carriage' don't <u>name</u> offence."*[121] Again: "'Mrs. Langtry's lover'—Surely other ways of expressing this. . . . Steer clear darling as much as you can of hurtful words."[122]

Magnus completed his book in August 1962.[123] Mackworth-Young vetted the typescript, suggesting only minor changes and selecting controversial passages for Queen Elizabeth to see. The biography sold more than twenty thousand copies and received good reviews, though most followed A. J. P. Taylor's lead in *The Observer* and wrote more about the subject, and especially his appetite for food, rather than the book.[124]

Bertie had done all he could to frustrate and block his biographers. By ordering his papers to be burned and by writing letters that were as discreet as they were dull, he sought to guard his private life from posterity. The result was not what he had intended. Destroying the historical record does not prevent the history being written. The official biographer, Sidney Lee, constructed an unreal image of the prince as anodyne political prodigy. Yet outside the control of the royal archives, there flourished an unofficial version of Bertie as libertine and playboy. Anita Leslie's excellent *Edwardians in Love* was based on family tradition preserved by her father, Shane Leslie. But there proliferated a genre of royal books about Bertie that recycled and repackaged tired old anecdotes, half-truths, and choice quotations in the manner of subprime debt. No one attempted to reconcile the two versions. Philip Magnus, writing in 1964, was unable to address the prince's private life, even if he had wished to do so. Not only were the papers

---

* She was referring to the scandal caused by Bertie's friend Valentine Baker, who was convicted of indecent assault on a young woman in a railway carriage.

missing; the stories were still too sensitive. Only recently has this changed.

We now know that Lord Knollys did not burn everything. He seems to have squirreled away compromising papers salvaged from the King's archive and kept them among his own papers. Packets tantalizingly labeled "The Aylesford Affair" or the letters of poor pathetic Susan Vane-Tempest or blackmail letters from the Paris courtesan La Barucci he kept, along with a mass of other correspondence.*

As King Edward subsides into history, the scandals of his early life are no longer seen as potential threats to the monarchy. At last it is possible to make connections between the public and the private, to show how it was that debauched Prince Hal evolved into the people's King Edward the Peacemaker.

---

* The Knollys Papers were first used by Giles St. Aubyn, in his excellent *Edward VII* (1979), and then deposited in the Royal Archives, where they are today.

ACKNOWLEDGMENTS

My first and greatest debt is to Her Majesty the Queen for granting me unrestricted access to the papers of Edward VII in the Royal Archives at Windsor Castle. This book is not an official biography. I was not commissioned to write it; the proposal was mine, and it has been an incredible privilege to work in Windsor's treasure house of papers. Pam Clark and Jill Kelsey guided my research, which must at times have seemed never ending. They painstakingly checked my transcriptions and rigorously examined the accuracy of my text. For this I am grateful, though any remaining errors are, of course, my own. I should like to thank the Royal Librarian Lady Roberts, Lord Luce, and Lady de Bellaigue.

The Hon. Georgina Stonor gave invaluable advice, especially on Queen Alexandra. Victoria Fishburn, an indefatigable researcher, accompanied me on trips to archives and dug away at Daisy Warwick's papers. I should like to thank Caroline Spurrier for permission to quote from her Daisy Warwick archive. Other descendants of Bertie's women friends who have been especially helpful are Anne Somerset, Sarah Lutyens, and Sir Philip Naylor-Leyland. Cara Lancaster generously lent the papers of Mabel Batten. For Emma Bourke, I thank James Collett-White. Miranda Villiers entertained me and helped me to understand the Keppels, and John Phillips provided encouragement and information. Anthony Camp's prompt and scholarly genealogical research has kept me right on mistresses and bastards.

The late Lord Aylesford was generous with his records and his time at Packington Hall. I am grateful to John Sandwich for permission to use the Mapperton Papers (Oliver Montagu), and for kindly allowing me to reproduce illustrations from his superb albums. Penny Crowe approached me with the forgotten story of her forebear James Mackenzie and made available his papers. Charles Sebag-Montefiore kindly allowed me to use the papers of Philip Magnus. Michaela Reid showed me the diaries of Sir James Reid. Henry Poole and Co. of Savile Row provided an insight into Tum Tum's waistline. Ian Shapiro generously allowed me to reproduce photographs from his collection at Argyll Etkin.

For advice on medical issues I am grateful to Carole Reeves of the Wellcome Library and to James Lefanu and Anthony Wright. My thanks to Philip Mansel and the Society for Court Studies, to whom I have given four papers on various aspects of this book. Working on a documentary for BBC2 about Bertie with Denys Blakeway and Rob Coldstream greatly helped to focus my thoughts. Edwina Ehrman enlightened me about Alexandra's clothes. Marina Vorobieva kindly helped with Russian sources. Yvonne Ward lent me her excellent PhD thesis.

I was awarded a Research Fellowship by the Leverhulme Trust in 2007–8. This was immensely valuable in enabling me to dedicate time to writing the book. The Leverhulme Trust also awarded me a research expenses grant to fund the translation from Danish of Alexandra's letters to her sister Minnie. Birgit Christensen, my translator in Copenhagen, opened up Alexandra's world for me.

The following people have lent me books and unpublished materials, provided information, and helped in all sorts of ways with the book: R. J. Q. Adams; Mark Amory; Nicolas Barker; Stephen Bartley; Richard Belfield; Mark Blackett-Ord; Vernon Bogdanor; Mark Bostridge; Fiona Campbell; Moyra Campbell; David Cannadine; Juliet Carey; Professor John Clarke; Miss Denise Critchley-Salmonson; Joe Mordaunt Crook; Sarah Cubitt; Angus Cundey; Mark Curthoys of the ODNB; Richard Davenport-Hines; Susannah Davis; Patric Dickinson; Frances Dimond; Martyn Downer; John Drew; Laura Dugdale; Sir William Dugdale; the late Charles Elwell; Jessica Fletcher; Nicholas Gibbs; Sir Martin Gilbert; Richard Grantley; the Dowager Lady Grimthorpe; Jennifer Holmes; Michael Holroyd; Simon Houfe; Kathryn Hughes; the late Mrs. Maud Hutton-Attenborough; Cindy Jansz; Mary Kenny; Judith Keppel; Anna Kirk; Jeremy Lewis; Lady Amabel Lindsay; Lucy and Andrew Lloyd Davies; Sarah Mahaffy; Clarissa Mitchell; Eoghain Murphy; Maggie Oliphant; Anthea Palmer; Clarissa Palmer; Hannah Palmer; Edward Pearce; Helen Rappaport; Josie Reed; Susanna Rickett; Adam Ridley; my namesake, Jane Ridley; Judy Ridley; Andrew Riley; John Rohl; Ian Scott; Mary Clare Scrope; Anne Sebbah; Thomas Seymour; Rupert Shortt; Nancy Sladek; William St. Clair; Gerard Stamp; Kate Strasdin; Bridget Taverner; Humphrey Thomas; Anna Thomasson; Hugo Vickers; Sheila Walton; Michael Wheeler-Booth; Andrew Wilson; Sue Woolmans; Mary Yule; Philip Ziegler.

Material from the Royal Archives is quoted by permission of Her Majesty Queen Elizabeth II. The Hon. Rupert Carington kindly gave permission to quote from the diaries and writings of Lord Carrington (Lincolnshire Papers) held by the Carington Estates at Bledlow and available on microfilm at the Bodleian Library. Passages from the Margot Asquith diaries in the Bodleian Library are reproduced by permission of Christopher Osborne. Edward Sandars and the Bodleian Library gave leave to quote from the Sandars Papers. For permission to quote from the Wilfrid Blunt diaries, I am grateful to the Fitzwilliam Museum, Cambridge. For permission to quote from the papers of Nathaniel Meyer, 1st Lord Rothschild, I am grateful to the Rothschild Archive, London. The Churchill Archives Centre allowed me to quote from Jennie Churchill's papers. The Esher Papers are reproduced by kind permission of the Churchill Archives Centre on behalf of the 5th Lord Esher. My thanks to the Marquess of Salisbury for permission to quote from the papers of the 3rd Marquess of Salisbury at Hatfield House. The Royal College of Physicians gave permission to quote from the diaries of Edward Sieveking.

My colleagues at the University of Buckingham have supported my research, especially Judith Bray, Angela Brown, Roy Davis, and Terence Kealey. Special thanks to my students on the Biography MA program, who have no doubt had more than their fill about royal biography.

My son, Toby Thomas, read the book in manuscript and in proof and provided valuable and incisive criticism. My mother, Clayre Percy, was, as always, my first and most encouraging reader.

The Heir Apparent began life as a gleam in the eye of my agent, Caroline Dawnay, and she has cheerfully supported me and the book through a long and sometimes bumpy gestation. Thank you also to Olivia Hunt and Maria Dawson at United Agents, and to my American agent, Emma Parry. Christopher Phipps did a brilliant job on the index.

I am so thankful to my publishers for standing by the book. Susanna Porter of Random House has been patient and trusting. At Chatto, I have benefited greatly from Becky Hardie's clearheaded support. My thanks also to Alison Samuel and Parisa Ebrahimi. Silvia Crompton's quiet efficiency has made working on the last stages of the book a delight. Most of all, I want to thank my editor, Penelope Hoare. She is wise, funny, and always right, and I am the luckiest of writers to have Penny as my editor.

NOTES

ABBREVIATIONS USED IN THE NOTES

B	Bertie, Albert Edward, Prince of Wales, King Edward VII
POW	Prince of Wales
QV	Queen Victoria
Alix	Princess of Wales, Queen Alexandra
Vicky	Victoria, Princess Royal, Crown Princess of Prussia, Empress of Germany
Alice	Princess Alice, Grand Duchess of Hesse
Affie	Prince Alfred, Duke of Edinburgh
Fritz	Frederick William, Crown Prince of Prussia
Minnie	Dagmar, Princess of Denmark, later Marie Feodorovna, Czarina of Russia
George	Prince George, later King George V
Eddy	Prince Albert Victor, Duke of Clarence
RA	Royal Archives
RA VIC	Papers of Queen Victoria (these include the papers of Edward VII)
RA GV	Papers of George V
QVJ	Queen Victoria's journal

RA QVJ   Queen Victoria's journal in the Royal Archives
                          (unpublished)
RA VIC/EVIID   Bertie's diary
RA VIC/Add C07   Knollys papers
RA VIC/Add36   Henry Ponsonby's letters to Mary Ponsonby
RA VIC/U143   Queen Victoria's letters to Alice (microfilm)
GV/AA   Bertie's correspondence with Prince George
GV/GG9   Papers concerning Sidney Lee's biography
RPC   Royal Photograph Collection, Windsor
Copenhagen Letters Letters from Alexandra to her sister Minnie.
                          Håndskriftsamlingen XVI Danica, 1862–85, 4555.
                          Centralarkiv for Oktoberrevolutionen, Moskva, Boxes
                          102–4, in the Danish National Archives. Photocopies.
ODNB   *Oxford Dictionary of National Biography,* Oxford University
                          Press, 2004–13
BL   British Library
Fitzwilliam   The Fitzwilliam Museum

CHAPTER 1: VICTORIA AND ALBERT 1841

1. RA QVJ, 17 October 1841.
2. RA QVJ, 18, 19, 25, 28, 29 October, 3 November 1841.
3. RA VIC/M11/20, Albert to Robert Peel, 26 October 1841.
4. Cecil Woodham-Smith, *Queen Victoria: Her Life and Times, 1819–1861* (Sphere, 1975), p. 287.
5. Lady Lyttelton, the children's governess, used the phrase "vein of iron": Monica Charlot, *Victoria: The Young Queen* (Blackwell, 1991), pp. 189, 217.
6. RA VIC/Y54/88, Memo by Anson (Albert's secretary), 21 October 1841.
7. John Tosh, *A Man's Place: Masculinity and the Middle-Class Home in Victorian England* (Yale, 1999), pp. 82–83.
8. RA VIC/M11/25, Henry Wheatley to Albert, 11 November 1841.
9. RA QVJ, 2 December 1841.
10. RA Y54/92, Anson's memo, 9 November 1841.
11. See Anthony Camp, *Royal Mistresses and Bastards* (privately printed, 2007), pp. 132–329.
12. See D. M. Potts and W. T. W. Potts, *Queen Victoria's Gene* (Alan Sutton, 1995), pp. 55–73.
13. See Camp, *Royal Mistresses,* pp. 273–87.
14. Ibid., pp. 287–88. Steve Jones, *In the Blood* (HarperCollins, 1996), pp. 249–57, 267–70. *Lord of the Dance: Diverse Writing of Sir Iain Moncreiffe of That Ilk,* ed. Hugh Montgomery-Massingberd (Debrett's Peerage, 1986), p. 65.
15. Ida Macalpine and Richard Hunter, *George III and the Mad Business* (Allen Lane, 1969).
16. Timothy M. Cox, Nicola Jack, Simon Lofthouse, John Watling, Janice Haines, and Martin J. Warren, "King George III and Porphyria: An Elemental Hypothesis and Investigation," *Lancet,* vol. 266 (2005), pp. 332–35.
17. John Rohl, Martin Warren, and David Hunt, *Purple Secret: Genes, "Madness" and the Royal Houses of Europe* (Bantam Press, 1998), pp. 79–83.

18. Woodham-Smith, *Queen Victoria*, p. 107.

19. Timothy Peters, "George III: A New Diagnosis," *History Today*, September 2009, pp. 4–5.

20. King Leopold of Belgium to QV, 22 January 1841, in *The Letters of Queen Victoria*, ed. A. C. Benson and Viscount Esher (John Murray, 1908), vol. 1, pp. 257–58.

21. Lynne Vallone, *Becoming Victoria* (Yale, 2001), pp. 29, 63–65, 165–67. Woodham-Smith, *Queen Victoria*, pp. 103–5. Charlot, *Victoria*, pp. 47–50.

22. Anson's memo, 15 January 1841, in Benson and Esher, *Letters of Queen Victoria*, vol. 1, p. 256.

23. QV to King Leopold, 15 July 1839, in ibid., vol. 1, p. 177.

24. QVJ, 10 October 1839, in *Queen Victoria in Her Letters and Journals*, ed. Christopher Hibbert (Sutton, 2000), p. 55.

25. QVJ, 15 October 1839, in ibid., p. 57.

26. Lytton Strachey, *Queen Victoria* (Chatto and Windus, 1921), pp. 98–99.

27. QV to Vicky, 21 April 1866, in *Your Dear Letter: Private Correspondence Between Queen Victoria and the Crown Princess of Prussia, 1865–1871*, ed. Roger Fulford (Evans, 1971), p. 69.

28. See Camp, *Royal Mistresses*, pp. 342–43. Another rumor alleges that Albert's father was, in fact, his uncle Leopold, who visited Coburg at Christmas 1818. Albert was born on 26 August 1819. Even if true, which seems unlikely, this would not bring an infusion of "fresh blood." See Yvonne Ward, "Editing Queen Victoria: How Men of Letters Constructed the Young Queen," (PhD dissertation, La Trobe University, 2004), p. 239.

29. A. N. Wilson, *The Victorians* (Arrow Books, 2003), p. 55.

30. Theodore Martin, cited in Stanley Weintraub, *Albert: Uncrowned King* (John Murray, 1997), p. 31.

31. QVJ, 22 October 1839, in Hibbert, *Letters and Journals*, p. 58.

32. RA VIC/MAIN is still organized by Albert's filing system.

33. QV to King Leopold, 11 February 1840, in Benson and Esher, *Letters of Queen Victoria*, vol. 1, p. 217.

34. QV to Vicky, 15 March 1858, in *Dearest Child: Letters Between Queen Victoria and the Princess Royal, 1858–1861*, ed. Roger Fulford (Evans, 1964), p. 77.

35. QV to Albert, 31 January 1840, in Benson and Esher, *Letters of Queen Victoria*, vol. 1, p. 213.

36. Albert to his brother Ernest, September 1840, in Charlot, *Victoria*, p. 193.

37. King Leopold to QV, 22 January 1841, in Benson and Esher, *Letters of Queen Victoria*, vol. 1, p. 257.

38. Albert to his brother Ernest [March 1841], in Weintraub, *Albert*, p. 118.

39. QV to Vicky, 15 June 1859, in Fulford, *Dearest Child*, p. 195.

40. QV to Vicky, 9 June 1858, in Fulford, *Dearest Child*, p. 112.

CHAPTER 2: "OUR POOR STRANGE BOY" 1841–56

1. Victoria's description of Bertie at age ten: RA VIC/Y97/23, QV to King Leopold, 29 June 1852.

2. Lord Melbourne to QV, 1 December 1841, in Benson and Esher, *Letters of Queen Victoria*, vol. 1, p. 365. RA VIC/M11/44, Duke Ernest of Saxe-Coburg-Gotha to Albert, 28 November 1841.

3. RA VIC/Y198/181, QV to King Leopold, 14 July 1843.

4. QV to King Leopold, 6 June 1843, refers to "Bertie (as we call the boy)," in Hibbert, *Letters and Journals,* p. 95.

5. RA VIC/Y54/88, Anson's memo, 21 October 1841. RA QVJ, 10 December 1841.

6. QV to Vicky, 5 March 1859, in Fulford, *Dearest Child,* p. 165.

7. QV to King Leopold, 7 December 1841, in Benson and Esher, *Letters of Queen Victoria,* vol. 1, p. 366.

8. RA VIC/Y54/100, Anson's memo, 26 December 1841.

9. Woodham-Smith, *Queen Victoria,* p. 300.

10. QV to Vicky, 17 November 1858, 4 May 1859, in Fulford, *Dearest Child,* pp. 144, 267.

11. RA VIC/Y198/140, QV to King Leopold, 14 December 1841. RA VIC/Y99/23, QV to King Leopold, 13 June 1854.

12. QV to Vicky, 1 August 1860, in Fulford, *Dearest Child,* p. 267. QV to King Leopold, 20 September 1842, in Benson and Esher, *Letters of Queen Victoria,* vol. 1, p. 431.

13. QV to Vicky, 15 March 1858, in Fulford, *Dearest Child,* p. 78.

14. Charlot, *Victoria,* pp. 193–95, 209–10. Roger Fulford, *Hanover to Windsor* (Fontana/Collins, 1966), p. 59.

15. Albert to Baron Stockmar, 15 January 1842, in Charlot, *Victoria,* pp. 209–10.

16. RA VIC/Y54/98, Anson's memo, 5 December 1841.

17. See Elizabeth Longford, *Victoria RI* (Weidenfeld and Nicolson, 1964), p. 149. For Albert's search for power, see Charlot, *Victoria,* pp. 210–16.

18. Charlot, *Victoria,* pp. 218–20. E. S. Turner, *The Court of St. James's* (Michael Joseph, 1959), pp. 305–7.

19. RA QVJ, 25 January 1842.

20. RA QVJ, 6 April 1842.

21. Charlot, *Victoria,* pp. 277–78.

22. RA VIC/M13/46, Lady Lyttelton to QV, 29 September 1843.

23. Lady Lyttelton to QV, 16 February 1844, in Lord Esher, *The Influence of King Edward* (John Murray, 1915), p. 6.

24. RA VIC/M13/68, Lady Lyttelton's Journal, 24 August 1845. RA VIC/M13/74, Lady Lyttelton's Journal, 3 September 1845.

25. Charlot, *Victoria,* p. 280.

26. *Correspondence of Sarah Spencer, Lady Lyttelton,* ed. Hon. Mrs. Hugh Wyndham (John Murray, 1912), pp. 362, 372.

27. Eleanor Stanley to her father, 26 September 1846, in *Twenty Years at Court: From the Correspondence of the Hon. Eleanor Stanley,* ed. Mrs. Steuart Erskine (Nisbet, 1916), p. 122.

28. QVJ, 3 November 1844, in Charlot, *Victoria,* p. 281.

29. Esher, *Influence of King Edward,* p. 6.

30. RA VIC/Add A5/22, Birch's Stray Leaves Amongst My Papers, June 1850, an extract from Birch's Journal, returned to QV in 1877.

31. Diary of Frederick Gibbs, 26 January 1851, in "The Education of a Prince," *Cornhill Magazine,* vol. 165 (1951), p. 107.

32. John C. G. Rohl, *Young Wilhelm: The Kaiser's Early Life 1859–1888* (Cambridge University Press, 1998), p. 116.

33. RA VIC/M12/14, Stockmar's memo, 8 March 1842.

34. See Jean Meyer, *L'Education des Princes en Europe du XVe Au XIXe Siècle* (Perrin,

2004), pp. 210–14. John Rogister's review in *Times Literary Supplement,* 18 March 2005.

35. RA VIC/M12/40, Stockmar's memo [June 1846].

36. RA VIC/M12/66, Miss Hildyard's timetable, Prince of Wales [January 1848].

37. RA VIC/M13/89, Lady Lyttelton to QV, 3 September 1847.

38. RA VIC/M13/51, Lady Lyttelton to QV, 11 September 1844.

39. Baron Bunsen, quoted in Sidney Lee, *King Edward VII* (Macmillan, 1925), vol. 1, p. 17.

40. RA VIC/M12/35, QV's memo, 4 March 1844.

41. Christopher Hibbert, *Edward VII* (Allen Lane, 1976), pp. 9–10.

42. RA VIC/Z442/43, Frederick Gibbs to Albert, 14 August 1857.

43. RA VIC/M12/35, QV's memo, 4 March 1844.

44. Royal College of Physicians, Diary of Sir James Clark, 8 June 1848.

45. RA VIC/M15/107, Birch's memo, 25 February 1852.

46. RA VIC/M14/37, Albert's memo, Education of the Prince of Wales, 12 April 1849.

47. RA VIC/Z444/68, Reverend Tarver to Albert, 9 March 1859.

48. *The Greville Diary,* ed. P. W. Wilson (William Heinemann, 1927), vol. 2, pp. 454–55 (22 January 1848).

49. RA VIC/EVIID/1849–51, note by Birch, 10 March 1877.

50. RA VIC/M15/1, Henry Birch to Albert, 26 October 1850.

51. Royal College of Physicians, Diary of Sir James Clark, 24 June 1849.

52. RA VIC/Add J1665/4, Notes by Andrew Thomson (Balmoral dancing teacher), 30 August 1849.

53. RA VIC/M14/49, Mr. Birch's Private Thoughts, 1 December 1849.

54. RA VIC/M15/19, Henry Birch to Baron Stockmar, 24 November 1850.

55. RA VIC/EVIID/1849–51, Journal Dictated by Me to Mr. Birch, Albert Edward, 2 May 1850, 31 October 1850, 5 November 1850, 11 November 1850, 26 December 1850, 3 January 1851.

56. RA VIC/M15/16, Henry Birch to Baron Stockmar, 20 November 1850.

57. RA VIC/M14/107, George Combe to James Clark, 22 June 1850. RA VIC/M12/2, George Combe to Albert, 21 October 1850.

58. Correspondence between Albert and George Combe, in Hibbert, *Edward VII,* p. 10.

59. RA VIC/M15/17, Albert's memo, n.d.

60. RA VIC/M15/60, George Combe to James Clark, 27 March 1851.

61. RA VIC/M15/98, 8 December 1851, Dr. Becker to George Combe.

62. RA VIC/EVIID/1851: 27 September, 26 December.

63. RA VIC/EVIID/1852: 7, 8, and 20 January.

64. RA VIC/M15/107, Birch's memo, 25 February 1852.

65. Diary of Frederick Gibbs, January 1852, *Cornhill Magazine,* vol. 165 (1951), p. 106.

66. RA GV/GG9/439, Lord Esher to Frederick Ponsonby, 19 April 1914. See p. 585.

67. Gibbs's Diary, 28 February 1852, *Cornhill Magazine,* vol. 165 (1951), p. 111.

68. RA VIC/Y97/23, QV to King Leopold, 29 June 1852.

69. RA VIC/M15/105, Becker's memo, 9 February 1852.

70. Nightingale Papers, Wellcome MS8993/104, Florence Nightingale to family, 20 September [1852]: I am indebted to Mark Bostridge for this reference.

71. Becker to Albert, 19 January 1852, in Philip Magnus, *King Edward VII* (John Murray, 1964), pp. 10–11.

72. Diary of Frederick Gibbs, 2 March 1853, cited in Magnus, *King Edward VII*, p. 15.

73. RA VIC/EVIID/1853: 13 May.

74. RA VIC/T1/34, Alice to B, n.d.

75. Cited in Gerard Noel, *Princess Alice: Queen Victoria's Forgotten Daughter* (Constable, 1974), p. 41.

76. Vicky to Fritz, 17 March 1864, in Rohl, *Young Wilhelm,* p. 84.

77. RA VIC/EVIID/1849: 20 September.

78. Duff Hart-Davis, *Monarchs of the Glen* (Jonathan Cape, 1978), p. 119.

79. Bodleian Library, MSS Film 1120, Papers of Charles Robert Wynn-Carrington, Marquess of Lincolnshire, "King Edward VII as I Knew Him for 55 Years" (typescript).

80. See Nancy Ellenberger, "Constructing George Wyndham: Narratives of Aristocratic Masculinity in Fin-de-Siècle England," *Journal of British Studies,* vol. 39 (2000), pp. 493–94. David Roberts, "The Paterfamilias of the Victorian Governing Classes," in Anthony S. Wohl, *The Victorian Family* (Croom Helm, 1978), pp. 59–81.

81. Quoted in George Plumptre, *Edward VII* (Pavilion, 1995), p. 38.

82. Bertie's diary, 16 April 1855, in Magnus, *Edward VII,* p. 18.

83. RA VIC/T1/88, Alfred to B, 20 August 1855.

84. Queen Victoria, *Leaves from a Journal: A Record of the Visit of the Emperor and Empress of the French to the Queen and of the Visit of the Queen and HRH the Prince Consort to the Emperor of the French 1855,* ed. Raymond Mortimer (André Deutsch, 1961), p. 51.

85. Quoted in ibid., p. 20.

86. Ibid., p. 85.

87. Stanley Weintraub, *The Importance of Being Edward* (John Murray, 2000), p. 28.

88. *The Greville Memoirs,* vol. 7, ed. Lytton Strachey and Roger Fulford (Macmillan, 1938), p. 157.

89. RA VIC/T1/94, Alfred to B, 13 December 1855.

90. RA VIC/T1/92, Alice to B, 11 December 1855.

91. RA VIC/T1/97, QV to B, 19 December 1855.

92. RA VIC/Y100/48, QV to King Leopold, 18 December 1855.

93. RA VIC/M17/31, Gibbs's Memo Containing the Reasons for the Separation of the Two Princes in the Spring of 1856.

94. RA VIC/M17/33, B to Albert, 25 March [1856]. RA VIC/M17/35, Albert to B, 25 March 1856.

95. Longford, *Victoria RI,* p. 275.

96. Royal College of Physicians, Diary of Sir James Clark, 5, 15 February 1856.

97. RA VIC/T1/118, Alice to B, 27 August 1856.

98. Albert to QV, 1 October 1856, in Weintraub, *Albert,* p. 330.

CHAPTER 3: "NEITHER FISH NOR FLESH" 1856–60

1. Albert's description of Bertie in a letter to his brother Ernest, 18 November 1858, in *The Prince Consort and His Brother,* ed. Hector Bolitho (Cobden-Sanderson, 1933), p. 188.

2. RA VIC/Add A5/470E, B's Notes on Lectures upon Attraction Delivered by Professor Faraday at the Royal Institution, December 1856 and January 1857.
3. RA VIC/Z444/63, Albert to Reverend Tarver, 26 February 1859.
4. Albert to his brother Ernest, 29 September 1857, in Bolitho, *Prince Consort and His Brother*, p. 177. See QV's memo, May 1856, in Benson and Esher, *Letters of Queen Victoria*, vol. 3, pp. 192–94.
5. Lee, *Edward VII*, vol. 1, p. 42.
6. RA VIC/Z459/35, QV's memo, 15 February 1877.
7. RA VIC/T1/185, QV to B, 4 September 1857.
8. RA VIC/Z459, QV's memo to Henry Ponsonby, 9 July 1872. Albert to his brother Ernest, 18 November 1858, in Bolitho, *Prince Consort and His Brother*, p. 188
9. RA VIC/Z459/92, QV's memo, 15 February 1877.
10. RA VIC/Y176/7, B's Essay on Friends and Flatterers [1857].
11. RA VIC/Z126: 1857, "Wit and Whoppers."
12. RA VIC/Z442/36, Frederick Gibbs to Albert, 7 August 1857.
13. RA VIC/Z442/32, Frederick Gibbs to Albert, 26 July 1857.
14. Magnus, *Edward VII*, p. 21.
15. RA VIC/T1/190, QV to B, 13 October 1857.
16. *Disraeli, Derby, and the Conservative Party: Journals and Memoirs of Edward Henry, Lord Stanley, 1849–1869*, ed. John Vincent (Harvester Press, 1978), p. 181.
17. RA QVJ, 20 October 1857.
18. RA VIC/T1/191, QV to B, 26 October 1857.
19. Albert to his brother Ernest, n.d., in Bolitho, *Prince Consort and His Brother*, p. 169.
20. RA VIC/Y176/26, Prince of Wales's History Paper, 1857.
21. Benjamin Disraeli to Mrs. Brydges Willyams, 23 January 1858, in *The Correspondence Between Mr. Disraeli and Mrs. Brydges Willyams*, ed. Andrew Roberts (Roxburghe Club, 2006), p. 84.
22. RA VIC/T2/1, Vicky to B, 26 January 1858.
23. Theodore Martin, *The Life of the Prince Consort* (Smith, Elder, 1880), vol. 4, p. 174.
24. Walburga, Lady Paget, *Embassies of Other Days* (Hutchinson, 1923), vol. 1, pp. 85–86.
25. Andrew Sinclair, *The Other Victoria: The Princess Royal and the Great Game of Europe* (Weidenfeld and Nicolson, 1981), p. 33. Vicky to Fritz, 17 March 1864, in Rohl, *Young Wilhelm*, p. 84.
26. RA VIC/Z463/50, QV to B, 28 August 1862.
27. Paget, *Embassies*, vol. 1, pp. 85–86.
28. Vicky to Albert [3 February 1858], in Fulford, *Dearest Child*, p. 31.
29. Albert to Vicky, 3 February 1858, in Hannah Pakula, *An Uncommon Woman: The Empress Frederick* (Phoenix, 1997), p. 6
30. QV to Vicky, 26 May 1858, 27 November 1858, 1 December 1858, in Fulford, *Dearest Child*, pp. 109, 147, 148.
31. RA VIC/T2/6, Vicky to B, 29 March 1858.
32. RA VIC/Y41/60, Feodora to QV, 29 March 1858.
33. RA VIC/Z261, QV's "Remarks Conversations Reflections," 2 May 1858.

34. Ibid.

35. Strachey and Fulford, *Greville Memoirs*, vol. 7, pp. 388–89 (12 December 1858).

36. RA VIC/Z443/33, QV's Memo for the Guidance of the Gentlemen Appointed to Attend on the Prince of Wales, n.d.

37. RA VIC/Z261, QV's "Remarks Conversations Reflections," 2 May 1858.

38. Elizabeth Longford, "Queen Victoria's Doctors," in *A Century of Conflict: Essays for A. J. P. Taylor*, ed. Martin Gilbert (Hamish Hamilton, 1966), p. 79. Longford, *Victoria RI*, p. 276.

39. RA VIC/Z443/56, Col. Robert Lindsay to Charles Phipps, 27 July 1858.

40. RA VIC/Z443/87, Reverend Tarver to Albert, 31 October 1858.

41. QV to Vicky, 10 November 1858, in Fulford, *Dearest Child*, p. 142.

42. RA VIC/Z443/90, QV and Albert's memo to B, 9 November 1858.

43. Esher's journal, 1 February 1909, in *Journals and Letters of Reginald Brett, Viscount Esher*, ed. Maurice Brett (Ivor Nicholson and Watson, 1934), vol. 2, p. 368.

44. Albert to his brother Ernest, 18 November 1858, in Bolitho, *Prince Consort and His Brother*, p. 188.

45. RA VIC/Z444/77, Colonel Bruce to Albert, 26 March 1859.

46. *The Letters of Elizabeth Barrett Browning to Her Sister Arabella*, ed. Scott Lewis (Wedgestone Press, 2002), vol. 2, pp. 396, 402.

47. RA VIC/Z141/50, Albert to B, 9 April 1859.

48. Jules Stewart, *Albert* (I. B. Tauris, 2012), p. 35.

49. RA VIC/EVIID, Prince of Wales's Journal, Rome, 7 February 1859.

50. RA VIC/Z444/62, Albert to B, 26 February 1859. RA VIC/Z461/92, B to Albert, 10 March 1859.

51. RA VIC/Z444/68, Reverend Tarver to Albert, 9 March 1859. The Prince of Wales's journal contains a lengthy revised account of his interview with the pope.

52. Albert to Vicky, 17 November 1858, in Weintraub, *Albert*, p. 367.

53. RA VIC/Z444/79, General Bruce to Albert, 2 April 1859. RA VIC/Z444/76, Albert to Bruce, 26 March 1859. RA VIC/Z141/50, Albert to B, 9 April 1859. RA VIC/Add A4/194, B to Vicky, 25 December 1900.

54. RA VIC/Z444/86, Albert to General Bruce, 26 April 1859.

55. RA VIC/Z445/24, Albert to Reverend Tarver, 8 September 1859.

56. QV to Vicky, 9 April 1859, 29 June 1859, in Fulford, *Dearest Child*, pp. 174, 198.

57. RA VIC/T2/88, QV to B, 7 September 1859.

58. RA VIC/Z445/38, Albert to General Bruce, 27 October 1859; see RA VIC/Z443/84, Albert to Dean Liddell, 20 October 1858.

59. Lord Clarendon to the Duchess of Manchester, 29 January 1860, in *"My Dear Duchess": Social and Political Letters to the Duchess of Manchester, 1858–1869*, ed. A. L. Kennedy (John Murray, 1956), p. 88.

60. RA VIC/Z445/55, Dean Liddell to General Bruce, 16 December 1859.

61. RA VIC/T3/2, QV to B, 22 January 1860.

62. RA VIC/Z445/61, General Bruce to Albert, 13 February 1860.

63. RA VIC/Z445/68, Dean Liddell to General Bruce, 30 March 1860; Lee, *Edward VII*, vol. 1, p. 78.

64. Magnus, *Edward VII*, p. 92. Fulford, *Hanover to Windsor*, pp. 118–19. For John-

stone, see *The New York Times*, 19 March 1914; Lee, *Edward VII*, vol. 1, p. 80; Elizabeth Hamilton, *The Warwickshire Scandal* (Michael Russell, 1999), p. 93.

65. Archive of Henry Poole and Co., Client Ledgers, Measurements of Prince of Wales.

66. RA VIC/T3/23, QV to B, 10 March 1860. RA VIC/T3/13, QV to B, 14 February 1860.

67. RA VIC/Add A3/8, B to QV, 23 February 1860.

68. RA VIC/T3/16, QV to B, 23 February 1860.

69. RA VIC/T3/20, B to QV, 29 February 1860.

70. RA VIC/T2/63, QV to B, 7 May 1859.

71. RA VIC/T2/107, Vicky to B, 21 December 1859.

72. Kennedy, *"My Dear Duchess,"* p. 106.

73. RA VIC/T2/96, Alice to B, 5 November 1859. RA VIC/T2/69, Alice to B, 15 July 1859. RA VIC/ T2/60, Alice to B, 3 April 1859.

74. RA VIC/T2/104, Alice to B, 13 December 1859.

75. RA VIC/T3/14, Alice to B, 18 February 1860.

76. Kennedy, *"My Dear Duchess,"* pp. 136, 197.

77. B to Alice, 17 August 1860, in Noel, *Princess Alice*, p. 38. Kennedy, *"My Dear Duchess,"* pp. 136, 197.

78. RA VIC/T3/50, B to QV, 13 June 1860.

79. RA VIC/Z141/64, Albert to B, 17 June 1860.

80. *The Times*, 21 June 1860.

81. Albert to Baron Stockmar, 27 April 1860, in Martin, *Prince Consort*, vol. 5, p. 87.

82. RA VIC/Z141/68, Albert to B, 17 August 1860.

83. RA VIC/Z461/113, B to Albert, 6 September 1860.

84. Woodham-Smith, *Queen Victoria*, p. 517.

85. RA VIC/T3/57, B to QV, 7 October 1860.

86. RA VIC/T3/58, B to Albert, 14 October 1860. Lee, *Edward VII*, vol. 1, p. 104.

87. QV to Vicky, 10 November 1860, in Fulford, *Dearest Child*, p. 279.

88. RA QVJ, 15, 16 November 1860. RA VIC/Add C24/7, Lord Torrington to Delane, 16 December 1860.

CHAPTER 4: BERTIE'S FALL 1861

1. RA VIC/Z446/5, Dean Liddell to General Bruce, 19 December 1860.

2. RA VIC/Z461/115, B to Albert, 9 February 1861. RA VIC/Z446/12, Charles Kingsley to Dean of Windsor, 9 February 1861. RA VIC/T3/61, B to QV, 19 January 1861.

3. Rothschild Archive, 000/12, Nathaniel Rothschild to his parents, n.d. [1861].

4. RA VIC/T3/58a, QV to B, 22 November 1860. RA VIC/T3/58b, B to QV, 23 November 1860.

5. RA VIC/Add MSS U143/Reel 4, 26 July 1861. QV to Vicky, 26 December 1860, in Fulford, *Dearest Child*, p. 295.

6. RA VIC/Z446/13, General Bruce to Albert, 10 March 1861. Rothschild Archive, 000/12, Nathaniel Rothschild to his parents, n.d. [1861].

7. Niall Ferguson, *The World's Banker* (Weidenfeld and Nicolson, 1998), p. 769.

8. Rothschild Archive, 000/12, Nathaniel Rothschild to his parents, n.d. [1861]. Stanley Weintraub, *Charlotte and Lionel: A Rothschild Love Story* (Simon and Schuster, 2003), pp. 159–60.

9. Albert to Stockmar, 5 April 1861, in Martin, *Prince Consort*, vol. 5, p. 335.

10. Ibid.

11. Charlot, *Victoria*, pp. 410–13. Woodham-Smith, *Queen Victoria*, pp. 523–24.

12. Kennedy, *"My Dear Duchess,"* pp. 143–44.

13. Vicky to QV, 4 April 1861; QV to Vicky, 10 April 1861; QV to Vicky, 17 April 1861, in Fulford, *Dearest Child*, pp. 318, 320–21.

14. RA VIC/Add A3/38, QV to B, 13 April 1861.

15. RA VIC/Add A3/40, B to QV, 16 April 1861.

16. RA VIC/Z462/between 101 and 102.

17. RA VIC/Z462/14, Vicky to QV, 1 March 1861. Vicky to QV, 20 April 1861, in Fulford, *Dearest Child*, p. 323.

18. RA VIC/Z462/22, Baron Stockmar to QV, 6 April 1861. Vicky to QV, 21 December 1860; Vicky to QV, 22 February 1861, in Fulford, *Dearest Child*, pp. 293, 311.

19. RA VIC/Z462/43,Vicky to Albert, 6 June 1861. Vicky to QV, 4 June 1861, in Fulford, *Dearest Child*, pp. 337–38. Pakula, *Uncommon Woman*, p. 48.

20. Vicky to QV, 6 September 1862, in *Dearest Mama: Letters Between Queen Victoria and the Crown Princess of Prussia, 1861–1864*, ed. Roger Fulford (Evans, 1968), p. 104.

21. QV to Vicky, 19 June 1861, in Fulford, *Dearest Child*, p. 342.

22. RA VIC/Z141/82, Albert to B, 10 June 1861. RA QVJ, 26 May 1861.

23. RA VIC/Z462/46, B to Albert, 11 June 1861. RA QVJ, 12 June 1861.

24. RA VIC/Z446/13, General Bruce to Albert, 10 March 1861. RA VIC/Z446/31, Bruce to Charles Phipps, 4 July 1861.

25. RA VIC/Add A3/56, B to QV, 17 July 1861.

26. RA VIC/Y107/2, QV to King Leopold, 16 July 1861.

27. RA VIC/Z446/38, General Bruce to Albert, 15 August 1861. RA QVJ, 24 August 1861.

28. RA VIC/EVIID/1861: 6, 9, 10 September.

29. RA VIC/Z141/94, Albert to B, 16 November 1861. According to Albert, this took place in another officer's tent; but it seems more likely that it was a hut.

30. Ulrik Langen, "Travelling Incognito," *Court Historian*, vol. 7 (2002), pp. 154–55.

31. RA VIC/Z462/73, QV's memo, 9 August 1861. Vicky to QV, 21 September 1861; Vicky to QV, 26 September 1861, in Fulford, *Dearest Child*, pp. 349–51. Magnus, *Edward VII*, pp. 48–49; Georgina Battiscombe, *Queen Alexandra* (Constable, 1969), p. 27.

32. QV to Vicky, 1 October 1861, in Fulford, *Dearest Child*, p. 353.

33. Vicky to QV, 12 October 1861, in ibid., p. 356.

34. QV to Vicky, 10 October 1861, in ibid., p. 357.

35. Albert's memo to B, 7 October 1861, in Magnus, *Edward VII*, pp. 49–50.

36. Albert to his brother Ernest, 22 July 1861, in Bolitho, *Prince Consort and His Brother*, pp. 364–66.

37. Baron Stockmar to Albert, 20 November 1861; QV to Vicky, 11 January 1862, in Fulford, *Dearest Mama*, p. 38.

38. Bodleian Library, MSS Film 1120, Lincolnshire Papers, B to Charles Carrington, 23 January 1862.
39. See Michael Mason, *The Making of Victorian Sexuality* (OUP, 1995), pp. 94–95, 119–22.
40. QV to Vicky, 12 November 1861, in Fulford, *Dearest Mama*, p. 132.
41. RA VIC/Z141/94, Albert to B, 16 November 1861.
42. Derby diary, 25 December 1861, in Vincent, *Disraeli, Derby*, p. 181.
43. RA VIC/Add C07/1/0313, Charles Phipps to General Knollys, 22 November 1864. Genealogical research has failed to produce a convincing identity for the Greens: author emails from Anthony Camp, 24 January, 3 February, 23 February 2010.
44. RA VIC/Z141/95, Albert to B, 20 November 1861.
45. RA VIC/Y43/7, Feodora to QV, 4 December 1861.
46. RA, VIC/Add C/24/18, Lord Granville to Delane, 19 December 1861.
47. Longford, *Victoria RI*, p. 288.
48. Helen Rappaport, *Magnificent Obsession: Victoria, Albert and the Death That Changed the Monarchy* (Hutchinson, 2011), pp. 25–38.
49. Bodleian Library, MSS Film 1120, Lincolnshire Papers, Carrington Diary, 25 November 1861.
50. QV to Vicky, 12 November 1862, in Fulford, *Dearest Mama*, p. 132.
51. QV to Vicky, 27 November 1861, in Fulford, *Dearest Child*, p. 370.
52. Albert to Vicky, 29 November 1861, in Pakula, *Uncommon Woman*, p. 56.
53. Rothschild Archive, 000/12, Nathaniel Rothschild to his parents, "Sunday" [15 December 1861].
54. Rothschild Archive, 000/12, Nathaniel Rothschild to his parents, "Sunday" [8 December 1861].
55. Lee, *Edward VII*, vol. 1, p. 123.
56. Rappaport, *Magnificent Obsession*, pp. 68–69.
57. RA VIC/Add C30/53, Account of the Prince Consort's death, possibly written by or for Sir Charles Locock. Martyn Downer, *The Queen's Knight* (Bantam Press, 2007), p. 121.
58. RA VIC/Add C30/53, Account of the Prince Consort's death, possibly written by or for Sir Charles Locock.
59. The date of Alice's telegram is not clear. According to one account (RA VIC/Add C30/53), Alice telegrammed Bertie after the conversation with Albert on Wednesday 11 December; however, Ponsonby suggests the telegram was sent on Thursday evening. (RA VIC/Add A36/5, Henry Ponsonby to his mother, Lady Emily Ponsonby, 14 December 1861.)
60. Rothschild Archive, 000/12, Nathaniel Rothschild to his parents, Sunday [15 December 1861].
61. RA VIC/Add A36/5, Henry Ponsonby to his mother, Lady Emily Ponsonby, 14 December 1861.
62. Quoted in Rappaport, *Magnificent Obsession*, p. 76.
63. RA VIC/Add A36/6, Henry Ponsonby to his mother, Lady Emily Ponsonby, 14 December 1861. RA VIC/Add C30/53, Account of the Prince Consort's death, possibly written by or for Sir Charles Locock.
64. Ibid. RA VIC/Add A36/6, Henry Ponsonby to his mother, Lady Emily Ponsonby, 14 December 1861.

65. RA VIC/Add C24/20, Lord Torrington to Delane, 23 December 1861. *The Times*, 24 December 1861.
66. RA VIC/Add C24/17, Lord Torrington to Delane, 18 December 1861. RA VIC/Add C30/53, Account of the Prince Consort's death, possibly written by or for Sir Charles Locock.
67. Longford, "Queen Victoria's Doctors," pp. 85–86. Longford, *Victoria RI*, pp. 295–96.
68. See Stanley Weintraub, "Prince Albert," *ODNB*.
69. Rappaport, *Magnificent Obsession*, pp. 249–60.
70. Martin, *Prince Consort*, vol. 5, p. 415. Vicky to QV, 29 December 1861, in Fulford, *Dearest Mama*, p. 32.
71. Royal College of Physicians, Diary of Sir James Clark, December 1861.

CHAPTER 5: MARRIAGE 1861–63

1. RA VIC/Add C10/49, Francis Seymour to his father, George Seymour, 25 December 1861.
2. Bodleian Library, MSS Film 1120, Lincolnshire Papers, B to Charles Carrington, 19 December 1861.
3. Mapperton, Sandwich Papers, B to Lord Hinchingbrooke, 20 December 1861.
4. *The Times*, 24 December 1861.
5. William Kuhn, "Queen Victoria's Civil List: What Did She Do With it?," *Historical Journal*, vol. 36 (1993), pp. 653–58.
6. Derby diary, 23 January 1862, in Vincent, *Disraeli, Derby*, p. 182. See David Cannadine, "The Last Hanoverian Sovereign?: The Victorian Monarchy in Historical Perspective, 1688–1988," in *The First Modern Society: Essays in English History in Honour of Lawrence Stone*, ed. A. L. Beier, David Cannadine, and James M. Rosenheim (Cambridge University Press, 1989), esp. pp. 143–45.
7. Derby diary, 16 December 1861, in Vincent, *Disraeli, Derby*, p. 180.
8. *The Times*, 17, 24 December 1861. Delane, the editor of *The Times*, was inspired by Lord Torrington and Lord Granville. See RA VIC/Add C24/17, Torrington to Delane, 18 December 1861; RA Vic/Add C24/18, Granville to Delane, 19 December 1861.
9. RA VIC/Add C10/49, Francis Seymour to his father, George Seymour, 25 December 1861.
10. QV to Vicky, 18 December 1861, in Fulford, *Dearest Mama*, p. 23.
11. RA VIC/Z261, QV's "Remarks Conversations Reflections," p. 230.
12. Magnus, *Edward VII*, p. 53. Longford, *Victoria RI*, p. 312.
13. Lord Clarendon to the Duchess of Manchester, 14 March 1862, in Kennedy, *"My Dear Duchess,"* p. 186.
14. QV to Vicky, 8 January 1862, in Fulford, *Dearest Mama*, p. 38.
15. QV to Vicky, 27 December 1861, in ibid., p. 30.
16. RA VIC/Add MSS U/16, Lord Hertford's Account of Queen Victoria, 12 February 1862.
17. RA VIC/Z446/49, QV's memo, 5 January 1862.
18. Lord Clarendon to the Duchess of Manchester, 24 January 1862, in Kennedy, *"My Dear Duchess,"* p. 181.

19. RA QVJ, 29 January 1862.

20. QV to Vicky, 11 January 1862, in Fulford, *Dearest Mama*, p. 38.

21. RA QVJ, 6 February 1862.

22. RA VIC/EVIID, Diary of Grand Tour, 17, 18 February 1862. Bodleian Library, MSS Film 1120, Lincolnshire Papers, B to Charles Carrington, 10 March 1862.

23. *A Victorian Dean: A Memoir of Arthur Stanley*, ed. Dean of Windsor and Hector Bolitho (Chatto and Windus, 1930), pp. 120–22.

24. Bodleian Library, MSS Film 1120, Lincolnshire Papers, B to Charles Carrington, 10 March 1862.

25. Dean of Windsor and Bolitho, *Victorian Dean*, p. 194.

26. RA VIC/EVIID, Diary of Grand Tour, 1 April 1862. Martin Gilbert, author information, November 2010.

27. Bodleian Library, MSS Film 1120, Lincolnshire Papers, B to Charles Carrington, 25 May 1862.

28. QV to Vicky, 11 January 1862, in Fulford, *Dearest Mama*, p. 5.

29. Vicky to QV, 19 January 1862, in ibid., pp. 43–44.

30. Vicky to QV, 11 April 1862, in ibid., p. 51.

31. RA VIC/Z462/102, Wally Paget to Countess Blucher, 5 January 1862. RA VIC/Z462/103, Augustus Paget to Countess Blucher, 8 January 1862. RA VIC/Z462/108, Augustus Paget to Baron Stockmar, 17 January 1862.

32. QV to Vicky, 16 April 1862, in Fulford, *Dearest Mama*, p. 62.

33. Vicky to QV, 21 June 1862, in Fulford, *Dearest Mama*, p. 82.

34. QV to Vicky, 25 June 1862, in Fulford, *Dearest Mama*, pp. 83–84.

35. Vicky to QV, 15 April 1862, in Fulford, *Dearest Mama*, p. 54.

36. QV to Vicky, 18 June 1862, in Fulford, *Dearest Mama*, p. 78.

37. RA VIC/Add U143/Reel 1, QV to Alice, 21 July 1862. QV to Vicky, 29 July 1862, in Fulford, *Dearest Mama*, p. 98.

38. Rappaport, *Magnificent Obsession*, p. 132.

39. Lord Clarendon to the Duchess of Manchester, 20 March 1862, in Kennedy, *"My Dear Duchess,"* p. 189. Rappaport, *Magnificent Obsession*, p. 133.

40. Lord Clarendon to the Duchess of Manchester, 25 December 1862, in Kennedy, *"My Dear Duchess,"* p. 207.

41. QV to Vicky, 2 July 1862, in Fulford, *Dearest Mama*, p. 85.

42. RA VIC/Z463/50, QV to B, 28 August 1862.

43. RA VIC/Z447/21, QV to B, 9 July 1862.

44. RA VIC/Z447/27, B to QV, 15 July 1862.

45. RA VIC/Z463/50, QV to B, 28 August 1862.

46. RA VIC/Z463/52, B to QV, 31 August 1862.

47. Bodleian Library, MSS Film 1120, Lincolnshire Papers, B to Charles Carrington, 7 August 1862.

48. QV to Vicky, 24 January 1862, in Fulford, *Dearest Mama*, p. 44.

49. RA VIC/T3/81, QV to B, 28 August 1862. RA VIC/T3/82, QV's memo of 23 August 1862.

50. RA QVJ, 3 September 1862.

51. RA VIC/T3/88, QV to B, 3 September 1862.

52. RA VIC/Z463/60, B to QV, 7 September 1862.

53. RA VIC/Z463/67, B to QV, 9 September 1862.

54. RA VIC/Z463/71, King Leopold to QV, 9 September 1862.

55. RA QVJ, 9 September 1862. RA VIC/Z463/59, the Duke of Newcastle to QV, 6 September 1862.

56. RA VIC/Z463/83, B to QV, 11 September 1863.

57. BL, Paget Papers, Add MS 51237, fols. 173–77, General Grey to Augustus Paget, 10 December 1862.

58. RA VIC/Z463/116, Lady Augusta Bruce to Wally Paget, 26 October 1862.

59. RA VIC/Z463/135, QV to Vicky, 12 November 1862.

60. Copenhagen Letters, Alix to Minnie, 10 November 1862.

61. Battiscombe, *Queen Alexandra*, p. 41. RA VIC/T3/105, General Grey to Augustus Paget, 27 November 1862.

62. QV to Vicky, 6 November 1862, in Fulford, *Dearest Mama*, pp. 125–26.

63. Lord Clarendon to the Duchess of Manchester, 14 September 1862, in Kennedy, *"My Dear Duchess,"* p. 201.

64. Vicky to QV, 15 November 1862, in Fulford, *Dearest Mama*, p. 134.

65. RA VIC/Add C24/37, Lord Torrington to Delane, 7 December 1862.

66. RA VIC/Add C24/35, Lord Torrington to Delane, 3 December 1862. RA VIC Add C24/36, Lord Torrington to Delane, 6 December 1862.

67. BL, Paget Papers, Add MS 51237, fols. 6–8, Augustus Paget to Wally Paget, 27 February 1863.

68. RA QVJ, 7 March 1863.

69. BL, Paget Papers, Add MS 51237, fols. 29–32, Augustus Paget to Wally Paget, 8 March 1863.

70. RA VIC/Z463/45, Lord Palmerston to QV, 6 March 1863. RA VIC/ Z463/46, QV to Lord Palmerston, 7 March 1863.

71. RA QVJ, 7 March 1863.

72. Lord Clarendon to the Duchess of Manchester, 10 March 1863, in Kennedy, *"My Dear Duchess,"* p. 214.

73. RA QVJ, 10 March 1863.

74. Lord Clarendon to the Duchess of Manchester, 10 March 1863, in Kennedy, *"My Dear Duchess,"* p. 214.

75. RA QVJ, 10 March 1863.

76. Battiscombe, *Queen Alexandra*, pp. 49–50.

77. Lord Clarendon to the Duchess of Manchester, 10 March 1863, in Kennedy, *"My Dear Duchess,"* p. 214.

78. RA QVJ, 10 March 1863. *Disraeli's Reminiscences,* ed. Helen M. Swartz and Martin Swartz (Hamish Hamilton, 1975), p. 78.

79. RA QVJ, 10 March 1863.

80. Bodleian Library, MSS Film 1120. Lincolnshire Papers, Carrington Diary, 10 March 1863. Magnus, *Edward VII*, p. 68.

81. Margaret Homans, *Royal Representations: Queen Victoria and British Culture, 1837–1876* (University of Chicago Press, 1998), pp. 60–61.

82. RA QVJ, 26 March 1863.

83. RA QVJ, 9 March 1863.

84. Homans, *Royal Representations,* pp. 171–74.

85. RA VIC/Add C10/73, Francis Seymour to his father, George Seymour, 3 December 1862.

CHAPTER 6: "TOTALLY TOTALLY UNFIT . . . FOR EVER BECOMING KING" 1863–65

1. RA VIC/Add U143/Reel 1, QV to Princess Alice, 7 July 1863.
2. RA VIC/Z464/72, Mrs. Bruce (widow of General Bruce) to QV, 29 March 1863.
3. Quoted in Battiscombe, *Queen Alexandra*, p. 56.
4. Copenhagen Letters, Box 102, Alix to Minnie, 2 April 1863.
5. RA VIC/Z464/73, Mrs. Bruce to QV, 1 April 1863.
6. Benjamin Disraeli to Lady Chesterfield, 15 December 1873, in *Letters of Disraeli to Lady Bradford and Lady Chesterfield*, ed. Marquis of Zetland (Ernest Benn, 1929), vol. 1, pp. 291–93.
7. RA VIC/Add U143/Reel 1, QV to Alice, 14 May 1863. The originals of QV's letters to Alice are in Darmstadt.
8. RA VIC/Add U143/Reel 1, QV to Alice, 15 May 1863.
9. QV to Vicky, 25 March 1863; QV to Vicky, 4 April 1863, in Fulford, *Dearest Mama*, pp. 186, 190.
10. QV to Vicky, 18 March 1863, 22 April 1863, in Fulford, *Dearest Mama*, pp. 183, 202.
11. QV to Vicky, 24 June 1863, 11 July 1863, in Fulford, *Dearest Mama*, pp. 236, 246–47.
12. RA VIC/Add U143/Reel 1, QV to Alice, 17 June 1863.
13. RA VIC/Add U143/Reel 1, QV to Alice, 7 July 1863.
14. RA VIC/Add C07/1/0121, Francis Knollys to General Knollys, 9 April 1863. RA VIC/Add C07/1/1022 and RA VIC/Add C07/1/1023, Francis Knollys to General Knollys, 10 April 1863.
15. RA VIC/Add C07/1/0007, B to General Knollys, 30 January 1863. RA VIC/Add C07/1/114, General Knollys to Francis Knollys, 5 April 1863. RA VIC/Add C07/1/115, Francis Knollys to General Knollys, 8 April 1863.
16. Nancy Ellenberger, "The Transformation of London 'Society' at the End of Victoria's Reign," *Albion*, vol. 22 (1990), pp. 640–41.
17. Lady Knightley's journal, quoted in Battiscombe, *Queen Alexandra*, p. 54.
18. Copenhagen Letters, Box 102, Alix to Minnie, 20 May 1863. *The Times*, 16, 19 May 1863.
19. Stanley Diary, 16 June 1863, in Vincent, *Disraeli, Derby*, p. 198.
20. Stanley Diary, 16 June 1863, in Vincent, *Disraeli, Derby*, pp. 198–99.
21. Alix's measurements for 1863 are in the Poole Archive under the Prince of Wales's entry.
22. QV to Vicky, 28 April 1863, in Fulford, *Dearest Mama*, p. 209.
23. QV to Vicky, 8 June 1863, in ibid., p. 22.
24. Royal College of Physicians, Shelfmark 718, Private Diaries of Sir Edward Sieveking of his Attendance on Edward Prince of Wales and Princess Alexandra (hereafter "Sieveking Diary"), 1 March 1863.
25. Sieveking Diary, 8 August 1863, 13 February 1864.
26. Ibid., 29, 30 May 1864.
27. RA VIC/Add U143/Reel 1, QV to Alice, 10 June 1863.
28. QV to Vicky, 11 July 1863, in Fulford, *Dearest Mama*, pp. 246–47.

29. Sieveking Diary, 10 August 1863.

30. Ibid., 13, 16 September 1863.

31. QV to Vicky, 5 September 1863, in Fulford, *Dearest Mama*, p. 261.

32. QV to King Leopold, 19 November 1863, in *Letters of Queen Victoria* (2nd series), ed. G. E. Buckle (John Murray, 1926), vol. 1, p. 117.

33. Fulford, *Dearest Mama*, p. 14.

34. RA VIC/T4/42, General Grey to B, 8 February 1864.

35. QV to King Leopold, 19 November 1863, in Buckle, *Letters* (2nd series), vol. 1, p. 117.

36. Quoted in Pakula, *Uncommon Woman*, p. 315.

37. RA VIC/Add U143/Reel 2, V to Alice, 24 August 1863.

38. W. E. Mosse, "Queen Victoria and Her Ministers in the Schleswig-Holstein Crisis 1863–64," *English Historical Review*, vol. 78 (1963), pp. 271–72.

39. Ibid., p. 282.

40. QV to Lord Russell, 1 January 1865, in Buckle, *Letters* (2nd series), vol. 1, p. 139.

41. RA VIC/Add U128/19, B to Philip of Flanders, 1 January 1864.

42. Frances Dimond, *Developing the Picture: Queen Alexandra and the Art of Photography* (Royal Collection Publications, 2004), p. 28.

43. Sieveking Diary, 8–9 January 1864. RA VIC/Z447/86, B to QV, 8 January 1864, 10:30 p.m.

44. Battiscombe, *Queen Alexandra*, p. 62.

45. RA VIC/Z447/89, Lord Granville to Charles Phipps, 8 January 1864.

46. Lord Stanley of Alderley, quoted in Fulford, *Dearest Mama*, p. 289.

47. RA VIC/Add U143/Reel 2, QV to Alice, 9 January 1864.

48. Battiscombe, *Queen Alexandra*, p. 62.

49. RA, QVJ, 8 January 1864.

50. RA VIC/Add U143/Reel 2, QV to Alice, 9 January 1864.

51. QV to Vicky, 11 January 1864, in Fulford, *Dearest Mama*, p. 289.

52. RA VIC/Z447/118, QV to B, 13 January 1864, Osborne, copy.

53. QV to Vicky, 12 March 1864, in Fulford, *Dearest Mama*, p. 306.

54. QV to Vicky, 30 January 1864, in Fulford, *Dearest Mama*, p. 296.

55. QV to Vicky, 13 February 1864, in Fulford, *Dearest Mama*, p. 35.

56. RA VIC/Add U143/Reel 2, QV to Alice, 27 April 1864.

57. RA VIC/Add U143/Reel 2, QV to Alice, 27–28 March 1864.

58. RA VIC/Add U143/Reel 2, QV to Alice, 30 May 1864.

59. RA VIC/Add U143/Reel 3, QV to Alice, 7 October 1864.

60. RA VIC/Y111/25, QV to King Leopold, 12 March 1864.

61. RA VIC/Z448/11, General Grey to Lord Russell, 25 May 1864. RA VIC/Z448/13, B to QV, 1 June 1864. RA VIC/Z448/17, QV to B, 3 June 1864.

62. E.g. Copenhagen Letters, Box 103, Alix to Minnie, 21 February 1870.

63. RA VIC/Add U143/Reel 2, QV to Alice, 25 February 1864.

64. QV to Vicky, 30 March 1864, in Fulford, *Dearest Mama*, p. 315.

65. RA VIC/Y111/24, QV to King Leopold, 11 March 1864.

66. Sieveking Diary, 22, 27 March 1864.

67. Ibid., 3 June 1865.

68. Ibid., 22 March 1864.

69. Ibid., 14, 29 February, 3 March 1864.
70. Ibid., 3 June 1865.
71. Downer, *Queen's Knight*, p. 146.
72. RA VIC/Add C24/17, Lord Torrington to Delane, 18 December 1861.
73. RA VIC/Add C24/27, Lord Torrington to Delane, 16 March 1862.
74. Downer, *Queen's Knight*, pp. 77, 145–46.
75. RA VIC/Add C07/1/0377, General Knollys to Francis Knollys, 3 April 1864.
76. RA VIC/Add U128/21, B to Philip of Flanders, 12 July 1864.
77. RA VIC/Add C07/1/0377, General Knollys to Francis Knollys, 3 April 1864.
78. RA VIC/Add U143/Reel 2, QV to Alice, 30 May 1864.
79. RA VIC/Add U143/Reel 2, QV to Alice, 16 May 1864.
80. RA VIC/Y111/25, QV to King Leopold, 19 April 1864, 12 March 1864.
81. RA VIC/Add U143/Reel 2, QV to Alice, 16 May 1864.
82. RA VIC/Z448/54, B to QV, 7 October 1864.
83. Sieveking Diary, 31 August 1864.
84. RA VIC/Z448/54, B to QV, 7 October 1864.
85. RA VIC/Add C07/1/0305, QV to B, 1 October 1864.
86. RA VIC/Z448/57, QV's note, n.d.
87. RA VIC/T4/45b, General Grey to Lord Cowley, 8 October 1864.
88. RA VIC/Add U143/Reel 3, QV to Alix, 12 November 1864.
89. RA VIC/Add U143/Reel 3, QV to Alix, 16 November 1864. Copenhagen Letters, Box 102, Alix to Minnie, 19 November 1864.
90. RA VIC/Add C18/93, Diary of Lady Macclesfield, 9 November 1864.
91. RA VIC/Add C07/1/0311, B to General Knollys, 20 November 1864. See RA VIC/Add C07/1/0309, Charles Phipps to General Knollys, 18 November 1864. RA VIC/Add C07/1/0310, Charles Phipps to Arnold White (solicitor), 20 November 1864.
92. RA VIC/Add C07/1/0313, Charles Phipps to General Knollys, 22 November 1864.
93. RA VIC/EVIID/1865: 1 January.
94. RA VIC/EVIID/1865: 3 January.
95. RA GV/GG9/1044, Frederick Ponsonby to Sidney Lee, 2 December 1924. Jonathan Garnier Ruffer, *The Big Shots* (Debrett, 1977), ch. 2.
96. RA VIC/Z446/61, Charles Phipps to QV, 4 February 1862.
97. Bodleian Library, Lincolnshire Papers, MSS Film 1120, Carrington Diary, 26 December 1864.
98. Poole Archive, Ledger Z, 12 April 1865.
99. RA VIC/EVIID/1865: 13 April.
100. RA VIC/Add C07/1/0435, Charles Phipps to General Knollys, 22 April 1865.
101. RA VIC/Add C07/1/0382, General Knollys to Francis Knollys, 15 December 1864.
102. RA VIC/EVIID/1865: 13 April. See John Martin Robertson, "Sandringham," *Country Life*, 29 May 2008.
103. Magnus, *Edward VII*, pp. 63–65. Kuhn, "Queen Victoria's Civil List."
104. RA VIC/Add C07/1/0412, General Knollys to B, copy, 28 February 1865.
105. RA GV/AA25/32, B to George, 25 March 1908.
106. RA VIC/Z447/60, QV to Lord Granville, 10 February 1863.

107. RA VIC/EVIID/1865: 16, 21 March.

108. BL, Sidney Lee Papers, Add MS 560787A, fol. 157, G. O. Trevelyan to Lee, 22 March 1923.

109. Stanley Diary, 30 October 1865, in Vincent, *Disraeli, Derby,* pp. 239–40.

110. RA VIC/EVIID/1865: 2 June.

111. Sieveking Diary, 5 February, 3, 4 June 1865.

112. RA VIC/Z448/109, QV to B, 13 June 1865.

113. RA VIC/Z447/118, QV to B, 13 January 1864. RA VIC/Z447/119, QV to B, 14 January 1864. RA VIC/Z447/121, B to QV, 15 January 1864.

114. RA VIC/Z448/110, B to QV, 16 June 1865. RA VIC/Z448/111, Charles Phipps to QV, 17 June 1865.

115. RA VIC/Add C07/1/0457, Charles Phipps to General Knollys, 14 July 1865.

116. RA VIC/Add U143/Reel 4, V to Alice, 5 August 1865; 19 July 1865.

CHAPTER 7: ALIX'S KNEE 1865–67

1. RA VIC/Add C07/1/0485, Charles Phipps to General Knollys, 6 December 1865. Fulford, *Your Dear Letter,* p. xvii.

2. RA VIC/T4/78, Affie to B, 10 December 1865.

3. Copenhagen Letters, Box 102, Alix to Minnie, 3 and 24 April 1864.

4. RA VIC/Add C07/1/0485, Charles Phipps to General Knollys, 6 December 1865.

5. RA VIC/T4/74, Alice to B, 19 November 1865.

6. Fulford, *Your Dear Letter,* pp. xv, 49.

7. QV to Vicky, 23 December 1865, in ibid., p. 51.

8. QV to Vicky, 15 December 1865, in Fulford, *Your Dear Letter* p. 47.

9. QV to Vicky, 1 August 1866, in Fulford, *Your Dear Letter* p. 86.

10. Fulford, *Your Dear Letter,* pp. 114–15.

11. RA VIC/J81/102, Lord Clarendon to QV, 2 May 1866. RA VIC/Add U292/13, General Grey to Lord Derby, 13 July 1866.

12. Vicky to QV, 10 August 1866, in Buckle, *Letters* (2nd series), vol. 1, pp. 366–67.

13. Ibid.

14. RA VIC/T4/109, Vicky to B, 29 October 1866.

15. Vicky to QV, 4 December 1866, in Fulford, *Your Dear Letter,* p. 110.

16. RA VIC/T4/125, QV to B, 21 December 1866.

17. QV to Vicky, 13 August 1866, in Fulford, *Your Dear Letter,* p. 91.

18. Paget, *Embassies,* p. 203.

19. *The Times,* 10 November 1866.

20. RA VIC/Z448/135, QV to B, 16 October 1866 (copy). RA VIC/ Z448/138, QV to B, 20 October 1866 (copy). QV to Vicky, 14 November 1866, in Fulford, *Your Dear Letter,* p. 105.

21. Vicky to QV, 7 December 1866, in Fulford, *Your Dear Letter,* p. 111.

22. RA VIC/T4/117, QV to B, 20 November 1866. QV to Vicky, 14 November 1866, in Fulford, *Your Dear Letter,* p. 105.

23. Copenhagen Letters, Box 102, Alix to Minnie, 21–22 November 1866.

24. Sir William Knollys's account of conversation with Princess Alice, 14 November 1867, in Magnus, *Edward VII,* p. 95.

25. RA VIC/Add C7/5–7, Knollys Diary, 11 February 1867.

26. Sieveking Diary, 15 February 1867.
27. RA VIC/Add C7/10–11, Knollys Diary, 15 February 1867.
28. RA VIC/Add C7/5–7, Knollys Diary, 16 February 1867.
29. *The Times,* 18, 19 February 1867.
30. RA VIC/Z448/154, B to QV, 20 February 1867.
31. Ibid. Sieveking Diary, 20 February 1867.
32. RA VIC/Add C7/12, Knollys Diary, 20 February 1867.
33. RA QVJ, 23 February 1867.
34. RA QVJ, 27 February 1867.
35. RA VIC/Add C18/3, Lady to Lord Macclesfield, 2 March 1867.
36. Quoted in Battiscombe, *Queen Alexandra,* p. 83.
37. RA QVJ, 8 March 1867.
38. RA VIC/Add C18/7, Lady to Lord Macclesfield, 9 March 1867.
39. RA QVJ, 6, 8 March 1867.
40. *The Times,* 15 April 1867.
41. RA VIC/Add C7/19, Knollys Diary, 18 March 1867.
42. RA QVJ, 23 March 1867.
43. RA QVJ, 4 April 1867.
44. RA VIC/Add A3/81, B to QV, 4 April 1867.
45. RA QVJ, 13 April 1867.
46. RA QVJ, 17 February 1867.
47. Private information.
48. RA VIC/Add C07/1/1487, Charles Phipps to General Knollys, 15 December 1865.
49. RA VIC/Add C07/1/0482, Charles Phipps to General Knollys, 3 December 1865.
50. See Deborah Hayden, *Pox: Genius, Madness, and the Mysteries of Syphilis* (Basic Books, 2003).
51. Sieveking Diary, 15 February 1867.
52. Author email from James Lefanu, 19 November 2009.
53. BL, Paget Papers, Add MS 51237, fols. 20–21, Augustus Paget to Walburga Paget, 3 March 1863.
54. Stanley Diary, 30 October 1865, in Vincent, *Disraeli, Derby,* p. 240.
55. QV to Vicky, 19 May 1863, in Fulford, *Dearest Mama,* p. 213.
56. Battiscombe, *Queen Alexandra,* pp. 86–87. Obituary, *The Guardian,* 2 March 2006.
57. Sieveking Diary, 30 March 1864.
58. Sieveking Diary, 31 March 1864. Neil Wear, "Joseph Toynbee," *ODNB.*
59. Author email from Anthony Wright, 10 April 2011.
60. Poole Archive, DD569, 1867.
61. RA VIC/Add A3/84, B to QV, 3 May 1867.
62. RA VIC/Add C7/8, Knollys Diary, 11, 12 February 1867. RA VIC/Z448/155, General Knollys to QV, 20 February 1867.
63. RA VIC/Z448/159, Mrs. Stonor to QV, 10 May 1867.
64. RA VIC/Add A3/86, B to QV, 11 May 1867.
65. Bodleian Library, Lincolnshire Papers, MSS Film 1120, B to Charles Carrington, 17 July 1865, November 1867. *Les Amours de Napoléon III par l'auteur de La Femme de César* [Pierre Vesinier], 4 vols. (Londres, 1864).

66. Émile Zola, *Nana* (Penguin, 1972), pp. 145, 151–52, 157.

67. RA VIC/Add C7/28, Knollys Diary, 20 May 1867.

68. Camp, *Royal Mistresses*, pp. 351–52.

69. Joanna Richardson, *The Courtesans* (Weidenfeld and Nicolson,1967), pp. 28–32. Katie Hickman, *Courtesans* (Harper Perennial, 2003), pp. 249–51.

70. Vicky to QV, 6 September 1870, in Pakula, *Uncommon Woman*, pp. 295–96.

71. QV to Vicky, 17 September 1870, in Pakula, *Uncommon Woman*, pp. 295–96.

72. QV to Vicky, 7 August 1867, in Fulford, *Your Dear Letter*, pp. 146–47.

73. RA VIC/Add C18/1, Lady to Lord Macclesfield, 28 February 1867.

74. RA VIC/Add C7/32, Knollys Diary, 6 June 1867.

75. Hibbert, *Edward VII*, p. 87. See Camp, *Royal Mistresses*, p. 351.

76. RA VIC/EVIID/1865: 13 October.

77. Stanley Diary, 18 June 1867, in Vincent, *Disraeli, Derby*, p. 312.

78. RA VIC/Add C7/35, Knollys Diary, 20 June 1867.

79. See Tolstoy's *Kreutzer Sonata* (1889) for a meditation on the sexual mores of the time.

80. RA VIC/Add C7/37, 39–40, Knollys Diary, 3, 5 July 1867.

81. RA VIC/Add C7/88–94, Knollys Diary, 18, 19, 20 August 1867. Sieveking Diary, 5 August 1867.

82. RA VIC/Add A3/94, B to QV, 2 September 1867.

83. RA VIC/Add C7/98–9, Knollys Diary, 23 August 1867. RA VIC/Y44/107, Feodora, Princess of Hohenlohe-Langenburg to QV, 28 September 1867.

84. RA VIC/Add A3/93, B to QV, 27 August 1867.

85. James Pope-Hennessy, *Queen Mary* (Phoenix Press, 2000), pp. 82–88.

86. RA VIC/Y110/4, QV to King Leopold, 23 July 1863.

87. Bodleian Library, Lincolnshire Papers, MSS Film 1120, Carrington Diary, 30 August 1867.

88. Hans A. Schmitt, "From Sovereign States to Prussian Provinces: Hanover and Hesse-Nassau, 1866–71," *Journal of Modern History*, vol. 57 (1985), pp. 28–29.

89. RA VIC/Add C7/125, Knollys Diary, 23 September 1867.

90. RA VIC/Add C7/126–7, Knollys Diary, 23 September 1867.

91. QV to Vicky, 1 October 1867, in Fulford, *Your Dear Letter*, pp. 152–53.

92. QV to Vicky, 5 October 1867, in Fulford, *Your Dear Letter*, p. 154.

93. RA VIC/Add A3/96, B to QV, 4 October 1867.

94. RA VIC/Add C7/140, Knollys Diary, 5 October 1867.

95. RA VIC/Add C7/143–44, Knollys Diary, 7 October 1867.

96. RA VIC/Add C7/149–50, Knollys Diary, 11 October 1867. See Battiscombe, *Queen Alexandra*, pp. 90–91.

97. RA VIC/Add C7/150, Knollys Diary, 11 October 67. RA VIC/Add A3/98, B to QV, 20 October 1867.

98. Copenhagen Letters, Box 103, Alix to Minnie, 2 October 1867.

99. Bodleian Library, Lincolnshire Papers, MSS Film 1120, B to Charles Carrington, 10 October 1867.

100. QV to Vicky, 9 November 1867, in Fulford, *Your Dear Letter*, p. 158.

101. RA VIC/Add A5/390, B to Madame Didier, 12 November 1867. Author email from Anthony Camp, November 2009.

102. RA VIC/Add A/5/391, B to Madame Didier, 4 February [1874].

103. RA VIC/Add A5/392, B to Madame Didier, 14–26 February [1874].

104. RA VIC/Add A5/393, Madame Didier to Stamfordham, 12 April 1921.

105. RA VIC/Add A5/394, Pryce Mitchell to Frederick Ponsonby, 25 April 1921.

106. RA VIC/Add A5/395, Pryce Mitchell to Frederick Ponsonby, 7 May 1921.

CHAPTER 8: MARLBOROUGH HOUSE AND HARRIETT MORDAUNT 1868–70

1. Walter Bagehot, *The English Constitution* (Sussex Academic Press, 1997), p. 31.

2. RA VIC/Z448/186, QV to B, 7 January 1868 (copy).

3. RA VIC/Z448/129, QV to General Knollys, 10 June 1866 (copy).

4. RA VIC/Add C26/11, QV to Lady Cardine, 5 January 1868.

5. RA QVJ, 17 June 1859.

6. Henry Vane, *Affair of State: A Biography of the 8th Duke and Duchess of Devonshire* (Peter Owen, 2004), pp. 13–27.

7. Erskine, *Twenty Years at Court*, p. 345 (5 January 1859).

8. RA VIC/Add U143/Reel 2, QV to Alice, 16 May 1864.

9. Vane, *Affair of State*, pp. 74–75.

10. RA VIC/EVIID/1865: 8 February.

11. Stanley Diary, 5 June 1864, in Vincent, *Disraeli, Derby*, pp. 218, 225.

12. RA VIC/Add A3/106, B to QV, 2 February 1868. Copenhagen Letters, Box 103, Alix to Minnie, 21 February 1870.

13. RA VIC/Z448/129, QV to General Knollys, 10 June 1866.

14. Vane, *Affair of State*, pp. 83–84. Frances, Countess of Warwick, *Life's Ebb and Flow* (Hutchinson, 1929), p. 176.

15. RA VIC/Add A3/77, B to QV, 28 January 1867 [sic] (actually 1868). RA VIC/Add A3/106, B to QV, 2 February 1868.

16. Alix to Louise, 3 February 1868, in *Darling Loosy: Letters to Princess Louise, 1856–1939*, ed. Elizabeth Longford (Weidenfeld and Nicolson, 1991), p. 101.

17. Bodleian Library, Lincolnshire Papers, MS Film 1120, Carrington Diary, 4, 8 February 1868.

18. Lee, *Edward VII*, vol. 1, pp. 154–55.

19. RA VIC/Z449/97, QV to B, 1 June 1870 (copy).

20. Ibid. Bodleian Library, Lincolnshire Papers, MS Film 1120, B to Carrington, 27 April 1866.

21. Bodleian Library, Lincolnshire Papers, MS Film 1120, Carrington Diary, 2 February 1870.

22. RA VIC/Z449/105, QV to B, 30 June 1870 (copy).

23. RA VIC/Z449/104, B to QV, 29 June 1870. RA VIC/Z449/106, B to QV, 2 July 1870.

24. *Survey of London: Parish of St. James's Westminster*, vol. 29 (Athlone Press, 1960), p. 344. Lee, *Edward VII*, vol. 1, pp. 170–71.

25. Samuel Beeton, *Jon Duan: A Twofold Journey with Manifold Purposes* (Weldon, 1874), p. 85.

26. Collie Knox, "End of a Royal Club," *Country Life,* 25 February 1954.

27. Vane, *Affair of State*, p. 92.

28. Rothschild Papers, 000/12, Nathaniel Rothschild to his mother, n.d. [1868].

29. RA VIC/Add C07/1/0442, Lord Spencer to General Knollys, 25 May 1865.

30. RA VIC/Add C07/1/0668A, Francis Knollys's memo, September 1869.

31. Christopher Sykes, "Behind the Tablet," in *Four Studies in Loyalty* (Collins, 1946), p. 23. RA VIC/Add A3/140, B to QV, 25 July 1869.

32. Sykes, "Behind the Tablet," pp. 27–28.

33. John Plunkett, *Queen Victoria: First Media Monarch* (Oxford, 2003), pp. 151–61.

34. Edwina Ehrman, unpublished paper, "Madame Elise," 2009. Author email from Kate Strasdin, March 2010.

35. RA VIC/Z449/51, QV to B, 4 May 1869 (copy).

36. RA VIC/Add A3/135, B to QV, 7 May 1869.

37. Diana de Marly, *Worth: Father of Haute Couture* (Elm Tree Books, 1980), pp. 26, 100, 136–37. Therese Dolan, "The Empress's New Clothes: Fashion and Politics in Second Empire France," *Women's Art Journal*, vol. 15 (1994).

38. Copenhagen Letters, Box 103, Alix to Minnie, 8 January 1873.

39. Magnus, *Edward VII*, p. 79.

40. Frank Prochaska, *Royal Bounty: The Making of a Welfare Monarchy* (Yale, 1995), p. 109.

41. RA VIC/T5/10, B to QV, 4 January 1868.

42. Disraeli to QV, 6 March 1868 in Buckle, *Letters* (2nd series), vol. 1, pp. 512–13.

43. QV to B, 9 March 1868, in ibid., vol. 1, pp. 514–15.

44. Quoted in Battiscombe, *Queen Alexandra*, p. 93.

45. *The Times*, 13 March 1868.

46. QV to Vicky, 22 April 1868, in Fulford, *Your Dear Letter*, p. 185.

47. QV to Vicky, 2 May 1868, in ibid., p. 186.

48. RA VIC/Add A3/108, B to QV, 1 May 1868.

49. RA VIC/Add A3/125, B to QV, 9 February 1869.

50. RA VIC/Add A3/128, B to QV, 26 February 1869.

51. QV to Vicky, 13 May 1868, in Fulford, *Your Dear Letter*, p. 189.

52. *The Times*, 20 May 1868. QV to Theodore Martin, 14 May 1868, in Buckle, *Letters* (2nd series), vol. 1, pp. 529–30.

53. Vicky to QV, 12 May 1868, in Fulford, *Your Dear Letter*, p. 187.

54. Hibbert, *Queen Victoria in Her Letters and Journals*, p. 1.

55. "The Donkey's Daughter: Early Memories of Mary Critchley–Salmonson," typescript, n.d.

56. *The Times*, 21 February 1870. Elizabeth Hamilton, *The Warwickshire Scandal* (Michael Russell, 1999), pp. 38–39.

57. Ibid., p. 38.

58. Ibid., pp. 70–74. *An Official Report of the Cause Célèbre Mordaunt v. Mordaunt, Cole and Johnstone* (Evans, Oliver, 1870), pp. 67, 71. *The Times*, 21, 26 February 1870.

59. QV to Vicky, 10 July 1868, in Fulford, *Your Dear Letter*, p. 201.

60. RA VIC/Add A3/113, B to QV, 27 September 1868. RA VIC Add A3/112, B to QV, 15 August 1868.

61. RA VIC/Z449/20, QV to B, October 1868 (copy).

62. Alix to QV, 28 October 1868, in Battiscombe, *Queen Alexandra*, p. 98.

63. RA VIC/Z449/27, B to QV, 5 November 1868.

64. RA VIC/Add A3/118, B to QV, 31 December 1868.

65. RA VIC/Add A3/117, B to QV, 24 December 1868.

66. QV to Vicky, 29 December 1868, in Fulford, *Your Dear Letter*, p. 208.

67. RA VIC/Add A3/128, B to QV, 26 February 1869.

68. RA VIC/Add A3/117, B to QV, 24 December 1868.
69. Vicky to QV, 23 January 1869, in Fulford, *Your Dear Letter*, p. 220.
70. QV to Vicky, 27 January 1869, in Fulford, *Your Dear Letter*, p. 221.
71. RA VIC/Add A3/121, QV to B, 18 January 1869 (copy).
72. RA VIC/Add A3/121, QV to B, 18 January 1869 (copy). RA VIC/Add A3/113, B to QV, 27 September 1868.
73. RA VIC/Add A3/125, B to QV, 9 February 1869.
74. Ibid.
75. RA VIC/Add A3/135, B to QV, 7 May 1869.
76. *The Times*, 17 February 1870, evidence of Elizabeth Hancox, nurse.
77. *The Times*, 19 February 1870, evidence of Sir Charles Mordaunt.
78. Hamilton, *Warwickshire Scandal*, pp. 128, 138.
79. Gail Savage, "Erotic Stories and Public Decency: Newspaper Reporting of Divorce Proceedings in England," *Historical Journal*, vol. 41 (1998), p. 513.
80. Hamilton, *Warwickshire Scandal*, pp. 166, 177.
81. Copenhagen Letters, Box 103, Alix to Minnie, 21 February 1870.
82. Gunton Bill of Fare, 10, 13, 14 January 1870 (Gerard Stamp).
83. Bodleian Library, Lincolnshire Papers, MS Film 1120, Charles Carrington to his mother, 10 January 1870.
84. Copenhagen Letters, Box 103, Alix to Minnie, 21 February 1870. Lord Suffield, *My Memories* (Herbert Jenkins, 1913), pp. 154–55.
85. Hamilton, *Warwickshire Scandal*, pp. 203, 223–24.
86. RA VIC/Z449/66, B to QV, 10 February 1870.
87. RA VIC/Z449/70, B to QV, 14 February 1870.
88. Copenhagen Letters, Box 103, Alix to Minnie, 21 February 1870.
89. Hamilton, *Warwickshire Scandal*, pp. 293–310.
90. *Kilvert's Diary*, ed. William Plomer (Jonathan Cape, 1938), vol. 1, p. 40.
91. RA VIC/Add A25/279, QV to Colonel Elphinstone, 24 February 1870.
92. Bodleian Library, Lincolnshire Papers, MS Film 1120, Carrington Diary, 16 February 1870.
93. *Official Report of the Cause Célèbre Mordaunt v. Mordaunt*, pp. 54–55.
94. RA VIC/Z449/74, B to QV, 17 [*sic—actually 18*] February 1870.
95. RA VIC/Z449/79, Lord Hatherley to QV, 21 February 1870.
96. RA VIC/Z449/77, General Knollys to QV, 18 February 1870.
97. RA VIC/Z449/79, Lord Hatherley to QV, 21 February 1870.
98. Alexander Cockburn to POW, 21 February 1870, in Giles St. Aubyn, *Edward VII* (Collins, 1979), pp. 161–62.
99. RA VIC/Add C07/9, Bundle "Mordaunt Case," B to Francis Knollys, n.d.
100. Hamilton, *Warwickshire Scandal*, pp. 350–51.
101. RA VIC/Z449/83, B to QV, 23 February 1870.
102. *The Gladstone Diaries*, vol. 7, ed. H. C. G. Matthew (Clarendon Press, 1982), p. 242, 23 February 1870.
103. RA VIC/Z449/93, Delane to Arthur Helps, 25 February 1870.
104. Copenhagen Letters, Box 103, Alix to Minnie, 21 February 1870.
105. See Hamilton, *Warwickshire Scandal*.
106. Hugh Montgomery-Massingberd, *Lord of the Dance* (Debrett's, 1986), pp. 90, 120.
107. QV to Vicky, 2 March 1870, in Fulford, *Your Dear Letter*, p. 263.

108. *Reynolds's Newspaper,* 20 March 1871.
109. QV to Vicky, 2 March 1870, in Fulford, *Your Dear Letter,* p. 263.
110. RA VIC/Z449/86, William Gladstone to B, 23 February 1870.
111. RA VIC/Z449/94, QV to Alix, 13 March 1870 (copy).
112. Bodleian Library, Lincolnshire Papers, MS Film 1120, Carrington Diary, 20 March 1870.
113. Hamilton, *Warwickshire Scandal,* pp. 386, 426.

CHAPTER 9: ANNUS HORRIBILIS 1870–71

1. Bodleian Library, Lincolnshire Papers, MS Film 1120, Carrington Diary, 13 June 1870.
2. Hamilton, *Warwickshire Scandal,* p. 381.
3. Camp, *Royal Mistresses,* p. 357; *The Times,* 21, 25 April 1870; *Reynolds's Newspaper,* 24 April 1870.
4. *A Selection from the Diaries of Edward Henry Stanley, 15th Earl of Derby (1826–93): Between September 1869 and March 1878* (hereafter *Derby Diaries 1869–78*), ed. John Vincent (Royal Historical Society, 1994), p. 77 (5 March 1871).
5. See Dorothy Thompson, *Queen Victoria* (Virago, 1990), ch. 4.
6. Fitzwilliam Museum, Wilfrid Blunt Papers, MS 33–1975, Diary, 18 August 1885.
7. *Selected Extracts from the Journal of Lewis Harcourt,* ed. Patrick Jackson (Fairleigh Dickinson University Press, 2006), pp. 81–82, 17 February 1885.
8. Downer, *Queen's Knight,* pp. 178, 183–84.
9. Ibid., p. 182.
10. RA VIC/Add A3/115, B to QV, 9 December 1868.
11. Fitzwilliam, Blunt Papers, MS 33–1975, Diary, 18 August 1885, Wilfrid Blunt's record of conversation with Catherine Walters, aka Skittles. Skittles is an unreliable witness, but this story seems to fit the facts. Bertie was at Abergeldie from 26 August to 13 September 1869. (*The Times,* 30 August, 13 September 1869.) Boehm was at Balmoral at the same time. See Mark Stocker, *Royalist and Realist: The Life and Work of Sir Joseph Edgar Boehm* (New York: Garland, 1988), pp. 80–88.
12. RA VIC/A17/496, B to Princess Louise, 13 September 1871.
13. RA VIC/A17/332, B to Princess Louise, 5 December 1869.
14. RA VIC/Z173/13, QV to Princess Louise, 21 February 1884.
15. Downer, *Queen's Knight,* p. 255. Jehanne Wake, *Princess Louise* (Collins, 1988), pp. 116–17. According to a story printed in *Reynolds's Newspaper* (26 March 1876), Duckworth himself informed the Queen of Louise's inappropriate feelings toward him, offering to resign in order to avoid scandal.
16. RA VIC/Z173/13, QV to Princess Louise, 21 February 1884.
17. RA VIC/Z173/12, Princess Louise to QV, 19 February 1884.
18. RA VIC/A17/381, B to Princess Louise, 10 October 1870.
19. RA VIC/A17/390, B to QV, 23 October 1870.
20. Copenhagen Letters, Box 103, Alix to Minnie, 6 March 1871.
21. RA VIC/Z449/114, B to QV, 21 July 1870.
22. Bodleian Library, Lincolnshire Papers, MS Film 1120, B to Charles Carrington, 4 September 1870.

23. Lee, *Edward VII*, vol. 1, pp. 308–10.

24. Bodleian Library, Lincolnshire Papers, MS Film 1120, Carrington Diary, 14 March 1871.

25. Ibid., 4 July 1871.

26. Camp, *Royal Mistresses*, pp. 357–58; Anita Leslie, *Edwardians in Love* (Hutchinson, 1972), p. 205; Simona Pakenham, *60 Miles from England: The English at Dieppe* (Macmillan, 1967), pp. 123–25.

27. Copenhagen Letters, Box 103, Alix to Minnie, 26 November 1870. *The Times*, 11 November 1870. John Martin Robinson, "Sandringham," *Country Life*, 29 May 2008.

28. *A Lonely Business: A Self-Portrait of James Pope-Hennessy*, ed. Peter Quennell (Weidenfeld and Nicolson, 1981), p. 230.

29. Copenhagen Letters, Box 103, Alix to Minnie, 26 November 1870. *The Times*, 3 December 1870.

30. Copenhagen Letters, Box 103, Alix to Minnie, 26 November 1870. RA VIC/Z449/128, Mrs. Stonor to QV, 8 April 1871.

31. Copenhagen Letters, Box 103, Alix to Minnie, 16 March 1871.

32. Copenhagen Letters, Box 103, Alix to Minnie, 17 February 1871.

33. RA VIC/T5/43, B to QV, 10 April 1871.

34. RA VIC/Z449/127, Mrs. Stonor to QV, 7 April 1871.

35. RA VIC/T5/36, B to QV, 6 April 1871.

36. RA VIC/Z449/127, Mrs. Stonor to QV, 7 April 1871.

37. RA VIC/T5/36, B to QV, 6 April 1871.

38. RA VIC/Add A8/43, Mrs. Stonor to the Duchess of Teck, 7 April 1871.

39. RA VIC/Z449/131, Mrs. Stonor to QV, 10 April 1871.

40. RA VIC/Z449/127, Mrs. Stonor to QV, 7 April 1871.

41. RA VIC/Z449/128, Mrs. Stonor to QV, 8 April 1871.

42. RA VIC/T5/40, B to QV, 8 April 1871.

43. RA VIC/Z449/132, Mrs. Stonor to QV, 11 April 1871. RA VIC/T5/42, B to QV, 9 April 1871.

44. RA VIC/Z449/132, Mrs. Stonor to QV, 11 April 1871.

45. Ibid.

46. Ibid.

47. RA VIC/Z449/140, Dean of Windsor to QV, 18 April 1871.

48. Copenhagen Letters, Box 103, Alix to Minnie, 10 September 1873.

49. RA VIC/T5/38, B to QV, 7 April 1871.

50. RA VIC/Z449/140, Dean of Windsor to QV, 18 April 1871.

51. Copenhagen Letters, Box 103, Alix to Minnie, 27 May 1871.

52. RA VIC/Z459/15, Orders from Lord Chamberlain's Office for Court Going into Mourning for Infant Prince John, 8 April 1871.

53. RA VIC/T5/43, B to QV, 10 April 1871.

54. *Reynolds's Newspaper*, 16 April 1871.

55. *Reynolds's Newspaper*, 7 May 1871.

56. *The New York Times*, 8 May 1871, quoted in *Reynolds's Newspaper*, 4 June 1871.

57. Richard Williams, *The Contentious Crown* (Ashgate, 1997), p. 38.

58. "The Monarchy and the People," *The Economist*, 22 July 1871, in *Collected Works of Walter Bagehot*, vol. 5, ed. Norman St. John Stevas (*The Economist*, 1974), p. 431.

59. Solomon Temple, Builder, *What Does She Do with It?* (Alfred Boot, 1871), p. 71.

60. Quoted in Rappaport, *Magnificent Obsession,* pp. 207–8.

61. William Gladstone to Lord Granville, 26 September 1870, in *The Political Correspondence of Mr. Gladstone and Lord Granville 1868–1876,* ed. Agatha Ramm (Royal Historical Society, 1952), vol. 1, p. 133.

62. William Gladstone to Lord Granville, 27 September 1871, in Ramm, *Political Correspondence,* vol. 2, p. 261.

63. *Reynolds's Newspaper,* 24 September 1871.

64. QVJ, 20, 28 September 1871, in Buckle, *Letters* (2nd series), vol. 2, pp. 160–61.

65. William Gladstone to Lord Granville, 1 October 1871, in Ramm, *Political Correspondence,* vol. 2, p. 264.

66. William Gladstone to Lord Granville, 5 October 1871, in ibid., vol. 2, p. 256.

67. RA VIC/Add A36/360, Henry Ponsonby to Mary Ponsonby, 27 September 1871.

68. RA VIC/Add A36/368, Henry Ponsonby to Mary Ponsonby, 4 October 1871.

69. RA VIC/Add A36/371, Henry Ponsonby to Mary Ponsonby, 7 October 1871.

70. RA VIC/Add C07/1/Vane-Tempest, Susan Vane-Tempest to B, "Tuesday" [26 September 1871].

71. Author email from Stephen Bartley, 9 April 2010. *The Times,* 26 September 1871.

72. QV to Vicky, 25, 28 April, 2, 5 May 1860, in Fulford, *Dearest Child,* pp. 249–52.

73. QV to Vicky, 18 June 1864, in Fulford, *Your Dear Letter,* pp. 347–48. Camp, *Royal Mistresses,* pp. 360–61.

74. RA VIC/Add C07/1/Vane-Tempest, Susan Vane-Tempest to B, "Tuesday" [26 September 1871]. St. Aubyn, *Edward VII,* p. 156.

75. Susan's friend Harriet Whatman told Bertie on 26 September that Susan was within two or three months of "the crisis." (Harriet Whatman to B, 26 September 1871, in St. Aubyn, *Edward VII,* pp. 156–57.) If the baby was due in early December, it was probably conceived in the second week of March.

76. RA VIC/Add C07/1/Vane-Tempest, Susan Vane-Tempest to B, "Monday" [?25 September 1871].

77. "I should indeed have written to Your Royal Highness soon after Your departure for abroad" (i.e. August), but instead she delayed until his return. (RA VIC/Add C07/1/Vane-Tempest, Susan Vane-Tempest to B, "Monday" [?25 September 1871].)

78. RA VIC/Add C07/1/Vane-Tempest, Susan Vane-Tempest to B, "Monday" [?25 September 1871].

79. RA VIC/Add C07/1/Vane-Tempest, Susan Vane-Tempest to Francis Knollys, "Tuesday" [?26 September 1871].

80. RA VIC/Add C07/1/Vane-Tempest, Susan Vane-Tempest to B, "Tuesday" [26 September 1871].

81. RA VIC/Add C07/1/Vane-Tempest, Susan Vane-Tempest to B, "Monday" [?25 September 1871].

82. Harriet Whatman to B, 26 September 1871, in St. Aubyn, *Edward VII,* pp. 156–57.

83. RA VIC/Add C07/1/Vane-Tempest, Susan Vane-Tempest to Dr. Clayton, 29 December 1871.

84. RA VIC/Add C07/1/Vane-Tempest, Susan Vane-Tempest to Francis Knollys, 3 February 1872.

85. Susan Vane-Tempest to B, 8 February 1872, in St. Aubyn, *Edward VII*, p. 159.

86. Author email from Anthony Camp, 18 March 2008.

87. Author email from James Lefanu, 26 November 2009.

88. Anthony Camp's *Royal Mistresses and Bastards*, pp. 349–78, is definitive: a meticulously researched examination of Bertie's mistresses and their alleged illegitimate children.

89. Dennis Friedman, *Inheritance: A Psychological History of the Royal Family* (Sidgwick and Jackson, 1993), pp. 50–51.

90. Peter Gay, *The Bourgeois Experience, vol.1, Education of the Senses* (Oxford University Press, 1984), pp. 252–53. Hickman, *Courtesans*, pp. 190–95.

91. RA VIC/Add C07/1/0691, B to Francis Knollys, 20 July 1871.

92. See St. Aubyn, *Edward VII*, pp. 151–55.

93. RA VIC/Add C07/1/Barucci, B to Knollys, 11 September 1871. RA VIC/Add C07/1/Barucci, telegram, Kanné to Francis Knollys, 7 November 1871.

94. RA VIC/Add C07/1/Barucci, Kanné to Francis Knollys, "Thursday evening" [9 November 1871].

95. RA VIC/Add C07/1/Barucci, B to Francis Knollys, 11 September 1871.

96. RA VIC/Add C07/1/Barucci, Kanné to Francis Knollys, "Thursday evening" [9 November 1871].

97. RA VIC/Add C07/1/Barucci, telegram, Francis Knollys to Kanné, 9 November 1871.

98. RA VIC/Add C07/1/Barucci, Kanné to Francis Knollys, n.d. [November 1871].

99. *Reynolds's Newspaper,* 26 November 1871.

100. *The Times,* 9 December 1871. Tom Cullen, *The Empress Brown* (Bodley Head, 1969), p. 151.

101. Bodleian Library, Lincolnshire Papers, MS Film 1120, Carrington Diary, 30 October 1871. *The Times,* 1 December 1871.

102. Wellcome Library, William Gull Papers, MS 5873, B/4, Gull's Notes on Prince of Wales's Illness, 13 November 1871.

103. Bodleian Library, Lincolnshire Papers, MS Film 1120, Carrington Diary, 14, 15, 16, 17 November 1871. The shoot was at Gayhurst, near Gerrards Cross.

104. Alix to Louise, 23 November 1871, in Longford, *Darling Loosy,* p. 158.

105. Wellcome, Gull Papers, MS 5873, B/4, Gull's Notes on Prince's Illness, 16–22 November 1871.

106. Wellcome, Gull Papers, MS 5873, B/4, Gull's Notes on Prince's Illness, 11 December 1871.

107. Alix to Louise, 29 November 1871, in Longford, *Darling Loosy,* p. 159. Copenhagen Letters, Box 103, Alix to Minnie, 22 November 1871.

108. Wellcome, Gull Papers, MS 5873, B/7, Gull's Notes on Prince's Illness, 27 November 1871.

109. Alix to Louise, 29 November 1871, in *Darling Loosy,* p. 159.

110. Lady Macclesfield, quoted in Battiscombe, *Queen Alexandra,* p. 115.

111. Ibid., p. 114.

112. *The Times,* 27, 28 November 1871.

113. QVJ, 27 November 1871, in Buckle, *Letters* (2nd series), vol. 2, p. 169.

114. RA QVJ, 29 November 1871.

115. RA VIC/Add A36/395, Henry Ponsonby to Mary Ponsonby, 29 November 1871.

116. Alice to Louis of Hesse, 29 November 1871, in Noel, *Princess Alice,* p. 172.

117. RA QVJ, 30 November 1871.

118. RA QVJ, 1 December 1871.

119. *The Times,* 2 December 1871.

120. RA VIC/T5/50, Lady Macclesfield to the Duchess of Teck, 4 December 1871.

121. Wellcome, Gull Papers, MS 5873, B/14, Gull's Notes on Prince's Illness, 4 December 1871.

122. Wellcome, Gull Papers, MS 5873, Gull's Notes on Prince's Illness, A/27, 8 December 1871; B/17, 8 December 1871.

123. *The Times,* 9 December 1871.

124. RA QVJ, 8 December 1871.

125. Wellcome, Gull Papers, MS 5873, J/3, 29 April 1889, MS page re 8 December 1871.

126. RA QVJ, 8 December 1871.

127. RA VIC/A36/401, Henry Ponsonby to Mary Ponsonby, 13 December 1871.

128. *The Graphic,* 9 December 1871.

129. *The Times,* 11 December 1871.

130. Wellcome, Gull Papers, MS 5873, A1/97, Gull's drafts of press bulletins, 10 December 1871. *The Times,* 11 December 1871.

131. Wellcome, Gull Papers, MS 5873, B/25, Gull's Notes on Prince's Illness, 11 December 1871.

132. RA QVJ, 11 December 1871. RA VIC/T5/64, Lady Macclesfield to Duchess of Teck, 13 December 1871.

133. RA VIC/Add A36/395, Henry Ponsonby to Mary Ponsonby, 29 November 1871.

134. QV to Arthur, 30 December 1871, in Downer, *Queen's Knight,* p. 266. RA VIC/Add A36/396, Henry Ponsonby to Mary Ponsonby, 30 November 1871.

135. Lady Macclesfield, quoted in Battiscombe, *Queen Alexandra,* p. 117.

136. William Gladstone to Lord Granville, 10 December 1871, in Ramm, *Political Correspondence,* vol. 2, p. 290.

137. QVJ, 13 December 1871, in Buckle, *Letters* (2nd series), vol. 2, p. 178.

138. RA VIC/Add A36/401, Henry Ponsonby to Mary Ponsonby, 13 December 1871.

139. RA VIC/T5/64, Lady Macclesfield to the Duchess of Teck, 13 December 1871.

140. QVJ, 14 December 1871, in Buckle, *Letters* (2nd series), vol. 2, p. 179.

141. Plomer, *Kilvert's Diary,* vol. 1, pp. 155, 157.

CHAPTER 10: RESURRECTION? 1871–75

1. RA VIC/Add A36/405, Henry Ponsonby to Mary Ponsonby, 16 December 1871.

2. RA VIC/T5/80, Francis Knollys to Henry Ponsonby, 19 December 1871.

3. Ibid.

4. RA VIC/Add A36/371, Henry Ponsonby to Mary Ponsonby, 7 October 1871.

5. QVJ, 21 December 1871, in Buckle, *Letters* (2nd series), vol. 2, p. 181.

6. Gladstone's Memorandum, 21 December 1871, in *The Gladstone Diaries,* vol. 8, ed. H. C. G. Matthew (Clarendon Press, 1982), p. 81.

7. Wellcome Library, Gull Papers, MS 5873, A/84, Gull's Bulletin, 27 December 1871; B/46, Gull's notes, 22 December 1871. RA VIC/Add A36/410, Henry Ponsonby to Mary Ponsonby, 31 December 1871.

8. QV to Vicky, 30 December 1871, in Fulford, *Darling Child,* p. 21.

9. RA VIC/Z450/41, James Paget to QV, 5 June 1872.

10. RA VIC/Add A17/531, QV to Princess Louise, 16 February 1872. RA QVJ, 12 February 1872. RA VIC/Z450/11, William Gull to QV, 25 February 1872.

11. RA VIC/Add A17/532, Leopold to Louise, 21 February 1872.

12. Alix to Louise, 7 February 1872, in Longford, *Darling Loosy,* p. 164.

13. Copenhagen Letters, Box 103, Alix to Minnie, 8 January 1873.

14. QV to Vicky, 14 February 1872, in Fulford, *Darling Child,* p. 28.

15. See RA Photograph Collection, Wales Family Photographs, RCINs 2108424–428, February 1872; RCIN 2108454, April 1872.

16. RA VIC/Add A17/532, Leopold to Louise, 21 February 1872.

17. Wellcome, Gull Papers, MS 5873, F/S/1–2, Alix to William Gull, 16 January 1872.

18. *The Economist,* 24 February 1874, in St. John Stevas, *Collected Works,* vol. 5, p. 439.

19. David Cannadine, "The Context, Performance and Meaning of Ritual: The British Monarchy and the 'Invention of Tradition,'" in *The Invention of Tradition,* ed. E. Hobsbawm and T. Ranger (Cambridge University Press, 1983), p. 118. William M. Kuhn, *Democratic Royalism* (Macmillan, 1996), pp. 43–44.

20. Kuhn, *Democratic Royalism,* pp. 43–44.

21. RA VIC/Z450/2, Alix to QV, 30 January 1872.

22. QV to Vicky, 28 February 1872, in Fulford, *Darling Child,* p. 32.

23. QVJ, 27 February 1872, in Buckle, *Letters* (2nd series), vol. 2, p. 194.

24. QV to Vicky, 28 February 1872, in Fulford, *Darling Child,* p. 31.

25. QVJ, 27 February 1872, in Buckle, *Letters* (2nd series), vol. 2, p. 195.

26. B to QV, 27 February 1872, in Buckle, *Letters* (2nd series), vol. 2, p. 196.

27. Alix to QV, n.d. [December 1871], in Lee, *Edward VII,* vol. 1, p. 323.

28. William Gladstone to Henry Ponsonby, 22 December 1871, in Philip Guedella, *The Queen and Mr. Gladstone* (Hodder and Stoughton, 1933), vol. 1, p. 321.

29. Matthew, *Gladstone Diaries,* vol. 8, p. 173, 2 July 1872.

30. William Gladstone to QV, 5 July 1872, in Guedella, *Queen and Mr. Gladstone,* vol. 1, pp. 351–8.

31. RA VIC/Z459/35, QV's memo dictated to Henry Ponsonby, 9 July 1872.

32. Guedella, *Queen and Mr. Gladstone,* vol. 1, pp. 359–61.

33. William Gladstone to QV, 5 July 1872, in ibid., vol. 1, p. 358.

34. Matthew, *Gladstone Diaries,* vol. 8, p. 173, 4 July 1873; William Gladstone to Lord Granville, 18 January 1872, in Ramm, *Political Correspondence,* vol. 2, p. 300.

35. QV to Vicky, 5 June 1872, in Fulford, *Darling Child,* p. 47.

36. William Gladstone to Lord Halifax, 28 August 1872, in Matthew, *Gladstone Diaries,* vol. 8, p. 202.

37. Lord Granville to William Gladstone, 4 September 1872, in Ramm, *Political Correspondence,* vol. 2, pp. 342–43.

38. William Gladstone to QV, 28 August 1872: QV to William Gladstone, 2 September 1872, in Guedella, *Queen and Mr. Gladstone,* vol. 2, pp. 376–79.

39. QV to William Gladstone, 18 November 1872, in ibid., vol. 2, p. 385.

40. Matthew, *Gladstone Diaries,* vol. 8, p. 251, 30 November, 1 December 1872.

41. Francis Knollys to Henry Ponsonby, 8 December 1872, in Magnus, *Edward VII,* pp. 123–24.

42. Lord Granville to Henry Ponsonby, 26 December 1871, in Arthur Ponsonby, *Henry Ponsonby* (Macmillan, 1943), p. 102.

43. RA VIC/Add A36/640, Henry Ponsonby to Mary Ponsonby, 17 September 1873.

44. William Gladstone to Lord Granville, 15 January 1873, in Ramm, *Political Correspondence,* vol. 2, p. 375.

45. QV to Vicky, 20 December 1871, in Fulford, *Darling Child,* p. 20.

46. Magnus, *Edward VII,* p. 125.

47. QV to Vicky, 3 April 1875, in Pope-Hennessy, *Queen Mary,* p. 74n.

48. Vincent, *Derby Diaries, 1869–78,* pp. 178–79 (2 September 1874), recording Disraeli's conversation with QV.

49. Diary of Lady Frederick Cavendish, 20 December 1872, in Battiscombe, *Queen Alexandra,* p. 127.

50. Tosh, *Man's Place,* ch. 4. Nancy Ellenberger, "George Wyndham," *Journal of British Studies,* vol. 39 (2000), pp. 493–94.

51. Rohl, *Young Wilhelm,* p. 117.

52. Vicky to QV, 6 June 1874, in Fulford, *Darling Child,* p. 141.

53. QV to Vicky, 16 June 1874, in Fulford, *Darling Child,* p. 143. Pope-Hennessy, *Queen Mary,* pp. 56–57.

54. QV to Vicky, 30 April 1870, in Fulford, *Your Dear Letter,* p. 277.

55. Letter from QV, 17 March 1872, in Battiscombe, *Queen Alexandra,* pp. 122–23.

56. Benjamin Disraeli to Lady Chesterfield, 15 December 1873, in *Letters of Disraeli to Lady Bradford and Lady Chesterfield,* ed. Marquis of Zetland (Ernest Benn, 1929), vol. 1, pp. 291–93.

57. RA VIC/Add A36/959, Henry Ponsonby to Mary Ponsonby, 12 September 1875.

58. See Richard Davenport-Hines, "John Dalton," *ODNB.*

59. RA VIC/Add A36/776, Henry Ponsonby to QV, 9 August 1874.

60. RA VIC/Add A36/474, Henry Ponsonby to Mary Ponsonby, 20 December 1872.

61. [A. A. Doughty and S. O. Beeton], *Beeton's Christmas Annual: The Coming K—* (Ward, Lock and Tyler, 1872), pp. 39–40.

62. Fitzwilliam, Wilfrid Blunt Papers, MS 398–1975, Diary, 5 March 1909. See Vane, *Affair of State,* pp. 49–69.

63. Fitzwilliam, Blunt Papers, MS 398–1975, Diary, 5 March 1909.

64. Ibid.

65. Stocker, *Royalist and Realist,* pp. 283–84.

66. Fitzwilliam, Blunt Papers, MS 7–1975, Diary, 15 April 1906.

67. Leo McKinstry, *Rosebery* (John Murray, 2005), pp. 43–44.

68. RA VIC/Add A36/588, Henry Ponsonby to Mary Ponsonby, 18 July 1873.

69. RA VIC/Add A36/623, Henry Ponsonby to Mary Ponsonby, 3 September 1873. For Mrs. Sloane-Stanley see Mrs. Hywfa Willliams, *It Was Such Fun* (Hutchinson, 1935), p. 23.

70. Lord Rossmore, *Things I Can Tell* (Eveleigh Nash, 1912). Leslie, *Edwardians in Love*, pp. 104–5. Camp, *Royal Mistresses*, pp. 362–63. Tim Coates claims that Patsy began an affair with Bertie in 1870, when she was sixteen, and repeats a story that "one, two or even three" of her children were Bertie's. (*Patsy*, Bloomsbury, 2004, p. 7.)

71. Copenhagen Letters, Box 103, Alix to Minnie, 2 May 1873.

72. Author email from Anna Kirk, 23 May 2011.

73. *Freeman's Journal*, 28 June 1873.

74. Copenhagen Letters, Box 103, Alix to Minnie, 16 September 1872. Pope-Hennessy, *Queen Mary*, p. 53.

75. Copenhagen Letters, Box 103, Alix to Minnie, n.d. [August 1873].

76. Copenhagen Letters, Box 103, Alix to Minnie, 10 September 1873.

77. Copenhagen Letters, Box 103, Alix to Minnie, 24 December 1872: "I must to bed as my Bertie, I think, will be coming immediately"; Alix to Minnie, 19 March 1874: "I now only hope that we are not, both of us, in a certain blessed condition."

78. RA VIC/Add C07/1/Cornwallis-West, Francis Knollys to Henry Ponsonby, 29 December 1873. See Ramm, *Political Correspondence*, vol. 2, p. 442.

79. Copenhagen Letters, Box 103, Alix to Minnie, 24 March 1874.

80. Copenhagen Letters, Box 103, Alix to Minnie, 22 November 1874.

81. RA VIC/Add A36/801, Henry Ponsonby to Mary Ponsonby, 1 September 1874.

82. *The Times*, 1 October 1874.

83. QV to Vicky, 20 October 1874, in Fulford, *Darling Child*, p. 158.

84. RA VIC/Add C07/1/0889, Henry Ponsonby to Francis Knollys, 15 October 1874.

85. RA VIC/T5/131, Benjamin Disraeli to B, 9 October 1874.

86. RA VIC/T5/133, B to Benjamin Disraeli, 7 October 1874. Marquis of Zetland, *Letters of Disraeli*, vol. 1, p. 160.

87. *The Times*, 19 October 1874. RA VIC/Add A36/826, Henry Ponsonby to Mary Ponsonby, 19 October 1874.

88. RA VIC/Z450/124, William Knollys to QV, 14 September 1874.

89. Hertford Record Office, Lytton Papers, DE/K/C40/41, Robert Lytton to John Forster, 29 October 1874.

90. Copenhagen Letters, Box 103, Alix to Minnie, 3 September–20 October 1874.

91. *The Times*, 19 October 1874, gives the list of names. See Richard Davenport-Hines, *A Night at the Majestic: Proust and the Great Modernist Dinner Party of 1922* (Faber, 2006), p. 111; Philippe Jullian, *Edward and the Edwardians* (Sidgwick and Jackson, 1967), pp. 98–99.

92. *The Times*, 10 October 1874, quoting *Le Figaro*.

93. Marquis of Zetland, *Letters of Disraeli*, vol. 1, pp. 166–67.

94. Quoted in George D. Painter, *Marcel Proust*, vol. 1 (Chatto and Windus, 1959), p. 162. See Camp, *Royal Mistresses*, pp. 361–62.

95. Hertford Record Office, Lytton Papers, DE/K/C40/41, Robert Lytton to John Forster, 29 October 1874.

96. Paris Police archives, cited in Hibbert, *Edward VII,* p. 122.

97. Painter, *Proust,* vol. 1, p. 162.

98. *The Daily News* (UK), 24 October 1874. Author email from Anthony Camp, 18 November 2009.

99. Hertford Record Office, Lytton Papers, DE/K/C40/41, Robert Lytton to John Forster, 29 October 1874.

100. Leslie, *Edwardians in Love,* pp. 70–72. Painter, *Proust,* vol. 1, pp. 154–55.

101. *The Times,* 23 March 1874.

102. RA VIC/T6/27, Benjamin Disraeli to Henry Ponsonby, 1 July 1875.

103. RA VIC/Add A36/960, Henry Ponsonby to Mary Ponsonby, 13 September 1875.

104. RA VIC/Add A36/921, Henry Ponsonby to Mary Ponsonby, 5 June 1875.

105. Vincent, *Derby Diaries 1869–78,* p. 221 (5 June 1875).

106. RA VIC/T6/22, Note by Henry Ponsonby, [7] June 1875.

107. RA VIC/T6/18, Francis Knollys to Henry Ponsonby, 4 June 1875.

108. RA VIC/T6/22, Note by Henry Ponsonby, June 1875.

109. Vincent, *Derby Diaries 1869–78,* p. 229 (14 July 1875).

110. Ibid., pp. 223, 227–28, 229–50 (9, 12 June, 3 July 1875).

111. Marquis of Zetland, *Letters of Disraeli,* vol. 1, p. 227.

112. Vincent, *Derby Diaries 1869–78,* pp. 203–4 (31 March 1875).

113. Copenhagen Letters, Box 103, Alix to Minnie, 5 April–8 May 1875; Marquis of Zetland, *Letters of Disraeli,* vol. 1, p. 224.

114. RA VIC/T6/48, B to Benjamin Disraeli, 13 September 1875.

115. RA VIC/Z468/46, Benjamin Disraeli to QV, n.d.

116. Benjamin Disraeli to Lady Chesterfield, 4 October 1875, in Marquis of Zetland, *Letters of Disraeli,* vol. 1, p. 224.

117. RA VIC/Z468/56, Helena to QV, 11 October 1875.

118. Copenhagen Letters, Box 103, Alix to Minnie, 26 October 1875.

119. RA VIC/Z468/67, Alix to QV, 14 October 1875.

CHAPTER 11: INDIA 1875–76

1. Bodleian Library, Lincolnshire Papers, MS Film 1120, Charles Carrington to his mother, 22 October 1875.

2. Copenhagen Letters, Box 103, Alix to Minnie, 26 October 1875.

3. B to Lord Granville, 29 October 1875, in Lee, *Edward VII,* vol. 1, p. 379.

4. QV to Vicky, 4 August 1875, in Fulford, *Darling Child,* p. 187.

5. RA VIC/T6/56, Sir Thomas Biddulph to Bartle Frere, 6 October 1875. RA VIC/Add A36/959, Henry Ponsonby to Mary Ponsonby, 12 September 1875.

6. RA VIC/Add A36/964, Henry Ponsonby to Mary Ponsonby, 17 September 1875. Turner, *Court of St. James's,* pp. 294–95.

7. RA VIC/Add A36/959, Henry Ponsonby to Mary Ponsonby, 12 September 1875.

8. Bodleian Library, Lincolnshire Papers, MS Film 1120, Charles Carrington to his mother, 5 November 1875.

9. BL, India Office Collections, Bourne and Shepherd's Royal Photographic Album, HRH's Tour in India (1876).

10. Bodleian Library, Lincolnshire Papers, MS Film 1120, Charles Carrington to

his mother, 22 October 1875. RA VIC/Z468/87, Francis Knollys to Henry Ponsonby, 7 November 1875.

11. BL, India Office, MSS Eur C144/12, Arthur Ellis to Lord Salisbury, 31 August 1875; Salisbury to Northbrook, 1 September 1875. *The Times,* 19 November 1875.

12. *The Times,* 19 November 1875. W. H. Russell, *The Prince of Wales's Tour* (Sampson Low, 1877), p. 7.

13. Bodleian Library, Lincolnshire Papers, MS Film 1120, Charles Carrington to his mother, 5 November 1875.

14. Lord Suffield, *My Memories* (Herbert Jenkins, 1913), p. 160. See Katherine Prior, "Edward Bradford," *ODNB.*

15. RA VIC/Add A2/6, QV to B, 26 November 1875. RA VIC/Add A2/11, QV to B, 31 December 1875.

16. Lord Northbrook to QV, 13 November 1875, in Buckle, *Letters* (2nd series), vol. 2, p. 431.

17. *The Times,* 6 December 1875.

18. Ibid., 7 December 1875.

19. Bodleian Library, Lincolnshire Papers, MS Film 1120, Charles Carrington to his mother, 22 November 1875. See David Gilmour, *The Ruling Caste: Imperial Lives in the Victorian Raj* (John Murray, 2005), pp. 196–97.

20. *The Times,* 20 December 1875.

21. BL, India Office, MSS Eur C144/12/64, Lord Salisbury to Lord Northbrook, 22 July 1875.

22. Bodleian Library, Lincolnshire Papers, MS Film 1120, Charles Carrington to his mother, 14 November 1875.

23. Russell, *Prince of Wales's Tour,* pp. 276–84. *The Times,* 13 December 1875.

24. Antony Taylor, "'Pig-Sticking Princes': Royal Hunting, Moral Outrage, and the Republican Opposition to Animal Abuse in 19th and early 20th c Britain," *History,* vol. 89 (2004), p. 44.

25. *Reynolds's Newspaper,* 19 December 1875.

26. Ibid., 16 January 1876.

27. QV to Vicky, 2 February 1876, in Fulford, *Darling Child,* p. 204.

28. Bartle Frere to QV, 10 February 1876, in Lee, *Edward VII,* vol. 1, p. 385.

29. Russell, *Prince of Wales's Tour,* p. 461.

30. RA VIC/Z469/29, Extract from Daly's Report, n.d.

31. *The Times,* 31 January 1876. Suffield, *Memories,* p. 215.

32. Barbara Strachey, *The Strachey Line* (Gollancz, 1985), p. 159.

33. *The Times,* 31 January, 6 March 1876.

34. B to Lord Granville, 30 November 1875, in Lee, *Edward VII,* vol. 1, p. 399.

35. Quoted in ibid., vol. 1, p. 399.

36. B to QV, 14 November 1875, in ibid. RA VIC/Add A2/8, QV to B, 9 December 1875.

37. BL, India Office, MSS Eur C144/12, Lord Salisbury to Lord Northbrook, 17 December 1875.

38. Lady Strachey's Diary, November 1875, in Diana Souhami, *The Trials of Radclyffe Hall* (Weidenfeld and Nicolson, 1998), p. 37.

39. Strachey, *Strachey Line,* p. 159.

40. Cara Lancaster Papers, B to Mabel Batten, 11 March 1876.

41. Cara Lancaster Papers, Running Order for Radio 4 Programme on Mabel Batten, 3 March 1999. Souhami, *Trials of Radclyffe Hall,* pp. 35–39. Camp, *Royal Mistresses,* pp. 363–64.
42. Battiscombe, *Queen Alexandra,* pp. 130–31.
43. RA VIC/Add A2/19, QV to B, 19 February 1876.
44. *Reynolds's Newspaper,* 13 February 1876.
45. *The Times,* 9 February 1876.
46. Walter L. Arnstein, "Queen Victoria Opens Parliament," *Historical Research,* vol. 63 (1990), pp. 185–87.
47. RA VIC/Add A2/18, QV to B, 18 February 1876.
48. RA VIC/Add A2/23, QV to B, 17 March 1876. Miles Taylor, "Queen Victoria and India, 1837–61," *Victorian Studies,* vol. 46 (2004), pp. 264–66.
49. RA VIC/Add C07/1/Ponsonby, Francis Knollys to Henry Ponsonby, 7 April 1876, "Confidential."
50. RA VIC/Add C07/1/0992, B to Benjamin Disraeli, 22 April 1876, copy.
51. Francis Knollys to Benjamin Disraeli, 22 April 1876, in Lee, *Edward VII,* vol. 1, p. 403.
52. Russell, *Prince of Wales's Tour,* pp. 469, 471–72, 476, 492.
53. RA VIC/Add A2/24, QV to B, 23 March 1876.
54. *Reynolds's Newspaper,* 5 March 1876.
55. RA VIC/EVIID/20 February 1876.
56. RA GV/AA13/14, B to George, 23 February 1876.

CHAPTER 12: THE AYLESFORD SCANDAL 1876

1. Edward Marjoribanks to the Duke of Marlborough, 1 March 1876, in Randolph Churchill, *Winston S. Churchill: Companion,* vol. 1 (Heinemann, 1967), part 1, p. 29.
2. QV to Ponsonby, [?11 May 1876], in ibid., part 1, p. 41.
3. Aylesford Papers, Packington Hall, Album on Royal Visit, 1874. Lord Aylesford letters to author, 30 October 2006, 3 December 2006. Copenhagen Letters, Box 103, Alix to Minnie, 22 November 1874.
4. Aylesford Papers, Packington Hall, Album on Royal Visit, 1874.
5. See B to Harriett Mordaunt, 30 November and 5 December 1867, in *The Times,* 21 February 1870.
6. Sir William Dugdale, author interview, 10 February 2007.
7. Statement by Lord Blandford, 27 July 1876, in Randolph Churchill, *Churchill: Companion,* vol. 1, part 1, p. 49.
8. Edith Aylesford to Jane, Countess of Aylesford, ?25 February 1876, in Randolph Churchill, *Churchill: Companion,* vol. 1, part 1, p. 27.
9. *The Times,* 4 July 1878.
10. Author interview with Lord Aylesford, November 2006. Randolph Churchill, *Churchill: Companion,* vol. 1, part 1, pp. 26ff. *The Times,* 4 July 1878.
11. Joe Aylesford to Edith Aylesford, 15 February 1876, in Randolph Churchill, *Churchill: Companion,* vol. 1, part 1, p. 26.
12. RA VIC/Add C07/1/1071, Joe Aylesford to Edith Aylesford, telegram (copy), 22 February 1876.

13. RA VIC/Add C07/1/1072, Joe Aylesford to Jane, Countess of Aylesford, telegram (copy), 22 February 1876.

14. Bodleian Libray, Lincolnshire Papers, MS Film 1120, Charles Carrington to his mother, 1 March 1876.

15. RA VIC/Add C07/1/1073, Alix to B, telegram, 23 February 1876.

16. RA VIC/Add C07/1/1075, Alix to B, telegram, 27 February 1876.

17. RA VIC/Add C07/1/1076, B to Alix, telegram, 29 February 1876.

18. RA VIC/Add C07/1/1078, Duchess of Manchester to B, telegram, 27 February 1876.

19. RA VIC/Add C07/1/1079, B to the Duchess of Manchester, telegram, 28 February 1876.

20. RA VIC/Add C07/1/1090, Duchess of Manchester to B, 27 March 1876.

21. Lord Blandford to Randolph Churchill, 5 April 1876, in Randolph Churchill, Churchill: Companion, vol. 1, part 1, p. 36.

22. Lord Lansdowne to B, 29 February 1876, in St. Aubyn, Edward VII, p. 175.

23. B to Lord Lansdowne, 11 May 1876, in ibid.

24. RA VIC/Add C07/1/1080, Randolph Churchill to B, telegram, 28 February 1876.

25. RA VIC/Add C07/1/1081, B to Randolph Churchill, telegram, 29 February 1876.

26. RA VIC/Add C07/1/1087, Randolph Churchill to B, telegram, 4 March 1876.

27. RA VIC/Add C07/1/1088, Randolph Churchill to B, telegram, 4 March 1876.

28. Henry Ponsonby to B, 4 April 1876, in Randolph Churchill, Churchill: Companion, vol. 1, part 1, pp. 33–34.

29. Battiscombe, Queen Alexandra, pp. 132–33. St. Aubyn, Edward VII, pp. 176–77.

30. Battiscombe, Queen Alexandra, pp. 133–34.

31. Ibid., p. 134.

32. The Court Circular for 6 March 1876 reports under both Buckingham Palace and Marlborough House that the princess visited the Queen. (The Times, 7 March 1876.)

33. RA VIC/Add A2/22, QV to B, 10 March 1876.

34. Lord Hardwicke to B, 4 April 1876, in St. Aubyn, Edward VII, p. 179: "I read to [Randolph] the passage in your letter as regarding himself, at the same time saying it was evidently written under great excitement, and that I could not press the mention of Your Royal Highness having a hostile meeting with him."

35. Randolph Churchill to B, 3 April 1876, in St. Aubyn, Edward VII, p. 179.

36. Copenhagen Letters, Box 103, Alix to Minnie, 26 October 1875.

37. Hardwicke to B, 4 April 1876, in St. Aubyn, Edward VII, pp. 178–79.

38. Ibid., p. 188. Francis Knollys to Henry Ponsonby, 17 December 1876, in Randolph Churchill, Churchill: Companion, vol. 1, part 1, p. 37.

39. Henry Ponsonby to Francis Knollys, n.d., in Randolph Churchill, Churchill: Companion, vol. 1, part 1, p. 37.

40. RA VIC/Add C07/1/1137, B to Edith Aylesford, 11 December [1873].

41. RA VIC/Add C07/1/1138, B to Edith Aylesford, 18 December 1873.

42. RA VIC/Add C07/1/1139, B to Edith Aylesford, 26 December 1873.

43. RA VIC/Add C07/1/1112, Lord Hartington to Lord Cairns, 24 July 1876.

44. RA VIC/Add A36/1051, Henry Ponsonby to Mary Ponsonby, 18 April 1876.

45. Randolph Churchill to Jennie Churchill, 20 April 1876, in Randolph Churchill, *Churchill: Companion*, vol. 1, part 1, pp. 39–40.

46. R. F. Foster, *Lord Randolph Churchill* (Oxford University Press, 1988), pp. 16–17; Mrs. George Cornwallis-West, *Reminiscences of Lady Randolph Churchill* (Edward Arnold, 1908), p. 61.

47. RA VIC/Add C07/1/1143, Randolph Churchill to Francis Knollys, "Monday 5th" [1873].

48. RA VIC/Add C07/1/1140, Randolph Churchill to Francis Knollys, "Wed 17th" [September 1873].

49. RA VIC/Add C07/1/1141 and 1142, Randolph Churchill to Francis Knollys, 24 and 26 September 1873.

50. Churchill College, Randolph Churchill Papers, CHAR 28/4/37, Randolph Churchill to Jennie Jerome, 9 March 1874.

51. Quoted in Magnus, *Edward VII*, p. 351.

52. See Anne Sebba, *Jennie Churchill* (John Murray, 2007), pp. 51–52.

53. Leslie, *Edwardians in Love*, p. 191.

54. RA VIC/EVIID/1875: 21 March, 4 April 1875, 15 August.

55. Leslie, *Edwardians in Love*, p. 191.

56. Cornwallis-West, *Reminiscences*, pp. 4–17, 39–49, 60–61.

57. Richard W. Davis, "'We Are All Americans Now!' Anglo-American Marriages in the Later 19th c," *Proceedings of the American Philosophical Society*, vol. 135 (1991), p. 142. See pp. 285–86.

58. Lord Aylesford letters to author, 30 October 2006, 3 December 2006; author interview with Lord Aylesford, 20 November 2006.

59. RA VIC/Add A2/24, QV to B, 23 March 1876.

60. Vincent, *Derby Diaries 1869–78*, p. 291 (19 April 1876). According to Derby's sources, "lodgings had been taken for the prince under an assumed name."

61. Bertie recorded two meetings with Mme. Murrieta in his diary. (RA VIC/EVIID/1875: 20, 23 April.) Author email from Anthony Camp, 17 May 2010.

62. Vincent, *Derby Diaries 1869–78*, p. 203 (31 March 1875). See above, p. 195.

63. Churchill Archives Centre, Jennie Churchill Papers, GBR/0014/CHAR 28/97, Jennie Churchill to Randolph Churchill, 19 April 1876. See J. Mordaunt Crook, *The Rise of the Nouveaux Riches* (John Murray, 1999), p. 241. Cornwallis-West, *Reminiscences*, p. 39.

64. Benjamin Disraeli to B, 20 April 1876, and B's reply, in Lee, *Edward VII*, vol. 1, p. 412.

65. RA VIC/Add C07/1, Arnold White to Francis Knollys, 29 June 1877. See RA VIC/Add C07/1, T. Gibson Bowles to B, 11 June 1877.

66. Quoted in Magnus, *Edward VII*, p. 147.

67. RA VIC/EVIID/1876: 11 May.

68. QV to Vicky, 16 May 1876, in Fulford, *Darling Child*, p. 211.

69. QV to Henry Ponsonby [11 May 1876], in Randolph Churchill, *Churchill: Companion*, vol. 1, part 1, p. 41. RA VIC/T6/88, Francis Knollys to Henry Ponsonby, 2 May 1876.

70. *The Times*, 12 May 1876.

71. Lord Hardwicke to Henry Ponsonby, 12 May 1876, 14 May 1876, in Randolph Churchill, *Churchill: Companion*, vol. 1, part 1, pp. 42–43.

72. Author letter from Lord Aylesford, 3 December 2006.
73. RA VIC/Add C07/1/1089, Lord Aylesford to B, 26 March 1876.
74. RA VIC/Add C07/1/1091, Lord Hardwicke to B, 4 April 1876.
75. Ibid.
76. RA VIC/EVIID/1882: 22–27 March and 31 March.
77. Bodleian Library, Lincolnshire Papers, MS Film 1120, Carrington Diary, New Year 1882.
78. Aylesford Papers, extract from *Parish Magazine,* n.d.
79. RA VIC/EVIID/1885: 14 January.
80. John Vincent, ed., *Later Derby Diaries* (Bristol, 1981), p. 103 (14 January 1885).
81. See Edward Marjoribanks to the Duke of Marlborough, 22 March 1876, in Randolph Churchill, *Churchill: Companion,* vol. 1, part 1, p. 32.
82. Edith Aylesford to Jane, Countess of Aylesford [25 February 1876], in Randolph Churchill, *Churchill: Companion,* vol. 1, part 1, pp. 27–28. *The Times,* 4 July 1878.
83. Williams, *It Was Such Fun,* pp. 75–76. Sophia Murphy, *The Duchess of Devonshire's Ball* (Sidgwick and Jackson, 1984), p. 69.
84. Cornwallis West, *Reminiscences,* p. 68.
85. Lord Cairns to Lord Beaconsfield, 20 September 1876, in Randolph Churchill, *Churchill: Companion,* vol. 1, part 1, p. 55.
86. RA VIC/Add C07/1/1136, Box 3, Lord Cairns to B, 23 July 1885.

CHAPTER 13: LILLIE LANGTRY 1877–78

1. Susan North, "John Redfern & Sons, 1847–1892," *Costume,* vol. 42 (2008). Author email from Kate Strasdin, 24 March 2011.
2. National Portrait Gallery, Photograph of Alix by James Russell, Chichester, August 1876.
3. RA VIC/Z452/9, Charlotte Knollys to QV, 24 March 1877.
4. Wellcome Library, Gull Papers, D/7/1, QV to William Gull, 31 March 1877.
5. RA VIC/Z452/25, Charlotte Knollys to QV, 10 April 1877.
6. Copenhagen Letters, Box 103, Alix to Minnie, 6 March 1874.
7. Copenhagen Letters, Box 103, Alix to Minnie, March 1877.
8. RA VIC/Z452/10, Alix to QV, 26 March 1877.
9. RA VIC/EVIID/1877: 23 March–3 April.
10. RA VIC/Z452/17, Alix to QV, 4 April 1877.
11. RA VIC/Z452/20, Alix to QV (telegram), 5 April 1877.
12. *The Times,* 5 May, 9 May 1877.
13. Sir Oliver Millar, quoted in *The Guardian,* 17 May 2007.
14. RA VIC/EVIID/1877: 11 May. *The Times,* 12 May 1877.
15. Laura Beatty, *Lillie Langtry: Manners, Masks and Morals* (Chatto and Windus, 1999), p. 38.
16. Lillie Langtry, *The Days I Knew* (Hutchinson, 1925), pp. 38–40, 60–61. Beatty, *Lillie Langtry,* pp. 38–39, 47.
17. Langtry, *Days I Knew,* p. 71.
18. RA VIC/EVIID/1877: 24 May.
19. Langtry, *Days I Knew,* p. 73.
20. Ibid., pp. 38–43.

21. National Portrait Gallery, Heinz Gallery, Lillie Langtry File, cutting "Interviewing Mrs. Langtry," 1882.

22. Beatty, *Lillie Langtry*, pp. 36, 101, 137. Cornwallis-West, *Reminiscences*, p. 105.

23. National Portrait Gallery, Heinz Gallery, Lillie Langtry File, Christie's *Catalogue*, Sant's Portrait of Lillie Langtry, auctioned 3 June 1999. The painting belonged to Bertie, and was left to his daughter Louise. *Whitehall Review*, 19 July 1879. Bertie visited Sant's studio in 1879 (RA VIC/EVIID/1879: 19 July).

24. Cornwallis-West, *Reminiscences*, p. 105.

25. Langtry, *Days I Knew*, p. 50.

26. Leslie, *Edwardians in Love*, p. 100. James Brough, *The Prince and the Lily* (Hodder and Stoughton, 1975), p. 140.

27. RA VIC/Z452/60, William Gull to QV, 3 July 1877.

28. Langtry, *Days I Knew*, p. 74. Beatty, *Lillie Langtry*, pp. 70–71, 86–77.

29. Copenhagen Letters, Box 103, Alix to Minnie, n.d. [1877].

30. RA VIC/Z452/74, Alix to QV, 2 August 1877.

31. See RA VIC/A2/28, QV to B, 16 August 1877. *The Times*, 23, 28 July; 2, 4, 7, 18, 20 August 1877.

32. Sir Seymour Fortescue, "King Edward as a Yachtsman," in Alfred E. T. Watson, *King Edward VII as a Sportsman* (Longmans, Green, 1911), pp. 296–97.

33. See, e.g., *Sheffield and Rotherham Independent*, 6 September 1877.

34. QV to Vicky, 6 November 1877, in Fulford, *Dearest Child*, p. 269.

35. RA VIC/Z452/128, Alix to QV, 22 November 1877. Copenhagen Letters, Box 103, Alix to Minnie, 4 August 1870.

36. *The Times*, 23, 24 November 1877.

37. Brough, *Prince and the Lily*, p. 154. Beatty, *Lillie Langtry*, pp. 88–89.

38. Bodleian Library, Harcourt Papers, MSS dep. 348, Lewis Harcourt Diary, 17 March 1881.

39. *Star*, 21 March, 11 April 1878. *Hampshire Telegraph*, 18 May 1878.

40. RA VIC/Add A2/23, QV to B. 17 March 1876.

41. Langtry, *Days I Knew*, pp. 155–57.

42. Beatty, *Lillie Langtry*, p. 97. Duchess of Manchester to Lord Beaconsfield, in Marquis of Zetland, *Letters of Disraeli*, vol. 2, p. 158. *The Times*, 21, 30 January 1878.

43. Ned Langtry was presented to the Queen by Bertie on 19 March 1878. (*The Times*, 20 March 1878.)

44. Langtry, *Days I Knew*, pp. 107–9. *The Times*, 10 May 1878.

45. Marquis of Zetland, *Letters of Disraeli*, vol. 2, p. 156.

46. *The World*, 6 September 1877.

47. RA VIC/Add A36/1314, Henry Ponsonby to Mary Ponsonby, 8 September 1877.

48. *The Times*, 6 May 1878.

49. *The Times*, 9, 11 May 1878. Lee, *Edward VII*, vol. 1, pp. 358–63.

50. *The Gladstone Diaries*, vol. 9, ed. H. C. G. Matthew (Clarendon Press, 1986), p. 317 (26 May 1878).

51. B to Lord Beaconsfield, 14 September 1876, in Lee, *Edward VII*, vol. 1, p. 420.

52. RA VIC/Add A36/1148, Henry Ponsonby to Mary Ponsonby, 7 October 1876. RA VIC/T6/115, Henry Ponsonby to Thomas Sanderson, 7 October 1876.

53. Lord Beaconsfield to QV, 13 April 1877, in Buckle, *Letters* (2nd series), vol. 2, p. 528.

54. RA VIC/Add A36/1340, Henry Ponsonby to Mary Ponsonby, 24 October 1877.

55. Dorothy Anderson, "Valentine Baker," *ODNB*.

56. Lee, *Edward VII*, vol. 1, p. 422.

57. RA VIC/Add A36/1140, Henry Ponsonby to Mary Ponsonby, 28 September 1876.

58. *The Times*, 2 May 1877.

59. RA VIC/Add A36/1140, Henry Ponsonby to Mary Ponsonby, 28 September 1876.

60. Vincent, *Derby Diaries 1869–78*, p. 412 (22 June 1877).

61. Ibid., p. 531 (25 March 1878).

62. RA VIC/T7/34, Salisbury to B, 24 July 1878. Lee, *Edward VII*, vol. 1, pp. 366–68.

63. Langtry, *Days I Knew*, pp. 152–53.

64. Beatty, *Lillie Langtry*, pp. 1–9.

65. RA VIC/Add C07/1, Lord Lytton to Francis Knollys, 12 December 1878.

66. Mark Girouard, *The Victorian Country House* (Oxford: Clarendon Press, 1971), p. 422. "Wadhurst Park," Wadhurst History Society, http://www.wadhurst.info/whs/newsletters/whs03/page5.htm.

67. Author email from Gerard Stamp, 9 April 2010.

68. Theo Aronson, *Royal Subjects* (Pan Books, 2001), p. 123.

69. Quoted in Battiscombe, *Queen Alexandra*, p. 100.

70. Mapperton Papers, Box 287, Oliver Montagu to Lord Sandwich, 26 October 1878. Alix's biographer, Georgina Battiscombe, reads the letter in this sense. (*Queen Alexandra*, pp. 138–39.)

CHAPTER 14: PRINCE HAL 1878–81

1. RA QVJ, 13 December 1878.

2. *The Times*, 13 December 1878.

3. RA QVJ, 13, 14 December 1878. *The Times*, 12, 20 December 1878.

4. RA QVJ, 14 December 1878.

5. Buckle, *Letters* (2nd series), vol. 2, pp. 654–55. RA QVJ, 14 December 1878.

6. RA QVJ, 14 December 1878.

7. *Alice, Grand Duchess of Hesse: Biographical Sketch and Letters*, ed. Dr. Sell (John Murray, 1884), pp. 370–71.

8. *The Times*, 12 December 1878.

9. RA VIC/T7/58, B to Lord Beaconsfield, 27 December 1878.

10. QV to Vicky, 10 January 1879, in *Beloved Mama: Private Correspondence of Queen Victoria and the German Crown Princess, 1878–1885*, ed. Roger Fulford (Evans, 1981).

11. Noel, *Princess Alice*, pp. 175–77.

12. Alice to QV, 6 September 1876, in Sell, *Alice*, p. 345.

13. QV to Vicky, 14, 18, 23 November 1878, in Fulford, *Beloved Mama*, pp. 28–29.

14. Alice to QV, 11 September 1876, in Sell, *Alice*, p. 346.

15. Alice to Grand Duke Louis of Hesse, December 1877, in Noel, *Princess Alice*, p. 224.

16. Alice to QV, 26 April 1874, in Sell, *Alice,* p. 321.
17. *The Times,* 17, 18 December 1878.
18. Copenhagen Letters, Box 104, Alix to Minnie, 1 January 1879.
19. Quoted in Lee, *Edward VII,* vol. 1, p. 592.
20. RA VIC/Add C07/1, B to Francis Knollys, 18 December 1878.
21. RA QVJ, 18 December 1878.
22. RA QVJ, 21 December 1878.
23. RA QVJ, 23 December 1878.
24. RA QVJ, 21 December 1878.
25. RA QVJ, 27 December 1878.
26. Downer, *Queen's Knight,* p. 275.
27. Inger-Lise Klausen, *Tak for Dansen, Louise* [*The First Glücksburg Royal Couple and All Their European Family*] (Copenhagen: Aschehoug, 2003), pp. 188–90, 198–203. Coryne Hall, *Little Mother of Russia* (Shepheard-Walwyn, 2006), pp. 67–80.
28. Pope-Hennessy, *Queen Mary,* p. 153.
29. Copenhagen Letters, Box 104, Alix to Minnie, 9 October 1878.
30. *The Times,* 23 December 1878.
31. Argyll Etkin Collection, B to Charles Wyke, 7 January 1879. See Lee, *Edward VII,* vol. 1, pp. 364–65.
32. RA VIC/S23/34, Vicky to B, 3 January 1879.
33. RA VIC/Z459/90, Dalton's Memorandum on Education of Prince Albert Victor and Prince George, 11 February 1877.
34. RA VIC/Z459/92, QV's Memorandum on Mr. Dalton's Memorandum on the Education of Prince Albert Victor and Prince George, 15 February 1877.
35. RA VIC/Z452/108, Alix to QV, 15 October 1877.
36. RA VIC/Z473A/1, Lord Ramsay to B, 3 December 1878.
37. RA VIC/Z453/9, John Dalton to B, 9 April 1879. Davenport-Hines, "John Dalton," *ODNB.*
38. Ponsonby's Memo, n.d., in Arthur Ponsonby, *Henry Ponsonby,* p. 105.
39. RA VIC/Z453/10, Lord Beaconsfield to QV, 19 May 1879.
40. RA VIC/Add C07/1, Francis Knollys to Henry Ponsonby, n.d. [1879].
41. *The Times,* 17 September 1879.
42. RA VIC/Z453/49, B to QV, 19 September 1879.
43. RA GV/AA13/61, B to George, 30 September 1879.
44. Copenhagen Letters, Box 104, Alix to Minnie, 23 December 1880.
45. See Theo Aronson, *Prince Eddy and the Homosexual Underworld* (John Murray, 1994), pp. 53–4.
46. Joanna Richardson, *Sarah Bernhardt and Her World* (Weidenfeld and Nicolson, 1977), pp. 78–84. Langtry, *Days I Knew,* pp. 120–23.
47. RA VIC/EVIID/1879: 19 June; 6, 9, 10, 11 July: records visits to Sarah Bernhardt's gallery or to the Comédie-Française.
48. Arthur Gold and Robert Fizdale, *The Divine Sarah* (HarperCollins, 1992), p. 153.
49. Lady Frederick Cavendish diary, quoted in Beatty, *Lillie Langtry,* p. 150. See Camp, *Royal Mistresses,* p. 367.
50. Beatty, *Lillie Langtry,* p. 145.
51. RA VIC/EVIID/1879: 6 April.

52. Brough, *Prince and the Lily*, p. 199. Typically, no source is given for this anecdote.
53. *Diaries of Edward Henry Stanley, 15th Earl of Derby (1826–93) Between 1878 and 1893*, ed. John Vincent (Leopard's Head Press, 2003), p. 221 (19 March 1880). Wilfrid Blunt heard the same story: See Theo Aronson, *The King in Love* (John Murray, 1988), pp. 86–87.
54. Lillie Langtry to Lord Wharncliffe, n.d. [June 1880], in Beatty, *Lillie Langtry*, p. 174.
55. Brough, *Prince and the Lily*, p. 200. *The Times*, 13 October 1879.
56. *The Times*, 13 October 1879.
57. QV to Vicky, 7 November 1879, in Fulford, *Beloved Mama*, p. 57.
58. Lee, *Edward VII*, vol. 1, pp. 416–17, 448–50.
59. Magnus, *Edward VII*, pp. 206–8.
60. Marquis of Zetland, *Letters of Disraeli*, vol. 2, p. 211 (1 April 1879).
61. Bertie's diary (RA VIC/EVIID/1880) records five visits by Louis Battenberg in May (30 April–3 May; 6–10 May; 14–17 May; 21–24 May; 25–31 May) and two in June (4–5 June, 27 June).
62. Anthony Lambton, *The Mountbattens* (Constable, 1989). Richard Hough, *Louis and Victoria* (Hutchinson, 1974), is based on taped interviews with Mountbatten. Count Egon Corti, *The Downfall of Three Dynasties* (Methuen, 1934). Author email from Anthony Camp, 3 May 2011.
63. Vicky to QV, 7 January 1885, in Fulford, *Beloved Mama*, p. 178.
64. Beatty, *Lillie Langtry*, p. 166, says the affair with Louis was conducted with "the apparent permission" of Bertie. Aronson says that "quite possibly" the Prince encouraged the liaison. (*King in Love*, p. 89.) According to Brough, it was "more than likely" that Bertie made the introduction knowing what would happen. (*Prince and the Lily*, pp. 194–95.)
65. Beatty, *Lillie Langtry*, p. 172.
66. Ibid., pp. 172–73. Aronson, *King in Love*, p. 87.
67. Langtry, *Days I Knew*, p. 68.
68. Lillie Langtry to Lord Wharncliffe, n.d., in Beatty, *Lillie Langtry*, p. 176.
69. Bertie's diary shows that Battenberg was staying at Marlborough House on 27 June, the likely conception time. (RA VIC/EVIID/1880: 27 June.)
70. Hough, *Louis and Victoria*, pp. 96–97.
71. Beatty, *Lillie Langtry*, p. 179.
72. Lillie Langtry to Lord Wharncliffe, n.d., in ibid., p. 184. Bertie does not mention this meeting in his diary, but this need not mean that it didn't take place; Lillie's letter to Lord Wharncliffe was written shortly after the event.
73. RA VIC/EVIID/1880: 17 October.
74. Beatty, *Lillie Langtry*, pp. 177, 187–210. Camp, *Royal Mistresses*, pp. 364–66.
75. Langtry, *Days I Knew*, p. 85.
76. Oscar Wilde, *Lady Windermere's Fan*, ebooks.adelaide.edu.au/w/wilde/oscar/lady_windermeres_fan, Act 3, Scene 1.
77. RA GV/AA14/3, B to George, 16 December 1881.
78. Bodleian Library, Harcourt Papers, Dep 364, MSS Diary, 10 February 1885.
79. RA VIC/Add C07/1, George Lewis to Francis Knollys, 4 November 1897. See also RA VIC/Add C07/1, Lewis to Knollys, 13, 18, 22 November 1897.
80. B to Lillie Langtry, 5 August 1885, in Beatty, *Lillie Langtry*, p. 269.

81. RA GV/ADD/Copy/86, B to Lillie Langtry, 19 January 1886.

82. Beatty, *Lillie Langtry*, p. 303.

83. RA GV/ADD/Copy/109, B to Lillie Langtry [n.d., 1890s].

84. *The Times*, 2 October 1879.

85. RA VIC/Z453/43, Charlotte Knollys to QV, 10 September 1879.

86. RA VIC/Z453/56, Charlotte Knollys to QV, 8 October 1879.

87. RA VIC/Z453/56, Charlotte Knollys to QV, 8 October 1879.

88. RA VIC/Z453/47, B to QV, 17 September 1879.

89. Ibid.

90. Marquis of Zetland, *Letters of Disraeli*, vol. 2, pp. 245–46 (9, 11 November 1879). See Magnus, *Edward VII*, pp. 161–62.

91. Copenhagen Letters, Box 104, Alix to Minnie, 3 November 1879.

92. Copenhagen Letters, Box 104, Alix to Minnie, 11 February 1880.

93. Copenhagen Letters, Box 104, Alix to Minnie, 23 December 1880.

94. Bodleian Library, Lincolnshire Papers, MS Film 1120, B to Carrington, 18 April 1879.

95. Mary Mackie, *The Prince's Thorn: Edward VII and the Lady Farmer of Sandringham* (Pegasus, 2008), pp. 190–242. David Duff, *Whisper Louise: Edward VII and Mrs. Cresswell* (Frederick Muller, 1974).

96. Marquis of Zetland, *Letters of Disraeli*, vol. 2, pp. 258–59 (13 January 1880).

97. QV to Henry Ponsonby, 4 April 1880, in Arthur Ponsonby, *Henry Ponsonby*, p. 184.

98. RA VIC/T8/6, B to Henry Ponsonby, 21 April 1880.

99. QV's minute of 22 April 1880, in Magnus, *Edward VII*, p. 166.

100. See Francis Knollys's letter to Lord Granville, in Lee, *Edward VII*, vol. 1, p. 514.

101. RA VIC/Z453/79, Henry Ponsonby to QV, 17 February 1880; RA VIC/Z453/95, Ponsonby to B, 21 May 1880; RA VIC/Z453/100, Francis Knollys to Ponsonby, 23 May 1880; RA VIC/Z453/103, Knollys to Ponsonby, 25 May 1880.

102. RA VIC/Add A15/3327, QV to Arthur, 27 May 1880.

103. RA VIC/Z453/112, B to QV, 7 June 1880.

104. RA VIC/EVIID/1881: 13 March.

105. Stephen Gwynn and Gertrude Tuckwell, *Life of Sir Charles Dilke* (John Murray, 1917), vol. 1, p. 414.

106. Bodleian Library, Harcourt Papers, MSS dep 348, Diary, 21 March 1881.

107. *The Times*, 28 March 1881. RA VIC/Z454/58, Charlotte Knollys to QV, 28 March 1881.

108. Lee, *Edward VII*, vol. 1, p. 505.

109. Lord Frederick Hamilton, quoted in Battiscombe, *Queen Alexandra*, pp. 160–61.

CHAPTER 15: PRINCE OF PLEASURE 1881–87

1. Magnus, *Edward VII*, p. 198.

2. RA VIC/Z162/10, B to QV, 22 January 1887.

3. Magnus, *Edward VII*, pp. 181–82.

4. RA VIC/EVIID/1881: 17 July. Bertie stayed at Waddesdon 14 July 1883, 21 July 1884, 18 July 1885, 17 July 1887 (see *The Times* for these dates).

5. McKinstry, *Rosebery*, p. 69.

6. Frances, Countess of Warwick, *Afterthoughts* (Cassell, 1931), pp. 88–89.

7. Michael Hall, *Waddesdon Manor: The Heritage of a Rothschild House* (New York: Abrams, 2002), pp. 149–69. Magnus, *Edward VII*, p. 106.

8. Warwick, *Afterthoughts*, pp. 44, 255.

9. Rosemary Baird, *Goodwood* (Francis Lincoln, 2007), pp. 193, 197.

10. RA VIC/EVIID/1881: 25 July. See *The Times*, 21 July 1881.

11. RA VIC/Z454/140, QV to B, 27 July 1881.

12. Gwynn and Tuckwell, *Dilke*, vol. 1, p. 415.

13. Hibbert, *Edward VII*, pp. 98–99.

14. Bodleian Library, Lincolnshire Papers, MS Film 1120, Charles Carrington to his wife, 20 December 1881.

15. RA VIC/EVIID/1882: 10–13 January. *The Times*, 13 January 1882. *Leicester Chronicle and Leicester Mercury*, 14 January 1882. Ruffer, *Big Shots*, pp. 130–31.

16. Amanda Mackenzie Stuart, *Consuelo and Alva* (HarperCollins, 2005), pp. 29–31, 49–50. Consuelo was always short of money, even after she became Duchess of Manchester in 1890. When she died in 1909, her inheritance from her father was valued at $120,000, not a large sum by ducal standards. She left an American fortune of $2.5 million. This was tied up in trust funds established in 1901–2 by her brother, who was a brother-in-law and business associate of William Kissam Vanderbilt.

17. Edith Wharton's *The Buccaneers* (Penguin, 1993); the original 1938 edition, which Wharton left unfinished at her death, can be read in the 1993 University Press of Virginia edition. Hermione Lee, *Edith Wharton* (Vintage, 2008), pp. 722–29.

18. Duke of Manchester, *My Candid Recollections* (Grayson and Grayson, 1932), pp. 28, 55–56. Rossmore, *Things I Can Tell*, pp. 110–11.

19. Vane, *Affair of State*, p. 186.

20. Richard W. Davis, "'We Are All Americans Now!,' *Proceedings of the American Philosophical Society*, vol. 135 (1991), pp. 140–99.

21. Wharton, *Buccaneers*, pp. 79, 122.

22. Vane, *Affair of State*, p. 187.

23. Williams, *It Was Such Fun*, p. 41.

24. RA VIC/EVIID/1882: 20 August–11 September. Herman Weber and F. Parkes Weber, *The Spas and Mineral Waters of Europe* (Smith, Elder, 1896), pp. 91–93.

25. Warwick, *Afterthoughts*, p. 39.

26. Hibbert, *Edward VII*, p. 236.

27. *Diary of Sir Edward Walter Hamilton*, ed. Dudley W. R. Bahlman (Oxford: Clarendon Press, 1972), vol. 2, p. 659. RA VIC/Add A/5/426, B to Alfred, 18 August 1884. Camp, *Royal Mistresses*, p. 368. Author email from Sir Philip Naylor-Leyland, May 2011.

28. Arthur Ponsonby, *Henry Ponsonby*, p. 129.

29. RA VIC/Z162/7, Alix to QV, 1 October 1883.

30. RA VIC/Z162/8, Alix to QV, 14 December 1883.

31. RA VIC/Z173/4, B to QV, 1 January 1884.

32. RA VIC/Z173/5, QV to B, 3 January 1884.
33. *The Gladstone Diaries,* vol. 10, ed. H. C. G. Matthew (Clarendon Press, 1990), p. clxv.
34. RA VIC/Z173/15, B to QV, 26 February 1884.
35. RA VIC/Z173/18, QV to B, 27 February 1884.
36. RA VIC/Z173/20, QV to B, 29 February 1884.
37. Arnstein, "Queen Victoria Opens Parliament," *Historical Research,* vol. 63 (1990), pp. 186–87.
38. RA VIC/Z460/140, B to QV, 6 February 1887.
39. RA VIC/Add C07/1/7, Francis Knollys to Henry Ponsonby, 16 January 1881.
40. Matthew, *Gladstone Diaries,* vol. 9, p. 619 (21 November 1880). See RA VIC/Add C07/1/9, Francis Knollys to Henry Ponsonby, 22 November 1880.
41. Bahlman, *Diary of Edward Hamilton,* vol. 1, p. 245 (1 April 1882).
42. Fitzwilliam, Blunt Papers, MS 333–1975, Diary, 17 May 1885.
43. RA VIC/EVIID/1882: 11 July.
44. Bahlman, *Diary of Edward Hamilton,* vol. 1, pp. 312, 314 (27, 30 July 1882). Henry Ponsonby to B, 31 July 1882, in Lee, *Edward VII,* vol. 1, pp. 457–58.
45. Henry Ponsonby to Mary Ponsonby, 5 April 1880, in Arthur Ponsonby, *Henry Ponsonby,* p. 185. Gwynn and Tuckwell, *Dilke,* vol. 1, pp. 302, 475.
46. Bodleian Library, Lincolnshire Papers, MS Film 1120, Carrington Diary, 18 February 1884.
47. RA VIC/EVIID/1884: 18 February.
48. *Hansard* (Lords), 22 February 1884.
49. Gwynn and Tuckwell, *Dilke,* vol. 2, p. 26. See Lee, *Edward VII,* vol. 1, pp. 547–51.
50. BL, Sidney Lee Papers, Add MS 56087B, fol. 9, Sir Charles Dilke to B, 26 July 1885. Gwynn and Tuckwell, *Dilke,* vol. 2, p. 166. See McKinstry, *Rosebery,* pp. 149–53.
51. Fitzwilliam, Blunt Papers, MS 333–1975, Diary, 4 August 1885.
52. RA VIC/Add C07/1, B to Francis Knollys, 28 September 1885.
53. RA VIC/EVIID/1884: 28 March. *The Times,* 29 March 1884.
54. QVJ, 28 March 1884, in Buckle, *Letters* (2nd series), vol. 3, p. 489.
55. QVJ, 29 March 1884, in ibid., vol. 3, p. 492.
56. *The Times,* 2 April 1884.
57. RA GV/AA14/58, B to George, 1 May 1884.
58. Frank Hardie, *The Political Influence of Queen Victoria, 1861–1901* (Oxford University Press, 1935), pp. 76, 192–93.
59. QV to Vicky, 29 March 1884, in Fulford, *Beloved Mama,* p. 162.
60. See Hermione Lee, *Virginia Woolf* (Vintage, 1997), pp. 64–65.
61. RA VIC/Z473/63, Report by J. K. Stephen, 30 August 1883.
62. *The World,* 20 October 1883.
63. See Lee, *Woolf,* p. 64. Andrew Cook, *Prince Eddy* (History Press, 2008), pp. 101–10.
64. *Standard,* 26 May 1884.
65. RA VIC/W64/64, Austen Chamberlain to B, 12 December 1905.
66. RA GV/AA6/333, B to John Dalton, 12 July 1884.
67. RA VIC/Z162/7, Alix to QV, 1 October 1883.

68. RA GV/AA14/52, B to George, 16 February 1884.

69. Copenhagen Letters, Box 104, Alix to Minnie, 3 October 1884.

70. Copenhagen Letters, Box 104, Alix to Minnie, 30 December 1884.

71. Alexander Mikhailovich, Grand Duke of Russia, *Once a Grand Duke* (Royalty Digest, 1995), p. 113.

72. RA VIC/Add C07/1, B to Francis Knollys, 3 May 1888.

73. Warwick, *Afterthoughts,* p. 41.

74. Marie, Queen of Romania, *The Story of My Life* (Cassell, 1934), vol. 1, p. 43.

75. Princess Louise to Francis Knollys [1885], in St. Aubyn, *Edward VII,* p. 103.

76. Magnus, *Edward VII,* p. 182.

77. Bodleian Library, Lincolnshire Papers, MS Film 1120, Carrington Diary, 21 July 1884. See *The Times,* 24 July 1884.

78. *The Times,* 14 April 1885.

79. RA VIC/Z455/20, B to QV, 19 April 1885.

80. RA VIC/Z455/17, Arthur Ellis to QV, 15 April 1885.

81. RA QVJ, 18 April 1885.

82. Bahlman, *Diary of Edward Hamilton,* vol. 2, p. 840 (16 April 1885).

83. Ibid., vol. 2, pp. 860–61 (10 May 1885).

84. BL, Sidney Lee Papers, Add MS 56087B, fol. 5, Francis Ponsonby to QV, 12 May 1885.

85. BL, Sidney Lee Papers, Add MS 56087B, fol. 7, Francis Ponsonby to QV, 18 May 1885.

86. Quoted in Leslie, *Edwardians in Love,* p. 120.

87. Battiscombe, *Queen Alexandra,* p. 173.

88. Copenhagen Letters, Box 104, Alix to Minnie, 23 December 1881.

89. Lady Geraldine Somerset's Diary, 21 February 1886, in Battiscombe, *Queen Alexandra,* pp. 172–73.

90. Hon. Georgina Stonor, letter to author, 30 April 2010. Robert Julian Stonor, *Stonor* (Newport: R. H. Johns, 1951), pp. 339–41.

91. Margot Asquith, *The Autobiography of Margot Asquith* (Thornton, Butterworth, 1920), vol. 1, pp. 63–65.

92. Bodleian Library, Margot Asquith Papers, MS Eng. P. 3198, fol. 167: Diary, 6 August 1885.

93. Bodleian Library, Margot Asquith Papers, MS Eng. D. 3268, fol. 29, B to Margot Tennant, 25 April 1886.

94. Bodleian Library, Margot Asquith Papers, MS Eng. D. 3268, fol. 32, B to Margot Tennant, 29 December 1886.

95. Bodleian Library, Margot Asquith Papers, MS Eng. D. 3268, fol. 33, B to Margot Tennant, n.d.

96. Bodleian Library, Margot Asquith Papers, MS Eng. D. 3268, fol. 34, B to Margot Tennant, n.d.

97. Quoted in Leslie, *Edwardians in Love,* p. 192.

98. *The Times,* 17 July 1886, 8 November 1886, 7 December 1886.

99. Churchill Archives Centre, Jennie Churchill Papers, CHAR 28/7/72, Randolph Churchill to Jennie Churchill, 10 January 1886; CHAR 28/8/85, Randolph Churchill to Jennie Churchill, 25 October 1888.

100. RA VIC/Z162/10, B to QV, 22 January 1887.

101. Sebba, *Jennie Churchill,* pp. 96–97.

102. Leslie, *Edwardians in Love,* p. 194.
103. Churchill Archives Centre, Jennie Churchill Papers, CHAR 28/49/18–19, B to Jennie Churchill, 26 March 1886. He didn't lunch with her on "Monday next."
104. Churchill Archives Centre, Jennie Churchill Papers, CHAR 28/49/12–13, B to Jennie Churchill, n.d.
105. Asquith, *Autobiography,* vol. 1, pp. 63–64.
106. Churchill Archives Centre, Jennie Churchill Papers, CHAR 28/48/5–6, B to Jennie Churchill, 23 March 1887.

CHAPTER 16: WILLIAM 1887–89

1. Sir Richard Holmes, *Edward VII: His Life and Times* (Amalgamated Press, 1911), vol. 2, p. 363.
2. *The Times,* 22 June 1887. Pakula, *Uncommon Woman,* p. 487.
3. Alix, quoted in Battiscombe, *Queen Alexandra,* p. 174. QVJ, 21 June 1887, in *Letters of Queen Victoria* (3rd series), ed. G. E. Buckle (John Murray, 1930), vol. 1, p. 322. *The Times,* 3 June 1887.
4. Holmes, *Edward VII,* vol. 2, p. 367.
5. *The Times,* 22 June 1887.
6. *Pall Mall Gazette,* 22 June 1887. Williams, *Contentious Crown,* p. 61.
7. Rohl, *Young Wilhelm,* pp. 675–80.
8. Hough, *Louis and Victoria,* p. 111.
9. Rohl, *Young Wilhelm,* p. 518.
10. Lee, *Edward VII,* vol. 1, pp. 473–81.
11. Thomas Kohut, "Kaiser Wilhelm II and His Parents," in *Kaiser Wilhelm II: The Corfu Papers,* ed. John Rohl and Nicholas Sombart (Cambridge University Press, 1982), p. 73.
12. Rohl, *Young Wilhelm,* pp. 388–89.
13. William to Alexander III, 13 March 1885, in Lee, *Edward VII,* vol. 1, p. 486.
14. William to Emperor William I, 30 September 1885, in Rohl, *Young Wilhelm,* pp. 481–82.
15. *The Holstein Papers,* ed. Norman Rich and M. H. Fisher, vol. 2 (Cambridge University Press, 1957), p. 254 (16 October 1885).
16. Lory Alder and Richard Dalby, *The Dervish of Windsor Castle: The Life of Arminius Vambery* (Bachman and Turner, 1979), pp. 231–32, 310–11.
17. Rich and Fisher, *Holstein Papers,* vol. 2, p. 254 (16 October 1885).
18. RA VIC/Add A5/479/6, B to Vicky, 9 March 1888.
19. Holmes, *Edward VII,* vol. 2, p. 370.
20. RA GV/AA16/56, B to George, 13 November 1887.
21. RA VIC/Add C07/1, Arthur Ellis to Francis Knollys, 18 March 1888.
22. RA VIC/Z68/34, Arthur Ellis to Henry Ponsonby, 16–17 March 1888.
23. RA VIC/EVIID/1888: 12–15 June.
24. QVJ, 15 June 1888, in Buckle, *Letters* (3rd series), vol. 1, p. 417.
25. B to QV, 18 June 1888, in ibid., vol. 1, p. 419.
26. RA VIC/Add A5/479/19, B to Vicky, 27 June 1888.
27. Ibid.
28. RA VIC/Add A5/479/20, B to Vicky, 29 June 1888.

29. RA VIC/Add A5/479/21, B to Vicky, 4 July 1888.

30. RA VIC/Add C07/9, Francis Knollys to Henry Ponsonby, 15 January 1889.

31. RA VIC/EVIID/1888: 22, 29 August, 1, 2, 5 September.

32. RA VIC/EVIID/1888: 10 September 1888. *The Times*, 11, 13 September 1888.

33. B to Prince Christian of Schleswig-Holstein, 3 April 1889, in Buckle, *Letters* (3rd series), vol. 1, p. 488.

34. See John Rohl, *Wilhelm II: The Kaiser's Personal Monarchy, 1888–1900*, trans. Sheila de Bellaigue (Cambridge University Press, 2004), p. 77ff. for a full account.

35. RA VIC/Z281/2, Arthur Ellis to Colonel Swaine, 12 September 1886.

36. Rohl, *Wilhelm II*, p. 73.

37. B to Prince Christian of Schleswig-Holstein, 3 April 1889, in Buckle, *Letters* (3rd series), vol. 1, p. 489.

38. Rohl, *Wilhelm II*, p. 75.

39. Arthur Ellis to Henry Ponsonby, 19 April 1889, in Arthur Ponsonby, *Henry Ponsonby*, pp. 110–12.

40. Rohl, *Young Wilhelm*, pp. 741–42.

41. QV to Lord Salisbury, 15 October 1888, in Buckle, *Letters* (3rd series), vol. 1, p. 441.

42. Judith Listowel, *A Habsburg Tragedy: Crown Prince Rudolf* (Ascent Books, 1978), p. 183.

43. Salisbury's Memo, 13 October 1888, in Buckle, *Letters* (3rd series), vol. 1, p. 440. Andrew Roberts, *Salisbury* (Weidenfeld and Nicolson, 1999), pp. 484–87.

44. QV to Salisbury, 15 October 1888, in Buckle, *Letters* (3rd series), vol. 1, pp. 440–41.

45. Alix to George, 17 October 1888, in Rohl, *Wilhelm II*, p. 84.

46. Magnus, *Edward VII*, p. 211. Roberts, *Salisbury*, p. 486.

47. QV to Henry Matthews, 13 November 1888, in Buckle, *Letters* (3rd series), vol. 1, p. 449.

48. *The Times*, 10 November 1888. Camp, *Royal Mistresses*, p. 370.

49. See Stephen Knight, *Jack the Ripper: The Final Solution* (Grafton, 1977).

50. Matthew Sturgis, *Walter Sickert: A Life* (HarperCollins, 2005), pp. 625–29. Camp, *Royal Mistresses*, pp. 383–85.

51. First suggested in 1962 by Philippe Jullian in a biography of Edward VII, this theory was elaborated in 1970 by Dr. T. E. A. Stowell. See "Prince Albert Victor," Casebook: Jack the Ripper, http://www.casebook.org/suspects/eddy.html.

52. See Aronson, *Prince Eddy*, pp. 93–102.

53. G. K. A. Bell, *Randall Davidson* (Oxford University Press, 1938), pp. 98–100.

54. RA VIC/EVIID/1889: 30 January.

55. Churchill Archives Centre, Jennie Churchill Papers, CHAR 28/48/13–14, B to Jennie Churchill, 11 February 1889.

56. Roberts, *Salisbury*, p. 537.

57. RA VIC/EVIID/1889: 1, 4, 12 February. Bertie saw Count Kinsky, the Austrian attaché, on these days.

58. B to QV, 12 February 1889, in Fritz Judtmann, *Mayerling: The Facts Behind the Legend* (George Harrap, 1971), p. 279.

59. RA VIC/T9/117, General Keith Fraser (British military attaché in Vienna, B's representative at Rudolf's funeral) to Dighton Probyn, 22 February 1889.

60. Magnus, *Edward VII*, p. 217.
61. QV to B, 7 February 1889, in Buckle, *Letters* (3rd series), vol. 1, p. 467.
62. Lord Salisbury to QV, 9 March 1889, in ibid., vol. 1, p. 477.
63. Rohl, *Wilhelm II*, p. 91.
64. Kohut, "Kaiser William II and His Parents," in Rohl and Sombart, *Corfu Papers*, pp. 84–85.
65. Vicky to QV, 7 March 1889, in Pakula, *Uncommon Woman*, p. 572.
66. RA VIC/Add A4/9, B to Vicky, 15 May 1889. RA VIC/Z281/45, Francis Knollys to Henry Ponsonby, 12 May 1889.
67. RA VIC/Add A4/6, B to Vicky, 24 April 1889.
68. QVJ, 23–7 April 1889, in Buckle, *Letters* (3rd series), vol. 1, pp. 495–97.
69. Lord Salisbury to QV, 11 May 1889, in Rohl, *Wilhelm II*, pp. 96–97.
70. RA VIC/Add A4/11, QV to Kaiser William, 25 May 1889 (copy). Rohl, *Wilhelm II*, pp. 97–98.
71. RA VIC/Add A4/12, B to Vicky, 29 May 1889.
72. RA VIC/T9/161, Kaiser William to QV, 28 May 1889 (copy extract).
73. Henry Ponsonby to Prince Christian, 1 June 1889, in Buckle, *Letters* (3rd series), vol. 1, p. 501.
74. RA VIC/Z281 contains drafts of letters to the kaiser from Marlborough House and Windsor, May 1889.
75. Francis Knollys to Prince Christian, 8 June 1889, in Buckle, *Letters* (3rd series), vol. 1, p. 501.
76. RA VIC/Add A4/14, B to Vicky, 18 June 1889.
77. Kaiser William to Edward Malet, 14 June 1889, in Buckle, *Letters* (3rd series), vol. 1, p. 505.
78. Kaiser William to QV, 23 June 1889, in ibid., vol. 1, p. 505.
79. RA VIC/EVIID/1889: 2–6 August. QVJ, 2, 5, 8 August 1889, in Buckle, *Letters* (3rd series), vol. 1, pp. 520–22.
80. Kaiser William to Herbert Bismarck, 7 August 1889, in John Rohl, *Wilhelm II* (Cambridge University Press, 2004), p. 104.
81. Kaiser William to QV, 17 August 1889, in ibid., p. 106.
82. Vicky to QV, 27 July 1889, in Pakula, *Uncommon Woman*, p. 574.

CHAPTER 17: SCANDAL 1889–90

1. Hatfield House, 3M/E, Lady C. Beresford to Lord Salisbury, 22 July 1891.
2. Frank Harris, "First Gentleman of Europe: Stories of Edward Prince of Wales," *Pearson's Magazine,* October 1916, p. 316. The articles Harris wrote for *Pearson's Magazine* in America during the First World War were based on information and letters supplied by Lady Warwick.
3. RA VIC/EVIID/1881: 30 April. Warwick, *Afterthoughts*, p. 61.
4. RA VIC/EVIID/1886: 19 June.
5. Warwick, *Life's Ebb and Flow,* p. 182. According to Lady Warwick, this story was related to her by Evelyn Paget, who was in waiting on Queen Victoria and was a great friend of her mother. But Queen Victoria doesn't mention the incident in her journal, nor is there any record that Lady Warwick ever stayed with Queen Victoria. (Information from Royal Archives.)
6. Roberts, *Salisbury*, p. 559.

7. Manchester, *Candid Recollections*, p. 64.

8. Warwick, *Afterthoughts*, pp. 65–66.

9. Sushila Anand, *Daisy* (Piatkus, 2008), p. 50. Margaret Blunden, *The Countess of Warwick* (Cassell, 1967), p. 67.

10. Hatfield House, Salisbury Papers, 3M/E, Lady C. Beresford to Lord Salisbury, 22 July 1891.

11. Hatfield House, 3M/E, Lady C. Beresford to Lord Salisbury, 22 July 1891.

12. John Juxon, *Lewis and Lewis* (Collins, 1983), pp. 236–37.

13. Hatfield House, 3M/E, Lady C. Beresford to Salisbury, 22 July 1891.

14. Ibid.

15. *Pearson's Magazine*, October 1916, p. 316. See Warwick, *Afterthoughts*, pp. 44–45, 255.

16. RA VIC/EVIID/1889: 9–13 December.

17. Caroline Spurrier Archive, B to Daisy Warwick [9 December 1899, copy].

18. Hatfield House, 3M/E, Lord C. Beresford to Lord Salisbury, 12 July 1891.

19. *Pearson's Magazine*, October 1916.

20. Ibid.

21. Hatfield House, 3M/E, Lady C. Beresford to Lord Salisbury, 22 July 1891.

22. Blunden, *Countess of Warwick*, p. 77.

23. RA VIC/Z50/48, Vicky to QV, 20 June 1891.

24. Bodleian Library, Lincolnshire Papers, MS Film 1120, Carrington Diary, 6 July 1891.

25. Hatfield House 3M/E, Copy of Proposed Letter from Lord C. Beresford to P. of Wales: sent to me July 23 by Lady Charles, apparently to obtain my advice [in Salisbury's hand: endorsed "Letter not sent at Lord S's advice."].

26. Hatfield House 3M/E, Lord Salisbury to Lord C. Beresford, 10 August 1891. Roberts, *Salisbury*, p. 559.

27. Hatfield House, 3M/E, Lord C. Beresford to B, 18 December 1891.

28. Warwick, *Afterthoughts*, p. 42.

29. Francis Knollys to Schomberg McDonnell, 19 December 1891, in Magnus, *Edward VII*, p. 296.

30. Arthur Balfour to Lady Salisbury, 23 December 1891, in *Salisbury–Balfour Correspondence: Letters Exchanged Between the Third Marquess of Salisbury and His Nephew A. J. Balfour 1869–92*, ed. Robin Harcourt Williams (Herts. Record Society, 1988), p. 321.

31. Roberts, *Salisbury*, p. 560.

32. Hatfield House, 3M/E, Schomberg McDonnell to Lord Salisbury, 17 December 1891.

33. Hatfield House, 3M/E, Lord C. Beresford to B, 21 December 1891.

34. Hatfield House, 3M/E, Duke of Portland to Lady C. Beresford, February 1892. Mina retained one copy.

35. Hatfield House, 3M/E, Lord C. Beresford to Lord Salisbury, 12 July 1891.

36. B to Lord Waterford, 6 April 1892, in Magnus, *Edward VII*, p. 236.

37. Manchester, *Candid Recollections*, pp. 62–63. See Vane, *Affair of State*, p. 187.

38. RA VIC/Add C07/1, B to Knollys, 8 April 1892. Bertie was referring here to the American Mrs. Arthur Paget: See p. 412.

39. Frederic Whyte, *Life of W. T. Stead* (Cape, 1925), vol. 2, p. 104.

40. Roberts, *Salisbury*, p. 558.

41. Kenneth Rose, *The Later Cecils* (Weidenfeld and Nicolson, 1975), p. 53.

42. Magnus, *Edward VII*, p. 217.

43. RA VIC/Add A5/468, Statement of Prince of Wales's Income 1881–1900.

44. Bahlman, *Diary of Edward Hamilton*, vol. 2, p. 539 (4 January 1884).

45. Ibid., vol. 2, p. 552 (3 February 1884).

46. Ibid., vol. 2, p. 598 (21 April 1884).

47. Williams, *Contentious Crown*, pp. 62–64.

48. *Hansard*, vol. 338, cols. 1291–95, Labouchere's speech, 25 July 1889.

49. Ibid., vol. 338, col. 1338.

50. Rothschild Archive RAL000/73 111/105, B to Natty Rothschild, 15 March 1885.

51. Rothschild Archive RAL000/73 111/105, Correspondence re Advance to Prince of Wales, 1889. Receipt for £60,000 advanced 25 July 1893 to Prince of Wales. See Niall Ferguson, *The World's Banker*, p. 771.

52. Penny Crowe Archive, Prince Albert Victor to James Mackenzie, 20 August 1889; B to James Mackenzie, 18 August 1889.

53. Penny Crowe Archive, B to James Mackenzie, 3 October 1889.

54. Penny Crowe Archive, B to James Mackenzie, March 1887. *The Times*, 23 August 1890.

55. Bertie's letters to James Mackenzie survive only for 1887–89, but Mackenzie clearly knew about Bertie's finances in 1884: Bahlman, *Diary of Edward Hamilton*, vol. 2, p. 538 (4 January 1884).

56. Author information, Penny Crowe, June 2010.

57. Vincent, *Derby Diaries 1878–93*, p. 867.

58. See Anthony Allfrey, *Edward VII and His Jewish Court* (Weidenfeld and Nicolson, 1991), pp. 70–97.

59. Vincent, *Derby Diaries 1878–93*, p. 867.

60. Allfrey, *Jewish Court*, p. 102. Pat Thane, "Maurice de Hirsch," *ODNB*.

61. Magnus, *Edward VII*, p. 219.

62. RA GV/AA18/32, B to George, 12 October 1890. RA VIC/EVIID/1890: 6–18 October.

63. RA GV/AA18/32, B to George, 12 October 1890.

64. Allfrey, *Jewish Court*, p. 101. Watson, *King Edward VII as a Sportsman*, p. 338.

65. RA GV/AA18/33, B to George, 19 October 1890.

66. Ruffer, *Big Shots*, p. 71.

67. Warwick, *Afterthoughts*, p. 40.

68. *Life with Queen Victoria: Marie Mallet's Letters from Court, 1887–1901*, ed. Victor Mallet (John Murray, 1968), p. 30 (28 July 1889).

69. RA VIC/Add A4/15, B to Vicky, 27 June 1889. See p. 137.

70. RA VIC/Z456/64, QV to B, 15 July 1889. RA VIC/Z456/69, QV to Princess Louise, 16 July 1889. RA VIC/Z456/67, QV to Lord Fife, 18 July 1889.

71. Bodleian Library, Lincolnshire Papers, MS Film 1121, Carrington Diary, 7 October 1906.

72. Pope-Hennessy, *Queen Mary*, p. 192.

73. Giles St. Aubyn, *The Royal George: The Life of Prince George, Duke of Cambridge* (Constable, 1963), p. 299.

74. Pope-Hennessy, *Queen Mary*, p. 193.

75. Churchill Archives Centre, Esher Papers, ESHR 12/3, Lord Arthur Somerset

to Reginald Brett, 10 September 1889. H. Montgomery Hyde, *The Cleveland Street Scandal* (W. H. Allen, 1976), p. 42.

76. Lord Arthur Somerset to Reginald Brett, 30 September 1889, in Hyde, *Cleveland Street,* p. 42.

77. James Lees-Milne, *The Enigmatic Edwardian: The Life of Reginald, 2nd Viscount Esher* (Sidgwick and Jackson, 1986), p. 78.

78. This is preserved in the Esher papers in the Churchill Archives Centre, reference ESHR 12/3.

79. Churchill Archives Centre, Esher Papers, ESHR 12/13, Lord Arthur Somerset to Reginald Brett, 5 October 1889. Hyde, *Cleveland Street,* p. 81.

80. Hamilton Cuffe to Lord Halsbury, Lord Chancellor, 16 October 1889, in Hyde, *Cleveland Street,* pp. 90–91.

81. Ibid., p. 90.

82. Knollys was accused of leaking against Salisbury. During the debate on 28 February 1890, the Liberal MP Henry Labouchere, the editor of *Truth,* was challenged to supply the name of his informant for the allegation that Salisbury had tipped off Probyn about the warrant for Lord Arthur Somerset's arrest. He theatrically wrote a name on a piece of paper, and then tore it up into tiny pieces. Afterward, an MP picked up the pieces, and revealed that the name was Sir Francis Knollys. This prompted Knollys to give an explanation to the PM in an interview with Schomberg McDonnell. According to McDonnell's memo, Knollys admitted that he had seen Labouchere in November, but claimed he had told him only one thing: that Lord Arthur had fled on the same day as the King's Cross meeting. "Sir Francis Knollys assures me that with the exception of the above remark he said literally nothing," noted McDonnell. (Hatfield House, 3M/E, Schomberg McDonnell's Memo of Conversation with Francis Knollys, 2 March 1890.)

83. Aronson, *Prince Eddy,* pp. 141–43.

84. Roberts, *Salisbury,* p. 546. A memo by Schomberg McDonnell, Salisbury's private secretary, appears to vindicate Salisbury. It records an interview with a certain General Marshall, who claimed to have been alerted by Colonel Pearson, the assistant commissioner of police, about the damning evidence against Lord Arthur Somerset. Marshall told Pearson to warn Probyn. This memo is minuted by Salisbury in red ink: "If General Marshall's impression is accurate Probyn played me an ugly trick for he did his best to make me assent to a letter which would have implied that he had obtained his information from my conversation. He told me that he had no communication with Somerset for several weeks before the flight." (Hatfield House, 3M/E, Schomberg McDonnell to Salisbury, 21 September 1891.)

85. B to Lord Salisbury, 25 October 1889, in Hyde, *Cleveland Street,* p. 96.

86. Oliver Montagu to Lady Waterford, 10 December 1889, in Hyde, *Cleveland Street,* p. 122.

87. Churchill Archives Centre, Esher Papers, ESHR 12/3, Lord Arthur Somerset to Reginald Brett, 10 December 1889.

88. Bodleian Library, Lincolnshire Papers, MS Film 1120, B to Charles Carrington, 2 January 1890.

89. Aronson, *Prince Eddy,* p. 170.

90. Cook, *Prince Eddy,* pp. 173–74, 197.

91. Oliver Montagu to Lady Waterford, December 1889, in Hyde, *Cleveland Street*, p. 124.
92. Broadlands Archive, Cassel Papers, T77, Eddy to Louis Mountbatten, 7 October 1889.
93. Quoted in Pope-Hennessy, *Queen Mary*, p. 194.
94. RA VIC/Z456/160, B to QV, 31 March 1890.
95. RA VIC/Add C07/9, Francis Knollys to Henry Ponsonby, 18 May 1890.
96. Arthur Balfour to Lord Salisbury, 30 August 1890, in Harcourt-Williams, *Salisbury–Balfour Correspondence*, p. 321.
97. QV to Eddy, 19 May 1890, in Pope-Hennessy, *Queen Mary*, p. 196.
98. Quoted in Pope-Hennessy, *Queen Mary*, p. 197.
99. RA VIC/EVIID/1890: 29 August.
100. QV's Memo, 29 August 1890, in Harcourt-Williams, *Salisbury–Balfour Correspondence*, p. 320.
101. Balfour's copy of Alix's letter to QV, in Harcourt-Williams, *Salisbury–Balfour Correspondence*, p. 322.
102. Arthur Balfour to Lord Salisbury, 30 August 1890, in Harcourt-Williams, *Salisbury–Balfour Correspondence*, p. 322.
103. Roberts, *Salisbury*, p. 550.
104. RA GV/AA18/38, B to George, 23 November 1890.
105. RA VIC/Add C07/1, Henry Ponsonby to Francis Knollys, 15 October 1890. RA VIC/Add C07/1, Ponsonby to Knollys, 30 October 1890.
106. Bodleian Library, Margot Asquith Papers, MSS Eng d3199, Diary, 22 June 1895.
107. Eddy to Lady Sybil St Clair Erskine, 21 June 1891, in Pope-Hennessy, *Queen Mary*, pp. 199–200.
108. See Cook, *Prince Eddy*, pp. 235–36.
109. Aronson, *Prince Eddy*, p. 199. Hyde, *Cleveland Street*, p. 57.

CHAPTER 18: NEMESIS 1890–92

1. RA GV/AA18/26, B to George, 26 August 1890.
2. RA VIC/Z456/85, B to QV, 17 August 1889. RA GV/AA21/25, B to George, 5 April 1897.
3. Magnus, *Edward VII*, p. 219. See RA EVIID/1890 (June, July).
4. Warwick, *Afterthoughts*, pp. 38–39, 93–94, 163.
5. RA VIC/Add C07/1, B to Francis Knollys, 7 November 1889.
6. RA GV/AA18/28, B to George, 9 September 1890. See Blunden, *Countess of Warwick*, p. 72.
7. Jason Tomes, "Sir William Gordon-Cumming," *ODNB*.
8. Vane, *Affair of State*, p. 189. Tomes, "Gordon-Cumming," *ODNB*. Bertie lunched at Harriet Street on 20 January 1880 and 6 February 1889. (RA VIC EVIID/1880: 20 January; RA VIC/EVIID/1889: 6 February 1889.) Gordon-Cumming stayed three times at Sandringham (*ODNB*).
9. RA GV/AA18/28, B to George, 9 September 1890. See Crook, *Nouveaux Riches*, pp. 27–28.
10. RA VIC/Y182/28, Hon. Arthur Somerset, "Tranby Croft Scandal," transcript, April 1940.

11. Allfrey, *Jewish Court*, pp. 52, 55. The London Library copy has a marginal note in pencil: "only when he was a very old man." See Roth, "Court Jews," *Jewish Social Studies* (1943), p. 361.

12. *The Baccarat Case*, ed. W. Teignmouth Shore (William Hodge, 1932), p. 115. *The Times*, 4 June 1891 (Baccarat Case: Stanley Wilson's evidence).

13. *The Times*, 4 June 1891.

14. George MacDonald Fraser wrote a story about Tranby Croft, which is published in *Flashman and the Tiger* (HarperCollins, 1999).

15. Michael Havers, Edward Grayson, and Peter Shankland, *The Royal Baccarat Scandal* (Souvenir Press, 1988), p. 123.

16. *The Times*, 4 June 1891.

17. Havers, Grayson, and Shankland, *Royal Baccarat Scandal*, p. 50.

18. Ibid., p. 32.

19. *The Times*, 3 June 1891 (evidence of Prince of Wales).

20. Shore, *Baccarat Case*, p. 181.

21. Ibid., p. 32.

22. RA VIC/Add U/32, QV to Vicky, 24 February 1891 [transcript].

23. Havers, Grayson, and Shankland, *Royal Baccarat Scandal*, p. 237.

24. Vincent, *Derby Diaries 1878–93* (3 February 1891), p. 867.

25. Leslie, *Edwardians in Love*, p. 141.

26. Havers, Grayson, and Shankland, *Royal Baccarat Scandal*, p. 269.

27. Ibid., p. 269. Vane, *Affair of State*, p. 189.

28. RA GV/AA18/29, B to George, 16 September 1890. RA VIC/EVIID/1890: 11 September.

29. RA VIC/EVIID/1890: 12 September.

30. Shore, *Baccarat Case*, p. 78.

31. William Gordon-Cumming to B, 12 September 1890, in Havers, Grayson, and Shankland, *Royal Baccarat Scandal*, p. 40.

32. *The Times*, 9 February 1911 (Letter from Daisy Warwick). Blunden, *Countess of Warwick*, pp. 72–73.

33. RA VIC/Y182/5, Redvers Buller to Henry Ponsonby, 13 February 1891. Magnus, *Edward VII*, p. 225.

34. RA VIC/Y182/22, Duke of Connaught to Henry Ponsonby, 22 February 1891.

35. See press comment in Havers, Grayson, and Shankland, *Royal Baccarat Scandal*, pp. 61–63.

36. RA VIC/Y182/23, Memo by Ponsonby, 22 February 1891.

37. Ibid., QV's note.

38. RA VIC/Y182/18, Lord Rowton to Henry Ponsonby, 19 February 1891.

39. RA VIC/Add U/32, QV to Vicky, 24 February 1891 [transcript].

40. RA VIC/Add A12/1774, Francis Knollys to Henry Ponsonby, 17 April 1891.

41. RA GV/AA18/55, B to George, 29 March 1891.

42. RA VIC/Add A4/29, B to Vicky, 20 May 1891.

43. RA VIC/Y182/28, Hon. Arthur Somerset, "Tranby Croft Scandal," transcript, April 1940.

44. T. H. S. Escott, *King Edward and His Court* (T. F. Unwin, 1903), p. 109. Richard Davenport-Hines, "Sir George Lewis," *ODNB*. Allfrey, *Jewish Court*, pp. 206–7.

45. Hatfield House, 3M/E, Lord Charles Beresford to B, 12 July 1891. RA VIC/EVIID/1890: 25 January. Juxon, *Lewis and Lewis*, pp. 96–97.

46. Bodleian Library, Lincolnshire Papers, MS Film 1120, Carrington Diary, 17 May 1891.

47. RA VIC/Add A12/1789, Henry Ponsonby to QV, 2 June 1891.

48. Havers, Grayson, and Shankland, *Royal Baccarat Scandal,* pp. 95–96.

49. *The Times,* 3 June 1891.

50. RA VIC/Add C07/9, Francis Knollys to Henry Ponsonby, 4 June 1891.

51. Ibid.

52. Havers, Grayson, and Shankland, *Royal Baccarat Scandal,* p. 154.

53. RA VIC/Add C07/9, Francis Knollys to Henry Ponsonby, 4 June 1891.

54. Havers, Grayson, and Shankland, *Royal Baccarat Scandal,* p. 203.

55. Ibid., p. 216.

56. RA VIC/Add C07/9, Francis Knollys to Henry Ponsonby, 8 June 1891.

57. Bodleian Library, Lincolnshire Papers, MS Film 1120, Carrington Diary, 10 June 1891.

58. RA GV/AA19/11, B to George, 17 June 1891.

59. Bodleian Library, Lincolnshire Papers, MS Film 1120, Carrington Diary, 12 June 1891.

60. RA VIC/Add U32/, QV to Vicky, 8 June 1891.

61. RA GV/AA19/11, B to George, 17 June 1891.

62. RA VIC/Add C07/1, Bundle labeled "June 1891, Cumming Case, letters and resolutions, none of which have been answered." St. Aubyn, *Edward VII,* pp. 171–72. *The Times,* 15 June 1891. Williams, *Contentious Crown,* pp. 66–67.

63. RA VIC/Add C07/1, Jennings to Knollys, 16 June 1891.

64. *Reynolds's Newspaper,* 14 June 1891.

65. RA VIC/Z50/45, Vicky to QV, 14 June 1891.

66. *Pall Mall Gazette,* 15 June 1891. RA VIC/Y182/28, Hon. Arthur Somerset, "Tranby Croft Scandal," transcript, April 1940.

67. Ross McKibbon, "Working-Class Gambling in Britain 1880–1939," *Past and Present,* no. 82 (1979).

68. *The Times,* 10 June 1891.

69. RA VIC/Add A4/32, B to Vicky, 14 June 1891.

70. Magnus, *Edward VII,* p. 229.

71. RA GV/AA19/10, B to George, 10 June 1891.

72. Ibid.

73. RA VIC/Add A4/33, B to Vicky, 23 June 1891.

74. RA GV/AA18/55, B to George, 29 March 1891.

75. Battiscombe, *Queen Alexandra,* p. 182.

76. Quoted in Pope-Hennessy, *Queen Mary,* p. 193.

77. Bodleian Library, Lincolnshire Papers, MS Film 1120, Carrington Diary, 19 May 1891.

78. Cook, *Prince Eddy,* p. 250.

79. RA VIC/Z475/16, QV to Salisbury, 4 August 1891 (draft).

80. Hatfield House, 3M/E, Francis Knollys to Lord Salisbury, 8 August 1891.

81. Pope-Hennessy, *Queen Mary,* p. 103. For Mary of Teck, see p. 280, note.

82. Pope-Hennessy, *Queen Mary,* pp. 114–18. *The Daily News,* 27 July 1883. *Dundee Courier,* 3 August 1883.

83. Pope-Hennessy, *Queen Mary,* p. 105.

84. Ibid., p. 186.

85. Ibid., p. 137.
86. Arthur Balfour to Lord Salisbury, 30 August 1890, in Harcourt-Williams, *Salisbury–Balfour Correspondence*, p. 321. Pope-Hennessy, *Queen Mary*, p. 52.
87. Mapperton Papers, 287, Oliver Montagu to Aunt E [August 1891].
88. *The Times*, 10, 20 October 1891.
89. Francis Knollys to Henry Ponsonby, 19 August 1891, in Magnus, *Edward VII*, p. 299.
90. Cook, *Prince Eddy*, pp. 253–54.
91. *The Times*, 2 November 1891.
92. RA VIC/Z457/32, Alix to QV, 4 November 1891.
93. RA VIC/Z457/31, Dighton Probyn to QV, 2 November 1891. *The Times*, 10 November 1891.
94. *The Times*, 18, 21 November 1891.
95. RA VIC/Add 4/38, B to Vicky, 16 November 1891.
96. RA VIC/Z457/42, Alix to QV, 17 November 1891.
97. Pope-Hennessy, *Queen Mary*, p. 210.
98. RA VIC/Add A4/42, B to Vicky, 9 December 1891.
99. Pope-Hennessy, *Queen Mary*, p. 213.
100. RA VIC/Z475/49, Alix to QV, 6 December 1891 (copy).
101. Francis Knollys to Schomberg McDonnell, 6 January 1892, in Cook, *Prince Eddy*, p. 263.
102. RA VIC/Z475/137, Alix to QV, telegram, 8:28 p. m., 8 January 1892.
103. RA VIC/Z475/140, B to QV, telegram, 11:10 a.m., 10 January 1892. See Buckle, *Letters* (3rd series), vol. 2, p. 91.
104. *The Times*, 14 January 1892.
105. RA VIC/Z475/154, B to QV, telegram, 11 a.m., 13 January 1892. See Buckle, *Letters* (3rd series), vol. 2, p. 92.
106. Cook, *Prince Eddy*, p. 268. *The Times*, 14 January 1892.
107. Pope-Hennessy, *Queen Mary*, pp. 222–23. Cook, *Prince Eddy*, pp. 269–70. Battiscombe, *Queen Alexandra*, pp. 189–90.
108. RA VIC/Z475/169, B to QV, telegram, 9:35 a.m., 14 January 1892.
109. RA VIC/Z95/5, B to QV, 14 January 1892.
110. RA VIC/Z95/11, George to QV, 18 January 1892.
111. RA VIC/Z475/188, B to QV, telegram, 11:13 a.m., 16 January 1892.
112. RA VIC/Z475/198, QV to B, telegram (draft), 18 January 1892.
113. RA VIC/Z475/199, B to QV, telegram (draft), 18 January 1892.
114. RA VIC/Z475/207, QV to B, telegram draft, 19 January 1892.
115. RA VIC/Z475/200, Alix to QV, telegram draft, 18 January 1892.
116. Bodleian Library, Lincolnshire Papers, MS Film 1120, Carrington Diary, 20 January 1892.

CHAPTER 19: DAISY WARWICK 1892–96

1. Quennell, *Lonely Business*, p. 231.
2. Alix to George, September 1902, in Pope-Hennessy, *Queen Mary*, p. 373.
3. Mapperton Papers, Alix to Lady Sydney, 13 January 1893.
4. RA GV/CC27/30, Duchess of Mecklenburg-Strelitz to Princess Mary of Teck, 16 May 1892.

5. QVJ, 2 February 1892, in Buckle, *Letters* (3rd series), vol. 2, p. 96.

6. RA VIC/Z457/62, Alix to QV, 12 February 1892. Pope-Hennessy, *Queen Mary,* pp. 231–32.

7. Williams, *Contentious Crown,* p. 67. *Reynolds's Newspaper,* 17 January 1892. *The Times,* 15 January 1892.

8. RA VIC/Add A12/1910, Francis Knollys to Henry Ponsonby, 15 August 1892.

9. William Gladstone to QV, 7 November 1892, and QV to Henry Ponsonby, 9 November 1892, in Buckle, *Letters* (3rd series), vol. 2, pp. 178–79.

10. Lord Salisbury to Henry Ponsonby, 14 November 1892, in Buckle, *Letters* (3rd series), vol. 2, p. 180.

11. RA VIC/L16/80, Henry Ponsonby to QV, 15 November 1892: QV's note.

12. Algernon West to Henry Ponsonby, 14 November 1892, in Buckle, *Letters* (3rd series), vol. 2, pp. 180–81. Francis Knollys to Henry Ponsonby, 13 November 1892, in Buckle, *Letters* (3rd series), vol. 2, p. 179.

13. Warwick, *Afterthoughts,* p. 31.

14. Lee, *Edward VII,* vol. 1, pp. 216–17, but the date is wrong. See Magnus, *Edward VII,* p. 237.

15. RA GV/GG9/924, Frederick Ponsonby to Sidney Lee, 19 December 1922.

16. RA VIC/Add C07/1, B to Francis Knollys, 20 September 1895.

17. RA GV/AA19/54, B to George, 16 March 1893.

18. Daisy Warwick to W. T. Stead, "May 19th," in Warwick, *Life's Ebb and Flow,* p. 116.

19. Warwick, *Life's Ebb and Flow,* p. 113. Frank Harris, "Love Stories of Edward VII," *Pearson's Magazine,* September 1916.

20. Warwick, *Life's Ebb and Flow,* pp. 192–93. The London Library copy is annotated: "Christopher Sykes's House in Mayfair, Francis Knollys arranged."

21. Fitzwilliam Museum, Wilfrid Blunt Papers, MS 398, Diaries, 4 April 1909.

22. Caroline Spurrier Archive, B to Daisy [May 1899] (transcript).

23. Leslie, *Edwardians in Love,* pp. 162–63.

24. Elinor Glyn, *Romantic Adventure* (Ivor Nicholson and Watson, 1936), pp. 66–76.

25. Warwick, *Life's Ebb and Flow,* p. 193.

26. Harris, "Love Stories of Edward VII."

27. Blunden, *Countess of Warwick,* p. 125.

28. Harris, "Love Stories."

29. Daisy Warwick to W. T. Stead, 10 September 1893, in Blunden, *Countess of Warwick,* p. 85.

30. Warwick, *Life's Ebb and Flow,* p. 145.

31. Ibid., pp. 155–57.

32. Daisy Warwick to W. T. Stead, October 1893, in Blunden, *Countess of Warwick,* p. 85.

33. Prochaska, *Royal Bounty,* p. 123.

34. Rosebery's diary, January 1898, in McKinstry, *Rosebery,* p. 479.

35. Copenhagen Letters, Box 104, Alix to Minnie, 30 December 1884. QV to Vicky, 24 November 1875, in Fulford, *Darling Child,* pp. 198–99.

36. Mapperton Papers, Box 319, F. Sandwith to Lord Sandwich, 26 January 1893. B to Lord Sandwich, 24 December 1892. Alix to Lord Sandwich, 4 January 1893. Alix to Lady Sydney, 13 January 1893.

37. Fitzwilliam Museum, Wilfrid Blunt Papers, MS 398–1975, Diaries, 4 April 1909.
38. Mapperton Papers, Box 319, Alix to Lady Sydney, 13 January 1893.
39. Mapperton Papers, Box 319, Alix to Lord Sandwich, 24 February 1893.
40. Pope-Hennessy, *Queen Mary*, p. 293.
41. Ibid., p. 247.
42. RA VIC/Z457/87, Alix to QV, 11 June 1892.
43. Pope-Hennessy, *Queen Mary*, p. 230.
44. RA GV/AA19/35, B to George, 24 August 1892.
45. Pope-Hennessy, *Queen Mary*, pp. 244, 248.
46. RA GV/AA20/7, B to George, 4 May 1893. RA VIC/Add C07/1, George to Francis Knollys, 3 May 1893.
47. RA GV/AA20/7, B to George, 4 May 1893.
48. RA VIC/Z457/135, Alix to QV, 5 May 1893.
49. Pope-Hennessy, *Queen Mary*, p. 261.
50. RA VIC/EVIID/1893: 6 July.
51. *Letters of Tsar Nicholas and Empress Marie*, ed. Edward Bing (Ivor Nicholson and Watson, 1937), pp. 71–72.
52. Pope-Hennessy, *Queen Mary*, pp. 275–83.
53. Kenneth Rose, *King George V* (Phoenix, 1983), p. 57.
54. RA GV/AA20/10, B to George, 10 July 1893.
55. Lord Carisbrooke, Princess Beatrice's son, interview with Harold Nicolson, in James Lees-Milne, *Harold Nicolson* (Chatto and Windus, 1981), vol. 2, p. 234.
56. Harold Nicolson, *Diaries and Letters, 1945–62* (Collins, 1968), p. 174 (17 August 1949).
57. Seymour Fortescue, "King Edward as a Yachtsman," in Watson, *Edward VII as a Sportsman*, pp. 311, 319.
58. RA VIC/EVIID/1894: 3 March.
59. Bodleian Library, Lincolnshire Papers, MS Film 1120, Carrington Diary, 3 February 1895. *The Gladstone Diaries*, vol. 13, ed. H. C. G. Matthew (Clarendon Press, 1994), p. 386.
60. RA VIC/Add C07/1, William Gladstone to B, 28 February 1894.
61. Battiscombe, *Queen Alexandra*, pp. 192–93.
62. RA GV/AA19/53, B to George, 8 March 1893.
63. McKinstry, *Rosebery*, pp. 358–66.
64. Bodleian Library, Lincolnshire Papers, MS Film 1120, Carrington Diary, 18 July 1896.
65. Leslie, *Edwardians in Love*, pp. 290–91. McKinstry, *Rosebery*, pp. 484–87.
66. Richard Davenport-Hines, "A Radical Lord Chamberlain at a Tory Court: Lord Carrington, 1892–95," *Court Historian*, vol. 16 (2011), pp. 217–18.
67. Pope-Hennessy, *Queen Mary*, p. 321.
68. QV to Vicky, 6 June 1894, in Magnus, *Edward VII*, p. 245.
69. Pope-Hennessy, *Queen Mary*, p. 322.
70. RA VIC/Z457/252, Charlotte Knollys to QV, 29 October 1895.
71. Princess Henriette de Lieven to the Marquis de Soveral, in Gordon Brook-Shepherd, *Uncle of Europe* (Collins, 1975), p. 147.
72. RA VIC/EVIID/1894: 30 October.

73. RA GV/AA20/42, B to George, 1 November 1894. Warwick, *Afterthoughts,* p. 13.

74. RA VIC/Add C07/1, Arthur Ellis to Francis Knollys, 5 November 1894.

75. Minnie to Nicky, 27 June 1894, in Bing, *Letters of Tsar Nicholas,* p. 86.

76. RA GV/AA20/43, B to George, 5 November 1894.

77. *A Lifelong Passion: Nicholas and Alexandra,* ed. Andrei Maylunas and Sergei Mironenko (Weidenfeld and Nicolson, 1996), p. 99.

78. RA GV/AA/20/43, B to George, 5 November 1894.

79. Greg King, *The Court of the Last Czar* (New Jersey: John Wiley, 2006), p. 331.

80. RA VIC/Add C07/1, Charlotte Knollys to Francis Knollys, 5 November 1894.

81. RA VIC/Add C07/1, Arthur Ellis to Francis Knollys, 5 November 1894.

82. RA VIC/Add C07/1, Charlotte Knollys to Francis Knollys, 11 November 1894.

83. RA VIC/Add C07/1, Arthur Ellis to Francis Knollys [7 November 1894].

84. Bodleian Library, Lincolnshire Papers, MS Film 1120, Carrington Diary, 15 November 1894.

85. Ibid. *The Times,* 27 November 1894.

86. RA VIC/Z274/50, B to QV, 28 November 1894.

87. King, *Court of the Last Czar,* pp. 384–88.

88. QV to Victoria Battenberg, 21 October 1894, in Hibbert, *Queen Victoria in Her Letters and Journals,* p. 329.

89. RA VIC/Z457/202, Alix to QV, 6 December 1894.

90. RA VIC/Add C07/1, Arthur Ellis to Francis Knollys [7 November 1894].

91. Warwick, *Life's Ebb and Flow,* pp. 89–92.

92. Bodleian Library, Margot Asquith Papers, MSS Eng d3202, Diary, 15 May 1897.

93. RA VIC/EVIID/1895: 11 October. Blunden, *Countess of Warwick,* pp. 92–95.

94. *The Times,* 16 March 1896.

95. Roy Strong, *The Roy Strong Diaries* (Phoenix, 1998), p. 106.

96. Whyte, *Life of W. T. Stead,* vol. 2, p. 104.

97. Leslie, *Edwardians in Love,* p. 171. Anand, *Daisy,* pp. 79–81.

98. RA PS/GV/O479B/23B/2, B to Lady Warwick, 4 January 1898. See p. 328.

99. Fitzwilliam, Wilfrid Blunt Papers, MS 9–1975, Diary, 7 February 1909. Theo Aronson, *The King in Love* (John Murray, 1988), pp. 246–47. Weintraub, *Edward,* pp. 365, 411–12.

100. Bodleian Library, Lincolnshire Papers, MS Film 1120, Carrington Diary, 8 May 1897.

101. Weintraub, *Edward,* p. 310.

102. Hibbert, *Edward VII,* p. 236.

103. Romi, *Maisons Closes* (Editions Serg, n.d.), pp. 96–97. *World of Interiors,* September 1991, pp. 114–23.

104. Weintraub, *Edward,* p. 311.

105. Celia and John Lee, *Winston and Jack* (Celia Lee, 2007), pp. 148–49.

106. Churchill Archives Centre, Jennie Churchill Papers, CHAR 28/48/30–1, B to Jennie Churchill, 27 December 1894.

107. Churchill Archives Centre, Jennie Churchill Papers, CHAR 28/48/33–4, B to Jennie Churchill, 24 January 1895.

108. Lee, *Winston and Jack,* pp. 157–61.

109. Churchill Archives Centre, Jennie Churchill Papers, CHAR 28/50/55–6, 63–4, B to Jennie Churchill [1890s].
110. Warwick, *Afterthoughts,* p. 81.
111. Warwick, *Life's Ebb and Flow,* p. 140.
112. Leslie, *Edwardians in Love,* pp. 319–20.
113. Churchill Archives Centre, Jennie Churchill Papers, CHAR 28/61/5, B to Jennie Churchill, 2 February 1897.
114. Churchill Archives Centre, Jennie Churchill Papers, CHAR 28/50/46, B to Jennie Churchill, 2 o'c Tuesday [1897].
115. Lee, *Winston and Jack,* pp. 161–64.
116. B to Jennie Churchill, 25 February 1898, in ibid., p. 166.
117. Churchill Archives Centre, Jennie Churchill Papers, CHAR 28/50/15, B to Jennie Churchill, n.d.
118. Churchill Archives Centre, Jennie Churchill Papers, CHAR 28/49/28–9, B to Jennie Churchill, 28 July 1900.
119. RA PP/EVII/A15800 (February 1903), J. T. Woods to Francis Knollys, 5 February 1903, asking about B's height; note dated 10 February 1903 says HM's height is about five feet nine inches.
120. Whyte, *Life of W. T. Stead,* vol. 2, pp. 106–7, 110, 116–17, 121.
121. RA VIC/Add C07/1, B to Francis Knollys, 22 September 1895.
122. Francis Knollys to Arthur Bigge, 18 April 1895, in Rohl, *Wilhelm II,* p. 771.
123. Ibid., p. 772.
124. St. Aubyn, *Edward VII,* pp. 132–34.
125. Watson, *Edward VII as a Sportsman,* p. 148.
126. RA VIC/Z458/2, B to QV, 4 June 1896. *The Times,* 4 June 1896.
127. RA VIC/Add A23/110, QV to Beatrice, 3 June 1896.
128. Buckle, *Letters* (3rd series), vol. 3, p. 79.
129. *Lady Lytton's Court Diary,* ed. Mary Lutyens (Rupert Hart-Davis, 1961), p. 37.
130. Turner, *Court of St. James's,* p. 335.
131. Frederick Ponsonby, *Recollections of Three Reigns* (Odhams Press [1951]), p. 22.
132. Ibid., pp. 12–13.
133. Arthur Ponsonby, *Henry Ponsonby,* p. 359.
134. Matthew Dennison, *The Last Princess* (Weidenfeld and Nicolson, 2007), p. 205.
135. Mallet, *Life with Queen Victoria,* p. 72.
136. Lutyens, *Lady Lytton's Court Diary,* pp. 73, 75.
137. RA VIC/EVIID/1896: 25 September.
138. Schomberg McDonnell to Arthur Bigge, 15 September 1896, in Buckle, *Letters* (3rd series), vol. 3, p. 75.
139. Roberts, *Salisbury,* pp. 643–44.
140. Nicky to Minnie, 2 October 1896, in Bing, *Letters of Tsar Nicholas,* pp. 119–20.
141. Lutyens, *Lady Lytton's Court Diary,* p. 82.
142. Mallet, *Life with Queen Victoria,* p. 80.

CHAPTER 20: "WE ARE ALL IN GOD'S HANDS" 1897–1901

1. *The Diary of Beatrice Webb,* ed. Norman and Jeanne MacKenzie (Virago, 1986), vol. 2, p. 108 (5 February 1898).
2. Prochaska, *Royal Bounty,* p. 154.

3. Rothschild Archive, RAL000/848, G. E. Buckle to Lord Rothschild, 3 February 1897.
4. Prochaska, *Royal Bounty*, pp. 153–55.
5. Henry Burdett, *Prince, Princess and People* (Longmans, Green, 1889), pp. 229, 336–47.
6. Prochaska, *Royal Bounty*, pp. 127–31.
7. "A Foreign Resident" [T. H. S. Escott], *Society in the New Reign* (Fisher, Unwin, 1904), pp. 118–19.
8. Allfrey, *Jewish Court*, p. 16. RA VIC/EVIID/1899: 18 July.
9. "A Foreign Resident," *Society in the New Reign*, p. 114.
10. *The Times*, 15 March, 1 April, 5 April, 8 April 1897.
11. Michaela Reid, *Ask Sir James* (Eland, 1996), p. 144: Reid's diary, 4 April 1897. Shrabani Basu, *Victoria and Abdul* (History Press, 2011), pp. 185–95.
12. Reid, *Ask Sir James*, p. 154: Reid's diary, 18 February 1898, conversation with Lord Salisbury.
13. Blunden, *Countess of Warwick*, pp. 112–13.
14. RA VIC/EVIID/1897: 11–14 April.
15. "A Foreign Resident," *Society in the New Reign*, p. 113.
16. RA VIC/Add C07/1, B to Francis Knollys, 19 June 1896.
17. Bodleian Library, Lincolnshire Papers, MS Film 1120, Carrington Diary, 26 January 1897.
18. RA VIC/Add C07/1, Duke of Portland to Francis Knollys, 1 June 1897 (copy). RA VIC/Add C07/1, Lord Charles Beresford to the Duke of Portland, 1 June 1897 (copy). See pp. 266–67.
19. RA VIC/Add C07/1, Daisy Warwick to Francis Knollys, 6 June [1897] (copy). RA VIC/Add C07/1, Knollys to the Duke of Portland, 1 June 1896 (copy).
20. *The Times*, 18 June 1897.
21. Bodleian Library, Lincolnshire Papers, MS Film 1120, Carrington Diary, 17 June 1897.
22. B to Daisy Warwick, 17 June [1897], in Theo Lang, *My Darling Daisy* (Michael Joseph, 1966), pp. 26–27.
23. Leslie, *Edwardians in Love*, p. 103. See pp. 314–15.
24. Warwick, *Afterthoughts*, p. 92.
25. Jamie Wilson in *The Guardian*, 26 July 2001.
26. Holmes, *Edward VII*, vol. 2, pp. 405–6. But see Kuhn, *Democratic Royalism*, pp. 62–66.
27. Pope-Hennessy, *Queen Mary*, p. 335.
28. QVJ, 22 June 1897, in Buckle, *Letters* (3rd series), vol. 3, p. 174.
29. Longford, *Victoria RI*, p. 689. Greg King, *Twilight of Splendour: The Court of Queen Victoria During Her Diamond Jubilee Year* (John Wiley, 2007), p. 266.
30. See Francis Knollys to Arthur Bigge, 25 February 1897, in Buckle, *Letters* (3rd series), vol. 3, p. 140.
31. Kaiser William to QV, 10 June 1897, in Rohl, *Wilhelm II*, p. 968.
32. Magnus, *Edward VII*, p. 257. Murphy, *Duchess of Devonshire's Ball*, pp. 30–31, 69.
33. Murphy, *Duchess of Devonshire's Ball*, p. 118.
34. Consuelo Vanderbilt Balsan, *The Glitter and the Gold* (William Heinemann, 1953), p. 96.

35. RA GV/AA21/32, B to George, 16 August 1897.
36. RA GV/AA21/34, B to George, 23 August 1897.
37. Sigmund Muntz, *King Edward VII at Marienbad* (Hutchinson, 1934), pp. 35, 40, 45, 50.
38. RA VIC/Add U/419/67, B to Mrs. Emma Bourke, 19 September [1897] (copy).
39. RA VIC/Add U/419/4, B to Mrs. Eddie Bourke, [26 March 1898] (transcript).
40. RA VIC/Add U/419/55, B to Mrs. Eddie Bourke, 3 July [1899] (copy).
41. RA VIC/EVIID/1897: 25, 26 September; 16, 30 October; 3, 21, 27 November; 19, 20 December. Ds are inscribed on all these days.
42. RA PS/GV/O479B/23B/2, B to Daisy Warwick, 4 January 1898 (copy).
43. Warwick, *Life's Ebb and Flow,* p. 185.
44. Caroline Spurrier Archive, Daisy Warwick to W. T. Stead, 20 February 1898.
45. RA PS/GV/O479B/53, Lady Warwick to Lord Stamfordham, 23 June 1915.
46. Fitzwilliam, Wilfrid Blunt Papers, MS 11–1975, Diaries, 14 December 1910.
47. Margot Asquith on Alix, in Sarah Bradford, *King George VI* (Weidenfeld and Nicolson, 1989), p. 9.
48. RA VIC/EVIID/1897: 16, 17, 20, 21, 24, 27 June; 2, 5, 12 [twice], 16 [twice], 19, 20, 23 [twice], 24 [twice], 25 [twice] July.
49. Caroline Spurrier Archive, B to Daisy Warwick, n.d. [1898], two letters (Daisy transcripts).
50. Anand, *Daisy,* p. 81.
51. Daisy Warwick to Lord Rosebery, May 1900, in McKinstry, *Rosebery,* p. 481.
52. RA VIC/EVIID/1898: 1, 9, 10, 26 May; 9, 22 [twice, staying Warwick], 23 [twice], 24 [twice], 25 [twice], 26 [twice], 27 June.
53. RA GV/AA21/60, B to George, 26 June 1898.
54. Blunden, *Countess of Warwick,* pp. 127–28. Warwick, *Life's Ebb and Flow,* pp. 124–25.
55. Caroline Spurrier Archive, B to Daisy Warwick, n.d., Petworth [9 December 1899] (Daisy transcript).
56. Caroline Spurrier Archive, B to Daisy Warwick, n.d. [1899] (Daisy transcript).
57. Caroline Spurrier Archive, B to Daisy Warwick, n.d. [August 1899], Marienbad (Daisy transcript).
58. RA VIC/EVIID/1898: 27 February.
59. Leslie, *Edwardians in Love,* p. 230.
60. Diana Souhami, *Mrs. Keppel and Her Daughter* (Flamingo, 1997), p. 22. Victoria, Lady Sackville, was the source for this story.
61. Fitzwilliam, Wilfrid Blunt Papers, MS 9–1975, Diary, 7 February 1909.
62. Violet Trefusis, *Don't Look Round* (Hutchinson, 1952), p. 28.
63. Ibid., pp. 27–28.
64. *The Times,* 26 April 1898.
65. *The Last Edwardians: An Illustrated History of Violet Trefusis and Alice Keppel,* ed. John Phillips (Boston Athenaeum, 1985), p. 17.
66. Trefusis, *Don't Look Round,* p. 20.
67. Souhami, *Mrs. Keppel,* p. 21. Michael Holroyd, *A Book of Secrets* (Chatto and Windus, 2010), p. 53. Raymond Lamont-Brown, *Edward VII's Last Loves: Alice Keppel and Agnes Keyser* (Sutton Publishing, 1998), p. 57.
68. Holroyd, *Book of Secrets,* pp. 44–54. The name of Beckett's mistress was José

Dale-Lace. In 1895, shortly after she had given birth to her illegitimate child, the Prince of Wales visited Beckett at Kirkstall, his house near Leeds. Beckett wrote to Bertie to ask if he could present José privately beforehand, in order that she could entertain him at Kirkstall. He proposed to appear at Marlborough House with José at three p.m. the very next day. (RA VIC/Add C07/1, Ernest Beckett to B, 28 September 1895.) This was stopped, but, unabashed by the royal snub, José appealed directly to HRH herself: "My great fault apparently Sir has been that I loved Ernest with all my heart and soul." (RA VIC/Add C07/1, José Dale-Lace to B, 1 October 1895.) So pushy was she that Bertie took advice from George Lewis, who counseled him to avoid all contact, else YRH may find "that her presentation to you may fan her powers of imagination into creating one more story." (RA VIC/Add C07/1, George Lewis to B, 4 October 1895.)

69. Author emails from Miranda Villiers and John Phillips, January–February 2011.
70. Author conversation, Michael Holroyd, June 2011.
71. RA VIC/EVIID/1898: 18 July.
72. Warwick, *Life's Ebb and Flow*, p. 147.
73. Lamont-Brown, *Edward VII's Last Loves*, pp. 73–74.
74. Bodleian Library, Lincolnshire Papers, MS Film 1120, Carrington Diary, 28 July 1898.
75. RA VIC/Add A4/68, B to Vicky, 20 July 1898.
76. QVJ, 31 July 1898, in Buckle, *Letters* (3rd series), vol. 3, p. 261.
77. RA GV/AA22/3, B to George, 13 September 1898. RA GV/AA22/2, B to George, 8 September 1898.
78. RA GV/AA22/7, B to George, 25 October 1898.
79. Caroline Spurrier Archive, Daisy Warwick to W. T. Stead, 6 September 1898.
80. RA GV/AA22/5, B to George, 16 October 1898. Christopher Sykes, *Four Studies in Loyalty*, pp. 36–37. Christopher Simon Sykes, *The Big House* (HarperCollins, 2004), pp. 243–44.
81. RA GV/AA22/20, B to George, 16 August 1899.
82. Leslie, *Edwardians in Love*, pp. 294–95. Murphy, *Duchess of Devonshire's Ball*, p. 107.
83. Lee, *Edward VII*, vol. 2, p. 62.
84. Allfrey, *Jewish Court*, p. 136. Fitzwilliam, Wilfrid Blunt Papers, MS 9–1975, Diary, 27 June 1909.
85. Janet Morgan, *Edwina Mountbatten* (HarperCollins, 1991), pp. 18–19.
86. Ibid., p. 20. Warwick, *Afterthoughts*, pp. 91–92.
87. Caroline Spurrier Archive, B to Daisy Warwick [May 1899] (Daisy transcript).
88. RA VIC/Add U/419/1, B to Emma Bourke, 20 September [1899] (transcript).
89. *The Times*, 10 August 1900.
90. Bodleian Library, Lincolnshire Papers, MS Film 1120, Carrington Diary (8 July 1900).
91. RA VIC/EVIID/1899: 2 December.
92. RA VIC/EVIID/1899: 4 December.
93. Wernher also bought Bath House in Piccadilly, which had previously belonged to Baron Hirsch. Raleigh Trevelyan, *Grand Dukes and Diamonds* (Secker and Warburg, 1991), pp. 99, 109, 127–29.

94. Buckle, *Letters* (3rd series), vol. 3, p. 440.

95. B to Arthur Bigge, 19 December 1899, in ibid., vol. 3, p. 442.

96. RA GV/AA22/31, B to George, 8 January 1900.

97. *The Times*, 30 March 1900.

98. *The Times*, 16 March 1900. Lee, *Edward VII*, vol. 1, p. 752.

99. *The Times*, 27 February 1900.

100. Magnus, *Edward VII*, p. 263. Battiscombe, *Queen Alexandra*, p. 212.

101. Kaiser William to B, 21 December 1899, in Lee, *Edward VII*, vol. 1, p. 754.

102. Kaiser William to B, 4 February 1900, in Lee, *Edward VII*, vol. 1, p. 756.

103. B to Kaiser William, 8 February 1900, in Lee, *Edward VII*, vol. 1, p. 759.

104. Arthur Bigge to Lord Salisbury, 25 March 1900, in Buckle, *Letters* (3rd series), vol. 3, p. 518.

105. Lord Rosebery to QV, 15 March 1900, in ibid., vol. 3, p. 513.

106. B to Arthur Paget, March 1900, in *Personal Letters of King Edward VII*, ed. J. P. C. Sewell (Hutchinson, 1931).

107. RA VIC/EVIID/1895: 8 October.

108. RA VIC/EVIID/1900: 21 February. Allfrey, *Jewish Court*, p. 182.

109. Murphy, *Duchess of Devonshire's Ball*, p. 117.

110. Balsan, *Glitter and Gold*, pp. 29–30.

111. Sewell, *Personal Letters*, p. 50. Author email from Sarah Lutyens, 20 March 2008.

112. Caroline Spurrier Archive, B to Daisy Warwick, 9 April 1900 (Daisy transcript).

113. *The Times*, 5, 6 April 1900.

114. RA GV/AA22/3, B to George, 13 September 1898.

115. RA VIC/Z458/68, Charlotte Knollys to QV, 8 April 1900.

116. *The Times*, 5 April 1900.

117. Magnus, *Edward VII*, p. 266.

118. RA VIC/Add A4/169, B to Vicky, 25 July 1900.

119. RA VIC/Add A4/173, B to Vicky, 8 August 1900.

120. RA VIC/Add A4/172, B to Vicky, 5 August 1900.

121. Bodleian Library, Lincolnshire Papers, MS Film 1120, Carrington Diary (18 May 1900).

122. RA VIC/EVIID/1900: 31 July.

123. RA GV/AA21/52, B to George, 16 March 1898.

124. QVJ, 31 July 1900 in Buckle, *Letters* (3rd series), vol. 3, p. 579.

125. RA VIC/Add A4/170, B to Vicky, 31 July 1900.

126. Pakula, *Uncommon Woman*, p. 652.

127. William to QV, 12 October 1900, in ibid., p. 658. RA VIC/Add A4/177, B to Vicky, 12 September 1900.

128. Pakula, *Uncommon Woman*, p. 659.

129. RA GV/AA22/55, B to George, 16 October 1900.

130. RA VIC/Add A4/188, B to Vicky, 19 November 1900.

131. Reid, *Ask Sir James*, p. 199. Tony Rennell, *Last Days of Glory* (Viking, 2000), pp. 48–53.

132. Reid, *Ask Sir James*, p. 200.

133. Rennell, *Last Days*, p. 114.

134. Reid, *Ask Sir James*, p. 203.

135. *The Times,* 21 January 1901.

136. Reid, *Ask Sir James,* p. 205.

137. Ibid., p. 203.

138. Ibid., p. 210.

139. Frederick Ponsonby, *Three Reigns,* p. 82.

140. Reid, *Ask Sir James,* pp. 210–11.

141. RA VIC/EVIID/1900: 22 January.

CHAPTER 21: KING EDWARD THE CARESSER 1901–2

1. Nicolas Barker, private information, 9 September 2008. See Frederick Ponsonby to Lady Lytton, 22 January 1901, in Lutyens, *Lady Lytton's Court Diary,* pp. 151–52.

2. *The Times,* 24 January 1901. Ponsonby, *Three Reigns,* p. 83.

3. *The Times,* 24 January 1901. RA VIC/EVIID/1901: 23 January. Roger Fulford, "The King," in *Edwardian England,* ed. Simon Nowell-Smith (Oxford University Press, 1964), p. 4.

4. Roberts, *Salisbury,* p. 797.

5. RA VIC/EVII/W36/1, Text of Declaration, n.d. This document, which is on Privy Council paper and endorsed "Appd ER," was written after the event with help from Rosebery. See Lee, *Edward VII,* vol. 2, pp. 4–5; Sir Almeric Fitzroy, *Memoirs* (Hutchinson, n.d.), vol. 1, p. 42; Bodleian Library, Lincolnshire Papers, MS Film 1121, Carrington Diary, 23 January 1901; Rennell, *Last Days,* pp. 176–77.

6. Reid, *Ask Sir James,* pp. 215–16 (25 January 1901).

7. Rennell, *Last Days,* pp. 185–88, 294–300.

8. Ponsonby, *Three Reigns,* p. 85.

9. Lee, *Edward VII,* vol. 2, p. 8.

10. Rennell, *Last Days,* pp. 241–42.

11. RA VIC/Add A4/199, B to Vicky [7 February 1901].

12. Ponsonby, *Three Reigns,* pp. 85–93. Kuhn, *Democratic Royalism,* pp. 124–25.

13. Henry James to O. Wendell Holmes, in Weintraub, *Edward VII,* p. 390. James to Ariana Curtis, 3 February 1901, in *Henry James Selected Letters,* ed. Leon Edel (Harvard University Press, 1987), p. 329.

14. *The Times,* 23 January 1901.

15. Fitzwilliam, Wilfrid Blunt Papers, MS 6–1975, Diary, 23 January 1901.

16. Fulford, *Hanover to Windsor,* pp. 128–31. Fulford, "The King," pp. 4–5. St. Aubyn, *Edward VII,* p. 382.

17. Balsan, *Glitter and Gold,* pp. 119–20.

18. Magnus, *Edward VII,* pp. 364–65.

19. Hibbert, *Edward VII,* p. 195.

20. Ponsonby, *Three Reigns,* p. 201. Private information, Hugo Vickers, April 2010.

21. RA GV/CC29/16, Duchess of Mecklenburg-Strelitz to Mary, Duchess of York, 13 June 1901.

22. Warwick, *Afterthoughts,* p. 17.

23. Fulford, *Hanover to Windsor,* p. 139.

24. See Fulford, "The King," p. 16.

25. *Journals and Letters of Reginald Viscount Esher,* ed. Maurice Brett (Ivor Nicholson and Watson, 1934–38), vol. 1, p. 285 (17 February 1901).

26. Sir Lionel Cust, *King Edward VII and His Court* (John Murray, 1930), pp. 34–35. See RA VIC/Add A4/208, B to Vicky, 3 April 1901. RA VIC/Add A4/209, B to Vicky, 10 April 1900. RA VIC/Add A4/221, B to Vicky, 3 July 1901.

27. Alix to Vicky, 14 May 1901, in Magnus, *Edward VII,* p. 290.

28. Brett, *Journals and Letters,* vol. 1, p. 279 (6 February 1901).

29. Longford, *Victoria RI,* p. 542. For the saga of the Munshi's letters, see p. 586.

30. RA VIC/EVIID/1901: 13 April.

31. RA VIC/Add C07/9, Lord Esher to Francis Knollys, 14 February 1901.

32. RA VIC/Add A4/201, B to Vicky, 17 February 1901.

33. Arnstein, "Queen Victoria Opens Parliament," *Historical Research,* vol. 63 (1990), pp. 186–87.

34. Anna Keay, *The Crown Jewels* (Thames and Hudson, 2011), pp. 158–63.

35. Princess Mary to the Duchess of Mecklenburg-Strelitz, 16 February 1901; Alix to Queen Mary, 6 February 1911, in Pope-Hennessy, *Queen Mary,* pp. 363, 437.

36. Alix to Queen Mary, 6 February 1911, in ibid., p. 437.

37. Fitzwilliam, Wilfrid Blunt Papers, MS 6-1975, Diary, 28 March 1901.

38. *The Times,* 15 February 1901.

39. Cannadine, "The British Monarchy and the 'Invention of Tradition,'" in *The Invention of Tradition,* ed. Hobsbawm and Ranger.

40. David M. Craig, "The Crowned Republic? Monarchy and Anti-monarchy in Britain, 1760–1901," *Historical Journal,* vol. 46 (2003), p. 173. Homans, *Royal Representations,* pp. xvii–xxvii.

41. Fulford, *Hanover to Windsor,* pp. 141–42.

42. C. W. Stamper, *What I Know* (Mills and Boon, 1913), p. 243.

43. Winston Churchill to Jennie Churchill, 22 January 1901, in Randolph Churchill, *Churchill: Companion,* vol. 1, part 1, p. 545.

44. B to Emma Bourke, 23 January 1901, telegram (transcript), in Humphrey Whitbread Archive, W/H 75/75. Fitzwilliam, Wilfrid Blunt Papers, MS 6–1975, Diary (28 March 1901).

45. B to Emma Bourke, n.d. [October 1901], transcript, Humphrey Whitbread Archive, W/H 75/77. Lee, *Edward VII,* vol. 2, p. 416.

46. Bodleian Library, Lincolnshire Papers, MS Film 1121, Carrington Diary (21 February 1902).

47. Fitzwilliam, Wilfrid Blunt Papers, MS 6–1975, Diary (12 July 1904). *The Times,* 23 May 1901. RA VIC/Add A4/216, B to Vicky, 29 May 1901.

48. Anand, *Daisy,* pp. 108–15.

49. Warwick, *Afterthoughts,* p. 276.

50. Ibid., pp. 275–76.

51. Brett, *Journals and Letters,* vol. 1, p. 279 (5 February 1901).

52. Lee, *Edward VII,* vol. 2, p. 54.

53. RA GV/CC29/16, Duchess of Mecklenburg-Strelitz to Princess Mary, 18 June 1901.

54. Princess Mary to the Duchess of Mecklenburg-Strelitz, 27 January 1901, in Pope-Hennessy, *Queen Mary,* p. 363.

55. Duchess of Mecklenburg-Strelitz to Princess Mary, 26 May 1901, Pope-Hennessy, *Queen Mary,* p. 371.

56. Ibid.

57. Brett, *Journals and Letters*, vol. 1, p. 305 (14 October 1901).

58. Prochaska, *Royal Bounty*, p. 126.

59. Frank Prochaska, "Queen Mary," *ODNB*.

60. *Louisa Lady in Waiting*, ed. Elizabeth Longford (Jonathan Cape, 1979), p. 87.

61. Brett, *Journals and Letters*, vol. 1, pp. 345–46 (28 July 1902).

62. Duchess of York to the Grand Duchess of Mecklenburg-Strelitz, 17 June 1901, in Pope-Hennessy, *Queen Mary*, p. 361.

63. Countess of Airlie, *Thatched with Gold* (Hutchinson, 1962), p. 107.

64. Ponsonby, *Three Reigns*, p. 105.

65. Brett, *Journals and Letters*, vol. 1, p. 290 (18 March 1901).

66. Alix to George, August 1901, in Pope-Hennessy, *Queen Mary*, p. 375.

67. Ibid., p. 423.

68. A. W. Purdue, "Alexandra," *ODNB*. See Purdue, "Queen Adelaide: Malign Influence or Consort Maligned?," in Clarissa Campbell Orr, *Queenship in Britain, 1660–1837* (Manchester University Press, 2002), pp. 267–87.

69. Longford, *Louisa*, p. 79. Battiscombe, *Queen Alexandra*, p. 225.

70. Brett, *Journals and Letters*, vol. 1, p. 318 (18 November 1901).

71. Ibid., vol. 1, p. 373 (9 February 1902).

72. RA VIC/Add U/28, Sir Frederick Treves, "An Account of the Illness of King Edward VII in June 1902" (typescript), pp. 115–16.

73. A. C. Benson, *Edwardian Excursions*, ed. David Newsome (John Murray, 1981), p. 75.

74. RA VIC/Add A4/200, B to Vicky, 13 February 1901.

75. RA VIC/Add A4/201, B to Vicky, 17 February 1901.

76. RA VIC/Add A4/202, B to Vicky, 21 February 1901.

77. Ponsonby, *Three Reigns*, p. 110.

78. Ibid., p. 112.

79. Rose, *George V*, p. 315.

80. Pakula, *Uncommon Woman*, p. 667. RA VIC/Add A4/216, B to Vicky, 29 May 1901. RA VIC/Add A4/217, B to Vicky, 5 June 1901.

81. RA VIC/EVIID/1901: 31 July 1901.

82. RA VIC/MAIN/X19/1a, Princess Helena to B, 6 August 1901.

83. RA GV/AA23/5, B to George, 7 August 1901.

84. RA VIC/MAIN/X19/1b, Princess Helena to B, 10 August 1901.

85. RA GV/CC45/248, Duke of Connaught to the Duchess of York, 21 August 1901.

86. Lee, *Edward VII*, vol. 2, p. 26.

87. *The Diary of Sir Edward Hamilton, 1885–1906*, ed. Dudley Bahlman (Hull University Press, 1993), pp. 398, 400 (10, 20 February 1901).

88. Bodleian Library, Sandars Papers, MS Eng Hist. c. 718, fols. 67–68, Francis Knollys to Lord Salisbury, 15 June 1901.

89. Magnus, *Edward VII*, p. 357. Allfrey, *Jewish Court*, pp. 191–95. Kuhn, "Queen Victoria's Civil List," *Historical Journal*, vol. 36 (1993), pp. 663–64.

90. *Hansard*, 9 May 1901, vol. 93, cols. 1199–1214.

91. RA GV/AA23/16, B to George, 9 December 1901.

92. Magnus, *Edward VII*, pp. 289–90. Matthew Dennison, *The Last Princess* (Weidenfeld and Nicolson, 2007), pp. 225–29.

93. Ponsonby, *Three Reigns*, pp. 151–52.
94. Battiscombe, *Queen Alexandra*, p. 220.
95. Brett, *Journals and Letters*, vol. 3, October 1911.
96. RA VIC/Add C13, Nurse Haines's Diary, 9 September 1902.
97. Lee, *Edward VII*, vol. 2, p. 411.
98. Battiscombe, *Queen Alexandra*, p. 201.
99. Brett, *Journals and Letters*, vol. 1, p. 300 (20 June 1901).
100. Hibbert, *Edward VII*, p. 223.
101. Sidney Holland, Viscount Knutsford, *In Black and White* (Edward Arnold, 1926), p. 181.
102. Warwick, *Afterthoughts*, p. 21.
103. Longford, *Louisa*, p. 87.
104. Cust, *Edward VII*, p. 28.
105. Information from Simon Houfe, June 2009.
106. Hibbert, *Edward VII*, pp. 197–98.
107. John Martin Robinson, *Buckingham Palace* (Royal Collection, 2000), p. 125.
108. Cust, *Edward VII*, p. 91. Brett, *Journals and Letters*, vol. 1, pp. 306–7 (Lord Esher to Arthur Ellis, 20 February 1901).
109. Ellenberger, "Transformation of London 'Society' at the End of Victoria's Reign: Evidence from the Court Presentation Records," *Albion*, vol. 22 (1990), esp. pp. 638–53.

CHAPTER 22: "EDWARD THE CONFESSOR NUMBER TWO" 1902

1. Lord Salisbury, quoted in Roberts, *Salisbury*, p. 798.
2. Lee, *Edward VII*, vol. 2, p. 51.
3. RA VIC/Add U/28, Treves, "Illness of King Edward VII," pp. 57–58. Hibbert, *Edward VII*, plates 45, 46.
4. RA VIC/Add U/28, Treves, "Illness of King Edward VII," p. 8. Hibbert, *Edward VII*, p. 223.
5. RA VIC/Add U/28, Treves, "Illness of King Edward VII," pp. 5–6.
6. Cust, *Edward VII*, pp. 32–33.
7. RA VIC/Add U/28, Treves, "Illness of King Edward VII," pp. 10–11, 86.
8. Ibid., pp. 6–7.
9. RA VIC/EVIID/1902: 15 June.
10. *Lancet*, 25 June 1902.
11. Ibid., 5 July 1902.
12. *Lancet*, 25 June 1902.
13. RA VIC/Add U/28, Treves, "Illness of King Edward VII," p. 47.
14. Hibbert, *Edward VII*, p. 282. According to one of the doctors present, the King ceased breathing twice. Stephen Trombley, *Sir Frederick Treves* (Routledge, 1989), p. 130.
15. *Lancet*, 25 June, 5 July 1902.
16. RA VIC/Add U/28, Treves, "Illness of King Edward VII," pp. 74, 79.
17. RA VIC/Add A5/472, B to Mrs. Keppel, "Wednesday 10 a.m." [25 June 1902].
18. RA VIC/Add A5/473, B to Mrs. Keppel, "Thursday 9 a.m." [26 June 1902].
19. RA VIC/Add U/28, Treves, "Illness of King Edward VII," pp. 60, 87, 89.
20. RA VIC/Add U/28, Treves, "Illness of King Edward VII," p. 93.

21. Kenneth James, *Escoffier: The King of Chefs* (Hambledon, 2002), pp. 186–88.

22. Yvonne Ward, "'Gosh! Man I've Got a Tune in my Head': Edward Elgar, A. C. Benson and the Creation of 'Land of Hope and Glory,'" *Court Historian*, vol. 7 (2002), pp. 17–39.

23. J. E. C. Bodley, *The Coronation of Edward the Seventh* (Methuen, 1903), p. 201.

24. Fitzroy, *Memoirs*, vol. 1, p. 96. Kuhn, *Democratic Royalism*, pp. 125–28.

25. Fitzroy, *Memoirs*, vol. 1, pp. 98–99. Kuhn, *Democratic Royalism*, p. 95. Holmes, *Edward VII*, vol. 2, p. 513.

26. Balsan, *Glitter and Gold*, p. 132.

27. Holmes, *Edward VII*, vol. 2, p. 513.

28. Keay, *Crown Jewels*, p. 164.

29. Holmes, *Edward VII*, vol. 2, p. 516.

30. See Camp, *Royal Mistresses*, p. 376, for the controversy as to who exactly was sitting in the box.

31. Balsan, *Glitter and Gold*, p. 132. Battiscombe, *Queen Alexandra*, pp. 249–50.

32. Magnus, *Edward VII*, p. 299.

33. Keay, *Crown Jewels*, p. 166. Alix's crown had four intersecting arches in the manner of continental crowns, including those of Denmark, rather than the pair of crossing arches found on English crowns.

34. For Alix's baldness, see Frank Harris, "Some New Stories of King Edward," *Pearson's Magazine* (1916), p. 317.

35. A. Escoffier, *A Guide to Modern Cookery* (William Heinemann, 1911), pp. 481–82, 667. James, *Escoffier*, pp. 92–93, 181, 189, 204–5.

36. Bodleian Library, Lincolnshire Papers, MS Film 1121, Carrington Diary (4 February 1901).

37. Ponsonby, *Three Reigns*, p. 139.

38. Rose, *George V*, pp. 145–46.

39. Ponsonby, *Three Reigns*, p. 140.

40. David Cannadine, "The Last Hanoverian Sovereign?: The Victorian Monarchy in Historical Perspective, 1688–1988," in *The First Modern Society: Essays in English History in Honour of Lawrence Stone*, ed. A. L. Beier, David Cannadine, and James M. Rosenheim (Cambridge University Press, 1989), pp. 156–58.

41. Brett, *Journals and Letters*, vol. 1, p. 415 (29 June 1903).

42. RA VIC/Add C07/1, Thomas Sanderson to Francis Knollys, 27 October 1902. RA VIC/Add C07/1, Lord Lansdowne to Knollys, 28 October 1902.

43. RA VIC/X29/76c, Lady Gwendolen Cecil to Sidney Greville, 27 August 1903.

44. BL, Sidney Lee Papers, Add MS 56087A, Lee's Notes of Interview with Balfour, 24 November 1911.

45. *The Crawford Papers*, ed. John Vincent (Manchester University Press, 1984), p. 39 (2 June 1897).

46. Lord Salisbury, quoted in Roberts, *Salisbury*, p. 798.

47. B to Lord Salisbury, 17 February 1901, in Lee, *Edward VII*, vol. 2, p. 23.

48. Roberts, *Salisbury*, p. 798.

49. Schomberg McDonnell's memo to Lord Salisbury, 13 February 1902, in Simon Heffer, *Power and Place: The Political Consequences of King Edward VII* (Phoenix, 1999), pp. 124–25.

50. Lord Salisbury's note on McDonnell's memo, 13 February 1902, in ibid., p. 125.

51. Lee, *Edward VII*, vol. 2, p. 97.

52. RA VIC/W38/1, Lord Esher to Francis Knollys, 22 May 1900.

53. B to Lord Salisbury, 20 April 1902, in Lee, *Edward VII*, vol. 2, p. 98.

54. Heffer, *Power*, pp. 128–29. Stanley Martin, *The Order of Merit* (Tauris, 2007).

55. Longford, *Louisa*, p. 97.

56. RA VIC/W36/9, A. J. Balfour to Lord Knollys, 10 May 1902. Francis Knollys was created Viscount Knollys in the Coronation Honours of 1902.

57. The society doctor Sir Douglas Powell advised Lord Salisbury not to attend the Coronation on account of "irritability of the bladder and liability to over distension which would result in serious trouble. I am quite sure that if the King had any idea of this risk he would wish you to avoid it." (RA VIC/ W36/18, Lord Salisbury to B, 29 July 1902, enclosing Sir D. Powell to Salisbury, 28 July 1902.)

58. Arthur Balfour to Lady Elcho, 10 February 1901, in *The Letters of Arthur Balfour and Lady Elcho, 1885–1917*, ed. by Jane Ridley and Clayre Percy (Hamish Hamilton, 1992), p. 177.

59. BL, Sidney Lee Papers, Add MS 56087A, Lee's Notes of Interview with Balfour, 24 November 1911.

60. Bodleian Library, Sandars Papers, MS Eng Hist 718, fols. 19–21, Arthur Balfour to Lord Knollys, 9 February 1901; fols. 26–28, Knollys to Balfour, 9 February 1901; fols. 19 21, Balfour to Knollys, 9 February 1901.

61. BL, Add MS 48371, Diary of Almeric Fitzroy (9, 11 February 1901).

62. BL, Sidney Lee Papers, Add MS 56087A, Lee's Notes of Interview with Balfour, 24 November 1911.

63. Bodleian Library, Sandars Papers, MS Eng Hist, c. 718, fols. 116–17, Lord Knollys to J. S. Sandars, 18 July 1902.

64. Ponsonby, *Three Reigns*, pp. 146–47.

65. RA GV/GG9/218, Frederick Ponsonby to Arthur Davidson, 15 January 1913.

66. Heffer, *Power*, p. 148.

67. Arthur Balfour to Lord Knollys, 3 November 1902, in ibid., pp. 150–51.

CHAPTER 23: KING EDWARD THE PEACEMAKER 1903–5

1. Ponsonby, *Three Reigns*, pp. 154, 159.

2. Roderick R. McLean, *Royalty and Diplomacy in Europe, 1890–1914* (Cambridge, 2001), pp. 143–44.

3. Ibid., p. 146.

4. Daisy, Princess of Pless, *From My Private Diary* (John Murray, 1931), pp. 91–92 (29 March 1901).

5. RA GV/AA23/38, B to George, 12 April 1903.

6. Ponsonby, *Three Reigns*, p. 155.

7. RA VIC/W43/77, Frederick Ponsonby to Lord Knollys, 22 April 1903.

8. Ponsonby, *Three Reigns*, p. 159.

9. BL, Sidney Lee Papers, Add MS 56087A, fols. 134–38, Charles Hardinge to Sidney Lee, 14 November 1920.

10. Ponsonby, *Three Reigns*, p. 161.

11. Magnus, *Edward VII*, p. 384.

12. Bodleian Library, Sandars Papers, MS Eng Hist c. 719, fols. 58–59, Lord Knol-

lys to Arthur Balfour, 16 March 1903; fols. 60–61, Knollys to Balfour, 19 March 1903; fols. 66–67, Knollys to Balfour, 23 March 1903; fols. 70–71, Knollys to J. S. Sandars, 26 March 1903.

13. Bodleian Library, Sandars Papers, MS Eng Hist, c. 719, fols. 77–78, Duke of Norfolk to Charles Hardinge, draft telegram [8 April 1903].

14. Ponsonby, *Three Reigns*, pp. 162–64. Lee, *Edward VII*, vol. 2, pp. 230–33.

15. Bodleian Library, Sandars Papers, MS Eng. Hist, c. 719, fols. 152–56, Charles Hardinge to Arthur Balfour, 29 April 1903.

16. Lee, *Edward VII*, vol. 2, p. 237.

17. For B's friendship with Jeanne Granier, see Frank Harris, *My Life and Loves* (privately printed, 1922–27), vol. 2, pp. 467–69. This book is still considered so obscene that readers at the London Library are required to sit at a special desk supervised by a librarian; it is disappointingly bland. Bertie stayed at Cannes 16 February–6 March 1889, and visited Monte Carlo, where he stayed for two nights: 21–22 February. (RA VIC/EDVIID/1889: 16 February–6 March.) Randolph Churchill, who was also in Monte Carlo, wrote to Jennie about Jeanne Granier. Churchill Archives Centre, Jennie Churchill Papers, CHAR 28/9/9, Randolph Churchill to Jennie Churchill, 19 February 1889.

18. BL, Sidney Lee Papers, Add MS 56087A, fols. 1–3, George Saunders to Lee, 22 November 1911.

19. Ponsonby, *Three Reigns*, p. 171.

20. Shane Leslie, *Long Shadows* (John Murray, 1966), p. 97.

21. Pless, *Diary*, p. 95 (15 May 1903).

22. Jullian, *Edward and the Edwardians*, p. 248.

23. McLean, *Royalty and Diplomacy*, p. 148.

24. Memorandum by Eyre Crowe, 1 January 1907, in *British Documents on the Origins of the War*, vol. 3, *The Testing of the Entente, 1904–6*, ed. G. P. Gooch and Harold Temperley (HMSO, 1928), p. 397.

25. BL, Sidney Lee Papers, Add MS 56087A, fols. 7–9, Lee's Note of Interview with Balfour, 24 November 1911.

26. McLean, *Royalty and Diplomacy*, pp. 141–42.

27. See ibid., p. 142, note 7, for a list of modern analyses of British foreign policy during the reign that virtually ignores King Edward VII.

28. H. C. G. Matthew, "Edward VII," *ODNB*.

29. BL, Sidney Lee Papers, Add MS 56087A, fols. 1–3, George Saunders to Sidney Lee, 22 November 1911.

30. Christopher Andrew, "France and the Making of the Entente," *Historical Journal,* vol. 10 (1967), esp. pp. 101, 103–4.

31. Roberts, *Salisbury*, p. 643.

32. W. C. Sellers and R. J. Yeatman, *1066 and All That: A Memorable History of England* (Methuen, 2005), pp. 164–65.

33. Fulford, "The King," p. 33.

34. RA VIC/X/19/23e, Kaiser William to B, telegram, 1 April 1905.

35. Miranda Carter, *The Three Emperors* (Fig Tree, 2009), pp. 319–20.

36. B to Lord Lansdowne, 15 April 1905, in Lee, *Edward VII*, vol. 2, p. 340.

37. B to Louis Battenberg, 15 April 1905, in McLean, *Royalty and Diplomacy,* p. 115.

38. Ponsonby, *Three Reigns*, p. 211.

39. McLean, *Royalty and Diplomacy*, p. 115.
40. *The Times*, 1 May 1905.
41. BL, Sidney Lee Papers, Add MS 56087A, fols. 1–3, George Saunders to Sidney Lee, 22 November 1911.
42. Ponsonby, *Three Reigns*, pp. 216–17.
43. Souhami, *Mrs. Keppel*, p. 72.
44. Ponsonby, *Three Reigns*, p. 216.
45. McLean, *Royalty and Diplomacy*, p. 118.
46. George Wyndham to Pamela Tennant, 26 July 1903, in J. W. Mackail and Guy Wyndham, *Life and Letters of George Wyndham* (Hutchinson, 1925), vol. 2, p. 462.
47. Fitzwilliam, Wilfrid Blunt Papers, MS 10–1975, Diary, 7 May 1910, reporting conversation with Lady Elcho.
48. *The Times*, 22 July 1903.
49. Mary Kenny, *Crown and Shamrock* (New Island, 2009), pp. 83–89.
50. Mackail and Wyndham, *George Wyndham*, vol. 2, pp. 462–65.
51. Vincent, *Crawford Papers*, p. 67 (15 June 1902).
52. Sonia Keppel, *Edwardian Daughter* (Hamish Hamilton, 1958), p. 23.
53. Trefusis, *Don't Look Round*, p. 33.
54. Fitzwilliam, Wilfrid Blunt Papers, MS 7–1975, Diary, 12 July 1904.
55 Vita Sackville-West, *The Edwardians* (Hogarth Press, 1930), p. 147.
56. Ponsonby, *Three Reigns*, p. 152.
57. Balsan, *Glitter and Gold*, p. 120.
58. Phillips, *Last Edwardians*, p. 21.
59. Fitzwilliam, Wilfrid Blunt Papers, MS 7–1975, Diary, 12 July 1904.
60. Sackville-West, *Edwardians*, pp. 204–5.
61. McKinstry, *Rosebery*, p. 496.
62. Fitzroy, *Memoirs*, vol. 1, pp. 160–61.
63. Diane Urquhart, *The Ladies of Londonderry* (I. B. Tauris, 2007), pp. 82–84.
64. Fitzroy's MSS diary, 18 October 1903, in Richard Davenport-Hines, *Ettie* (Weidenfeld and Nicolson, 2008), p. 152.
65. See Warwick, *Afterthoughts*, pp. 46, 256.
66. *The Times*, 6 January 1904.
67. Pless, *Diary*, pp. 126–27 (10, 12 January 1904). Vane, *Affair of State*, p. 241.
68. Bodleian Library, Lincolnshire Papers, MS Film 1121, Carrington Diary, 2 February 1906.
69. Magnus, *Edward VII*, p. 316.
70. Bodleian Library, Lincolnshire Papers, MS Film 1121, Carrington Diary, 12 September 1903.
71. Magnus, *Edward VII*, p. 318.
72. Fitzroy, *Memoirs*, vol. 1, p. 146.
73. Bodleian Library, Lincolnshire Papers, MS Film 1121, Carrington Diary, 29 September 1903.
74. Magnus, *Edward VII*, pp. 318–19.
75. Heffer, *Power*, p. 180.
76. RA VIC/Add C7/2/S, B to Lord Knollys, 28 August 1903.
77. David Gilmour, *Curzon* (John Murray, 1994), pp. 291–92.
78. Earl of Midleton, *Records and Reactions* (John Murray, 1939), pp. 159–62.

79. Lord Esher to Maurice Brett, 21 September 1903, in Brett, *Journals and Letters,* vol. 2, p. 14.

80. Lord Esher to Arthur Balfour, 25 September 1903, in ibid., vol. 2, p. 19.

81. Lord Esher to Maurice Brett, 11 October 1903, in ibid., vol. 2, p. 27.

82. Lees-Milne, *Esher,* pp. 16, 136.

83. Lord Esher to Admiral John Fisher, 6 August 1904, in Arthur J. Marder, ed., *Fear God and Dread Nought: The Correspondence of Admiral of the Fleet Lord Fisher of Kilverstone* (Cape, 1952–59), vol. 1, p. 324.

84. Lord Esher to Arthur Balfour, 16 January 1904, in Brett, *Journals and Letters,* vol. 2, p. 38.

85. W. S. Hamer, *The British Army: Civil-Military Relations, 1885–1905* (Oxford: Clarendon Press, 1970), pp. 13–14, 36–37.

86. Ibid., pp. 243–44.

87. Ibid., p. 225.

88. Bodleian Library, Sandars Papers, MS Eng Hist. c. 720, fols. 80–90, Lord Salisbury to Arthur Balfour, 21 April 1905.

89. Bodleian Library, Lincolnshire Papers, MS Film 1121, Carrington Diary, 11 December 1905.

90. Lord Esher to Maurice Brett, 5 March 1906, in Brett, *Journals and Letters,* vol. 2, p. 149.

91. Lees-Milne, *Esher,* p. 161.

92. B to Lord Knollys, 16 April 1904, in Lee, *Edward VII,* vol. 2, p. 253.

93. Fulford, "The King," pp. 26–27.

94. Bodleian Library, Sandars Papers, MS Eng Hist, c. 719, Lord Knollys to J. S. Sandars, 22 December 1903.

95. Bodleian Library, Sandars Papers, MS Eng Hist, c. 719, fols. 247–48, J. S. Sandars to Lord Knollys, 27 December 1903 (draft).

96. Lee, *Edward VII,* vol. 2, p. 243.

97. Bodleian Library, Sandars Papers, MS Eng Hist, c. 720, fol. 37, Lord Knollys to Arthur Balfour, 16 February 1905.

98. Bodleian Library, Sandars Papers, MS Eng Hist, c. 720, fol. 109, Lord Knollys to Arthur Balfour, 25 July 1905.

99. Gilmour, *Curzon,* pp. 217, 236.

100. Lord Knollys to Arthur Balfour, 1 September 1905 (telegram), in St. Aubyn, *Edward VII,* p. 391.

101. Bodleian Library, Sandars Papers, MS Eng Hist, c. 720, fol. 128b, Arthur Balfour to Lord Knollys, 1 September 1905 (copy).

102. See Gilmour, *Curzon,* p. 348.

103. Bodleian Library, Sandars Papers, MS Eng Hist, c. 720, fols. 129–30, Lord Knollys to J. S. Sandars, 2 September 1905.

104. RA VIC/Add C07//P, Arthur Balfour to Lord Knollys, 6 September 1905.

CHAPTER 24: UNCLE OF EUROPE 1905–7

1. Census Records, 1881, 1891, 1901. *The Times,* 22 April 1914.

2. Stamper, *What I Know.*

3. Rose, *George V,* p. 296.

4. Keppel, *Edwardian Daughter,* p. 20.

5. Bodleian Library, Lincolnshire Papers, MS Film 1121, Carrington Diary, 5 February 1905.

6. Ponsonby, *Three Reigns*, p. 204. *The Times*, 6, 7, 9, 11 December 1905.

7. RA GV/AA24/29, B to George, 30 November–1 December 1905.

8. RA GV/AA24/30, B to George, 8 December 1905.

9. Asquith, *Autobiography*, vol. 2, p. 72.

10. Lord Knollys to B, 8 December 1905, in Heffer, *Power*, p. 208.

11. Fitzroy, *Memoirs*, vol. 1, p. 272.

12. RA VIC/Add A17/1033, B to Louise, 11 December 1905.

13. RA GV/AA24/31, B to George, 15 December 1905.

14. Brett, *Journals and Letters*, vol. 2, pp. 126–27.

15. Frank Hardie, *The Political Influence of the British Monarchy, 1868–1952* (Batsford, 1970), p. 83.

16. R. B. Haldane to Lord Knollys, 12 September 1905, and Knollys's reply, in John Wilson, *CB: A Life of Sir Henry Campbell-Bannerman* (Constable 1973), pp. 427–30.

17. Ponsonby, *Three Reigns*, p. 234.

18. Wilson, *CB*, p. 426.

19. RA VIC/Add U417, B to the Marquis de Soveral, 27 August 1905. Wilson, *CB*, pp. 144–45, 427.

20. Heffer, *Power*, p. 208.

21. RA VIC/Add C07/9, Lord Esher to Lord Knollys, 10 October 1905.

22. RA GV/AA24/32, B to George, 22 December 1905.

23. BL, Sidney Lee Papers, Add MSS 56087A, fols. 134–38, Charles Hardinge to Sidney Lee, 14 November 1920.

24. Carter, *Three Emperors*, pp. 306–8.

25. RA VIC/Add C07/2/Q, Charles Hardinge to Lord Knollys, 27 September 1905.

26. RA GV/AA23/27, B to George, 17 November 1905.

27. Quoted in Harold Nicolson, *Sir Arthur Nicolson, First Lord Carnock* (Constable, 1930), p. 214.

28. Ibid., pp. 171, 212.

29. Williams, *It Was Such Fun*, pp. 223–24.

30. Zara Steiner, "The Last Years of the Old Foreign Office, 1898–1905," *Historical Journal*, vol. 6 (1963), p. 80.

31. Ibid., p. 82.

32. Charles Hardinge to Lord Knollys, 25 May 1904, in Lee, *Edward VII*, vol. 2, p. 291.

33. RA VIC/Add C07/2/Q, Charles Hardinge to Lord Knollys, 17 November 1905.

34. Steiner, "Last Years," pp. 82–85.

35. Zara Steiner, "Grey, Hardinge and the Foreign Office, 1906–1910," *Historical Journal*, vol. 10 (1967), pp. 415–17.

36. RA VIC/Add C07/2/Q, Charles Hardinge to Lord Knollys, 21 June 1906.

37. RA GV/GG9/661, Arthur Davidson to Frederick Ponsonby, 27 November 1914.

38. RA GV/CC24/43, Mary, Princess of Wales to Augusta, Grand Duchess of Mecklenburg-Strelitz, 22 February 1906.

39. RA VIC/R27/36, Note by B on CB's letter of 9 March 1906.

40. Brett, *Journals and Letters,* vol. 2, p. 265 (1 December 1907).

41. RA VIC/R27/78, Memo by B, 18 July 1906.

42. RA VIC/R27/79, Sir Henry Campbell-Bannerman to Lord Knollys, 19 July 1906.

43. RA VIC/R27/80, Memo by B, 19 July 1906.

44. Bodleian Library, Sandars Papers, MS Eng Hist, c. 720, fol. 109, Lord Knollys to Arthur Balfour, 25 July 1905.

45. RA VIC/X16/3, B to Winston Churchill, 20 August 1906. Randolph Churchill, *Winston S. Churchill,* vol. 2, *Young Statesman* (Heinemann, 1967), pp. 158–61.

46. Robert Benson to Robert Witt (secretary of the NACF), 19 January 1906, in Mary Yule, "The Acquisition of Velazquez's Rokeby Venus" (typescript, 2007). See Edmund Gosse, letter to *The Times,* 15 March 1906.

47. Lady Colin Campbell in *The World,* 15 November 1905, in Yule, "Acquisition of Velazquez's Rokeby Venus," p. 9.

48. Ibid., p. 12.

49. RA VIC/R28/27, B to Lord Knollys, 12 March 1907.

50. B to Sir Henry Campbell-Bannerman, 29 March 1907, in Lee, *Edward VII,* vol. 2, p. 468.

51. Caroline Spurrier Papers, B to Daisy Warwick, n.d. [1899].

52. Stamper, *What I Know,* p. 157.

53. RA GV/AA24/37, B to George, 26 January 1906.

54. *Autobiography of Sir Felix Semon,* ed. Henry Semon and Thomas McIntyre (Jarrold, 1926), p. 280.

55. RA GV/AA24/43, B to George, 8 March 1906. B to Lady Londonderry, 26 March 1906, in Lee, *Edward VII,* vol. 2, pp. 510–11.

56. Keppel, *Edwardian Daughter,* p. 44.

57. Vane, *Affair of State,* p. 187.

58. RA VIC/W64/87, Lord Loreburn to B, 27 February 1906.

59. Stamper, *What I Know,* pp. 42–44. Lee, *Edward VII,* vol. 2, pp. 511–14.

60. B to Prince Charles of Denmark, 11 August 1905, in Lee, *Edward VII,* vol. 2, p. 321.

61. Carter, *Three Emperors,* p. 324.

62. Ibid., p. 325.

63. Lord Lansdowne to Frank Lascelles, 25 September 1905, in McLean, *Royalty and Diplomacy,* p. 123.

64. BL, Sidney Lee Papers, Add MSS 56087A, fols. 134–38, Charles Hardinge to Sidney Lee, 14 November 1920.

65. Thomas A. Kohut, "Kaiser Wilhelm and His Parents," in *Kaiser Wilhelm II,* ed. John Rohl and Nicolaus Sombart (Cambridge University Press, 1982), pp. 84–88.

66. B to Kaiser William, 27 January 1906, in Lee, *Edward VII,* vol. 2, p. 525.

67. Kaiser William to B, 1 February 1906, in ibid., vol. 2, pp. 525–26.

68. RA VIC/Add C07/2/S, B to Lord Knollys, 19 March 1906.

69. McLean, *Royalty and Diplomacy,* p. 126.

70. Carter, *Three Emperors,* p. 331.

71. John Phillips Archive, Transcript of Menu Hôtel du Palais Biarritz, in King's handwriting, ER le 2 Avril 1906.

72. Pope-Hennessy, *Queen Mary,* p. 400.

73. RA VIC/W50/33 Charles Hardinge to Lord Knollys, 20 October 1906.

74. McLean, *Royalty and Diplomacy,* p. 200.

75. Magnus, *Edward VII,* p. 122.

76. RA VIC/W49/75, Charles Hardinge to Lord Knollys, 16 July 1906.

77. RA VIC/W49/82, Charles Hardinge to Lord Knollys, 28 July 1906.

78. *The Times,* 16 August 1906.

79. RA VIC/W49/93, Charles Hardinge to Lord Knollys, 19 August 1906.

80. Ponsonby, *Three Reigns,* p. 181.

81. Ibid., p. 182.

82. RA VIC/W49/93, Charles Hardinge to Lord Knollys, 19 August 1906.

83. RA VIC/W49/95, Charles Hardinge to Edward Grey, 16 August 1906.

84. Ponsonby, *Three Reigns,* p. 272.

85. Stamper, *What I Know,* pp. 73, 141.

86. RA VIC/X32/264, Stanley Clarke (equerry) to Lord Knollys, 24 September 1906. Ponsonby, *Three Reigns,* pp. 235–36.

87. RA VIC/Add U/28, Treves, "Illness of King Edward VII," p. 13. The rodent ulcer had apparently been cured by X-ray before the Coronation, but "the malignant growth returned and by January 1906 had assumed serious proportions and had become adherent to the bone."

88. Lee, *Edward VII,* vol. 2, p. 404. Prochaska, *Royal Bounty,* pp. 152–53: Sir Ernest Cassel and Lord Iveagh founded a Radium Institute on Portland Place that opened in 1911.

89. *Crawford Papers,* p. 153 (8 May 1910).

90. Hibbert, *Edward VII,* pp. 229–30. *The Times,* 11, 12 July 1906.

91. Bodleian Library, Lincolnshire Papers, MS Film 1121, Carrington Diary, 10 July 1906.

92. Bodleian Library, Lincolnshire Papers, MS Film 1121, Carrington Diary, February 1907.

93. Stamper, *What I Know,* p. 102. Ponsonby, *Three Reigns,* p. 225.

94. Stamper, *What I Know,* p. 102.

95. Semon and McIntyre, *Autobiography,* p. 283.

96. *The Times,* 8 March 1907.

97. RA VIC/X32/286, G. de Reuter to Arthur Davidson, 6 March 1908 [*sic—actually 1907*].

98. Winston Churchill to Lord Elgin, 27 March 1907, in Randolph Churchill, *Winston S. Churchill: Companion,* vol. 2 (Heinemann, 1969), part 1, p. 653.

99. Morgan, *Edwina Mountbatten,* p. 28.

100. Lee, *Edward VII,* vol. 2, p. 534. Stamper, *What I Know,* pp. 109, 111.

101. Lee, *Edward VII,* vol. 2, p. 544.

102. RA VIC/W51/22, Charles Hardinge to Lord Knollys, 17 February [1907]. RA VIC/W51/23, Hardinge to Knollys, 18 February 1907.

103. *The Times,* 9 April 1907.

104. RA VIC/W52/9, Charles Hardinge to Lord Knollys, 19 July [1907].

105. *The Times,* 19 April 1907.

106. Frank Lascelles to Edward Grey, 19 April 1907, in *British Documents on the Origin of the War,* ed. C. P. Gooch and H. Temperley (HMSO, 1930), vol. 6, p. 28.

107. Frederick Ponsonby to Charles Hardinge, 25 April 1907, in Magnus, *Edward VII,* p. 479.

108. Carter, *Three Emperors,* p. 345.

109. RA VIC/Add U417, B to the Marquis de Soveral, 19 September 1907.

110. Bodleian Library, Lincolnshire Papers, MS Film 1121, Carrington Diary, 13 August 1906.

111. RA VIC/W51/71, Charles Hardinge to Lord Knollys, 6 April 1907.

112. RA VIC/W52/9, Charles Hardinge to Lord Knollys, 19 July [1907].

113. RA VIC/W52/12, Charles Hardinge to Lord Knollys, 22 August 1907. Lee, *Edward VII,* vol. 2, pp. 546–47. Ponsonby, *Three Reigns,* p. 184.

114. RA VIC/Add U417, B to the Marquis de Soveral, 19 September 1907.

115. RA VIC/Add U417, B to the Marquis de Soveral, 20 September 1907.

116. Stamper, *What I Know,* p. 137.

117. Leslie, *Edwardians in Love,* p. 301. Lady Cunard, with others, lunched with the King on 1 September 1907 (RA VIC/EVIID/1907: 1 September).

118. B to Lord Knollys, 31 October 1907, in Lee, *Edward VII,* vol. 2, p. 554.

119. John Rohl, "The Emperor's New Clothes," in Rohl and Sombart, *Wilhelm II,* p. 48. See Lamar Cecil, *Wilhelm II* (University of North Carolina Press, 1996), vol. 2, pp. 112–15.

120. RA VIC/W50/18, Charles Hardinge to B, 9 October 1906.

121. RA VIC/W52/43, Edward Grey to Lord Knollys, 11 October 1907.

122. Edward Grey to Frank Lascelles, 1 November 1907, in Gooch and Temperley, *British Documents,* vol. 6, p. 88. McLean, *Royalty and Diplomacy,* p. 204.

123. RA VIC/W52/53, Edward Grey to Lord Knollys, 1 November 1907.

124. Charles Hardinge to Frank Lascelles, 2 October 1907, in Gooch and Temperley, *British Documents,* vol. 6, p. 84.

125. Kaiser William to B, 20 June 1907, in Lee, *Edward VII,* vol. 2, pp. 546–47.

126. Jonathan Steinberg, "The Kaiser and the British," in Rohl and Sombart, *Wilhelm II,* pp. 133–34.

127. Brett, *Journals and Letters,* vol. 2, p. 255 (16 November 1907).

128. Edward Grey to Francis Bertie, 20 November 1907, in Gooch and Temperley, *British Documents,* vol. 6, p. 102.

CHAPTER 25: KING CANUTE 1908–9

1. RA VIC/EVIID/1908: 6 March.

2. Auguste Rodin to Daisy Warwick, 7–8 March 1908, Rodin Archive: I am grateful to Victoria Fishburn for this reference.

3. Marion J. Hare, "Rodin and His English Sitters," *Burlington Magazine,* vol. 129 (1987), pp. 374–75.

4. Battiscombe, *Queen Alexandra,* p. 261.

5. RA PS/GV/O/479B/23A, Charles Russell's Memo for Lord Stamfordham, 21 July 1914.

6. RA PS/GV/O/479B/109, Lady Algernon Gordon-Lennox, n.d., fragment.

7. Ibid. Warwick, *Afterthoughts,* p. 29. Warwick, *Life's Ebb and Flow,* p. 158.

8. RA PS/GV/O/479B/23A, Charles Russell's Memo for Lord Stamfordham, 21 July 1914.

9. RA PS/GV/O/479B/12, Lord Stamfordham to George, 6 July 1914.

10. Warwick, *Afterthoughts,* pp. 21–22.

11. Daisy claimed in her memoirs in 1929 that the marble bust had been bought

by the Rodin Gallery in New York, but according to Hare it never reappeared after she sold it. (Warwick, *Life's Ebb and Flow,* p. 165. Hare, "Rodin," pp. 374–75.)

12. RA VIC/EVIID/1908: 4 March. Wilson, *CB,* p. 621.

13. RA VIC/Add C07/2/G, B to Lord Knollys, 21 March 1908. Warwick, *Afterthoughts,* p. 33.

14. H. H. Asquith to Margot Asquith, 4 March 1908, in *Life of Herbert Henry Asquith, Lord Oxford and Asquith,* ed. J. A. Spender and Cyril Asquith (Hutchinson, 1932), vol. 1, p. 195. This conversation is dated as taking place on 29 February 1908 after the Privy Council by Margot Asquith. (Bodleian Library, MS Eng d3206, Margot Asquith Diary, 29 February 1908.) See Fitzroy, *Memoirs,* vol. 2, p. 341 (29 February 1908).

15. RA VIC/X33/373, Arthur Davidson to Francis Bertie, 17 November 1908. Lee, *Edward VII,* vol. 2, pp. 577, 687.

16. Keppel, *Edwardian Daughter,* pp. 44–45. Stamper, *What I Know,* pp. 175–85.

17. RA VIC/Add C07/2/G, B to Lord Knollys, 25 March 1908.

18. B to Sir Henry Campbell-Bannerman, telegram, 3 April 1908, in Lee, *Edward VII,* vol. 2, p. 580.

19. H. H. Asquith to Margot Asquith, 6 (actually 8) April 1908, in Spender and Asquith, *Life,* vol. 1, p. 197.

20. *The Times,* 7, 9 April 1908.

21. Lee, *Edward VII,* vol. 2, p. 582. Bodleian Library, Lincolnshire Papers, MS Film 1121, Carrington Diary, 8, 16 April 1908. Brett, *Journals and Letters,* vol. 2, pp. 300–301 (5 April 1908).

22. RA VIC/Add C07/2/G, Arthur Davidson to Lord Knollys, 30 March 1908.

23. Bodleian Library, Lincolnshire Papers, MS Film 1121, Carrington Diary, 16 April 1908.

24. RA VIC/W39/115, Lord Esher to Lord Knollys, 6 September 1905. RA VIC/W39/131, Lord Esher to Lord Knollys, 30 December 1905. Admiral John Fisher to Lord Esher, 23 December 1908; Fisher to Esher, 15 March 1909, in Brett, *Journals and Letters,* vol. 2, pp. 363, 375.

25. RA VIC/W39/117, Lord Esher to Lord Knollys, 10 September 1905.

26. Bodleian Library, Lincolnshire Papers, MS Film 1121, Carrington Diary, 15 March 1907.

27. *The Times,* 6 February 1908.

28. Kaiser William to Lord Tweedmouth, 14 February 1908, in Lee, *Edward VII,* vol. 2, p. 605.

29. B to Kaiser William, n.d., in ibid., vol. 2, p. 606.

30. Brett, *Journals and Letters,* vol. 2, pp. 287–88.

31. Admiral John Fisher to Lord Esher, 19 April 1908, in Marder, *Fear God and Dread Nought,* vol. 2, p. 174.

32. RA VIC/EVIID/1908: 5 June.

33. Admiral John Fisher to his wife, 7 June 1908, in Marder, *Fear God and Dread Nought,* vol. 2, p. 180.

34. RA VIC/W52/118, Charles Hardinge to Lord Knollys, 16 February 1908.

35. Ponsonby, *Three Reigns,* p. 196. Carter, *Three Emperors,* pp. 353–54.

36. Nicolson, *Sir Arthur Nicolson,* pp. 269–73.

37. King, *Last Czar,* pp. 430–31.

38. Frances Welch, *The Romanovs and Mr. Gibbs* (Short Books, 2002), p. 14.

39. Admiral John Fisher to R. McKenna, 12 June 1908, in Marder, *Fear God and Dread Nought,* vol. 2, p. 181.

40. Prince von Bülow, *Memoirs* (Putnam, 1931), vol. 2, p. 309.

41. Kaiser William's minute, 25 June 1908, in Lee, *Edward VII,* vol. 2, p. 596.

42. McLean, *Royalty and Diplomacy,* pp. 166–67.

43. Lord Knollys to H. H. Asquith, 15 June 1908, in Magnus, *Edward VII,* p. 409.

44. RA VIC/W66/26, Alexander Murray of Elibank to Lord Knollys, 17 June 1908.

45. RA VIC/W66/31, Alexander Murray of Elibank to Lord Knollys, 26 June 1908.

46. RA VIC/W66/29, Arthur Ponsonby to Lord Knollys, 23 June 1908. RA VIC/W66/38, Ponsonby to Knollys, 1 July 1908. RA VIC/W66/39, Note by B, 3 July 1908.

47. Matthew, "Edward VII," *ODNB.*

48. RA VIC/W66/25, Lord Northcliffe to Lord Knollys, 2 June 1908.

49. RA VIC/X33/366c, Schomberg McDonnell to Lord Knollys, 5 June 1908. RA VIC/X33/366d, Note by B, 7 June 1908.

50. RA VIC/X34/414, Arthur Davidson to Lord Althorp, Lord Chamberlain, 26 March 1908.

51. RA VIC/X34/405, Colonel Hon. Charles Gathorne-Hardy to Frederick Ponsonby, 24 February [1908].

52. Turner, *Court of St. James's,* p. 344.

53. Ibid. p. 345.

54. The message was conveyed by Lord Churchill, not Winston, as Magnus suggests. (*Edward VII,* p. 497.) RA VIC/W66/22, Lord Churchill to Lord Knollys, 31 May 1908. RA VIC/W66/23, Knollys to Lord Churchill, 1 June 1908. Winston Churchill wrote to the King begging that the duke, who was a Knight of the Garter, should be permitted to attend the dinner after the Garter ceremonies; this was granted. (Mary Lovell, *The Churchills,* Little, Brown, 2011, p. 263.)

55. Bodleian Library, MS Eng. d. 3206, Margot Asquith Diary, 20 June 1908. This passage was cut from Margot's published autobiography.

56. Broadlands Archive, Cassel Papers, XI, Emma Bourke to B, n.d. [1907].

57. Broadlands Archive, Cassel Papers, XI, B to Cassel, 5 April [1907].

58. RA VIC/Add U/419/100, B to Emma Bourke, 4 August 1908.

59. For B's letters to Mabel Batten, see Cara Lancaster Archive.

60. Fitzwilliam, Wilfrid Blunt Papers, MS 9–1975, Diary (8 December 1908).

61. Fitzwilliam, Wilfrid Blunt Papers, MS 7–1975, Diary (15 April 1906); MS 9–1975, Diary (8 December 1908).

62. Grey's memorandum, 6 August 1908, in Gooch and Temperley, *British Documents,* vol. 6, p. 173.

63. B's minute, 6 August 1908, in Magnus, *Edward VII,* p. 503.

64. Minute by B on F. Cartwright to Edward Grey, 14 August 1908, in Gooch and Temperley, *British Documents,* vol. 6, p. 180.

65. Edward Grey to Lord Knollys, 8 August 1908, in Lee, *Edward VII,* vol. 2, p. 617.

66. RA GV/AA25/41, B to George, 20 August 1908.

67. RA VIC/W54/7 Charles Hardinge to Lord Knollys, 17 August 1908.

68. Charles Hardinge to Edward Grey, 15 August 1908, in Gooch and Temperley, *British Documents*, vol. 6, p. 183.

69. RA GV/AA25/41, B to George, 20 August 1908.

70. RA VIC/W54/7, Charles Hardinge to Lord Knollys, 17 August 1908.

71. Charles Hardinge to Lord Knollys, 17 August 1908, in Lee, *Edward VII*, vol. 2, p. 626.

72. Ponsonby, *Three Reigns*, pp. 246–47. Lee places this story in 1907. (*Edward VII*, vol. 2, p. 549.)

73. Charles Hardinge to Lord Knollys, 17 August 1908, in Lee, *Edward VII*, vol. 2, p. 626.

74. Miklos Banffy, *They Were Found Wanting* (Arcadia Books, 2009), pp. 157–59.

75. RA VIC/W54/71, Charles Hardinge to B, 3 October 1908.

76. RA VIC/EVIID/1908: 5 October.

77. Bülow, *Memoirs*, vol. 2, p. 148.

78. Lord Redesdale, *King Edward VII: A Memory* (privately printed, 1915), p. 28.

79. R. R. McLean, "Monarchy and Diplomacy in Europe 1900–1910," (PhD dissertation, University of Sussex, 1996), pp. 123–25.

80. RA VIC/EVIID/1908: 11 October.

81. *The Times*, 20, 21, 24, 26 October 1908.

82. RA VIC/W54/115, Charles Hardinge to B, 20 October 1908.

83. RA VIC/W54/116, Charles Hardinge to B, 22 October 1908.

84. Carter, *Three Emperors*, p. 360.

85. B to Nicholas II, 27 October 1908, in Lee, *Edward VII*, vol. 2, p. 642.

86. RA VIC/W54/119, Charles Hardinge to B, 24 October 1908.

87. Edwin Lutyens to Lady Emily Lutyens, 15 March 1902, in *The Letters of Edwin Lutyens to His Wife Lady Emily*, ed. by Clayre Percy and Jane Ridley (Collins, 1985), p. 97.

88. Caroline Spurrier Archive, B to Daisy Warwick, 7 January 1898.

89. Stamper, *What I Know*, pp. 209–11.

90. RA VIC/W54/123, Charles Hardinge to B, 28 October 1908.

91. RA VIC/W54/124, Charles Hardinge to B, 28 October 1908.

92. Cecil, *Wilhelm II*, vol. 2, p. 140.

93. *The Observer*, 22 November 1908.

94. RA VIC/Add C07/2/Q, Charles Hardinge to Lord Knollys, 12 November 1908.

95. McLean, *Royalty and Diplomacy*, p. 359.

96. B to Lord Knollys, 25 November 1908, in Lee, *Edward VII*, vol. 2, p. 622.

97. RA VIC/Add C07/2/Q, Charles Hardinge to Lord Knollys, 7 November 1908.

98. RA VIC/Add C07/2/Q, Note by B on Charles Hardinge to Lord Knollys, 18 November 1908.

99. Brett, *Journals and Letters*, vol. 2, p. 360.

100. Bodleian Library, MS Eng. d. 3206, Margot Asquith Diary, November 1908.

101. Lord Howard de Walden to Holbrooke, 22 November 1908, Thomas Seymour collection.

102. Stamper, *What I Know*, pp. 214–15.

103. Allfrey, *Jewish Court*, p. 53.

104. Ponsonby, *Three Reigns*, p. 207.

105. Fitzroy, *Memoirs*, vol. 1, pp. 368–70 (8, 19 December 1910).

106. Stamper, *What I Know*, pp. 231–32. Bertie's diary shows Mrs. Keppel dining. RA VIC/EVIID/1908: 10, 17 December.

107. Stamper, *What I Know*, pp. 231–32.

108. Ibid., pp. 225, 230.

109. Bodleian Library, Lincolnshire Papers, MS Film 1121, Lord Knollys to Charles Carrington, 23 January 1909.

110. Edward Grey to Francis Bertie, 7 January 1909, in Gooch and Temperley, *British Documents*, vol. 6, p. 227.

111. Bodleian Library, MS Eng. d. 3206, Margot Asquith Diary, 1 April 1909.

112. *The Times*, 10 February 1909. Ponsonby, *Three Reigns*, p. 256. Reid, *Ask Sir James*, p. 236.

113. Bodleian Library, MS Eng. d. 3206, Margot Asquith Diary, 1 April 1909.

114. Daisy Fürstin von Pless, *Daisy, Princess of Pless, by Herself* (John Murray, 1928), pp. 176–77 (Diary: 10 February 1909).

115. Lee, *Edward VII*, vol. 2, p. 676. Magnus, *Edward VII*, p. 512.

116. Reid, *Ask Sir James*, pp. 237–38.

117. Bodleian Library, MS Eng. d. 3206, Margot Asquith Diary, 1 April 1909.

118. Ponsonby, *Three Reigns*, pp. 256–58.

119. B to Charles Hardinge, 28 March 1909, in Magnus, *Edward VII*, p. 513.

CHAPTER 26: KING OF TRUMPS 1909–10

1. B's comment on Asquith's letter of 19 December 1908, 20 December 1908, in Lee, *Edward VII*, vol. 2, p. 678.

2. RA VIC/Add C07/2/K, Lord Knollys to B, 18 December 1908.

3. Winston Churchill, *Great Contemporaries* (Thornton Butterworth, 1937), p. 137.

4. Magnus, *Edward VII*, p. 421.

5. Bodleian Library, MS Eng. d. 3206, Margot Asquith Diary, 15 November 1909.

6. Cameron Hazlehurst, "Asquith as Prime Minister," *English Historical Review*, vol. 85 (1970), p. 508.

7. Lee, *Edward VII*, vol. 2, p. 678.

8. Ponsonby, *Three Reigns*, pp. 260–61.

9. Ibid., pp. 262–63.

10. RA VIC/R30/7, Frederick Ponsonby to H. H. Asquith, 1 May 1909.

11. RA VIC/X35/506, W. E. Grey to Frederick Ponsonby, 9 May 1909.

12. Daisy Pless to Kaiser William [June 1910], in *Daisy, Princess of Pless*, p. 185.

13. Stamper, *What I Know*, pp. 252–53.

14. Brett, *Journals and Letters*, vol. 2, p. 387.

15. Stamper, *What I Know*, pp. 252–54, 263–64, 267, 278–79. Rose, *George V*, p. 319.

16. Fitzroy, *Memoirs*, vol. 1, p. 379.

17. Stamper, *What I Know*, pp. 256, 268. Rhodes James, *Chips*, p. 241.

18. Stamper, *What I Know*, pp. 272–73.

19. Bodleian Library, Lincolnshire Papers, MS Film 1121, Lord Knollys to Charles Carrington, 10 July 1909.

20. Fitzwilliam, Wilfrid Blunt Papers, MS 9–1975, Diary (5 March 1909).

21. Phillips, *Last Edwardians*, pp. 20–21.

22. RA VIC/W66/88, Lewis Harcourt to Lord Knollys, 25 July 1909. RA VIC/ W66/89, Knollys to Harcourt, 26 July 1909. Lee, *Edward VII*, vol. 2, pp. 665–66.

23. Lord Knollys to Lord Crewe, 1 August 1909, in Magnus, *Edward VII*, pp. 430–31.

24. RA VIC/W55/50, Edward Grey to Lord Knollys, 25 July 1909.

25. H. H. Asquith to David Lloyd George, 3 August 1909, in John Grigg, *LG: The People's Champion* (Methuen, 1991), pp. 208–9. *The Times*, 3 August 1909.

26. See Grigg, *People's Champion*, pp. 209–11, for the exchange of letters between B and David Lloyd George.

27. Rhodes James, *Chips*, pp. 234–35.

28. Esher's Journal, 8 September 1909, in Lees-Milne, *Esher*, p. 197.

29. Camp, *Royal Mistresses*, p. 377. Hibbert, *Edward VII*, pp. 244–45. McKinstry, *Rosebery*, pp. 487–88. Winston Churchill to his wife, 25 June 1911, in Randolph Churchill, *Churchill: Young Statesman*, pp. 356–57.

30. Muntz, *Edward VII at Marienbad*, pp. 238–40.

31. Esher's Journal, 8 September 1909, in Lees-Milne, *Esher*, p. 197.

32. Randolph Churchill, *Churchill: Young Statesman*, pp. 326–27.

33. Esher's Journal, 8 September 1909, in Lees-Milne, *Esher*, pp. 197–98.

34. Churchill Archives Centre, Esher Papers, 2/11, Journal, 24 July 1908.

35. RA VIC/X5/12a, Lord Esher to Lord Knollys, 11 February 1909.

36. RA VIC/Add C07/1/9, Lord Esher to Lord Knollys, 13 October 1909.

37. RA VIC/X5/12a, Lord Esher to Lord Knollys, 11 February 1909.

38. *The Times*, 11 September 1909.

39. Winston Churchill to his wife, 12 September 1909, in Randolph Churchill, *Churchill, Young Statesman*, p. 327.

40. B to Lord Esher, 10 September 1909, in Lees-Milne, *Esher*, p. 198.

41. RA VIC/Add C07/1/9, Lord Esher to Lord Knollys, 26 September 1909.

42. Brett, *Journals and Letters*, vol. 2, p. 411 (4 October 1909).

43. Moscow: State Archive of the Russian Federation, Fond 1126—op 1—delo 152, Count Benckendorff to his wife, 16–29 September 1909. For this reference, I am indebted to Marina Vorobieva.

44. Moscow: State Archive of the Russian Federation, Fond 1126—op 1—delo 152, Count Benckendorff to his wife, 23 September–6 October 1909.

45. Asquith's Memo of Conversation with King, 6 October 1909, in Spender and Asquith, *Life*, vol. 1, p. 257.

46. Bodleian Library, MS Eng. d. 3206, Margot Asquith Diary, H. H. Asquith to Margot Asquith, 30 September 1909.

47. H. H. Asquith to David Lloyd George, 7 October 1909, in Grigg, *People's Champion*, p. 221.

48. RA GV/AA25/65, B to George, 13 October 1909.

49. Ibid. RA VIC/EVIID/1909: 12 October.

50. Bodleian Library, Lincolnshire Papers, MS Film 1121, Carrington Diary, 15 October 1909.

51. RA VIC/Add C07/1/9, Lord Esher to Lord Knollys, 13 October 1909.

52. Bodleian Library, MS Eng. d. 3206, Margot Asquith Diary, 15 November 1909.

53. Knutsford, *In Black and White*, p. 230.

54. Rose, *George V*, pp. 293–94.

55. Knutsford, *In Black and White*, pp. 234–37.

56. Magnus, *Edward VII*, pp. 437–38.

57. Fitzroy, *Memoirs*, vol. 1, p. 389.

58. Knutsford, *In Black and White*, p. 245.

59. Ibid., p. 246.

60. *Daisy, Princess of Pless*, pp. 187, 201.

61. See James Lees-Milne, *Deep Romantic Chasm: Diaries 1979–81*, ed. Michael Bloch (John Murray, 2000), p. 205.

62. Knutsford, *In Black and White*, pp. 250–51.

63. Watson, *King Edward as Sportsman*, p. 219.

64. Lord Esher to Lord Knollys, 1 December 1909, in Brett, *Journals and Letters*, vol. 2, pp. 423–25.

65. Lord Knollys to Lord Esher, 2 December 1909, in Heffer, *Power*, p. 285.

66. Ibid.

67. Memo by Vaughan Nash, 15 December 1909 in Spender and Asquith, *Life*, vol. 1, pp. 261–62.

68. Magnus, *Edward VII*, p. 441. See Vernon Bogdanor, *The Monarchy and the Constitution* (Oxford: Clarendon Press, 1995), pp. 113–15; Hardie, *Political Influence of the British Monarchy*, p. 112.

69. Stamper, *What I Know*, p. 321.

70. *Daisy, Princess of Pless*, p. 202.

71. Ibid., pp. 203–4.

72. RA VIC/Add A5/475, B to Mrs. Keppel, 1 January 1910.

73. Elizabeth Countess of Fingall, *Seventy Years Young* (Collins, 1937), p. 296.

74. Ibid., pp. 298, 303. Rhodes James, *Chips*, pp. 21, 347.

75. Bodleian Library, Lincolnshire Papers, MS Film 1121, Carrington Diary, 3, 4 January 1910.

76. Fingall, *Seventy Years Young*, p. 298.

77. Ibid., pp. 298, 305–6.

78. Stamper, *What I Know*, pp. 300–301.

79. Vincent, *Crawford Papers*, p. 570.

80. Hibbert, *Edward VII*, p. 285.

81. RA VIC/EVIID/1910: 14 January.

82. Brett, *Journals and Letters*, vol. 2, pp. 435–36 (Journal, 9 January 1910).

83. Lord Esher to his son, 23 January 1910, in Brett, *Journals and Letters*, vol. 2, p. 439.

84. Lord Esher to his son, 25 January 1910, in Brett, *Journals and Letters*, vol. 2, p. 442.

85. Bodleian Library, MS Eng. d. 3208, Margot Asquith Diary, 1 February 1910.

86. RA VIC/W66/112, Margot Asquith to Lord Knollys, 2 February 1910.

87. RA VIC/W66/113, Margot Asquith to Lord Knollys, n.d.

88. RA VIC/W66/114, Lord Knollys to Margot Asquith, 4 February 1910.

89. Warwick, *Afterthoughts*, p. 33.

90. Bodleian Library, MS Eng. d. 3208, Margot Asquith Diary, 17 February 1910.

91. RA VIC/R30/84, B's Note on Vaughan Nash to Lord Knollys, 12 January 1910.

92. Bodleian Library, MS Eng. d. 3208, Margot Asquith Diary, 15 February 1910.

93. Redesdale, *King Edward VII: A Memory,* p. 33. RA VIC/EDVIID/1910: 17 February.

94. Lee, *Edward VII,* vol. 2, p. 702.

CHAPTER 27: THE PEOPLE'S KING: MARCH–MAY 1910

1. *The Times,* 7 March 1910.

2. RA GV/AA25/70, B to George, 16 March 1910.

3. Physicians' Report, *The Times,* 12 May 1910.

4. BL, Sidney Lee Papers, Add MSS 56087A, fols. 1–3, George Saunders to Sidney Lee, 22 November 1911. *The Times,* 8 March 1910.

5. Leslie, *Edwardians in Love,* p. 337. RA VIC/EVIID/1910: 8 March.

6. RA VIC/EVIID/1910: 11 March.

7. Mrs. Keppel to the Marquis de Soveral, n.d., in Brook-Shepherd, *Uncle of Europe,* p. 350.

8. *The Times,* 15 March 1910.

9. RA VIC/EVIID/1910: 14–18 March.

10. Reid, *Ask Sir James,* p. 239.

11. *The Times,* 12 May 1910.

12. Reid, *Ask Sir James,* p. 239.

13. RA GV/AA25/71, B to George, 22 March 1910.

14. RA GV/GG9/33, Arthur Davidson to Dighton Probyn, 3 August 1912. Reid, *Ask Sir James,* p. 239.

15. RA GV/CC42/79, Alix to Princess of Wales, 26 November 1910.

16. "I am afraid he must have been very bad, much worse than we in England had any idea of": Reid Papers, Arthur Bigge to James Reid, 22 March 1910.

17. Stamper, *What I Know,* pp. 332, 334.

18. Ponsonby, *Three Reigns,* p. 267.

19. RA GV/GG9/189, Arthur Davidson to Dighton Probyn, 5 December 1912.

20. RA VIC/EVIID/1910. 20 March, 4 April.

21. RA GV/GG9/189, Arthur Davidson to Dighton Probyn, 5 December 1912.

22. RA GV/AA25/72, B to George, 29 March 1910.

23. RA VIC/Add C07/2/H, B to Lord Knollys, 26 March 1910. Stamper, *What I Know,* pp. 335, 340–41.

24. RA VIC/Add C07/2/H, B to Lord Knollys, 9 April 1910. Stamper, *What I Know,* pp. 344–45.

25. Battiscombe, *Queen Alexandra,* p. 268.

26. RA VIC/Add C07/2/H, B to Lord Knollys, 9 April 1910.

27. Lord Esher to B, 10 April 1910, in Brett, *Journals and Letters,* vol. 2, pp. 433–35.

28. RA VIC/Add C07/1/9, Lord Esher to Lord Knollys, 10 April 1910.

29. H. H. Asquith to B, 13 April 1910, in Magnus, *Edward VII,* pp. 451–52.

30. RA VIC/X11/29, B to H. H. Asquith (draft), 16 April 1910. Lee, *Edward VII,* vol. 2, p. 706.

31. RA VIC/Add C07/2/H, B to Lord Knollys, 16 April 1912.

32. *Hansard,* 14 April 1910, vol. 16, cols. 1547–51.

33. RA VIC/Add C07/2/H, B to Lord Knollys, 16 April 1910.

34. Colin Matthew, "Herbert Henry Asquith," *ODNB.* G. H. L. Le May, *The Victorian Constitution* (Duckworth, 1979), pp. 198–99.

35. Lord Knollys to Lord Esher, 17 April 1910, in Magnus, *Edward VII*, p. 453.
36. RA VIC/Add C07/2/H, B to Lord Knollys, 23 April 1910.
37. Stamper, *What I Know*, pp. 350–51.
38. Ibid., pp. 351. Kenny, *Crown and Shamrock*, pp. 107–8.
39. Lee, *Edward VII*, vol. 2, p. 709.
40. Ponsonby, *Three Reigns*, p. 267.
41. RA VIC Add C07/2/H, B to Lord Knollys, 23 April 1910. RA VIC/Add C07/2/H, Prince of Wales to Knollys, 24 April 1910. RA VIC/EVIID/1910: 27 April. *The Times*, 28 April 1910.
42. Esher's memorandum of a Conference at Lambeth, 27 April 1910, in Brett, *Journals and Letters*, vol. 2, pp. 456–59.
43. Bogdanor, *Monarchy and the Constitution*, pp. 115–19.
44. RA VIC/Add C07/2/H, B to Lord Knollys, 23 April 1910. H. H. Asquith to Margot Asquith, 28 April 1910, in Asquith, *Autobiography*, vol. 2, p. 135.
45. *The Times*, 6 May 1910.
46. Redesdale, "King Edward VII: A Memory," p. 34.
47. Churchill Archives Centre, Esher Papers, 2/12, Journal, 7 May 1910.
48. *The Times*, 6 May 1910.
49. RA VIC/EVIID/1910: 30 April. *The Times*, 12 May 1910. Ponsonby, *Three Reigns*, p. 268.
50. Ponsonby, *Three Reigns*, p. 268.
51. Reid, *Ask Sir James*, p. 240.
52. Ibid.
53. Esher's Memorandum, 3 May 1910, in Lee, *Edward VII*, vol. 2, p. 713. Ponsonby, *Three Reigns*, p. 268.
54. Ponsonby, *Three Reigns*, p. 268.
55. Fitzroy, *Memoirs*, vol. 2, p. 409.
56. Ibid., vol. 2, p. 409. Lee, *Edward VII*, vol. 2, p. 715. Redesdale, "King Edward VII: A Memory," p. 35.
57. Public Record Office of Northern Ireland, Schomberg McDonnell Papers, D/4091/A/6/1, "Schomberg McDonnell's Journal of Death and Funeral of King Edward VII," May 1910, p. 11.
58. George to Alix, 4 May 1910, in Battiscombe, *Queen Alexandra*, p. 270.
59. RA VIC/EVIID/1910: 4 May.
60. Ponsonby, *Three Reigns*, p. 269.
61. Ibid. Reid, *Ask Sir James*, p. 241.
62. Asquith, *Autobiography*, vol. 2, p. 137.
63. Reid, *Ask Sir James*, p. 241.
64. Quoted in Longford, *Louisa*, p. 203.
65. *The Times*, 6 May 1910.
66. Fitzroy, *Memoirs*, vol. 2, p. 402.
67. Reid, *Ask Sir James*, p. 241. Bodleian Library, MS Eng. d. 3208, Margot Asquith Diary, 6 May 1910.
68. Ernest Cassel to Mrs. Wilfrid Ashley, 6 May 1910, in Lee, *Edward VII*, vol. 2, pp. 716–17.
69. Souhami, *Mrs. Keppel*, p. 91.
70. Bodleian Library, MS Eng. d. 3208, Margot Asquith Diary, 6 May 1910.
71. Leslie, *Edwardians in Love*, p. 338.

72. RA VIC/Add A5/471, B to Mrs. Keppel, May 1901 [sic]. Why Bertie should have written this letter in 1901, rather than 1902, when he was ill, is unclear. Royal Librarian Robin Mackworth-Young annotated: "He must have felt very out of sorts to feel it necessary to write it but there is no record of any grave illness at this time."

73. Churchill Archives Centre, Esher Papers, 2/12, Journal, 12 June 1910. Sir Francis Laking, who was one of the doctors in attendance, told Skittles that the King said to the Queen, "You must kiss Alice," and Alix obeyed. (Fitzwilliam, Wilfrid Blunt Papers, MS 11–1975, Diary, 14 December 1910.)

74. Rhodes James, Chips, p. 32.

75. See p. 408.

76. Churchill Archives Centre, Esher Papers, 2/12, Journal, 12 June 1910.

77. Fitzwilliam, Wilfrid Blunt Papers, MS 11–1975, Diary, 14 December 1910.

78. Lee, Edward VII, vol. 2, p. 717.

79. Vincent, Crawford Papers, p. 153 (9 May 1910). Holmes, Edward VII, vol. 2, p. 599.

80. Churchill Archives Centre, Esher Papers, 2/12, Journal, 7 May 1910.

81. Charles Sebag-Montefiore Archive, Philip Magnus Papers, Shane Leslie to Magnus, 24 August 1961. Shane Leslie is a key source for this story, which has also been handed down in Father Forster's family, and still lingers today. See Mary Kenny, The Irish Catholic, 24 September 2009.

82. Charles Sebag-Montefiore Archive, Philip Magnus Papers, Shane Leslie to Magnus, 19 July 1961.

83. Philip Magnus heard a story from Evelyn Waugh that King Edward underwent a deathbed conversion to Roman Catholicism. (Charles Sebag-Montefiore Archive, Philip Magnus Papers, Philip Magnus to Lady Magnus, 6 February 1962.) A search by Magnus in the archives of the Archbishop of Westminster yielded nothing, and Magnus does not mention the story in his biography. (Charles Sebag-Montefiore Archive, Philip Magnus Papers, David Norris, Private Secretary to Archbishop of Westminster, 14 July 1961.)

84. Bell, Davidson, p. 608. Churchill Archives Centre, Esher Papers, 2/12, Journal, 7 May 1910.

85. Holmes, Edward VII, vol. 2, p. 599.

86. Bodleian Library, MS Eng. d. 3208, Margot Asquith Diary, 6 May 1910.

87. Bodleian Library, MS Eng. d. 3208, Margot Asquith Diary, 7 May 1910.

88. The Times, 10 May 1910.

89. Fitzwilliam, Wilfrid Blunt Papers, MS 10–1975, Diary, 6 May, 13 May 1910.

90. Fitzwilliam, Wilfrid Blunt Papers, MS 10–1975, Diary, 15 August 1910.

91. The Times, 12 May 1910. Before leaving for Biarritz, the King complained to Daisy Warwick about the effect of the injections against influenza he was being given. (Life's Ebb and Flow, p. 158.)

92. Fitzwilliam, Wilfrid Blunt Papers, MS 11–1975, Diary, 13 May, 16 June 1910.

93. Vincent, Crawford Papers, p. 154 (10 May 1910).

94. Ibid., p. 153 (9 May 1910). See George Dangerfield, The Strange Death of Liberal England (New York: Perigree, 1980), pp. 5–6.

95. A Liberal Chronicle: Journals and Papers of J. A. Pease, ed. Cameron Hazlehurst and Christine Woodland (Historians' Press, 1994), p. 176 (10 May 1910).

96. The Times, 10 May 1910 (British Medical Journal extract). The Times, 12 May 1910 (Physicians' Report).

97. Felix Semon and Francis Laking to Lord Knollys, 23 February 1907, in Lee, *Edward VII*, vol. 2, pp. 685–86.

98. Felix Semon to Lord Knollys, 7 May 1910, in St. Aubyn, *Edward VII*, p. 475.

99. *The Times*, 13 May 1910.

100. Ponsonby, *Three Reigns*, p. 271.

101. Churchill Archives Centre, Esher Papers, 2/12, Journal, 10 May 1910.

102. McKinstry, *Rosebery*, p. 496.

103. Keppel, *Edwardian Daughter*, p. 53.

104. Allfrey, *Jewish Court*, p. 247. Souhami, *Mrs. Keppel*, p. 92.

105. Fitzwilliam, Wilfrid Blunt Papers, MS 10–1975, Diary, 13 May 1910.

106. Reid, *Ask Sir James*, p. 243.

107. Mrs. Keppel to Lady Knollys, n.d., in Souhami, *Mrs. Keppel*, p. 96.

108. Churchill Archives Centre, Esher Papers, 2/12, Journal, 12 June 1910. For the house in Grosvenor Street, see Osbert Lancaster, *Great Morning* (Reprint Society, 1949), pp. 216–17.

109. McKinstry, *Rosebery*, p. 496.

110. Admiral John Fisher to Reginald McKenna, 14 May 1910, in Marder, *Fear God and Dread Nought*, vol. 2 p. 325.

111. Queen Alexandra's Message, *The Times*, 23 May 1910. Battiscombe, *Queen Alexandra*, pp. 272–73.

112. Reid, *Ask Sir James*, p. 242.

113. St. Aubyn, *Edward VII*, p. 475, quoting Alix's remarks to Theodore Roosevelt.

114. Diary of George V, 11 May 1910, in Kuhn, *Democratic Royalism*, p. 101.

115. *The Times*, 14 May, 16 May 1910.

116. PRO Northern Ireland, D/4091/A/6/1, Schomberg McDonnell's journal, "Edward VII," May 1910, p. 13.

117. *The Times*, 17 May 1910.

118. Holmes, *Edward VII*, vol. 2, p. 614.

119. *The Times*, 13 May 1910.

120. Holmes, *Edward VII*, vol. 2, p. 615. *The Times*, 18 May 1910.

121. RA GV/CC25/59, Queen Mary to Augusta Grand Duchess of Mecklenburg-Strelitz, 22 May 1910.

122. Carrington Diary, 17 May 1910, in Hibbert, *Edward VII*, pp. 312–13.

123. Holmes, *Edward VII*, vol. 2, p. 620.

124. Lord Esher to Schomberg McDonnell, 9 May 1910, in Kuhn, *Democratic Royalism*, p. 103.

125. Schomberg McDonnell to Arthur Bigge, 10, 11 May 1910, in ibid., p. 104.

126. John Wolffe, *Great Deaths* (British Academy, 2000), p. 252.

127. PRO Northern Ireland, D/4091/A/6/1, Schomberg McDonnell's journal, "Edward VII," May 1910, p. 26.

128. Holmes, *Edward VII*, vol. 2, p. 625.

129. PRO Northern Ireland, D/4091/A/6/1, Schomberg McDonnell's journal, "Edward VII," May 1910, p. 26.

130. Carrington Diary, 18 May 1910, in Hibbert, *Edward VII*, p. 313.

131. Ibid.

132. PRO Northern Ireland, D/4091/A/6/1, Schomberg McDonnell's journal, "Edward VII," May 1910, pp. 35–36.

133. Carrington Diary, 18 May 1910, in Hibbert, *Edward VII*, p. 313.

134. PRO Northern Ireland, D/4091/A/6/1, Schomberg McDonnell's journal, "Edward VII," May 1910, pp. 39–41.
135. PRO Northern Ireland, D/4091/A/6/1, Schomberg McDonnell's journal, "Edward VII," May 1910, pp. 42–3.
136. Holmes, *Edward VII*, vol. 2, p. 625. Kuhn, *Democratic Royalism*, p. 105. There was no official count of attendance, and estimates vary. See Wolffe, *Great Deaths*, pp. 252–53.
137. Vincent, *Crawford Papers*, p. 155 (19 May 1910).
138. *The Times*, 13 May 1910.
139. Arthur Davidson to Arthur Bigge, 7 May 1910, in Kuhn, *Democratic Royalism*, p. 101.
140. Asquith, *Autobiography*, vol. 2, p. 140.
141. Ibid.
142. Ibid., vol. 2, p. 141.
143. St. Aubyn, *Edward VII*, p. 477.
144. *The Times*, 21 May 1910. Holmes, *Edward VII*, vol. 2, p. 628.
145. Vincent, *Crawford Papers*, p. 156 (20 May 1910).
146. *The Times*, 21 May 1910.
147. Vincent, *Crawford Papers*, pp. 155–56 (20 May 1910).
148. Ibid.
149. BL, Sidney Lee Papers, Add MS 56087A, fols. 1–3, George Saunders to Sidney Lee, 22 November 1911.
150. Leslie, *Edwardians in Love*, p. 340.
151. PRO Northern Ireland, D/4091/A/6/1, Schomberg McDonnell's journal, "Edward VII," May 1910, p. 27. See Wolffe, *Great Deaths*, pp. 247–48, for a more positive assessment of Norfolk's role.
152. Asquith, *Autobiography*, vol. 2, p. 142. Kuhn, *Democratic Royalism*, p. 129.
153. Fitzroy, *Memoirs*, vol. 1, p. 142.
154. PRO Northern Ireland, D/4091/A/6/1, Schomberg McDonnell's journal, "Edward VII," May 1910, p. 47.
155. Holmes, *Edward VII*, vol. 2, p. 644. *The Times*, 23 May 1910.
156. Pope-Hennessy, *Queen Mary*, p. 422.
157. Bodleian Library, MS Eng. d. 3208, Margot Asquith Diary, 20 May 1910.
158. Asquith, *Autobiography*, vol. 2, p. 143.

CONCLUSION

1. Owen Morshead, quoted in Lees-Milne, *Harold Nicolson*, vol. 2, p. 230.
2. Bodleian Library, MS Eng. d. 3206, Margot Asquith Diary, 20 June 1908.
3. Strachey's review of Sidney Lee's *Edward VII* in *Daily Mail*, 11 October 1927, cited in Hardie, *Political Influence of the British Monarchy*, p. 115.
4. Logan Pearsall Smith, *Afterthoughts* (Cassell, 1931), p. 34. Rose, *George V*, p. 303.
5. McLean, *Royalty and Diplomacy*, p. 138.
6. Cannadine, "The Last Hanoverian Sovereign?," pp. 156–57. Peter Clarke, *Hope and Glory: Britain 1900–1990* (Penguin Books, 1997), pp. 34, 36.
7. Heffer, *Power*, pp. 2–3, 304.
8. I am indebted to Bogdanor, *Monarchy and the Constitution*, pp. 32–41.

9. Lord Fisher, *Memories* (Hodder and Stoughton, 1919), p. 3.
10. Esher quoted in Hibbert, *Edward VII*, p. 205.
11. RA GV/GG9/76, Arthur Davidson to Dighton Probyn, 15 September 1912. RA GV/GG9/82, Davidson to Probyn, 4 October 1912.
12. Alexander Mikhailovich, Grand Duke of Russia, *Always a Grand Duke* (Royalty Digest, 1995), pp. 202–3.
13. Battiscombe, *Queen Alexandra*, p. 274.
14. Quoted in Leslie, *Edwardians in Love*.
15. Rose, *George V*, p. 291.
16. Author interview, Mrs. Maud Hutton-Attenborough, née Ponsonby, 8 March 2004.
17. T. E. Lawrence, *The Mint* (Cape, 1973).
18. RA VIC/Add A21/159, Alix to Bertie, Duke of York, 15 March 1921.

AFTERWORD: BERTIE AND THE BIOGRAPHERS

1. RA VIC/Z505/11, QV to Alice, 12 January 1875.
2. Ponsonby, *Three Reigns*, pp. 67–70.
3. RA VIC/Add C07/2/S, Fleetwood Edwards to Lord Knollys, 24 February 1901.
4. Charles Sebag-Montefiore Archive, Philip Magnus Papers, Robin Mackworth-Young to Philip Magnus, 5 July 1963. See Dennison, *Last Princess*, pp. 216–23.
5. Theodore Martin, *Queen Victoria as I Knew Her* (William Blackwood, 1908), pp. 143–46.
6. RA VIC/W41/2, Lord Esher to Lord Knollys, 14 October 1907.
7. Churchill Archives Centre, Esher Papers, ESHR/11/3, Lord Knollys to Lord Esher, 21 December 1903.
8. Benson Diary, 20 November 1903, in Ward, "Editing Queen Victoria," p. 305.
9. RA VIC/W39/41, B's note on Lord Esher to Lord Knollys, 3 April 1904.
10. Benson Diary, 17, 23 May, 25 June 1904, in Ward, "Editing Queen Victoria," pp. 149–50, 190.
11. See ibid., pp. 294–96.
12. RA VIC/Add C07/1/9, Lord Esher to Lord Knollys, 17 August 1905.
13. Ward, "Editing Queen Victoria," p. 264.
14. Lord Knollys to Lord Esher, 25 August 1906, in ibid., p. 267.
15. Ibid., p. 285.
16. Ibid., p. 322.
17. Churchill Archives Centre, Esher Papers, ESHR/11/3, Arthur Bigge to Lord Esher, 22 August 1906.
18. RA VIC/W41/37, B's note, 28 March 1908. RA VIC/W41/36, Lord Esher to B, 23 March 1908.
19. Robin Mackworth-Young, "The Royal Archives, Windsor Castle," *Archives*, vol. 13 (1978), p. 120.
20. RA GV/GG9/439, Lord Esher to Frederick Ponsonby, 19 April 1914.
21. Fitzroy, *Memoirs*, vol. 1, pp. 166–67 (16 November 1903).
22. RA VIC/W64/8, B's note, 23 November 1904.
23. RA VIC/W41/5, Lord Knollys to Lord Rothschild, 28 October 1907.
24. RA VIC/X33/336, Lord Rothschild to Lord Knollys, 31 October 1907.

25. RA VIC/X33/337, Lord Esher to Lord Knollys, 1 November 1907.
26. Mackworth-Young, "Royal Archives," p. 122.
27. Brett, *Journals and Letters,* vol. 2, p. 256 (16 November 1907). Mackworth-Young, "Royal Archives," p. 123. Magnus, *Edward VII,* p. 462.
28. Reid, *Ask Sir James,* pp. 227–28.
29. RA VIC/Add C07/2/P, B to Lord Minto, 17 March 1909 (copy).
30. Magnus, *Edward VII,* p. 461.
31. Rose, *George V,* pp. 140–41.
32. Lord Knollys to George, 14 February 1913, in Magnus, *Edward VII,* p. 461.
33. Ibid.
34. RA GV/GG9/76, Arthur Davidson to Dighton Probyn, 15 September 1912.
35. RA GV/GG9/476, Frederick Ponsonby to Arthur Davidson, 12 May 1914. RA GV/GG9/527, Ponsonby to Davidson, 16 July 1914.
36. Eckardstein quoted in Mackworth-Young, "Royal Archives," p. 124.
37. Cited in Magnus, *Edward VII,* p. 462.
38. Carolyn W. White, "The Biographer and Edward VII: Sir Sidney Lee and the Embarrassments of Royal Biography," *Victorian Studies,* vol. 27 (1984), pp. 301–19.
39. "Edward VII," *Dictionary of National Biography: Supplement 1901–1911* (Smith, Elder, 1912), pp. 606–7.
40. RA GV/GG9/58, Arthur Davidson to Alix, 10 September 1912. RA GV/GG9/76, Davidson to Dighton Probyn, 15 September 1912.
41. RA GV/GG9/27, Lord Esher to Arthur Davidson, 28 July 1912.
42. RA GV/GG9/58, Arthur Davidson to Alix, 10 September 1912.
43. RA GV/GG9/39b, Arthur Davidson to Lord Knollys, 23 August 1912.
44. Charles Sebag-Montefiore Archive, Philip Magnus Papers, Owen Morshead to Philip Magnus, 7 April 1964.
45. RA GV/GG9/64, Dighton Probyn to Lord Knollys, 13 September 1912.
46. Churchill Archives Centre, Esher Papers, ESHR/6/4, Alix to Lord Esher, 29 September 1912.
47. RA GV/GG9/82, Arthur Davidson to Dighton Probyn, 4 October 1912.
48. RA GV/GG9/114, Alix to Dighton Probyn, telegram, 22 October 1912.
49. RA GV/GG9/140, Alix to Dighton Probyn, 25 October 1912.
50. RA GV/GG9/175a, Davidson to Dighton Probyn, 16 November 1912.
51. RA GV/GG9/165, Frederick Ponsonby to Arthur Davidson, 8 November 1912.
52. RA GV/GG9/172A, Arthur Davidson to Lord Knollys, 12 November 1912. RA GV/GG9/171, H. H. Asquith to Arthur Davidson, 11 November 1912.
53. RA GV/GG9/139, Davidson's Note, 25 October 1912.
54. BL, Balfour Papers, Add MS 49685, fols. 147–53, Short to Davidson, 4 November 1912. I am indebted to Professor R. J. Q. Adams for this reference.
55. RA GV/GG9/183, Arthur Davidson to Dighton Probyn, 3 December 1912.
56. BL, Sidney Lee Papers, Add MSS 56087A, Lee's Notes of Conversation with Balfour, 24 November 1911.
57. RA GV/GG9/183, Arthur Davidson to Dighton Probyn, 3 December 1912.
58. RA GV/GG9/184, Frederick Ponsonby to Arthur Davidson, 4 December 1912.
59. RA GV/GG9/338, Arthur Balfour to Arthur Davidson, 13 December 1913.

60. RA GV/GG9/183, Arthur Davidson to Frederick Ponsonby, 3 December 1912.

61. *DNB: Supplement,* p. 603.

62. RA GV/GG9/183, Arthur Davidson to Frederick Ponsonby, 3 December 1912.

63. RA GV/GG9/253, Davidson's Note on Interview with Morley and Lee, 1 July 1913. RA GV/GG9/258, Arthur Davidson to Lord Knollys, 4 July 1913.

64. RA GV/GG9/258, Arthur Davidson to Lord Knollys, 4 July 1913.

65. White, "The Biographer," p. 312.

66. RA GV/GG9/447, Sidney Lee to Lord Knollys, 12 July 1913. RA GV/GG9/447, Lee to Ponsonby, 11 May 1914.

67. RA GV/GG9/429, Frederick Ponsonby to Arthur Davidson, 7 April 1914.

68. RA GV/GG9/512, Frederick Ponsonby to Arthur Davidson, 15 June 1914.

69. BL, Balfour Papers, Add MS 49685, Frederick Ponsonby to J. S. Sandars, 1 August 1914.

70. Ibid.

71. RA GV/GG9/516, Frederick Ponsonby to Arthur Davidson, 20 June 1914. RA GV/GG9/518, Arthur Davidson to Frederick Ponsonby, 20 June 1914.

72. RA GV/GG9/465, Arthur Davidson to Frederick Ponsonby, 5 May 1914.

73. RA GV/GG9/539, Note by Davidson, 8 October 1914.

74. See Theo Lang, *My Darling Daisy* (Michael Joseph, 1966). Blunden, *Countess of Warwick,* pp. 236–44.

75. RA PS/GV/O/479B/4, Blanche Gordon-Lennox to Lord Stamfordham, 2 July 1914.

76. RA GV/GG9/527, Frederick Ponsonby to Arthur Davidson, 16 July 1914.

77. RA PS/GV/O/479B/23, Memo by Charles Russell for Stamfordham, 21 July 1914.

78. RA PS/GV/O/479B/36, Charles Russell's Report, 30 July 1914.

79. H. H. Asquith to Venetia Stanley, 13 February 1915, in *H. H. Asquith: Letters to Venetia Stanley,* ed. Michael and Eleanor Brock (Oxford University Press, 1982), pp. 428–29.

80. RA PS/GV/O/479B/48, Charles Russell to Lord Stamfordham, 2 March 1915.

81. RA PS/GV/O/479B/52, Stamfordham's Note, 17 June 1915. RA PS/GV/O/479B/55, Stamfordham's Note, n.d. [c. 29 June 1915].

82. RA PS/GV/O/479B/54, Affidavit by Lady Warwick [1915]. See RA PS/GV/O/479B/53, Lady Warwick to Lord Stamfordham, 23 June 1915.

83. RA PS/GV/O/479B/61, Alice Keppel to Frederick Ponsonby, n.d. [1921].

84. Lang, *My Darling Daisy,* p. 186.

85. RA PS/GV/O/479B/63, Lord Stamfordham to George, 5 January 1921. RA GV/O/479B/48A, Lady Warwick to solicitors Langton and Passmore, 26 February 1915.

86. Lees-Milne, *Esher,* p. 347.

87. RA PS/GV/O/479B/71, Stamfordham's Note for George V, 8 December 1927.

88. RA GV/GG9/552, Arthur Davidson to Frederick Ponsonby, 29 April 1920.

89. RA GV/GG9/556, Frederick Ponsonby to Arthur Davidson, 16 July 1920. RA GV/GG9/570, Arthur Davidson to Frederick Ponsonby, 1 August 1920.

90. Robert Faber and Brian Harrison, "The *Dictionary of National Biography*: A Publishing History," in *Lives in Print,* ed. Robin Myers, Michael Harris and Giles Mandelbrote (Oak Knoll Press and BL, 2002), pp. 174–75.

91. RA GV/GG9/514, Arthur Davidson to Frederick Ponsonby, 16 June 1914.

92. RA GV/GG9/492, Admiral John Fisher to Frederick Ponsonby, n.d. [May 1914].

93. BL, Sidney Lee Papers, Add MSS 56087A, fol. 121, Frederick Ponsonby to Sidney Lee, 5 September 1920.

94. RA GV/GG9/868, Arthur Davidson to Frederick Ponsonby, 16 May 1922.

95. RA GV/GG9/568, John Fortescue to Frederick Ponsonby, 24 July 1920.

96. RA GV/GG9/623, Arthur Davidson to Sidney Lee, 9 November 1920.

97. RA GV/GG9/629, Arthur Davidson to Frederick Ponsonby, 12 November 1920.

98. RA GV/GG9/707, Charles Hardinge to Lord Stamfordham, 20 January 1921.

99. RA GV/GG9/909, Lord Stamfordham to Frederick Ponsonby, 29 November 1922.

100. RA GV/GG9/631, Frederick Ponsonby to Arthur Davidson, 13 November 1920.

101. RA GV/GG9/913, Frederick Ponsonby to Lord Rosebery, 15 December 1922. RA GV/GG9/924, Ponsonby to Lee, 19 December 1922. Lee, *Edward VII,* vol. 1, pp. 216–17

102. RA GV/GG9/1032, Frederick Ponsonby to H. H. Asquith, 18 November 1924.

103. RA GV/GG9/1062 [Stamfordham's Memo for Ponsonby], 11 April [1925].

104. BL, Sidney Lee Papers, Add MSS 56087A, fol. 114, Lytton Strachey to Sidney Lee, 31 December 1918.

105. RA GV/GG9/1048, Ponsonby s memo to Stamfordham, 16 February 1925, RA GV/GG9/1049, Stamfordham's memo to Ponsonby, 16 February 1925. Here Stamfordham says: "Would it not be unusual for a personal presentation. It would be a pity to associate the King too much with the work, especially as, unless I am mistaken, a predominant note in it will be, disparagement of Queen Victoria."

106. RA GV/GG9/1170, Lionel Cust to Frederick Ponsonby, 3 November 1927.

107. RA GV/GG9/833, Frederick Ponsonby to Arthur Davidson, 8 September 1921. White, "The Biographer," p. 315.

108. RA GV/GG9/1091, Frederick Macmillan to Frederick Ponsonby, 23 February 1926.

109. RA GV/GG9/1170, Lionel Cust to Frederick Ponsonby, 3 November 1927. White, "The Biographer," p. 115.

110. Lee, *Edward VII,* vol. 2, p. 408.

111. David Cannadine, "From Biography to History: Writing the Modern British Monarchy," *Historical Research,* vol. 77 (2004), p. 295.

112. *King's Counsellor: The Diaries of Sir Alan Lascelles,* ed. Duff Hart-Davis (Phoenix, 2007), pp. 72–73.

113. Wheeler-Bennett quoted in Cannadine, "From Biography to History," p. 296.

114. Charles Sebag-Montefiore Archive, Philip Magnus Papers, Robin Mackworth-Young to Philip Magnus, 6 April 1960, and 7 December 1960.

115. Charles Sebag-Montefiore Archive, Philip Magnus Papers, Robin Mackworth-

Young to Philip Magnus, 10 September 1958, 27 May 1960, and 10 October 1961.

116. Charles Sebag-Montefiore Archive, Philip Magnus Papers, Robert Blake to Philip Magnus, 20 May 1962 and 27 August 1962.

117. Colin Matthew, "Philip Magnus," *ODNB*. Charles Sebag-Montefiore Archive, Philip Magnus Papers, Hugh Trevor-Roper to Philip Magnus, 21 November 1960 and 30 March 1961.

118. Charles Sebag-Montefiore Archive, Philip Magnus Papers, Philip Magnus to his mother, Mrs. Magnus, 3 May 1959.

119. Charles Sebag-Montefiore Archive, Philip Magnus Papers, Mrs. Magnus to Philip Magnus, 28 November 1960.

120. Charles Sebag-Montefiore Archive, Philip Magnus Papers, Elliott B. Macrae to Philip Magnus, 17 February 1960.

121. Charles Sebag-Montefiore Archive, Philip Magnus Papers, Mrs. Magnus to Philip Magnus, 29 August 1960.

122. Charles Sebag-Montefiore Archive, Philip Magnus Papers, Mrs. Magnus to Philip Magnus, 18 November 1961.

123. Charles Sebag-Montefiore Archive, Philip Magnus Papers, Philip Magnus to Mrs. Magnus, 24 August 1962.

124. *The Observer,* 15 March 1964.

INDEX

About the Author

JANE RIDLEY is professor of history at the University of Buckingham in England, where she teaches a course on biography. Her previous biographies include *The Young Disraeli* and *The Architect and His Wife: A Life of Edwin Lutyens,* which won the prestigious Duff Cooper Prize. A Fellow of the Royal Society of Literature, Ridley writes book reviews for *The Spectator* and other newspapers, and has also appeared in several television and radio documentaries. She lives in London and Scotland.